Textbook on
International Law

Seventh Edition

Martin Dixon, MA, PhD (Oxon, Cantab)

Reader in Law, University of Cambridge
Fellow, Queens' College, Cambridge
Visiting Professor of Law, City University, London

OXFORD
UNIVERSITY PRESS

OXFORD

UNIVERSITY PRESS

Great Clarendon Street, Oxford, OX2 6DP,
United Kingdom

Oxford University Press is a department of the University of Oxford.
It furthers the University's objective of excellence in research, scholarship,
and education by publishing worldwide. Oxford is a registered trade mark of
Oxford University Press in the UK and in certain other countries

Fourth edition 2000
Fifth edition 2005
Sixth edition 2007
Impression: 1

British Library Cataloguing in Publication Data
Data available

ISBN 978-0-19-957445-2

Printed in Great Britain by
Ashford Colour Press Ltd, Gosport, Hampshire

PREFACE

This latest edition of the *Textbook* has been long in the making and much has been re-written in order to bring the text up to date for 2013. Every chapter has been updated and the impact of significant cases before the International Court of Justice and other international tribunals has been woven into the text. While the fundamental nature of the international legal system has not changed, there is no doubt that international law has had to respond to new and deeper challenges. Old conceptions about the nature of statehood and sovereignty have had to be re-thought in the light of a revitalised international judicial system and a widespread perception that a shrinking and complex world *needs*, rather than just *chooses*, an effective international legal order.

While the text has changed, the aim remains the same: to present an accurate and reasonably detailed exposition of international law for the interested student. The deeper theoretical debates that abound in international law are left for further reading and a signpost is provided at the end of each Chapter. The complexity of the subject is not minimised, but the aim is to enlighten and explain. In this task, I have benefitted greatly from the advice, guidance and research of Robert McCorquodale and Sarah Williams and the publication of the 5th edition of *Cases & Materials on International Law*.

As ever, thanks are due to many, not least the staff of OUP whose patience I stretched and stretched. I hope it was worth the wait. Finally, I cannot sign off without marking the passing of two of the greatest scholars of international law of the modern era. I was lucky enough to be taught by both Derek Bowett and Ian Brownlie. Much that is in this *Textbook*, and in the courses studied by students around the world, has been influenced by the work of these Titans of international legal scholarship and practice. Much of the international legal order that shapes the modern world and protects the people in it is of their making.

Martin Dixon
Queens' College
Ash Wednesday 2013

NEW TO THIS EDITION

- Recent developments in the law relating to the use of force, including Security Council responses to terrorism and civil war.
- Consideration of the ICJ's analysis of the concept of independence and sovereignty (*Accordance with international law of the unilateral declaration of independence in respect of Kosovo (Request for Advisory Opinion)*).
- Recent developments in territorial sovereignty and jurisdictional sovereignty.
- The developing law of immunity and its relationship to human rights – *Jurisdictional Immunities of the State (Germany* v *Italy: Greece intervening)* and *Questions relating to the Obligation to Prosecute or Extradite (Belgium* v *Senegal)*.
- The first cases tried by the International Criminal Court and the developing law of individual personal responsibility for violations of human rights.

OUTLINE CONTENTS

1   The nature of international law and the international system   1

2   The sources of international law   24

3   The law of treaties   55

4   International law and national law   90

5   Personality, statehood and recognition   115

6   Jurisdiction and sovereignty   148

7   Immunities from national jurisdiction   182

8   The law of the sea   217

9   State responsibility   252

10   The peaceful settlement of disputes   286

11   The use of force   321

12   Human rights   354

DETAILED CONTENTS

Preface   v
New to this edition   vi
List of abbreviations   xii
Table of cases   xiv
Table of treaties   xxiv
Table of other documents   xxix
Table of statutes   xxxi

1 The nature of international law and the international system   1

1.1 The role of international law   *3*
1.2 The existence of international rules as a system of law   *4*
1.3 The enforcement of international law   *6*
1.4 The effectiveness of international law   *11*
1.5 The weakness of international law   *14*
1.6 The juridical basis of international law   *16*
1.7 The future of international law   *21*
    Further reading   *22*
    Summary   *23*

2 The sources of international law   24

2.1 Article 38 of the Statute of the International Court of Justice   *24*
2.2 International treaties ('conventions')   *28*
2.3 Custom   *32*
2.4 General principles of law   *42*
2.5 Judicial decisions   *45*
2.6 Writings of publicists   *49*
2.7 Resolutions and decisions of international organisations   *49*
2.8 Soft law   *52*
    Further reading   *53*
    Summary   *54*

3 The law of treaties   55

3.1 What is a treaty?   *56*
3.2 Acts lacking an intention to create legal relations   *57*
3.3 Other 'non-treaty' circumstances giving rise to legally binding obligations   *58*
3.4 The Vienna Convention on the Law of Treaties 1969   *62*
3.5 Vienna Convention on the Succession of States in Respect of Treaties 1978   *85*
3.6 Vienna Convention on the Law of Treaties between International Organisations or between States and International Organisations 1986   *86*
    Further reading   *87*
    Summary   *88*

4 International law and national law   90

4.1 Theories   *91*
4.2 National law before international courts and tribunals   *94*
4.3 Theories about international law in the national legal system: incorporation, transformation and implementation   *98*
4.4 International law in the national law of the United Kingdom   *100*

4.5 National courts applying international law   *111*
4.6 Executive certificates and ministerial discretion   *112*
Further reading   *113*
Summary   *114*

5 Personality, statehood and recognition   115

Part One: Personality and statehood in international law   *115*
5.1 The concept of personality in international law   *115*
5.2 The subjects of international law   *117*

Part Two: Recognition   *131*
5.3 Recognition in international law   *132*
5.4 Recognition of states and governments in national law   *136*
Further reading   *146*
Summary   *147*

6 Jurisdiction and sovereignty   148

6.1 General principles of jurisdiction   *148*
6.2 Civil and criminal jurisdiction   *150*
6.3 The acquisition of sovereignty over territory   *161*
6.4 Rights over foreign territory   *174*

6.5 Areas outside the exclusive jurisdiction of any state   *175*
6.6 Jurisdiction over airspace and aircraft   *178*
Further reading   *180*
Summary   *181*

7 Immunities from national jurisdiction   182

Part One: State immunity   *183*
7.1 General conception of immunity and rationale in international law   *183*
7.2 State immunity in international law   *187*
7.3 The UN Convention on Jurisdictional Immunities of States and their Property 2004 (the ILC Draft Articles)   *194*
7.4 State immunity in the United Kingdom   *196*
7.5 Heads of state   *206*

7.6 The European Convention on State Immunity 1972   *207*
7.7 State immunity in the UK and human rights   *207*
Part Two: Diplomatic and consular immunities   *208*
7.8 International law   *209*
7.9 The United Kingdom   *213*
7.10 A note on the immunities of international organisations   *214*
Further reading   *215*
Summary   *216*

8   The law of the sea   217

8.1   Sources of the law of the sea   *217*
8.2   The territorial sea and
        contiguous zone   *220*
8.3   The Exclusive Economic Zone   *224*
8.4   The continental shelf   *228*
8.5   The deep sea bed   *236*
8.6   The high seas   *241*

8.7   Miscellaneous matters   *242*
8.8   Conclusion   *246*
        Further reading   *247*
        Summary   *248*
        Appendix: Guide to the 1982
        Convention on the Law of
        the Sea and 1994 Agreement
        on the Deep Sea Bed   *249*

9   State responsibility   252

9.1   General issues of state
        responsibility   *254*
9.2   The treatment of foreign
        nationals   *266*
9.3   Expropriation of foreign-owned
        property   275
9.4   The internationalisation
        of contracts   281

9.5   Protection for private investors   283
9.6   Other forms of responsibility
        in international law   *284*
        Further reading   *284*
        Summary   *285*

10   The peaceful settlement of disputes   286

10.1 Negotiation   *287*
10.2 Mediation and good offices   *288*
10.3 Inquiry   *288*
10.4 Settlement by the
        United Nations   *289*
10.5 Conciliation   *291*
10.6 Settlement by regional
        machinery   *292*

10.7 Arbitration   *292*
10.8 The International Court
        of Justice   *294*
10.9 Advisory Opinions   *316*
        Further reading   *319*
        Summary   *320*

11   The use of force   321

      Part One: The unilateral use
        of force   *322*
11.1 The law before 1945   *322*
11.2 The law after the UN Charter   *324*
      Part Two: The collective
        use of force   *341*

11.3 The United Nations   *342*
11.4 Regional organisations   *348*
11.5 Peacekeeping   *350*
        Further reading   *352*
        Summary   *353*

12   Human rights   354

12.1 The role and nature of human
        rights law   *354*

12.2 The development of the law
        of human rights   *357*

12.3 The protection of human rights
under the United Nations   *359*

12.4 The European Convention on
Human Rights and Fundamental
Freedoms 1950   *365*

12.5 Other regional machinery   *369*

12.6 Success and failure   *370*

Further reading   *371*

Summary   *373*

Glossary   375
Index   377

LIST OF ABBREVIATIONS

AHG	Assembly of Heads of State and Government, OAU
AJIL	American Journal of International Law
BYIL	British Yearbook of International Law
Carricom	Caribbean Common Market
CLCS	Commission on the Limits of the Continental Shelf
CMLR	Common Market Law Reports
CRAMRA	Convention on the Regulation of Antarctic Mineral Resource Activities
CSC	Continental Shelf Convention 1958
EC	European Community
ECOSOC	Economic and Social Council (UN)
EEZ	Exclusive Economic Zone
EFTA	European Free Trade Association
EFZ	Exclusive Fisheries Zone
EHRR	European Human Rights Reports
EJIL	European Journal of International Law
EU	European Union
GA Res.	General Assembly Resolution
GATT	General Agreement on Tariffs and Trade
HSC	High Seas Convention 1958
IAEA	International Atomic Energy Agency
ICAO	International Civil Aviation Organisation
ICC	International Criminal Court
ICCPR	International Covenant on Civil and Political Rights
ICJ	International Court of Justice
ICJ Rep	Reports of Judgments, Advisory Opinions and Orders of the International Court of Justice
ICLQ	International Comparative Law Quarterly
ILC	International Law Commission
ILM	International Legal Materials
ILO	International Labour Organisation
ILQ	International Law Quarterly
ILR	International Law Reports
IMF	International Monetary Fund
IRC	Inland Revenue Commissioners
ITLOS	International Tribunal for the Law of the Sea
LNOJ	League of Nations Official Journal
LOS 1982	Law of the Sea Convention 1982
OAS	Organisation of American States
OAU	Organisation of African Unity, now the African Union
OSCE	Organisation for Security and Co-operation in Europe
PCIJ	Permanent Court of International Justice
PLO	Palestine Liberation Organisation
RIAA	Reports of International Arbitral Awards
SC Res.	Security Council Resolution
SWAPO	South West Africa People's Organisation
TRNC	Turkish Republic of Northern Cyprus
TSC	Territorial Sea Convention 1958
UN	United Nations

UNDOF	United Nations Disengagement Observations Force
UNEF	United Nations Emergency Force
UNESCO	United Nations Educational, Scientific and Cultural Organisation
UNFICYP	United Nations Force in Cyprus
UNIFIL	United Nations Interim Force in Lebanon
UNRWA	United Nations Relief and Works Agency
VC	Vienna Convention
WHO	World Health Organization

TABLE OF CASES

A v Secretary of State for the Home
Department [2006] 2 AC 221 ... 48, 100,
111, 355

Aaland Islands Case [1920] LNOJ Special
Supp. No. 3 ... 78

AAPL v Sri Lanka ... 256, 261, 263, 293

Adams v Adams [1970] 3 All ER 572 ... 140,
141

Admissions Case 1948 ICJ Rep 57 ... 73

Advisory Opinion on the Accordance
with international law of the unilateral
declaration of independence in respect of
Kosovo (2008) ... 10, 291, 298, 316–19,
340

Advisory Opinion on the Accordance
with international law of the unilateral
declaration of independence in respect
of Kosovo (2010) ... 32, 51, 62, 122, 124,
127, 171, 172, 294

Advisory Opinion on the applicability of Art
VI, section 22 of the Convention on the
Privileges and Immunities of the United
Nations (1989) ICJ Rep 177 (Immunities
Case) ... 127, 317, 318

Advisory Opinion on the Constitution of
the Maritime Safety Committee of IMCO
Case 1960 ICJ Rep 150 ... 73

Advisory Opinion on the Difference
Relating to Immunity from Legal
Process of a Special Rapporteur of the
Commission of Human Rights, 20 April
1999 ... 214

Advisory Opinion on the Interpretation of
the Treaty of Lausanne Case (1925) PCIJ
Ser. B No. 12 ... 293

Advisory Opinion on the Jurisdiction of the
European Commission of the Danube,
PCIJ Ser. B No. 14 ... 127

Advisory Opinion on the Legal
Consequences of the Construction of a
Wall in the Occupied Palestinian Territory
July 2004 ICJ Rep ... 10, 29, 290

Advisory Opinion on the Legality of the
Threat or Use of Nuclear Weapons (WHO
Case) 1996 ICJ Rep 66 ... 37, 45, 116, 297,
328

Advisory Opinion on Nuclear Weapons
(WHO Case) ... 127

Advisory Opinion on Reservations to
Certain Commonwealth of Independent
States Agreements 127 ILR 1 ... 72

Aerial Incident Case (Israel v Bulgaria)
(Preliminary Objections) 1959 ICJ Rep
127 ... 311

A-G for Canada v A-G for Ontario [1937] AC
326 ... 101

A-G of Israel v Eichmann (1961) 36 ILR 5 ...
154, 156, 160, 260, 341

A-G v Guardian Newspapers Ltd (No. 2)
[1990] 1 AC 109 ... 106

Ahmadou Sadio Diallo (Republic of Guinea
v Democratic Republic of the Congo)
Merits, Judgment, (ICJ 2010) ... 9

Ahmadou Sadio Diallo Republic of Guinea v
Democratic Republic of the Congo
(ICJ 2012) ... 9

Ahmed v Government of the Kingdom of
Saudi Arabia [1996] 2 All ER 248 ... 197

AIG Capital Partners Inc v Kazakhstan ...
201

Air Services Agreement Case (France v
United States) 18 RIAA 416 (1978) ... 85

Al Skeini and others v Secretary of State for
Defence (2009) ... 153

Alabama Claims Arbitration (1872) Moore 1
Int. Arb. 495 ... 94

Al-Adsani v Government of Kuwait 107 ILR
536 ... 193, 194, 197, 200, 201, 207

Al-Adsani v UK (2002) 34 EHRR 273 ... 194,
208

Alcom v Republic of Colombia [1984] 2
WLR 750 ... 205

Ambatielos Case (Jurisdiction) 1952 ICJ Rep
28 ... 74, 312

Ambatielos Arbitration (Greece v UK) (1956)
12 RIAA 83 ... 272

Amco v Indonesia (1985) 24 ILM 1022 ...
279

Amoco Finance v Iran 15 Iran–US CTR 189
(1987) ... 263, 275, 278, 279, 280

Anglo-French Continental Shelf Case (1979)
18 ILM 397; 54 ILR 6 ... 41, 69, 76, 231,
244

Anglo-Iranian Oil Co. Case (Jurisdiction)
1952 ICJ Rep 93 ... 58, 61

Anglo-Norwegian Fisheries Case 1951 ICJ
Rep 116 ... 32–5, 47, 90, 96, 220, 222,
223, 244, 245

Animoil Case (1982) 21 ILM 976 ... 277,
278, 282

Application of the Interim Accord of 13
September 1995 (The Former Yugoslav
Republic of Macedonia v Greece) (2011)
... 10, 63, 74, 75, 76, 82, 84, 85, 291, 298,
316

Application for Revision of the Judgment of
11 September 1992 ... 295

Arab Monetary Fund v Hashim [1991] 1 All
ER 871 ... 102–4, 113, 145
Aramco Case (1963) 27 ILR 117 ... 276
Arantzazu Mendi, The [1939]
AC 256 ... 139
Armed Activities on the Territory of Congo
Case (New Application 2002: Congo v
Rwanda) ... 70, 306
Armed Activities on the Territory
of the Congo (Democratic Republic
of the Congo v Uganda) Case 2005 ICJ
Rep ... 324, 330, 331, 333
Asian Agricultural Products Ltd (AAPL) v
Republic of Sri Lanka (1992) 30 ILM
577 ... 75, 255
Asylum Case (Columbia v Peru) 1950 ICJ
Rep 266 ... 35
Attorney-General v Associated Newspapers
[1994] 2 AC 238 ... 108
Avena Case see Case Concerning Avena
and other Mexican Nationals (Mexico v
United States of America) 2004 ICJ Rep
AY Bank (in liquidation) v Bosnia &
Herzegovina (2006) ... 101, 104

B v B (2000) 2 FLR 707 ... 140, 141
Banković and others v Belgium
and 16 other Contracting States
ECHR 2001 ... 152
Barbados/Trinidad & Tobago Maritime
Delimitation Arbitration (April
2006) ... 217, 227, 228, 230, 231, 233,
234, 236, 246, 292
Barcelona Traction Case (Preliminary
Objections) 1964 ICJ Rep 6 ... 273, 312
Barcelona Traction Case (Belgium v Spain)
1970 ICJ Rep 3 ... 44, 270, 271
Bat v Germany [2011] EWHC
2029 ... 25, 48
Beagle Channel Arbitration (Chile v
Argentina) 17 ILM 638 ... 75, 293
Behrami v France; ECHR Grand Chamber
(2007) 22 BHRC 477 ... 116, 127
Benin v Niger see Frontier Dispute Case
(Benin v Niger) (2005)
Berrehab v Netherlands (1989) 11
EHRR 322 ... 366
Bleir v Uruguay, 1 Selected Decisions
HRC 109 ... 361
Bolivar Railway Case (Great Britain v
Venezuela) (1903) 9 RIAA 445 ... 261
Border and Transborder Armed Actions Case
(Nicaragua v Honduras) (Jurisdiction and
Admissibility) 1988 ICJ Rep 69 ... 298
Bosnia Serbia Genocide Case ... 5
Botswana v Namibia Case ... 166, 169
BP v Libya (1974) 53 ILR 329 ... 276, 277

Brannigan and McBride v United Kingdom
ECHR Series A (1993) No. 258-B ... 366
Brazilian Loans Case (France v Brazil) (1929)
PCIJ Ser. A No. 21 ... 97
Brind v Secretary of State for the Home
Department [1991] 1 All ER 720 ... 108
Brogan v UK (1989) 11 EHRR 117 ... 95, 366
Brown (R.E.) Case (US v Great Britain)
(1923) 6 RIAA 120 ... 273
Buck v A-G [1965] Ch 745 ... 183, 184
Buttes Gas and Oil Co v Hammer [1981] 3
All ER 616 ... 184
Buvot v Barbuit (1737) Cases t. Talbot
281 ... 109

Caire Claim (1929) 5 RIAA 516 ... 256
Cameroon v Nigeria (Application for
Intervention) (21 October 1999) ... 302
Cameroon v Nigeria Case (Equatorial
Guinea intervening) ... 161, 162, 169,
311, 312
Camouco Case (Panama v France) ... 272
Campaign for Nuclear Disarmament v
Prime Minister [2002] EWHC 2777 ... 92,
100
Canada/France Maritime Delimitation
Arbitration (1992) 31 ILM 1145 ... 231–3,
244, 292, 294
Carl Zeiss Stiftung v Rayner and Keeler
(No. 2) [1967] 1 AC 853 ... 138, 140–3
Caroline Case ... 327, 328, 331
Case Concerning Ahmadou Sadio Diallo
(Republic of Guinea v Democratic
Republic of the Congo) Preliminary
Objections, (2007) ... 271, 273
Case Concerning Armed Activities on the
Territory of the Congo (Congo v Uganda)
(Provisional Measures),
1 July 2000 ... 290
Case Concerning Armed Activities on the
Territory of the Congo (New Application:
2002) (Democratic Republic of the Congo
v Rwanda) ... 300, 305
Case Concerning Avena and other Mexican
Nationals (Mexico v United States of
America) 2004 ICJ Rep ... 274, 298, 299,
301, 303, 305
Case concerning Certain Phosphate Lands
in Nauru (Nauru v Australia) (Preliminary
Objections) 1992 ICJ Rep 240 ... 299
Case Concerning Certain Questions
Relating to Secession of Quebec from
Canada 161 DLR (4th) 385 ... 173
Case Concerning East Timor (Portugal v
Australia) 1995 ICJ Rep 89 ... 42, 46, 171,
302
Case Concerning Kasikili/Sedudu Island
(Botswana v Namibia) (1999) ... 28, 60

Case Concerning Maritime Delimitation and Territorial Questions between Qatar and Bahrain (Qatar v Bahrain) (Jurisdiction and Admissibility) 1994 ICJ Rep 112 ... 56

Case Concerning Maritime and Territorial Questions between Qatar and Bahrain 2001 ICJ Rep ... 218

Case Concerning Oil Platforms (Islamic Republic of Iran v United States of America) (2003) ... 26

Case Concerning Questions of Interpretation and Application of the 1971 Montreal Convention arising from the Aerial Incident at Lockerbie (Libya v United States; Libya v United Kingdom) (Request for the Indication of Provisional Measures) 1992 ICJ Rep 114 ... 315

Case Concerning Sovereignty over Pedra Branca (Malaysia v Singapore) 2003 ICJ Rep ... 304

Case Concerning Sovereignty over Pedra Branca/ Pulau Batu Puteh, Middle Rocks and South Ledge (Malaysia v Singapore) (2008) ... 244

Case Concerning Sovereignty over Pulau Ligitan and Pulau Sipadan (Indonesia v Malaysia) 2002 ICJ Rep ... 62, 162

Case Concerning the Aerial Incident of 10 August 1999 (Pakistan v India) (Jurisdiction) 2000 ICJ Rep ... 304

Case concerning the Application of the Convention on the Prevention and Punishment of the Crime of Genocide (Bosnia and Herzegovina v Yugoslavia (Serbia & Montenegro)) (Indication of Provisional Measures) 1993 ICJ Rep 325 ... 10, 44, 296

Case Concerning the Application of the Convention on the Prevention and Punishment of the Crime of Genocide (Bosnia and Herzegovina v Serbia & Montenegro) ICJ 2007 ... 5, 28, 43, 47, 48, 60, 64, 117, 118, 134, 155, 253, 254, 258–60, 262, 290, 294, 296, 299, 300, 305, 314, 315, 355

Case Concerning the Application of the Convention on the Prevention and Punishment of the Crime of Genocide (Preliminary Objections) (Bosnia and Herzegovina v Yugoslavia) 1996 ICJ Rep 1 ... 259

Case Concerning the Arrest Warrant of 11 April 2000 (Congo v Belgium) 2002 ICJ Rep 14 ... 193, 208

Case Concerning the Arrest Warrant of 11 September 2000 (Congo v Belgium) 2002 ICJ Rep ... 154

Case Concerning the Frontier Dispute (Benin/Niger) 2005 ... 165

Case Concerning the Gabcikovo-Nagymaros Project (Hungary v Slovakia) (1998) 37 ILM 162; 1997 ICJ Rep ... 28, 31

Case Concerning the Land and Maritime Boundary (Cameroon v Nigeria) (Preliminary Objections) 1998 ICJ Rep 275 ... 306, 307

Case Concerning the Land and Maritime Boundary between Cameroon and Nigeria: (Cameroon v Nigeria, Equatorial Guinea Intervening) (2002) ... 166

Case Concerning the Land, Island and Maritime Frontier Dispute (El Salvador v Honduras) 2003 ICJ Rep ... 295

Case Concerning the Territorial Dispute (Libyan Arab Jamahiriya v Chad) 1994 ICJ Rep 6 ... 57, 58, 163

Case Concerning the Vienna Convention on Consular Relations (Paraguay v US) (Provisional Measures) 1998 ICJ Rep 248 ... 13

Central Bank of Yemen v Cardinal Finance Investments Corp [2000] EWCA Civ 266 ... 190, 198

Certain Activities carried out by Nicaragua in the Border Area (Costa Rica v Nicaragua) (2010) ... 262, 300, 305

Certain Activities carried out by Nicaragua in the Border Area (Costa Rica v Nicaragua) (2011) ... 301

Certain Criminal Proceedings in France Case (Congo v France) (2003) ... 304

Certain Expenses of the United Nations Case 1962 ICJ Rep 151 ... 74, 316, 347

Certain German Interests in Polish Upper Silesia Case (1926) PCIJ Ser. A No. 7 ... 96, 276, 279

Certain Phosphate Lands in Nauru Case (Nauru v Australia) (Preliminary Objections) (1993) 32 ILM 46 ... 45, 46

Certain Property Case (Lichtenstein v Germany) (2006) ... 303, 305

Certain Questions Concerning Mutual Assistance in Criminal Matters (Djibouti v France) (2006) ... 304

Chamizal Arbitration (US v Mexico) (1911) 5 AJIL 785 ... 75, 166

Charkieh, The (1873) LR 4 A & E 59 ... 196

Chattin Claim (1927) 4 RIAA 282 ... 266, 267

Chorozow Factory Case (Merits) (Germany v Poland) (1928) PCIJ Ser. A No. 17 ... 43, 263, 264, 277

Chung Chi Cheung v R [1939] AC 160 ... 109

City of Berne v Bank of England 9 Ves. 347 ... 140

Civil Air Transport v Central Air Transport [1953] AC 70 ... 140

Clipperton Island Arbitration (France v Mexico) (1932) 26 AJIL 390 ... 163–5, 169, 293

CND v Prime Minister [2002] EWHC 2759, QB ... 101, 184

Commissioners of Customs and Excise v Ministry of Industries and Military Manufacturing, Republic of Iraq (1994) 43 ICLQ 194 ... 198

Committee of US Citizens Living in Nicaragua v Reagan 859 F.2d. 929 ... 42

Compania Naviera Vascongado v Steamship 'Cristina' [1938] AC 485 ... 152

Company, A v Republic of X (1989) *The Times* ... 197, 201

Conditions for the Admission of a State to Membership in the UN Case 1948 ICJ Rep 57 ... 317, 319

Congo Case (1 July 2000) ... 298, 301

Congo Case (New Application: 2002) ... 301

Congo v Rwanda 2002 ICJ Rep 1999 ... 301

Construction of a Road in Costa Rica along the San Juan River (Nicaragua v Costa Rica) Case (2011) ... 305

Continental Shelf Case (Libya v Malta) 1984 ICJ Rep 3; 1985 ICJ Rep 13 ... 219, 228, 232, 313

Continental Shelf Case (Tunisia v Libya) 1982 ICJ Rep 18 ... 219, 224

Convention arising from the Aerial Incident at Lockerbie (Libya v United States; Libya v United Kingdom) (Request for the Indication of Provisional Measures) 1992 ICJ Rep 114 ... 315

Corfu Channel Case 1949 ICJ Rep 4 ... 219, 221, 224, 242, 255, 256, 296, 303, 305, 326

Croatia v Serbia [2010] 2 WLR 555 ... 101

Danube Dam Case ... 29, 41, 43, 62, 64, 81, 82, 84, 86, 265, 266

Decision on Challenge to Jurisdiction, Prosecutor v Kallon and Kamara Appeals Chamber, Special Court for Sierra Leone (2004) ... 56

Delimitation of Maritime Areas Arbitration (France/Canada) (1992) 31 ILM 1145 ... 219

Delimitation of Maritime Areas between Canada and France (St Pierre and Miquelon) Case (1992) ... 227

Demjanjuk v Petrovsk (1985) 776 F.2d. 571 ... 154

Democratic Republic of the Congo v Rwanda (2002) ... 300

Derbyshire CC v Times Newspapers [1992] QB 770; [1992] 3 WLR 28 ... 106, 108

Diplomatic Claim, Ethiopia's Claim 8, (2006), Eritrea/Ethiopia Claims Commission ... 209

Dispute Concerning Delimitation of the Maritime Boundary between Bangladesh and Myanmar in the Bay of Bengal, (Bangladesh/Myanmar) (2012) ... 223, 227, 229–31, 234, 235

Donegal v Zambia (2007) ... 197, 201

DPP v Doot [1973] AC 807 ... 155

DPP v Joyce [1946] AC 347 ... 156

Duff Development Corp v Kelantan [1924] AC 797 ... 112, 202

Earl Russel, Trial of [1901] AC 446 ... 154

East Timor Case ... 50

Eastern Carelia Case (1923) PCIJ Ser. B No. 5 ... 317, 318

Eastern Greenland Case (Denmark v Norway) (1933) PCIJ Ser. A/B No. 53 ... 59, 65, 163, 164, 169

EC Arbitration Commission on Yugoslavia [1993] 92 ILR 162 ... 133, 170

Egypt v Gamal-Eldin [1996] 2 All ER 237 ... 192, 197, 199, 200, 206

Eichmann Case *see* A-G of Israel v Eichmann

El Salvador v Honduras (1987) ... 165, 304

El Salvador v Honduras 1992 ICJ Rep 92 ... 313

Elettronica Sicula Case (US v Italy) 1989 ICJ Rep 15 ... 96, 272, 273, 275, 283, 295

Ellerman Lines v Murray [1931] AC 126 ... 106

Emin v Yeldag [2002] 1 FLR 956 ... 141

Empson v Smith [1966] 1 QB 426 ... 211

Eritrea Ethiopia Claims Commission, Final Award, 17 August 2009 (Ethiopia's Damages Claims), Permanent Court of Arbitration, The Hague ... 254, 263, 264

Eritrea/Yemen, Barbados/Trinidad & Tobago Maritime Delimitation Arbitration ... 236

Eritrea/Yemen Arbitration 1999 ... 218

Ethiopia/Eritrea Claims Commission Award (2005) ... 168

European Road Transport Agreement Case (22/70) [1971] CMLR 335 ... 127

Exchange of Greek and Turkish Populations Case (1925) PCIJ Ser. B No. 10 ... 46

Farouk v Yemen (2005) ... 197

Federal Democratic Republic of Ethiopia v The State of Eritrea (2006) 45 ILM 430 ... 324

Finnish Ships Arbitration (Finland v Great Britain) (1934) 3 RIAA 1479 ... 273, 274

Fisheries Jurisdiction Case (UK, Federal Republic of Germany v Iceland) (1972) ... 300, 303

Fisheries Jurisdiction Case (Jurisdiction) (UK v Iceland) 1973 ICJ Rep 3 ... 168

Fisheries Jurisdiction Case (Preliminary Objections) (Spain v Canada) 1998 ICJ Rep ... 58, 59, 224, 302, 308–10

Fisheries Jurisdiction Case (UK v Iceland) (Jurisdiction) 1974 ICJ Rep 3 ... 44, 58, 64, 83

Flegenheimer Claim (1958) 25 ILR 91 ... 269, 270

Fogarty v UK (2001) 34 EHRR 302 ... 194, 208

Fothergill v Monarch Airlines Ltd [1980] 2 All ER 696 ... 105

Free Zones of Upper Savoy and Gex Case (1932) PCIJ Ser. A/B No. 46 ... 78

Frontier Dispute (Burkina Faso/Niger) (2010) ... 26, 169, 304

Frontier Dispute (Burkina Faso v Niger) Case (2012) ... 78

Frontier Dispute Case (Benin v Niger) (2005) ... 96, 163, 164, 169

Frontier Dispute Case (Burkina Faso v Mali) 1985 ICJ Rep 6 ... 295, 302

Frontier Dispute Case (Burkina Faso v Mali) 1986 ICJ Rep 545 ... 44, 163, 169, 170

Gamel-Eldin ... 204

Gdynia Ameryka Linie v Boguslawski [1953] AC 11 ... 140

Genoa Ships Case (1883) 4 C Rob 388 ... 74

Genocide Convention (Reservations) Case 1951 ICJ Rep 15 ... 69

Golder Case 57 ILR 200 ... 74, 75

Grand Prince Case (Belize v France), Case No. 8, 2001 ... 269

Great Belt Case ... 301

Grovit v De Nederlandsche Bank (2005) ... 199, 203

Guinea/Guinea-Bissau Maritime Delimitation Case 77 ILR 636 (1983) ... 222–4, 227, 293

Gulf of Maine Case (Canada v USA) (1984) ICJ Rep 246 ... 32, 37, 227, 232, 233, 314

Gulf of Maine Case (US v Canada) 1982 ICJ Rep 3 ... 295

Gur Corp v Trust Bank of Africa [1986] 3 WLR 583 ... 138, 142, 143

Haile Selassie v Cable & Wireless Co. (No. 2) [1939] Ch 182 ... 140

Hartford Fire Insurance Co. v California US Supreme Court 113 S. Ct 2891 (1993) ... 157

Haya de la Torre Case (1951) ICJ Rep 71 ... 312

Hesperides Hotels v Aegean Turkish Holidays [1978] QB 205 ... 140, 141

Hispano Americana Mercantile SA v Central Bank of Nigeria [1979] 2 Lloyd's Rep 277 ... 196

Hogg v Toye & Co. Ltd [1935] Ch 497 ... 106

Holland v Lampen-Wolfe [2000] 1 WLR 1573 ... 183, 185–7, 192, 196, 198–200, 205–7

Home Missionary Society Case (1920) 6 RIAA 42 ... 256

Hostages Case (US v Iran) [1980] ICJ Rep 3 ... 263

I Congreso del Partido [1981] 2 All ER 1064 ... 189, 191, 192, 196, 204, 206

I'm Alone (Canada v US) 3 RIAA 1609 ... 255, 263, 272

Interhandel Case (Switzerland v USA) 1959 ICJ Rep 6 ... 273, 308

International Registration of Trademark (Germany) Case (1959) 28 ILR 82 ... 133

International Status of South West Africa Case 1950 ICJ Rep 128 ... 44

International Tin Council – J. H. Rayner (Mincing Lane) Limited v Department of Trade and Industry [1990] 2 AC 418 ... 94, 100

Interpretation of Peace Treaties Case 1950 ICJ Rep 65 ... 46, 74

IRC v Collco Dealings Ltd [1962] AC 1 ... 107

Island of Palmas Case (1928) 2 RIAA 829 ... 162, 164–7, 169, 173, 292

Jalapa Railroad Claim (1948) 8 Whiteman 908 ... 281

James Buchanan & Co. v Babco Forwarding and Shipping (UK) [1977] 3 All ER 1048 ... 104

Jan Meyen Case (Denmark v Norway) 1993 ICJ Rep 38 ... 227, 229, 231–5, 244, 306, 314

Jan Meyen Conciliation Commission (Iceland v Norway) (1981) 20 ILM 797 ... 291

Janes Claim (US v Mexico) (1926) 4 RIAA 82 ... 255, 263

Janes Claim and Massey Claim (1927) 4 RIAA 155 ... 266

Jones v Saudi Arabia [2006] 2 WLR 1424 ... 91, 92, 95, 185, 186, 193, 194, 197, 200–2, 207, 208

Joyce v DPP [1946] AC 347 ... 149

Jurisdictional Immunities of the State (Germany v Italy) Case (2008) ... 314

Jurisdictional Immunities of the State (Germany v Italy: Greece Intervening) (2012) ... 33, 34, 36, 37, 41, 42, 80, 182, 183, 185, 186, 193

Jus Ad Bellum Ethiopia's Claims 1–8 (The Federal Democratic Republic of Ethiopia v The State of Eritrea) (2006) ... 330

Kahan v Pakistan Federation [1951] 2 KB 1003 ... 197

Kasikili/Sedudu Island Case (Botswana v Namibia) 13 December 1999 ... 57, 62, 64, 74, 75, 77, 78, 96, 162

Kuwait Airways Corp v Iraqi Airways Co [1995] 1 WLR 1147 ... 184, 189, 199, 203–5

Kuwait Airways Corp v Iraqi Airways Co. (No. 3) 1998 (1999) CLS 31 ... 183

Kuwait Airways Corp v Iraqi Airways Co. (No. 4 & 5) [2002] UKHL 19 ... 184

Kuwait v M.S. Fenzi (1999) ... 206

La Grand case (Case Concerning the Vienna Convention on Consular Relations (Germany v US) 1999 ICJ Rep) ... 13

La Grand Case (Germany v United States) 2001 ICJ Rep ... 274, 299, 301

Laker v Sabena Airways (1984) 731 F.2d. 909 ... 157

Lampen-Wolfe *see* Holland v Lampen-Wolfe

Land and Maritime Boundaries Case (El Salvador v Honduras) 1987 ICJ Rep 10 ... 295

Land and Maritime Boundary Case (Cameroon v Nigeria) (Provisional Measures) 1996 ICJ Rep 13 ... 301

Land and Maritime Boundary Case (Cameroon v Nigeria) 2002 ICJ Rep ... 302

Land Island and Maritime Frontier Dispute Case (El Salvador v Honduras) 1992 ICJ Rep 92 ... 163, 313

Land, Island and Maritime Frontier Dispute Case (El Salvador v Honduras) (Merits) 1992 ICJ Rep 35 ... 162

Larivière v Morgan (1872) 7 Ch App 550 ... 196

Legal Consequences of the Construction of a Wall in the Occupied Palestinian Territory Case ... 47

Legality of the Use of Force Case (Provisional Measures) Yugoslavia v Belgium etc (1999) 39 ILM 950 ... 286, 301, 310

Legality of the Use of Force Cases (Serbia v NATO countries) (2004) ... 134, 290, 296, 297, 303, 314, 337

Legality of the Use of Nuclear Weapons Case 1996 ... 127, 316, 318, 319

Leroy Simmonds v Jamaica (1994) 1 IHRR 94 ... 362

Liamco Case (1977) 20 ILM 1 ... 276

Liangsiriprasert v US [1990] 2 All ER 866 ... 156

Libya v Malta 1985 ICJ Rep 13 ... 314

Libya v UK ... 179

Libya v US ... 179

Littrell v United States of America (No. 2) [1994] 2 All ER 3 ... 192, 199, 200, 204, 206

Lockerbie Case (Libyan Arab Jamahiriya v UK and US 1992 ICJ Rep para 22) ... 10, 298

Loewen Group, Inc. and Raymond L. Loewen v United States of America (2006) ... 266

London Branch of the Nigerian Universities Commission v Bastians [1995] ICR 358 ... 197

Lotus Case (1927) PCIJ Ser. A No. 10 ... 32, 33, 148, 149, 159

Lusitania Claims 7 RIAA 32 ... 263

Luther v Sagor [1921] 3 KB 532 ... 137

Maclaine Watson v Dept of Trade and Industry [1988] 3 All ER 257; [1989] 3 All ER 523 ... 30, 99, 127, 197

Malaysian Industrial Redevelopment Authority v Jeyasingham [1998] ICR 307 ... 197

Maritime and Territorial Dispute Case (Qatar v Bahrain) ... 75, 76

Maritime Delimitation and Territorial Questions Case (Qatar v Bahrain) 1994 ICJ Rep 112 ... 65, 95, 303, 304

Maritime Delimitation and Territorial Questions between Qatar and Bahrain (Qatar v Bahrain) (2001) ... 227

Maritime Delimitation in the Area between Greenland ... 227, 229

Maritime Delimitation in the Black Sea (Romania v Ukraine) Case (2009) ... 223, 227, 234, 235

Mavrommatis Palestine Concessions Case (Jurisdiction) (1924) PCIJ Ser. A No. 2 ... 268, 305

Mavrommatis Palestine Concessions Case (1925) PCIJ Ser. A No. 5 ... 44

McElhinney v Ireland (2001) ... 194, 208

McElhinney v Williams and Her Majesty's Secretary of State for Northern Ireland (1995) ... 192

McKerr, Re [2004] UKHL 12 ... 92, 94, 99, 104

Mellenger v New Brunswick Development
Corp [1971] 1 WLR 604 ... 202
Mergé Claim (1955) 22 ILR 443 ... 270
Military Affairs Office of the Embassy of the
State of Kuwait v Caramba-Coker
(2003) ... 198
Military and Paramilitary Activities in and
against Nicaragua Case (Nicaragua v USA)
(Merits) 1986 ICJ Rep 14 ... 253, 260
Minquiers and Ecrehos Case (France v UK)
1953 ICJ Rep 47 ... 165, 169, 304
Molyneaux, ex parte [1986] 1 WLR
331 ... 184
Monetary Gold Removed from Rome Case
(Preliminary Question) 1954 ICJ Rep 19
... 302
Mortensen v Peters (1906) 8 F (J) 93 ... 109
MV Saiga (No. 1) ... 246
MV Saiga (No. 2) Case (St Vincent and the
Grenadines v Guinea) (1999) 38 ILM 1323
... 224–6, 242

Namibia Case 1971 ICJ Rep 16 ... 82, 316
Naulilaa Case (1928) 2 RIAA 1012 ... 335
Nauru v Australia (Jurisdiction) 1992 ICJ
Rep 240 ... 25, 26, 47, 302
Neer Claim (1926) 4 RIAA 60 ... 256, 267
New Zealand Banking Group v Australia
(1990) 39 ICLQ 950 ... 192, 198, 199
Nicaragua v Honduras (Jurisdiction and
Admissibility) 1988 ICJ Rep 69 ... 301,
305
Nicaragua v USA 1984 ICJ Rep 392 ... 58,
59, 300
Nicaragua v USA 1986 ICJ Rep 14 ... 25, 26,
29, 32, 33, 37, 39, 40, 42, 43, 46, 50, 79,
262, 303, 307, 309, 311, 314, 321, 329–33
North American Dredging Company Case
(US v Mexico) (1926) 4 RIAA 26 ... 274
North Atlantic Fisheries Arbitration (US v
Great Britain) (1910) 11 RIAA 167 ... 174
North Sea Continental Shelf Cases 1969 ICJ
Rep 3 ... 30, 32, 34, 36, 228, 231, 232
Northern Cameroons Case 1963 ICJ
Rep 15 ... 298
Norwegian Fisheries Case ... 38
Norwegian Loans Case (France v Norway)
1957 ICJ Rep 9 ... 308, 311
Nottebohm Case 1955 ICJ Rep 4 ... 47, 96,
269, 270
Noyes Claim (US v Panama) (1933) 6 RIAA
308 ... 261, 263
Nuclear Test Case (New Zealand v France)
1995 ICJ Rep 288 ... 45, 60, 241, 300
Nuclear Test Cases (Australia v France, New
Zealand v France) 1974 ICJ Rep 253 ... 59,
60, 241, 300

Nuclear Test Cases (Interim Protection)
1973 ICJ Rep 99 ... 300
Nulyarimma v Thompson (2000) 39
ILM 20 ... 103, 129

Obligation to Arbitrate on UN Headquarters
Agreement Case 1988 ICJ Rep 12 ... 131
Oil Platforms (Islamic Republic of Iran v
United States of America) Case
(2003) ... 330–2, 335, 337

Pakistan v India (2000) ... 307, 312
Palestinian Wall Advisory Opinion (2004
ICJ Rep para. 88) ... 64, 96, 121, 124, 126,
127, 129, 168, 171–3, 265, 298, 307, 312,
316–19, 324, 329, 330, 339, 340, 347, 348
Panevezys Railway Case (Estonia v
Lithuania) (1939) PCIJ Ser. A/B
No. 76 ... 273
Paquete Habana, The (1900) 175
US 677 ... 48, 49, 94
Paraguay v USA (Provisional Measures)
(1998) 37 ILM 810 ... 258
Parlement Belge (1879) 4 PD 129 ... 101
Passage through the Great Belt Case
(Finland v Denmark) Provisional
Measures 1992 ICJ Rep 3 ... 300
Pedra Branca/Pulau Batu Puteh Case ... 164
Pepper v Hart [1992] 3 WLR 1033 ... 105
Philippine Admiral, The v Wallem Shipping
(Hong Kong) [1977] AC 373 ... 196
Pinochet see R v Bow Street Metropolitan
Stipendiary Magistrate, ex parte Pinochet
(No. 3)
Piracy Jure Gentium, Re [1934]
AC 586 ... 154
Pocket Kings Ltd v Safenames Ltd
(2009) ... 202
Polish Postal Service Case (1925) PCIJ Ser. B
No. 11 ... 73
Prevention of Genocide Case (1993) ... 300,
301, 303
Prevention of Genocide Case (Bosnia-
Herzegovina v Yugoslavia (Serbia and
Montenegro)) (1993) 32 ILM 888) ... 66
Prevention of Genocide Case 1993 ... 305,
316
Pritchard v Gloucestershire CPS
(2004) ... 109
Privileges and Immunities Case ... 127
Propend Finance v Singh (1999) ... 202
Prosecutor v Thomas Lubanga Dyilo
(2012) ... 9, 128
Public Service Alliance of Canada
Case ... 190
Pulau Islands Case (Indonesia v Malaysia)
(2002) ... 64, 74–7, 169, 171

Pulau Ligitan and Pulau Sipadan
Case ... 164, 168

Pulp Mills on the River Uruguay Case
(Uruguay v Argentina) (2007) ... 300, 301

Qatar v Bahrain 2001 ICJ Rep
para 174 ... 58, 220, 223, 244, 303

Questions relating to the Obligation to
Prosecute or Extradite Case (Belgium v
Senegal) 2009 ... 151, 152, 159

Questions relating to the Obligation to
Prosecute or Extradite (Belgium v Senegal)
(ICJ 2012) ... 30, 40, 64, 65, 68, 95, 96,
254, 255

R (on the application of Hilal Abdul-Razzaq
Ali Al-Jedda) v Secretary of State for
Defence [2006] 3 WLR 954 ... 90

R (on the application of HRH Sultan of
Pahang) v Secretary of State for the Home
Department [2011] EWCA
Civ 616 ... 112, 202, 206

R (on the application of North Cyprus
Tourism Centre Ltd) v Transport For
London (2005) UKHRR 1231 ... 137, 144

R (on the application of) Kibris Türk Hava
Yollari v Secretary of State for Transport
(2010) ... 112, 137, 141, 145

R v Abu Hamza [2006] EWCA Crim 2918
... 156

R v Bow Street Metropolitan Stipendiary
Magistrate, ex parte Pinochet (No. 3)
[1999] 2 All ER 97 ... 4, 5, 48, 91, 103,
110, 111, 186, 189, 193, 206, 207

R v Charrington (unreported) ... 161

R v CPS, ex parte Pepushi (11 May
2004) ... 106

R v Governor of Belmarsh Prison, ex parte
Martin [1995] 2 All ER 548, CA ... 152,
153

R v Horseferry Magistrates' Court, ex parte
Bennett [1993] 3 All ER 138 ... 160

R v IRC, ex parte Camacq Corp [1990] 1 All
ER 173 ... 206

R v Jones [2006] UKHL 16; [2006] 2 WLR
772 ... 5, 37, 90, 93, 99, 100, 103, 104,
108, 110

R v Keyn (1876) 2 Exch D 63 ... 90, 109

R v Lyons [2002] UKHL 44 ... 100, 106, 107

R v Mills (1995) 44 ICLQ 949 ... 242

R v Mullen [1999] 3 All ER 777 ... 160

R v Sansom [1991] 2 All ER 145 ... 156

R v Secretary of State for Foreign and
Commonwealth Affairs, ex parte Samuel
The Times, 17 August 1989 ... 90, 113, 214

R v Secretary of State for Foreign and
Commonwealth Affairs, ex parte Trawnik,
The Times, 20 February 1986 ... 112

R v Secretary of State for Transport, ex parte
Factortame (No. 2) [1990] 3
WLR 818 ... 97, 106

R v Staines Magistrates' Court, ex parte
Westfallen [1998] 4 All ER 2101 ... 160, 161

R v The Commissioners for the Inland
Revenue, ex parte Resat Caglar ... 137

R v The Minister of Agriculture, Fisheries &
Food, ex parte S.P. Anastasiou (Pissouri)
and Others (not reported) ... 143

R (Abbasi) v Secretary of State for Foreign
and Commonwealth Affairs and Secretary
of State for the Home Department
[2003] ... 90, 184, 268

R (European Roma Rights Centre and
others) v Immigration Officer at Prague
Airport ... 104, 105

R (on the application of Hilal Abdul-Razzaq
Ali Al-Jedda) v Secretary of State for
Defence [2006] 3 WLR 954 ... 90

R (on the application of HRH Sultan of
Pahang) v Secretary of State for the Home
Department [2011] EWCA
Civ 616 ... 112, 202, 206

R (on the application of North Cyprus
Tourism Centre Ltd) v Transport For
London (2005) UKHRR 1231 ... 137, 144

R (on the application of) Kibris Türk Hava
Yollari v Secretary of State for Transport
(2010) ... 112, 137, 141, 145

Rafidian Bank [1992] BCLC 301, Re ... 200,
203–5

Rahimtoola v Nizam of Hyderabad [1958]
AC 379 ... 185

Rainbow Warrior Arbitration (1987) 26 ILM
1346 ... 258

Rainbow Warrior Arbitration (New Zealand
v France) 82 ILR 499 ... 64, 82–4, 265

Rann of Kutch Arbitration (India v Pakistan)
(1968) 50 ILR 2 ... 44

Reparations Case 1949 ICJ Rep 174 ... 74,
126

Reparations for Injuries Suffered in the
Service of the United Nations Case 1949
ICJ Rep 174 ... 116

Republic of Ecuador v The United States
(2011) ... 292

Request for interpretation of the Judgment
of 15 June 1962 in the case concerning
the Temple of Preah Vihear (Cambodia v
Thailand) (Cambodia v Thailand)
(2011) ... 301, 312

Resat Calgar Case ... 141

Responsibilities and obligations of States
sponsoring persons and entities with
respect to activities in the
Area (2011) ... 240

Rights of Passage Case (Portugal v India)
1960 ICJ Rep 6 ... 35, 174

Rights of Passage over Indian Territory Case (Preliminary Objections) 1957 ICJ Rep 125 ... 306–8

Rights of US Nationals in Morocco Case (US v France) 1952 ICJ Rep 176 ... 126

Rio Martin Case 2 RIAA 615 ... 65

River Meuse Case (Netherlands v Belgium) (1937) PCIJ Ser. A/B No. 70 ... 44

River Oder Case (1929) PCIJ Ser. A No. 23 ... 77

Roberts Claim (1926) 4 RIAA 77 ... 256, 266

Salem Case (Egypt v US) (1932) 2 RIAA 1161 ... 270

Salomon v Commissioners of Customs and Excise [1967] 2 QB 116 ... 106

Sambaggio Case (Italy v Venezuela) (1903) 10 RIAA 499 ... 261

Schering v Iran (1984) 5 Iran–US CTR 361 ... 259

Schooner Exchange v McFaddon (1812) 7 Cranch 116 ... 150, 185

Scotia, The (1871) 14 Wallace 170 ... 111

Senegal/Guinea-Bissau Arbitral Award Case (1992) 31 ILM 32 ... 294

Sengupta v Republic of India [1983] ICR 221 ... 192, 200

Serbian Loans Case (1929) PCIJ Ser. A No. 20 ... 97

SerVaas Incorporated (Appellant) v Rafidian Bank and others (Respondents) (2012) ... 201, 205

Shahin Shane Ebrahim v Iran (1995) Iran–US Claims Tribunal ... 275, 277–9

Short v Iran (1987) 16 Iran–US CTR 76 ... 261

Sierra Leone Telecommunications v Barclays Bank plc [1998] 2 All ER 821 ... 113, 139

Somalia (Republic) v Woodhouse Drake & Carey (Suisse) SA [1993] 1 All ER 371 ... 113, 132, 138, 139

South West Africa Cases of 1962 and 1966 (Preliminary Objections) 1962 ICJ Rep 319; (Second Phase) 1966 ICJ Rep 6 ... 46

Southern Pacific Properties (Middle East) Ltd v Arab Republic of Egypt (1993) 32 ILM 933 ... 258, 278, 280, 284, 293

South-West Africa Cases (Preliminary Objections) 1962 ICJ Rep 319 ... 298

Sovereignty over Pedra Branca/Pulau Batu Puteh, Middle Rocks and South Ledge (Malaysia/Singapore) Case 2008 ... 162, 163, 166, 170

Sovereignty over Pulau Ligitan and Pulau Sipadan Case (Indonesia v Malaysia) 2002 ICJ Rep ... 304

Spanish Zone of Morocco Claims Case (1925) 2 RIAA 615 ... 49

St Pierre and Miquelon Case (Canada/France) ... 223

Standard Chartered Bank v International Tin Council [1987] 1 WLR 641 ... 214

Starrett Housing Corp v Iran, Interlocutory Proceedings, (1984) 23 ILM 1090 ... 275

Starrett Housing v Iran 4 Iran–US CTR 122 ... 279

State v Ebrahim (1991) 31 ILM 888 ... 160, 341

Svenska Petroleum v Lithuania (2006) ... 197, 201

Taba Area Boundary Arbitration (Egypt v Israel) (1988) 27 ILM 1421 ... 165

Tadic Case 1999 ILM 1518 ... 260, 262

Temple of Preah Vihear Case 1962 ICJ Rep 6 ... 44, 80, 263

Territorial and Maritime Dispute between Nicaragua and Honduras in the Caribbean Sea (Nicaragua v Honduras) (2006) ... 227

Territorial and Maritime Dispute between Nicaragua and Honduras in the Caribbean Sea (Nicaragua v Honduras) (2007) ... 169, 170, 244

Territorial Dispute Case (Libya v Chad) 1994 ICJ Rep 6 ... 47, 64, 74, 77, 305

Texaco v Libya (1977) 53 ILR 389 ... 25, 61, 95, 97, 130, 263, 266, 279, 281, 282, 286

Texas v White 74 US 700, 1868 ... 141

Thai Europe Tapioca Service Ltd v Government of Pakistan [1975] 3 All ER 961 ... 109, 185

Thakrar v Secretary of State for the Home Dept [1974] QB 684 ... 109

Threat or Use of Nuclear Weapons Case ... 47, 51

Timberlane Lumber Co. v Bank of America ... 157

Tin Council Cases ... 99, 101–4, 107, 108

Tinoco Arbitration (Great Britain v Costa Rica) (1923) 1 RIAA 369 ... 132, 293

Trademark Case ... 134

Trendtex Trading Corp. v Central Bank of Nigeria [1977] QB 529; [1977] 1 All ER 881 ... 109, 189, 190, 196, 204

Triquet v Bath (1746) 3 Burr 1478 ... 109, 110

Tunisia v Libya 1982 ICJ Rep 18 ... 30, 47, 226, 232, 244, 314

United States Diplomatic and Consular Staff in Tehran Case (United States v Iran) 1980 ICJ Rep 3 ... 315

United States v Alvarez-Machain (1992) 31 ILM 902 ... 160

United States v The Public Service Alliance of
Canada (1993) 32 ILM 1 ... 189, 192, 200

United States v Yousef (2003) ... 155

US Diplomatic and Consular Staff in Tehran
Case (US v Iran Hostages Case) 1980 ICJ
Rep 3 ... 209, 314

US Diplomatic and Consular Staff in Tehran
Cases (US v Iran) 1979 ICJ Rep 7 ... 300

US Diplomatic and Consular Staff in Tehran
Case (US v Iran) 1980 ICJ Rep 3 ... 43,
209, 211, 213, 314

US v Alvarez-Machain (1992) 31 ILM
902 ... 73, 341

US v Neil (2002) ... 159

US v Yunis (1988) 681 F.Supp 896 ... 155, 159

Victory Transport Inc v Comisaria General
De Abastecimientos y Transpertos, 35 ILR
110 (1963) ... 189, 190

Volga Case (Russian Federation v Australia)
(2002) ... 225

West Rand Central Gold Mining Co. v R
[1905] 2 KB 391 ... 109

Western Sahara Case 1975 ICJ
Rep 12 ... 119, 171, 317, 318

Westland Helicopters Ltd v Arab
Organisation for Industrialisation [1995]
2 All ER 387 ... 101–4, 110, 145

Westminster CC v Islamic Republic of Iran
[1986] 3 All ER 284 ... 205, 211

Wilhelm Finance Inc v Ente Administrator
Del Astillero Rio Santiago (2009) ... 202,
204, 205

Wimbledon Case (1923) PCIJ Ser. A
No. 1 ... 46, 174

Yeager v Iran (1987) 17 Iran–US CTR 92 ...
260

Youmans Claim (US v Mexico) (1926) 4
RIAA 110 ... 258, 266

Young, James and Webster Case (1983) 5
EHRR 201 ... 367

Zafiro Case (Great Britain v US) (1925) 6
RIAA 160 ... 260

Zamora, The [1916] 2 AC 77 ... 111

TABLE OF TREATIES

Treaties

African Charter on Human and Peoples' Rights 1981
  Art 1 ... 370
  Art 18 ... 370
  Arts 19–24 ... 370
  Art 27 ... 370
  Art 28 ... 370
  Art 29 ... 370
Agreement on the Future of Hong Kong 1984 ... 28
Agreement Governing the Activities of States on the Moon and other Celestial Bodies 1979 ... 176
Agreement for the Prosecution and Punishment of Major War Criminals 1945 ... 365
American Convention on Human Rights 1969
  Art 45 ... 369
  Art 62 ... 369
Antarctic Treaty 1959 ... 28, 81, 176
  Art 4 ... 177
  Art 7 ... 177
Brussels Convention on the Unification of certain rules relating to the Immunity of State Owned Vessels 1926 ... 196
Charter of Economic Rights and Duties of States 1974 ... 51, 277
Chicago Convention on International Civil Aviation 1944, Art 6 ... 178
Chicago International Air Services Transit Agreement 1944 ... 178
Convention on the Continental Shelf 1958 ... 41
Convention on the Contract for the International Carriage of Goods by Road 1956 (Warsaw Convention) ... 104
Convention on the Elimination of All Forms of Discrimination Against Women 1979 ... 365
Convention between Great Britain and the Netherlands 1891 ... 78
Convention against Illicit Traffic in Narcotic Drugs and Psychotropic Substances 1988 ... 242
Convention on International Civil Aviation 1944 ... 112
  Art 17 ... 179
  Art 18 ... 179

Convention on the Prevention and Punishment of the Crime of Genocide 1948 ... 31, 365
  Art IX ... 305
Convention on the Privileges and Immunities of the United Nations 1946 ... 214
Convention on the Regulation of Antarctic Mineral Resource Activities 1988 ... 177
Convention on the Settlement of Investment Disputes 1964 ... 130
Convention on the Suppression and Punishment of the Crime of Apartheid 1973 ... 365
Convention Against Torture 1984 ... 103, 365
Convention on Treaties between International Organisations etc. 1986 ... 63
Convention on Valuation of Goods for Customs Services 1950 ... 105
Double Taxation Agreement between the UK and Eire 1926 ... 107
Environmental Protection Protocol ... 177, 178
European Convention on Human Rights 1950 ... 95, 108, 129, 365–8
  Art 1 ... 366
  Arts 1–12 ... 366
  Art 4(1) ... 366
  Art 5(3) ... 366
  Art 6 ... 207, 208
  Art 15 ... 366
  Arts 27–30 ... 368
  Art 35 ... 368
  Art 43 ... 368
  Art 46 ... 368
  Art 47 ... 368
  Art 50 ... 367
  Protocol 10 ... 366
  Protocol 11 ... 366, 367
  Protocol 14 ... 368
European Convention for the Peaceful Settlement of Disputes 1957 ... 305
European Convention on State Immunity 1972 ... 196, 207
European Social Charter 1961 ... 369
Four Powers Treaty for the Governance of Berlin 1946 ... 125

General Act for the Pacific Settlement of
  Disputes 1928 ... 291
General Convention on the Privileges and
  Immunities of the Specialised Agencies of
  the UN 1947, s 30 ... 317
General Treaty for the Renunciation of War
  1928 (Kellogg–Briand Pact) ... 168
  Art 1 ... 323
Geneva Conventions 1949 ... 96, 365
  Protocol 1977 ... 365
Geneva Convention on the Continental
  Shelf 1958 ... 218, 219, 228–234
  Art 1 ... 229
  Art 2 ... 228
  Art 2(2) ... 228
  Art 3 ... 228
  Art 6 ... 231, 244
Geneva Convention on the Fishing and
  Conservation of Living Resources of the
  High Seas 1958 ... 218, 219
  Art 1 ... 241
  Art 2 ... 241
  Art 6 ... 241
  Art 11 ... 242
  Art 22 ... 242
  Art 23 ... 242
  Art 24 ... 245
  Art 25 ... 245
  Art 145 ... 241
Geneva Convention on the Protection of
  Victims of International Armed Conflicts
  Protocol 1 ... 57
Geneva Convention on the Territorial Sea
  and Contiguous Zone 1958 ... 218, 219
  Art 1 ... 220
  Art 4 ... 223
  Art 7 ... 245
  Art 10 ... 243
  Art 12 ... 223
  Art 14 ... 221
  Art 14(4) ... 221
  Art 16(4) ... 221, 242
  Art 19 ... 220
  Art 20 ... 220
  Art 24 ... 224
Hague Convention for the Pacific
  Settlement of Disputes 1899 ... 291
Hague Convention for the Pacific
  Settlement of Disputes 1907 ... 291
Hague Convention for the Suppression of
  Unlawful Seizure of Aircraft 1970,
  Art 7 ... 179
International Air Transport Agreement
  1944 ... 312

International Convention on Civil Liability
  for Oil Pollution Damage 1969 ... 246
International Convention for the
  Prevention of Pollution of the Sea by Oil
  1954 ... 245
International Convention for the
  Prevention of Pollution from Ships
  1973 ... 245
International Convention for the Safety of
  Life at Sea 1974 ... 220
International Convention on the
  Elimination of All Forms of Racial
  Discrimination 1966 ... 364
  Art 14 ... 365
International Convention for the
  Settlement of Investment Disputes
  1964 ... 283, 293
International Covenant on Civil and
  Political Rights 1966 ... 28, 69, 129, 358,
  363, 366
  Art 2 ... 52
  Art 2(2) ... 360
  Art 2(3) ... 360
  Art 4 ... 360
  Art 6 ... 360
  Art 7 ... 360
  Art 8 ... 360
  Art 9 ... 360
  Art 15 ... 360
  Art 16 ... 360
  Art 18 ... 360
  Art 21 ... 360
  Art 27 ... 360
  Art 40 ... 360
  Art 41 ... 361
Optional Protocol ... 361
Second Optional Protocol 1989 ... 362
International Covenant Economic, Social
  and Cultural Rights 1966 ... 358, 362
  Art 2 ... 52, 363
  Art 3 ... 363
Optional Protocol 2008 ... 363
Italian Peace Treaty 1947 ... 270
Law of the Sea Convention 1982 ... 31, 41,
  52, 66, 81, 217–49, 287, 288, 291
  Art 1(1) ... 238
Pt II The territorial sea and contiguous
  zone ... 249
  Art 2 ... 220, 249
  Art 3 ... 222
  Art 5 ... 249
  Art 7 ... 223, 249
  Art 10 ... 245, 249
  Art 15 ... 223, 249
  Art 17 ... 221, 249

Art 18 ... 249
Art 18(2) ... 221
Art 19 ... 221, 249
Art 27 ... 221, 249
Art 28 ... 221
Art 33 ... 224, 249
Pt III Straits used for international navigation ... 249
Art 36 ... 243, 249
Art 37 ... 249
Art 38 ... 243, 249
Art 38(2) ... 243
Art 42 ... 243
Art 44 ... 243, 249
Art 45 ... 221, 242
Pt IV Archipelagic states ... 249
Art 46 ... 243, 249
Art 47 ... 249
Art 49 ... 249
Art 52 ... 243
Art 53 ... 249
Art 54 ... 243
Pt V Exclusive Economic Zone ... 30, 249
Art 56 ... 225, 249
Art 56(3) ... 227, 235
Art 57 ... 249
Art 58 ... 226, 249
Art 58(3) ... 226
Art 61 ... 225, 249
Art 62 ... 249
Art 62(2) ... 225
Art 73 ... 225
Art 74 ... 226, 236, 249
Pt VI The Continental Shelf ... 228, 249
Art 76 ... 229, 249
Art 76(1) ... 229, 230
Art 76(5) ... 229
Art 77 ... 228, 249
Art 77(3) ... 228
Art 78 ... 228, 249
Art 82 ... 230, 249
Art 83 ... 233, 236, 249
Art 83(1) ... 233
Pt VII High seas ... 249
Art 86 ... 241, 250
Art 87 ... 241, 250
Art 91 ... 269
Art 92 ... 241, 250
Art 97 ... 242
Art 100 ... 241
Art 105 ... 250
Art 109 ... 241, 250

Art 110 ... 242, 250
Art 111 ... 242, 250
Pt VIII Islands ... 250
Art 121 ... 244, 250
Art 121(3) ... 244
Art 135 ... 239
Pt XI Deep sea bed (The Area) ... 218, 219, 237, 250
Art 136 ... 239, 240, 250
Art 137 ... 239, 240, 250
Art 140 ... 239, 240, 250
Art 141 ... 240, 250
Arts 143–145 ... 239
Art 144 ... 250
Art 145 ... 250
Pt XII Protection of marine environment ... 245, 250
Arts 186–191 ... 246
Pt XV Settlement of disputes ... 246
Art 220 ... 241
Art 221 ... 242
Pt XVIII Final provisions ... 250
Art 306 ... 67, 250
Art 308 ... 67, 250
Art 311 ... 250
Arts 311–316 ... 80
Montevideo Convention on Rights and Duties of States 1933 ... 122, 123, 136, 172
Art 1 ... 119, 147
Art 9 ... 267
Montreal Convention for the Suppression of Unlawful Acts against the Safety of International Civil Aviation 1971 ... 179
Nuclear Test Ban Treaty 1963 ... 241
Permanent Neutrality and Operation of Panama Canal Treaty 1978 ... 78
Refugee Convention 1951 ... 104–6
Art 32 ... 106
Single European Act ... 57
Statute of the International Court of Justice
Ch IV ... 316
Art 2 ... 295
Art 26 ... 295
Art 31 ... 295
Art 34 ... 295
Art 35(1) ... 296
Art 35(2) ... 296, 297, 306
Art 36 ... 309, 310
Art 36(1) ... 303–6
Art 36(2) ... 58, 88, 306, 320
Art 36(5) ... 311, 312

Art 36(6) ... 308

Art 37 ... 312

Art 38 ... 24–7, 35, 43, 47–9, 54

Art 38(1)(a)–(d) ... 24

Art 38(1) ... 26, 44

Art 38(1)(c) ... 42, 43, 45, 94

Art 38(1)(d) ... 94

Art 38(2) ... 26, 44

Art 41 ... 299

Art 59 ... 45–7, 302

Art 60 ... 312

Art 62 ... 302, 312, 313

Art 63 ... 302, 312

Statute of the International Criminal Court 1998 ... 28

Art 5 ... 129, 155

Art 17 ... 156

Tokyo Convention on Offences and Certain Other Acts Committed on Board Aircraft 1963 ... 179

Treaty on European Union 1992 (Maastricht Treaty) ... 369

Treaty between Hungary and Czechoslovakia 1977 ... 31

Treaty of Paris ... 167

Treaty on Principles Governing the Activities of States in the Exploration of Outer Space, including the Moon and Other Celestial Bodies 1966 ... 176

UK/China Bilateral Treaty on Hong Kong 1984 ... 18, 55, 57

UK/France Territorial Sea Boundary Agreement 1988 ... 223

UK/India Agreement 1994 ... 277, 278

UK/Ireland Continental Shelf Boundary Agreement 1988 ... 55

UK/Latvia Agreement 1993 ... 280

UK/Netherlands Agreement 1999 ... 149

UK/Peru Agreement 1994 ... 276, 277, 278

UK/Ukraine Agreement 1993 ... 277, 278

UN Charter 1945 ... 37, 78

Ch VI ... 289

Ch VII ... 7, 8, 51, 95

Art 1 ... 324

Art 2(1) ... 183, 185

Art 2(3) ... 286, 320

Art 2(4) ... 73, 322, 324–7, 334–8, 340, 341, 349, 351, 353

Art 2(7) ... 150, 356

Art 7 ... 339

Art 12(1) ... 10

Arts 11–14 ... 347

Art 14 ... 289

Art 24 ... 347

Art 33 ... 286

Art 36(3) ... 290

Art 39 ... 7, 290, 342–4

Art 41 ... 342, 343

Art 42 ... 342–4

Art 43 ... 344

Art 51 ... 325–9, 332, 345, 349, 351, 353

Art 53 ... 348, 349, 353

Art 55 ... 357

Art 56 ... 357

Art 96 ... 297, 316

Art 96(1) ... 318

Art 102 ... 57, 58

Art 103 ... 69, 349

Art 105 ... 126

Art 107 ... 325

Art 109 ... 80

UN Convention on Jurisdictional Immunities of States and their Property 2004 ... 182, 187

Art 2 ... 189, 194

Art 2(1) ... 195

Art 2(3) ... 195

Art 5 ... 195

Arts 10–12 ... 194

Art 18 ... 194

Art 19 ... 194

UN Headquarters Agreement between the United Nations and the United States 1947 ... 56

Unification Treaty 1990 ... 125

Universal Declaration of Human Rights 1948 ... 358, 359

Vienna Convention on Consular Relations 1963 ... 209, 213

Art 35(3) ... 212

Optional Protocol ... 305

Vienna Convention on Diplomatic Relations 1961 ... 28, 29, 55, 92, 104, 209

Art 1 ... 210, 211

Art 22 ... 211

Arts 22–24 ... 214

Art 24 ... 211

Art 26 ... 211

Art 27 ... 211, 212

Art 27(4) ... 211

Arts 27–40 ... 214

Art 29 ... 210

Art 30 ... 211

Art 31 ... 210

Art 32 ... 213

Art 37 ... 211

Art 41 ... 212

Art 45 ... 211, 214
Vienna Convention on the Law of Treaties
  1969 ... 29, 56, 62–85
Pt II ... 64, 68
Art 1 ... 62
Art 2 ... 56, 62
Art 2(1) ... 88
Art 2(1)(d) ... 69
Art 3 ... 63, 72
Art 3(c) ... 63
Art 4 ... 62, 63
Art 6 ... 64
Art 7 ... 66
Art 7(2) ... 66
Art 8 ... 64, 66
Art 11 ... 66
Art 12 ... 66
Arts 12–17 ... 66
Art 14 ... 66
Art 15 ... 67
Art 18 ... 67
Art 19 ... 70, 72
Arts 19–23 ... 64
Art 20(1) ... 70
Art 20(2) ... 70
Art 20(3) ... 71
Art 20(4) ... 70, 71
Art 20(4)(b) ... 72
Art 21 ... 71
Art 21(3) ... 72
Art 24 ... 67
Art 24(2) ... 67
Art 26 ... 64, 68
Art 27 ... 64, 68, 95
Art 30(1) ... 79

Art 30(3) ... 79
Art 30(4)(b) ... 79
Art 31 ... 29, 47, 64, 74–6, 88
Art 31(4) ... 76
Art 32 ... 74, 76, 77, 88, 105
Art 34 ... 77
Art 35 ... 78
Art 36 ... 78
Art 40 ... 64, 81
Art 41 ... 64, 79
Art 43 ... 63
Art 46 ... 80, 95
Art 46(2) ... 65
Art 48 ... 80
Art 49 ... 80
Art 50 ... 80
Art 51 ... 80
Art 52 ... 80, 168
Art 53 ... 41, 42, 79, 81, 89
Art 55 ... 81
Art 57 ... 81
Art 59 ... 79, 89
Art 60 ... 64, 79, 81, 82, 84
Art 60(4) ... 82, 84
Art 61 ... 81–4
Art 62 ... 81, 84
Art 64 ... 79, 81, 89
Art 69 ... 41
Art 73 ... 63, 86
Art 85 ... 87
Vienna Convention on State Succession in
  Respect of Treaties 1978 ... 85, 86
Art 11 ... 78, 86
Art 12 ... 78, 86
Art 16 ... 86

TABLE OF OTHER DOCUMENTS

Agreement Governing the Activities of States on the Moon and other Celestial Bodies ... 176

Agreement for the Prosecution and Punishment of Major War Criminals 1945 ... 365

Agreement Relating to the Implementation of Part XI of the United Nations Convention on the Law of the Sea 1994

Art 1 ... 251

Art 2 ... 251

Art 7 ... 251

s 1 ... 239, 251

s 2 ... 239, 251

s 3 ... 251

s 4 ... 251

s 5 ... 239, 251

s 6 ... 251

s 7 ... 251

s 8 ... 239, 251

s 9 ... 238, 251

Brezhnev Doctrine 1989 ... 341

Chicago International Air Services Transit Agreement 1944 ... 178

Commonwealth Statement on Apartheid in Sport 1977 (Gleneagles Agreement) ... 51

Conference on Security and Cooperation in Europe 1975 (Helsinki Accords) ... 51, 52, 57

Covenant of the League of Nations 1919, Arts 10–16 ... 323

Declaration on the Establishment of the New International Economic Order 1974 ... 51

Declaration on the Granting of Independence to Colonial Peoples and the right of self-determination 1960 ... 51

Declaration on the Inadmissibility of Intervention in the Domestic Affairs of States 1965 ... 50

Definition of Aggression 1974 ... 50

Final Act of the Conference on Security and Co-operation in Europe 1975 (the Helsinki Final Act of the CSCE) ... 369

General Assembly Resolutions ... GA Res 217A (1948) ... 358

GA Res 377 (V) ... 347

GA Res XVIII (1962) ... 176, 278

GA Res 42/22 (1987) ... 324

GA Res 45/90 ... 21

GA Res 1803 (XVII) ... 275

GA Res 2131 (XX) (1965) ... 324, 333

GA Res 2574D (XXIV) ... 237

GA Res 2625 (XXV) ... 324, 335, 339

GA Res 2749 (XXV) ... 237

GA Res 3201 (S–VI) ... 276

GA Res 3281 (XXIX) ... 276

GA Res 3314 (XXIX) ... 322, 324

International Law Commission (ILC) Draft Articles on the Diplomatic Courier and the Diplomatic Bag

Art 28 ... 212

Art 28(2) ... 212

Draft Articles on Jurisdictional Immunities ... 187, 189, 194

Draft Articles on State Responsibility ... 84, 182, 252

Art 1 ... 254

Art 2 ... 255

Art 3 ... 254, 255

Art 4 ... 47, 253, 259

Arts 4–11 ... 258

Art 7 ... 259

Art 8 ... 47, 253

Art 10 ... 261

Art 12 ... 254

Art 13 ... 255

Art 16 ... 47, 253, 254

Arts 20–26 ... 264, 265

Art 21 ... 265

Art 22 ... 273

Art 23 ... 265

Art 24 ... 265

Art 25 ... 265

Art 28 ... 254

Art 29 ... 256, 264

Art 30 ... 256, 264

Art 31 ... 254, 263

Art 32 ... 265

Art 33 ... 256

Art 35 ... 263

Art 38 ... 263

Art 40 ... 253

Art 40(2) ... 257

Art 41 ... 253, 257

Art 44 ... 272, 273

Art 48 ... 257

Arts 49–52 ... 264

Art 54 ... 257

Art 58 ... 253, 257
Harvard Research Draft on State
    Responsibility 1929 ... 151, 156, 158
Art 9 ... 266
Security Council Resolutions
    SC Res 232 (1966) ... 343
    SC Res 235 (1968) ... 343
    SC Res 418 (1977) ... 343, 360
    SC Res 541 (1983) ... 118
    SC Res 550 (1984) ... 118
    SC Res 678 (1990) ... 344
    SC Res 687 (1991) ... 254
    SC Res 748 (1992) ... 10
    SC Res 787 (1992) ... 348
    SC Res 827 (1993) ... 155

SC Res 918 (1994) ... 343
SC Res 955 (1994) ... 155
SC Res 1031 (1995) ... 344, 348
SC Res 1244 (1999) ... 52, 62
SC Res 1264 (1999) ... 344
SC Res 1304 (2000) ... 290, 298
SC Res 1390 (2002) ... 7
SC Res 1464 (2003) ... 348
SC Res 1528 (2004) ... 348
SC Res 1718 (2006) ... 7
SC Res 1973 (2011) ... 344, 349
Truman Proclamation 1945 ... 228
Vienna Declaration and Programme of
    Action 1993 ... 358, 370

TABLE OF STATUTES

UK

Antarctic Act 1994 ... 177, 178
Asylum and Immigration Appeals
Act 1993 ... 104
Aviation Security Act 1982 ... 179
Broadcasting Act 1990 ... 149, 156, 241
Carriage By Air Act 1961 ... 105
Carriage of Goods by Road Act 1965 ... 104
Civil Aviation (Amendment)
Act 1996 ... 153
Constitutional Reform and Governance Act
2010
s 20 ... 65
s 22 ... 65
Consular Relations Act 1968 ... 214
Criminal Justice Act 1993, ss 1–3 ... 153
Customs and Excise Act 1952 ... 105
Diplomatic and Consular Premises
Act 1987 ... 214
s 2(2) ... 90, 112
Diplomatic Privileges Act 1964 ... 95, 97,
104, 206, 214
s 7 ... 214
Sch 1 ... 214
European Communities Act 1972,
s 2 ... 106
Extradition Act 1989 ... 160
Family Law Act 1986
s 46 ... 144
s 49 ... 144
Finance (No. 2) Act 1955, s 4(2) ... 107
Foreign Compensation
Act 1950 ... 280
Foreign Compensation (Amendment) Act
1993 ... 280
Foreign Corporations
Act 1991 ... 143, 145
Hijacking Act 1971 ... 179
Human Rights Act 1998 ... 100, 107, 108,
355, 366
Immigration Act 1971 ... 109
Immigration and Asylum Act 1999 ... 105
s 31 ... 106
International Organisations Act 1968 ... 214
International Organisations Act 1981 ... 214
Merchant Shipping Act 1988 ... 97
Prevention of Terrorism Act 1984 ... 95
Prevention of Terrorism (Temporary
Provisions) Act 1984 ... 366

Protection of Trading Interests
Act 1980 ... 157
State Immunity Act 1978 ... 95, 189, 192,
194, 196
s 1 ... 197
s 2 ... 197
ss 2–11 ... 197, 204
s 3 ... 198, 199, 203, 206
s 3(3)(a)–(c) ... 198
s 3(3)(b) ... 199
s 3(3)(c) ... 199, 204, 206
ss 3–11 ... 202, 203
s 4 ... 199, 206
s 4(2)–(4) ... 200
s 5 ... 199, 200
s 6 ... 199, 200
s 10 ... 200
s 11 ... 200
s 12 ... 205
s 13(3) ... 201
s 13(4) ... 201
s 14 ... 199, 201–5, 216
s 14(1) ... 202
s 14(1)(a) ... 206
s 14(2) ... 204
s 14(2)(a) ... 203
s 14(2)(b) ... 203
s 15 ... 197
s 16(1) ... 205
s 16(1)(a) ... 200
s 16(2) ... 206
s 16(5) ... 206
s 18 ... 207
s 21 ... 112, 202
Territorial Sea Act 1987 ... 34, 222
Terrorism Act 2000
s 59 ... 153
s 62 ... 153
s 63 ... 153
United Nations Act 1946 ... 95
United Nations Arms Embargoes
(Amendment) (Rwanda) Order 1994 (SI
1994/1637) ... 343
War Crimes Act 1991 ... 111

Canada

State Immunity Act 1985 ... 192, 200

Germany
Basic Law, Art 25 ... 98

South Africa
Status of Ciskei Act 1981 ... 142, 143

USA
Anti-Apartheid Act 1988 ... 156

Cuban Liberty and Democratic Solidarity
 Act 1996 ... 157
International Anti-Trust Enforcement
 Assistance Act 1994 ... 158
Iran-Libya Sanctions Act 1996 ... 158

1

The nature of international law and the international system

In the following chapters, much will be said about the substance of international law, the method of its creation and the legal persons or 'subjects' who may be governed by it. The purpose of this first chapter is, however, to examine the very nature and quality of this subject called 'international law'. For as long as it has existed, international law has been derided or disregarded by many jurists and legal commentators, not always because of their own ideology or the political imperatives of the states of which they are nationals. They have questioned, first, the existence of *any* set of rules governing inter-state relations; second, its entitlement to be called 'law'; and, third, its effectiveness in controlling states and other international actors in 'real life' situations. In the first two decades of the twenty-first century, this theoretical rejection of the prescriptive quality of international law by some jurists may appear to have been borne out by the practice of states, groups and individuals who have engaged in internationally 'unlawful' action without even the remotest possibility of their conduct being checked by the international legal system. Whatever the legal merits of the US-led invasions of Iraq and Afghanistan, or the detention of 'terrorist' suspects without trial, or the unhindered resort to indiscriminate violence against civilians by groups based in existing states (with or without the support of another state's government), or the rejection by some of international minimum standards for the protection of the environment, the *perception* has been that international law is failing in one of its primary purposes – the maintenance of an ordered community where the weak are protected from arbitrary action by the strong. Some commentators have even suggested that the twenty-first century needs to accept a new reality where international law is accepted as a political and moral force, but not a *legal discipline*. Others would argue that the *content* of international law should change in order to be less prescriptive and more permissive, especially as the world faces challenges undreamt of when international law first began to be regarded by some as genuinely 'legal' in quality.

There is, of course, some truth in these criticisms, but let us not pretend that we are arguing that international law is a perfect legal system. It is not, but neither is the national legal system of any state. Historically, there have been successes and failures for the international legal system, as there are for the national legal systems of all states. The invasion of Kuwait by Iraq in 1990 and the situation in Libya in 2011 produced a significant and lawful response from the international community, but the United Nations failed in Bosnia, Somalia and Sudan and most recently in Syria in 2012. Likewise, the denial of procedural and substantive rights to those being held in detention by the USA at Guantanamo Bay during the Bush Presidency constituted a violation of the international law of human rights worthy of much criticism, but it pales beside the activities of Pol Pot in Cambodia in the late 1970s or the Rwandan genocide of the 1990s. On the other hand, these episodes can be contrasted with the successful UN-led efforts to bring self-determination and then independence to East Timor in 2002, the groundbreaking establishment and operation of the International Criminal Court responsible for prosecuting individuals for violation of fundamental international human rights, the protection of civilian populations during the Libyan civil war of 2011 and the continuing impact of the International Court of Justice in regulating states' use of the world's oceans and their natural resources. In other words, the story of international law and the international legal system, like so many other legal systems, is one of achievement and disappointment. So, in much the same way that we would not suggest that the law of the UK is somehow 'not law' because it is currently proving impossible to control cross-border internet crime, it does not necessarily follow that international law should be dismissed as a system of law because there are international actors that seem determined to ignore it.

The way in which the international system deals with these high-profile crises, and the many other less headline-grabbing incidents that occur on a daily basis whenever the members of the international community interact, goes to the heart of the debate about whether 'international law' exists as a *system of law*. However, to some extent, this debate about the nature of international law is unproductive and perhaps even irrelevant. The most obvious and most frequently used test for judging the 'existence' or 'success' of international law is to compare it with national legal systems such as that operating in the UK or Russia or anywhere at all. National law and its institutions – courts, legislative assemblies and enforcement agencies – are held up as *the* definitive model of what 'the law' and 'a legal system' should be like. Then, because international law sometimes falls short of these 'standards', it is argued that it cannot be regarded as 'true' law. Yet, it is not at all clear why *any* form of national law should be regarded as the appropriate standard for judging international law, especially since the rationale of the former is fundamentally different from that of the latter. National law is concerned primarily with the legal rights and duties of legal persons (individuals and companies) within a body politic – the state or similar territorial entity. This 'law' commonly is derived from a legal superior (e.g. a parliament or person with legislative power), recognised as legally competent by the society to whom the law is addressed (e.g. in a constitution), and in situations where the governing power has both the authority and practical competence to make and enforce that law. International law, at least as originally conceived, is different. It is concerned with the rights and duties of the states themselves. In their relations with each other, it is neither likely nor desirable that a relationship of *legal* superiority exists. States are legal equals and the legal system which regulates their actions between themselves must reflect this. Such a legal system must *facilitate* the interaction of these legal equals rather than control or compel them in a poor imitation of the control and compulsion that national law exerts over its subjects. Of course, as international law develops and matures it may come to encompass the legal relations of non-state entities, such as 'peoples', territories, international organisations (governmental and non-governmental), individuals or multinational companies, and it must then develop institutions and procedures which imitate in part the functions of the institutions of national legal systems. Indeed, the re-casting of international law as a system based less on state sovereignty and more on individual liberty is an aim of many contemporary international lawyers and there is no doubt that very great strides have been made in this direction in recent years. The establishment of the International Criminal Court is perhaps the most powerful evidence of this development. However, whatever we might hope for in the future for international law (see section 1.7), it is crucial to remember that at the very heart of the system lies a set of rules designed to regulate states' conduct with each other, and it is this central fact that makes detailed analogies with national law misleading and inappropriate.

1.1 The role of international law

In simple terms, international law comprises a system of rules and principles that govern the international relations between sovereign states and other institutional subjects of international law such as the United Nations, the Arab League and the African Union (formerly the Organisation of African Unity). As we shall see, that is not to say that international law is unconcerned with the rights and obligations of the individual or non-governmental organisation and, indeed, it may be becoming more concerned with them. Rather, it is that the rules of international law are created primarily by states, either for their own purposes or as a means of facilitating and controlling the activities of other actors on the international plane. Rules of international law cover almost every facet of inter-state and international activity. There are laws regulating the use of the sea, outer space and Antarctica. There are rules governing international telecommunications, postal services, the carriage of goods and passengers by air and the transfer of money. International law is a primary tool for the conduct of international trade. It is concerned with nationality, extradition, the use of armed force, human rights, protection of the environment, the dignity of the individual and the security of nations. In short, there is very little that is done in the international arena that is not regulated by international law and it can now govern some aspects of relations between distinct units *within* a sovereign state, such as the territories of federal Canada or the devolved regions of the UK. International law is the vital mechanism without which an interdependent world could not function. In this sense, international law *facilitates* the functioning of the international community, of which we are all a part and on which we all depend. However, that is not all. Modern international law also seeks to *control* states by inhibiting or directing their conduct both in their relations with other states (e.g. the law prohibiting the use of armed force to settle disputes) and in relation to individuals, both individuals of other states (e.g. issues concerning the exercise of criminal jurisdiction) and its own nationals (e.g. the law of human rights). It is the evolution of international law from a system that was concerned primarily with facilitating international cooperation among its subjects (states), to a system that is now much more engaged in the control of its subjects that is the pre-eminent feature of the history of international law in the last seventy-five years.

It is also important to realise that the practice of international law is intrinsically bound up with diplomacy, politics and the conduct of foreign relations. It is a fallacy to regard international law as the only facilitator or controller of state conduct. It cannot be this and, more significantly, it is not designed to do it. International law does not operate in a sterile environment and international legal rules may be just one of the factors which a state or government will consider before deciding whether to embark on a particular course of action. In fact, in many cases, legal considerations will prevail, but it is perfectly possible that a state may decide to forfeit legality in favour of self-interest, expediency or 'humanity', as with the Iraqi invasion of Kuwait in 1990 and the US-led invasion of Iraq some thirteen years later. There is nothing surprising in this and it is a feature of the behaviour of every legal person in every legal system, including that of the UK. If it were not so, there would be, for example, no theft and no murder. Indeed, in international society, where politics are so much a part of law, it may be that contextual and flexible rules, so evident in international law, are a strength rather than a weakness.

1.2 The existence of international rules as a system of law

The most cogent argument for the existence of international law as a *system of law* is that members of the international community recognise that there exists a body of rules binding upon them as law. States believe international law exists. When Iraq invaded Kuwait in 1990, or earlier when Tanzania invaded Uganda in 1978/79, the great majority of states regarded the action as 'unlawful', not merely 'immoral' or 'unacceptable'. The same is true of the war crimes committed in Bosnia and Rwanda, and this is given concrete form when the United Nations Security Council imposes sanctions or takes action against a delinquent state, as with that against Libya in 2011 in order to protect civilian populations. The criticism of the US-led invasion of Iraq in March 2003 and of Israel's forceful intervention in Lebanon in July 2006 followed a similar pattern, both being cast by a majority of the international community as a violation of law, not merely as unethical, immoral or undesirable. Similarly, those arguing in support of these uses of force do not dismiss international law as irrelevant, but seek instead to justify the invasions as lawful under the legal rules concerning collective security and self-defence. In other words, even the international actors who engage in potentially unlawful activity do not deny the relevance of international law or its prescriptive quality. This acceptance of the reality of international law by the very persons to whom it is addressed exposes the weakness of those who argue that international law does not exist. Of course, this does not answer questions about its effectiveness, nor does it settle whether it is 'law' in the same sense as that of the UK or of other states. Yet, it does reflect accurately the reality of international relations. How then do we know that states believe that there is a set of rules binding on them as law? What evidence is there of this 'law habit'?

(a) International law is practised on a daily basis in the Foreign Offices, national courts and other governmental organs of states, as well as in international organisations such as the United Nations and the Organisation of American States. Foreign Offices have legal departments whose task is to advise on questions of international law and to assist in the drafting of international agreements and the like. National courts are frequently concerned with substantive questions of international law, as with the series of *Pinochet* cases in the UK concerning questions of immunity and human rights (*R v Bow Street Metropolitan Stipendiary Magistrate, ex parte Pinochet*

(No. 3) [1999] 2 All ER 97) and the House of Lords judgment in *R v Jones* [2006] 2 WLR 772 concerning the meaning of the international crime of aggression and its impact on domestic law. In reading the judgment of Lord Bingham in that case, no-one could doubt the legal validity of the system of international law. Similarly, international organisations, in all their forms (both inter-governmental and non-governmental), use lawyers, employing the language of the law, to conduct their everyday business. These organisations and their members accept that they are 'legally bound' to behave in a certain way and will pursue claims against each other alleging a 'breach' of international law.

(b) It is a fact of the utmost significance that states – still the most important of the subjects of international law – do not claim that they are above the law or that international law does not bind them. When Iraq invaded Kuwait it did not claim that the law prohibiting armed force did not apply to it or was irrelevant. Rather, Iraq argued that international law 'justified' its action; in other words, that it was 'legal' by reference to some other rule of international law. Likewise, in the *Case Concerning the Application of the Convention on the Prevention and Punishment of the Crime of Genocide (Bosnia and Herzegovina v Serbia & Montenegro)* (ICJ 2007), Serbia did not deny the existence of rules of law concerning genocide, but contended rather that it was not internationally responsible for the violations of international law that had taken place. In fact there is no modern day example of a state claiming that it is not bound by general rules of international law, although there is often a great deal of debate as to the precise obligations imposed by that law (as in the *Bosnia Serbia Genocide Case* where there was argument over the precise obligations imposed by the Genocide Convention). This is powerful evidence that states follow rules of international law as a matter of obligation, not simply as a matter of choice or morality. If this were not so, there would be no need for states to justify their action in legal terms when they departed from a legal norm.

(c) Further convincing evidence of the existence of international law is that the overwhelming majority of international legal rules are consistently obeyed. Of course, there will be occasions when the law is ignored or flouted, just as there will be murder and theft in national law. Indeed, the *apparent* ineffectiveness of international law stems from the fact that it is the occasions of law-breaking that receive the most publicity. Some of the modern day and notorious failures of international law, such as the US invasion of Grenada in 1983, the genocide of the Kurds at the hands of the Iraqis and the invasions of Afghanistan and Iraq in pursuit of 'the war on terrorism' are not representative of the whole. Outside of the exceptional cases, the everyday operation of international law goes on in a smooth and uninterrupted fashion. The occasions when a state disregards its treaty or customary law obligations are but a small fraction of the occasions on which those obligations are observed. The same is true of the law of diplomatic immunities, state responsibility and the law of the sea. In short, the vast majority of the rules of international law are obeyed most of the time. Such observance is not headline news.

(d) It is a function of all legal systems to resolve disputed questions of fact and law. International law has to do this and, because it has only a limited number of developed legal institutions, it sometimes fails. That, however, is no reason to doubt its validity as a system of law. Rather, it suggests that *if* international law is to be on a par with national law, it needs to develop better institutions responsible for law creation and enforcement. In comparison with national law, international

law may be regarded as 'weak' law, not because of a problem with its binding quality, but because of its less organised approach to the problems of adjudication and
enforcement. On the other hand, it has been suggested earlier that the existence of
such institutions is a feature of national law that cannot be adopted wholesale into
international law or at least not without modifcation to suit the requirements of the
international system. For example, given that international law regulates the conduct of legal equals, it might be unwise to have a formal and coercive process of law
enforcement such as an international 'police force'. All states are powerful in some
measure and all have the practical ability to inflict harm on each other whether
that be economic, political or military. For example, were the majority of the international community to have taken enforcement action against the Syrian government in 2012 for its gross violations of human rights, what would have been the
practical response of Syria's supporters, China and Russia? Those individuals caught
in the middle of any resulting conflict might not be comforted by the knowledge
that the majority were enforcing international law. The potential for widespread
harm beyond those engaging in the unlawful activity is something which national
law does not have to deal with. With such a reality, it may be that the best way to
regulate state conduct is to proceed on the basis of a system of law that is voluntarily accepted and voluntarily enforced. This does not mean that international law
forfeits the right to be called law – because it still obliges states to do certain things.
It means, rather, that it is not the same kind of law as national law. Indeed, in those
areas where international law does function in a similar manner to national law – as
where individuals are given enforceable rights or are subject to personal obligations
(e.g. war crimes) – international law has developed institutional mechanisms similar to those existing in national legal systems. The well-established European Court
of Human Rights, the War Crimes Tribunals for Bosnia, Rwanda and Somalia and
the International Criminal Court are good examples. In other words, when thinking about what 'law' is, and what its purpose is, there is not one measure and not
one perfect model.

1.3 The enforcement of international law

Many jurists claim that the hallmark of a system of law is that its rules are capable of being enforced against malefactors. Consequently, one of the most frequent
arguments used against international law is that it is not 'true' law because it is not
generally enforceable. This raises two issues. First, as a matter of principle, does the
existence of any system of law depend on the chances of effective enforcement?
Secondly, is it true that international law is not enforceable or effective?

In national legal systems it is assumed that the law will be enforced. If someone
steals, provided they are caught, they will be punished. In international law this
may not be the case. There was, for example, no formal enforcement action taken
against the USA after its illegal invasion of Grenada and no formal condemnation of
Israel for invading Lebanon in 2006. We might even suggest that on those occasions
when the United Nations has acted (e.g. against Iraq after its invasion of Kuwait),
it is more in the way of keeping or restoring the peace than of enforcing the law.
Yet is it really true that the test of the binding quality of any 'law' is the presence or

absence of assured enforcement of its rules? It may be that the assumed certainty of enforcement of *national* law masks its true basis and, in the same way, enforcement may be irrelevant to the binding quality of international law. For example, a better view of national law may be that it is 'law' not because it will be enforced, but because it is generally accepted as such by the community to whom it is addressed: the local population. The national society recognises that there must be some rules governing its life and, so long as these come into existence in the manner accepted as authoritative (e.g. in the UK through Act of Parliament), they are binding. In other words, the validity of 'law' may depend on the way it is created, that being the method regarded as authoritative by the legal subjects to whom it is addressed. The fact of enforcement may be a reason why individuals obey the law (and that is not certain), but it is not the reason why it is actually law. In international law, then, the fact that rules come into being in the manner accepted and recognised by states as authoritative (see the 'sources of law' in Chapter 2) is enough to ensure that 'law' exists. Less effective enforcement procedures may encourage states to flout the law more frequently than the individual does in national legal systems (although this is arguable), but that is a question about motives for compliance with law, not about its quality as 'law'.

If international law is regarded as a system of 'law', it is axiomatic that all states are under a legal obligation to abide by its rules. Evidence of the existence of this obligation has been presented in section 1.2. What, however, of the methods which international law does possess for enforcing these legal obligations? While international law has never been wholly dependent on a system of institutionalised enforcement, the absence of a 'police force' or compulsory court of general competence does not mean that international law is impotent. In fact there are a range of enforcement procedures and these are considered immediately below. Reference should also be made to section 1.4 on the reasons for compliance with international law.

1.3.1 The Security Council

Most legal systems provide for the use of forceful sanctions or penalties against malefactors. Under the Charter of the United Nations, the Security Council may take 'enforcement action' against a state when it poses a threat to the peace, or has committed an act of aggression or breach of the peace (Art. 39 and Chapter VII UN Charter). Enforcement action is authorised by resolution of the Council and may comprise military action, as with the use of force by the UN in Korea in 1950, against Iraq in 1990/91 and as authorised (but barely used) against Indonesia over East Timor in 1999/2000; or economic sanctions, as with the trading restrictions and embargoes against South Africa in 1977 and Serbia/Montenegro in 1992; or other similar measures, be they diplomatic, political or social, such as the mandatory severance of air links with Libya (as a result of the Lockerbie incident) in 1992 and April 1993 and the partial embargo imposed on North Korea by SC Res. 1718 (2006) following the latter's nuclear test. The Security Council may even act against non-state entities, as with SC Res. 1390 (2002) imposing financial and economic sanctions against the Al-Qaida organisation and the Taliban.

Of course, there are limitations to the exercise of this power, both political and legal. Until the end of the 'cold war' between the (then) USSR and the USA, enforcement action under the UN Charter was largely impossible, even if there was a serious outbreak of violence as with the many Arab–Israeli wars since 1945. Obviously, the veto power still enjoyed by the five permanent members of the Security Council, whereby any one negative vote can defeat a draft resolution, was the major cause of this. Indeed, this is not all history, for the threat of a veto, or its use, has meant that the Security Council has been unable to pronounce on the invasions of Afghanistan and Iraq and on the internal crisis in Syria in 2012 (where resolutions were vetoed three times by Russia and China). However, despite these setbacks, it is apparent that the emergence of general, if cautious, cooperation among the five permanent members of the Security Council has led in recent times to the adoption of more 'enforcement resolutions' under Chapter VII of the Charter than at any other time in the Organisation's history and many of the sanctions regimes put in place by these resolutions are ongoing. Moreover, Council action has encompassed many different and diverse conflicts: the straightforward Iraqi aggression against Kuwait, the breakup of the sovereign state of Yugoslavia, the civil wars in Somalia and Sudan, the alleged Libyan sponsorship of aircraft terrorism, the denial of East Timor's independence by Indonesia and conduct likely to cause the proliferation of nuclear weapons. Of course, it is to be remembered that the Security Council's powers are exercised in response to a breach of the peace, threat to the peace or act of aggression and they are not specifically intended to meet the non-fulfilment of general legal obligations. Constitutionally, the powers of the Council are designed primarily to preserve the peace rather than to enforce the law, although sometimes these can coincide, as with Iraq and Kuwait. In fact, in an armed conflict, the first task of the Security Council is to stop the fighting and not necessarily to apportion blame or act only against the guilty party. That said, it seems that the Security Council will act more readily in support of international legal principles, although not consistently when one of the permanent members' vital interests is at stake. However, we must not lose perspective. Ultimately, the issue turns on the political will of states and the degree of cooperation among the five permanent members. As the crisis in Syria demonstrates, the Council (i.e. its members) is not always prepared to enforce even the most fundamental of international norms, even if the threat to international society is obvious and severe and the harm to individuals evident to the world. We also know that when the Big Five's vital interests are engaged – for example, in Afghanistan, Iraq, the Falkland Isles, Tibet, Chechnya and Lebanon – the Security Council is paralysed politically and legally.

1.3.2 Loss of legal rights and privileges

Another method of enforcing legal obligations is to ensure that any violation of law results in the loss of corresponding legal rights and privileges. For example, if State A violates the terms of a commercial treaty with State B, the latter may be entitled to rescind the whole treaty or suspend performance of the obligations it owes to State A. Of course, this is no hardship to State A if its whole purpose is to avoid the obligations contained in the treaty, but the loss of legal rights or privileges may go further. Thus, on a bilateral level, there may be termination of diplomatic relations, restriction of economic aid or cancellation of supply agreements. In 1982, for example, the UK broke diplomatic relations with Argentina after its invasion of the Falkland Islands, in 1979/80 the USA froze Iranian assets after the unlawful seizure of its embassy in Tehran and in 2012 the USA froze assets and took other measures against a range of persons and bodies associated with the Syrian government, even though there was not primarily a bilateral dispute between the two countries. Similarly, a state's unlawful action may cause the community at large to impose penalties. Again, this can take various forms, including the expulsion or suspension from inter-governmental organisations, as when the International Atomic Energy Agency suspended Israel after the latter's unlawful attack on an Iraqi nuclear facility in 1981. Likewise, when Iranian students occupied the US embassy in Tehran, several Western industrialised powers cut back on their diplomatic contacts and in 1992 the European Community as a whole imposed trading restrictions on Serbia and Montenegro. Again, in 1995 Nigeria was suspended from the Commonwealth as a result of its violation of human rights. More strikingly, in 1999/2000 the EU imposed limited penalties (now lifted) on Austria – itself an EU member – following the election of what was seen as an extremist government, although whether any breach of 'international law' had occurred is not clear.

These methods of enforcement should not be underestimated for they can cause embarrassment and hardship to the delinquent state. Of course, such methods are overlaid with political and economic considerations and they cannot be regarded as a wholly trustworthy mechanism for the enforcement of legal obligations. They are often more appropriate for dealing with violations of international good practice rather than law and, of course, a state may choose to ignore a blatant violation of international law if it is in its interests to do so. However, on the whole, the loss of legal rights and privileges can have a greater practical effect on a delinquent state than overt displays of force, especially in today's highly interdependent international community.

1.3.3 Judicial enforcement

As we shall see in Chapter 10, there are various procedures for the settlement of disputes by judicial means. As well as ad hoc tribunals, there is the International Court of Justice (ICJ), being the principal judicial organ of the United Nations, and the relatively recent International Criminal Court for dealing with serious violations of international law by individuals (see, for example, the sentence of fourteen years' imprisonment imposed in *The Prosecutor* v *Thomas Lubanga Dyilo* (2012) for war crimes, the first conviction before the ICC). Moreover, while a state cannot be compelled to use the ICJ for the resolution of a legal dispute, if a matter is referred to it, its award is binding on the parties and must be carried out. For a recent example see, *Ahmadou Sadio Diallo (Republic of Guinea* v *Democratic Republic of the Congo)*, *Merits*, Judgment, (ICJ 2010), where the ICJ ordered monetary compensation to be paid and which has been assessed at USD 95,000, payable by August 2012 (*Ahmadou Sadio Diallo Republic of Guinea* v *Democratic Republic of the Congo)* (ICJ 2012). In this sense, the ICJ is primarily concerned with the enforcement of international rights and duties, even though the procedure by which states can be compelled to carry out awards of the Court is limited. Such compulsion is by reference to the Security Council and it suffers from all of the defects associated with that body. The procedure has never yet been successfully invoked, although the occasions on which resort to the Council is actually needed are relatively few as the majority of ICJ awards are carried out by the parties voluntarily, at least where the Court's jurisdiction was not seriously disputed. Of more general concern, however, is the ICJ decision in the *Lockerbie Case* (*Libyan Arab Jamahiriya* v *UK and US* 1992 ICJ Rep para. 22). In this case, Libya had applied to the Court for the indication of interim measures of protection (similar to temporary injunctions) because of alleged threats made by the UK and USA as a response to allegations that Libyan nationals were responsible for the destruction of the aircraft over Lockerbie in 1988. During the hearing of Libya's application, the Security Council adopted enforcement measures and the Court took the view that it was bound to dismiss Libya's claim because of the mandatory Council resolution which decisively characterised Libya's conduct as a threat to international peace (SC Res. 748). This acceptance by the Court of Security Council supremacy in what was clearly a legal dispute, and one that was already before the Court, illustrates very powerfully that matters of legal obligation can become entwined with political necessity in the system of international law. It is likely, however, that the Court will not renounce its jurisdiction if the Council is only considering a dispute, as opposed to when it has actually made a concrete determination of the very question before the Court: see e.g. Judge Lauterpacht's Separate Opinion in the First Phase of the *Case Concerning the Application of the Convention on the Prevention and Punishment of the Crime of Genocide (Bosnia and Herzegovina* v *Yugoslavia (Serbia and Montenegro))* 1993 ICJ Rep 325, and the exercise of jurisdiction in the *Congo Case* (2000). Certainly, this seems to be the path being taken in cases after the *Lockerbie Case* and this is a welcome, and proper, assertion of the independence of the Court. In its *Advisory Opinion on the Legal Consequences of the Construction of a Wall in the Occupied Palestinian Territory* July 2004 ICJ Rep, the ICJ considered the argument that the General Assembly of the United Nations lacked the power to request an Advisory Opinion on a matter while that issue was being dealt with by the Security Council (see Art. 12(1) UN Charter). This was rejected, one reason being that the mere presence of an item on the Council's agenda did not prevent the Assembly from dealing with an issue that otherwise fell within its responsibilities (see *Opinion on the Legal Consequences* paras. 27–28). Although the point of contention involved the constitutional relationship of the Assembly and the Council, the parallels with the relationship between the Council and the Court are clear and, after all, the Court did not decline to give the Advisory Opinion just because the matter of Israeli/ Palestinian relations was constantly before it. This was followed up in the *Advisory Opinion on the Accordance with international law of the unilateral declaration of independence in respect of Kosovo* (2008) with a strong statement about the Court's power, and willingness, to rule on a legal question even if this concerned contentious matters before the Assembly and Security Council and in respect of a dispute where the Security Council had indeed taken concrete measures, although not on the legal question itself. Neither is this new found vigour limited to Advisory Opinions because in the *Application of the Interim Accord of 13 September 1995 (The Former Yugoslav Republic of Macedonia* v *Greece)* (2011), the ICJ decided that the case was admissible despite the fact, as argued by Greece, that aspects of the dispute between it and the Former Yugoslav Republic of Macedonia were subject to the Security Council attempts at a negotiated settlement. So, although there were raised eyebrows at the reluctance shown by the ICJ in the *Lockerbie Case*, it now seems that that case should be regarded as 'decided by reference to its own special facts' rather than being indicative of the ICJ's general approach. The ICJ has since proven itself willing and able to rule on a legal question despite even strong political overtones (such as state independence and sovereignty!) and despite parallel action having been taken by the Council. It might be otherwise if the Council is actually taking action when the matter is referred to the ICJ, but even then it may well turn on the nature of the questions being asked, rather than the mere fact that the Council is currently dealing with the issue.

A second welcome development is the growth of specialised judicial institutions concerned with discrete issues of international law. The Iran–US Claims Tribunal, charged with unravelling the legal morass left by the ejection of the USA from Iran in 1979, provides a model for the judicial settlement of inter-state disputes and the Ethiopia/Eritrea Claims Commission is operating in much the same way to resolve issues arising from the separation of these two countries. Similarly, the Yugoslavia, and Rwanda War Crimes Tribunals and the International Criminal Court (ICC) reflect the growing importance of individuals as subjects of international legal disputes. Both the Yugoslavia and the Rwanda Tribunals have tried and convicted and sentenced individuals, and the ICC has laid charges in a number of cases and four trials are underway. In June 2012, after the ICC's first trial, Thomas Dyilo was sentenced to fourteen years' imprisonment for international crimes committed in the Democratic Republic of Congo.

Thirdly, many problems of international law arise in the national courts of states. Usually, this involves a dispute between a state and a private individual but sometimes simply between two nationals. In either case, the national court may decide a substantive question of international law, which will then be binding on the parties. Moreover, awards of domestic tribunals, even if not voluntarily complied with, may be enforced by the normal enforcement machinery of the national legal system, subject only to certain immunities which foreign states enjoy (see Chapter 7). Again, in practice, such awards are seldom ignored because of the effect this would have on the relations between the state of jurisdiction and the state against whom the order was made.

1.4 The effectiveness of international law

It has already been suggested that the great majority of the rules of international law are followed consistently every day as a matter of course. It is normal to obey international law. This is something that is overlooked by some critics of the system and it goes a long way to refute their claims that international law is nothing more than a haphazard collection of principles that can be ignored at will. In this section we will examine some of the reasons why international law does work.

1.4.1 The common good

There is no doubt that a very important practical reason for the effectiveness of international law is that it is based on common self-interest and necessity. Today, international society is more interdependent than ever and the volume of inter-state activity continues to grow. International law is needed in order to ensure a stable and orderly international society. It is in every state's interest to abide by the rules of international law, for they lay down orderly and predictable principles for the conduct of international relations and international commerce. For example, it is vital that the allocation of the scarce resources of the high seas and ocean floor is achieved smoothly and equitably and it is only through rules of international law – binding on all states – that this can be achieved. Likewise with the protection of the environment and the management of climate change. Thus, a major reason why international law works is that it provides a stable and authoritative regime for the conduct of international relations and the regulation of global issues in an increasingly interdependent world.

1.4.2 The psychological Rubicon

Law has a self-perpetuating quality. When it is accepted that the principles governing the activities of a society amount to 'law', as is the case with states and international law, the rules of that system assume a validity and force all of their own. For example, if a state is presented with a choice of action, one which is legal and one which is not, it will take pressing reasons for the state to act consciously in violation of 'the law'. Breaking international law, like breaking national law, is not a matter to be taken lightly and certainly it is not the *preferred* course of conduct for a state. There is, in other words, a psychological barrier against breaking international law simply because it is law. If a state does embark on such a course of conduct, its action will be described as 'unlawful' or 'illegal', and these are regarded as more powerful forms of criticism than behaviour which is simply 'immoral' or 'unacceptable'. The psychological force of international rules as a *system of law* is a reason in itself why international law is obeyed.

1.4.3 The practitioners of international law

International law operates hand in glove with international politics and diplomacy. Its most potent field of operations is, in fact, in the Foreign Offices and legal departments of the world's governments and in international organisations. While it is tempting to think of international law as operating in the abstract and impersonal terms of 'governments', 'organisations' and 'states', in practice the application of international law is a matter for the considered judgment of some individual somewhere. This may be a judge of the ICJ or national court, a legal adviser at the UN or a government official. Along with the army of legal advisers available to non-governmental organisations, these are the actual practitioners of international law. The crucial point is that the great majority of these officials will have been trained in the national law of their own countries and they are likely to approach international law in the same way as they would any other legal system. The practitioners of international law may have a 'habit of obedience' derived from their own training as national lawyers which serves to encourage respect for international law.

1.4.4 The flexible nature of international law

International law is not an 'adversarial' system of law. As we shall see when considering the sources of international law, many of its rules have evolved from the practice of states and often these do not stipulate rigid obligations or confer overriding legal rights. Indeed, in some circumstances, the substance of a rule may be unclear, as was the case with the law on the breadth of the territorial sea until the deliberations of the Third UN Conference on the Law of the Sea. It is a fact of the system that in many areas it may not be possible to achieve a clear and unambiguous statement of a state's legal position. This is the flexible nature of international law.

This flexibility may be perceived as a weakness, for states need to know with some degree of certainty the precise scope of their legal obligations and the extent of their legal rights. Uncertainty is the mother of instability. In international law, however, the flexible or open-ended nature of the rules means that disputes are less likely to be seen as 'right' versus 'wrong'. The absence of rigid and precise obligations leads to modest claims and, because there may be no objectively 'right' answer, there is a premium on compromise. Moreover, the flexible nature of international law means that a state may be able to choose from a range of policies, all of which will be legal. It will not be hamstrung or feel 'boxed in'. The fact that international law rarely leaves the state with only one course of action is a great advantage for a system so bound up with politics and diplomacy.

1.4.5 The political cost

There is much a state can lose through a violation of international law. Apart from the legal sanctions that might be imposed (see section 1.3), there are other political and economic costs to be paid. The loss of influence and the loss of trust consequent upon a breach of the law may mean a reduction in overseas trade, loss of foreign aid or a refusal to enter into negotiations over some other matter. Similarly, many states may not be prepared to enter into new treaties with a state if it has a history of violating existing agreements. When the USA invaded Grenada, for example, the loss of influence and trust throughout the states of the non-aligned world was a cost that hampered future US policy in the Caribbean. The same is true of its use of force in Panama in 1989, especially in respect of Latin American states, and the true international cost of US and UK intervention in Iraq and Afghanistan is still not known. Similarly, New Zealand may doubt the bona fides of France after the *Rainbow Warrior* affair and the UK was for many years wary of Argentinian promises after the latter's invasion of the Falkland Islands. Who will listen to a US lecture on human rights while prisoners are detained without trial at Guantanamo Bay and what chance does the current Syrian government have of operating effectively in the international arena after the civil war of 2012? Moreover, apart from these more tangible considerations, one should not underestimate the very public and embarrassing criticism which flows from a breach of international law, especially in such fields as human rights and crimes against humanity. In November 1998, the USA issued an apology 'to the Government and people of Paraguay' following its violation of the Vienna Convention on Consular Relations, as highlighted by the *Case Concerning the Vienna Convention on Consular Relations (Paraguay v US) (Provisional Measures)* 1998 ICJ Rep 248. Unfortunately, this embarrassment was not enough to prevent the USA apparently violating the same Convention in a similar way in the *La Grand* case (*Case Concerning the Vienna Convention on Consular Relations (Germany v US)* 1999 ICJ Rep). Evidently, some states are more easily embarrassed than others.

1.4.6 Sanctions

The types of sanction and the enforcement machinery known to international law have been considered previously. These also will play some part in ensuring that the law is obeyed. They represent one more motive for compliance, as they do in national law.

1.5 The weakness of international law

It would be a mistake to conclude that international law is a perfect system. There is much that could be reformed and enhanced. However, as a practical matter, the development of international law can be achieved only by states themselves. The United Nations, other international organisations and the International Law Commission may propose substantive changes in the law or changes in procedure, but the development of the system depends ultimately on the political will of sovereign states. If the system is believed to work satisfactorily for most of the time, as most states appear to believe, there will be no great movement to reform, especially if this involves a diminution of state power. This is not to underestimate the role that non-governmental organisations play in pushing for reform, but in the final analysis it is only states that can enter into effective multilateral treaties concerning questions of global significance and only states whose practice can influence the speedy development of customary rules of international law. The creation of the International Criminal Court is a good example of when this succeeds, but we still wait for effective international rules on such matters as climate change and the protection of ethnic minorities in existing states.

1.5.1 Lack of institutions

International law lacks many of the formal institutions present in national legal systems. There is no formal legislative body, no court machinery with *general* compulsory jurisdiction and no police force. Of course, this does not mean that the functions typically carried out by such bodies are neglected in international law, for new rules can be created, disputes can be settled judicially and obligations can be enforced. It does mean, however, that international law does not operate in the systematic manner so typical of, say, the legal system of the UK. While this may not be a serious defect because of the different purpose of international law, there will always be some difficulties, especially if malefactors are perceived to be able to violate the law with impunity. The impact of events in Afghanistan and Syria may well cause many states to ponder these weaknesses and it remains to be seen whether the result is a general willingness to violate the law more often (because it is apparent that the system is imperfect) or a desire to do something about the structural enforcement weaknesses of the system. Again, the absence of a central organisation responsible for law creation may be a disadvantage when there is a need to develop a comprehensive and general body of rules, as with the law concerning protection of the international environment. The customary law-making process may be too slow when new rules are needed quickly or circumstances change rapidly, as in the area of international communications. Lastly, the absence of a compulsory court structure means that some disputes may persist for decades to the detriment of all concerned, as with Argentina and the UK over the Falkland Islands, and India and Pakistan over Jammu-Kashmir.

1.5.2 Lack of certainty

The disadvantage of a system of flexible and open-ended rules is a lack of certainty. It sometimes seems that many of the disputes between states occur precisely because the rule of international law governing their conduct is not clear, rather than that one state is deliberately behaving illegally. For example, disputes generated by trans-boundary pollution (e.g. the Chernobyl incident) are only made worse by the lack of clear rules defining the ambit of state responsibility for apparently lawful acts. On the other hand, if lack of certainty does mean less entrenched disputes, this may be advantageous in a system of law that does not have many formal institutions.

1.5.3 Vital interests

It is true of all legal systems that the vital interests of its subjects may prevail over the dictates of the law. Sometimes this is recognised by the legal system itself, as with the law of self-defence and necessity in international law, but usually it is not. International law is no different from national law in this respect and it is unrealistic to expect perfect obedience. However, it may be that because international law lacks formal enforcement machinery, the temptation and opportunity to violate the law is greater than in other systems. In this sense, international law is 'weaker' than the law of the UK or other states. When a state believes its 'vital interests' to be threatened, it is not certain that international law will be able to prevent illegal conduct. Such was the case, for example, with the invasions of Afghanistan, Iraq and Lebanon, the use of the veto to prevent the Security Council acting in respect of Syria in 2012 and the Israeli violation of Argentinian sovereignty in seizing the war criminal, Adolf Eichmann, in 1960. Yet, this is not to say that international law is irrelevant in times of crises. Importantly, it may serve to modify a state's conduct to bring it closer to the legal norm, if not actually within it. The US bombing of Libya in 1986, for example, appears to have been limited to military targets because this was less likely to be condemned by other states, and the same is true of NATO's bombing of Serbia in 1999. So, while international law may not prevent a state from engaging in illegal conduct when its vital interests (or vital community goals?) are at stake, it may soften that state's reaction to a crisis. Also, on a more general level, it may be that the purpose of international law is not to resolve major political and diplomatic problems at all or to be 'inhibitive' in the same way as national law. One view of international law is that its first task should be to ensure that the international community runs on orderly and predictable lines. In this it largely succeeds.

1.5.4 Vital rules

Every system of law contains rules prohibiting certain conduct which, if unchecked, would destroy the society regulated by that system. In national legal systems there are rules prohibiting murder and other forms of violence, and in international law there is a general prohibition against the use of force. For some critics, the validity of the legal system as a whole stands or falls by the degree to which these vital rules are obeyed or enforced. International law has had a poor record in this regard and many of the infamous incidents referred to earlier involve the use of force by one state against another. International law often seems powerless to prevent these major ruptures of the fabric of international society and, again, it is weak law because of it. Dealing with the consequences of a violation of these rules is often too late, as the peoples of Kuwait, Bosnia, Iraq, The Sudan and Syria will bear witness.

This is a valid criticism of international law and needs to be recognised as such. However, the inability of international law to prevent or control outbreaks of violence is not as destructive as it would be if it occurred in national legal systems. The factual context of international law is quite different from the operational field of national law and aggression between states is something quite different from acts of violence between individuals. The violence used by an individual in a society can be overwhelmed easily by the forces at the disposal of the central authority with very little chance of major disruption to the state itself. In international society, an act of aggression by one state against another state has far greater consequences and the costs of controlling it *forcefully* are exceptionally high. It is quite possible, for example, for the forces available to the aggressor to outweigh the forces available to the enforcers of the law and, even if they do not, the loss of life and consequential economic damage caused by inter-state violence is quantitatively and qualitatively different from anything likely to occur within national boundaries. This is perhaps the reason why more determined action was not taken in the territory of the former Yugoslavia in the early stages of the dispute. Of course, this is not an argument advocating that international law should have no rules prohibiting acts of violence. Rather, it is a suggestion that because of the field of operation of international law, rules of physical enforcement are not as desirable or practical as they are in other legal systems. This is a fact of international life, albeit not a palatable one.

1.6 The juridical basis of international law

If, then, we accept that international law is 'law', albeit a very different kind of law from that which we find in national legal systems, from where does it derive its legal validity? What is the juridical origin or source of international law? Why is it law? These are questions that have vexed jurists for many years and a number of theories have been developed. These are now considered.

1.6.1 The command theory

John Austin was one of the greatest legal philosophers of the nineteenth century. His view of 'law' was that it comprised a series of commands or orders, issued by a sovereign, and backed by the threat of sanctions (enforcement) if the commands were disobeyed. Consequently, unless the rules of a system amounted to a collection of orders backed by threats, emanating from a sovereign, they were not 'positive law'. This theory has had a profound and, perhaps, unwarranted impact on the search for the juridical origin of international law. According to Austin, 'international law' is not 'positive law' because it does not result from the commands of a sovereign. Customary law, for example, develops through state practice and treaty law develops through consent. Thus, international law, because it is not made up of commands, is properly to be regarded as a species of 'positive morality' and is not within the province of jurisprudence.

As a general description of what law is, this theory has now been largely discredited. The picture of law as a series of commands issued by a sovereign and backed by threats does not even describe national law accurately, let alone international law. Moreover, Austinian theory may be dismissed in so far as it suggests that international law is the same sort of animal as national law. The sovereignty theory misinterprets the function of international law because its primary purpose is not to coerce or command states, but to enable them to interact freely by laying down orderly, predictable and binding principles. Austinian theory cannot explain why states themselves regard international law as binding even when there is no 'sovereign'.

1.6.2 The consensual theory

The basic tenet of the consensual theory is that the binding quality of international law – its existence as 'law' – flows from the consent of states. It is said to be a 'positivistic' system of law based on the actual practice of states. In its pure form, this consensual or positivist theory stipulates that no international law can be created without the consent of the state which is to be bound. Thus, 'new' states would not be bound by pre-existing rules because consent is the source of all legal obligations. International law is said to flow from the will of the state. It is formed from the realities of international life rather than its desirabilities. It is created by what actually goes on (consent), rather than according to some higher moral principles.

This theory recognises that a state's consent may be given in a variety of ways – express in treaties or implied in custom – but essentially the system of international law is based on voluntary self-restriction. In this regard, the consensual theory has certain attractions, for it appears to reflect accurately what goes on in international society. The rule that states are bound by their treaty obligations (*pacta sunt servanda* – treaties must be observed) seems to be based on consent because, as we shall see, treaties are generally binding on a state only if it deliberately and positively accepts the terms. Similarly, it is not inconceivable to regard customary law as being consensual, for consistent state practice may be tantamount to agreeing to be bound by the rule that then develops.

However, there are certain difficulties with the consensual approach to international law, both theoretical and practical. First, as a matter of legal theory, it is not at all clear why states can be bound *only* by self-imposed obligations. There seems to be no necessary reason why this should be so, especially since many rules are not really referable to consent. Indeed, if there exists a rule that says 'states can create law only by consent', where did that rule come from? Where is the legal authority for the *pacta sunt servanda*/consent rule? If we say that states have always behaved as if consent was fundamental to the creation of legal norms, we can ask further why it is that customary practice should have the authority to validate legal rules. In fact, the search for the legal source of the consent rule can go on *ad infinitum*, for we can always ask one more question and take one more step up the 'ladder of authority'.

Secondly, on a practical level, consent does not explain the existence of all legal obligations. The last twenty-five years have witnessed the birth of many 'new' states, including former dependencies of colonial powers and former members of defunct federations (Yugoslavia, USSR). If consent is the basis of international law, how is it that these new states are bound by pre-existing rules of customary law? There is no doubt that they are bound by the general obligations of international law, yet they have not had the opportunity to accept or reject them. It has been suggested that consent for new states is implied, either specifically by their 'first act' of state practice under an existing rule, or generally by acceptance of membership of the international community. This is, however, no more than a fiction, since it would allow states to 'opt out' of certain rules if the intention not to be bound was made known. This simply does not happen, nor would it be acceptable to the existing members of the international community. To talk of consent in such circumstances is unrealistic and ignores the pre-existing validity of international law for new states. Similarly, a change in circumstances may expose an existing state to rules of customary law with which previously it was unconcerned, yet it is still bound without its prior consent. For example, Panama and Liberia did not have the chance of objecting to customary maritime law before they became influential maritime states. In fact, even the binding quality of the ultimate consensual instrument – the treaty – cannot be explained fully by use of the consent theory. There is, for example, a limited class of treaties, known as dispositive treaties, which are mainly concerned with territorial issues and which bind all states. After the UK ceded to China by treaty in 1997 that part of the Hong Kong colony which was sovereign UK territory, no other state claimed (or could claim) that the UK was still the sovereign by alleging that they were not a party to the UK/China bilateral treaty. Other states have not consented to this transfer of jurisdiction but they are bound by it. More importantly, there are certain fundamental rules of customary law (rules of *jus cogens*) which cannot be altered by the express agreement of states, even if in treaty form. If consent was the basis of international law, nothing would be unalterable by treaty.

In general, then, the consensual theory is attractive but it does not describe accurately the reality of international law. When we consider the sources of international law in Chapter 2, it will become apparent that consent is a method for creating binding rules of law, rather than the reason why they are binding.

1.6.3 Natural law

In almost complete contrast to the consensual approach is the theory of international law based on natural law doctrines or 'the law of nature'. This presupposes an ideal system of law, founded on the nature of man as a reasonable being. Thus, rules of law are derived from the dictates of nature as a matter of human reason. International law is said to derive its binding force from the application of 'the law of nature' to the methods of law creation used by states. Natural law can be contrasted with positive (consensual) law, the latter being based on the actual practice of states while the former is based on objectively correct moral principles.

Empirically, natural law theory finds little support in international law. Given that the method of law creation in international law is so heavily dependent on consent or practice, it is difficult to maintain that there is some guiding body of principles to which states defer when creating law. In general, concrete rules of international law are derived from what states actually do, rather than what 'the law of nature' supposes they should do. However, 'natural law' may be a good *descriptive* label for such concepts as equity, justice and reasonableness which have been incorporated in substantive rules of law, such as those dealing with the continental shelf, human rights, war crimes and rules of *jus cogens*. In this sense, natural law may be part of the sources of international law under the category 'general principles recognised by civilised nations' (see Chapter 2). Natural law does not, however, explain why international law is binding, especially if we remember that the states of the world are so diverse that it is impossible to find any universal moral or ideological thread tying them together.

1.6.4 *Ubi societas, ubi jus*

It may be that the juridical origin of international law lies in practical necessity. It can be argued that 'law' is the hallmark of any political community which exists for the common good. Law is necessary for the society to function and, because it is necessary, it is *ex hypothesi* binding. Therefore, because international society is a community of interacting and interdependent states, it also needs rules governing its life. These are the rules of international law which provide a set of stable, orderly and predictable principles by which the society can operate.

   Obviously, this view of international law is a pragmatic and uncomplicated one. To a certain extent it is tautologous because it stipulates that international law is binding because it has to be binding. Apart from this objection, is it also true that states form a 'community' at all? There appear to be few shared values and each state seems more concerned with the interests of itself and its nationals than with the common good. Yet, this is a rather one-sided view of international society and, whatever the practice of a minority of states, isolationism is a thing of the past. There is little alternative to cooperation and compromise in most areas of international activity. The merit of this pragmatic view is that it roots the binding quality of international law in an 'extra-legal' concept. It does not seek to explain international law in terms of the way its rules are created, their substance, or by reference to some higher authority. Rather, the legal quality of international law lies in the fact that it is needed and that this is recognised by states themselves, the legal persons to whom it is addressed.

1.6.5 **Variations on a theme**

As well as the general theories of international law considered in the previous sections, there are many variations of these themes. These relate both to the structure of international law as a whole and to specific topics within the body of substantive international law. Some of these truly discuss the juridical origins of international law, while others argue for one or other philosophical or theoretical approach to the interpretation or application of existing rules. The following is a selection:

   (a) *Deconstructionist theories*. Some jurists (e.g. Koskenniemi) argue that international law has no legal objectivity at all. It is not a system of 'law' in the sense that it can be used to justify or criticise international behaviour on a rational or objective basis. It is, rather, a conjunction of politics, morality and self-interest that can be used alternatively to justify or condemn any behaviour according to the standpoint of the critic. Legal language and the apparent habit of obedience are seen as smokescreens for behaviour that would have occurred in any event and for reasons unrelated to the existence of a so-called legal rule.

(b) *'Value' orientated theories*. Some jurists (e.g. McDougal, Lasswell and Feliciano) see the role of international law as the pursuit of certain pre-existing community values. All rules should be interpreted and applied consistently with these values. Of course, this presupposes that there is agreement as to what these 'values' actually are, although 'world public order' is a favourite starting point.

(c) *Realist theories*. Some jurists argue that the real importance of international law lies not in the validity or otherwise of its claim to be law, but in the impact it makes on the conduct of international relations (see the analysis in Scott, (1994) 5 *EJIL* 313). It is enough to justify the existence of international law that it is accepted as a major influence on international politics; whether or not it is accepted as law is neither here nor there, nor whether it is disobeyed or obeyed. Its function as the oil in the engine of international politics is what matters.

(d) *Non-statist theories*. Some jurists reject the fundamental concept of international law as a system of law created primarily by states for states. They argue, from differing starting points, that this is far too narrow a view of international law, especially in the modern era (see e.g. Allot in *Eunomia*). Such jurists often stress the importance of international law for individuals, or as a means of achieving justice (sometimes at the expense of stability) or as a means of accommodating the cultural and ethnic diversity of a modern international society that is no longer centred on Europe. This is a favourite theme of the modern era and gains many supporters because of the possibility that international law could be used to check the excesses of otherwise sovereign states. Whether such a view of international law would be possible without the foundations laid by legal rules that were undoubtedly created by states, for states, is an open question.

Any attempt to reach a conclusion about the nature of international law or its claim to be a 'system of law' is bound to attract criticism from all sides. Yet it must not be forgotten that the origin of the binding character of law is a *general* problem. It is an issue for national law as well as international law. Usually, in national legal systems there are formal institutions, like the UK Parliament, whose task is to create law and which may be regarded as a 'source of law'. However, while the existence of such institutions enables us to identify what is or is not 'a law', they do not explain why it is law. It may be that the constitution authorises Parliament to make law, but from where does the constitution derive its authority? This is a problem we have seen before. In national systems, the search for the juridical origin of law goes beyond the existence of institutions or constitutions and international law loses nothing in this respect by their absence. The juridical origin of law is a large question and it is a mistake to think that only international law fails to find an answer. In the end, if an answer to this question is needed, the first and most powerful reason why international law is to be regarded as law is that it is recognised as such by the persons whom it controls, the states and other subjects of international law. If this begs the question somewhat, we should remember that international law is not the only system to be unsure of the answer.

1.7 The future of international law

The 'decade of international law' (GA Res. 45/90) has come and gone and the international community has entered the twenty-first century. At the start of the 1990s, the end of the 'cold war' brought uncertainty but actually heralded a new era of cooperation among the five permanent members of the Security Council and a consequential increase in the influence of the United Nations. The world is too uncertain to predict whether the present decade will witness further fundamental changes in the organisation of the international community, but the challenges facing international law are no less pressing.

The next few years will see the wider exercise of jurisdiction by the International Criminal Court and, no doubt, a widening of the scope of international law to embrace in even more detail non-state entities such as individuals, organisations and corporations. This is nothing new, but perhaps the pace of this development will gather speed. Likewise, to give but a few examples, there will be significant advances in international environmental law (see, for example, the ongoing ICJ cases, *Construction of a Road in Costa Rica along the San Juan River (Nicaragua v Costa Rica)* (2011) and *Whaling in the Antarctic (Australia v Japan)* (2010)), in the law of international communications and more treaty codification of customary law. In the United Nations itself, calls for the abolition of the 'veto' and/or an increase in the number of permanent members of the Security Council are becoming louder and more persistent. In contrast, many international lawyers believe that 'regionalisation' will replace 'universality' as the most effective template for managing the international community. So, perhaps, there will be different rules of international law for Europe, and Africa or North America. Certainly, regional organisations seem more prepared to take on the task of regulating the conduct of its members rather than submit to 'outside' regulation. There is uncertainty, but the world is changing and international law must change with it.

All this will have an impact on a system of law that was conceived originally as a set of rules to govern sovereign states in their international relations. Of course, it remains true that the majority of concrete rules of international law are created by states for states and that conceptions of 'sovereignty' and independence are deeply rooted in the fabric of international society. Nevertheless, it seems that the institutions of international law are changing, and will have to change further, to accommodate the slow but steady move to rules aimed at controlling states (even in their dealings with their own nationals inside their own territory) instead of rules which simply facilitate their interaction. Much will depend on how international law copes with the issue of effective enforcement. A set of rules that *facilitates* interaction between states without over-prescribing a particular course of action can survive with little or weak enforcement machinery. A set of rules that seeks to *control* states in their actions needs a stronger enforcement mechanism if it is to achieve its goals. Is this likely, or will the attempt fail and bring the whole edifice of international law into disrepute?

FURTHER READING

Fitzmaurice, G., 'The Foundations of the Authority of International Law and the Problem of Enforcement', (1956) 19 *MLR* 1.

Hart, H. L. A., *The Concept of Law*, Chapter X (Oxford University Press, 1961).

Lauterpacht, H., *The Function of Law in the International Community* (Clarendon Press, 1933), pp. 385–438.

Mullerson, R., 'Sources of International Law: New Tendencies in Soviet Thinking', (1989) 83 *AJIL* 494.

Perreau-Saussine, A., 'The Character of Customary Law: An Introduction' in Amanda Perreau-Saussine and James Murphy (eds), *The Nature of Customary Law: Philosophical, Historical and Legal Perspectives* (Cambridge University Press, 2009).

For some alternative theories

Allott, P., *Eunomia: New Order for a New World*, 1st edn. (Oxford University Press, 1990).

Charlesworth, H., Chinkin, C. and Wright, S., 'Feminist Approaches to International Law', (1991) 85 *AJIL* 613.

Charney, J., 'Universal International Law', (1993) 87 *AJIL* 529.

McCorquodale, R., 'An Inclusive International Legal System' (2004) 17 *Leiden Journal of International Law* 477.

Marks, S., *Exploitation as an International Legal Concept* in S. Marks (ed), *International Law on the Left* (Cambridge University Press, 2008).

Scobbie, I., 'Some Common Heresies About International Law' in Malcolm Evans (ed.), *International Law* (Oxford University Press, 2003).

Scobbie, I., *Theory and International Law: An Introduction* (British Institute of International and Comparative Law, 1991).

Scobbie, I., 'Towards the Elimination of International Law: Some Radical Scepticism about Sceptical Radicalism', (1990) *BYIL* 339.

Scott, S., 'International Law as Ideology', (1994) 5 *EJIL* 313.

Simpson, G. (ed.), *The Nature of International Law* (Dartmouth, 2001).

SUMMARY

The nature of international law and the international system

- International law comprises a system of rules and principles that govern the international relations between sovereign states and other institutional subjects of international law. It operates alongside international diplomacy, politics and economics.

- The most cogent argument for the existence of international law as a *system of law* is that members of the international community recognise that there exists a body of rules binding upon them as law. States believe international law exists. This acceptance of the reality of international law by the very persons to whom it is addressed exposes the weakness of those who argue that international law does not exist.

- While international law has never been wholly dependent on a system of institutionalised enforcement, the absence of a 'police force' or compulsory court of general competence does not mean that international law is impotent.

- There is no doubt that a very important practical reason for the effectiveness of international law is that it is based on common self-interest and necessity. Today, international society is more interdependent than ever and the volume of inter-state activity continues to grow. International law is needed in order to ensure a stable and orderly international society.

- It would be a mistake to conclude that international law is a perfect system. There is much that could be reformed and enhanced. There is a general lack of institutions; the content of the rules of international law can be uncertain; states may elect to ignore international law when their vital interests are at stake; states are able to violate basic rules, such as the prohibition of violence without fear of being coerced.

- The juridical force of international law does not derive from a traditional conception of law, nor is it based on consent, or derived from natural law. Its force comes from the fact that it is needed to ensure that international society operates efficiently and safely. 'Law' is the hallmark of any political community and is necessary for the society to function and, because it is necessary, it is *ex hypothesi* binding.

2

The sources of international law

Every legal system must have some criteria by which legal norms or 'laws' are recognised. It must have reasonably clear sources of law. Generally speaking, these sources of law are either 'law creating' or 'law identifying'. In the UK, for example, the passage of a Bill through Parliament plus the Royal Assent is the primary means by which law is created and whether any alleged rule is a legal rule can be determined by reference to the statute book. In this sense, both the process of law creation and the statute book are 'sources' of law. Similarly, even though international law does not possess formal institutions responsible for law creation, there are recognised and accepted methods by which legal rules come into existence, as well as several ways in which the precise content of legal rules can be identified. These are the sources of international law. The related question of the origin of the binding quality of international law – its juridical source – is discussed in Chapter 1.

2.1 Article 38 of the Statute of the International Court of Justice

The traditional starting-point for a discussion of the sources of international law is Art. 38 of the Statute of the International Court of Justice. This provides that:

(1) The Court, whose function is to decide in accordance with international law such disputes as are submitted to it, shall apply,
  (a) international conventions, whether general or particular, establishing rules expressly recognised by the contesting States;
  (b) international custom, as evidence of a general practice accepted as law;
  (c) the general principles of law recognised by civilised nations;
  (d) subject to the provisions of Article 59, judicial decisions and the teachings of the most highly qualified publicists of the various nations, as a subsidiary means for the determination of rules of law.
(2) This provision shall not prejudice the power of the Court to decide a case *ex aequo et bono*, if the parties agree thereto.

It is immediately apparent that Art. 38 does not, in terms, purport to be a list of the sources of international law. Rather, it is a direction to the Court authorising it to consider various materials when deciding disputes submitted to it. Moreover,

Art. 38 does not even provide a complete list of the matters which the Court in fact considers when determining the rights and duties of states. For example, Art. 38 makes no reference to resolutions of the United Nations General Assembly or to diplomatic correspondence, both of which figure prominently in the Court's judgments (e.g. *Nicaragua* v *USA* 1986 ICJ Rep 14 and *Nauru* v *Australia (Jurisdiction)* 1992 ICJ Rep 240) and which may tell us a great deal about the substance of the rules binding each disputant. Similarly, Art. 38 concentrates primarily on the activities of *states*. However, non-state actors in international law may well contribute to law creation in a number of ways: for example, when international organisations conclude treaties (e.g. Status of Forces Agreements between the United Nations and countries hosting UN forces) or when the actions of individuals, groups or even multinational companies (see e.g. *Texaco* v *Libya* (1977) 53 ILR 389) contribute to the development of customary practice. As we shall see, one reason for these various omissions may be that these matters are not regarded universally as 'true' sources of law, but merely 'evidence' of state practice and thus subsumed under the head of customary law. However, it is obvious that this merely begs the question as to what we mean by 'sources' and it does not help explain why the activities of non-state actors can have such an important practical impact on the content of international law.

Similarly, there is no indication in Art. 38 of the priority or hierarchy of the sources of international law. Apart from the single reference to 'subsidiary means' in Art. 38(1)(d), we do not know the order in which the sources of law are to be applied. Words of priority were included in preliminary drafts of the Article, but ultimately these were rejected because it was intended that the Court should consider each 'source' simultaneously as in *Nicaragua* v *USA*. Indeed, there is no difficulty if the actual content of the rules derived from the various sources is complementary and, of course, this will usually be the case. However, in cases of conflict it is vital to determine which 'source' shall prevail. Does a later treaty prevail over earlier customary law and can subsequent customary law detract from an earlier but explicit treaty obligation? These matters, and especially the interaction of treaty and custom, are considered later after the nature of treaties and customary law have been explored more fully. Subject to what will be said then about fundamental rules (rules of *jus cogens*), the better view is that in those rare cases where it is important, the priority of sources follows the order of Art. 38, that is from (1)(a) to (1)(d).

Article 38 of the Statute does not provide a complete and unambiguous statement of the sources of international law and it leaves several questions unanswered. Still, it would be a mistake to underestimate the importance of Art. 38, not least because it is vital that a reasonably clear and precise statement of the sources be available. It is because Art. 38 more or less fulfils this role that it has been accepted as authoritative by the Court, by states themselves and by national courts (e.g. in the UK, *Bat* v *Germany* (2011)). It is also arguable that Art. 38 is mandatory in the sense that states cannot ask the Court to decide a dispute on the basis of selected sources only. It is important that states accept that international law is an integrated body of rules and not merely an amalgam of various unrelated principles; hence the fact that the priority of the sources in Art. 38(1) is rarely in issue. However, some caution must be exercised here. Although it could be seen as a violation of a treaty to which the state is a party (the ICJ Statute) and as a denial of the prescriptive authority of validly created rules of international law, the consensual nature of the Court's jurisdiction can be taken to imply a power for states to pick and choose the law relevant to a dispute. So, just as the Court may be asked to decide a case *ex aequo et bono* (Art. 38(2): see later), it is possible that the Court would permit two states to agree that rules from a certain 'source' were inapplicable to that particular dispute. If this were permissible, it should be seen as an issue going to the jurisdiction of the Court – as with the exclusion of multilateral treaty disputes by the US reservation in *Nicaragua* v *USA* – rather than as a denial of the 'legal' quality of the excluded rules. However, it is clear that the ICJ is reluctant to accept that certain sources of law or types of obligation are excluded from its determination of a dispute concerning international law – *Case Concerning Oil Platforms (Islamic Republic of Iran v United States of America)* (2003) – and it is likely that such an exclusion would have to be clearly and unequivocally expressed before it was accepted. By way of contrast, in the *Frontier Dispute (Burkina Faso/ Niger) Case* (2010), the parties have agreed specifically that the ICJ shall apply the sources of law specified in Art. 38(1), 'including the principle of the intangibility of boundaries inherited from colonization and the Agreement of March 1987'. It is not clear what will be the result if this 'principle' contradicts the sources of law specified in Art. 38 itself.

This leads us to consider the reasons for singling out the particular sources identified in Art. 38. As we have seen, the Article makes no reference to General Assembly resolutions, diplomatic correspondence, publications of international organisations, the activities of non-state actors or the many other materials which may reflect current international law. One reason may be the alleged distinction between 'formal', 'material' and 'evidentiary' sources of international law.

2.1.1 Formal and material sources

In order to understand the distinction between formal and material sources it is necessary to concentrate on the *function* which 'sources of law' can perform within a legal system. Thus, the procedures or methods by which rules become legally binding are formal sources of law. A formal source of law is a process by which a legal rule comes into existence: it is law creating. In the UK, for example, the passage of a Bill through Parliament is a formal source of law. In international law, 'custom' is a formal source of law as it is one way legal rules can be created. Similarly, if treaties create 'law' for the parties, and not merely 'obligations' (on which, see subsequent paragraph), they are formal sources of law. The same may be true of 'general principles of law' if they encompass rules having pre-existing legal validity; that is, rules which are not dependent for their binding effect on treaty or custom. This is discussed in more detail in the sections dealing specifically with each limb of Art. 38.

Material sources, on the other hand, are not concerned with the formal act of law creation. Material sources are those sources of law concerned with the substance and content of legal obligations. They are law identifying and perform the vital function of enabling the 'subjects of international law' – the legal entities to whom the law is addressed – to be reasonably certain about what the law requires in a practical context. So, to sum up, the function of formal sources is to create law, the function of material sources is to identify the substance of the obligations which become law. In this sense, state practice, the practice of international organisations, the practice of non-state actors, judicial decisions, the writings of jurists and General Assembly resolutions are all material sources for they indicate what a state's obligations actually are, rather than the method by which those obligations became legally binding. Similarly, treaties may be material sources if (and this is controversial) they create 'obligations' rather than 'law', on which see section 2.2.1.

2.1.2 Material and evidentiary sources

It has been suggested that there is a difference between material and evidentiary sources of international law. To call something a material source describes *solely* the function it performs – the provision of the substance of the rules which formal sources turn into law. By way of contrast, evidentiary sources of international law have nothing to do with functions and everything to do with substance. Evidentiary sources of international law, such as state activity, diplomatic memoranda, statements of government representatives in international organisations and the actual text of treaties, tell us the precise content of the legal obligations which bind states. In a sense, evidentiary sources are the most important 'sources' of international law for they tell us exactly what a state or other international legal person can or cannot do. We must not, however, make the mistake of treating theory as a substitute for analysis and it may well be that there is nothing profound in the distinction between 'material' and 'evidentiary' sources other than a reminder that what amounts to the 'sources of law' depends greatly on the reason why we need to know. Are we engaged in a theoretical analysis in order to construct a 'doctrine of sources' or are we looking for the answer to a practical problem in the relations between members of the international community? Each question is important, but the answers may be different.

In theory then, it may be possible to maintain a distinction between these three concepts of the sources of international law. For example, in the case of custom we could say that the process of customary law formation is a formal source because it describes the way rules become legally binding; that state practice is a material source of custom, because it describes the way in which the substance of customary rules is identified; and that diplomatic correspondence and actual state activity etc. comprise the evidence of state practice. However, in reality, these supposed distinctions are highly artificial and difficult to maintain. They distort the function of the sources of international law because all 'sources' are, in some way, both law creating and law identifying. State practice, for example, is part of the definition of custom and to describe it merely as a material source ignores this. Similarly, judicial decisions can define absolutely the legal obligations of parties in a particular and specific situation and, in this sense, they are law creating. Furthermore, it is difficult to see any real difference between material and evidentiary sources, especially since both are concerned ultimately with the substance of the rules which bind states. A better way to look at the sources of international law is to examine each in turn and to recognise that all of the 'sources' specified in Art. 38 can, of themselves, provide an answer to the question 'what is the international law on this subject?' In this sense, Art. 38 provides a useful, although incomplete, list of the sources of international law.

2.2 International treaties ('conventions')

International conventions, or treaties, are the only way states can create international law consciously. Treaties may be bilateral (between two states) or multilateral
(between many) and usually they are the outcome of long and difficult negotiations. A treaty is, in essence, a bargain between legal equals and it may cover any
aspect of international relations. Treaties range from those defining the status of
territory, such as the 1984 Agreement on the future of Hong Kong between the UK
and China, to those dealing with the rights or obligations of individuals such as the
International Covenant on Civil and Political Rights 1966 and the Statute of the
International Criminal Court 1998, to those multilateral treaties instituting specific
legal regimes such as the 1959 Antarctic Treaty and the 1961 Vienna Convention on
Diplomatic Relations. Treaties are the means by which states can create certain and
specific obligations and, because they are the result of a conscious and deliberate
act, they are more likely to be respected. International treaties, whether general or
particular, are now the most important source of international law and this is likely
to remain so given the continuing efforts of the International Law Commission to
codify customary law in treaty form.

The precise rules dealing with the creation of treaties are discussed elsewhere
(Chapter 3). Here, we are concerned with the treaty as a source of law – that is, with
the nature of a treaty once it has satisfied all the formal requirements for its existence
and has entered into force. When that is the case, a treaty imposes obligations on the
state-parties which must be carried out and failure to conform to the terms of a binding treaty will incur international responsibility unless a defence is available (*Case
Concerning the Gabcikovo-Nagymaros Project (Hungary v Slovakia) (1998) 37 ILM 162,
Case Concerning the Application of the Convention on the Prevention and Punishment of the
Crime of Genocide (Bosnia and Herzegovina v Serbia & Montenegro) (ICJ 2007)*). In fact,
however, it is evident that the great majority of treaties are respected by state-parties
most of the time. This should not come as a surprise given that a treaty will have
been entered into voluntarily and only after due and serious consideration.

As a source of law, the treaty is governed by a number of principles which will
now be considered.

(I) Treaties are voluntary in the sense that no state can be bound by a treaty without
having given its consent to be bound by one of the methods recognised as effective in
international law for this purpose (e.g. signature, ratification, accession). Only parties
to the treaty are bound by its terms. There are limited exceptions to this rule, dealing
with practical matters such as the delimitation of territorial boundaries which must
necessarily bind all states, but such treaties are exceptional in international law and
they operate in the same way as formal conveyances of land in national law. They are
said to be valid *ergo omnes*, i.e. effective against the whole world, as noted in the *Case
Concerning Kasikili/Sedudu Island (Botswana v Namibia) (1999)*.

(II) Once a state has signified its consent to a treaty, it is bound by its terms
vis-à-vis all other parties to that treaty. A state is not bound by a treaty to which
it is a party in its relations with a state which is not a party to that treaty. Thus,
treaties are a source of binding law exclusively for the parties in their relations
inter se. However, this simple picture is complicated by the fact that treaties may

codify or develop customary law (for example, the Vienna Convention on the Law of Treaties itself), and then non-parties to the treaty may come to be bound by *customary* rules having the same content as the treaty. However, even then, the primary rule remains that a state cannot be bound by a treaty to which it is not a party, even if its obligations under customary law are identical to those contained in treaty form.

(III) When a treaty codifies existing customary law, as was the case with much of the Vienna Convention on Diplomatic Relations and the Vienna Convention on the Law of Treaties (*Danube Dam Case*, para. 46), the substance of the obligations specified in the treaty may be binding on all states, because:

(i) those states that are parties to the treaty are bound by the treaty in the normal way (rule II); and

(ii) states that are not parties to the treaty cannot be said to be bound by it (rule I), but because the treaty codifies existing customary law, these states are bound by the same obligations as expressed in the treaty, only this time because they are rooted in customary law. The substance of the obligation is the same for parties and non-parties, even if the origin of that obligation is different. Again, a recent example is provided by the ICJ's *Advisory Opinion on the Legal Consequences of the Construction of a Wall in the Occupied Palestinian Territory* where the Court notes that 'customary international law as expressed in Article 31 of the Vienna Convention on the Law of Treaties' should be applied (2004 ICJ Rep para. 94). However, the fact that the origin of a state's obligation lies in customary law (and not the codifying treaty) can have some practical consequences, as where the ICJ has jurisdiction over disputes arising under one 'source' but not the other. In *Nicaragua* v *USA*, despite its objections, the USA was held subject to the Court's jurisdiction in respect of its dispute with Nicaragua because although the Court lacked jurisdiction to decide matters arising under a treaty binding both states, it *did* have jurisdiction to decide a matter of customary law between the parties – and the customary law was very similar in content to the non-justiciable treaty. The existence of 'parallel obligations' arising simultaneously in treaty and customary law is a by-product of the diffuse methods of law creation that exist in international law. As long as there is no single legislature, there will exist the possibility of overlap between the 'sources' of law.

(IV) Many multilateral treaties are a mixture of codification of current customary law and progressive development of that law. Often, it is the intention of the state-parties to such a treaty that the rules contained therein will regulate the future conduct of *all* states although once again, this cannot be guaranteed.

(i) Parties to the treaty are bound in the normal way by *all* of the obligations in the treaty, but non-parties are bound only by those obligations which have *in fact* attained the status of customary law.

(ii) More importantly, the fact that the treaty is intended to lay down a code of conduct for all states in the future may mean that added impetus is given to the formation of customary law. If state practice develops along the lines of the code established by the treaty, the result can be that new rules of custom, similar in content to the obligations of the treaty, come into being. If this happens, non-parties to the treaty will be bound by the new customary law. For example, the 1982 Law of the Sea Convention, which is now in force for its parties, crystallised the concept of the Exclusive Economic Zone (EEZ) to such an extent that it can now be regarded as part of customary law (see e.g. *Tunisia* v *Libya* 1982 ICJ Rep 18) and the concept of the EEZ now exists in parallel in treaty and customary law. However, not all treaty provisions can give rise to customary law in this way. According to the ICJ in the *North Sea Continental Shelf Cases* 1969 ICJ Rep 3, in order to extrapolate a general customary norm from a treaty provision, that treaty provision 'should be of a fundamentally norm creating character such as could be regarded as forming the basis of a general rule of law'. In other words, the treaty provision which is said to give rise to the custom must be capable of general application and must be intended to be the basis for future state practice, as well as being supported by the necessary *opinio juris* (see later) and by acts of practice by non-parties to the treaty. It is unlikely, for example, that the detailed rules regulating the working of the EEZ, found in Part V of the 1982 Law of the Sea Convention, will become part of customary law even though the concept itself has done so. This is because the detailed treaty obligations were designed to be part of the treaty's particular code of law and were not intended to be of general application. Indeed it is unlikely that such *detailed* state practice would occur sufficient enough to establish a rule of customary law. However, when a treaty sets general standards – such as the Convention Against Torture 1984 – the impetus given to customary law formation may be considerable (*Questions relating to the Obligation to Prosecute or Extradite (Belgium* v *Senegal)* (ICJ 2012)).

The legal effect of treaties is not difficult to understand if it is remembered that only parties are bound by the treaty itself. If the treaty reflects customary law, non-parties may have identical obligations, but only because they exist in customary law. If the treaty is intended to develop the law, non-parties *may* come under similar obligations to those found in the treaty if the intention of the treaty and the effect of state practice is to give rise to new customary law.

2.2.1 Law or obligations

The fact that only parties to treaties are bound by them has given rise to a debate about whether treaties create *law* or whether they impose *obligations* which 'the law' says must be carried out. The debate is often expressed in terms of a distinction between 'contract treaties' and 'law-making treaties'. Typically, bilateral treaties are said to be examples of the former, and multilateral treaties examples of the latter. However, since we have the rule that *all* treaties, whether bilateral or multilateral, only bind the parties to them, this is an unhelpful distinction. Rather, the issue is whether all treaties are 'contracts' and impose obligations, or all treaties are 'law-making' and create international law.

2.2.1.1 The treaty as a contract

It is said that treaties are like contracts in national law. According to Lord Templeman in *Maclaine Watson* v *Dept of Trade and Industry* [1989] 3 All ER 523 (the Tin Council litigation), a 'treaty is a contract between the governments of two or more sovereign states'. Treaties are the result of direct negotiations between legal equals and each party is bound by the terms of the agreement because they have consented deliberately to the obligations contained therein. Thus, just as national contracts create specific obligations which 'the law' says must be fulfilled, so international treaties create specific obligations which international law says must be fulfilled. Furthermore, the 'law' which requires treaties to be obeyed is itself a rule of customary international law and is expressed by the maxim *pacta sunt servanda*. Consequently, according to this view the only 'law' involved in a treaty is the customary law that says that states must fulfil their treaty obligations. All of the specific matters detailed in the treaty are not law, but legal obligations. Treaties are a material source of law.

2.2.1.2 The treaty as a source of law

The reason why treaties are described as a source of obligation rather than as a source of law is in an attempt to explain *why* treaties are binding. Allegedly, the answer is that 'customary law says they are'. Yet, even if this is true, this is not a complete or convincing answer because we are faced with the problem discussed in Chapter 1 – namely, where is the legal authority for the customary rule that says treaties are binding? Indeed, to regard treaties purely as a source of obligation conceals the vital function they perform in the system of international law. They are the only method by which states consciously can create binding law and they are routinely used for that very purpose. When a state acts contrary to a treaty, it is said that it has violated international law as well as having violated its obligations towards the other parties. If a state is bound by the terms of the treaty, it is legally bound to act in a certain way and, in a practical sense, it has created law for itself. In fact, given that the purpose of all treaties is to govern the future conduct of the parties, it is difficult to see why they cannot be regarded as creating law for those parties.

It is clear, then, that the legal effect of treaties is identical whether we regard them as law creating or obligation creating. In all cases, a state is bound to act in accordance with the terms of a treaty to which it is a party, whether we call this a 'law' or an 'obligation'. The distinction is, in fact, a theoretical one which is used to help answer the question 'why is international law binding?' Even then, the contract theory of treaties does not provide a solution because it merely moves the question one step up the ladder of authority – it does not tell us why the customary rule (*pacta sunt servanda*) is binding. In fact, the reason why we might like to make a distinction between different types of treaty has nothing to do with their legal effect at all. In practice, a 'treaty contract' or bilateral treaty will terminate either when the particular object for which it was entered into has been achieved or if other unforeseen circumstances intervene, as with the 1977 treaty between Hungary and Czechoslovakia concerning the River Danube which led to the *Case Concerning the Gabcikovo-Nagymaros Project (Hungary v Slovakia)* 1997 ICJ Rep. A 'law-making' or multilateral treaty, on the other hand, may be intended to endure and lay down rules for the conduct of states for the indefinite future. It might give rise to general customary law for all states (e.g. the Law of the Sea Convention 1982, the Convention on the Prevention and Punishment of the Crime of Genocide 1948). In other words, the distinction between the various types of treaty is not one of legal effect but one of purpose and aim, and this is the only reason why we might like to describe some treaties as contracts and some as law-making.

2.3 **Custom**

Customary international law is that law which has evolved from the practice or customs of states. It is the foundation stone of the modern law of nations. Although in the last three decades the treaty has replaced custom as the primary source of international law, a great part of the rules which govern states and other international legal persons today still comes from this source. As was pointed out in the *Gulf of Maine Case* 1984 ICJ Rep 246, custom is ideally suited to the development of general principles and it is always available to fill the void should the detailed legal regime of a treaty fail to gain universal acceptance. The process of customary law formation, being derived from the practice of states and occasionally the practice of other legal persons, is an ongoing phenomenon and its great advantage is that it enables international law to develop in line with the needs of the time. Of course, along with this flexibility comes a certain amount of uncertainty and a lack of speed in the development of new law and here treaties have a definite advantage. Yet the scope of custom is as varied as the activities of states and for this reason its potential as a source of international law is virtually unlimited. It is, quite literally, what states make of it.

2.3.1 **Elements of customary law**

When we say that customary law has evolved from the practice of states, this is exactly what we mean. The activities of states in the international arena may give rise to binding law. For example, if all maritime nations declare a territorial sea 12 miles seaward from the coastline, a customary law may develop to this effect. Obviously, however, it is not all acts (or omissions) that can give rise to customary law and there are certain conditions which must be fulfilled before practice crystallises into law. These may be described conveniently as the elements of customary law and they derive mainly from a series of decisions of the Permanent Court of Justice and its successor, the International Court of Justice. Principal among these are the *North Sea Continental Shelf Cases*, the *Lotus Case* (1927) PCIJ Ser. A No. 10, the *Anglo-Norwegian Fisheries Case* 1951 ICJ Rep 116 and *Nicaragua* v *USA* 1986 ICJ Rep 14, although many other precedents could be given. It should be emphasised, however, that these criteria are not absolute or exclusive and the weight to be given to each factor will depend ultimately on the subject matter of the rule that is in dispute.

2.3.1.1 State practice

As well as being unduly formalistic, any attempted definition of 'state practice' would almost certainly be incomplete. Necessarily, of course, the complete absence of state practice in relation to an alleged rule of customary law is fatal (*Advisory Opinion on the Accordance with international law of the unilateral declaration of independence in respect of Kosovo* (2010)). As a guideline, state practice includes, but is not limited to, actual activity (acts and omissions), statements made in respect of concrete situations or disputes, statements of legal principle made in the abstract (such as those preceding the adoption of a resolution in the General Assembly), national legislation and the practice of international organisations. In fact, some scholars argue that *any* activity of the state can amount to state practice for the purpose of identifying the content of a legal rule; it is merely that different types of activity carry different weight. In this regard, documentary records of 'practice', such as the Repertory of Practice of UN Organs and UK Materials on International Law, are of considerable practical importance. Although views vary about the relative importance of different types of state practice – for example, some states such as the United States argue that an analysis of what states do is more important than what they say – it is clear that *not* doing something (especially when action might reasonably be expected) also carries weight, especially where the claim is that a state is under a new customary law obligation or limitation. This was emphasised strongly by the ICJ in *Jurisdictional Immunities of the State* (*Germany* v *Italy: Greece Intervening*) (2012) where the near total absence of state practice denying immunity to states in the courts of other countries for tortious conduct was regarded as critical in establishing that Italy had violated international law when it did deny Germany immunity in its local courts.

2.3.1.2 Consistency of practice

One of the most important factors in the formation of customary law is that the state practice must be reasonably consistent. It must, in the words of the Permanent Court in the *Lotus Case*, be 'constant and uniform', or what the ICJ in *Jurisdictional Immunities of the State Case* called 'settled practice'. For example, if the maritime nations declared territorial seas of varying seaward limits, then no general customary rule could develop. However, there need not be total consistency, for it is clear that this criterion is satisfied if there is substantial, rather than complete, consistency in the practice of states. It is also clear from the *Anglo-Norwegian Fisheries Case* that the degree of consistency required may vary according to the subject matter of the rule in dispute. Thus, if we are dealing with positive obligations, as where a state is obliged to do something (such as the duty to protect foreign nationals in its territory), a greater degree of consistency may be needed for the formation of a customary norm than in the case of passive obligations where a state is obliged to refrain from doing something (such as not to interfere in the free communication between a diplomatic envoy and his government). Likewise, any alleged change to a customary rule having the character of *jus cogens* (for which, see section 2.3.2.2) would need to be supported by almost universally consistent state practice before it could take effect. Simply put, the more fundamental the customary rule, the more consistent any contrary state practice must be before a change in that rule could be recognised. Similarly, it is clear from the *Nicaragua Case* that the mere existence of some state practice which appears to be contrary to an existing or emerging rule of customary law should not be taken without more to be destructive of that rule. According to that case, contrary state practice should, without evidence of greater intent, be presumed to be action in breach of the rule. This must be correct, for otherwise any state acting contrary to an existing customary rule, without more, could argue that it was 'merely' engaged in developing a new rule rather than breaking an existing one. (See section 2.3.1.6 on changing an existing rule.) Unlawful practice cannot be excused by arguing that it was intended 'merely' to change or clarify existing customary law.

2.3.1.3 Generality of practice

In order for a universal norm of customary law to develop (as opposed to a 'local custom' binding only a few states) the practice must be fairly general. That is, the practice must be common to a significant number of states. Once again, however, it is clear that the practice need only be 'generally adopted in the practice of states' (*Anglo-Norwegian Fisheries Case*) and, as the *North Sea Continental Shelf Cases* illustrate, not all states need participate before a general practice can become law. Conversely, where consistent practice is widespread, the almost irresistible conclusion is that (subject to establishing *opinio juris* – section 2.3.1.5) a rule of customary law does exist – *Jurisdictional Immunities of the State Case*. It is, of course, impossible to determine exactly how many states must participate in a practice, for international law is not concerned with percentages, nor does it operate by way of majority vote. Again, the degree of generality required will vary with the subject matter, so that an onerous customary law obligation may require a more general practice than a norm which gives a state limited privileges. Rules enhancing state sovereignty are often more easily established than rules limiting sovereignty.

However, the concept of generality is subject to some important qualifications that are inherent in the nature of customary law.

(a) In assessing whether a customary rule has come into existence, special weight may be given to the practice of those states whose interests are specifically affected by the subject matter of the rule (*North Sea Continental Shelf Cases*). For example, the practice of major maritime powers will have more significance in the formation of rules on the law of the sea than, for example, that of landlocked Austria. It is not that some states are necessarily more 'important' or more powerful than others; it is, rather, that some states will be directly affected by certain rules and thus their practice is more significant. Indeed, in some cases, it may be that complete local uniformity is required among a group of specially interested states before a rule can develop binding that group.

(b) When a state from the outset objects to a particular practice carried on by other states or adopts a contrary practice, it seems that it may not be bound by an evolving customary rule. This is known as the concept of the 'persistent objector'. In other words, *initial and sustained* objection will prevent a state being bound by a customary rule, as with Norway and the '10 mile rule' in the *Anglo-Norwegian Fisheries Case*. Moreover, while it is generally true that an objection from one state will not prevent the formation of customary law for other, non-objecting states, in some cases it may be that the persistent objector is such an important operator in a particular field that its continued objection prevents customary law developing for all states. Of course, this could happen in special circumstances only, for example, if the USA objected to a certain practice in the field of space exploration. However, while in theory a persistent objector can opt out of *evolving* customary law, in practice there is very little evidence to suggest that a persistent objector can remain outside the scope of a new customary rule for very long. The pressure to conform to the new standard, as well as the disadvantages of being outside the legal orthodoxy, ensure that the objecting state does not long maintain a position contrary to the overwhelming practice of other states. This was true, for example, in respect of the UK's former objection to the extension of the territorial sea from 3 to 12 miles, the latter limit now established for the UK by the Territorial Sea Act 1987. It is also clear that *subsequent* objection to an established rule of customary law cannot prevent that rule binding a state, for it is a matter of principle that states cannot avoid legal obligations once they have come into being. Some scholars argue that there may be an exception to the principle of the validity of pre-existing customary law in respect of 'new' states, that is those that were not in existence at the time of the formation of the custom, at least if the particular customary law can be said to be discriminatory or 'colonial' in origin. An example may be the duty to pay compensation for the nationalisation of foreign-owned property, which is alleged to exist by capital-exporting countries such as the UK and USA, but which is denied by the countries of the less developed world. On the other hand, it should be appreciated that the ability of new states to opt out of 'colonial' or 'imposed' international law is a matter of considerable controversy and the better view may be that the contrary practice of newly independent states should be regarded as of especial significance in assessing whether a new customary law has developed, at least where the 'old' rule is fundamentally contrary to their interests. This would avoid the dangerous claim that some states have a pre-existing inherent exemption from current customary law, as well as allowing each case to be judged on its merits according to all the criteria for the formation of a customary norm. Of course, it is not that subsequent objection is entirely irrelevant whether from a 'new' or established member of the international community: rather that subsequent objection cannot excuse unlawful conduct. Finally, it remains true that persistent objection may, over time, have a significant impact on the substance of customary international law. First, other states may acquiesce in the deviation from the customary norm, so that the subsequent objector is absolved from legal liability towards them. An example is the UK's acquiescence in the Norwegian system of territorial sea delineation in the *Anglo-Norwegian Fisheries Case* 1951 ICJ Rep 116. Secondly, subsequent objections or deviations may become so widespread that the previous rule is destroyed and replaced by a new rule, as with the extension of the territorial sea seaward from the coastline from 3 to 12 miles.

(c) In the *Asylum Case (Columbia v Peru)* 1950 ICJ Rep 266, the Court recognised that Art. 38 of the Statute of the ICJ encompassed local custom as well as general custom, in much the same way as it encompasses bilateral and multilateral treaties. Local customary law may exist where a practice has developed between two or more states, both or all of whom recognise the practice as binding. An example was Portugal's right of transit over Indian territory recognised in the *Rights of Passage Case* 1960 ICJ Rep 6. However, the state alleging the existence of local custom will be under a heavy burden to show that the practice was regarded as legally binding, rather than merely habitual or born of the desire for amicable relations. Subject to this, and to what will be said later about rules of *jus cogens*, local customary law can supplement or derogate from general custom. In practice, local or regional custom is most likely to develop between states sharing the same economic and political ideology (e.g. the EU), although, as the *Rights of Passage Case* shows, this is not essential.

2.3.1.4 Duration of practice

The ICJ has not presented any clear guidelines on the time required for consistent, general state practice to mature into customary law. Indeed, it would be strange if there was a precise rule about how long a practice must continue before it could become law because the process of customary law creation is inherently fluid. The

North Sea Continental Shelf Cases suggest that the length of time needed will vary from subject to subject and, further, that the passage of only a brief period of time is not necessarily a bar to the formation of customary law. If this is true, it raises the possibility that even a single act, without subsequent repetition, can be the basis for custom, although the situations where this could happen must be very limited in practice. So, although 'instant custom' is a possibility, it would require very strong evidence that states regarded the new 'practice' as legally binding. A possible example is the law of outer space where the necessary *opinio juris* may be found in a series of General Assembly resolutions. Outer space does not (yet) admit of widespread and repeated state activity.

2.3.1.5 *Opinio juris*

It is not enough for the formation of customary law that there is general, uniform and consistent state practice. In order that this practice constitutes law, states must recognise it as binding upon them *as law*. State practice must be accompanied by a belief that the practice is obligatory, rather than merely convenient or habitual. This belief in the obligatory nature of the practice is called the *opinio juris*.

In the *Lotus Case*, the PCIJ emphasised that *opinio juris* was an essential element in the formation of customary law. This was reiterated in the *North Sea Continental Shelf Cases* and has been accepted ever since, most recently by the ICJ in the *Jurisdictional Immunities of the State Case* (2012). This is not surprising given that there must be some hallmark by which we can distinguish state practice amounting to law from other kinds of state activity, such as acts of comity or friendship. Yet, while it is easy enough to understand the need for *opinio juris*, it is not so easy to see how it can be established. Rarely is it the case that a state will explain in detail why it has pursued a particular course of conduct. On this point, a majority of the Court in the *North Sea Continental Shelf Cases* said that 'the frequency or even habitual character' of a practice is not enough to establish *opinio juris*. So, it seems that *opinio juris* cannot be inferred from the fact of practice alone because it is a distinct requirement that has to be independently and positively established. Unfortunately, the majority did not go on to tell us how this was to be done. A contrary view was expressed by the dissenting judges in that case precisely because they appreciated the difficulty of proving *opinio juris* if it could not be implied from the fact of repeated activity. Their view was that *opinio juris could* be presumed from consistent practice, unless a contrary intention was apparent. In other words, in the absence of any other evidence or explanation, the minority suggest that we are to assume that states behave in a certain way because they feel legally obliged to do so.

Obviously, these two approaches have important consequences for the formation of customary law. The former, if it were rigidly applied, would make it difficult to establish any reasonably certain rules, while the latter could result in the formation of customary law with little evidence that this was ever intended by the states concerned. There is no advantage in imposing customary law on states, for it would not be respected, but equally the development of international law through the customary law-making process must not be hindered by impossibly strict conditions. In fact, these two theories represent different views about the importance of customary law and its relationship to state sovereignty. Happily, it seems that in practice the ICJ has veered away from either extreme. It is clear that the Court will not accept the simple fact of state activity as evidence of *opinio juris*, at least where it is contended that a state is subject to onerous duties, but neither will it put the state alleging the existence of general custom under a heavy or impossible burden of proof. In the *Jurisdictional Immunities of the State Case*, the ICJ found the *opinio juris* in the very consistent practice of domestic courts and the repeated, and unvarying, public statements of governments. A possible way forward is to recognise that the degree of proof required for *opinio juris* will vary according to the subject matter of the disputed customary rule. Thus, a claim that a rule has attained the status of *jus cogens* might require very clear evidence of *opinio juris* independent of the actual fact of consistent state practice. Conversely, for an alleged rule that grants rights or privileges to all states, it might be possible to infer *opinio juris* from the simple fact of repeated state activity – such as in immunity cases. However, if the alleged rule places burdens on all states, clear extrinsic evidence of *opinio juris* might be required. For example, the lack of use of nuclear weapons cannot provide the *opinio juris* for a rule banning their use because such abstinence may be referable to many other factors (*Advisory Opinion on the Legality of the Threat or Use of Nuclear Weapons* 1996 ICJ Rep 66). In essence, the matter is one of judgement, but in the same way that national law does not require the same *mens rea* for every criminal offence, so international law might require different levels of *opinio juris* and different degrees of proof for different substantive rules of customary law.

It is easy to criticise the requirement of *opinio juris* as a theoretical construct which actually plays no part in the development of international law. In a sense, the concept is tautologous for it suggests that something must be considered as law before it can become law. Yet, without the requirement it would be impossible to determine where habit stopped and law began. Its importance has been affirmed in ICJ decisions such as *Nicaragua* v *USA*, the *Gulf of Maine Case* and the *Jurisdictional Immunities of the State Case*. In this regard, however, it is important to note that the Court in *Nicaragua* v *USA* came face to face with one of the mysteries surrounding the concept of *opinio juris*. In that case, the ICJ determined that the content of customary law on the use of force was virtually identical to that contained in the UN Charter (see section 2.3.2.1 and Chapter 11). A majority of the Court found the state practice and *opinio juris* necessary to support this conclusion in the fact that most states had abstained from the use of force since the advent of the UN Charter in 1945. Indeed, the majority determined that the prohibition on the use of force had attained the status of a customary rule of *jus cogens* – a view now widely adopted (see e.g. *R* v *Jones* [2006] UKHL 16 per Lord Bingham). However, as Judge Jennings pointed out in his Dissenting Opinion in *Nicaragua*, most states are parties to the UN Charter and their conduct/state of mind in refraining from the use of force was surely due to their observance of this paramount treaty obligation rather than because of some view they had about the content of customary law. This paradox, which is always present when treaty and custom cover the same ground, was not resolved by the Court and perhaps it never could be. However, what this aspect of *Nicaragua* v *USA* does illustrate is the flexible way in which the requirement of *opinio juris* can be satisfied when the need arises. The majority in *Nicaragua* also went on to say that it was permissible to find *opinio juris* in, among other things, General Assembly resolutions, statements made by state representatives and in the simple fact that treaties covering similar ground as customary law had been concluded.

Consequently, it seems that the same state activity may be evidence of a general, uniform and consistent state practice as well as the evidence of *opinio juris* necessary to turn that practice into law.

2.3.1.6 How does customary law change?

It is inherent in what has been said already that in order for a new customary law to develop in place of an existing customary law, there must be sufficient state practice contrary to the existing rule supported by *opinio juris*. Necessarily, however, much of this contrary state practice (at least initially) will be regarded as action in breach of the existing law because the customary norm will not yet have changed. It is an unusual feature of the international legal system that only through prima facie illegal conduct can some rules be modified or abandoned. Clearly, in such cases, *opinio juris* will play a pivotal role: in particular, the manner in which the contrary conduct is received by interested members of the international community and any applicable judgment of the ICJ or other international judicial body (such as the International Tribunal for the Law of the Sea in maritime matters). Continued and sustained criticism of the contrary conduct is clear evidence that no replacement rule of customary law is emerging. Of course, it is difficult to define with precision the moment the contrary conduct ceases to be unlawful (if ever) and becomes the manifestation of a new rule, but such nuances are inherent in the concept of customary law and are a mark of its flexibility. Importantly, however, two further points should be noted. First, even if the contrary conduct has not been accepted by the international community at large, a state which accepts or 'acquiesces' in the conduct of another state that is ostensibly in breach of an existing customary norm, will be taken to have forfeited the right to complain of the breach. The 'new' practice will be taken to embody the rule between these two states. A good example is the UK's acquiescence in Norway's use of the 'straight baseline' method of maritime delimitation in the *Norwegian Fisheries Case*, which meant that even if customary law had not changed in Norway's favour, the UK could not complain of it. Secondly, it will be very difficult to establish that a rule of *jus cogens* has been changed by contrary state practice. Rules of *jus cogens* are fundamental rules of customary law that not even a treaty can contradict: for example, the customary prohibition of the use of aggressive force and the prohibition of genocide (see section 2.3.2.2). Although in theory such customary rules can change, it is difficult to imagine how in normal circumstances any contrary state practice will be accepted as the emergence of a new rule. Any contrary conduct is likely to be regarded itself as a serious breach of international law, and this can lead in practice to rules of *jus cogens* having *de facto* permanence – a fact that might explain why there is a reluctance to endow many rules with this status. Perhaps such rules can be changed only when there is a fundamental change in the nature of the international system to which the rule relates: for example, the dissolution of the United Nations and the proliferation of nuclear weapons might generate sufficient state practice and *opinio juris* to justify a change in the *jus cogens* rule prohibiting the use of aggressive force; or the use of force for a specific purpose (e.g. to combat 'terrorism') might become so prevalent that the rule of *jus cogens* prohibiting general force is modified. As can be imagined, however, this would herald more than just a change in *jus cogens* rules.

Custom has been a source of international law for as long as states have been governed by legal rules. There is no agreed explanation as to why customary practice is capable of constituting binding law. Some jurists have suggested that custom is based on the consent of states, explicit or implied, but this does not explain why new states are bound by existing law for they have never had the opportunity of forming any intention in respect of the practice. Neither does it explain the ineffectiveness of subsequent objection to an existing rule. Once again, the real question is why any international law is binding and this is considered in Chapter 1.

Lastly, we must note that the primary reason why custom has been supplanted in recent years as the major source of international law is the ability of treaty law to lay down definite and precise legal rules. Of course, this does not mean that custom has no advantages. It develops by spontaneous practice and reflects changing community values so that, unlike a treaty, it need not go out of date. In addition, the often flexible or vague nature of customary law means that conflicts can be avoided and a practical solution to disputes worked out according to legal guidelines rather than definite legal obligations. On the negative side, customary law cannot meet the needs of a rapidly changing international society, especially in more technical fields where detailed rules may be required or where it is impossible to divine any consistent or durable practice. Again, while local custom can deal with local problems, the diverse political, economic and social nature of states makes customary law an impractical tool for the development of major legal regimes, such as those regulating use of ocean resources, Antarctica and protection of the environment.

2.3.2 The relationship between customary and treaty law

It should not be thought that custom and treaty are in competition. They are the two major – some would say the only – sources of international law and they are both necessary components of the international legal order. Usually, they serve different purposes and are quite complementary, as illustrated by the customary and treaty rules on the use of force discussed in *Nicaragua* v *USA*. The relationship between treaty and custom has been considered briefly already and we have seen that a treaty may codify custom or may lead to the development of new customary law through the impetus it gives to state practice. This overlap causes no problems when the treaty and custom are complementary but difficulties can arise if the treaty and customary law stipulate contradictory or dissimilar obligations.

2.3.2.1 Where custom and treaty are complementary

Where customary law and treaty law stipulate the same or similar legal obligations there are few problems. Parties to the treaty will be bound by the treaty and non-parties will be bound by custom. More importantly, the case of *Nicaragua* v *USA* makes it clear that custom does not cease to bind a state even if it is a party to a treaty stipulating the same obligation. If this is the case, the state is bound by both custom and treaty law. The importance of this parallel obligation was illustrated in the *Nicaragua Case* itself, where both the USA and Nicaragua were bound by the prohibition on the use of armed force contained in the UN Charter (the treaty) and by a similar obligation in customary law. However, the ICJ did not have jurisdiction in respect of a dispute concerning treaty obligations, but was able to pass judgment on the merits of the dispute because of the parallel and virtually identical obligation existing in customary law over which it did have jurisdiction. As the Court indicated, it may be that different rules of interpretation apply to custom and treaty law respectively, and the latter may embroider the central obligation with more detail, but that does not alter the fact that a state which is party to a treaty is bound by both that treaty and any similar customary law.

It is as yet unclear, however, whether 'parallel obligations' can exist in *all* cases where treaty and custom overlap. In *Nicaragua*, the particular customary law at issue was a rule of *jus cogens* – a rule fundamental to the system – and it is hardly surprising that the ICJ should take the view that it had an existence independent of treaty law. Thus, if the treaty should fall away, this rule of custom would still regulate states' conduct and the use of force would still be unlawful. Yet, the pertinent question is whether a 'normal' rule of customary law would have survived a treaty covering the same subject matter in the same circumstances. After all, while there is a premium on the continued existence of a customary rule prohibiting the use of force, irrespective of any treaty, can the same be said of, say, a customary rule stipulating the width of the territorial sea? In other words, not only were there jurisdictional problems which compelled the Court in *Nicaragua* to develop the theory of parallel obligations (and hence to assert jurisdiction), that theory has not been tested where less fundamental rules of customary law are said to be superseded by an all-embracing treaty. That said, however, in the *Questions relating to the Obligation to Prosecute or Extradite (Belgium v Senegal) Case* (ICJ 2012), Belgium alleged that Senegal had violated both customary international law and the Convention Against Torture in relation to the prosecution of persons alleged to have committed torture. The Court held that there was no dispute in relation to a breach of customary law concerning an obligation to prosecute (partly because it was not clear that the customary rule contended for by Belgium in fact existed), but nevertheless the Court determined that such an obligation did exist under the Convention. Again, this might have been influenced by the fact that the prohibition of torture is a rule of *jus cogens* (as distinct from the obligation to prosecute individuals), but it is the converse of *Nicaragua*, with treaty law filling the potential void of customary law. As one might expect, the ICJ sees the sources of law as complementary rather than in competition.

2.3.2.2 When custom and treaty conflict

Where custom and treaty law conflict, there is some disagreement as to the effect this has on the legal relations of the parties to a dispute.

(a) If the treaty is later in time than the custom, subject to the operation of rules of *jus cogens* (at (c)), the treaty will prevail. This is because treaties represent a deliberate and conscious act of law creation. The parties to the treaty will be governed by the terms of the treaty, while the relations of non-parties (including parties and non-parties) will be governed by customary law. Thus, it is perfectly possible for states to have different rights and duties with different states in respect of the same subject matter or the same dispute.

(b) Where contrary customary law has developed subsequent to the adoption of a treaty, the position is unclear. Because the custom is later in time than the treaty, it might be thought that this should prevail, especially since non-parties to the treaty will be bound by the new custom. However, this cuts against the certainty and vitality of obligations freely and deliberately undertaken in a treaty. In practice, it is likely that subsequent custom can modify treaty obligations for state-parties to the treaty only in very exceptional circumstances, perhaps only where there is a manifest and overwhelming consensus among parties that it should be abandoned. The better view is that the treaty continues to govern the relations between parties even though a new practice has developed. A practical example of this has occurred with the delimitation of the continental shelf between opposite and adjacent states, where parties to the 1958 Convention on the Continental Shelf (not also being parties to the 1982 Law of the Sea Convention) are still bound by the 'equidistance principle' even though customary law has developed in a different direction. It should be noted, however, that the ICJ will strive to avoid this kind of conflict. So, even though at first sight a treaty and custom may appear to conflict, the ICJ will attempt to interpret the treaty as complementary to the new custom as far as is possible. Again, this has happened with respect to continental shelf delimitation, where the 'equidistance principle' has been interpreted in such a way as not to impinge too greatly on developing customary law (see e.g. *Anglo-French Continental Shelf Case* (1979) 18 ILM 397). Similarly, in the *Danube Dam Case*, the ICJ was able to synthesise later developments in customary law with the obligations contained in the (earlier) disputed treaty between Hungary and Slovakia on the ground that the terms of the treaty specifically allowed 'new' norms of customary law to impact upon its application. These attempts to find consistency are not surprising given that international law is intended to be an integrated system of legal rules.

(c) The general superiority of treaties is displaced where rules of *jus cogens* are concerned. Article 53 of the Vienna Convention on the Law of Treaties 1969 states that:

[A] treaty is void if, at the time of its conclusion, it conflicts with a peremptory norm of general international law. For the purposes of the present Convention, a peremptory norm of general international law is a norm accepted and recognised by the international community of States as a whole as a norm from which no derogation is permitted and which can be modified only by a subsequent norm of general international law having the same character.

Rules of *jus cogens* are rules of customary international law that are so fundamental that they cannot be modified by treaty. Any treaty provision which conflicts with a rule of *jus cogens* is void and this is true whether or not the rule of *jus cogens* developed before or after the treaty came into force (Art. 64 Vienna Convention on the Law of Treaties 1969). This is a fundamental principle of international jurisprudence, and undisputed by states, organisations and other persons subject to international law. However, it is important to understand its proper scope. The rule is that a treaty must not contradict the *obligation or norm* which has attained the status of *jus cogens*. It is *not* that a treaty cannot regulate how that obligation or norm is upheld. We are concerned with treaties which contradict the substance of the rule (void) not with treaties which deal with procedural or peripheral matters. So, while it is a rule of *jus cogens* that war crimes and crimes against humanity are unlawful, a treaty which provides that a state enjoys immunity from the local courts of another state in respect of such matters is not void – *Jurisdictional Immunities of the State (Germany v Italy: Greece Intervening)* (2012) – because the treaty is regulating how the obligation is to be enforced; it is not a denial of that obligation.

Although according to Art. 53 these fundamental or peremptory norms can be changed by new and convincing practice (leading to a new fundamental rule), in reality this is unlikely to happen, and this makes identification of such rules very important. Quite simply, because these rules are fundamental, any conduct contrary to the rule of *jus cogens* will usually be regarded as 'illegal' no matter how often it is repeated. In this sense, rules of *jus cogens* are self-perpetuating and it would take almost unanimous agreement and very weighty evidence of *opinio juris* before such a rule could be replaced, at least where it is claimed that the 'new' rule now allows that which was previously prohibited. It may be otherwise, if the 'new' rule of *jus cogens* is said to modify the old rule without changing its essential purpose (see section 2.3.1.6).

Unfortunately, there is not universal agreement as to which rules of customary law have attained this exalted status and this is why no examples are given in Art. 53 of the Vienna Convention. Following the judgment in *Nicaragua* v *USA*, one certain example is the prohibition of the use of armed force in international relations, as in the prohibition of war crimes and crimes against humanity *Jurisdictional Immunities of the State Case*. Other possibilities include the sovereign equality of states, freedom of the high seas and, more specifically, the right of self-determination (*Case Concerning East Timor (Portugal* v *Australia)* 1995 ICJ Rep 89) and the prohibition of genocide and torture. So, for example, a treaty between State A and State B whereby each undertook to help the other in an armed attack on State C would be unlawful and void. It could not be enforced by either party and no liability would arise for non-performance. Treaties establishing military alliances such as NATO are not contrary to rules of *jus cogens* because they are concerned with mutual defence, which is lawful. Note, however, in the US domestic law case of *Committee of US Citizens Living in Nicaragua* v *Reagan*, 859 F.2d. 929, the national court was of the opinion that the obligation to abide by an ICJ judgment issued in respect of compulsory jurisdiction was not itself a rule of *jus cogens*.

2.4 General principles of law

According to para. 1(c) of Art. 38, the Court may consider 'the general principles of law recognised by civilised nations'. As far as the reference to 'civilised nations' is concerned, possibly this was meant to exclude consideration of 'primitive' or 'underdeveloped' legal systems, rather than being a reference to the economic or political status of different countries. Today it is irrelevant and can be ignored.

Article 38(1)(c) is an intriguing provision and it has generated much academic comment. Some regard the reference to 'general principles' as truly ground-breaking, arguing that it represents an acknowledgement by states that there are sources of international law outside state control. Others take a narrower view, contending that para. 1(c) merely describes general, non-specific principles that have already been validated as 'law' by the 'real' formal sources: viz. custom and treaty. We now consider some of the alternatives.

2.4.1 Natural law doctrines

Some jurists (e.g. Verdross) believe that the effect of Art. 38(1)(c) is to incorporate natural law doctrines into the corpus of international law. Rules derived from natural law are said to have a pre-existing legal validity – that is, they are already law irrespective of treaty or custom – and reference should be made to Chapter 1 to see how these differ from 'positive law'. Almost certainly, this was not the original purpose of para. 1(c) because states were (and are) reluctant to give up control over the creation of 'law', although in recent years it has been alleged that this provision is the 'source' of those legal rules dealing with moral issues, such as the protection of human rights and the prohibition of genocide. However, while such principles as these may well have a universal appeal, in practice the source of a state's concrete obligations in these fields is firmly based in treaty and custom. Respect for the individual and similar moral doctrines may be examples of 'general principles' and this may explain why they *should* be law, but as far as states are concerned such principles form part of the corpus of international law only if they are 'enacted' by treaty or custom.

2.4.2 Material sources

Following from section 2.4.1, it can be argued that para. 1(c) adds nothing to Art. 38, for everything which is 'law' is covered already by treaty or custom. This was the view of Art. 38 favoured by the now defunct USSR in line with its general jurisprudence that international law can be created only with the express or implied consent of states. So, while para. 1(c) could encompass general principles of international law, such as 'freedom of the high seas' or 'sovereign equality', the actual obligations incumbent on states in these areas derive from treaty or custom. General principles may, therefore, be purely *descriptive* of general doctrines or bundles of rights which form part of international law, but they are nothing to do with the law creating sources of international law. On this view, general principles are material sources only.

2.4.3 Rules and principles common to all legal systems

Perhaps a better view of Art. 38 1(c) is that its purpose is to ensure that international law includes rules and principles common to all legal systems because such rules are part of the structure of 'the law'. If international law is to be accepted as a system of law, it must incorporate those procedural and administrative rules which are inherent in the concept of every legal system and, therefore, part of the law of every state. Examples are the right of legal persons to go to court to settle disputes and, perhaps, the right to be heard by a court before judgment is pronounced. Indeed, the latter has been emphasised by the Court in cases where one party has not participated formally in its proceedings, with the result that the Court takes it upon itself to consider all the points that the absent state would have raised, as in the *US Diplomatic and Consular Staff in Tehran Case (US v Iran)* 1980 ICJ Rep 3 and *Nicaragua v USA*. Also in this category are evidential rules such as the exclusion of circumstantial evidence (*Corfu Channel Case* 1949 ICJ Rep 4), the general principle that a claimant is entitled to receive compensation for proven injury (*Chorzow Factory Case* (1928) PCIJ Ser. A No. 17 and *Danube Dam Case*, para. 152) and the principle of *res judicata*, applied with such effect in the *Case Concerning the Application of the Convention on the Prevention and Punishment of the Crime of Genocide (Bosnia and Herzegovina v Serbia & Montenegro)* (ICJ 2007) to prevent Serbia challenging the jurisdiction of the ICJ given that an earlier judgment between the parties had decided that it did have jurisdiction. These are 'principles' which must form part of international law because it is a system of law. In addition, it was suggested by Judge McNair in the *International Status of South West Africa Case* 1950 ICJ Rep 128, that certain substantive national law concepts may be incorporated in international law under this paragraph. The point here is not that national law concepts should be imported in to international law wholesale, but rather that national law can provide an indication of the types of rule, based on public policy, which might be of assistance in international law. These might include, for example, the concept of trusts (*South West Africa Case*), the concept of subrogation (*Mavrommatis Palestine Concessions Case* (1925) PCIJ Ser. A No. 5), the concept of limited liability (*Barcelona Traction Case* 1970 ICJ Rep 3) and, controversially, the principle that decisions of executive organs (the Security Council) can be reviewed by a competent judicial authority (the ICJ) (first phase, *Case Concerning the Application of the Genocide Convention (Bosnia v Yugoslavia)* 1993 ICJ Rep 325, per Judge Lauterpacht). However, whether substantive legal concepts from diverse legal systems are brought into the corpus of international law under this view of Art. 38(1)(c), or whether that effect is given only to those procedural and administrative rules inherent in every system of law, it is clear that the concepts or rules (as the case may be) have a pre-existing legal validity. They do not need to be validated by either custom or treaty to have legal effect.

2.4.4 Principles of equity

According to Judge Hudson in the *River Meuse Case (Netherlands v Belgium)* (1937) PCIJ Ser. A/B No. 70, 'principles of equity have long been considered to constitute a part of international law, and as such they have often been applied by international tribunals'. Such principles, being general principles of fairness and justice, appear to be within the ambit of Art. 38(1)(c) and certainly have been applied by the ICJ and other international judicial bodies. Examples include the *River Meuse Case* itself (equitable principle of estoppel), the *Temple of Preah Vihear Case*, 1962 ICJ Rep 6 (acquiescence) and the *Frontier Dispute Case (Burkina Faso v Mali)* 1986 ICJ Rep 554 (equity in territorial delimitation). Perhaps the most prominent use of equity as a source of international law has been in the law of the sea in the context of the delimitation of maritime zones between opposite and adjacent states (see Chapter 8). Here, the ICJ has sought 'an equitable solution derived from the applicable law' (*Fisheries Jurisdiction Case (UK v Iceland)* 1974 ICJ Rep 3) and has elevated the use of equity to an art form. The essential point is that the concept of equity is a source of international law in the sense that it may influence the manner in which more substantive rules are applied. It is a 'form of equity which constitutes a method of interpretation of the law in force, and is one of its attributes' (*Frontier Dispute Case* at p. 58). This is important, as the judges of the ICJ and other tribunals must be seen to be applying rules of law, rather than exercising an individual discretion based on their own personal predilections. Consequently, the ICJ has made great efforts to distinguish the use of equitable principles from its power to decide a case *ex aequo et bono* (according to fair dealing and good conscience) under Art. 38(2) of its Statute. The Court has emphasised that equity is not an abstract concept, but denotes the application of substantive rules of international law with due regard to fairness and reasonableness (*Rann of Kutch Arbitration (India v Pakistan)* (1968) 50 ILR 2). Unlike the power to decide a case *ex aequo et bono*, the use of equitable principles means a decision according to law, not one taken outside it by means of a sense of abstract justice.

2.4.5 General principles of international law

It is also possible that Art. 38(1)(c) may include 'general principles of international law'. These are similar to general principles of law common to national legal systems, save that they have a distinct international character because of the context in which they apply. Examples include the 'sovereign equality of nations' and the exclusiveness of a state's jurisdiction within its own territory. It is apparent that these 'principles' are in the nature of bundles of rights and this has led some commentators to argue that they comprise political goals rather than enforceable legal rules. Following this argument, the detail and precise scope of the principles of 'sovereign equality' and 'exclusive domestic jurisdiction' must be provided by 'real' norms of treaty and customary law. Nevertheless, even if these 'principles' do not qualify as binding law (and some would argue that they do), it is clear that such general principles may have a profound impact on the development of international law, either as furnishing a reason why specific norms *should* be adopted or as the catalyst for state practice leading to the creation of customary and treaty law. A good illustration is provided by the strong (but controversial) dissent of Judge Weeramantry in the *Nuclear Test Case (New Zealand v France)* 1995 ICJ Rep 288. He stated that there is 'a fundamental principle of environmental law which must be noted. It is well entrenched in international law ... This basic principle [is] that no nation is entitled by its own activities to cause damage to the environment of any other nation.' It is not certain that Judge Weeramantry is justified in reaching this conclusion, but if his 'basic principle' is a 'general principle of international law', it is apparent that its generality will need to be tempered with rules of more focused content and it may well be that custom, or even only treaty law, can provide this.

Without doubt, Art. 38(1)(c) has eroded the strict positivist view of international law. It permits the Court to apply principles which do not seem to have their origin in either custom or treaty, although they may later become embodied in such. Moreover, the fact that there is little agreement about the precise content of these 'general principles' does not seem to have inhibited the Court and other tribunals from making full use of them. As in all systems of law, judges fear a *non liquet* – an absence of rules in novel situations – and Art. 38(1)(c) clearly helps reduce this risk although it has not eliminated it (see *Advisory Opinion on the Legality of the Threat or Use of Nuclear Weapons* 1996 ICJ Rep 66). Perhaps this is the ultimate justification for their use in international law which, after all, does not benefit from the certainty provided by institutional methods of law creation.

2.5 Judicial decisions

2.5.1 The International Court of Justice

Judicial decisions are described in Art. 38 as a 'subsidiary' means for the determination of law. In theory, they do not make law but are declaratory of pre-existing law. They are law identifying or material sources of law. This appears to be confirmed by Art. 59 of the ICJ Statute, which states that 'the decision of the Court has no binding force except between the parties and in respect of that particular case'. Indeed, in the *Certain Phosphate Lands in Nauru Case (Nauru v Australia) (Preliminary*

Objections) (1993) 32 ILM 46 the ICJ specifically relied on Art. 59 when rejecting Australia's objection to the exercise of jurisdiction. In the majority's view, provided the immediate dispute before the Court did not form the 'very subject matter' of a dispute involving an unrepresented state, 'the interests of a third State which is not a party to the case are protected by Art. 59'. Thus, even though the UK and New Zealand had also constituted the Administering Authority of Nauru under a UN Trusteeship Agreement, and even though Nauru's claims related to acts done during that Administration, the Court would not decline to exercise jurisdiction in a dispute concerning Australia because neither the UK nor New Zealand could be bound by the decision of the Court. In fact, this rather literal approach to Art. 59 seems to rest on two complementary assumptions: first, that Art. 59 allows the Court to ignore the actual decision in one case, even when deciding another case about similar subject matter, both when the subsequent case is between different states (as illustrated by the *Nauru Case*) or even when it is between the same two states (see e.g. the two *South West Africa Cases* of 1962 and 1966 (Preliminary Objections) 1962 ICJ Rep 319; (Second Phase) 1966 ICJ Rep 6); and secondly, that Art. 59 allows the Court to ignore a prior determination as to the substance or content of a rule of international law on a specific matter (irrespective of the parties) simply because it was elucidated in a previous decision.

While it is true that Art. 59 deliberately excludes a formal doctrine of *stare decisis* (or binding precedent) from the international legal system, at least in the sense just discussed, we need to be wary. In essence, to adopt a strict application of Art. 59 ignores the practical effect which an ICJ decision may have on the legal obligations of very many other states, and this was the core of the argument of the four judges who dissented (agreeing with the Australian objection) in the *Nauru Case*. So, in the *Case Concerning East Timor (Portugal v Australia)* 1995 ICJ Rep 90, a substantial majority of the Court (14:2) declined jurisdiction precisely because Indonesia's international obligations would be called into question by consideration of the case, irrespective of the 'safeguard' provided by Art. 59. Perhaps the difference in these two attitudes turns not so much on the ambit of Art. 59 but on whether the obligations of the 'third state' would form the 'very subject matter' of the dispute. In *Nauru* they did not and jurisdiction could have been exercised; in *East Timor* they would have and jurisdiction was declined, but the line is a fine one. In any event, it is clear that the ICJ pays great regard to both the actual decisions it has reached in previous cases and to the law it has declared therein. For example, in the *Interpretation of Peace Treaties Case* 1950 ICJ Rep 65, the Court felt obliged to distinguish the earlier decision of the PCIJ in the *Eastern Carelia Case* (1923) PCIJ Ser. B No. 5, when, if one were to take Art. 59 at face value, this was not at all necessary. Similarly, the Court will follow its earlier decisions, as in the *Exchange of Greek and Turkish Populations Case* (1925) PCIJ Ser. B No. 10, where it referred to the 'precedent afforded by the *Wimbledon Case*'. Likewise, if the *Nauru Case* had gone to a hearing on the merits (the case was settled out of court), it is difficult to see how the UK and New Zealand could have avoided being tarnished by any finding of Australian responsibility given that they were joint administrators of the territory with Australia before it became independent. It is not simply that the Court regards its earlier judgments as examples or guidelines, but rather that they are seen as *authority* for future decisions, just as in the *Nauru Case* itself the principles of *Nicaragua* v *USA* were relied on by the majority. Similarly, in a series of decisions, the

Court has developed a set of principles regarding the delimitation of the disputed maritime zones and, practically speaking, these have no validity other than the fact that they have been incorporated in formal judgments and followed in subsequent cases. In this sense, 'judicial decisions' are the source of much international maritime law. Indeed, the fact that the Court largely circumvents Art. 59 in practice (except where its applicability is useful in order to *assert* jurisdiction over a reluctant state, e.g. *Nauru Case*) is not surprising given that, as a court of law, it will seek to develop and maintain a coherent and consistent body of legal principles.

This leads us to another issue, namely whether the Court's function really is limited to the determination of disputes according to pre-existing legal rules. Whatever the theory, the better view is that the ICJ is more involved in the process of law creation than either Art. 38 or Art. 59 of its Statute suggests. First, it is obvious that the Court will decide, once and for all, the substance of a dispute submitted to it and, under the Statute, states are bound by this decision. In a practical sense, therefore, the decision of the Court has created law for the parties, for they are obliged to do or not to do something which previously was in doubt. Indeed, this may be so even if the judgment of the Court is technically an Advisory Opinion, as in the *Legal Consequences of the Construction of a Wall in the Occupied Palestinian Territory Case* where the Court's conclusion necessarily placed Israel under international obligations in connection with the removal of the wall – obligations which if not fulfilled will involve Israel in international responsibility, (2004 ICJ Rep paras. 149–153). Secondly, and of more significance, a decision of the Court may have a profound impact on customary law. It is often the case that the Court will bring the process of crystallisation of customary law to a swift conclusion. It may accelerate the creation of customary law by confirming trends in state practice and by 'discovering' the necessary *opinio juris*. This seems to have happened in the *Anglo-Norwegian Fisheries Case* and in *Tunisia* v *Libya* in respect of the Exclusive Economic Zone. Likewise, the Court may confirm that a principle first adumbrated in a treaty or even draft treaty has now attained the status of general customary law, as in the *Territorial Dispute Case (Libya* v *Chad)* 1994 ICJ Rep 6 and the *Palestinian Wall Case* with respect to Art. 31 of the Vienna Convention on the Law of Treaties, in the *Danube Dam Case* concerning the ILC's Draft Articles on 'defences' on the law of State Responsibility and in the *Case Concerning the Application of the Convention on the Prevention and Punishment of the Crime of Genocide (Bosnia and Herzegovina* v *Serbia & Montenegro)* (ICJ 2007) concerning Draft Articles 4, 8 and 16 of the ILC's Draft on State Responsibility. Moreover, decisions of the Court may have a decisive effect on subsequent state practice, for they can indicate how the law is developing or how it should develop. If states then order their affairs to meet the standard identified by the Court, new customary law may come into existence, as in the *Nottebohm Case* 1955 ICJ Rep 4. By way of contrast, a decision of the Court can determine that a rule of customary law does *not* exist, as in the *Threat or Use of Nuclear Weapons Case*, itself a 'mere' Advisory Opinion, which determined that there was no rule either prohibiting or permitting the use of nuclear weapons per se. In conclusion then, although the Court technically is disbarred from participating in the law-making process, in practice this is a wholly unrealistic view. The better view is that the decisions of the Court have a similar impact in international law as do decisions of the Supreme Court in UK law, without the formal doctrine of binding precedent, and this is likely to be the case with the decisions of the International Criminal Court within its sphere of activity. The attempt to protect state sovereignty by limiting the function of the ICJ (and the ICC) to one of simple adjudication rather than law creation largely has failed.

2.5.2 Other tribunals

It is tempting to think of judicial decisions only in terms of those emanating from the ICJ and its predecessor the PCIJ. However, as we shall see when considering in detail the peaceful resolution of disputes in international law, only three or so cases a year go to the 'World Court' while many more disputes are settled elsewhere. In fact, the reference to 'judicial decisions' in Art. 38 is not qualified and there is no reason why the decisions of other judicial bodies should not be regarded as 'sources' of international law in the same way as those of the ICJ itself. Thus, we may make reference to decisions of arbitration panels, national courts, specialised institutions and regional courts such as the International Criminal Court, the Inter-American Court of Human Rights, the European Court of Human Rights, the Yugoslav War Crimes Tribunal (much relied on in the *Case Concerning the Application of the Convention on the Prevention and Punishment of the Crime of Genocide (Bosnia and Herzegovina* v *Serbia & Montenegro)* (ICJ 2007)), the Law of the Sea Tribunal, the African Court of Human and Peoples' Rights and the Centre for the Settlement of Investment Disputes. Not only are decisions of these and similar bodies generally binding between the parties or in respect of the international culpability of individuals, they may also help considerably in the development of certain areas of the law. The awards of Mixed-Claims Commissions, for example the Iran–US Commission, have done much to clarify and develop the law of state responsibility and the Yugoslav War Crimes Tribunal is adding to our understanding of this developing area of state and individual responsibility. Further, national courts deal regularly with matters of international law and provide important evidence as to the practice of states, particularly in fields such as state immunity, neutrality, extradition, international personality and the protection of human rights. The *Pinochet* litigation in the UK concerning the scope of Head of State immunity, *Bat* v *Germany* (2011) on the scope of immunity for other state personnel and *A* v *Secretary of State for the Home Department* [2006] 2 AC 221 concerning the admissibility of evidence obtained in violation of international law are prime examples. Generally, of course, decisions of national courts cannot be regarded as a means of law creation, but they may provide authoritative guidance as to the status of existing customary law. They are law identifying or material sources. Occasionally, however, they may have an even greater impact, as in *The Paquete Habana* (1900) 175 US 677, a US Supreme Court case which did much to clarify the concept of customary law itself.

In any system of law, those institutions whose function is to decide disputed questions in concrete situations will necessarily play a major role. This is no less true in international law than it is in national law. The judgments of the ICJ have great political and legal importance (as will those of the International Criminal Court) and their contribution to the development of international law should not be underestimated. Similarly, any other judicial body which pronounces on substantive questions of law affecting the rights and duties of states or other international legal persons can, in some measure or other, be regarded as a source of international law.

2.6 Writings of publicists

The writings of the 'most highly qualified publicists' are also to be regarded as a 'subsidiary' means for the determination of rules of law, although it is clear that they are material or evidential sources only. Today, the writings of even the most respected international lawyers cannot create law.

It is true, however, that during the formative period of international law, the writings of jurists such as Grotius, Vattel and Gentili were instrumental in establishing the very idea that there was a set of binding rules that could govern the relations of sovereign and independent states. This may account for their inclusion in Art. 38 today. Of course, the development of the positivist theory of international law, with its emphasis on state practice and consent, necessarily meant that the opinions of writers on substantive questions became less important and this has continued now that states have so many opportunities of expressing their views in bodies such as the United Nations. Yet, even if the writings of publicists are of purely evidential weight, they may be of great importance where a rule is vague or uncertain, as demonstrated by the use of publicists in *The Paquete Habana Case*. Moreover, like judicial decisions, the writings of publicists can have a direct impact on customary law, for they can help establish state practice by predicting trends and encouraging states to follow the predicted – and desirable – path. In addition, as a purely literary 'source', the writings of publicists are used frequently in the Foreign Offices and legal departments of most governments. There is no statute book for international law and textbooks and publications represent a quick and easy way to discover the current content of the law.

Of course, a certain amount of judgment must be used when choosing which publicist to rely on, and much will depend on the time of writing, the political orientation of the author and even his nationality. In the *Spanish Zone of Morocco Claims Case* (1925) 2 RIAA 615, Judge Huber warned that writers 'are frequently politically inspired' and caution must be exercised when the country of the author has a special interest in a particular matter. The views of UK and Argentinian jurists on the sovereignty of the Falkland Islands, for example, would have to be treated with some care, although the same need not be true of more disinterested observers. In fact, there is very little evidence as to the degree to which judges of the International Court rely on the writings of jurists, apart from their own, but it may be that they are used more frequently in the actual practice of international law than Art. 38 would otherwise suggest. While they can only be material or evidential sources, they may have a tangible effect on state practice as well as being the everyday first reference of the practising international lawyer.

2.7 Resolutions and decisions of international organisations

Resolutions of international organisations are omitted from the list of materials that the court may consider when deciding disputes submitted to it and this may be because such resolutions do not usually, of themselves, create binding law. Generally speaking, the principles contained in the resolutions of most international organisations cannot be regarded as rules of law simply by reason of their incorporation in such a formal text. They are material or evidential sources. However, as before, formal resolutions may accelerate the formation of customary law as well as providing crucial evidence of the elusive *opinio juris* (see e.g. the use of General Assembly resolutions by the ICJ in *Nicaragua v USA*). Much of the debate about the legal effect of resolutions has been concerned with those of the General Assembly and special reference is made to these at section 2.7.1. It should be remembered, however, that much of what is said in respect of these resolutions applies to those of other bodies also, especially where the organisation is concerned with a specific area of international law. Thus, the resolutions and decisions of the International Labour Organisation and the Atomic Energy Agency have done much to develop the law relating to workers' rights and the use of nuclear materials respectively.

2.7.1 The General Assembly

The General Assembly is essentially a political body, and even though it produces many resolutions dealing with questions of international law this is not its main function. The primary rule is that resolutions of the General Assembly are not binding, even if they are adopted unanimously (see the discussion in the *East Timor Case* at p. 261). States are not legally obliged to follow the conduct stipulated in a General Assembly resolution even if they voted in favour of it. However, as with many of the 'sources' of international law, this simple statement of principle conceals the considerable practical importance of Assembly resolutions.

It is clear that there is one exception to this rule that resolutions are not binding, namely those resolutions concerned with the internal working of the United Nations or matters peculiarly within its competence. For example, resolutions on the admittance of new states, on election to the Security Council, on request for ICJ Advisory Opinions, on the budget and on the appointment of judges to the ICJ are all legally binding. They have full legal effect for all members of the Organisation. Some of these resolutions may have an external effect, in the sense that they create a state of affairs that even non-members must respect. This is the case with resolutions concerning UN-administered territories, as was once the case with what is now Namibia, which bind all states in much the same way as territorial treaties bind non-parties. Of course, it can be argued that these resolutions do not create international law at all, for they are concerned with the competence of the Organisation itself, but this would seem to be a misdescription, at least where 'external effect' resolutions are concerned. As the ICJ said when considering the General Assembly's termination of the trusteeship of Nauru by resolution in 1967, '[s]uch a resolution had definitive legal effect.'

While General Assembly resolutions dealing with substantive questions of international law (e.g. on the Definition of Aggression 1974) are not binding, there is an interplay between these and customary international law. As with treaties, General Assembly resolutions may be declaratory of existing customary law and, even though it is not the resolution itself that creates the binding obligation, this may be where the principles are found. An early example is the 1965 Declaration on the Inadmissibility of Intervention in the Domestic Affairs of States. Similarly, Assembly resolutions may crystallise state practice so that a new rule of custom is created, although this may be more obvious where the resolution is adopted unanimously, as with the resolutions on the law of outer space. With contentious resolutions, care must be taken to distinguish between those which are *evidence* of existing custom and those which express a hope or wish of the majority but which do not embody customary law. A good example of the latter is provided by the Assembly resolutions stigmatising the use of nuclear weapons. These have neither created nor embody customary law (see the *Threat or Use of Nuclear Weapons Case*). Of course, that is not to prevent General Assembly resolutions stipulating a voluntary course of conduct which is subsequently followed by states and becomes a rule of customary law, as seems to have happened with the 1960 Declaration on the Granting of Independence to Colonial Peoples and the right of self-determination. Importantly, a vote in favour of a resolution *may* be an indication of *opinio juris*, although this must be treated with considerable caution because of the political nature of the Assembly.

In a similar vein, General Assembly resolutions may be used deliberately to attack and eventually destroy an existing rule of customary law. This seems to have been the purpose behind the 1974 Declaration on the Establishment of the New International Economic Order and the 1974 Charter of Economic Rights and Duties of States. Of course, there is considerable danger in the use of Assembly resolutions for this purpose, for it may lead to a system of law creation (or rather destruction) by majority vote. That would be unacceptable to many states and is contrary to the spirit of international law. The better view is that the destruction of customary law through Assembly resolutions can happen only in the most exceptional circumstances.

Apart from legal considerations, General Assembly resolutions do much to raise the political expectations of states. A vote in favour of a resolution implies that the state will act according to its terms, even if it is not legally bound to do so. If this were not so, there would be little point in voting against it. Obviously, the political expectation raised by a positive vote will have a considerable impact on the behaviour of states and, therefore, on the development of customary law. Often, political necessity is more compelling than legal nicety. A similar effect can, indeed, be attributed to those inter-state agreements which are not actually treaties, such as the 1977 Commonwealth Statement on Apartheid in Sport (Gleneagles Agreement) and the 1975 Final Act of the Conference on Security and Cooperation in Europe (Helsinki Accords). Like Assembly resolutions, these are not binding in law but once had a considerable impact on state practice because of their political import. Such matters are sometimes referred to as creating 'soft law', being an attempt to indicate their importance despite the absence of binding legal obligation.

2.7.2 Other bodies, including the Security Council

It should be remembered that the Assembly is not the only organ of the United Nations to pass formal resolutions. 'Decisions' of the Security Council under Chapter VII of the Charter, for example, are binding on states, although rarely do they deal with abstract points of law. They are concerned more with mandatory enforcement action against delinquent states. However, as was made clear in the ICJ *Advisory Opinion on the Accordance with international law of the unilateral declaration of independence in respect of Kosovo* (2010), Security Council resolutions can make special law (*lex specialis*) for those to whom it is addressed which will govern the international legal responsibility of the entity. So, in the Kosovo situation, SC Res. 1244 (1999) and the Constitutional Framework for Provisional Self-Government established under it constituted, together with general international law, the applicable international law in the situation. Again, there are many organisations outside of the UN which are concerned with matters of legal principle and one must not discount the contribution they make to the development of international law. This is especially true of regional organisations such as the Organisation of American States, the Organisation of African Unity and the Arab League or with organisations exercising influence in specific areas, such as the Atomic Energy Agency, the International Labour Organisation and the institutions established under the Law of the Sea Convention. Even though resolutions of these and other bodies are not mentioned in Art. 38, their role in the formation of international law – both customary and treaty – should not be underestimated and they can be viewed as similar in their effect to General Assembly resolutions.

2.8 Soft law

'Soft law' is a term of art used to describe two different but related phenomena in international law. First, soft law is the name given to those rules of international law that do not stipulate concrete rights or obligations for the legal persons to whom they are addressed. Such rules are normative – they are rules of law – but their content is inherently flexible or vague. Many examples exist in non-traditional areas of international law, such as treaties concerned with human rights and environmental protection, where states are wary of establishing clear-cut norms in novel situations. Such soft law often creates incremental or relative obligations, such as Art. 2 of the Covenant on Economic, Social and Cultural Rights 1966, which obliges parties to 'take steps, individually and through international assistance ... with a view to achieving progressively' the rights recognised in the treaty. Likewise, the obligation may be vague in what it requires states to do in order to avoid international responsibility, such as the alleged customary law obligation to pay 'appropriate' compensation following an expropriation of foreign-owned property. Undoubtedly, such rules lessen the chances of conflict between competing ideologies and, of course, may lead to the development of 'harder' law in due course, as with later human rights treaties. The disadvantage is that such law may be so vague or imprecise as to have no practical legal content at all.

A second, less helpful, use of the term 'soft law' is as a description of those values, guidelines, ideas and proposals that may develop into rules of international law but have not yet done so. This is not really law at all, soft or otherwise, but is another name for principles *de lege ferenda*, or principles which *could* become normative in the future. Often such principles emerge from the codified conclusions of international conferences or are embodied in non-binding agreements, such as the Helsinki Agreement establishing the original Conference on Security and Cooperation in Europe. Nevertheless, these are only proposals for development or agreed, non-binding plans of action. They will become law only by the action of the customary, treaty or other law-making process, which they often precede.

FURTHER READING

Akehurst, M., 'Custom as a Source of International Law', (1974–5) 47 *BYIL* 53.

Akehurst, M., 'Equity and General Principles of Law', (1976) 25 *ICLQ* 801.

d'Aspremont, Jean, *Formalism and the Sources of International Law: A Theory of the Ascertainment of Legal Rules* (Oxford University Press, 2011).

Caplan, L., 'State Immunity, Human Rights, and Jus Cogens: A Critique of the Normative Hierarchy Theory', (2003) 97 *Am. J. Int'l L.* 741.

Charney, J., 'The Persistent Objector Rule and the Development of Customary International Law', (1985) *BYIL* 1.

Christenson, G., 'The World Court and *Jus Cogens*', (1987) 81 *AJIL* 93.

Czaplinski, W., 'Sources of Law in the Nicaragua Case', (1989) 38 *ICLQ* 151.

Fitzmaurice, G., 'Some Problems Regarding the Formal Sources of International Law', (1958) *Symbolae Verzijl*, p. 153.

Kammerhofer, J., 'Uncertainty in the Formal Sources of International Law: Customary International Law and Some of Its Problems', (2004) *Eur. J. Int. Law* 15(3) 523.

Mullerson, R., 'Sources of International Law: New Tendencies in Soviet Thinking', (1989) 83 *AJIL* 494.

Schachter, O., 'The Twilight Existence of Non-binding International Agreements', (1977) 71 *AJIL* 296.

Schachter, O., 'New Custom: Power, Opinio Juris and Contrary Practice', in J. Makarczyk (ed.), *Theory of International Law at the Threshold of the 21st Century* (Kluwer Law International, 1996).

Shelton, D., 'International Law and Relative Normativity', in Malcolm Evans (ed.), *International Law* (Oxford University Press, 2003).

Sloan, B., 'General Assembly Resolutions Revisited', (1987) 58 *BYIL* 93.

Thirlway, H., 'The Sources of International Law', in Malcolm Evans (ed.), *International Law* (Oxford University Press, 2003).

Weil, P., 'Towards Relative Normativity in International Law', 77 (1983) *AJIL* 413.

SUMMARY

The sources of international law

- The traditional starting-point for a discussion of the sources of international law is Art. 38 of the Statute of the International Court of Justice.

- International treaties – International treaties are the only way states can create international law consciously. Treaties may be bilateral (between two states) or multilateral (between many) and usually they are the outcome of long and difficult negotiations. Treaties only bind states that become parties, but treaties may promote the development of customary law.

- Customary international law – Customary international law is that law which has evolved from the practice or customs of states. It is the foundation stone of the modern law of nations. Customary law is derived from general, uniform and consistent state practice, together with a belief that the practice is obligatory (*opinio juris*). Generally, a treaty may modify or replace customary law, but there are some fundamental rules of customary law (rules of *jus cogens*) that may not be changed by treaty.

- General principles of law – This may comprise law from a number of sources: natural law doctrines; rules common to all legal systems; principles of equity; general principles of international law.

- Judicial decisions – Judicial decisions are said to be a 'subsidiary means' for the determination of law, although in practice such decisions play a much more direct role in clarifying the sources of law. They include decisions of the International Court of Justice; decisions of other international tribunals such as the International Criminal Court, the Permanent Court of Arbitration and the International Tribunal for the Law of the Sea; decisions of national courts on questions of international law.

- The writings of publicists – These provide support for the other sources of international law and may provide clarification in cases of doubt. They are certainly subsidiary.

- Resolutions of international organisations – These are omitted from Art. 38 of the ICJ Statute but they can play a significant role in the elucidation of customary law, the development of customary law, the identification of *opinio juris* and in settling matters relating to the constitution of the organisation. They include resolutions of the Security Council and General Assembly of the United Nations, and may include resolutions of regional organisations.

3

The law of treaties

As we have seen in Chapter 2, treaties are one of the most important – if not the most important – sources of international law. They are the only way in which states may create binding legal obligations in a deliberate and conscious manner. It is not surprising, therefore, that international law should have developed a specific set of rules whose sole purpose is to regulate the creation, operation and termination of these legally binding instruments. The law of treaties is the name given to that body of international law which deals with the procedural and substantive rules governing the use of treaties as a source of international law. Although the analogy is far from perfect, the law of treaties is similar to those rules of national law which lay down the requirements for the creation and operation of contracts or trusts.

The law of treaties covers a wide variety of matters. There are rules dealing with entry into force, termination, interpretation, reservations (being exceptions to specific obligations in a treaty) and the relationship of treaty law to custom. In addition, it should be appreciated that the law of treaties is one of the least 'political' areas of international law, although one does not have to search long to find various academic theories about how treaties should work. In reality, however, the treaty is the vehicle through which much of the business of international law is conducted and it is in the interests of every state that there should exist a comprehensive, certain and stable legal code regulating their operation. This need for certainty and clarity is the primary reason why the International Law Commission has made great efforts to produce a code of treaty law that itself can be formalised in a multilateral treaty. Thus, much of the law of treaties is itself to be found in treaty form, supported by custom.

One of the most striking features of the law of treaties is that it appears to assume that broadly similar legal rules can be applied to all types of treaty, irrespective of their purpose. If we go back to our analogy with the law of contract and the law of trusts, national law does not lay down the same formal requirements for the creation of a valid contract and a trust because they serve different roles within the national legal system. Yet, as has been frequently pointed out (see e.g. McNair, 11 BYIL 100), the treaty also performs a variety of functions in the international legal system, but there is a widespread assumption that the *same* set of rules will serve for treaties of all types. So, a treaty transferring title to territory (e.g. the 1984 UK/China Agreement on Hong Kong), a treaty regulating an international boundary (e.g. UK/Ireland Continental Shelf Boundary Agreement 1988) and a multilateral treaty codifying an entire area of international law (e.g. Vienna Convention on Diplomatic Relations 1961) are all to be regulated by the same legal rules. While this uniformity has its own advantages, it is not necessarily appropriate that, for example, treaties regulating frontiers should be dealt with in the same way as treaties regulating trade. It is perhaps for this reason that treaty and customary law covering the 'law of treaties' is not always prescriptive or absolute. As we shall see, the Vienna Convention on the Law of Treaties is quite flexible in that it will often defer to the particular requirements of a treaty by permitting the parties to agree to modify, restrict, enhance or exclude the 'standard' rules of the law of treaties. This at least ensures that the 'treaty law' applicable to different types of treaty in practice can be moulded in part to fit their unique subject matter.

3.1 What is a treaty?

Before we examine the law of treaties in detail, we must be sure that we understand what a treaty actually is. Generally, a 'treaty' can be regarded as a legally binding agreement deliberately created by, and between, two or more subjects of international law who are recognised as having treaty-making capacity. A treaty is an instrument governed by international law and, once it enters into force, the parties thereto have legally binding obligations in international law. In this sense, a treaty creates rights and obligations distinct from those arising under the national law of any state. Obviously, the great majority of treaties will be made between states, but there are many examples of other international persons – such as international organisations – entering into treaty arrangements either with states or with each other (e.g. UN Headquarters Agreement between the United Nations and the United States 1947). Treaties are, then, legally binding agreements, governed by international law, made between those international legal persons recognised as having treaty-making capacity. In the absence of this, the agreement may be effective in other ways, but it is not a treaty. See, for example, the *Decision on Challenge to Jurisdiction, Prosecutor* v *Kallon and Kamara* Appeals Chamber, Special Court for Sierra Leone (2004), which determined that the Lome Agreement between the Govenrment and insurgents did not create obligations at international law, and was not a treaty. Nevertheless, it was still effective between the parties in that Court.

There are no obligatory formal requirements which must be satisfied before a 'treaty' can come into existence, although the Vienna Convention on the Law of Treaties 1969 applies only to treaties in written form (see Art. 2 VC 1969). Under general international law, treaties can be oral, in a single written instrument or in several written instruments. Similarly, a treaty may arise from the deliberations of an international conference, from direct bilateral negotiations or informal governmental discussions, from an 'exchange of notes' or an 'exchange of letters' or any other means which the parties choose. In the *Case Concerning Maritime Delimitation and Territorial Questions between Qatar and Bahrain (Qatar* v *Bahrain) (Jurisdiction and Admissibility)* 1994 ICJ Rep 112, this issue arose directly when Bahrain claimed that the agreed record of a meeting with Qatar (known as the Doha Minutes) did not constitute a 'treaty' in international law. The Court thought otherwise, and in confirming the existence of a treaty, noted that Art. 2 of the Vienna Convention on the Law of Treaties 1969 does not lay down a definition of what constitutes a treaty and that the matter should be judged objectively. This must be correct, not least because a judicial assessment of the effect of actions in international law must result from the application of legal principle rather than depend on the characterisation of the parties to a dispute. This was one reason why the 'agreement' of Britain and South Africa concerning the boundary between present-day Botswana and Namibia was not 'a treaty' (see *Kasikili/Sedudu Island Case (Botswana v Namibia)* 13 December 1999). It is also evident that there is no set nomenclature for a 'treaty'. The *Covenant* of the League of Nations, the Vienna *Convention* on Diplomatic Relations, the *Charter* of the UN, the *Statute* of the ICJ, the Single European *Act* and *Protocol I* to the Geneva Convention on the Protection of Victims of International Armed Conflicts are all treaties in international law. In addition, there is no equivalent in international law to the doctrine of 'consideration' found in the UK law of contract. In order to create a valid and binding agreement, the parties to the treaty need not provide each other with a counter-promise or benefit. A treaty can create obligations or rights for one party only. For example, one part of the Agreement between the UK and China regarding Hong Kong provided for the transfer of sovereign UK territory to China without any monetary or other quid pro quo. In conclusion, then, the method by which the agreement is formulated and the name given to it by the parties are irrelevant. The instrument will be a treaty so long as it is intended to be legally binding in the sense of creating rights and duties enforceable under international law, and this is to be judged objectively according to the nature and content of the agreement and the circumstances in which it was concluded.

3.2 Acts lacking an intention to create legal relations

It is obvious that states and other subjects of international law will interact on the international plane in a variety of situations. Not all of these activities, whether they result in 'agreements' or not, can be regarded as giving rise to 'treaties'. For a treaty to come into existence, it is clear that the parties must have intended to create rights or duties binding under international law, judged objectively. This is a vital precondition to the formation of treaties, bearing in mind that international law does not stipulate any set form for their creation. For example, communiqués issued at the end of summit meetings, declarations of common policy by members of regional organisations and general diplomatic correspondence usually will not constitute binding treaties. The same is true of General Assembly resolutions. Moreover, it is quite possible for states to conclude a quite complicated 'agreement', encompassing formal procedures for future action, without establishing a legally binding treaty. This was, for example, the position with the Final Act of the Conference on Security and Cooperation in Europe 1975 (the Helsinki Declaration), which was not intended to take effect as a treaty under international law but which has given rise to a whole host of formal procedures and institutions. One useful indicator as to whether an 'agreement' constitutes a treaty is whether it is registered with the United Nations as such under Art. 102 of the Charter. However, one must be careful in applying this practical test, for the UN Secretariat will accept for registration any matter regarded by a state as a treaty, without determining whether this is in fact the position in international law. Likewise, non-registration of an agreement under Art. 102 does not mean that the agreement cannot be a treaty in international law, although in the *Case Concerning the Territorial Dispute (Libyan Arab Jamahiriya v Chad)* 1994 ICJ

Rep 6, Judge ad hoc Sette-Camara in his Dissenting Opinion appeared to suggest that a non-registered treaty may not be binding between the parties. This is a dubious proposition as Art. 102 merely regulates the circumstances in which the United Nations as an Organisation should have regard to a treaty; it says nothing about the validity of a treaty between the parties. Consequently, it is no surprise that the ICJ in *Qatar* v *Bahrain* made it clear that an 'unregistered' treaty remains legally binding between the parties.

3.3 Other 'non-treaty' circumstances giving rise to legally binding obligations

In common form, the treaty involves a binding agreement between two or more subjects of international law, but it is uncontroversial that states in particular may place themselves under obligations binding in international law by means other than the 'treaty'. The following examples illustrate how states may assume obligations in international law in circumstances that can easily be confused with the creation of a treaty but which in reality involve legally distinct situations.

3.3.1 Declarations under Article 36(2) of the Statute of the ICJ

In Chapter 9, the mechanism provided for in Art. 36(2) of the ICJ Statute by which states may unilaterally declare their acceptance, in advance, of the jurisdiction of the ICJ is discussed in some detail. The question to be discussed here is whether these declarations of acceptance under the 'optional system' are to be regarded as 'treaties'. As will be seen, the consensual bond created by deposit of declarations has full legal effect and creates legally binding obligations between all states making such declarations, irrespective of the sequence in which they are made. In this sense they are similar to treaties and, in *Nicaragua* v *USA* 1984 ICJ Rep 392, some members of the Court indicated that states could not withdraw their declarations made under Art. 36(2) of the ICJ Statute without reasonable notice, by analogy with the requirements of good faith in the law of treaties.

These obiter dicta in the *Nicaragua Case* seem to suggest that declarations under the optional system are to be regarded as treaties in international law, or at least as 'treaty-like'. That, however, ignores the fact that such declarations are unilateral acts, unlike treaties which are bilateral or multilateral. In fact, evidence from the case law is equivocal on this issue. In the *Fisheries Jurisdiction Cases (Jurisdiction)* 1973 ICJ Rep 3, the Court did appear to treat optional clauses as treaty provisions. This was also the provisional view of the International Law Commission when drafting the Vienna Convention on the Law of Treaties, although this recommendation was not adopted in their final proposals. Likewise, the UN Secretariat is prepared to register optional declarations under Art. 102 of the Charter, although again this cannot be regarded as conclusive. On the other hand, in the *Anglo-Iranian Oil Co. Case (Jurisdiction)* 1952 ICJ Rep 93, a majority of the Court refused to apply the rules relating to the interpretation of treaties to the Iranian declaration of acceptance on the ground that it 'is not a treaty text resulting from the negotiations between two or more states'. This was restated forcefully in the *Fisheries Jurisdiction*

Case (Spain v Canada) (Jurisdiction) 1998 ICJ Rep, where the Court was explicit that it should not interpret a Declaration as if it were a treaty. Moreover, if the essence of a treaty is that it is a legally binding instrument, created between two subjects of international law, then clearly these unilateral and voluntary obligations cannot be included. The better view is that declarations under the Optional System cannot be regarded as treaties per se, because they are so firmly rooted in unilateral action. For example, whereas a state may not withdraw from its treaty obligations except in certain defined situations, a state may withdraw from the optional system (subject to the terms of its own Declaration) simply because it no longer chooses to be a party thereto, as with the USA in 1985. In the final analysis, a binding treaty is essentially compulsory, in that an unlawful termination may give rise to liability to another state. A binding declaration remains voluntary in the sense that it can be unilaterally terminated according to its terms without international responsibility, irrespective of the wishes of any other state. Of course, declarations may be subject to rules similar in content to those applicable to treaties (*Nicaragua Case*), but that does not make them treaties in law.

3.3.2 Unilateral statements

One question of some importance in international law is whether the unilateral pronouncements of a state can result in binding international obligations. In the *Eastern Greenland Case* (1933) PCIJ Ser. A/B No. 53, the Foreign Minister of Norway had declared in conversation with the Danish Ambassador that Norway would not create any difficulties in respect of the Danish claim of sovereignty over Eastern Greenland. When the matter came before the PCIJ, Denmark alleged that this statement was binding on Norway and prevented any objection to the Danish claim. A majority of the Court decided that the statement did not amount to a recognition of Danish sovereignty but did amount to a legally binding commitment to refrain from occupying Greenland. This would seem to suggest that unilateral statements can create internationally binding obligations for a state. Unfortunately, the matter is far from certain because the Court in this case appeared to regard the Norwegian statement as being given in return for a Danish commitment not to oppose a Norwegian claim to Spitzbergen. If this is the correct interpretation, then there is no obligation arising from a *unilateral* statement – Norway and Denmark can be seen to have entered into an oral treaty binding in the normal way.

However, later judicial decisions have brought some clarity to the matter and in the *Nuclear Test Cases (Australia v France, New Zealand v France)* 1974 ICJ Rep 253, the Court confirmed that unilateral statements of states can become legally binding in appropriate circumstances. The essence of the case was that Australia and New Zealand brought a claim against France in respect of the latter's atmospheric nuclear tests conducted in the South Pacific. Before a hearing on the merits could proceed, the French President and Foreign Minister made a series of statements making it clear that France would cease atmospheric testing and the Court considered briefly whether these statements could have created a binding obligation for France. In the opinion of the majority, '[i]t is well recognised that declarations made by way of unilateral acts concerning legal or factual situations, may have the effect of creating legal obligations'. So, if it is the intention of the state when making a unilateral declaration that it should become binding, this is enough to confer upon it the character of a legal obligation. Moreover, the majority judgment makes it clear that a quid pro quo is not required, neither is the acceptance, reply or reaction of any other state. It is enough if the declaration is given publicly with an intent to be bound, either orally or in written form.

This decision has been criticised widely on the grounds that the evidence for the supposed rule of law about the bindingness of unilateral statements was not as clear as the Court suggested. On the other hand, there is no evidence that states have become wary in their policy statements or public pronouncements because of a fear of binding themselves in the future and it may be that the practical impact of the Court's judgment has been over exaggerated. The Court made it plain that clear evidence will be required before unilateral statements can have binding effect and, further, that any statement which would restrict a state's sovereignty or freedom of action must be viewed with extreme caution. In the *Nuclear Test Cases*, it may have been significant that the French statements were made at a time when France was subject to a pending legal action. Subsequently, in the *Frontier Dispute Case (Burkina Faso v Mali)* 1986 ICJ Rep 554, a Chamber of the Court confirmed the possibility that unilateral statements could create binding legal obligations, but warned that this would normally happen only when there was clear evidence of an intention to be legally bound. In that case, an undertaking by the Mali Head of State did not fulfil this requirement, especially since it was made in the context of bilateral nego-tiations and not to the world at large, unlike the statement in the *Nuclear Test Cases*. Likewise, in the *Case Concerning the Application of the Convention on the Prevention and Punishment of the Crime of Genocide (Bosnia and Herzegovina v Serbia & Montenegro)* (ICJ 2007), the majority held that a statement issued by the *new* Serbian authorities condemning atrocities in Bosnia could not be taken as an admission of responsibil-ity for such actions, the Court noting the political rather than legal import of the statement. Although Vice-President Al-Khasawneh specifically dissented from this finding in the *Bosnia Case*, believing that the statement did, and was intended to, have legal effect, it seems that the majority view is more in conformity with the Court's previous jurisprudence that stresses the need for certainty before attributing legal effect to statements made in a non-legal context. That said, however, the *Case Concerning Kasikili/Sedudu Island (Botswana v Namibia)* provides another example of a statement having such effect. In that case, the Court decided that a joint com-muniqué issued by the Presidents of Botswana and Namibia concerning the con-tinuation of navigation rights for nationals of both states irrespective of which was held to have sovereignty over the disputed river, should be adhered to. This is a rare example of a joint, non-treaty statement definitively modifying the legal obliga-tions of the parties. What is clear, then, is that unilateral (or even joint) statements can result in binding legal obligations for the state(s) making them, although this is not likely to happen in anything other than exceptional circumstances. Of course, even if such statements are effective at international law, they are not 'treaties'.

3.3.3 Legally binding acts in national law

Not all legally binding agreements entered into by states (or other international legal persons) can be regarded as 'treaties'. States usually are competent to act as legal persons in the national law of other countries and they may enter into a variety of legal relationships that have nothing to do with international law. For example, states can enter into legally binding contracts with other states, companies and even individuals. A contract between State A and X Co. (a company registered in State B) for the supply of cement will not be a treaty – it will be an ordinary contract governed by the domestic law of the parties' choice, sometimes the law of either State A or State B and sometimes the law of a third jurisdiction (e.g. many such contracts are governed by the law of England). The point is that states are not limited to creating legal obligations for themselves on the international plane. They can and do behave like any other legal person, entering into legal relationships in national law. It is only when such obligations take effect in international law that the source of that obligation might be regarded as a treaty.

There is, however, one qualification to this. As will be seen in Chapter 9 on State Responsibility, states often enter into 'concessionary' agreements with companies whereby the latter are given exclusive rights to develop and exploit the natural resources of a state. Good examples are the early contracts concerning oil exploitation such as that between Iran and the Anglo-Iranian Oil Co., and that between Libya and Texaco. In the *Anglo-Iranian Oil Co. Case*, the Court indicated that these types of agreement were not to be regarded as treaties because they were mere contracts. Yet this only begs the question, for one of the touchstones of a treaty is whether the agreement creates obligations enforceable under international law. Subsequently, the decision in *Texaco* v *Libya* (1977) 53 ILR 389 confirmed that certain types of concessionary contract could be regarded as 'internationalised', so that the rights and duties arising under them were regulated in accordance with international legal principles. If the 'contract' is of this form, it is an agreement that takes effect in international law and it should properly be regarded as a treaty. In effect, it is a treaty between the state and the company, the latter having international treaty-making capacity for the limited purpose of the agreement. In other words, the essence of a treaty is not the identity of the parties, but the substance of the obligations created and the law that governs them.

3.3.4 Acts giving rise to customary law

It is clear from the earlier discussion that states may engage in a variety of activities which do not actually create legally binding obligations at international law, let alone amount to a treaty. An obvious example is a state's participation in the discussions and then the vote leading to the adoption of a United Nations General Assembly resolution. However, it should not be forgotten that state practice, which may include the adoption of Assembly resolutions, can give rise to norms of customary law. In this very general sense then, all state activity on the international plane may have legal significance. Acts which do not of themselves give rise to a specific legal obligation may eventually contribute to the formation of customary law.

3.3.5 Formal Acts of international organisations

In special cases, a formal act or decision of an international organisation may give rise to binding international law for the persons to whom the act or decision is addressed. This is discussed more fully in Chapter 2 (Sources), but the point is that in such (unusual) cases, the act or decision creates *lex specialis* (special law) for the relevant persons. Often, this will look like a treaty obligation, although it is juridically distinct. For example in the *Advisory Opinion on the Accordance with international law of the unilateral declaration of independence in respect of Kosovo* (2010), the ICJ noted that SC Res 1244 (1999) and the Constitutional Framework for Provisional Self-Government established under it constituted, together with general international law, the applicable international law in the situation.

3.4 The Vienna Convention on the Law of Treaties 1969

The work undertaken by the International Law Commission that led to the adoption of The Vienna Convention on the Law of Treaties 1969 is one of the Commission's most important contributions to the development of international law. The Convention was adopted by the Vienna Conference in 1969, but it did not enter into force until January 1980. This is perhaps surprising given the importance of the law of treaties in international law, but it does reflect the fact that this Convention is quite comprehensive in scope and that it deals with a number of controversial issues. As at 1 September 2012 there were 112 parties, including the UK (one of the earliest parties from 1971) and Malta (one of the newest from January 2012). The Convention itself is not retroactive (Art. 4) and does not, therefore, apply to treaties concluded before its own entry into force. To be clear then, it applies only to treaties concluded after its entry into force *and* for states that have become bound by the Vienna Convention itself. In the *Kasikili/Sedudu Island Case*, neither Botswana nor Namibia were parties to the Vienna Convention (and still are not), so it was inapplicable to the disputed treaty. However, this does not prevent any customary rules similar to those found in the Convention from applying to pre-Convention treaties or where the disputants have not accepted the Vienna Convention. Thus, in the *Kasikili/Sedudu Island Case*, the *Danube Dam Case*, and the *Case Concerning Sovereignty over Pulau Ligitan and Pulau Sipadan (Indonesia/Malaysia)* 2002 ICJ Rep the state-parties were prepared to accept that the content of the applicable Articles of the Vienna Convention had passed into customary law.

There is no doubt that the conclusion and entry into force of the Vienna Convention is a success in itself, although as has been pointed out, 'satisfaction must be tempered with realism' (Sinclair, *The Vienna Convention on the Law of Treaties*, 2nd edn. (1984)). For the parties to it, the Convention has settled many areas of considerable difficulty but, as with all 'law-making' treaties, many of its provisions reflect compromise rather than legal principle. Consequently, a number of the provisions of the Convention are deliberately open-ended and flexible and may give way to different rules where such are expressed in the treaty to which the Convention is said to apply. On the whole the Convention is to be warmly welcomed as a reasonably successful attempt to clarify an area of international law that is vital to the operation of the entire legal system.

3.4.1 Definitions and exclusions

The Vienna Convention does not apply to all international treaties. It is made clear in Arts 1 and 2 that the Convention applies only to treaties between states and only to treaties 'in written form ... governed by international law'. This last exclusion ('governed by international law') is largely superfluous for, as discussed previously, a legal instrument cannot properly be regarded as a 'treaty' in the first place unless it operates under international law. However, treaties between states and other international persons, or between those persons alone, are excluded from the scope of this Convention, as are oral treaties. A separate Convention deals with treaties made between international organisations or between states and international organisations and this is considered later. Likewise, the Vienna Convention does not deal with state succession to treaties as this is also governed by a separate Convention. Note, however, if non-states are parties to a multilateral treaty, relations between states under that multilateral treaty will be governed by the 1969 Vienna Convention (Art. 3(c) and see 1986 Convention on Treaties between International Organisations etc. Art. 73). In other words, the fact that non-states are party to a treaty does not prevent the application of the Vienna Convention to that treaty for states that have accepted the Vienna Convention.

3.4.2 The Vienna Convention and customary law

As with all treaties, the Vienna Convention only regulates the legal relations of those states that are parties to it. In this sense, the law of treaties as spelt out in the Vienna Convention applies only to the legal relations between states under a treaty concluded after the Convention came into force and where those states are also parties to the Convention, as in *Application of the Interim Accord of 13 September 1995 (The Former Yugoslav Republic of Macedonia v Greece)* (2011). As for all other states (and treaties), the position is governed by rules of customary international law. Yet, as was explained in Chapter 2, this does not mean that non-parties to the Convention necessarily will be under different legal obligations in relation to the application and interpretation of treaties. The Vienna Convention may have accelerated the formation of new customary law in similar terms to the provisions of the Convention or might even be taken to have codified existing customary law.

The *exact* relationship of the Vienna Convention to customary international law is a matter of debate simply because it is difficult to identify precisely all of those provisions of the Convention which also form part of customary law, and even more difficult to determine whether this is because the provision in question was already customary law before the Convention or is now so because of the impetus to practice given by the Convention. That said, numerous pronouncements by the ICJ have clarified the *general* position and the following matters are reasonably clear:

(a) The Convention itself preserves the operation of customary international law. Thus, in Arts 3 and 4, the Convention states that nothing shall preclude the operation of rules set forth in the Convention to treaties outside its scope if such rules exist 'independently of the Convention' – that is, in customary law. What these and other provisions make clear (e.g. Art. 43) is that the Vienna Convention is in part a codification of customary international law – and thus the substance of specific obligations will be binding on non-parties – and in part a progressive development of that law. Of course, as time goes by, those parts of the Vienna Convention that *were* 'progressive development' may have actually developed into customary law!

(b) There are clearly certain areas of the Convention which were intended to be a codification of existing customary international law or which have now achieved that status. For example, the rules on fundamental change of circumstance (Art. 62; *Fisheries Jurisdiction Case* 1974 ICJ Rep 3) and material breach (Art. 60; *Namibia Case* 1971 ICJ Rep 16) are identified by Sinclair (op. cit. p. 20) as areas of codification rather than progressive development, and this has been confirmed by the *Danube Dam Case*. To this we may add Art. 61 on supervening impossibility (*Rainbow Warrior Arbitration (New Zealand v France)* 82 ILR 499; *Danube Dam Case*). In the *Territorial Dispute Case (Libya v Chad)* 1994 ICJ Rep 6, the ICJ confirmed that Art. 31 of the Vienna Convention on principles of treaty interpretation now represented customary law, and this was accepted without demur by the parties and the Court in the *Kasikili/Sedudu Island Case*, the *Pulau Islands Case (Indonesia v Malaysia)* (2002), the *Palestinian Wall Advisory Opinion* (2004) and the *Case Concerning the Application of the Convention on the Prevention and Punishment of the Crime of Genocide (Bosnia and Herzegovina v Serbia & Montenegro)* (ICJ 2007). Similarly, the more procedural aspects of the Convention, such as the rules relating to capacity (Art. 6), effect of unauthorised agreement by a representative (Art. 8), observance of treaties (Art. 26) and relationship with national law (Art. 27 – see *Questions relating to the Obligation to Prosecute or Extradite (Belgium v Senegal)* ICJ (2012)) also can be regarded as codification of customary law. As noted earlier, it is not possible to identify with certainty all of the provisions of the Convention which did codify customary international law or which now represent it. In any event, as the number of signatories to the Convention increases, the need to identify 'customary law provisions' will fall away.

(c) Sir Ian Sinclair also identifies a number of Convention Articles that the International Law Commission regarded as matters for progressive development rather than codification. This is not to say, of course, that such areas will not come (or have not already come) to represent customary international law, for they may pass into the general corpus of international law because of the impetus to state practice provided by their incorporation in the Convention. All that is asserted here is that originally these provisions did not represent customary international law. The most striking of these is the law on reservations (Arts 19–23) which, as we shall see, did not represent universal practice at the time of its adoption and which still causes difficulties although its 'customary' status is becoming more certain. Similarly, the Articles on modification (Arts 40–41) and certain of the Articles on invalidity and termination appeared *at the time* to be more about standard setting for the future rather than as representing the current state of international law. Once again, however, so much of this is open to debate that it is impossible to say with complete certainty where codification stopped and progressive development began. It is even more difficult to be clear whether those matters that were 'developmental' have now passed into the corpus of customary international law.

3.4.3 The inception of treaties

The provisions of Part II of the Vienna Convention deal with rules pertaining to the creation of treaties in international law. Within this framework are matters relating to the authority of state representatives, compliance by a state with its own national law, adoption of treaties, entry into force, signature and ratification. It will be appreciated that much of the material considered in this Part of the Vienna Convention relates to the procedural aspects of treaty formation. For this reason, this is one area where many of the Convention Articles are drafted in such a way as to yield to an alternative rule if such has been expressly incorporated in the particular treaty that is being considered.

3.4.3.1 Authority to conclude treaties

It is a matter for the national law of each state to decide which government official or entity is competent to enter in to international treaties on its behalf. For example, in the UK, treaties are concluded by the Crown – in effect, the government acting under the Royal Prerogative – and do not need to be formally ratified or accepted by Parliament (unless otherwise provided). However, under section 20 of the Constitutional Reform and Governance Act 2010, a treaty 'is not ratified' (excepting special cases, s. 22) unless it is laid before Parliament under what has become known as the 'Ponsonby Rule' which requires treaties to be laid before Parliament with an Explanatory Memorandum for twenty-one days (or longer if extended) for inspection and information. In the USA, 'treaties' require the consent of at least two thirds of the Senate, but the President may make 'executive agreements' (which in international law also qualify as binding treaties) without the need to consult any other body.

It must be remembered that these are *national law* provisions and usually they affect the validity of the treaty in national law only. Under Art. 46 of the Convention, a state may not claim that a violation of its internal law concerning competence to create treaties is a reason for invalidating its consent to that treaty in international law 'unless that violation was manifest and concerned a rule of its internal law of fundamental importance'. In other words, simple non-compliance with national law is not enough to invalidate a state's consent to a treaty. This will happen only if such non-compliance concerns a 'fundamental rule' and is manifest in the sense of being 'objectively evident to any state conducting itself ... in accordance with normal practice' (Art. 46(2)). This must be a question of fact in each case, although it does seem that international law will refuse to accept a claim of lack of consent on this ground in all but the most clear-cut and notorious cases. The point is that if consent is given on behalf of the state by the body competent *under international law* to do so, then other matters are largely irrelevant. This was certainly the position adopted by Judge Huber in the *Rio Martin Case* 2 RIAA 615, and is supported by the Court's approach in the *Eastern Greenland Case*, where the majority implicitly rejected Norway's claim that its Foreign Minister was not competent under national law to give the promise referred to in section 3.3.2. In the *Maritime Delimitation and Territorial Questions Case (Qatar v Bahrain)* 1994 ICJ Rep 112, the Court rejected the argument that the 'Doha Minutes' were not a treaty, deciding in passing that it was irrelevant that the Bahrain Foreign Minister claimed to have no constitutional authority to conclude a treaty per se. The existence of a valid treaty was to be judged objectively. These cases are in line with the general principle expressed in Art. 27 of the Convention that a state cannot invoke its national law as a ground for non-fulfilment of *any* obligation in *any* treaty (*Questions relating to the Obligation to Prosecute or Extradite Case (Belgium v Senegal)* ICJ (2012)).

How, then, do we determine which 'official or entity' is competent under international law to give consent on behalf of a state? The answer to this question is very much related to the question of statehood and the legitimacy of governments considered in Chapter 5. However, assuming a legitimate state or government to exist, the question whether any particular person or body is entitled to act on behalf of the state is governed by the doctrine of 'full powers'. A 'full power' is simply a formal document containing the authority given by a state to its representatives (e.g. diplomats, Prime Minister, etc.) to conclude treaties on its behalf. Modern practice is to dispense with formal full powers as such and this is recognised by the Convention. Under Art. 7, a person is to be considered as being authorised to consent to a treaty on behalf of a state if he or she does possess full powers or it appears from state practice that the person does represent the state and it was intended to dispense with full powers. In any event, under Art. 7(2), certain persons are deemed to be representing their state without presenting full powers, and these include Heads of State or Government (see, for example, the first phase of *The Prevention of Genocide Case (Bosnia-Herzegovina v Yugoslavia (Serbia and Montenegro))* (1993) 32 ILM 888), Foreign Ministers and delegates to international conferences convened for the purpose of adopting the text of a treaty. By way of balance, under Art. 8, consent to a treaty is 'without legal effect' if made by a person not authorised under Art. 7, unless afterwards confirmed by the state.

The Convention, then, lays down rules by which we are to determine who is competent under international law to give consent to a treaty on behalf of a state. If these conditions are met, usually the treaty will be valid irrespective of the position in domestic law because international law is slow to invalidate a treaty on the grounds of lack of compliance with national rules.

3.4.3.2 Modes of consent and entry into force

Before a treaty can create legally binding obligations for a state, two distinct criteria must be met. First, the state must have given its consent to be bound and, secondly, the treaty must have entered into force. In international law, just because a state has consented to a treaty does not mean that it becomes binding upon it automatically. It will do so only if the treaty has entered in to force according to its own terms. As a practical matter, therefore, entry into force – the start date for the legal effect of the treaty – usually occurs at some time after the initial negotiating parties actually gave their consent. For example, in January 1989, over 100 states had signed the 1982 Law of the Sea Convention, but this treaty did not enter into force until November 1994, one year after sixty states had ratified it. These are the two distinct stages in the inception of treaties as binding legal instruments: consent and entry into force.

(a) *Consent*. Article 11 of the Convention stipulates that the consent of a state to be bound by a treaty may be expressed 'by signature, exchange of instruments constituting a treaty, ratification, acceptance, approval or accession or by any other means if so agreed'. Obviously, this provision is open-ended, although it lists the most common ways by which a state may give its consent to a treaty. The more detailed aspects of each 'mode' are then dealt with in Arts 12–17.

There are many technical issues in these Articles, but perhaps the most significant point here is the relationship between 'signature' and 'ratification'. Ratification is the process whereby a state finally confirms that it intends to be bound by a treaty that it has previously signed, consent not being effective until such ratification. Usually, the treaty itself will indicate whether signature or ratification is the appropriate mode of consent and this is recognised in Arts 12 and 14. Yet, where the treaty itself is silent, it is a matter of some debate whether signature alone is sufficient or whether some requirement for ratification should be implied. The Vienna Convention deals with this issue only superficially by providing that the appropriate mode of consent is to be determined by reference to the intention of the parties, save that if a state's representative declares that signature is subject to ratification, this takes precedence. Obviously, this is a matter of considerable practical importance and it is unfortunate that the Convention does not deal with the matter more conclusively. It is just as well, therefore, that the majority of treaties spell out the precise steps that must be taken in order for consent to be given. The Law of the Sea Convention, for example, makes it clear that ratification, and not signature, amounts to consent to be bound (LOS 1982 Art. 306).

States that did not participate in the negotiations leading to the treaty usually express their consent to be bound by 'accession' (Art. 15). Moreover, although there is some doubt, the better view is that states may accede to a treaty that has not yet entered into force. Indeed, this is in line with the preceding analysis, which sees the creation of binding obligations under a treaty as a two-stage process – consent and entry into force.

(b) *Entry into force.* Under Art. 24 of the Vienna Convention, a treaty enters into force 'in such manner and upon such date as it may provide or as the negotiating states may agree'. Thus, as with so much of the Convention, primacy is given to each individual treaty and it is normal practice for treaties to contain a provision dealing with these matters. Once again, for example, the 1982 Law of the Sea Convention entered into force twelve months after the deposit of the 60th instrument of ratification or accession (LOS Art. 308), in effect in November 1994, some twelve years after the treaty was finalised and opened for ratification. In those cases where the treaty does not specify its own rules, Art. 24(2) of the Vienna Convention indicates that the treaty will enter into force as soon as consent to be bound has been established for all the negotiating states.

Lastly, it should be noted that under Art. 18 a state is legally obliged 'to refrain from acts which would defeat the object and purpose of the treaty' in the period between signature and ratification (if required) until it has indicated that it will not be a party to the treaty, *and* also in the period between consent to be bound and entry into force of the treaty, provided the latter is 'not unduly delayed'. This last proviso is somewhat unclear for many multilateral treaties involving a large number of states may take some time to come into force, as with the Law of the Sea Convention. It would seem to be a question of fact in each case whether the entry into force has been *unduly* delayed. Article 18 provoked considerable debate at the ILC, but it seems that the obligation to abstain from pre-treaty acts prejudicial to the treaty is necessary if states wish to conduct their international relations with certainty and in good faith. It follows logically that if this pre-treaty obligation carries legal force, a breach of it will itself involve international responsibility. Note, however, that this pre-treaty obligation does not mean that a state must conform with the very terms of the treaty before it has entered into force. If it did, it would effectively mean that the treaty became binding as soon as consent was given, irrespective of entry into force. Instead, it encompasses an obligation not to act (possibly deliberately) to defeat the very purpose of the treaty. Although this obligation stands apart from the treaty itself, it is very general and there are no clear cases of a state having violated it.

Part II of the Vienna Convention clearly gives primacy to the terms of each treaty in determining what rules shall apply to its inception as a legally binding instrument. However, as the ILC pointed out in its commentary on the Vienna Convention, the rules in a treaty relating to its own entry into force etc. cannot be regarded as legally binding under that treaty. This is simply because the treaty in which they are contained will not yet have entered into force! Such rules are logically prior to the treaty itself and it seems that their legal validity stems purely from the act of signature to the treaty or the states' participation in the negotiations leading to the treaty.

3.4.4 The scope of legal obligation

The Vienna Convention deals quite comprehensively with the scope of the legal obligation that a state accepts when it expresses its consent to be bound by a treaty and that treaty has entered into force. Again, these matters are essentially procedural in that they tell us how the substance of the treaty obligation is to be applied in a particular case. However, there are some rules having more substantive effect, as with the doctrine of *jus cogens*.

3.4.4.1 The fundamental rule

Article 26 of the Convention states what is rightly regarded as one of the most fundamental rules of international law. Thus, '[e]very treaty in force is binding in good faith upon the parties to it and must be performed by them in good faith'. This is the rule *pacta sunt servanda*, which expresses the essential binding quality of treaties and without which it would be impossible to operate a system of treaty law. The rule itself is also a rule of customary law. Similarly, Art. 27 of the Convention stipulates that the dictates of national law cannot be invoked as a reason for failure to perform a treaty obligation and this preserves the objective validity of international law as a *system of law* distinct from the local laws of each state (*Questions relating to the Obligation to Prosecute or Extradite (Belgium v Senegal)* ICJ (2012)). Consequently, failure to perform a treaty obligation involves international responsibility (*Interpretation of Peace Treaties Case* 1950 ICJ Rep 65; *Danube Dam Case*, para. 47) even if the act in breach is consistent with, or even required by, national law.

3.4.4.2 Reservations

In the negotiations leading to a bilateral treaty, the two participating states may disagree over the precise terms of the treaty that is to bind them. If this is the case, they may renegotiate the treaty in order to reach a compromise or abandon the attempt altogether. In multilateral treaties, however, it is too much to expect that all the negotiating states will agree on every provision and it is unlikely that all differences can be resolved through changes of emphasis or substance in the proposed draft. Therefore, international law recognises that states may be able to become parties to treaties without accepting all the provisions thereof. This is achieved by means of 'reservations' to the treaty, and their validity and effect are dealt with at some length in the Vienna Convention.

Reservations can properly be regarded as unilateral statements made by a state at the time it gives its consent to be bound (or later if the treaty permits) and which are intended to modify or exclude an otherwise binding treaty obligation. In some cases the reservation may not be effective (i.e. may not exclude or modify the obligation) until it has been accepted by other parties to the treaty, but this does not destroy its essential character as a unilateral act (VC Art. 2(1)(d)). Importantly, so-called 'interpretative declarations', whereby a state makes a declaration concerning some aspect of the treaty at the time of its signature etc., are not reservations for the purposes of the Convention. Such statements are merely indications of the view that the state holds about the substance of the treaty, rather than being an attempt to derogate from the full legal effect of its provisions. Obviously, the line between such statements and reservations proper may be a thin one and it will be a matter for construction in each case, as in the *Anglo-French Continental Shelf Case* 54 ILR 6. In the words of the UN Human Rights Committee in its 1994 General Comment on the effect of reservations made to the International Covenant on Civil and Political Rights (34 ILM 840), the distinction between reservations and interpretative declarations should be made according:

> to the intention of the State, rather than the form of the instrument. If a statement, irrespective of its name or title, *purports* to exclude or modify the legal effect of a treaty in its application to the State, it constitutes a reservation. Conversely, if a so-called reservation merely offers a State's understanding of a provision but does not exclude or modify that provision in its application to that State, it is, in reality, not a reservation.

Prior to the 1969 Vienna Convention, there was some disagreement as to the effect of a reservation on a state's consent to a multilateral treaty. The approach adopted in the practice of the League of Nations was that if a state made a reservation to a multilateral treaty, that reservation had to be accepted by all the other parties to the treaty. If it was not, the state making the reservation could not be regarded as a party to the treaty at all, even in respect of those states that did accept the reservation. This rule of unanimity was designed to ensure the integrity and uniformity of multilateral treaty obligations, especially in relation to those matters where it was desirable to create a uniform and certain legal regime. However, in the practice of other states, particularly those of the Pan-American Union, such an approach was thought too rigid, for it could exclude many states from the operation of a treaty when their reservations had little to do with the central object and purpose of the treaty. There was, then, a tension between maintaining the uniformity of treaty obligations and encouraging the widest possible participation in a 'law-making' exercise even if all the peripheral matters could not be agreed upon.

In 1950, when several states attempted to make reservations to the Convention on the Prevention and Punishment of the Crime of Genocide 1948, the General Assembly requested an Advisory Opinion from the ICJ on the legal effect of reservations. In the *Genocide Convention (Reservations) Case* 1951 ICJ Rep 15, the Court was asked to consider first, whether a state can be a party to a multilateral treaty even though it has made a reservation which is objected to by other parties and, secondly, if this is possible, what is the legal effect of such a reservation for those states that have accepted or rejected the reservation. The Court ruled by a majority broadly in favour of the Pan-American approach. A state could be regarded as a party to a treaty, even if its reservation had not been accepted by all other parties, so long as that reservation 'is compatible with the object and purpose of the Convention'. On the other hand, if a state actually did object to another's reservation it could consider that the reserving state was not a party to the treaty in respect of itself. Eventually, after some vacillation in the ILC, this became the substance of the rule adopted in the Vienna Convention. Again, however, the Vienna Convention gives primacy to the particular treaty in question when determining the precise effect of reservations made to it. The Convention provides as follows:

(a) Under Art. 19, a state has liberty to make reservations to a multilateral treaty unless all reservations are prohibited, or the specific attempted reservation is prohibited, or the specific attempted reservation is incompatible with the object and purpose of the treaty. The effect of this is that a prohibited reservation is without legal effect and the term of the treaty to which the invalid reservation related applies in full between all the parties. It is as if the reservation had never been made. In the Human Rights Committee's General Comment referred to earlier, the Committee identify potential reservations to the International Covenant on Civil and Political Rights which would be impermissible in this sense, being reservations offending rules of *jus cogens* and reservations to specific protected human rights, the denial of which would be incompatible with the object and purpose of the Covenant. In fact, the list is quite extensive, demonstrating how these procedural rules about reservations may be crucial in ensuring the efficacy or otherwise of a multilateral treaty. In the *Armed Activities on the Territory of Congo Case (New Application 2002: Congo v Rwanda)*, Judges Higgins, Kooijmans, Elarby, Owada and Simma noted in a Joint Separate Opinion that a reservation may be contrary to the object and purpose of a treaty if it goes to the substance of a treaty obligation (as one might expect) or if it goes to a question of jurisdiction (e.g. where a treaty requires a state to submit a dispute to the ICJ). This raises the intriguing prospect that for some treaties (e.g. those protecting fundamental human rights) a state may be required to accept compulsory dispute settlement as the price of joining that treaty. It would mean that a reservation ousting the compulsory jurisdiction of a tribunal dealing with a dispute could, in the right circumstances, be incompatible with the object and purpose of a treaty. This is a controversial view, not yet widely accepted and contrary to the long-established practice in international law that submission to the jurisidction of an international tribunal is essentially voluntary.

(b) Under Art. 20(1), a reservation expressly authorised by the treaty does not require acceptance by any other party (unless otherwise provided). The reserving state is a party to the treaty and its obligations are modified according to the terms of the reservation in its relations with all other parties.

(c) Under Art. 20(2), if it appears from the limited number of negotiating states and the object and purpose of the treaty that the treaty obligations are to be accepted in their entirety by all prospective parties, then a reservation requires acceptance by all those parties. In other words, for those classes of treaty that are intended to create a completely uniform set of obligations, the unanimity rule still prevails. A state whose reservation is accepted by all states is a party to the treaty on the terms of its reservation, whilst a state whose reservation is objected to by any one of the prospective parties cannot be a party to the treaty at all. In the normal case, it should be apparent from the negotiating history of the treaty whether it is of this special class. General multilateral treaties will not usually be governed by this provision, but by Art. 20(4) (see subsequently).

(d) Under Art. 20(3), a reservation to a treaty which is the constituent instrument of an international organisation must be accepted by the competent organ of that organisation before it can have legal effect.

(e) Under Art. 20(4), if the reservation is not prohibited ((a)), or not expressly permitted ((b)) and the multilateral treaty is not in one of the special classes ((c) and (d)), then:

(i) Acceptance of one state's reservation by another state means that the multilateral treaty comes into force between the reserving state and the accepting state. Thus, if State A makes a reservation to the X Convention and State B accepts it, States A and B are parties to the X Convention in their relations with each other. The treaty is in force between the two states, as modified for both parties by the terms of the reservation (Art. 21).

(ii) Objection to a state's reservation by another state does not prevent the entry into force of the treaty between the reserving state and the objecting state unless a contrary intention is definitely expressed by the objecting state. Thus, if State A makes a reservation to the X Convention and State B objects to it, the X Convention may still be in force between State A and State B, so long as State B has not expressly declared otherwise. It should be noted here that this goes further than the *Genocide Case*. Whereas the Vienna Convention clearly dispenses with the unanimity rule per se, it also provides that even if a state does object to a reservation, the multilateral treaty may still be in force between it and the reserving state. In other words, the rules of the Vienna Convention strongly encourage extensive participation in multilateral treaties.

(iii) Of course, if the objecting state has declared that it does not regard the reserving state as a party to the treaty, then the treaty does not govern their relations. The treaty is not in force between them, although it will remain in force in their relations with other states. Yet, if the entry into force of the treaty between the two states is *not* opposed by the objecting state, then the treaty will govern their relations inter se save only that 'the provisions to which the reservation relates do not apply as between the two states to the extent of the reservation' (Art. 21). This last provision has caused some difficulty.

 Example

Let us assume that State A and State B are intending to be parties to the X Multilateral Convention, which has three Articles. If State B makes a reservation that it 'does not accept Art. 3', we must first determine whether this reservation is permitted by the treaty, whether it is incompatible with its object and purpose ((a)), whether it is expressly authorised ((b)) or whether the treaty is one of the special classes ((c) and (d)). Assuming none of these conditions applies, then if this reservation is accepted by State A, the X Convention comes into force between State A and State B as modified – i.e. Art. 3 does not apply in their relations inter se: Art. 20(4)(a); para (e)(i).

If, on the other hand, State B makes the same reservation but State A objects then two things may happen – para (e)(ii). First, if State A declares that it does not regard State B as a party to the treaty, then the X Convention is not in force between these two states at all:

→

➞

Art. 20(4)(b). Second, State A may object to the reservation, but allow the treaty to enter into force, so that the X Convention applies, except that 'the provisions to which the reservation relates do not apply ... to the extent of the reservation': Art. 21(3). This means that the X Convention applies, but Art. 3 does not, for it is the very provision to which the non-accepted reservation relates. This is somewhat strange, for it will be apparent that the effect of accepting the reservation and of objecting to it (but allowing the treaty to operate) can be exactly the same – in our case, that Art. 3 does not apply.

In such circumstances, the choice facing the state which is minded to object to a reservation is a poor one – it can either determine that the treaty does not apply at all or realise that even if it does object, the reserving state may still get its own way. This is certainly true in respect of reservations which seek to 'exclude' a treaty provision entirely (as in our example), although it may be different where the reservation seeks to 'modify' an obligation. As was pointed out in the *Anglo-French Continental Shelf Case*, a provision in respect of which a reservation has been made and objected to by another state (the treaty remaining in force), does not apply 'to the extent of the reservation': Art. 21(3). This would seem to envisage that not all of the provision to which the reservation relates is void. Yet, in practice, the substance of a reservation 'modifying' an obligation may be little different from a reservation 'excluding' one and this still does not tell us what is meant by the phrase 'to the extent of the reservation' in Art. 21(3).

So, once again, as far as reservations are concerned, the Vienna Convention gives primacy to the particular terms of each treaty. The treaty may authorise or prohibit certain reservations and may determine their legal effect. Likewise, it is clear that the Convention is designed to ensure that as many states as possible become parties to multilateral treaties, especially those which are intended to lay down a comprehensive legal regime. This is the reason behind dispensing with the unanimity rule. In the normal case this must be correct, for many reservations deal with peripheral matters only and do not derogate from the central obligations under a treaty. In any event, reservations which are incompatible with the object and purpose of the treaty are void under Art. 19 (see for example, the Economic Court of the Commonwealth of Independent States' *Advisory Opinion on Reservations to Certain Commonwealth of Independent States Agreements* 127 ILR 1). Of course, it must be appreciated that one important consequence of the Vienna Convention approach is that it is not possible to determine the precise ambit of a party's legal obligations simply by looking at the terms of the treaty. One must examine also the reservations made by that state and whether they have been accepted or rejected by other parties. Moreover, it also means that the truly multilateral treaty is rare indeed. The possibility of valid reservations and valid objections ensures that each state can have different levels of obligation with the other parties. In one sense, then, the reservations regime of the Vienna Convention means that each party to a multilateral treaty is bound by a series of bilateral obligations, albeit under a general umbrella. This is, perhaps, an extreme view, for it ignores the fact that the framework of a multilateral treaty may be as important as the precise legal obligations undertaken. Yet it serves to remind us that the web of obligations under a multilateral treaty is more complicated than might first appear.

The ability of states to make reservations to treaties reminds us of the flexible and dynamic way in which international law works. However, the varied practice in relation to reservations and the rule that each treaty may stipulate its own scheme for reservations can create problems of inconsistency and uncertainty. Since the early

1990s, the International Law Commission has been considering the issue of reservations to multilateral treaties, including human rights treaties, and have received and considered a number of reports on the topic. In 2011, the ILC adopted a *Guide to Practice on Reservations to Treaties,* which is partly an attempt to solidify the existing law with a view to creating consistent practice and perhaps even a treaty. The current text is, therefore, a reflection of existing practice (some of which is already codified in the Vienna Convention), good future practice in areas not covered by the Convention and possible future developments. The Guide is far from being prescriptive and continues to generate controversy, with diverse states having varying concerns. Of course, as is the way with international law, it may well be that in due course these guidelines will help crystallise and promote consistent state practice and lead to the formation of customary law.

3.4.4.3 Interpretation

It is inherent in the application of any treaty to any situation that some element of 'interpretation' of the provisions of that treaty will be required. In most cases, this is nothing more than the usual problem of applying clear or reasonably clear treaty provisions to diverse facts. For example, in deciding whether a state has resorted to the use of force 'against the territorial integrity or political independence' of another state under Art. 2(4) of the UN Charter, it is necessary to determine, on the facts, whether a use of force has been directed against these objects. However, it may also be necessary, as a preliminary matter, to determine what 'territorial integrity or political independence' actually means. The rules concerning treaty interpretation in the Vienna Convention are directed towards this second question – the meaning and scope of the terms of the treaty. Of course, in practice the two issues often become confused, but it should be remembered that treaty interpretation is more concerned with the objective meaning of the treaty than its application in any given case.

Prior to the adoption of the Vienna Convention, it was said that international law knew several 'principles' or 'rules' of interpretation, rather like the rules of statutory construction in UK law. Not surprisingly, these did not command universal acceptance and, in any event, they were not mutually exclusive. Treaty interpretation was, and is, a complex matter and a court or other body charged with the interpretation of a treaty provision may have cause to refer to a variety of aids to interpretation suitable to the particular circumstances before it. The various approaches may be summarised as follows:

(a) The literal or textual approach – the terms of the treaty are to be interpreted according to their natural and plain meaning, as in the *Admissions Case* 1948 ICJ Rep 57, the *Advisory Opinion on the Constitution of the Maritime Safety Committee of IMCO Case* 1960 ICJ Rep 150 and the *Polish Postal Service Case* (1925) PCIJ Ser. B No. 11. This, of course, assumes that it is possible to determine what the 'natural' or 'plain' meaning of words and phrases is. In *US v Alvarez-Machain* (1992) 31 ILM 902, the literal approach was applied by the US Supreme Court with considerable vigour, largely to the exclusion of any other principle of interpretation. In that case, the Supreme Court had to consider whether the US–Mexican extradition treaty prohibited the forceful abduction of a Mexican national from Mexico and his subsequent indictment in the USA. If it did, the US court would have no jurisdiction because the Mexican national would not have been passed to the USA in conformity with the treaty. The majority took the view that because the extradition treaty did not specifically and deliberately prohibit abduction, an abduction did not constitute a violation of the treaty and hence US jurisdiction was well founded. This is the literal approach *par excellence*, for one might legitimately ask what the 'object and purpose' of the extradition treaty actually was if it was not to regulate totally the transfer of citizens from one jurisdiction to another. Indeed, there is every suspicion that the USA was eager to assert jurisdiction over the alleged drug dealer and torturer at any price, and that difficult issues of treaty interpretation were not going to stand in its way. In the normal case, the 'natural/plain meaning' of words in a treaty can be understood only in the context in which they are used, and it is a mistake to believe that any treaty phrase has one 'true' meaning.

(b) The intentions of the parties – the terms of the treaty are to be interpreted according to the intention of the parties at the time the treaty was adopted, as in the *Genoa Ships Case* (1883) 4 C Rob 388. Again, this assumes that all the parties had the same intention and that it is possible to divine what it was.

(c) The object and purpose or teleological approach – the terms of the treaty are to be interpreted so as to facilitate the attainment of the objectives of the treaty, as in the *Ambatielos Case* 1952 ICJ Rep 28, and in the *Golder Case* 57 ILR 200 (European Court of Human Rights). As it was put in the *Application of the Interim Accord of 13 September 1995 (The Former Yugoslav Republic of Macedonia v Greece)* (2011), the key is to intepret the treaty 'in context and in light of the object and purpose of the treaty'. As a matter of principle, however, the 'object and purpose' is that desired by the parties (rather than the court), but this must be assessed by reference to the time the treaty was entered into and not when the alleged breach occurred.

(d) The principle of effectiveness (*ut res magis valeat quam pereat*, it is better for a thing to have effect than to be made void) – is closely allied to the teleological approach and means that the treaty should be interpreted in order to ensure maximum effectiveness in achieving the object and purpose of the treaty, as in the *Certain Expenses Case* 1962 ICJ Rep 151 and the *Reparations Case* 1949 ICJ Rep 174. In the *Interpretation of Peace Treaties Case* however, the Court refused to apply the principle of effectiveness so as to overrule the plain meaning of the text of the 1947 Peace Treaties then under consideration.

It is clear that these principles overlap to a considerable extent, although in any given case they may either confirm or conflict with each other. For example, one way to determine the 'object and purpose' of the treaty is to look to the parties' intentions. On the other hand, it seems that the ICJ is reluctant to ignore the plain meaning of the text, at least where substantive rights of individual states are in issue, if this is not supported by clear evidence that to apply such meaning would lead to a manifestly absurd result. Again, however, if the treaty is the constituent instrument of an international organisation, the favoured interpretation may well be that which enables the organisation to achieve its objectives most effectively, as in the *Certain Expenses Case*.

The Vienna Convention tackles these problems by composite provisions in Art. 31 and Art. 32 and these are now taken to reflect customary law – see the *Territorial Dispute Case (Libya v Chad)*, the *Kasikili/Sedudu Island Case* and the *Pulau Islands Case*. According to Art. 31, treaties 'shall be interpreted in good faith in accordance with the ordinary meaning to be given to the terms of the treaty in their context and in the light of their object and purpose'. This is obviously another open-ended provision, but perhaps it is the best guidance that could be obtained given the breadth of views in the ILC about treaty interpretation. Its merit is that it reflects the reality of the situation, in that no 'rule' of treaty interpretation can be absolute or mandatory. Indeed, given that Art. 31 reflects customary law, it can be used as the foundation for treaty interpretation even for states who are not parties to the Vienna Convention (*Asian Agricultural Products Ltd (AAPL) v Republic of Sri Lanka* (1992) 30 ILM 577 at 594) and even in the interpretation of investment agreements between companies and states (*AAPL Case*).

Preference is given, then, to the ordinary meaning of the terms of the treaty in their context. Of course, this in itself involves a degree of subjectivity on the part of those interpreting the treaty. For example, in the *Maritime and Territorial Dispute Case (Qatar v Bahrain)*, the ICJ believed that the Doha Minutes (the treaty) did have an 'ordinary meaning' in the light of its context and object and purpose and so rejected any supplementary means of treaty interpretation. However, as it turned out, an examination of the 'supplementary means' of treaty interpretation under Art. 32 of the Convention (in this case referring to the *travaux préparatoires* – discussed later in this section) revealed that this 'ordinary meaning' was not necessarily the best interpretation (see Dissenting Opinion of Judge Schwebel). Another approach is revealed by the *Kasikili/Sedudu Island Case*, where the Court first decided what the treaty meant according to the ordinary meaning of the words and then checked this against the treaty's object and purpose, an approach adopted again in the *Application of the Interim Accord of 13 September 1995 (The Former Yugoslav Republic of Macedonia v Greece) Case*. In the *Pulau Islands Case*, the Court used the 'supplementary means' to check its own interpretation of the treaty *after* using the 'object and purpose' test to resolve the uncertainties.

In addition, under Art. 31, the 'context' in which the 'ordinary meaning' is to be divined includes the preamble to a treaty (as in the *Golder Case* and the *Beagle Channel Arbitration*) and even agreements between the parties made in connection with the treaty (see Art. 31(a)(b) and the *Pulau Islands Case* where a map was held *not* to be such an agreement). Clearly, this has the potential to generate uncertainty, as both sides in a dispute are likely to be able to find *some* evidence or 'context' to suggest that the 'true' ordinary meaning is the one that they favour. Similar concerns are raised by the use of subsequent practice of the parties or a subsequent agreement between them as an aid to treaty interpretation. Although consideration of these matters is expressly authorised by Art. 313(b), and was used in the *Application of the Interim Accord of 13 September 1995 (The Former Yugoslav Republic of Macedonia v Greece) Case*, there will be difficulties in determining what kind of 'subsequent practice' is relevant and how far this, and any subsequent 'agreement', can affect the ordinary meaning of the terms. In the *Chamizal Arbitration (US v Mexico)* (1911) 5 AJIL 785, subsequent practice was an important factor, but in the *Kasikili/Sedudu Island Case*, the ICJ adopted a strict approach to what amounted to 'subsequent practice' and disallowed the unilateral acts of the previous authorities in Botswana on the grounds that the cited actions (the preparation of reports concerning the frontier with present-day Namibia) were purely for the internal purposes of those authorities and were not made known to the authorities in Namibia. This seems to suggest that 'subsequent practice' can be relevant only when it is 'shared' subsequent practice and operated (or was intended to operate) internationally. Note, however, in the *Application of the Interim Accord of 13 September 1995 (The Former Yugoslav Republic of Macedonia v Greece) Case*, most of the subsequent practice relied on by the Court was that of Greece alone whose behaviour supported the inter-pretation of the treaty put forward by the Court, even though they (Greece) were now arguing for a different meaning of the contested obligation. In such circum-stances, perhaps it is not surprising that the Court were happy to rely on only one party's subsequent practice because it did contradict the interpretation they were now advancing, but it does illustrate that there is no consistent approach to the use of 'subsequent practice' in treaty interpretation.

Similar difficulties exist with respect to 'subsequent agreement', and there is doubt about what amounts to 'an agreement' for these purposes. Clearly, it cannot mean that there must be a subsequent enforceable international treaty, as the provi-sion would be redundant. But, it is not clear what it does mean. In the *Kasikili Case* the 'agreement' between the previous authorities in Namibia and Botswana was no more than collaboration between the two authorities over practical matters affect-ing the border and was held by the Court not to have an impact on interpretation of the treaty itself. It seems, indeed, as if there has to be something approaching a real consensus, and in the *Pulau Islands Case* reliance on an alleged agreed map as an aid to interpretation was disallowed because, in the Court's opinion, this was never accepted by Malaysia's predecessor as an 'agreement relating to' the disputed treaty and so could not be used to interpret it. Much turns on the intention with which the subsequent actions are done or the subsequent agreements made, though it may be going too far to say that such practice or agreement must be intended spe-cifically to clarify the meaning of the treaty per se. Perhaps it is enough if the activ-ity is intended to be in application of the treaty, so that its application in a concrete case can tell us how the treaty was meant to be interpreted. Note also that under Art. 31(4) of the Vienna Convention, a 'special meaning', different from its 'ordinary meaning', may be given to a term if it is established that this was the intention of the parties, as in the *Anglo-French Continental Shelf Case*.

In Art. 32, the Convention deals with the use of the *travaux préparatoires* of a treaty as an aid to its interpretation. These are expressed to be 'supplementary means of interpretation' which may be used to confirm the meaning resulting from Art. 31 or, more vaguely, to determine the meaning according to Art. 31 when that mean-ing is obscure or leads to a manifestly absurd or unreasonable result. Once again, however, the language of Art. 32 makes treaty interpretation appear to be a lot more clinical than it really is. As noted previously, in the *Maritime and Territorial Dispute Case (Qatar v Bahrain)*, a majority in the ICJ took the view that the main treaty text had a clear meaning (and hence gave it jurisdiction to try the case) and would not resort to the *travaux préparatoires* to confirm or deny that meaning, an approach followed in the *Application of the Interim Accord of 13 September 1995 (The Former Yugoslav Republic of Macedonia v Greece) Case* (2012).

This robust approach to the text of the treaty emphasises that it is for the Court, not the parties, to interpret a treaty and the Court will seek to give the text an objective meaning, rather than follow that which the parties (or one of them) now wishes or which the *travaux* appear to reveal. Of course, just because the parties to a treaty are contesting the meaning of the text does not mean that it has no clear, objective meaning, but neither should the Court rush to place its own 'objective' meaning on the text by simply asserting that there is one, thereby ignoring other aids to interpretation. As *Qatar v Bahrain* illustrates, the sharp distinction drawn by Arts 31 and 32 between the materials which a court may rely on to interpret a treaty is probably too rigid in practice, for there is little doubt that courts and tribunals do regard preparatory material as a considerable aid to treaty interpretation in appropriate cases (see e.g. the comments in the *Kasikili/Sedudu Island Case* and the use of *travaux préparatoires* as a 'check' in the *Pulau Islands Case*). Likewise in this chapter repeated reference has been made to the ILC Commentary on the Vienna Convention itself as a means of understanding its scope and this is pure *travaux préparatoires*. In any event, it would seem that the wording of Art. 32 is flexible enough to allow resort to the preparatory material in all but the most clear-cut cases, or those which are thought to be clear-cut. In this context, the distinction promoted by the Court in the *River Oder Case* (1929) PCIJ Ser. A No. 23, whereby any *travaux préparatoires* could not be used against states that did not participate in the preparatory work leading to the conclusion of a treaty, is not expressly preserved in the Vienna Convention, although that does not necessarily mean that a tribunal will use such material when the rights of a non-participating state are in issue. However, given that a state must be presumed to have fully understood the nature of its obligations when it acceded to a treaty, the better view is that interpretation of treaty provisions by use of preparatory material is not necessarily excluded when the rights of a state that did not participate in the preliminary negotiations are at stake. It is recognised that this is somewhat circular (after all, the question is 'what are those obligations?'), but to deny the value of preparatory material in such circumstances seems unduly legalistic.

It is apparent then, that the Vienna Convention gives a great deal of latitude to the body or court charged with the interpretation of a treaty. It does not attempt to settle the dispute between the various 'schools' of interpretation, neither does it purport to lay down any absolute rules. The leaning towards the textual approach, as determined in the context of the treaty, is more a reflection of a desire for certainty in treaty relations than a philosophical statement. It asks also that the terms of a treaty be interpreted in good faith, again in order to promote the integrity of treaty obligations (see e.g. the *Territorial Dispute Case (Libya v Chad)* and the *Kasikili/Sedudu Island Case*). Obviously, the more that the actual text of a treaty is regarded as the primary reference point, the less likely it is that courts can engage in judicial legislation. Hopefully, recognition that the text is most important will lead to better draftsmanship, with states defining their obligations with clarity and precision.

Lastly, as already made clear, the interpretation of a treaty is a matter to be decided according to international law and it does not rest with the unilateral decision of one party. For example, on the occasion of the ratification of the Intermediate Nuclear Forces Treaty between the US and USSR, the US Senate indicated that its consent had been given on the basis that *its* interpretation of various provisions of the treaty was operative. As US President Reagan pointed out in his reply, 'treaties are agreements between sovereign states and must be interpreted in accordance with accepted principles of international law': 82 AJIL 811. Treaty interpretation is a matter for international law according to the principles of interpretation just discussed.

3.4.4.4 Third states

As a general rule, treaties are binding only on the parties – see Chapter 2. As recognised in Art. 34 of the Convention, treaties create rights and obligations only for those states that have consented to be bound (*pacta tertiis nec nocent nec prosunt* – agreements are not prejudicial to third parties and do not benefit them). However, it is sometimes the case that parties to a treaty may intend to confer rights or obligations on third states (i.e. non-parties) without the latter becoming 'treaty states'. Whether a provision in a treaty is *intended* to confer a right (or an obligation) on a third state is a matter of interpretation in the light of all the circumstances (*Free Zones of Upper Savoy and Gex Case* (1932) PCIJ Ser. A/B No. 46). But can it be done in the sense of giving the third state a right that can be enforced against the treaty states, or of imposing an obligation which if not performed involves international responsibility?

Under Art. 35 of the Convention, if the parties to a treaty intend an *obligation* arising from a treaty to be binding on a third state, it becomes binding only if the third state expressly accepts that obligation in writing. This is, in effect, nothing more than a reiteration of the rule that treaties cannot bind third parties without their consent. Here, the consent is to a specific provision rather than the entire treaty. If, on the other hand, the parties intend to confer a *right* on a third state, the third state shall be presumed to have consented to accepting that right unless the contrary is indicated (Art. 36). So burdens imposed by a treaty have to be expressly accepted by non-parties, whereas benefits are presumed to have been accepted, without more. In both cases consent – express or implied – is at the root of the transfer of the treaty provisions to the third party.

In contrast to these rules, there are some treaties (known as 'dispositive' treaties) which create legal regimes valid for the whole world (*erga omnes*). For example, treaties dealing with territorial matters such as the delimitation of boundaries, international waterways (e.g. Permanent Neutrality and Operation of Panama Canal Treaty 1978) and territorial status (e.g. *Aaland Islands Case* [1920] LNOJ Special Supp. No. 3; *Kasikili/Sedudu Island Case*) establish a factual situation that must, in practice, be recognised by all states whether or not they are parties to the treaty. A similar thread runs through the *Libya* v *Chad* decision, where the ICJ was concerned to uphold the stability of international frontiers, this time by means of judicious treaty interpretation and a sensible approach to the enforcement of a treaty between the parties. Likewise, the Charter of the UN may have created an Organisation with 'objective' legal personality, opposable to members and non-members alike, irrespective of whether they have signed the Charter. Such is the reasoning in the *Reparations Case* (see Chapter 4).

Unfortunately, the Vienna Convention itself is silent on the issue of dispositive treaties, but this does not mean that such treaties cannot exist. The Vienna Convention on State Succession in Respect of Treaties 1978, provides that the succession of a new state in the territory of a former state does not affect certain treaty rights and obligations concerning boundaries and other territorial matters which the 'old' state had accepted (VC on State Succ. Arts 11 and 12 and see the principle of *uti possedetis* referred to in Chapter 6). This is supported by the practice of the new states that have emerged from the dissolution of Yugoslavia and is a feature of the *Kasikili/Sedudu Island Case*, where Botswana and Namibia accepted that a treaty of 1870 between Germany and Britain (the former colonial powers) provided the basis for determining the line of the frontier. A similar view was taken by Indonesia and Malaysia in the *Pulau Islands Case* in respect of a 1891 Convention between Great Britain and the Netherlands which the Court held partially demarcated sovereignty in the disputed area and in the *Frontier Dispute (Burkina Faso v Niger) Case* (2012) the parties have asked the ICJ expressly to apply the 'the principle of the intangibility of boundaries inherited from colonization and the Agreement of 28 March 1987'.

In fact, even a brief survey of state practice makes it clear that certain treaties, by their very nature, create a situation that other states are forced to accept. For example, it is not open to any state to claim that the UK is still the legitimate sovereign of Hong Kong now that the treaty of cession with China has taken effect. Ultimately, there-fore, whether these types of treaty are binding on third states because of some sort of deemed consent or, more radically, because they are valid for third parties *ipso facto* due to the nature of their subject matter, does not alter the practical effect that a third state cannot dispute the objective validity of the state of affairs created by the treaty.

Lastly, it should be remembered that none of the rules considered earlier dimin-ishes or alters the validity of 'treaty' obligations which become binding on all states because they subsequently become part of customary international law.

3.4.4.5 Inconsistent treaties

Under Art. 59 of the Convention, if *all* the parties to a treaty conclude a later treaty dealing with the same subject matter, then the prior treaty is considered terminated if this is the intention of the parties or the provisions of the earlier treaty are so incompatible with the terms of the later treaty that it is impossible to apply the two treaties at the same time. However, where the earlier treaty is not terminated under this Article, then the matter falls to be considered under Art. 30. If *all* the parties to the earlier treaty are parties to the later treaty, then only those provisions of the ear-lier treaty which are compatible with the later treaty remain effective (Art. 30(3)). On the other hand, if the parties to the later treaty do not include all the parties to the earlier treaty, then as between states that are parties to both, Art. 30(3) applies (as discussed earlier). As between states that are not parties to both treaties, the treaty to which they are both parties governs their relations inter se (Art. 30(4)(b)). Of course, nothing in these provisions prevents two states modifying their rights inter se under a multilateral treaty (see later, Art. 41) and the treaty may still be ter-minated under Art. 60 (termination or suspension as a consequence of breach).

These somewhat complicated provisions really do no more than reflect the prin-ciple that in the event of a conflict of obligations the rights of the parties under two different treaties are usually to be determined by reference to the treaty latest in time or by reference to the treaty to which they are both parties. It should be noted, however, that under Art. 103 of the UN Charter, in the event of any conflict between the obligations of a state under the UN Charter and any other 'international agree-ment', the Charter is to prevail. This primacy of the Charter is recognised by Art. 30(1) of the Vienna Convention.

3.4.4.6 Rules of jus cogens

It has been suggested earlier that reference to the concept of *jus cogens* in the Convention originally was more in the nature of progressive development than codification. Of course, matters have developed considerably since 1969, so much so that some members of the Court in *Nicaragua* v *USA* felt able to identify the cus-tomary prohibition against the use of force as a rule of *jus cogens*.

Under Art. 53 of the Convention, a treaty is void if it conflicts with an existing rule of *jus cogens* and, under Art. 64, a treaty becomes void if it conflicts with an emerg-ing rule of the same quality. As discussed in Chapter 2, there is some disagreement as to which customary rules fall into this category and, further, it is only if the treaty actually contradicts the principle that it will be void. A treaty regulating how an obligation of *jus cogens* may be implemented is not void (*Jurisdictional Immunities of the State* (*Germany* v *Italy: Greece Intervening*) (2012)). In general terms, rules of *jus cogens* tend to encompass rules based more on 'morality' or 'natural law' than the traditional 'positivist' rules springing from state practice. Examples include the prohibition of the use of force, the prohibition of the crime of genocide and torture, the right of self-determination, freedom of the seas and the sovereign equality of states. The first four encompass obligations having a reasonably defined content, whereas the last three describe 'bundles' of rights which are endemic in the system of international law and may qualify as 'general principles of international law' (see Chapter 2).

3.4.5 The validity, amendment and termination of treaties

3.4.5.1 Problems in formation

The Vienna Convention has a great deal to say about matters which may affect the validity of a state's consent to be bound by a treaty. We have discussed previously the fact that non-compliance with the requirements of national law does not of itself mean that the treaty is void on the international plane (Art. 46). Conversely, a state can invoke 'error' as a ground for invalidating its consent, if the error related to a fact or situation which formed 'an essential basis' for that consent (Art. 48). There are, of course, many circumstances which may prompt a state to plead 'error' as a circumstance vitiating consent and it is not inconceivable that non-compliance with national law requirements may be such an error, albeit in rare cases. Consequently, Arts 46 and 48 should be read together. What is certain, as the *Temple of Preah Vihear Case* 1962 ICJ Rep 6 indicates, is that error will not vitiate consent if the state relying on it contributed to that error or circumstances were such that it should have realised that it was operating under a material mistake. Other grounds for vitiating consent are fraud (Art. 49), corruption of representatives (Art. 50), coercion of representatives (Art. 51) and, significantly, a treaty is void under Art. 52 if it is procured by the unlawful use or threat of force. It should be noted, however, that it will be rare for a treaty to be declared invalid on one of these grounds, save perhaps that it was procured by the use of force. Even then, treaties which regularise the situation after resort to force (e.g. peace treaties) are not void on this ground. Rather, Art. 52 is intended to invalidate 'normal' treaties where benefits are extracted by the use or threat of aggressive force. Thus, *if* Kuwait had been forced to surrender some of its territory by treaty to Iraq as a result of the latter's use of force in 1990, the treaty would have been void. However, a post-conflict treaty between these states regularising the border would not be void.

3.4.5.2 Amendment and modification

Article 39 of the Vienna Convention sets forth the unexceptional rule that a treaty may be amended by agreement between the parties. Similarly, Art. 40 recognises that any treaty may stipulate for itself the conditions and procedures for its amendment and these will displace the Convention. In fact the normal practice for multilateral treaties is that they create their own regime dealing with these matters, as with Arts 311–316 of the 1982 Law of the Sea Convention and Art. 109 of the UN Charter.

In default of a multilateral treaty establishing its own regime, the Vienna Convention lays down some general rules. The Convention recognises that it may be difficult to secure the agreement of all parties to the amending instrument for a multilateral treaty and therefore does not require complete unanimity among treaty states before an amendment can be effective. Thus, under Art. 40, an amending instrument to a treaty will be effective to amend the obligations inter se for those parties to the treaty that have consented to that amendment. For states that have not consented to the amending instrument, the unamended treaty will continue to apply between themselves and in their dealings with states that did consent. The complementary Art. 41 is really no more than a specific application of this principle, in that it allows just two state-parties to a multilateral treaty to modify their rights inter se, so long as the possibility of modification is provided for in the treaty or the specific attempted modification is not prohibited by the treaty. Lastly, in much the same way as the Convention deals with reservations, such two-party modifications are not permitted if they affect the rights of other parties to the treaty or derogate from a provision necessary for the achievement of the object and purpose of the treaty. Bilateral treaties may, of course, be amended by direct negotiation between the two states.

3.4.5.3 Termination and suspension

It is axiomatic that a treaty is necessarily terminated as soon as its object and purpose is achieved. Of course, not all treaties have a definite, once and for all aim, as with those laying down a durable legal regime such as the 1982 Law of the Sea Convention or the Antarctic Treaty 1959. For such treaties, and in cases where the object has not yet been achieved, it is necessary to decide when a state may lawfully withdraw from a treaty or when it can consider the treaty terminated.

3.4.5.4 Termination by consent

Once again, the Convention recognises that a state may withdraw from a treaty or that the treaty may be terminated or suspended according to its own terms (Arts 55 and 57). In addition, we have already noted that termination may occur by reason of the conclusion of a later inconsistent treaty under Art. 59 or by inconsistency with a rule of *jus cogens* (Arts 53 and 64). Similarly, since treaties are based on consent, all the parties can at any time agree that it will cease to bind them, although this will usually be recorded in a formal instrument. Further, two or more states may agree to suspend the operation of a multilateral treaty in their relations inter se under similar conditions as apply to inter se modifications of the treaty (Art. 58).

3.4.5.5 Termination by other parties' conduct

These are all essentially consensual terminations. What of termination or suspension by reason of the conduct of other parties? These include material breach of the terms of the treaty (Art. 60), supervening impossibility of performance (Art. 61) and fundamental change of circumstance – *rebus sic stantibus* (Art. 62). Again, as noted previously, these three provisions can be taken to represent customary law (*Danube Dam Case*).

(a) *Material breach.* Under Art. 60, a 'material breach' of a treaty is defined as a repudiation of the treaty in a manner not authorised by the Vienna Convention or a violation of a provision essential to the accomplishment of the object and purpose of the particular treaty. In a bilateral treaty, such a breach enables the injured party to terminate or suspend a treaty at its election. A material breach of a multilateral treaty enables all the parties by unanimous action to terminate the treaty altogether or to terminate it for the defaulting state only. Similarly, a single state which is specifically affected by a material breach may suspend the multilateral treaty between itself and the defaulting state, or any single state (not including the defaulting state) may suspend the treaty for itself entirely if the treaty is such that a material breach by one state radically alters the obligations under the treaty for all states. Again, however, these rules are subject to any rule stipulated in the treaty itself (Art. 60(4)). For a practical example, we can look to the *Namibia Case*, where a majority of the Court were of the opinion that South Africa had effected a material breach of its Mandate over the territory, thus justifying termination of that Mandate by the United Nations. Of course, it is central to this ground of termination that the breach be 'material', and this seems to be a question of mixed fact and law – that is, whether an unauthorised repudiation has taken place or whether the provision violated is central to the 'object and purpose' of the treaty.

In the *Danube Dam Case*, Hungary argued that it was entitled to terminate the relevant treaty because of a prior breach of treaty by Czechoslovakia (for whose actions Slovakia was now responsible). While agreeing that Art. 60 now represented customary law, the ICJ held (unsurprisingly) that only a breach of the treaty itself (i.e. *not* other rules of international law) by Czechoslovakia could justify Hungary's termination and that no breach (of any kind) had occurred prior to Hungary's purported termination. Moreover, the Court also noted that Hungary could not rely on a material breach by Czechoslovakia when Czechoslovakia's alleged breach was a response to Hungary's undoubted earlier breaches: as in national law, a party cannot take advantage of its own wrong. Similarly, in the *Application of the Interim Accord of 13 September 1995 (The Former Yugoslav Republic of Macedonia v Greece) Case* (2011), the firmly rejected Greece's argument that its violation of the Interim Accord was justified by reason of the FYRM's prior breach, noting that a material breach was one in relation to 'a provision essential to the accomplishment of the object or purpose of the treaty' and not the relatively trivial matter raised by Greece (the wearing of emblems of 'Macedonia' by state officials of the FYRM). Both cases demonstrate clearly just how reluctant the ICJ is to admit termination by material breach, although it must be noted that, factually, neither case was particularly strong. We still await clearer guidance on when a breach is 'material' and when it is not.

(b) *Supervening impossibility*. In their Commentary on the Vienna Convention, the ILC recognise that there are few examples in state practice of termination on the ground of supervening impossibility. Termination by reason of impossibility of performance arises under Art. 61 when there is a 'permanent disappearance or destruction of an object indispensable for the execution of the treaty', so long as this is not caused by breach of the treaty by the party claiming to terminate or suspend. That this Article now reflects customary law seems certain (*Rainbow Warrior Arbitration* and *Danube Dam Case*). Once again, however, the Court in the *Danube Dam Case* adopted a restrictive interpretation (in line with the *travaux préparatoires* of the Vienna Conference which preceded the Vienna Convention), noting that any supervening impossibility of performance must concern the destruction of something 'indispensable' for the performance of the treaty obligations. That later circumstances had made execution of the treaty more difficult was not caught by Art. 61 and no reliance could be placed on the Article if the state had contributed to the impossibility by its own actions.

(c) *Rebus sic stantibus: fundamental change of circumstance*. Although termination on the ground of fundamental change of circumstance was a matter of some controversy in the ILC, there is now no doubt that international law recognises such a doctrine. Occasions will arise where circumstances have altered so radically that performance of the treaty becomes something far removed from that which was originally intended. On the other hand, it is obvious that too wide a doctrine would provide states with an easy escape from obligations that have turned out to be more onerous than it was anticipated when they consented to the treaty. A balance must be struck. The purpose of the *rebus sic stantibus* doctrine is to excuse states from obligations that have changed out of all recognition rather than to provide an escape from what has turned out to be a hard bargain.

The rule found in Art. 62 of the Convention provides that fundamental change of circumstance can be invoked to terminate a treaty only when the original circumstances constituted an essential basis for the state's consent to the treaty *and* if the effect is to transform radically the extent of its obligations. However, fundamental change of circumstance cannot be invoked to challenge the validity of a treaty establishing a boundary or if the change results from the breach of the party claiming to be released. In the *Fisheries Jurisdiction Case (UK v Iceland)*, the Court considered that Art. 62 'embodied' international law on this matter. In this case, the alleged change of circumstances did not radically alter Iceland's obligation to submit the fisheries dispute to the Court for peaceful settlement. Moreover, according to the Court, a fundamental change of circumstance would be effective as a ground for termination only if it meant that obligations to be performed under the treaty would be radically altered 'to the extent of rendering the performance something essentially different from that originally undertaken'. In other words, the change of circumstance must affect future as well as past obligations. In fact, termination under the *rebus sic stantibus* doctrine is no more than an expression of the rule that treaties are based on consent. If the circumstances have changed so radically that the parties cannot be taken to have consented to the performance of the treaty in those circumstances, the treaty will be terminated. In practice, this is likely to be the exception rather than the rule. So, in the *Danube Dam Case*, which also accepted that Art. 62 represented customary law, Hungary could not terminate on this ground because the alleged changes in environmental knowledge and environmental law since the Dam Treaty's conclusion in 1977 (which would indeed affect the treaty's execution) would not *radically* affect the parties' obligations, nor were such developments unforeseen by the treaty itself. As the Court says, a 'fundamental change of circumstances must have been unforeseen; the existence of the circumstances at the time of the treaty's conclusion must have constituted an essential basis of the consent of the parties to be bound by the treaty. The negative and conditional wording of Article 62 of the Vienna Convention on the Law of Treaties is a clear indication moreover that the stability of treaty relations requires that the plea of fundamental change of circumstances be applied only in exceptional cases.'

(d) *State responsbility defences*. It is convenient to mention at this point other ways in which a state may escape from an existing treaty obligation or, to put it more accurately, other ways in which a state may escape liability for breaching an existing treaty obligation. Prior to the *Rainbow Warrior Arbitration*, it was commonly believed that a state could escape liability for breach of a treaty only if its conduct fell within the strict 'excuses' identified in the Articles of the Vienna Convention itself: viz. material breach by another party (Art. 60), supervening impossibility (Art. 61), fundamental change of circumstance (Art. 62) and conflict with rules of *jus cogens*. However, the *Rainbow Warrior Arbitration* suggested that a state will not incur liability for breach of a treaty if it can show that it has a defence under the general law of state responsibility, and this has now been confirmed in the *Danube Dam Case*. In other words, a state will not be deemed to have violated a treaty at all if it can avail itself of the 'circumstances precluding wrongfulness' (i.e. defences) identified by the ILC in its Draft on State Responsibility, even though none of the Vienna Convention grounds is made out. For example, in *Rainbow Warrior*, France successfully relied on 'duress' (as defined in the ILC Draft) as a partial defence where it might not have had any defence under the Vienna Convention. Likewise, in the *Danube Dam Case*, Hungary pleaded 'necessity' as an excuse for its breach of treaty, and although not made out on the facts, the ICJ were clear that such a defence was available in principle. Importantly, however, the ICJ in the *Danube Dam Case* were concerned to differentiate between pleas based on 'treaty law' and pleas based on defences ('circumstances precluding wrongfulness') in the law of state responsibility. Thus, reliance on Arts 60–62 of the Vienna Convention on the Law of Treaties was a plea that the alleged treaty violator had not in fact violated the treaty at all: reliance on defences in the law of state responsibility accepted that a treaty violation had occurred, but precluded the 'wrongfulness' of this conduct if the defence existed. So if necessity was made out (a defence under the law of state responsibility), the relevant treaty obligation remained applicable but the violator could not be responsible while the necessity existed. Once the necessity ceased, the obligation revived. In contrast, a successful plea under Arts 60–62 terminates the obligation permanently.

There is, of course, merit in not 'pigeon-holing' international obligations, and one of the hallmarks of a coherent legal system is that its defences to alleged unlawful conduct apply universally, irrespective of the source of the particular legal obligation in issue. So, as in *Rainbow Warrior*, even though France's particular legal obligation arose from a treaty, this did not mean that a general (state responsibility) defence was denied. Rather, the concern is that it may be unrealistic to 'pigeon-hole' the conduct of states in the manner suggested by the ICJ in the *Danube Dam Case*. The Court there suggests that it is possible to separate that state conduct which relates to 'treaty law' matters, being conduct relating to the conclusion, adoption and entry into force of the treaty as originally conceived, from that conduct which is referable to 'state responsibility' matters, being matters arising while the treaty is being carried out. This seems highly artificial and may well lead to difficulties in the future. Might it not have been more accurate to accept that the same state conduct *could* trigger both a 'treaty' and a 'state responsibility' defence?

(e) *Exceptio non adimpleti contractus* – non-performance by the other party. In the *Application of the Interim Accord of 13 September 1995 (The Former Yugoslav Republic of Macedonia v Greece) Case* (2011), Greece also argued that its violation of the Interim Accord was justified because of non-performance of the treaty by the FYRM. This is distinct from the claim that there has been a material breach of a central provision by the other party. Rather, it is that non-performance is excused by reason of simple non-performance by the other party, though perhaps only in relation to 'fundamental provisions'. In the words of Greece in that case, it is the ability 'to withhold the execution of its own obligations which are reciprocal to those not performed by [the Applicant]'. Essentially, it sees obligations within a treaty as inter-dependent. Such a general excuse for non-performance is not found in the Vienna Convention itself and the question is whether there is such a rule of customary law. In the *Application of the Interim Accord Case*, the ICJ found that Greece had failed to establish the factual conditions which *it* alleged were necessary to establish this excuse in the first place, and so it was 'unnecessary for the Court to determine whether that doctrine forms part of contemporary international law'. Suffice it to say that, without the support of the Vienna Convention, proof that such a principle exists will be challenging.

(f) *Countermeasures*. A matter related to excuses for non-performance is whether a state that has been the victim of a breach of treaty can take measures falling short of the termination of the treaty against the 'delinquent' state. These are so-called 'countermeasures', being measures which, if standing alone, would themselves be in breach of international law, either under the treaty in issue or under general international law, may be permitted if they are proportionate to the breach suffered (*Air Services Agreement Case (France v United States)* 18 RIAA 416 (1978)). Whether actual countermeasures are proportionate must be a question of fact in each case, although once again care must be taken not to encourage action which deliberately contradicts treaty obligations. The law concerning the legitimacy of countermeasures is discussed more fully in Chapter 9 and certainly the ILC in its Draft Articles on State Responsibility posutlates that there may well be customary principle. Greece also relied on this doctrine in the *Application of the Interim Accord Case* but, once again, failed to establish on the facts that action by the FYRM amounted to a sufficently serious breach to even trigger consideration of the principle.

The Vienna Convention represents a reasonably comprehensive statement of the law of treaties and there is no doubt that it has exerted a great influence on customary law, as well as regulating matters for the parties to it. Of course, in many areas, the Vienna Convention gives primacy to the terms of each treaty, but this is perfectly in accordance with the nature of treaties as instruments flowing from the consent of states. In addition to the matters identified already as falling outside the scope of this Convention we must add the effect of hostilities on treaties and state succession. State succession is dealt with by a separate Convention, as is the position of treaties made by international organisations. On the whole, however, the 1969 Convention has been a success. It is especially important in view of the fact that the treaty is likely to become the major form for the creation of rules of international law in the future.

3.5 Vienna Convention on the Succession of States in Respect of Treaties 1978

Succession of states occurs where one state replaces another as the international person responsible for a particular area of territory. Thus, when former colonies become independent, there is a succession in favour of the 'new' state and the colonial power ceases to have any international responsibility for the territory. A similar issue arises when a once federal state – as was Yugoslavia – breaks into several new states, each having sovereignty over a part of the old state. Another example is the peaceful separation of Czechoslovakia into the Czech and Slovak Republics. The question addressed by the 1978 Convention on the Succession of States in Respect of Treaties is whether 'new' states are bound by the treaties made on behalf of the territory by the former sovereign. Generally, the answer provided by the Convention is that they are not. The new state starts with a 'clean slate' (Art. 16), although it may expressly agree to be bound by treaties formerly concluded on its behalf. The exception to this principle is in respect of treaties establishing boundaries or concerning other territorial matters. These are binding on the new state, as detailed in Arts 11 and 12, which now seem to reflect customary law (*Danube Dam Case*). Note, however, that it is the *territorial regime* established by the treaty which is binding on successor states under Art. 12, rather than the treaty itself (*Danube Dam Case*). Of course, even if it is not the treaty per se which binds a successor, it is perfectly possible that the *regime* established by the treaty will include many of the detailed obligations contained in the treaty.

The break-up of the Soviet Union and Yugoslavia has revealed just how much pressure can be exerted on 'new' states to comply with the international treaty obligations of their predecessors. Thus, the newly independent Soviet states were urged repeatedly to comply with various arms limitation treaties concluded in respect of their territories by the Soviet Union, and the new 'Yugoslavian' states have accepted voluntarily many of the treaty obligations of their predecessor (e.g. the Genocide Convention). Some other states even suggested that recognition of the independence of these ex-federal states turned on whether they would accept such obligations. Of course, this does not contradict the Convention on State Succession as such, for that itself allows 'new' states to adopt existing treaties freely, but it does suggest that the rather absolute rule of 'clean slate' found in the Convention simply does not match up to the realities of life as a member of the international community. The Convention came into force on 6 November 1996 and as at 1 September 2012 there were twenty-two parties, which did not include the UK, but did include many states of the former Yugoslavia and both the Czech and Slovak Republics. Thus, although participation in this Convention is not widespread, there are indications that it is useful in resolving practical difficulties that occur when former federal states break apart.

3.6 Vienna Convention on the Law of Treaties between International Organisations or between States and International Organisations 1986

This Convention is designed to regulate the treaty relations of the other major subject of international law, the international organisation. It will apply to treaties made between international organisations or between organisations and states. The applicability of the 1969 Convention is preserved for states that are parties to it in their relations inter se, no matter that an international organisation may also be a party to the particular treaty at issue (Art. 73). In fact, the most remarkable feature of the new Convention is the extent to which it follows the 1969 Convention. In the greater part, the 1986 Convention lays down rules identical or substantially similar to its predecessor, save for necessary drafting changes. This can serve only to confirm that the 1969 Convention is now broadly reflective of customary international law. The 1986 Convention will enter into force thirty days after the 35th ratification or accession by *states*. The 'act of formal confirmation' by an international organisation does not count towards this requirement (Art. 85). As at 1 September 2012, there were forty-two parties, including the UK, but only thirty of these were states. The United Nations itself is a party to the treaty.

FURTHER READING

Bowett, D., 'Reservations to Non-Restricted Multilateral Treaties', (1976) 48 *BYIL* 67.

Cannizzaro, E., *The Law of Treaties Beyond the Vienna Convention* (Oxford University Press, 2011).

Christenson, G., 'The World Court and *Jus Cogens*', (1987) 81 *AJIL* 93.

Corten, O., and Klein, P., *The Vienna Conventions on the Law of Treaties: A Commentary* (Oxford Commentaries Intl Law, 2011).

Fitzmaurice, G., 'The Law and Procedure of the International Court of Justice: Treaty Interpretation', (1951) 28 *BYIL* 1.

Fitzmaurice, M., 'The Practical Working of the Law of Treaties', in Malcolm Evans (ed.), *International Law* (Oxford University Press, 2003).

Higgins, R., 'Derogation under Human Rights Treaties', (1976–77) 48 *BYIL* 281.

Higgins, R., *The Development of International Law* (Oxford University Press, 1963), pp. 328–36.

Marks, S., 'Reservations Unhinged', (1990) 39 *ICLQ* 300.

Sinclair, I., 'The Principles of Treaty Interpretation', (1963) 12 *ICLQ* 508.

Sinclair, I., *The Vienna Convention on the Law of Treaties*, 2nd edn. (Manchester University Press, 1984).

SUMMARY

The law of treaties

- The law of treaties covers a wide variety of matters. There are rules dealing with entry into force, termination, interpretation, reservations (being exceptions to specific obligations in a treaty) and the relationship of treaty law to custom. The law of treaties is one of the least 'political' areas of international law.

- A 'treaty' can be regarded as a legally-binding agreement deliberately created by, and between, two or more subjects of international law who are recognised as having treaty-making capacity. A treaty is an instrument governed by international law and, once it enters into force, the parties thereto have legally binding obligations in international law.

- There are a number of other examples of acts creating legal relations that do not amount to treaties as such. These include declaration under Art. 36(2) of the Statute of the ICJ; unilateral statements intended to have legal effect; acts having legal effect in national law; and acts giving rise to customary international law.

- The Vienna Convention on the Law of Treaties 1969 governs written treaties for state-parties to this Convention. However, much of the content of the Vienna Convention is now replicated in customary international law.

- The provisions of Part II of the Vienna Convention deal with rules pertaining to the creation of treaties in international law including authority to conclude treaties, modes of consent and entry into force.

- Reservations – Reservations can properly be regarded as unilateral statements made by a state at the time it gives its consent to be bound (or later if the treaty permits) and which are intended to modify or exclude an otherwise binding treaty obligation. In some cases the reservation may not be effective (i.e. may not exclude or modify the obligation) until it has been accepted by other parties to the treaty, but this does not destroy its essential character as a unilateral act (VC Art. 2(1) (d)). Reservations may be prohibited by a treaty and they may be objected to, or accepted by, other states. An objection to a reservation may prevent the entry into force of the treaty between the two states or it may merely modify the obligation.

- Treaty interpretation is governed by Arts 31 and 32 of the Vienna Convention, and these represent customary law. Preference is given to the ordinary meaning of the terms of the treaty in their context. The 'context' in which the 'ordinary meaning' is to be divined includes the preamble to a treaty and even agreements between the parties made in connection with the treaty. In Art. 32, the Convention deals with the use of the *travaux préparatoires* of a treaty as an aid to its interpretation. These are expressed to be 'supplementary means of interpretation' that may be used to confirm the meaning resulting from Art. 31.

- Third states – As a general rule, treaties are binding only on the parties. However, it is sometimes the case that parties to a treaty may intend to confer rights or obligations on third states (i.e. non-parties) without the latter becoming 'treaty states'.

- Inconsistent treaties – Under Art. 59 of the Convention, if *all* the parties to a treaty conclude a later treaty dealing with the same subject matter, then the prior treaty is considered terminated if this is the intention of the parties or the provisions of the earlier treaty are so incompatible with the terms of the later treaty that it is impossible to apply the two treaties at the same time.

- *Jus cogens* – Under Art. 53 of the Convention, a treaty is void if it conflicts with an existing rule of *jus cogens* and, under Art. 64, a treaty becomes void if it conflicts with an emerging rule of the same quality.

- A treaty may be terminated by a number of methods: consent; material breach by another party; supervening impossibility; fundamental change of circumstance.

4

International law and national law

One of the most important areas of international law for the practising lawyer is
the question of its relationship with national law, such as the domestic law of the
UK. While it is generally true that international law is concerned with the legal
relations between sovereign states and national law is concerned with the legal
relations of individuals within a state, there is considerable overlap between the
two legal systems. This can occur in a number of ways, some of which are discussed
later. Recent examples include whether UK nationals held in detention by the USA
at Guantanamo Bay in apparent violation of international law can use the domestic
legal system and principles of UK law to secure redress – see *R v Secretary of State for
Foreign Affairs, ex parte Abbasi* [2002] EWCA Civ 1598 – or whether UK courts can
use principles of international law in the resolution of civil or criminal matters – for
example, *R v Jones* [2006] 2 WLR 772 where the House of Lords considered whether
the prevention of an alleged crime under international law could be a defence to a
charge of criminal damage under national law. Indeed, now that international law
confers rights and obligations directly on individuals – as with human rights, war
crimes and crimes against humanity – it is becoming even more important to know
precisely how the rules of one system will affect the decision-making process in the
courts of another. For example, we need to know whether the courts of a national
legal system can recognise the *international* scope of human rights obligations, as in
R (on the application of Hilal Abdul-Razzaq Ali Al-Jedda) v Secretary of State for Defence
[2006] 3 WLR 954 where a UK court determined that detention of individuals in
pursuance of a Security Council resolution could modify (i.e. limit) the protection
given to that individual under the domestic law as embodied in the Human Rights
Act 1998.

In this chapter, we shall examine how these issues are resolved in theory and in
practice. First, how does national law affect decisions before international courts
and, secondly, how does international law affect decisions before national courts.
As to the first question, for example, national law may be cited before an international court as evidence of compliance with international obligations, as in the
Anglo-Norwegian Fisheries Case 1951 ICJ Rep 116. As to the second, for example, the
international law of the sea may be relevant in determining the territorial extent of
national criminal jurisdiction (e.g. *R v Keyn* (1876) 2 Exch D 63) or a government
minister may be given certain powers which may only be exercised in conformity
with international law (e.g. Diplomatic and Consular Premises Act 1987, s. 2(2),
R v Secretary of State for Foreign and Commonwealth Affairs, ex parte Samuel (1989)
The Times, 17 August 1989). More importantly, it may be contended that international law gives an individual certain rights or obligations which can be enforced

directly in national courts, as was alleged in the *Pinochet* cases (see e.g. *R v Bow Street Metropolitan Stipendiary Magistrate, ex parte Pinochet (No. 3)* [1999] 2 All ER 97) or it may be argued that alleged breaches of international law permit a court to override statutory defences in UK law, a view recently rejected in the UK by the House of Lords in *Jones* v *Saudi Arabia* [2006] 2 WLR 1424. As we shall see, these matters may be resolved in a variety of ways, principally because the manner in which international law is employed in the national courts of any particular country is largely determined by the national law of that country. Each state will have its own rules of internal constitutional law as well as specific legislative provisions that tell us how international law is to be utilised in practice in the national courts of that state. Consequently, different rules will apply for different countries. In this chapter, we shall discuss how the UK deals with the problem. However, before we examine these practical matters, we must consider the theories that have been developed to explain the relationship of international law and national law at a general level.

4.1 Theories

4.1.1 Monism

The monist theory supposes that international law and national law are simply two components of a single body of knowledge called 'law'. 'Law' is seen as a single entity of which the 'national' and 'international' versions are merely particular manifestations. Thus, both sets of rules operate in the same sphere of influence and are concerned with the same subject matter. Moreover, because they operate concurrently over the same subject matter, there may be a conflict between the two systems: international law may require one result and the provisions of national law another. If this happens in a concrete case, international law is said to prevail. For example, if the international law of human rights stipulates that no person may be imprisoned without trial, under the monist theory a national court would be *obliged* (rather than have a choice whether) to give effect to this even though a clear rule of national law said otherwise.

Although all 'monists' suppose the superiority of international law in cases of conflict with national law, there are several different explanations as to why this should be so. Hans Kelsen, a noted legal theorist, sees the superiority of international law as a direct consequence of his 'basic norm' of all law. This basic norm – or fundamental principle from which *all* law gains its validity – is that 'states should behave as they customarily have behaved'. Kelsen is 'monist-positivist' in that international law derives from the practice of states and national law derives from the state as established in international law. International law is, therefore, a 'higher' legal order. In contrast, Hersch Lauterpacht, a former judge of the ICJ, sees international law as superior because it offers the best guarantee for the human rights of individuals. Indeed, the 'state' itself is seen as a collection of individuals, rather than a legal entity in its own right. International law is said to control or override national law because the latter cannot be trusted to protect individuals and, more often than not, because it is used to persecute them. International law prevails because it is the guarantor of individual liberty, and clearly this echoes the current thinking of lawyers involved in the everyday practice of law. A similar view sees the relationship between international law and national law as monist, with international law being relatively superior, but with both systems subject to a higher legal order – the law of nature. This is the 'monist-naturalist' theory and it roots the validity of all law in natural law (see Chapter 1). According to this view there is a hierarchy of legal orders, with natural law at the summit, followed by international law, followed by national law.

Obviously, these diverse opinions about why international law should take priority over national law cannot all be correct. They are part of the wider debate about the validity of international law as a 'legal' system (see Chapter 1). However, what they have in common is the basic monist tenet that international law and national law are part of the same hierarchical legal order. Consequently, norms of international and national law must be ranked in order of priority should a conflict occur in a concrete case. In this sense, international law is superior. In practice, this means that the legal institutions of a state, such as its courts and legislature, should ensure that national rights and obligations conform to international law and that citizens can rely on international law in national courts. Most importantly, in cases of conflict, the national court should both recognise and give effect to international law and not its own domestic law.

4.1.2 Dualism

Dualism denies that international law and national law operate in the same sphere, although it does accept that they deal with the same subject matter. For dualists, international law regulates the relations between states whereas national law regulates the rights and obligations of individuals within states. International law deals with that subject matter on the international plane whereas national law deals with the subject matter internally. Consequently, if an individual is denied a right in a national court which is guaranteed under international law, the national court will apply the national law. Likewise, action by a state that might be unlawful under international law may nevertheless attract validity and protection in national law if there is a clear rule of national law to that effect – for example, in the UK, *Jones* v *Saudi Arabia* permits state immunity for alleged acts of torture, even though torture is unlawful under international law. The state itself may be in breach of its obligations on the international plane (i.e. for permitting or instigating torture), but that is a matter for an international court. There are, in other words, dual legal systems operating simultaneously in respect of the same rights and obligations and the national court should not concern itself 'with the meaning of an international instrument operating purely on the plane of international law' – per Simon Brown LJ in *Campaign for Nuclear Disarmament* v *Prime Minister of the United Kingdom* [2002] EWHC 2777 (QB). The effect of such a doctrine is that a government may be behaving perfectly lawfully within its own territory, even though it is behaving unlawfully under international law and may incur international responsibility. To take an extreme example, if the UK were to confiscate the Embassy of France under some valid domestic law, this could be perfectly lawful *within* the UK at the same time as being a violation at international law of the UK's obligations under the Vienna Convention on Diplomatic Relations 1961. In *Re McKerr* [2004] UKHL 12, Lord Steyn in the House of Lords noted that the rationale for the dualist theory – at least in its application in the UK – was to prevent the Executive from being able to create law for its citizens without observing the domestic constitutional requirements necessary for law creation (i.e. to prevent law creation without an Act of Parliament), a view echoed by Lord Bingham in *R v Jones* [2006] 2 WLR 772 rejecting the view that crimes under international customary law are automatically crimes under UK law. However, in *McKerr*, Lord Steyn also notes that the constitutional objections might not apply where the effect of international law is to confer a right on individuals, as opposed to obligations. Thus, he questions whether the dualist theory can stand scrutiny when it seeks to exclude international laws from effect in the UK if those laws are created for the *benefit* of those same citizens and he hints that human rights obligations might become an exception to dualist theory in the UK. This is explored more fully later. For the present, however, the impact of the dualist theory is that international law cannot invalidate domestic law, or vice versa, and rights and obligations arising under one system cannot automatically be transferred to the other. This theory does accept that the systems can come into conflict – because they deal with the same subject matter – but recognises that each system applies its own law unless the rules of that system say otherwise. International courts apply international law and national courts apply national law.

4.1.3 Different subject matter

Both monism and dualism accept that international law and national law deal with the same subject matter; that they are in fact concerned with the same substantive issues. Monism simply accepts that the international rule takes priority, whereas dualism insists that each system deals with the matter in its own way. A third view, promoted by Fitzmaurice and Anzilotti, denies that international law and national law ever operate in the same sphere or that they are concerned with the same subject matter. According to this view, the relationship between international law and national law is like the relationship between English law and French law: they never contradict each other as *systems of law*. It may be that the 'obligations' of each system come into conflict – as where national law allows imprisonment without trial and international law does not – but then which obligation is to prevail is to be settled by the 'conflict of laws' rules of whichever court the matter is being dealt with. So, rules of national law may or may not say that international law is to prevail (and vice versa), but the solution is still dictated by national law or international law, as the case may be.

Essentially, this is a less theoretical approach to the problem of the relationship of international and national law. Each system of law is seen as completely independent of the other because it is argued that this is how the systems relate in practice. If obligations do conflict, national courts give effect to national law obligations, unless a national rule says otherwise, and international law gives effect to international obligations, unless an international rule says otherwise. It will be appreciated that in this regard the third approach is similar to the dualist theory, and in terms of practical consequences there is little difference between the two. The distinction lies primarily in the theoretical point that this is a theory of 'coordination' (the two systems do not conflict *as systems*), whereas both monism and dualism are theories of 'confrontation'.

These theories have occupied the minds of legal philosophers ever since international law emerged as a coherent body of rules that could affect national legal systems. However, this is not the full picture. An analysis of the many cases dealing with the relationship of international and national law where a concrete issue needed to be resolved reveals that, whatever theoretical approach to this problem we consider the most appropriate, courts and tribunals rarely reach their decisions by applying monism, dualism or any other theory. Courts have looked for practical answers to practical problems. Of course, it is possible to analyse cases *ex post facto* and decide which applied monism and which applied dualism (as does Lord Steyn in *Re McKerr* when describing the UK decision in the *International Tin Council – J. H. Rayner (Mincing Lane) Limited* v *Department of Trade and Industry* [1990] 2 AC 418), but it is clear that these theories are not used as *reasons* for decisions. Actual decisions may be described in these terms, but cases are not usually decided *because* a court adopted a monist or dualist approach. In this sense, the effect of international law in national law depends on the particular constitutional rules of each state and the precise effect of domestic legislation. It is not dictated by the precepts of any pre-conceived theory. The effect of national law in international law depends on the competence of the international court, its terms of reference and its immediate task. In this sense, the third theory may be the most accurate from a descriptive point of view, but it tells us only how the systems interact, not why they do it in a particular way.

4.2 National law before international courts and tribunals

In this section, we shall examine the circumstances in which national law may be an issue before international courts and tribunals. Obviously, the purpose of international tribunals is to decide matters according to international law, but this does not mean that questions of national law are irrelevant.

4.2.1 Sources

As we have seen in Chapter 2, the decisions of national courts (e.g. *The Paquete Habana* (1900) 175 US 677) and certain national law concepts (e.g. limited liability in the *Barcelona Traction Case* 1970 ICJ Rep 3) may be used as 'sources' of international law. Strictly speaking this is more a question of using national law to help determine the content of international law than of using national law directly to resolve a dispute. However, we should not forget that the ICJ can utilise these 'sources' under Art. 38(1)(c) and (d) of its Statute as a way of elucidating the precise scope of a state's rights and duties under international law.

4.2.2 National law and international obligations

It is clear that a state cannot plead the provisions of its national law as a valid reason for violating international law. In the *Alabama Claims Arbitration* (1872) Moore 1 Int. Arb. 495, Great Britain could not rely on the absence of domestic legislation as a reason for non-fulfilment of its obligations of neutrality in the

American Civil War. Likewise, a state 'may not invoke its internal law as justification for its failure to perform a treaty' (Art. 27 of the Vienna Convention on the Law of Treaties 1969, *Questions relating to the Obligation to Prosecute or Extradite (Belgium v Senegal)* (ICJ 2012)), nor may it rely on non-compliance with national law in order to deny that it has consented to be bound by a treaty (Art. 46 of the Vienna Convention, *Maritime Delimitation and Territorial Questions Case (Qatar v Bahrain)* 1994 ICJ Rep 112). Conversely, a state cannot plead before an international court that its national law authorises it to do something which amounts to an internationally unlawful act. So, for example, the existence of authorising national law (even if passed specifically for the purpose) cannot justify an internationally unlawful expropriation of foreign-owned property, as in *Texaco v Libya* (1977) 53 ILR 389.

In essence, then, when a binding international obligation exists for a state, it must fulfil that obligation irrespective of whether its national law permits it to do so or forbids it from doing so. Indeed, this logic is at the heart of human rights obligations for the very point is that international human rights standards may engage responsibility for a state precisely because its national law permits it to do, or not to do, something which then contravenes an internationally protected human right. If a change in national law is required in order that a state may fulfil its international obligations, then the state is under an international duty to make that change or otherwise mitigate its international responsibility. In the UK, for example, the obligation to grant immunities and privileges to foreign diplomats under the 1961 Vienna Convention on Diplomatic Relations was implemented by the Diplomatic Privileges Act 1964 (changing national law) and, as a result of the decision of the European Court of Human Rights in *Brogan v UK* (1989) 11 EHRR 117, the UK had to enter a reservation to the European Convention on Human Rights mitigating its international responsibility to ensure that the detention provisions of the (then) Prevention of Terrorism Act 1984 did not continue to violate international law. Similarly, the observance of mandatory sanctions ordered by the Security Council against delinquent states under Chapter VII of the Charter may be enforced in UK national law under the United Nations Act 1946, as was the case with the Orders in Council implementing sanctions against Serbia and Montenegro in June 1992. If, however, a state does not make the necessary changes in its domestic law, it does not incur international responsibility simply because it has failed to bring its national law 'into line' with its international obligations. International responsibility arises only when the state fails, in a concrete case, to fulfil its international obligations. For instance, in the diplomatic privileges example, the UK would not have incurred liability simply by refusing to make changes in its national law, but only when a diplomat was arrested or detained in violation of the privileges guaranteed by international law even if this was permitted under national law. The converse is also true: national law may give more rights to an individual than international law permits, again engaging the state in international responsibility if the state then permits the enforcement of those rights. For example, in *Jones v Saudi Arabia*, the UK State Immunity Act 1978 provided the foreign sovereign with immunity from the judicial process for alleged acts of torture against a UK citizen occurring outside the UK, irrespective of whether such immunity was available in international law. As it happens, it is not clear whether immunity is available under *international law* for such an offence, but if it is not, then the UK would incur international responsibility by granting such privileges even though justified under UK law.

4.2.3 Defining concepts for use in international law

Although an international tribunal will normally be required to settle a dispute between two states according to international law, it may be able to do so only by reference to concepts defined in the national law of either party. For example, if an international court is asked to determine whether State A had jurisdiction over a crime committed in State B, it may be essential to know whether the alleged offender or victim was a 'national' of State A. Nationality is something determined by national law and, as the *Nottebohm Case* 1955 ICJ Rep 4 makes clear, 'it is for every sovereign state, to settle by its own legislation the rules relating to acquisition of nationality'. That does not mean, of course, that the proven fact of nationality will have the desired effect on the international plane (as in the *Nottebohm Case*), but it is for national law to decide who may be 'a national'. In this type of situation, the international court is determining the obligations of the state on the international plane, but because the substantive issue involves national law concepts, it must make reference to that national law.

4.2.4 Evidence before international tribunals

It is clear also that national law may serve as evidence of 'facts' before international tribunals. So the extent of a state's claim of maritime jurisdiction may be evidenced by its national law, as in the *Anglo-Norwegian Fisheries Case*, or national law (or its absence) may be a factor in territorial disputes (*Kasikili/Sedudu Island Case*, *Frontier Dispute Case (Benin v Niger) (2005)*), or national law may be evidence that a state has accepted the applicability of international law to a given state of affairs, as when the Israeli Supreme Court accepted that the Geneva Convention 1949 on the protection of civilians applied in the Palestinian occupied territories (*Palestinian Wall Advisory Opinion* 2004 ICJ Rep para. 100). More importantly, national law may be very weighty evidence of state practice, so helping to decide whether any rule of customary law has developed. For example, whether many states assume criminal jurisdiction under the 'passive personality' principle (see Chapter 6) can be determined only by reference to their national law and this will be crucial in determining whether sufficient state practice exists to generate a customary rule to this effect. Similarly, national law can be evidence of compliance with international obligations, and so may be used to prove that the state has not ignored its duties under treaty or customary law. Good examples are the *Certain German Interests in Polish Upper Silesia Case* (1926) PCIJ Ser. A No. 7 and the *Elettronica Sicula Case* 1989 ICJ Rep 15. However, in such cases, it still remains for the international court to determine whether the national law is *sufficient* to fulfil an international obligation: mere existence of the national law is not enough, see the *Questions relating to the Obligation to Prosecute or Extradite (Belgium v Senegal) Case* (ICJ 2012) where, despite the existence of national laws concerning investigation of torture, Senegal was held in violation of its international obligations under the Torture Convention 1984.

Although national law can be used as evidence by an international tribunal in a variety of ways, like any other 'fact', the precise content of national law must be proven before an international tribunal before it is considered, as in the *Brazilian Loans Case (France v Brazil)* (1929) PCIJ Ser. A No. 21, and for this the international tribunal will hear evidence from local law experts. It is clear also, as noted earlier, that an international court may judge the adequacy of a rule of national law in meeting the international obligation it was designed to satisfy. In the UK, for example, the Diplomatic Privileges Act will be evidence of the UK's compliance with its obligations under the Vienna Convention on Diplomatic Relations and, if the Act does not give the degree of protection required by international law, the UK may find itself internationally responsible. This is not an interference in the domestic affairs of the UK because the international court is concerned only with international obligations. Consequently, an international court could not declare the offending national legislation invalid or void for this would be an interference in domestic affairs and so the 'inadequate' Act would still be effective in national law. The point is that the offending local law would not be effective to meet the state's international obligations. That does not mean, of course, that a *national court* cannot declare a local Act void for want of conformity with international law, but that is a matter for the competence of the national court, as determined by national law. An example of this may be the decision in *R v Secretary of State for Transport, ex parte Factortame (No. 2)* [1990] 3 WLR 818, where the House of Lords declared void those parts of the Merchant Shipping Act 1988 that contradicted EC law (this does, of course, assume that EC law is international law and not a species of national law).

4.2.5 National law as a basis for a tribunal's decision

It is not impossible for an international tribunal to be given jurisdiction to decide a dispute solely or primarily on the basis of national law. This will be rare, simply because international law usually concerns supranational issues, but it is not unknown. For example, in the *Serbian Loans Case* (1929) PCIJ Ser. A No. 20, the Permanent Court of International Justice (the predecessor to the ICJ) was called upon to determine the validity and application of certain loan agreements made between French nationals and the Serbian government. This was a matter of national law, the Court eventually deciding the substantive issue according to Serbian law. Although the Court would normally only decide matters which called for the application of international law, its jurisdiction in this case rested on the fact that the dispute was submitted to it by 'special agreement' within the terms of its Statute. Similarly, mineral concession agreements between states and commercial corporations (e.g. for oil extraction) may provide that disputes are to be settled by an arbitration panel who may apply both the national law of the state and relevant rules of international law, as in *Texaco v Libya*. When an international court is called upon to apply national law directly, it will pay 'the utmost regard to decisions of the municipal courts of a country' (*Brazilian Loans Case*) because it is not sensible to adopt an interpretation of that law different from that which applies inside the state itself. If, however, the correct interpretation of national law is unclear, the international court will 'select the interpretation which it considers most in conformity with the law' of that state (*Brazilian Loans Case*).

4.3 Theories about international law in the national legal system: incorporation, transformation and implementation

In theoretical terms, the use of international law in national courts is often explained in terms of the doctrines of incorporation and transformation. Under the doctrine of incorporation, a rule of international law becomes part of national law without the need for express adoption by the local courts or legislature. The rule of international law is incorporated in national law simply because it is a rule of international law. This 'automatic' adoption is said to operate unless there is some clear provision of national law, such as a statute or judicial decision, which precludes the use of the international law rule by the national court. Consequently, once it is established that an international law rule exists and would be relevant to the case in hand, under the doctrine of incorporation it is, without more, part of national law and may be applied by the national court. For example, if a state follows the incorporation doctrine, then international rules on diplomatic privileges will automatically and without more allow a diplomat to plead immunity before national courts. Usually, where a country adopts the incorporation approach it is because of some constitutional provision of its own, as with Art. 25 of the Basic Law of the Republic of Germany. The UK *appears* to adopt the incorporation approach for rules of international customary law, although whether this is in fact the case is discussed more fully later.

The doctrine of transformation, on the other hand, stipulates that rules of international law do not become part of national law until they have been expressly adopted by the State. International law is not *ipso facto* part of national law. Therefore, a national court cannot apply a particular rule of international law until that particular rule has been deliberately 'transformed' into national law in the appropriate manner, as by legislation. Consequently, international law and national law are kept separate by the state and it is only if the state has taken the conscious step of utilising rules of international law that the rules so chosen can be said to be 'part of' national law. For example, if a state follows the transformation doctrine, then international rules on diplomatic privileges do not operate in favour of the diplomat until legislation has been passed authorising national courts to give effect to such privileges. Until that point, the diplomat is subject to the jurisdiction of the national court irrespective of what international law says. As we shall see, this appears to be the position in the UK in respect of international law derived from treaties.

In essence, then, the difference between incorporation and transformation is that the former adopts international law into national law just because it is international law, whereas the latter requires a deliberate act on the part of the state concerned. Under the former, rules of international law are part of national law unless excluded, under the latter they are part of national law only if deliberately included. Moreover, it is often said that the doctrines of incorporation and transformation match up to monism and dualism respectively. The idea is that, under monism, international law and national law are part of the same unified system and this is reflected by the fact that international law is automatically incorporated into national law. By way of contrast, dualism says that each system operates in its own area of competence, and thus rules of international law can operate in national law only if they are deliberately transformed into that system by the appropriate national process.

Unfortunately, this neat theoretical symmetry is not entirely accurate, although it is adopted by Lord Steyn in the case of *Re McKerr* when describing the effect of international treaties in UK law. It is clear, as indicated previously, that whether any state adopts the incorporation or transformation doctrine is to be determined by its own national law, usually its 'constitution'. Therefore, to say that a state adopts incorporation or transformation tells us only what *method* that state has chosen as its way of giving effect to international law in its national courts. It does not necessarily tell us whether the state is monistic or dualistic. For example, in the *Tin Council Cases* in the Court of Appeal (*Maclaine Watson* v *Dept of Trade and Industry*) [1988] 3 All ER 257, one of the questions facing the court was whether there was a rule of international law which stipulated that state-members of international organisations (i.e. the Tin Council) could be sued directly for the liabilities of the organisation. If there was such a rule, the next question was whether that rule was part of UK national law, with the alleged consequence that states could be sued for those liabilities in UK courts. Both Kerr and Nourse LJJ proceeded on the basis that there was such a rule of international law and, further, that this was a customary rule. Both judges also agreed on the method by which this rule of international law could become part of UK law – under the doctrine of incorporation. However, for Nourse LJ, the existence of the rule – 'that state-members of organisations can be sued for the liabilities of the organisation' – plus the doctrine of incorporation meant that such states could be sued directly in UK courts. This is a monist approach, for it sees liability under international law as being equivalent to liability under national law. Incorporation was simply the method by which the liability was transferred from one system to the other. Kerr LJ, on the other hand, adopted a dualist approach. For him, the rule of international law that needed to be incorporated was *not* 'can states be sued for the debts of international organisations', but rather 'can states be sued for the debts of international organisations in *national law*'. In his view, there was no such rule and so no liability in national law. For Kerr LJ, liability under one system cannot be transferred to another system per se. The only way for an international customary rule to authorise suit in national courts – even if that customary rule was incorporated – was where the international rule gave that right specifically. This is the dualist position *par excellence* and it was again manifested in the UK by the House of Lords in *R* v *Jones* where Lord Bingham and Lord Hoffmann (with whom the other judges agreed) rejected the submission that the international customary law crime of 'aggression' was *automatically* a crime in UK law. This was not because they denied that the international crime of aggression existed (in fact, they were clear that it did exist), nor because they disagreed in principle with the incorporation theory (thus the judgments deliberately avoid commenting on matters of UK civil law), but because the substance of the alleged incorporated customary law would have had a profound effect on the rights of UK citizens and the UK legal system without going through the normal legislative process for similar laws. Thus, what the judgments in these cases illustrate is that there is no necessary correlation between incorporation and monism or transformation and dualism. In the Court of Appeal in the *Tin Council* case, both judges recognised the existence of a customary rule (although the House of Lords later decided that the relevant rule was one found in treaty [1989] 3 All ER

523) and confirmed the incorporation theory, but one was monist and the other dualist. In *R* v *Jones*, both judges accepted incorporation, but reached an essentially dualist conclusion.

The theories of incorporation and transformation are an attempt to rationalise how international law is used within a national legal system. As we shall see subsequently, the UK *appears* to adopt incorporation for customary international law but *appears* to prefer transformation for treaty law. It must be remembered, however, that these are *theories*. In practice, a state may adopt a variety of approaches to using rules of international law within its legal system that do not fit neatly into these two categories. Consequently, a purely pragmatic approach is to think in terms of implementation: how does the national court implement rules of international law that have a bearing on the subject matter of a dispute? This empirical approach may well reveal an uneven pattern in the application of international law that does not turn on the origin of the international rule (i.e. *not* whether the rule originates in custom or treaty) but on its subject matter or likely impact on the local legal system (see section 4.4.5). Moreover, it may well reveal that both incorporation and transformation are too absolute in their result: after all, they are rather 'all or nothing'. In the UK, for example, the Human Rights Act 1998 has brought the substantive rights and jurisprudence of the European Convention for the Protection of Human Rights and Fundamental Freedoms 1959 into national law. Yet the manner of this adoption is neither incorporation nor transformation; it is a peculiarly UK form of implementation designed to ensure that the rights of the Convention are workable within the existing matrix of rights and processes of UK law (a point made with some force by Lord Hoffmann in *R* v *Lyons* [2002] UKHL 44). This is not a large issue but it serves to remind us that the interaction between international law and national law may be rather more complex than the solutions offered by the two major theories of incorporation and transformation.

4.4 International law in the national law of the United Kingdom

4.4.1 Treaties and similar international instruments – general rule

In the UK, the general rule is that rights and obligations arising from treaties (and Security Council resolutions) have to be transformed into national law by Act of Parliament before they can create any rights or obligations enforceable in national courts (*J. H. Rayner (Mincing Lane) Ltd* v *Department of Trade and Industry, Tin Council Cases* (1990), *R* v *Lyons* (2002), *Campaign for Nuclear Disarmament* v *Prime Minister* [2002] EWHC 2777 and *A* v *Secretary of State for the Home Department* [2006] 2 AC 220). Treaties are concluded by the Crown under the Royal Prerogative and a treaty cannot change the substance or nature of individual rights guaranteed under common law or statute. Thus, if a treaty is to operate in national law, it must be enacted by Act of Parliament. The only limited exceptions to this are treaties of cession or those pertaining to the conduct of war. These are treaties which, by their nature, indirectly affect the rights of individuals but they may do so without Act of Parliament.

It will be appreciated that this is very much a constitutional rule of the UK, stemming from the fight for legislative supremacy between the Crown and Parliament. Although it does, on one view, support the dualist approach to international law, it was not developed for that reason. It is purely a national law rule that has been applied without demur in a great many cases, such as *The Parlement Belge* (1879) 4 PD 129; *A-G for Canada* v *A-G for Ontario* [1937] AC 326, and recently by the House of Lords and Court of Appeal in the cases referred to earlier.

In the *Tin Council Case*, the House of Lords confirmed explicitly that a 'treaty to which Her Majesty's Government is a party does not alter the laws of the United Kingdom ... Except to the extent that a treaty becomes [transformed] into the laws of the United Kingdom by statute, the courts of the United Kingdom have no power to enforce treaty rights and obligations at the behest of a sovereign government or at the behest of a private individual' (per Lord Templeman). In this case, as Lord Templeman went on to point out, the treaty establishing the International Tin Council was not transformed by a statute and thus any matters arising from it could not be settled in UK courts and it is now settled that this applies with equal forms to other similar international instruments, such as Security Council resolutions (*CND* v *Prime Minister*). Moreover, according to Lord Oliver in the *Tin Council Case*, the non-justiciability of untransformed treaties meant that UK courts should be wary of even referring to such treaties when deciphering the legal relations of parties to a dispute. In this sense, he agreed with the trial judge and Gibson LJ in the Court of Appeal that a UK court should not have reference to the unenacted treaty in order to adjudicate on the substantive claims of the parties. His approach was, therefore, much stricter than that of Kerr and Nourse LJJ in the Court of Appeal, both of whom treated the non-justiciable rule in a liberal fashion and made reference to the unenacted treaty quite freely.

It is clear that Lord Oliver in the *Tin Council Case* would not permit the use of an unenacted treaty to identify the legal rights of the state-parties to that treaty – that would be going beyond the permissible use of the treaty as evidence of the factual background of the parties' dispute. As it was put in general terms in *AY Bank (in liquidation)* v *Bosnia & Herzegovina* (2006), the courts in England have no power to interpret or enforce treaties between foreign sovereign states that have not been incorporated into the domestic law of England. Such treaties are governed by public international law, which alone determine their validity, interpretation and enforcement. Nevertheless, it will be appreciated that the distinction which Lord Oliver seeks to draw in *Tin Council* between a permissible and non-permissible use of an unenacted treaty is a fine one. In *Westland Helicopters Ltd* v *Arab Organisation for Industrialisation* [1995] 2 All ER 387, Coleman J was faced with an unenacted treaty establishing the Arab Organisation. In his view, and citing Lord Oliver extensively, he could not determine whether the state-parties to the treaty had violated its terms (the treaty being unenacted in UK law), but he could examine the terms of the treaty, as a matter of fact, in order to distil the constitution of the Organisation it created. This generous use of the unenacted treaty – on the ground that it provided evidence of certain facts – does not stand comfortably with Lord Oliver's refusal in *Tin Council* to use the treaty in order to determine the rights of the parties to it. Similarly, in *Croatia* v *Serbia* [2010] 2 WLR 555, the High Court agreed that the Land Registry could make entries in the register dealing with title to land, even though the dispute as to ownership arose out of an unenacted treaty between the two states.

While a determination about the merits of the dispute would be non-justiciable because of the unenacted treaty, issues relating to administrative acts concerning the land register could be dealt with. We might legitimately ask whether there is any real difference between use of an unenacted treaty to determine the rights of the parties (*Tin Council*, not permitted) and use of an unenacted treaty to determine the constitution of an international organisation created by the treaty (*Westland*, permitted) or recognition of the state of affairs created by the unenacted treaty when deciding matters of administration falling under private law (*Crotatia*, permitted).

This leads us to a second problem created by unenacted treaties, an issue addressed by the House of Lords in *Arab Monetary Fund* v *Hashim* [1991] 1 All ER 871 and by Coleman J in *Westland Helicopters*. The Arab Monetary Fund was an international organisation that had been established by an international treaty to which the UK was not a party. That treaty had not been transformed into UK law and hence (following the *Tin Council Cases*), the Monetary Fund had no existence in UK law and could not sue the defendant. However, the Monetary Fund had been incorporated in the domestic law of the United Arab Emirates (UAE), a sovereign state with whom the UK enjoyed full diplomatic relations. According to the House of Lords, this meant that although the Monetary Fund *as an international organisation* could not be accorded legal status in the UK – because it was created by an untransformed treaty – the Monetary Fund *as a legal person of the UAE* could be recognised under the normal conflict of laws rules which gave UK recognition to legal entities created by the laws of other states. Obviously, this is a neat solution to the particular problem in the *Hashim* case, but it is not altogether clear why the House of Lords could not apply 'the normal conflict of laws' rules to an organisation created under international law. The question the House of Lords did *not* answer in *Hashim* is why entities created under the domestic law of other countries will be recognised while entities created under international law will not. The House of Lords also failed to give clear guidance on the exact nature of the organisation which the UK court would now recognise. What did it mean to say that it was recognised as existing under the law of the 'host' state, and how would a UK court deal with an organisation created by an unenacted treaty but incorporated by the law of several states? Would such an organisation have several personalities in UK law, one for each of the states in which it was incorporated, and which would be pre-eminent? This was exactly the problem in *Westland Helicopters*. The Arab Organisation for Industrialisation was incorporated under the law of Egypt, having been created by a number of Arab states by a treaty not transformed into UK law. Following *Hashim*, it was argued that this meant that the Organisation had personality as an Egyptian corporation and, moreover, that the Organisation's Egyptian representatives could sue on its behalf in the UK. This was resisted by Westland, who claimed that the Egyptian representatives did not actually represent the Organisation at all. Coleman J followed *Hashim* to the extent that he agreed that the Organisation had an existence in UK law, despite the unenacted treaty, because of its incorporation in the law of a state which the UK recognised. However, in his view, this did not make the Organisation an Egyptian corporation for all purposes, for otherwise the Organisation would have multiple personalities depending on which states had incorporated it and, indeed, there could be disputes between the different personalities. According to Coleman J, once the Organisation's personality in UK law had been established through the medium of another state's law, the true nature of the organisation as a *public international law* organisation should be recognised, as defined by the treaty which established it. This is an ingenious gloss on *Hashim*, itself a neat sidestep of the consequences of *Tin Council*. In effect, it means that an international organisation created by a treaty which is not enacted in the UK will be treated as an *international* organisation in UK law provided it is incorporated in any state that the UK recognises. Not only does this mean that a UK court will have regard to the unenacted treaty (in order to find the 'true' nature of the organisation), it means in effect that UK law will recognise the personality of nearly every international organisation – for nearly all are incorporated somewhere. This raises the obvious question of why it is not possible simply to recognise that entities created under international law can be entities in UK law as stemming from a recognised legal system, instead of engaging in the fiction that they can be recognised because they are incorporated in some state's national law? To accept the personality in UK law of international organisations per se would be more straightforward and more intellectually defensible.

A third problem surrounding 'unenacted' (or perhaps 'unimplemented' is a more accurate description) treaties is a jurisdictional one. In the *Pinochet Case (No. 3)*, one issue was whether the crimes allegedly committed by Senator Pinochet were 'extradition crimes' so as to trigger the UK court's jurisdiction over the Senator. In turn, this depended on whether the (alleged) act of torturing a non-UK citizen outside the UK was nevertheless a crime under UK law. The UK was a party to the Convention Against Torture 1984, but this was only implemented (i.e. 'enacted') in UK law for acts occurring after 28 September 1988. Consequently, as most of the events for which the Senator was allegedly responsible had occurred before this date, the UK court had jurisdiction only over relatively few of the alleged crimes because the Torture Convention was unenacted during most of the relevant period. As we shall see in Chapter 6 (Jurisdiction), there was a possible way around this problem by seeing the alleged crimes as giving rise to 'universal jurisdiction' thus authorising the local court to try the matter – this being a rule of customary law that could be incorporated without a statute. However, apart from Lord Millett, the judges in *Pinochet* were unwilling to take this route and preferred to follow the traditional rule about unenacted treaties. This led to a lack of jurisdiction over many of the alleged offences. A similar reluctance was evident in the Australian case of *Nulyarimma* v *Thompson* (2000) 39 ILM 20, where the admittedly international crime of genocide (giving universal jurisdiction) was not a crime under Australian federal law because of the absence of local legislation. Likewise, when the issue arose again in *R* v *Jones*, the House of Lords took the view that, even accepting the existence of a customary international law crime of genocide, that crime was not 'incorporated' directly (as discussed previously) into UK law because it would have the effect of creating a new criminal offence, for which individuals would suffer punishment, without legislative approval. This was something that a UK court could not countenance and demonstrates that the real issue is not whether the source of international law is unenacted treaty or customary law, but the potential impact it would have on the domestic legal system.

What this means then in practice is that, at present, constitutional principle appears to require that the unenacted treaty is without legal effect in UK law. It may not create rights or obligations for the parties in national law and its substantive provisions cannot be made the subject of litigation in national courts. Furthermore, the Court cannot make reference to the treaty in order to determine the extent of individual rights because this raises a non-justiciable issue, and it may even lack jurisdiction in respect of events arising before (if ever) the treaty is transformed. However, as cases since *Tin Council* have illustrated, that does not mean that the unenacted treaty can have no impact on UK law at all and in *Hashim* and *Westland* we can see how the unfortunate consequences of the rule can be avoided altogether. So also in *AY Bank (in liquidation)* v *Bosnia & Herzegovina* (2006), where in the end the court did feel able to adjudicate on the dispute about ownership of assets of the former Yugoslavia because, it was held, the issue was essentially a private law matter concerned with proof of debts that did not require the court to go into details of the unenacted treaty. Finally, as noted earlier, given that the constitutional principle is designed to *protect* UK citizens from law creation without Parliamentary approval, Lord Steyn has suggested, in *Re McKerr*, that treaties conferring and protecting human rights might have direct effect in the UK whether they are transformed by domestic legislation or not. Such treaties, he suggests, are of their nature supportive of individuals and not oppressive. It remains to be seen whether this radical approach gains currency, and the tenor of later judgments particularly *R v Jones* is against it, for the issue is not simply about the effect of international on individuals, but also about the constitutionality of law making. However, as the following sections illustrate, we should not discount the influence that treaties (whether transformed or not) are able to exert over national law in other ways.

4.4.2 The enacted treaty

The corollary of what we have just discussed is that if a treaty is transformed by statute into UK law it has full legal effect to the extent of its enactment. Such transformation is often achieved by means of a general enabling Act to which a Schedule is attached containing the provisions of the treaty to be enacted. For example, the Diplomatic Privileges Act 1964 enacts the Vienna Convention on Diplomatic Relations 1961, and the Carriage of Goods by Road Act 1965 enacts the Convention on the Contract for the International Carriage of Goods by Road 1956 (the Warsaw Convention). Both of these Acts were necessary if the terms of the respective treaties were to have force and effect in national law, as was the legislation giving jurisdiction over non-territorial torture in the *Pinochet* case. However, as was pointed out by Lord Steyn in *R (European Roma Rights Centre and others)* v *Immigration Officer at Prague Airport*, legislation may 'enact' a treaty in a variety of ways, not only by inclusion of the entire treaty or parts of it in a Schedule. So, in that case, the Asylum and Immigration Appeals Act 1993 made reference to the Refugee Convention 1951 which Lord Steyn took to be 'enaction by reference' of its principles.

Obviously, if the treaty is an integral part of the enabling Act (as where contained in a Schedule) then any interpretation of the Act will automatically encompass interpretation of the terms of the treaty. The treaty and the Act are as one. However, when an enabling Act needs to be interpreted, we need to know what principles of interpretation the court may use and whether it may make reference to any extraneous material, such as the *travaux préparatoires* of the enacted treaty or alternative language texts. In *James Buchanan & Co.* v *Babco Forwarding and Shipping (UK)* [1977] 3 All ER 1048, the House of Lords were concerned with the interpretation of the Carriage of Goods by Road Act referred to previously. This enacted the Warsaw Convention in Schedule 1. In the opinion of the majority, when the court was called on to interpret an Act which enacted a treaty, it should apply the rules appropriate to the interpretation of an international convention, unconstrained by technical rules of English law or by legal precedent. The court should proceed on the basis of rules of general application, not on peculiarly English rules because, in essence, the court was interpreting the treaty itself. Moreover, if the treaty had more than one official language, the court was able to look to the other language even though it was not formally enacted by the Act. According to Lord Wilberforce, reference could be made to the alternative language text even if there was no ambiguity in the English text, although the majority thought such reference permissible only if there was prior ambiguity.

These principles were applied by the House in the later case of *Fothergill v Monarch Airlines Ltd* [1980] 2 All ER 696, although here the alternative language text (French) was also enacted in the Schedule. In this case, the House of Lords adopted a purposive interpretation to the Carriage By Air Act 1961 (enacting the Warsaw Convention for the Unification of Certain Regulations concerning International Air Travel of 1929 and Hague Protocols 1955) even though the result achieved was at odds with the normal English meaning of the words under consideration. Furthermore, Lord Wilberforce was prepared to allow use of the *travaux préparatoires* of a treaty as an aid to interpretation where those materials were public and accessible and pointed to a definite legislative intention and (per Lord Diplock) where this would clear up any ambiguities. This was, as the court noted, the rule found in Art. 32 of the Vienna Convention on the Law of Treaties 1969 (see Chapter 3) and it should be applied where a court was performing a similar function. Moreover, reference to the *travaux préparatoires* was permissible even though a UK court could not at that time have had regard to the legislative history of 'ordinary' Acts of Parliament when interpreting their terms (but see now *Pepper v Hart* [1992] 3 WLR 1033).

Consequently, not only do treaties which are enacted have full legal effect to the extent of their enactment, the enabling Act is to be treated in the same way as an international treaty would be treated before an international court. Again, although the majority view in *Buchanan v Babco* and *Fothergill v Monarch* suggests that reference to extraneous material should not be made unless the terms of the 'treaty-Act' are ambiguous, Lord Wilberforce favours a more liberal approach and would resort to such materials as a primary source of reference on the ground that the Act was intended to fulfil international obligations and should, therefore, be interpreted as doing so.

4.4.3 The unenacted treaty and the interpretation of statutes

4.4.3.1 Statutes intended to give effect to treaty obligations

Even if a treaty is not enacted, either in the traditional way by a Schedule or by Lord Steyn's more generous sense of 'enaction by reference' (4.4.2, *R (European Roma Rights Centre and others) v Immigration Officer at Prague Airport*), it may be that the Act was intended to give effect to the terms of the treaty in national law. For example, the Customs and Excise Act 1952 was intended to give effect to the Convention on Valuation of Goods for Customs Services 1950, even though it did not contain the treaty or make reference to it, and the Immigration and Asylum Act 1999 in part is intended to give effect to provisions in the Convention Relating to the status of Refugees 1951. In such cases, the question arises whether a UK court may have regard to the treaty when interpreting the Act and, if it does, whether the court may adopt an interpretation which achieves the purpose of the treaty despite an apparently different meaning. Obviously the situation is different from that just considered because now the treaty is not part of the Act – it is unenacted and may raise non-justiciable issues. This was the question considered by the Court of Appeal in *Salomon* v *Commissioners of Customs and Excise* [1967] 2 QB 116 in respect of the Customs and Excise Act just referred to and in *R* v *CPS, ex parte Pepushi* (11 May 2004) in relation to the Refugee Convention.

In the leading judgment in *Salomon*, which has been approved on many occasions since, Diplock LJ developed three principles which the court should apply in this type of case. First, if the terms of the Act are clear and unambiguous, they must be given effect to by the court even if they do not carry out the obligations which are found in the treaty. UK courts are subject to the doctrine of parliamentary sovereignty and although it may be presumed that Parliament does not intend to legislate contrary to international obligations, it may do so. So, if the terms of the Act clearly require an interpretation contrary to the treaty they were designed to implement, the court follows the Act, as in the earlier case of *Ellerman Lines* v *Murray* [1931] AC 126. Likewise, if the relevant Act is clear and is narrower in scope than the corresponding enacting treaty, a UK court must give effect to the Act rather than the wider provision found in the treaty. So, in *ex parte Pepushi*, the court followed the narrower provision of s. 31 of the Immigration and Asylum Act 1999, rather than the wider scope of Art. 32 of the Refugee Convention. Indeed, if the UK court is required to follow an Act that is either contrary to or narrower than the counterpart unenacted treaty, the UK will be responsible in international law for any treaty violations, but this is not the concern of the national court. It should be noted, however, that this first proposition does not hold good if the particular treaty concerned is one of the treaties establishing the European Union. In that case, it is clear from *R* v *Secretary of State for Transport, ex parte Factortame (No. 2)* [1990] 3 WLR 818, that the law of the EU Treaties (i.e. the law of Europe) must prevail even in the face of a clearly contrary Act of Parliament. This is because of the special status of this version of international law within the UK legal system, a matter confirmed by s. 2 of the European Communities Act 1972.

Secondly, if the domestic legislation which is intended to give effect to treaty obligations is not clear and is reasonably capable of more than one meaning, the unenacted treaty is relevant and may be referred to by the court. If there is then a choice between a meaning which implements the treaty and a meaning which does not, the former should be adopted because Parliament does not intend to legislate contrary to international obligations in the absence of clear language. *A-G* v *Guardian Newspapers Ltd (No. 2)* [1990] 1 AC 109 and *R* v *Lyons* (2002). Similarly, the common law should be interpreted and applied, wherever possible, in a manner consistent with those obligations (*Derbyshire CC* v *Times Newspapers* [1992] QB 770). Thirdly, the rule that the court may refer to the unenacted treaty in cases of ambiguity applies whether or not the Act makes reference to the treaty in its preamble or elsewhere. It is enough if extrinsic evidence establishes that the Act was intended to implement the UK's international obligations under a Convention, as in *Hogg* v *Toye & Co. Ltd* [1935] Ch 497.

These rules apply, then, to Acts which do not enact a treaty 'but which are intended to give effect to its terms in national law, always bearing in mind the special status of law derived from the EU Treaties. It has been suggested (e.g. Brownlie, *Principles of International Law*, 1998, p. 48) that the need for prior ambiguity before reference can be made to the unenacted treaty is unnecessary, because of the already established intention to give effect to that treaty. However, the reluctance of UK courts to use extraneous materials when the terms of an Act are clear has been noted earlier in those cases where the Act *did* enact a treaty (or one version of it) and it would be surprising if the court imposed a less strict test in cases where the Act did not enact the treaty. Indeed, as Lord Hoffmann makes clear in *R v Lyons*, an interpretation of a statute in a manner consistent with the UK's international obligation is desirable, but should be undertaken only when the court is free to do so because the 'sovereign legislator in the UK is Parliament. If Parliament has plainly laid down the law, it is the duty of the courts to apply it, whether that would involve the Crown in breach of an international treaty or not' (*R v Lyons* at para. 28.) Indeed, it may be argued that the lack of express enactment of the treaty indicates that Parliament may have contemplated making modifications to the obligations of the treaty as they take effect in national law. This can be done by clear words. In the *Tin Council Case*, Lord Oliver confirmed that where a statute is intended to give effect to a treaty without direct enactment, 'the terms of the treaty may have to be considered and, if necessary, construed *in order to resolve any ambiguity or obscurity* as to the meaning or scope of the statute' (emphasis added).

To some extent, the Human Rights Act 1998 falls into this category, being a statute which does not actually 'enact' a treaty in full (the European Convention on Human Rights) but the purpose of which is to ensure the protection of the substantive rights of the Convention in UK law. In fact, however, the Human Rights Act is much more than an attempt to ensure that the UK meets its international obligations: it is the willing adoption of the substance of an international treaty in local law. Clearly, the rules discussed earlier will have a role in the interpretation of this Act but it is clear that a whole new jurisprudence is developing around the Human Rights Act, drawing much of its support from the jurisprudence of the European Court at Strasbourg.

4.4.3.2 Other statutes

In the previous two sections, we have discussed statutes which enact the treaty expressly and statutes which are intended to give effect to international treaty obligations even though no reference is made to the treaty. There is, of course, a third category comprising those Acts of Parliament which were not intended to give effect to any specific international obligation but which in fact deal with the same subject matter as a treaty to which the UK is a party and which, therefore, binds the UK in international law. The question is whether a UK court can have regard to the international obligations of the UK when interpreting an 'ordinary' domestic statute. Once again, we must note that European Union law will have priority over UK law, whatever the context.

In *IRC v Collco Dealings Ltd* [1962] AC 1, the appellants argued that the application of s. 4(2) of the Finance (No. 2) Act 1955 would involve a breach of the Double Taxation Agreement 1926 between the UK and Eire. This was an unenacted treaty and the Finance Act was not passed in order to give effect to its terms. According to Viscount Dilhorne, the fact that the application of clear and unambiguous statutory provisions would involve a breach of the UK's international obligations under a valid treaty should not affect the court's interpretation of the statute. Parliament legislates for national law and this normally takes priority.

However, this case is not authority for the general proposition that a court should disregard a treaty in interpreting a statute simply because the statute was enacted for reasons that had nothing to do with the treaty. This was a case where the statute was clear and unambiguous and it would have been a surprise if the court had ignored the statutory language in such circumstances. Again, we must not forget the general rule of construction that Parliament will be presumed not to have legislated contrary to international obligations and it seems that this principle can operate in the case of ambiguous statutes that are not intended to implement a treaty at all. Formerly, this issue arose most frequently in respect of the European Convention on Human Rights before its implementation in UK law by the Human Rights Act 1998 (see section 4.4.3.1). Historically, UK courts sought to interpret statute (and common law) in conformity with the European Convention unless this was impossible due to the clear words of the legislation. See, for example, *Derbyshire CC* v *Times Newspapers* [1992] 3 WLR 28; *Brind* v *Secretary of State for the Home Department* [1991] 1 All ER 720; and *Attorney-General* v *Associated Newspapers* [1994] 2 AC 238. It would thus be reasonable to suppose that UK courts would continue to follow this approach in respect of the interpretation of all Acts of Parliament where they touch upon the international obligations of the UK.

4.4.4 Customary international law

As has been indicated earlier, customary international law may form part of the law of the UK under the doctrine of incorporation. In principle, this means that unless there is a contrary statutory provision, rules of customary international law may be operative in the national legal system. However, as we have seen with the judgments in the Court of Appeal in the *Tin Council Case* and of the House of Lords in *R* v *Jones*, this does not necessarily mean that rights or obligations founded in customary international law can be enforced directly in national courts. In particular, Lord Bingham in *Jones* is not prepared 'to accept this proposition in quite the unqualified terms in which it has often been stated' and sees international customary law as one of the sources of UK law rather than automatically 'part' of it. Thus, it may be more accurate to say that incorporation of a customary rule can occur automatically only if it is of a type that can be made justiciable in the national legal system and is of a kind where automatic implementation would not offend a basic constitutional precept of that system. In other words, it must be a right or obligation of customary international law that is intended to operate within the national legal system and whose existence therein is compatible with rules of that system.

It has not always been the case that UK courts have accepted so unequivocally the incorporation doctrine in respect of customary international law, even in the modified form it now takes. Earlier cases seem to have suggested that customary international law could not operate at all in the UK without express adoption – i.e.

transformation. For example, in *R* v *Keyn*, several of their Lordships appear to suggest that customary rules on the territorial sea were not part of UK law unless specifically adopted. Similarly, there are dicta in cases such as *West Rand Central Gold Mining Co.* v *R* [1905] 2 KB 391; *Mortensen* v *Peters* (1906) 8 F (J) 93; *Chung Chi Cheung* v *R* [1939] AC 160; and *Thakrar* v *Secretary of State for the Home Dept* [1974] QB 684, which seem to confirm this transformation view. However, as has been repeatedly pointed out (see Collier, (1989) 38 ICLQ 924), these cases can be explained on other grounds. In *R* v *Keyn* there is much to suggest that there was doubt about the very existence of the customary rule; in *West Rand*, the action failed on the ground that the petitioner was seeking to use 'act of state' as a sword against the Crown; and in *Mortensen* v *Peters* there was a statute which clearly prevented the court from applying the customary rule. In fact, none of these cases, except perhaps the decision in *Thakrar*, clearly rejects the incorporation theory.

In *Thakrar* v *Secretary of State*, Lord Denning rejected the incorporation theory in respect of a claim by the applicant to be allowed entry into the UK under the rules of international law concerning the obligation of states to accept its own nationals. Of course, this might be explained by the fact that the alleged rule of international law appeared to be contrary to the Immigration Act 1971, which would obviously take precedence. Subsequently, however, in *Trendtex Trading Corp.* v *Central Bank of Nigeria* [1977] QB 529 Lord Denning changed his mind and both he and Shaw LJ reasserted the efficacy of customary rules of international law within the UK legal system without express adoption. In *Trendtex*, the Bank of Nigeria claimed to be immune from the jurisdiction of the court under the rules of sovereign immunity and, at that time, there was clear precedent that a UK court was bound by the doctrine of absolute immunity (see Chapter 7). However, the majority of the court (Stephenson LJ dissenting) applied the theory of restrictive immunity on the ground that international law had changed in the intervening years from one to the other. It mattered not that the Court of Appeal was apparently bound by higher authority to apply the absolute theory of immunity in the UK because, under the incorporation doctrine, new customary international law rules could be used in the UK from the moment of their creation (see also dicta to the same effect in the Court of Appeal decision in *Pritchard* v *Gloucestershire CPS* (2004)). Thus, it seems from *Trendtex* that not only do customary rules become part of UK law as soon as they exist (assuming that the limitations discussed in *R* v *Jones* do not apply), but they do so even if previous decisions of UK courts have applied a different rule of customary law. It is *not* the case that such incorporated rules have to comply with the normal UK rules of binding precedent, contrary to the dicta of Scarman and Lawson LJJ in *Thai Europe Tapioca Service Ltd* v *Government of Pakistan* [1975] 3 All ER 961.

An unkind observer might venture to suggest that Lord Denning's *volte-face* in *Trendtex* had little to do with his allegiance to one theory or the other and more to do with his desire to achieve what he believed to be the 'just' result in the case before him. However, whatever his motives, the House of Lords have confirmed in general terms that the UK follows the incorporation theory with regard to customary international law, albeit that the practical effect may be muted because of the substance of the allegedly incorporated customary rule. Indeed, as much was settled in the eighteenth century in a number of cases dealing with the law of diplomatic privileges, such as *Buvot* v *Barbuit* (1737) Cases t. Talbot 281 and *Triquet* v

Bath (1746) 3 Burr. 1478. In the UK, then, customary international law may be used by a court *in appropriate cases* without express authorisation from Parliament.

4.4.5 Transformation and incorporation in the UK: food for thought

The simple picture presented by the transformation theory (treaties) and the incorporation theory (customary law) is superficially attractive. All we need do is identify the origin of a rule of international law and that will tell us how it relates to the UK legal system. This is because there is, apparently, a constitutional objection to the automatic use of treaties in UK law (no Parliamentary approval). In reality, however, there is no Parliamentary approval of customary international law either and at least the government of the UK decides whether to ratify a treaty whereas the role of the UK in the formation of customary international law may be minimal or non-existent. From this perspective, there are at least as strong objections to customary law as there are to treaties, especially as customary law emerges from the practice of all states. Indeed, if we are truly concerned to see that the effect of international law within the UK does not compromise accepted notions of Parliamentary sovereignty, we should object with as much vigour to customary law as we do to treaty law and this is implicit in Lord Bingham's judgment in *R v Jones* as well as being evident in the *Pinochet* case.

Perhaps, however, this is the wrong argument, or at least the wrong analysis. There is a plausible case that it is not (and never has been) the *source* of a relevant rule of international law that determines its effect within the UK legal system. Rather we can argue that it is the *substance* of the international rule that determines its impact on UK law – not its juridical origin. So we might argue that international rules which deal with general concepts, such as the extent of maritime jurisdiction and the status of international organisations, will be adopted in UK law without any transforming local law, irrespective of whether the international rule is found in custom or treaty (see e.g. the *Westland* case). On the other hand, rules which affect the concrete rights of legal persons in defined ways – such as war crimes, human rights or crimes of aggression – will *not* be accepted in the national legal system without transforming local law, irrespective of their international root. For example, there is no universal jurisdiction over acts of torture (*Pinochet*) and no crime of aggression (*Jones*) in UK law without Parliamentary approval even though both are rooted in customary international law. In other words, perhaps UK courts really are concerned with the substance of rules of international law – both in terms of their precise content and in terms of what their adoption in the UK would actually require – when deciding how those rules affect the UK, rather than a simplistic assessment of where the international rules came from. To many commentators, including this author, this seems to be an eminently sensible approach because it divorces the impact of international law on UK law from the arbitrary and accidental matter of how the relevant rule of international law came into being. It does not mean, of course, that every rule of international law – whether deriving from treaty or custom – should have an effect in the UK legal system. It means, rather, that only those rules which are certain as to content and which can meaningfully be translated into the national legal system without compromising local constitutional principles should be so translated. It also reveals that the relationship between international law and local law is complex and multifaceted.

4.5 National courts applying international law

It is perfectly possible for UK courts to be authorised by UK statute to apply international law directly to cases coming before them. This is the position in respect of prize courts, whose function is to apply the international law of prize (law of the sea), as in *The Scotia* (1871) 14 Wallace 170. In fact, following dicta in *The Zamora* [1916] 2 AC 77, it seems that prize courts may ignore UK delegated legislation, such as an Order in Council, if this is contrary to a relevant rule of international law. However, as the judgments in *The Zamora* also make clear, a UK court would be bound by a contrary Act of Parliament, for this is primary legislation which must be respected. Indeed, it may be that the better view of this case is that the delegated legislation then under consideration did not represent a statement of law binding on the court but was merely evidence of particular facts, which the court chose to disregard in the light of stronger contrary evidence.

A more interesting example of UK courts applying (and enforcing) international law is to be found in the recent War Crimes Act 1991. This domestic statute makes it possible for a person who is now a British citizen or who is now resident in the UK to be tried for murder and related crimes in respect of violations of the laws and customs of war committed during World War II. This could be regarded simply as an example of the creation of a new offence under national law, but in reality it is the UK giving its courts jurisdiction over matters which are offences under international law. So, in order to assess whether an individual is guilty of a violation of the laws and customs of war, it will be necessary to examine and apply the relevant international law, whether that be found in treaty or custom. It is a good example of a national court being authorised by national law to apply substantive provisions of international law.

A third example of this type of interaction between national and international law is provided by the *Pinochet* cases. Here, the UK court was authorised by statute to apply international legal concepts. In the particular example, the UK court was concerned with the meaning and scope of the international crime of torture. Of course, this has long been a crime under national law, but traditionally national courts could only exercise their jurisdiction when the torture was committed in the UK or perhaps by a UK national abroad. In seeking to determine whether Senator Pinochet was liable for extradition, the court was required to divine the meaning of 'torture' as prohibited by international law, because the UK court effectively was exercising an international jurisdiction by virtue of its responsibilities under the Torture Convention. Such cases are, indeed, likely to increase as the reach of international law encompasses more and more of what goes on *inside* a state rather than what goes on between them.

A final example of how national courts might take direct notice of rules of international law arises in the UK law of evidence. In *A v Secretary of State for the Home Department* [2006] 2 AC 221, a full bench of seven House of Lords judges had to determine whether the Special Immigration Appeals Commission (deciding the immigration status of the applicant) could consider evidence concerning the applicant's alleged terrorist activities when that evidence might have been procured by torture in a foreign state. Although two of their Lordships dissented on the precise burden of proof to be applied in such case, all seven agreed that evidence obtained by torture was not admissible in any UK court or tribunal. This was because such evidence was abhorrent to the common law and also because torture was a crime under international law and the prohibition of torture one of its most important principles, being a rule of *jus cogens*.

4.6 Executive certificates and ministerial discretion

4.6.1 Certificates

It is a feature of the UK legal system that certain questions of fact or mixed law and fact which arise before national courts can be determined on the basis of a certificate issued by the government. Such matters usually concern areas of international law and international relations in respect of which the Executive has peculiar competence or knowledge. Generally, these certificates are conclusive of the issue to which they relate, whether they be concerned with factual matters or questions of international law (see *Duff Development Corp.* v *Kelantan* [1924] AC 797). If a certificate is validly issued (see e.g. *R* v *Secretary of State for Foreign and Commonwealth Affairs, ex parte Trawnik, The Times*, 20 February 1986), a court cannot inquire into the merits or otherwise of the government's statement or make its own determination. For example, whether an entity is to be treated as a 'state' for the purposes of UK law, is to be determined conclusively by Executive certificate under s. 21 of the State Immunity Act 1978 (see Chapter 7) and the domestic court cannot examine international law to see if the international rules relating to statehood are satisfied. So too, in those cases where the status of a person as representative of a state is in issue. Thus, in *The Queen on the Application of HRH Sultan of Pahang v SSHD* [2011] EWCA Civ 616, the court regarded as conclusive a certificate from the Foreign Office that made it clear that the Sultan was not Head of State of Malaysia with the consequence that he was not entitled to immunity. In these special cases, the relationship of international law and national law is determined by the conclusive Executive certificate.

4.6.2 Discretionary action on the basis of international law

It is another feature of domestic legislation that certain discretionary powers may be exercised only in a manner consistent with international law, especially where the discretion is connected with a treaty obligation. In *R (on the application of) Kibris Türk Hava Yollari* v *Secretary of State for Transport* (2010), the Court of Appeal noted that it was 'common ground' that the Secretary of State's discretion to issue air operating licences had to be exercised in conformity with the Convention on International Civil Aviation 1944, a treaty to which the UK is a party and which imposes international obligations in respect of air transport. This is another aspect of the general rule that national law will not countenance a breach of international law unless the national law is specific and clear.

Moreover, it may be that a statutory discretion specifically refers to principles of international law which should be considered. For example, under s. 2(2) of the Diplomatic and Consular Premises Act 1987, the Foreign Secretary has the power to have diplomatic premises vested in him provided a number of conditions are satisfied, one of which is that 'he shall only exercise the power conferred ... if he is satisfied that to do so is permissible under international law'. This raises the question of whether the national court is competent to oversee the Minister in the exercise of his statutory power should a decision be challenged as being *ultra vires* for want of conformity with international law. Necessarily, a thorough examination of the issue would require the domestic court to consider all the relevant international rules. In *R* v *Secretary of State for Foreign and Commonwealth Affairs, ex parte Samuel* (1989) *The Times*, 17 August 1989, the Court of Appeal considered an application for judicial review of the Minister's exercise of this power of vesting in respect of the premises of the former Cambodian Embassy in London. In rejecting the application, Fox LJ noted that the Act merely required the Minister to be satisfied that international law had been complied with. The court would not examine the correctness of that determination, although it could interfere if the power was exercised in bad faith or if a particular decision was so unreasonable that no reasonable Minister could have made it. Moreover, while the court stated that it would not readily accept that a Minister could determine his own conformity with a rule of domestic law, 'international law is another matter', apparently because the court is reluctant to compromise the Executive in foreign affairs. Presumably, if the statute had employed objective language, such that conformity with international law was a condition precedent to the exercise of statutory power, the court would have assessed the correctness of the Minister's decision for this would have been the will of Parliament. For present purposes, however, the importance of the decision is that it illustrates UK judges' reluctance to adjudicate on matters which they believe are both outside their competence and constitutional role (although see *Somalia (Republic)* v *Woodhouse Drake & Carey (Suisse) SA* [1993] 1 All ER 371 and *Sierra Leone Telecommunications* v *Barclays Bank plc* [1998] 2 All ER 821, Chapter 5). Once again, like the decision in *Arab Monetary Fund* v *Hashim*, *ex parte Samuel* is an example of a UK court treating international law very differently from the way it treats its own law or, indeed, the domestic law of another country. It is unfortunate that UK courts are not always prepared to regard international law as a system of law in its own right.

FURTHER READING

Bianchi A., 'International Law and US Courts: The Myth of Lohengrin Revisited' (2004) 15(4) *EJIL* 751.

Collier, J., 'Is International Law Really Part of the Law of England?', (1989) 38 *ICLQ* 924.

Fitzmaurice, G., 'The General Principles of International Law Considered From the Standpoint of the Rule of Law', (1957) 92 *Rec de Cours*, pt. II, pp. 68–99.

Sinclair, I., 'The Interpretation of Treaties before Municipal Courts', (1963) 12 *ICLQ* 508.

Warbrick, C., 'The Governance of Britain' (2008) 57(1) ICLQ 209.

SUMMARY

International law and national law

- Monism – The monist theory supposes that international law and national law are simply two components of a single body of knowledge called 'law'. 'Law' is seen as a single entity of which the 'national' and 'international' versions are merely particular manifestations.

- Dualism – Dualism denies that international law and national law operate in the same sphere, although it does accept that they deal with the same subject matter.

- Different subject matter – Both monism and dualism accept that international law and national law deal with the same subject matter; that they are in fact concerned with the same substantive matters. This view says that the relationship between international law and national law is like the relationship between English law and French law: they never contradict each other as *systems of law*. It may be that the 'obligations' of each system come into conflict but then which obligation is to prevail is to be settled by the 'conflict of laws' rules of the particular court.

- National law may be used before international courts in a number of ways: as sources of law; as evidence of compliance with international obligations; to define concepts used in international law; as evidence of facts; as a component in the decision of the international tribunal.

- Incorporation and transformation – Under the doctrine of incorporation, a rule of international law becomes part of national law without the need for express adoption by the local courts or legislature. The rule of international law is incorporated in national law simply because it is a rule of international law. The doctrine of transformation, on the other hand, stipulates that rules of international law do not become part of national law until they have been expressly adopted by the state. International law is not *ipso facto* part of national law.

- International law in UK courts – Treaties do not form part of UK law without express adoption in a statute and cannot generally be pleaded in UK courts if not adopted. Customary international law may be incorporated directly into UK law. However, this simple picture disguises the fact that the relationship may depend on the content of the alleged rule of international law rather than its origin.

5

Personality, statehood and recognition

Much has been said already of the fact that international law is concerned primarily with the rights and duties of states and there is no doubt that states are the major legal persons (or 'subjects') of international law. However, since the inception of the United Nations, international law increasingly has become concerned with the rights and duties of non-state actors in the international arena and these other subjects now play a significant role in international relations and have a measurable impact on the development and application of international law. They include international organisations (e.g. the UN itself), ethnic groups within and across national boundaries (e.g. the Kurds), pre-independent territorial entities (e.g. the territory controlled by the Palestinian Authority), individuals (e.g. those charged with war crimes, heads of state) and multinational companies (e.g. those concerned with the extraction of natural resources). In this chapter we shall examine the concept of personality in international law and examine some of its subjects in more detail. As we shall see, one of the most important issues when discussing international personality is the role of 'recognition' and Part Two of this chapter will examine some of the problems arising in international and national law from the concept of 'recognition' of foreign states, governments and international organisations.

Part One: **Personality and statehood in international law**

5.1 **The concept of personality in international law**

Generally speaking, a subject of international law is a body or entity that is capable of possessing and exercising rights and duties under international law. Yet, as Professor Brownlie has pointed out (*Principles of International Law*, 1998, p. 57), this is a somewhat circular definition, for the answer to the question 'who has international rights and duties?' is 'the subjects of international law'. This circularity has led some commentators to suggest that it is impossible to define or explain legal personality purely by reference to rules of international law because of the *a priori* nature of the concept. In other words, in the final analysis personality may depend on some 'extra-legal' concept such as 'effective existence' or 'political recognition' rather than pre-determined legal criteria. However, the short answer to the problem is to assert that a subject of international law is a body or entity recognised or accepted as being capable, or as in fact being capable, of exercising international rights and duties. Although this does not take the search for a theory of international personality a great deal further, it does enable us to examine the actual practice of international law in our search for its 'subjects'.

The main capacities of an international legal person are first, the ability to make claims before international (and national) tribunals in order to vindicate rights given by international law. Secondly, to be subject to some or all of the obligations imposed by international law. Thirdly, to have the power to make valid international agreements binding in international law. Fourthly, to enjoy some or all of the immunities from the jurisdiction of the national courts of other states, this being an attribute of an international legal person that is not available to the subjects of each state's national legal system. As we shall see, it is only states and certain international organisations (e.g. the UN) that have all of these capacities to the fullest degree. Other subjects may have some of the capacities or all of the capacities in varying degrees. The most important point about international personality is, indeed, that it is not an absolute concept. International personality operates as if on a sliding scale, with various subjects of international law having various capacities for particular purposes. Thus, a 'state' is the subject of international law *par excellence* and will have all of the capacities in full measure. Other subjects, such as most international organisations and individuals, will have personality in such measure and for such purposes as is necessary for the achievement of their roles within the international legal system and as is recognised by the system of international law.

This leads us to the question of how international personality is achieved. We shall see later that there are various criteria laid down by international law which must be satisfied before a 'state' can come into existence. Subject to what will be said then about the role of recognition, when these criteria are met, a 'state' exists and has all the capacities previously outlined. However, as far as the other subjects of international law are concerned, they seem to achieve their personality because it has been conferred, accepted or recognised by states. It may be that in time this personality acquires an objective status, as with the UN (see e.g. the *Reparations for Injuries Suffered in the Service of the United Nations Case* 1949 ICJ Rep 174 and *Behrami v France*, European Court of Human Rights (2007) 22 B.H.R.C. 477), but its source can be traced back ultimately to the action of states. It may be said, then, that there are two types of personality in international law: *original* personality, which belongs to states *ipso facto* once they satisfy the criteria of statehood; and *derived* personality, which flows from the recognition by states that other entities may have some competence in the field of international law. Once an entity is a 'state' it has legal personality under international law, but this is not necessarily true of individuals, companies or any of the other subjects of international law. As the ICJ said in their *Advisory Opinion on the Legality of the Threat or Use of Nuclear Weapons (WHO Case)* 1996 ICJ Rep 66, 'international organisations are subjects of international law which do not, unlike states, possess a general competence. International organisations … are invested by the states which create them with powers, the limits of which are a function of the common interests whose promotion those states entrust to them.' This explains clearly the concept of derived personality, and as such equally is applicable to other non-state subjects such as individuals. Note, however, that personality, once given, may be more difficult to take away. While an international organisation may be dissolved (and its derived personality with it), can the enforceable human rights of individuals be so easily subtracted?

Personality, then, is a relative concept. Generally, it denotes the ability to act within the system of international law as distinct from national law. However, the fact that the degree of personality accorded by international law can vary with each 'subject' means that one must be careful in drawing broad categories. It is equally valid to classify the subjects of international law by reference to what they may do, rather than what they are called. This should be remembered in the following discussion.

5.2 **The subjects of international law**

5.2.1 **States**

International law was conceived originally as a system of rules governing the relations of states amongst themselves. Consequently, states are the most important and most powerful of the subjects of international law. They have all of the capacities referred to previously and it is with their rights and duties that the greater part of international law is concerned. It is vital, therefore, to know when an entity qualifies as a state. Or, to put it another way, when is an entity entitled to all of the rights and subject to all of the duties assigned by international law to 'states'?

To produce a satisfactory definition of statehood is not easy. The answer does not necessarily lie in a roll call of the United Nations or any other international organisation. At present, there are 193 members of the UN, but only in 2002 did Switzerland become a member and there is no doubt that it was a state before membership. Likewise, a state may be suspended from the rights of membership of the United Nations, but this does not necessarily mean that it was not a state (see, for example, the position of Yugoslavia (Serbia & Montenegro) when it was suspended from the rights of membership between 1992–2000, discussed at length in the *Legality of the Use of Force Cases* (2004) and the *Case Concerning the Application of the Convention on the Prevention and Punishment of the Crime of Genocide (Bosnia and Herzegovina* v *Serbia & Montenegro)* ICJ 2007). In other words, membership of the UN is not synonymous with statehood. In fact, at one time, it was not even correct to say that membership of the UN was a sure mark of statehood; thus, the Ukraine and Byelorussia have been members of the UN since 1945, although both were undeniably part of the Soviet Union until 1991. Necessarily, membership of the United Nations depends on political considerations as well as legal facts (hence the entity known as the Republic of Kosovo is not a member of the UN, due to Russian opposition, despite being regarded as a state by some ninety-two other UN members and being a member of the IMF), although it appears to have taken on a much more important role since the end of the cold war. In this context reference must be made to the discussion of 'recognition' at section 5.2.1.6. So, it now seems that the admittance of a 'new' member to the UN is to be treated as a sign that they have achieved statehood in international law, although such status may have arisen prior to admission. Recent examples include the cases of North and South Korea, the former republics of the Soviet Union, the 'former Yugoslavian Republic of Macedonia', Estonia, Latvia and Lithuania, Timor-Leste and most recently in September 2011, South Sudan. Timor- Leste was admitted to membership of the UN in September 2002 and marked the transition of East Timor from a former territory of Indonesia to independence under UN auspices and South Sudan is a result of the agreed cession of that territory from The Sudan following years of internal strife.

Consequently, perhaps the best way to look at the role of UN membership in identifying statehood is to conclude that membership entails an almost irrebuttable presumption of statehood, while suspension of *membership rights* says nothing of statehood per se (as explained in the Dissenting Opinion of Vice-President Al-Khasawneh in the *Case Concerning the Application of the Convention on the Prevention and Punishment of the Crime of Genocide (Bosnia and Herzegovina v Serbia & Montenegro)* ICJ 2007). Conversely, it remains true that non-membership of the UN does not necessarily constitute a denial of statehood, for there may be many reasons why a state chooses or is forced to stay outside the UN system. An example of the former was Switzerland and of the latter, Taiwan. Of course, some entities may be deliberately excluded from membership by the UN itself as a sign that statehood is not accepted – as with the territory known as the 'Turkish Republic of Northern Cyprus' (TRNC) whose alleged statehood is explicitly denied by Security Council Resolutions 541 (1983) and 550 (1984) because its 'independence' flowed from the illegal invasion of Northern Cyprus by Turkish troops in 1974. In respect of membership of other international organisations, attendance at multilateral conferences or participation in multilateral treaty regimes, each organization will have its own rules concerning membership or participation and these may not even pretend to be limited to states.

In fact, a brief trawl through the history of the United Nations reveals just how complex the question 'What is a state?' actually is. If we were to conduct a straw poll of every existing government (assuming we could agree on how many there were), we would find that opinions as to the number of states varied, albeit within reasonably clear outer parameters. For example, what of Taiwan, the TRNC, the Palestinian territory and the Republic of Srpska in the Serbian enclaves of Bosnia and the Republic of Kosovo? This is not surprising in the political world of international law, but it does reveal that it is difficult to identify criteria for statehood that are universally accepted, even in principle. Moreover, even if this were possible, each state's application of those criteria to the facts of any given case would vary considerably. This would, in turn, affect the scope of the disputed entity's rights in international law. If, for example, the UK considered Taiwan to be an independent state then, in its relations with the UK, Taiwan would have the rights and duties of a state. If, however, the People's Republic of China took the opposite view, then Taiwan would not have the full capacities of statehood in its relations with China. This is the reciprocal and bilateral nature of international law and it can give rise to several different degrees of personality for the same territory in respect of its relations with different states.

These are factors that must be borne in mind in the following discussion of the definition of statehood. They do not mean that questions of statehood are purely subjective which each established state might answer for itself when a new candidate is presented. What they do reveal is that states may pick and choose whether to have *full* relations with any other subject of international law. If a territory qualifies as a state according to the criteria discussed subsequently, we can say that it has the legal ability to exercise all of the rights and duties of a state under international law. It will be subject to all the general obligations and have all the general rights of states in international law. On the other hand, whether the new state actually exercises all of its capacities on an individual level with every other state will depend on whether, in the estimation of those existing states, it has satisfied the criteria.

The starting point for a discussion of the criteria of statehood is Art. 1 of the Montevideo Convention on Rights and Duties of States 1933. This stipulates that the 'state as a person of international law should possess the following qualifications: (a) a permanent population; (b) a defined territory; (c) a government; and (d) a capacity to enter into relations with other states'.

5.2.1.1 Permanent population

It is not entirely clear what is meant by a permanent population. Obviously, it does not mean that there can be no migration of peoples across territorial boundaries, nor does it mean that a territory must have a fixed number of inhabitants. Rather, it seems to suggest that there must be some population linked to a specific piece of territory on a more or less permanent basis and who can be regarded in general parlance as its inhabitants. The territory of the Western Sahara, for example, is populated by nomadic tribes who roam freely across the desert without regard to land boundaries, yet their link with the territory is such that they may be regarded generally as its 'population' (*Western Sahara Case* 1975 ICJ Rep 12). It is also unclear whether the population has to be indigenous in the sense of originating in the territory. For example, the Falkland Islands are populated primarily by the descendants of UK nationals who arrived as a consequence of colonisation in the mid-nineteenth century. Is this sufficient to constitute a 'population' for our criteria? The question becomes of great significance if the Islands are to be regarded as candidates for self-determination, for generally that concept has been applied to indigenous peoples gaining liberty from 'foreign' masters.

5.2.1.2 Defined territory

It would seem to be essential that for a 'state' to exist there should be a defined territory. A state must have some definite physical existence that marks it out clearly from its neighbours. This does not mean that there must be complete certainty over the extent of territory. Even today there are innumerable border disputes between states over the precise line of the frontier, but this says nothing about their status as states. For example, the dispute between India and Pakistan over Jammu-Kashmir has continued since both states gained independence from the UK, but this has not affected their statehood. Similarly, a refusal to define the extent of the state precisely is not fatal to statehood. Israel has traditionally refused to put maximum limits on her claims to territory in 'Palestine' and this might be thought to come close to having no defined territory at all. In practice, however, there is no doubt that Israel is a state for there is a certain core of territory that undoubtedly is 'Israel'. Similarly, the fact that an existing or emerging state's territory is under threat or even factually subsumed by an aggressive neighbour does not destroy or prevent the existence of statehood. Kuwait was no less a state for its occupation by Iraq, and Iraq, Afghanistan and Syria are in law no less states despite the fractures in their territorial integrity caused by internal and external forces.

5.2.1.3 Government

In order for a state to function as a member of the international community it must have a practical identity on the international plane – a projection of its existence internationally. This is the government, which is primarily responsible for the vindication of, and ensuring compliance with, the international rights and duties of the state. It is not surprising, therefore, that one criterion of statehood is that a territory should have an effective government. This executive authority must be effective within the defined territory and exercise control over the permanent population. However, it does not mean that the 'government' must be entirely dominant within the territory, so long as it is capable of controlling the affairs of the 'state' in the international community. In addition, some commentators have argued that there is a further requirement that the government is likely to become permanent, although there is little support for this in the practice of states, and even less agreement about how it would be assessed.

While it is clear that the criterion of effective government must be satisfied *before* a territory can become a state, this does not mean that an established state loses its statehood when it ceases to have an effective government. There are numerous examples where a government does not have complete or even substantial control over the territory but its statehood on the international plane is not in issue, the situation in Syria in 2012 being typical. Civil war may mean that there is no effective government over the entire population and territory, but the state per se continues to exist as a subject of international law with all of its capacities intact. Indeed, during a civil war it may be that a state has two 'governments', each of which is recognised by (different) other states as being entitled to represent it. In these circumstances, the conduct of international relations on behalf of the state becomes complicated and in practical terms may disintegrate into a pattern of bilateral arrangements between the competing governments and their respective supporters.

5.2.1.4 Capacity to enter into legal relations

This is a requirement that often causes great difficulty, at least as a matter of theory. It has been suggested that it denotes 'independence', so that a territory cannot be regarded as a state so long as it is under the control, direct or indirect, of another state. Yet, if this is what this criterion means, it is quite unrealistic, for there is scarcely a state that does not depend to some degree on the goodwill, financial aid or political support of others. Are we to say that the territories of Central America are not states because of the influence of their powerful neighbour, or that the former Soviet republics are not states because of their close links with Russia? It is unlikely that this is what is meant by 'capacity to enter into relations'. The better view is that this criterion means 'legal independence', not factual autonomy. Thus, a 'state' will exist if the territory is not under the lawful sovereign authority of another state. Hong Kong is under the legal authority of China and, whatever else it is (it has a territory, population and 'government'), it is not a state. On the other hand, Slovakia and the Czech Republic are no longer legally united and, despite being heavily dependent on each other, both are regarded as sovereign states. In this sense, states with legal independence have the legal capacity to enter relations with other states on their own behalf as a matter of right. Whether they are able to exercise that legal capacity in practice is not relevant to the principled decision of whether they qualify as a state.

5.2.1.5 Manner of attainment of capacity to enter into legal relations

One of the more interesting questions in this regard is whether it matters how a state gains its separate existence. In other words, is the legal independence which is sufficient to justify statehood to be presumed from factual independence or are other criteria applicable? If, for example, Hong Kong declared its own independence and China was unable to reassert its authority, would this be sufficient to raise the presumption of legal capacity thus leading to statehood? Likewise, how is the international community to assess the claims of independence of the Turkish Republic of Northern Cyprus or the Republic of Kosovo? This is a problem that in recent years has come to the fore, not least because of the break up of the former federal states of Yugoslavia and the Soviet Union. The vital question is whether factual 'independence', however achieved, will give rise to a presumption of legal independence (legal capacity), or whether any illegality in the attainment of factual independence necessarily prevents such legal capacity arising? At the outset, it must be appreciated that this is a many-sided issue and that rules of international law are just one of a number of factors that may influence a final decision about the 'statehood' of an aspirant territory. Politics and economics are just two of the other relevant considerations.

(a) If the territory declaring factual independence is able to claim the right of self-determination, then it seems that this is sufficient to attain legal independence and (subject to the other criteria) 'statehood'. A former colonial territory has the right to achieve independence by virtue of this principle and it seems not to matter whether this is done voluntarily with the assent of the former colonial power or against its wishes. A relatively recent example is the emergence of the Federated State of Micronesia, arising out of the old Pacific Trust Territory which had been administered by the USA following the defeat of Japan in World War II and there is no doubt that the peoples of the *occupied* Palestinian territory have the right to self-determination and any action which may infringe that right is itself a violation of international law (*Palestinian Wall Advisory Opinion* (2004) ICJ Rep). As ever, however, matters are not cut and dried and many international lawyers would argue that the right of self-determination is available in circumstances far beyond the 'old colonial' situations. Thus, if self-determination is now to be regarded as a right of 'peoples', any ethnic group qualifying as a 'people' could claim self-determination and, if desired, independence and statehood. The natural consequence of this is the acceptance of a right of secession, whereby defined groups in an existing state declare independence under self-determination and claim statehood in international law. Effectively, this is the position in respect of the former federal republics of the Soviet Union and Yugoslavia, whose constituent territories have seceded and obtained independence in their own right, and, in a non-federal context, with the secession of an independent Eritrea from Ethiopia. In this respect, the opinions of the EC Arbitration Commission on Yugoslavia (which dealt with matters arising from the dissolution of the federal state) are instructive. Contrary to what many international lawyers would argue, the Commission has adopted a relatively narrow view of self-determination, secession and statehood. Thus, while accepting that former territories of federal states which fulfilled the other traditional requirements of statehood (the Montevideo conditions) enjoyed the right of self-determination, leading to statehood if desired, the Commission rejected the idea that ethnic groups and minorities *as such* enjoyed a right of self-determination. Simply put, 'peoples' enjoyed the right of self-determination as a step to statehood if linked to a pre-existing territorial unit (e.g. Palestine). Otherwise, such peoples enjoyed the right under international law to have their identity as a separate ethnic group recognised by the 'mother' state, but not in a way that guaranteed them independent statehood. So, coming back to our initial question, *lawful* self-determination is an appropriate way in which a territory may achieve legal capacity and hence statehood in international law bearing in mind that what amounts to 'lawful' self-determination is a matter of controversy. In the *Advisory Opinion on the Accordance with international law of the unilateral declaration of independence in respect of Kosovo* (2010), the ICJ specifically declined to comment on whether the right of self-determination extended beyond colonial or analogous situations noting that '[w]hether, outside the context of non-self-governing territories and peoples subject to alien subjugation, domination and exploitation, the international law of self-determination confers upon part of the population of an existing State a right to separate from that State is, however, a subject on which radically different views were expressed by those taking part in the proceedings and expressing a position on the question'.

(b) If we are prepared to accept that the method by which factual independence is achieved is relevant in determining statehood in international law, there is a further problem to be addressed. What if the factual criteria of statehood (population, territory, government) are established but they have been achieved in a manner regarded as unlawful under international law? In this sense, it may be that the criteria of the Montevideo Convention are not of themselves enough to establish statehood in international law. They may be necessary but are they sufficient? There is some evidence to suggest that states must achieve their statehood lawfully before it will be fully effective in international law, and there are several general principles of international law that could have an impact here. Note, however, that we are suggesting that a state might not arise out of a breach of international law, rather than the current local law then governing it. It is almost certainly the case that a population/administration seeking to achieve non-consensual independence from its current sovereign will be violating its domestic law. For example, international law prohibits the use of armed force and the practice of racial discrimination as well as laying down the principle of self-determination. If a territory satisfies the factual criteria of statehood but also violates one of these general principles, it may not qualify as a state. The area known as the Turkish Republic of Northern Cyprus appears to have a population, territory and government, but it is not regarded as a state in international law because it was born of an illegal use of force by Turkey in 1974. Similarly, Southern Rhodesia was not regarded as a state because of the violation of the principle of self-determination (in that it was the white minority, not the black majority, that achieved power) and the homelands of Venda, Ciskei, Transkei and Bophuthatswana were never regarded as states in international law because their establishment by South Africa in pursuance of apartheid violated the principle of non-racial discrimination. On the other hand, there is the case of Bangladesh. Following serious internal disturbances in 1971, India invaded East Pakistan, then part of a Pakistan federal state. Although India herself did not annex the territory, the result of its intervention was the emergence of the independent state of Bangladesh. If it matters how independence is achieved, this would seem to be an example of the creation of a state by unlawful means – the use of armed force. Yet, within three months Bangladesh had been recognised by over ninety other states and in the following year it was admitted as a full member of the United Nations. It is true that in Bangladesh that there was a population, territory and an effective government (although the latter was maintained initially by Indian force of arms), but how can we ignore the illegality in the manner of the state's creation? Once again, we are faced with the hard reality that principles of international law do not always govern state conduct or community reaction to it, and that, even in the field of statehood, principle can give way to pragmatism.

5.2.1.6 Recognition

One of the most important ways in which this pragmatism takes effect is through the concept of international recognition, discussed more fully in Part Two of this chapter. However, for the moment it is important to realise that subsequent recognition of the 'statehood' or 'sovereignty' of an aspirant state by members of the international community may be sufficient to cure a defect in an otherwise imperfect claim to statehood. In other words, even if a people within a territory have not satisfied in full the objective criteria of the Montevideo Convention, or have achieved them through unlawful means, they may still acquire statehood in international law because the formal defect or the violation of international law is 'waived' by the community at large. Effectiveness, that is the ability to operate as a state may, in certain circumstances, take priority over formal legality. Recent examples of collective recognition playing an important role in statehood, even perhaps where the factual criteria of the Montevideo Convention have not been satisfied, include the admission of some of the former Yugoslav republics to the United Nations. It should also be noted that recognition may be relevant for determining subsidiary questions connected with statehood. Thus, Russia has been universally accepted as capable of succeeding to the Soviet Union's place on the UN Security Council and this was done purely informally through acquiescence of the old Soviet Republics and acceptance by other members of the Council and UN.

Of course, we must be very careful not to accept the principle of the curative effect of recognition without some refinement. As a matter of principle, it is undesirable that recognition should be able to cure defects in any of the criteria of statehood other than that of lawful legal independence. Territory, population and government are in essence factual prerequisites which really do need to be established before there can be any possibility of statehood. Is it desirable, for example, that recognition could promote the statehood of a territory where there was no effective government that could fulfil that state's international obligations? The situation in the recognised state of Bosnia in 1992/3 is a poignant reminder of this. On the other hand, legal capacity and legality of creation are conditions rooted in law, not fact, and there is no reason why they may not be waived by those entitled to enforce a breach of the law – that is, by other states. While this may be a practical solution that has been applied in some cases (e.g. the international recognition of Bangladesh, despite the unlawful use of force), it will not be applicable universally. The current status of the Republic of Kosovo is in point. This territory has declared its independence from Serbia and the ICJ has (without deciding any issue of statehood) determined that the *making* of the Declaration was not in violation of international law, *Advisory Opinion on the Accordance with international law of the unilateral declaration of independence in respect of Kosovo*. It has been recognised as independent by some states and roundly rejected as such by others. It is not a member of the United Nations because of Russia's objection and veto power, but it does operate internationally and factually independently from Serbia. Is it a state and what has been the role of recognition and deliberate non-recognition in this process? In short, there are concerns about the potential curative effect of recognition at an international level and these mirror those we shall encounter when examining the constitutive theory of recognition in more detail (see Part Two).

5.2.1.7 Extinction of statehood

Lastly, one must note the near practical impossibility of an involuntary loss of statehood. If an entity ceases to possess any of the qualities of statehood examined earlier, this does not mean that it ceases to be a state under international law. For example, the absence of an effective government in Syria in 2012 during the period of civil unrest did not mean that there were no such state, and the same is true of Somalia where there still appears to be no entity governing the country effectively. Likewise, if a state is allegedly 'extinguished' through the illegal action of another state, it will remain a state in international law. The occupation and acquisition of territory through the use of force is illegal and territory gained in this manner does not belong to the conqueror (*Palestinian Wall Advisory Opinion* ICJ Rep). The UN enforcement action which successfully evicted Iraq from Kuwait in 1990/1 was based upon this principle and it was the reason why Estonia, Latvia and Lithuania's claim to statehood was successful after the collapse of the Soviet Union in 1991. Similarly, as previously discussed, suspension of the rights of membership of the UN does not entail loss of statehood. Usually, however, it is governments rather than states that cease to exist through the illegal use of force and then it becomes very much a question of international politics as to whether the 'new' government is accepted by the community at large as capable of acting on behalf of the state. Cambodia, for example, did not cease to exist by reason of Vietnam's invasion in 1979, but for many years there was a difference of opinion among the international community as to which body was its lawful government.

Of course, it is possible for an entity to cease to be an independent state through lawful means. This may take the form of a voluntary submission to the sovereignty of another state or the merger of two states in an entirely new body. Into this latter category comes the aborted attempt of Egypt and Syria to form the United Arab Republic and the successful union of the small Gulf States to form the United Arab Emirates. Similarly, the unification of West and East Germany and of North and South Yemen fall into this category. Note here, that the unification of North and South Vietnam also produced the modern state of Vietnam, and although this was through the use of force, there seems to have been little doubt at the time that the 'new' state existed under international law.

5.2.2 **Other territorial entities**

The relative nature of international personality, whereby a 'subject' may have certain rights and duties for certain purposes, means that states are not the only territorial entities that can be regarded as subjects of international law.

5.2.2.1 Treaty creations

There have been several examples of the creation by international treaty of artificial territorial entities having international personality. Former examples include the cities of Danzig, Berlin and Vienna. Such territories may be granted limited international personality by the states who would otherwise be entitled to exercise sovereign authority and they may have some or all of the capacities of 'a state' in international law. The nature and extent of their personality will depend on the terms of the treaty by which they were created. In the case of Berlin, for example, its status was regulated by the Four Powers Treaty for the Governance of Berlin 1946 between France, the USSR, the USA and the UK, although now, of course, Berlin is part of the sovereign state of Germany. In fact, it was not until the Unification Treaty of November 1990 that full sovereignty was restored to Germany in the measure in which it had existed before the Second World War. However, whatever the content of the personality of such special entities, it is clearly a form of derived personality and will depend entirely on the acquiescence of the states involved in their administration. Neither should it be thought that these entities are necessarily of historical interest only. There is no reason, for example, why the territory of Northern Cyprus should not be subject to a special territorial regime – perhaps with Greek, Turkish and UN involvement – as part of a practical solution to the problems facing the divided island.

5.2.2.2 Territorial entities as agencies of states

Although there are no current examples, it is possible that two states might agree to administer jointly a territory through an autonomous local administration. This local body could be granted limited capacities in international law to act on behalf of the territory. Such a joint exercise of sovereign authority, or condominium, would be suitable where sovereignty was disputed or unresolved, as with the Falkland Islands or Northern Cyprus. The most recent example was the New Hebrides, where authority was shared between France and the UK until it became independent as the state of Vanuatu.

5.2.2.3 Territories per se

As well as those entities just described, there are several other types of territory that may enjoy some measure of international personality. In fact, because of the relative nature of international personality, each territorial entity aspiring to international personality should be judged on its own merits and the categories of international legal persons should not be regarded as closed or exhausted by previous examples. Once common were protectorates, whereby an established state assumed responsibility for certain of the international activities – usually foreign affairs – of another territory or state. In the *Rights of US Nationals in Morocco Case (US v France)* 1952 ICJ Rep 176, the ICJ confirmed that Morocco had not lost its international personality by virtue of the protectorate agreement, but merely that it had entered into a contractual relationship with France whereby the latter would conduct some of its international responsibilities. Also in this category were the former Mandated territories of the League of Nations and the equivalent Trusteeship territories of the United Nations. These territories were home to 'non self-governing peoples' who had personality for the special purpose of achieving independence and ensuring that the mandate/trusteeship was properly administered (*Namibia Case* 1971 ICJ Rep 16). With the independence of the islands of the Pacific Trust Territory (see now the Federated States of Micronesia, the Republic of the Marshall Islands and the Republic of Palau) and the independence of Namibia in 1990, the UN Trusteeship scheme has ended. Nevertheless, other examples remain. The Palestinian Authority, exercising jurisdiction over the Palestine Autonomous Area, has a large degree of international personality, and concludes treaties and agreements with other states (and the United Nations) and both sends and receives diplomatic representatives. Clearly, it enjoys many of the capacities or attributes of states, as noted in the *Palestinian Wall Advisory Opinion* 2004 ICJ Rep. Nevertheless, it is not yet *universally* regarded as the government of an independent state despite its link to a clearly defined territory and so it appears, at least for the present, to be an international legal person *sui generis*. So too the Republic of Kosovo, recognised by some, rejected by others, but operating within a defined territory and with a broad measure of international personality of some kind.

5.2.3 International organisations

There are now more international organisations – being organisations whose members include or are limited to states – than at any time previously in the history of international law. They are concerned with a wide variety of matters of international import, ranging from the maintenance of international peace and security, to effective management of maritime affairs, to the regulation of international communications and to international cooperation in matters of civil and criminal justice. In order that they may be able to carry out their allotted tasks, it is apparent that they must enjoy some measure of international personality. This will vary according to the organisation, its objectives and the terms of its constitution or constituent treaty. In the *Reparations Case* 1949 ICJ Rep 174, one of the issues was whether the United Nations could recover reparations in its own right for the death of one of its staff while engaged on UN business. The Court confirmed that personality was essential if the UN was to discharge its functions effectively. This included the capacity to bring claims, to conclude international agreements and to enjoy privileges and immunities from national jurisdictions (see also UN Charter Art. 105). According to the Court, when the UN was created in 1945, its founding members conferred upon it an objective personality such that it became a subject of international law even in respect of those states coming into being after its creation. So, it seems that the UN is to be regarded as a subject of international law even in respect of non-members, for the Court's emphasis on objective legal existence suggests that the personality of the UN is no longer dependent on the recognition of states. The independent legal personality of the UN has again been confirmed by the ICJ in its *Advisory Opinion on the Applicability of Article VI of the Convention on the Privileges and Immunities of the United Nations* (1989) ICJ Rep 177, wherein the immunity of a UN officer was confirmed, even in respect of action taken against him by his own government. See also *Behrami* v *France;* ECHR Grand Chamber, (2007) 22 B.H.R.C. 477, where the actions of UN forces in Kosovo were held attributable to the Organisation itself, as a legal person, rather than attributable to the states of nationality of the personnel serving with those forces. Conversely, of course, it is quite possible for the current members to dissolve the Organisation, as they did with the League of Nations in 1945.

It is not only the UN itself that enjoys international personality. The European Communities (e.g. *Re European Road Transport Agreement Case* (22/70) [1971] CMLR 335; *Maclaine Watson* v *Dept of Trade* [1988] 3 All ER 257, though not, it seems, the European Union per se, see (1994) 65 BYIL 597), the Organisation of American States (OAS), the African Union and the specialised agencies of the UN all have some separate capacity to act on the international plane in order to achieve their purposes. For example, many UN organs have the power to request an Advisory Opinion from the ICJ: e.g. the General Assembly in *The Legality of the Use of Nuclear Weapons Case* 1996, *Palestinian Wall Case* 2004 and the *Advisory Opinion on the Accordance with international law of the unilateral declaration of independence in respect of Kosovo* (2010), and the Economic and Social Council in the *Privileges and Immunities Case*, and many subsidiary organs enter into treaties and agreements with states, as with UNRWA and its host agreements with Syria, Egypt, Jordan and Israel. Once again, this is not a closed list and we must examine the precise powers and responsibilities of any international organisation to see if it has international personality and in what degree.

The *Advisory Opinion on Nuclear Weapons (WHO Case)* also provides valuable guidance on the *content* of the personality of international organisations. As noted at the outset of this chapter, the personality of organisations is not one of 'general competence': it is not a personality for all purposes. As a form of derived personality, the 'constitution' of the organisation (usually a treaty) will set out explicitly some of the attributes of international personality that the organisation is to enjoy (e.g. PCIJ *Advisory Opinion on the Jurisdiction of the European Commission of the Danube*, PCIJ Ser. B No. 14). This may include, for example, the power to make treaties, to bring claims, etc. In addition, however, it is now settled law that an international organisation will enjoy implied powers, being that degree of international competence that is required to enable it to achieve its purposes even if these are not explicitly stated in the constituent treaty. As stated in the *WHO Case*, 'the necessities of international life may point to the need for organisations, in order to achieve their objectives, to possess subsidiary powers which are not expressly provided for in the basic instruments which govern their activities. It is generally accepted that international organisations can exercise such powers, known as implied powers.' So, in the *WHO Case* itself, the World Health Organisation undoubtedly had the international competence to request the ICJ to give an Advisory Opinion, but only in respect of matters explicitly or impliedly within its competence. In fact, this did not include the power to request an Advisory Opinion on the legality of the threat or use of nuclear weapons, although the General Assembly of the UN did possess such a power.

5.2.4 **Individuals**

It has been emphasised elsewhere that international law is concerned primarily with the relations of states. Historically, this has meant that there has been little scope for the international personality of individuals, and states have guarded jealously their right to deal with their own nationals while honouring the right of other states to deal with theirs. So it was that despite some isolated examples, it was not until after the Second World War that individuals could be regarded as having international personality in any meaningful sense, and then substantially because international law began to impose personal obligations on individuals separately from those attaching to the state which they represented. While this personality has grown both in quality and quantity, it remains true that states approach issues concerning the personality of individuals with some hesitation. Its future development depends on the continuing agreement of states, tacit or express.

The clearest example of the personality of individuals in modern international law is the responsibility that each individual bears for war crimes (acts contrary to the law of war), crimes against the peace (planning illegal war etc.) and crimes against humanity (genocide etc.). These are matters for which the individual is responsible personally under international law, irrespective of the laws of his own country and has become know as international criminal law. Thus an individual may be tried according to that law by an international court, as with the Nuremberg and Tokyo War Crimes Tribunals and their modern equivalents, the International Criminal Court (the ICC, formally established in 2002), the International Tribunal for the Prosecution of Persons Responsible for Serious Violations of International Humanitarian Law Committed in the Territory of the Former Yugoslavia (1993), the International Tribunal for Rwanda (1994) and the Special Court for Sierra Leone (2002). Indeed, these most recent examples, especially the ICC, are a concrete manifestation of the readiness of international law to encompass the international personality of the individual by way of the imposition of obligations. It is the natural counterpart to the granting of international protection through the law of human rights. Of course, the important point here is not that the individual is responsible as such (he may well be responsible in national law), but that responsibility is founded in international law, independent of the law of any state, including his state of nationality. In 2012, a sentence of fourteen years' imprisonment was imposed in *The Prosecutor* v *Thomas Lubanga Dyilo* (2012) for war crimes, the first conviction before the ICC.

In fact, as well as these modern manifestations of the personality of individuals, it has long been true that certain other criminal acts can give rise to international personality and responsibility because of the destructive effect they have on the international order. The most established of these is piracy. A pirate is *hostis humani generis* (an enemy of all mankind) and he may be arrested and tried by any state regardless of his nationality. The state of which the pirate is a national cannot complain, because under international law piracy is a crime of universal jurisdiction. The same may be true of aircraft hijackers, although there are specific treaty regimes regulating jurisdiction over such persons.

As has been noted already in passing, this form of individual international personality has undergone a radical transformation in recent years. Formerly, these international crimes generally were prosecuted in national courts (albeit according to international law) and then only if the local law had accepted the possibility of the exercise of such a jurisdiction (see e.g. the *Pinochet* cases in the UK and *Nulyarimma* v *Thompson* in Australia, Chapter 4). This was supported by limited international tribunals having competence over specific situations created only for those situations, as with the Yugoslavian, Rwandan and Sierra Leone tribunals. However, it is now the case that there is a permanent international tribunal having the competence to exercise a general jurisdiction over individuals as subjects of international law in respect of serious violations of international criminal law. On 1 July 2002, the International Criminal Court came into existence following the 60th state ratification of the Statute of the Court. This Court exercises a general international criminal jurisdiction over individuals of the nationality of state parties to the Statute (but only such nationals) and is the first permanent international court of its kind. The jurisdiction of the ICC extends to 'the most serious crimes of concern to the international community as a whole' (Art. 5 of the Statute) and includes the crimes of genocide, crimes against humanity and war crimes. Although the ICC will not normally exercise its jurisdiction if a state is proceeding with a matter in its national courts, it is clear that the establishment of the Court is a major advance in terms of deterring and punishing individuals charged with the most grievous violations of human rights. Of course, it necessarily implies that individuals have a large measure of international personality and illustrates just how far international law has come since the time when it was concerned only with relations between sovereign states. At 1 September 2012, there were 121 state-parties to the Statute of the ICC, including the UK (see the International Criminal Courts Act 2001) but not the USA or Russia. As well as securing the first conviction in 2012, the ICC Prosecutor is currently investigating a number of situations and this includes several indictments against named persons held in detention.

In addition to the imposition of duties and responsibilities on individuals, international law also grants personality in the form of rights. The most obvious is the ever expanding law of human rights. In some cases, these rights exist in the abstract, devoid of mechanisms for enforcement, but in others they are accompanied by a procedural capacity for the individual to initiate or partake in proceedings before an international tribunal by which the rights may be vindicated in concrete form. Such substantive and procedural rights are commonly granted by treaty, as with the European Convention on Human Rights 1950 and its Protocols (see generally Chapter 12). A similar procedural personality exists under the International Covenant on Civil and Political Rights 1966, whereby an individual has the right to petition the Human Rights Committee directly if his state of nationality has signed the Optional Protocol. Likewise, the individual's or group of individuals' rights may be vindicated indirectly, as where the subject matter of an international dispute necessarily resolves concerns over such rights, as in the *Palestinian Wall Advisory Opinion* 2004 ICJ Rep and the violation of the rights of the Palestinian population by the building of the security wall in occupied Palestinian territory.

It is clear that such international personality as individuals do have is contingent on the agreement of states and its content and scope will derive from their will. However, although it is *possible* for such capacity to be withdrawn, it would be politically very damaging, and consequently practically very difficult, to remove capacity once granted, especially in the field of human rights. Indeed, perhaps it is not going too far to suggest that the vitality of human rights provisions in international law and the status of some rights as rules of *jus cogens* have generated an objective personality for individuals in these matters that states cannot derogate from. Similarly, it is hardly credible to maintain – as some commentators have done previously – that individuals are objects of the law (benefiting from its protection) rather than 'true' subjects, for this misses the point that the individual is subject to a jurisdiction that is purely international. This jurisdiction is not rooted in the national laws of any state, even though identical local laws may exist. Thus, the individual is a subject of international law when certain duties are placed upon him directly by that law and when he is accorded certain rights.

5.2.5 **Corporations**

In the course of their commercial activities, states will deal not only with each other but with companies and trading concerns from around the world. Normally, their legal relations with such bodies will be governed by national law and the state will be in the same position as any other litigant acting in the domestic courts. In other words, just because a state chooses to act with a non-state body does not confer any degree of international personality on the latter. International personality exists only when relationships are governed by international law. So a contract between the UK government and a German company for the construction of a battleship would not ordinarily confer international legal personality on the company. The contract would be governed by the national law of either Germany or the UK, and both the government and the company would be subject to the national law.

However, that said, there are circumstances in which the contractual relationship between a state and a corporation will be governed by international law. For example, a concession agreement for the extraction of oil might be an 'internationalised' contract subject to rules of international law (e.g. *Texaco* v *Libya* (1977) 53 ILR 389) or states may have agreed that certain types of dispute with companies be settled by an international panel of judges applying international rules. Thus, the Convention on the Settlement of Investment Disputes 1964 establishes a permanent machinery whereby participating states and corporations can settle any differences arising out of investment agreements. Participation in such bodies, where the rights and duties of the company may be judged according to international law, entails international personality. Once again, the existence and extent of this personality depends ultimately on the agreement and recognition of states.

5.2.6 **Miscellaneous**

The relative nature of international personality means that the subjects of international law are many and varied. Moreover, because so much depends on the actions of states, new subjects are quite likely to arise as international law becomes more sophisticated. Governments in exile, belligerent or insurgent communities (e.g. Kurdish nationalists), representative organisations (e.g. the Palestine Liberation Organisation (PLO) and its successor, the Palestinian Authority) and historical bodies (e.g. Holy See, Order of St John) may all have personality of one degree or another. Obviously, the further one moves away from the established subjects of international law, the more international personality depends on recognition and acceptance by states. Indeed, it is quite possible for a body to have different degrees of international personality with different states. For example, before the emergence of a defined Palestinian territory, the PLO enjoyed a varied status according to the political orientation of the states with whom it had relations: see, for example, the US Congress's legislative moves against PLO facilities at UN Headquarters in New York which led to an Advisory Opinion (*Obligation to Arbitrate on UN Headquarters Agreement Case* 1988 ICJ Rep 12) addressing the international responsibility of the USA for failing to recognise the limited international personality of the PLO at the UN. This case is a good illustration of how it may be *practically* impossible for a state to ignore completely the personality of an emerging subject of international law whatever its own political position.

Personality, then, denotes the capacity to act in some measure under international law. It is a flexible and open-ended concept that can mean different things in different circumstances. States have international personality in the fullest measure and the United Nations is not far behind. Other organisations will have that degree of personality that enables them to discharge their functions effectively. The degree of personality enjoyed by the other subjects of international law will depend on many factors – a constituent treaty, a constitution and, importantly, recognition by states.

Part Two: **Recognition**

In international society, historically it has been the practice for one state to recognise formally the existence of another state or government. As far as recognition of states is concerned, this may be because a former colonial territory has gained independence, as with many countries of the Commonwealth, or because part of an existing state has gained its independence from the federal authorities, as with Bangladesh and the former constituent republics of the Soviet Union and Yugoslavia, or because a former disputed territory has achieved independence through self-determination, as with Timor-Leste. Similarly, recognition of a government may be necessary when a new administration comes to power unconstitutionally or a civil war gives rise to competing administrations. Recognition may be either *de jure* (as of right) or *de facto* (accepting the fact of). The latter implies that there may have been something unlawful in the manner of creation of the new state or government but that its effective existence demands that it be treated as an international person. An example was the UK's *de facto* recognition of the Bolshevik government of the USSR in 1921. In practice, however, the distinction between *de jure* and *de facto* recognition is diminishing in importance and, indeed, in the case of states it is hardly relevant.

The act of recognition itself may take various forms. It may consist of a formal pronouncement, an official letter to the newly recognised entity, a statement before a national court or it may be inferred from the opening of full diplomatic relations. Generally, participation in a multilateral conference with an unrecognised state (or an unrecognised government of an established state) does not amount to implied recognition, although it is certainly evidence that the entity in question has achieved some measure of international personality. A vote in favour of the admission of a new state to the UN may amount to implied recognition, as was the case with the UK's vote in favour of the admission of the former Yugoslav Republic of Macedonia to the United Nations on 8 April 1993.

Essentially, the act of recognition is a political act although it may well be based on legal criteria, or partly based thereon. Thus, the decision whether to recognise will be one for the executive authorities of each state and will be influenced by political, economic and legal considerations. Morocco, for example, refused to recognise the Saharan Arab Democratic Republic (Western Sahara) because it has a claim to that territory, even though the 'state' is a member of the African Union. However, as we shall see, it is more likely that disputes of this nature will occur in respect of governments rather than states, especially where an existing state suffers a civil war or similar upheaval, as with Somalia in 1993 (see *Somalia (A Republic)* v *Woodhouse Drake & Carey (Suisse) SA* [1993] 1 All ER 371). In this section we are not concerned primarily with the political motivation for recognition. We are interested in the legal effects of recognition and will attempt to discover the legal consequences of an act of recognition in international and national law.

5.3 Recognition in international law

As far as their relations inter se are concerned, the fact that State A has recognised State B means that each accepts the other as entitled to exercise all the capacities of statehood in international law. Again, if State A has recognised a new government in State B, this means that it will treat the latter as entitled to represent that state in international law. Between two states, then, recognition is a necessary precondition to full optional bilateral relations, such as diplomatic representation and treaty agreements. Conversely, the lack of diplomatic relations between two states need not say anything about recognition. This may be the by-product of a completely different dispute between the states – as with the lack of diplomatic relations between Libya and the UK through much of the 1990s after the Lockerbie bombing. Furthermore, on a more general level, there is a debate as to the effects of recognition on the legal status of the body being recognised. Essentially, this has resolved itself into two theories: the declaratory theory and the constitutive theory of recognition.

5.3.1 Declaratory theory

According to the declaratory theory, the general legal effects of recognition are limited. When an existing state 'recognises' a new state, this is said to be nothing more than an acknowledgment of pre-existing legal capacity. The act of recognition is not decisive of the new entity's claim to statehood, because that status is conferred by operation of international law. The international legal personality of a state does not depend on its recognition as such by other states. It is conferred by rules of international law and, whether or not a state or government is actually recognised by other states, it is still entitled to the rights and subject to the general duties of the system. For example, in the *Tinoco Arbitration (Great Britain* v *Costa Rica)* (1923) 1 RIAA 369, Great Britain made certain claims against Costa Rica arising out of obligations undertaken by the Tinoco government. This government had not been recognised by Great Britain, but the arbiter, Judge Taft, held that the fact of non-recognition did not preclude the claim. In his opinion, non-recognition was evidence, perhaps strong evidence, that the entity had not yet attained the alleged status in international law, but the ultimate test was a factual one based on internationally accepted criteria. So, if the unrecognised entity was effective, it could still be the object of international claims and was bound by the duties imposed by international law. Recognition itself did not determine personality under international law. A similar view was taken by the *EC Arbitration Commission on Yugoslavia* [1993] 92 ILR 162, in its opinions on the status of the former Yugoslavian republics. Although noting the importance of recognition by such bodies as the European Community, the Commission affirmed in general the declaratory theory and its application to the situation in Yugoslavia (but see, however, the EC Guidelines discussed in connection with the constitutive theory).

In general, this theory accords with significant, though not uniform, international practice. For example, the fact that certain Arab states at one time did not recognise Israel did not prevent them making international claims against her, and the same is true of North and South Korea although both are now members of the UN. Of course, the fact that one state has not recognised another may have consequences in national law (see section 5.4) and it may mean that the non-recognising state is not prepared to enter into treaties, diplomatic relations or other bilateral arrangements with the non-recognised body. Yet, this is merely an example of the relative nature of the rights and duties of international law: it does not mean that the unrecognised body has no international personality. If the entity satisfies the criteria for statehood or personality discussed earlier, especially those concerning actual and effective control, it will be a 'state' or 'government', irrespective of recognition. According to the declaratory theory of recognition, the effective body will be subject to, and be able to claim, the general duties and rights accorded to a state or government under international law.

5.3.2 Constitutive theory

The constitutive theory denies that international personality is conferred by operation of international law. On the contrary, the act of recognition is seen as a necessary precondition to the existence of the capacities of statehood or government. So, under this theory, if Taiwan is not recognised as a state, it is not a state; and apparently Eritrea became a state only when it was recognised as such by the international community in 1993. The practical effect of the constitutive theory is that if a 'state' or 'government' is not recognised by the international community, it cannot have international personality. Recognition is said to 'constitute' the state or government. For example, in the *International Registration of Trademark (Germany) Case* (1959) 28 ILR 82, a West German national court ruled that a trademark originating in East Germany was not entitled to protection (under International Conventions of 1883 and 1934) in its territory. The reason was that West Germany did not recognise the statehood of East Germany. According to the court, an entity which actually exists does not thereby become a state in international law without some form of recognition of its existence. In other words, recognition of statehood was essential to international personality.

The main strength of the constitutive theory is that it highlights the practical point that states are under no obligation to enter into bilateral relations with any other body or entity. West Germany did not have to recognise East Germany and, if it did not, there would be no bilateral relations between the 'states'. However, non-recognition did not mean that West Germany could ignore general rules of international law in its dealings with East Germany, nor on a proper analysis did it mean that East Germany was not a state. The *Trademark Case* was decided by a national court and was concerned with the protection by West German law of rights originating in East Germany and non-recognition of East Germany meant that such rights would not be protected *in West Germany*. It did not mean that an international court, applying international law, would find that West Germany had no *international* obligation to protect trade-marks originating in East Germany. In fact, in this case, non-recognition said nothing about the state-hood of East Germany, merely its status in West German courts. Likewise, the fact that the African Union may admit a new member by simple majority vote, as they did in the case of the Saharan Arab Democratic Republic, does not sup-port the constitutive theory. It means, rather, that this entity is entitled to the privileges of membership. It may be evidence of statehood but it does not consti-tute it. In principle, the same is true of admission to membership of the United Nations which is open only to states. *Ex hypothesi*, they must be states before they are admitted, not emerge as such as a consequence of being admitted. Of course, that does not diminish a new state's desire to be accepted as such by the international community through membership of the UN – as with the Republic of Kosovo's as yet unsuccessful attempts to gain admission – but acceptance of statehood through recognition is different from constituting statehood through recognition.

Furthermore, it is clear that the constitutive theory raises insoluble theoretical and practical problems. First, there is no doubt that recognition is a political act, governed only in part by legal principle. For example, the USA did not recognise the Soviet government until 1933, even though it had been effective within the state for at least ten years. Likewise, how long will it be possible to maintain that Taiwan is simply the 'real' China, the respective 'governments' of which are in dispute as to which is the legitimate authority of the whole. Secondly, we must ask ourselves whether it is consistent with the operation of *any* system of law that legal personality under it should depend on the subjective assessment of third parties. Surely, legal personality must be an objective fact capable of resolution by the application of rules of law. As Vice-President Al-Khasawneh pointed out in his Dissenting Opinion in the *Case Concerning the Application of the Convention on the Prevention and Punishment of the Crime of Genocide (Bosnia and Herzegovina v Serbia & Montenegro)* (ICJ 2007), the problem is that there is 'a relativism inher-ent in the constitutive theory of recognition [that] itself prevents the drawing of any firm inferences' about statehood and international capacity. Indeed, in that case, the suspension of Serbia & Montenegro from the United Nations between 1992–2000, coupled with a constitutive view taken by some ICJ judges, led to opposite conclusions about the ability of Serbia & Montenegro to have access to the Court (*Legality of the Use of Force Case* (2004), no access as no capacity for this purpose; *Case Concerning the Application of the Convention on the Prevention and Punishment of the Crime of Genocide (Bosnia and Herzegovina v Serbia & Montenegro)*

(ICJ 2007), access and capacity approved). Thirdly, assuming we accept the constitutive theory, in practical terms what degree of recognition is required in order to 'constitute' a state? Must there be unanimity among the international community (cf. Palestine and Kosovo), or is it enough that there is a majority, a substantial minority or just one recognising state? Again, is membership of an international organisation tantamount to collective recognition and, if so, which organisations? What if membership of the organisation is suspended? Are some states or groups of states (e.g. USA, the EU) more 'important' when it comes to recognition? These are practical problems that the constitutive theory must answer, yet cannot. Some commentators have attempted to meet these criticisms by supposing that there is a 'duty' to recognise once a state or government has fulfilled the criteria laid down by international law. However, not only is it impossible to find any support for the existence of this 'duty' in state practice, in real terms it is little different from the declaratory theory. If there really is a legal duty to recognise, then recognition itself is irrelevant to international personality.

5.3.3 Some conclusions

As far as the constitutive and declaratory theories are concerned, the latter seems to be more in accord with the bulk of international practice, although in this regard significant developments have occurred with the dissolution of the Soviet and Yugoslavian Federations. There is no doubt that the constituent republics of both of these federal states craved international recognition, both during and after the break up of their respective metropolitan countries. This continues still in relation to Kosovo in its attempts to break away from Serbia, itself a former constituent of Yugoslavia. This is significant because clearly the authorities in these territories regarded recognition as important, if only as means to gain international aid and access to international institutions. In response to these demands, the European Community issued Guidelines on the Recognition of New States in Eastern Europe and the Soviet Union and a Declaration on Yugoslavia. In these, the EC indicated its approach to the recognition of new states arising out of the turmoil in eastern Europe (see (1991) 62 BYIL 559). What is so interesting about these guidelines is that the EC put forward requirements for recognition that went far beyond the conditions of statehood found in the Montevideo Convention. Thus, recognition was to be dependent on respect for established frontiers, respect for human rights, guarantees of minority rights, acceptance of nuclear non-proliferation and a commitment to settle disputes peacefully. Of course, this does not necessarily mean that the EC was suggesting that a territory could not be a state until these conditions were complied with. Possibly, the point was that the EC would not *treat* a territory as a state until such conditions and concerns were met. However, even if these Guidelines were not meant to reiterate a constitutive theory of recognition (and on one reading they were), they are important because formal recognition of statehood was no longer to be dependent simply on the fulfilment of the factual Montevideo conditions, but rather on the quality of the political and economic life within a territory (expressed in terms of its commitment to certain values, e.g. human rights guarantees, etc.). This certainly was a novel departure for the UK government, whose practice in the past had been to recognise statehood on the basis of the Montevideo rules, these being more or less objective in character. A similar approach was evident in the UK's recognition of Yugoslavia (Serbia and Montenegro) on 9 April 1996, where much was made of the fulfilment of certain value-laden conditions by the new state. Of course, the EC position might have been no more than an exceptional response to an exceptional situation, but the near affirmation of the constitutive theory and the definite use of 'subjective' criteria perhaps indicate an increased use of recognition as a weapon to achieve political ends. In this respect, perhaps it is significant that there is no agreed EU position on the status of the Republic of Kosovo and each European state is being left to itself to determine whether or not it will recognise the independence of this territory (currently, some twenty-two EU members, including the UK, out of twenty-seven, do recognise Kosovo in some way).

There is a further problem with the constitutive theory in that it fails to clarify that there is a difference between the *exercise* of bilateral relations and the *capacity* to act under international law. The former may well depend on recognition (and this is what the EC may have meant when dealing with the former USSR and Yugoslavia) whereas the latter generally does not. An unrecognised entity may not be able to make a treaty with the UK (exercise of rights) even though formally it has the power to do so (capacity). As international lawyers, our prime concern is the latter, although, as ever, a word of caution is needed. We must remember that it is practice rather than theory which is important. The range and efficacy of rights and duties under international law depends ultimately on what states themselves actually do. We have seen in Part One of this chapter that collective recognition (typically through admission to the UN) may cure defects in the mode of creation of a state, but we have also seen that non-recognition of Israel by some Arab states did not prevent them from claiming that Israel had violated international law. Likewise, the dissolution of the federal states of Eastern Europe has brought new life to an old argument and has highlighted just how important recognition and admission to the UN are regarded by emerging states themselves. The fluid situation in relation to Kosovo, where some states have recognised it, others have expressly not recognised and some have recognised that it is moving towards statehood, reminds us that definitive answers are not to be found. In short, while the declaratory theory may hold more water, it is not watertight.

5.4 Recognition of states and governments in national law

There is a very real distinction between the effects of recognition in international law and its effects in national law. In international law, State A may have no choice other than to accept the fact of existence of State B, but national law is a different legal system. Whether the executive, administrative or judicial authorities of State A pay any regard to the acts of State B (or its government) on the national plane may depend entirely on whether it has been formally recognised. In practice, the legal effects or consequences of recognition in national law depend on the laws of each state. In this section we will be concerned primarily with the effects of recognition (or rather non-recognition) in the UK, but some reference will be made to the practice of other countries.

5.4.1 Types of recognition in the United Kingdom

5.4.1.1 States

International law generally leaves the question of the existence of a state in *national law* to the rules of the national legal system concerned – as explained in *R (on the application of North Cyprus Tourism Centre Ltd) v Transport For London* (2005) UKHRR 1231. In UK national law, whether a territorial entity claiming to be a state is recognised as such by the UK is a matter for the executive authorities. Numerous examples exist, but the formal recognition by the UK of Eritrea in 1993 and Yugoslavia (Serbia and Montenegro) in 1996 are good illustrations, as is the UK's refusal to recognise Chechen claims to independence from the Russian Federation and the UK's non-recognition of an independent state in Northern Cyprus (see the most affirmation of this, *R (on the application of) Kibris Türk Hava Yollari v Secretary of State for Transport* (2010)). As a matter of UK constitutional law, the conduct of foreign affairs is for the government and not for the judiciary and it is imperative that all the organs of the state 'speak with one voice'. Consequently, in domestic legal proceedings where there is some doubt about the status of an entity as a 'state', a request will be made by the court to the Foreign office, who may issue an executive certificate. This certificate will specify whether or not the 'state' is recognised as such by the UK and it is conclusive (e.g. *Luther v Sagor* [1921] 3 KB 532). Any attempts to circumvent this exclusive competence are dealt with firmly, as in *R v The Commissioners for the Inland Revenue, ex parte Resat Caglar* where the Foreign Office made it clear that 'Her Majesty's Government views with concern the suggestion that the "TRNC" [Turkish Republic of Northern Cyprus] should be held by the court to be a "foreign state" [within s. 321 of the Income and Corporation Tax Act 1988] notwithstanding that it is not recognised as such by her Majesty's Government'. Neither the court nor the parties can challenge the determination made in the certificate and the court is bound to act on the basis of the information supplied.

5.4.1.2 Governments

It frequently happens that a new government may come to power in an existing state by unconstitutional means – for example, by civil war or *coup d'état*. If this happens, it is essential to know whether the new administration is to be treated as a 'government' for the purposes of UK national law. Previously, the practice of the UK in respect of governments was the same as that for states: a request was made to the Foreign Office and a conclusive certificate was issued (e.g. *Luther v Sagor*). Essentially, the criterion applied by the UK in deciding whether to recognise a new government was whether the alleged government was in effective control of the territory it claimed to represent, although only *de facto* recognition would be accorded if there was some doubt about the permanence of the new administration or some concern as to the manner in which it came to power. Although UK practice was not entirely consistent, generally recognition of a new government by the UK did not signify approval, merely that it was effective within the territory. However, despite repeated government statements clarifying the point, the practice of recognising governments was often misunderstood as signifying approval of particular governments and the distinction between *de jure* and *de facto* recognition did not seem to clarify matters. This led to a change in practice.

In 1980, the UK joined many other states, including the USA, in adopting the so-called Estrada Doctrine. This means that the UK no longer accords formal recognition to governments. It will continue to recognise states in accordance with international practice and the requirements of national law but, when a new government comes to power unconstitutionally, the UK will not formally make a statement of recognition. According to the practice statement issued in 1980, Her Majesty's Government has 'concluded that there are practical advantages in following the policy of many other countries in not according recognition to governments. Like them, we shall continue to decide the nature of our dealings with regimes which come to power unconstitutionally in the light of our assessment of whether they are able to exercise effective control of the territory of the State concerned, and seem likely to do so.'

This does not mean, of course, that the substantive issue goes away. It will still be necessary for many purposes in national law to decide whether a body is entitled to be regarded as the 'government' of a state. The point is, rather, that national courts will not have the benefit of an executive certificate to settle the matter. It seems then that UK courts will have to decide the matter for themselves on the basis of the nature of the dealings which the UK government has with the new administration. That this is not necessarily an easy task is illustrated by two cases decided after the change in UK practice, although as we shall see the approach of the second is much to be preferred and now seems to be settled law. In the first case, *Gur Corp.* v *Trust Bank of Africa* [1986] 3 WLR 583, the court had to determine whether the 'Government of Ciskei' was a sovereign government so that it could act as claimant in a UK court. The court twice requested guidance from the Foreign Office and twice were met with the answer that the UK no longer recognised governments and that 'the attitude of Her Majesty's Government is to be inferred from the nature of its dealings with the regime concerned and in particular whether [the UK] deals with it on a government to government basis'. This did not deter the court from utilising the answers contained in the Foreign Office replies as a means of determining the issue and they purportedly followed the earlier case of *Carl Zeiss Stiftung* v *Rayner and Keeler (No. 2)* [1967] 1 AC 853. These two cases are discussed later in more detail, but for now the important point is that the UK court seemed reluctant to make its own decision. It was quite obviously predisposed to rely on an executive statement, even though there was no prospect of formal recognition of the 'government'. This was not surprising given the traditional reluctance of UK courts to interfere with matters connected with foreign affairs, but it is unfortunate that the court missed the opportunity to lay down guidelines for other cases. In fact, the case seemed to imply that when in future the Foreign Office supplied details of the 'course of dealings' which Her Majesty's Government had with a disputed 'government', a UK court would regard such evidence as virtually conclusive of the entity's status. In other words, *Gur* suggested simply that express recognition of governments had been replaced by implied recognition of governments.

Fortunately, an opportunity arose for a UK court to re-examine the matter. In *Somalia (Republic)* v *Woodhouse Drake & Carey (Suisse) SA* [1993] 1 All ER 371, an interim government of Somalia sought control over certain funds belonging to the Republic of Somalia. Somalia was at that time in a state of civil war, with no faction in effective control of the state. The judge had to decide whether the claimants were the 'government of Somalia' in order that they might recover the funds and, of course, due to the change in practice, there was no executive certificate to aid him. There was evidence before the court that the UK government had virtually no dealings with the claimants as a government and that, in fact, the UK view was that there was no effective government in Somalia at all. In the end, Hobhouse J agreed that there was no effective government of Somalia and the claimants' application was refused. Importantly, however, the judge identified the factors that a court should take into account when deciding whether an alleged 'government' was a sovereign government for the purpose of an action in UK courts. These were:

(a) whether the entity was the constitutional government of the state;

(b) the degree, nature and stability of administrative control, if any, which it exercised over the territory of the state;

(c) whether the British government had any dealings with that government and, if so, the nature of those dealings; and

(d) in marginal cases the extent of international recognition that it had as the government of that state.

Clearly, this is an important statement of principle in a number of respects. First, it makes it clear that a UK court is able, and willing, to make its own determination as to the status of an alleged foreign government. The court is not bound by the UK government's unofficial view, nor even by the 'nature of the dealings' that the UK has with the alleged government. Secondly, a UK court will pay regard to those factors that are important when sovereignty is in issue as a matter of international law, viz. legality, effectiveness and, in marginal cases, recognition. This is also to be greatly welcomed, not least because it is pleasing to see a UK court recognise the validity of principles of international law. Thirdly, there is the possibility – although it did not occur in this case – that a UK court would take a different view of the status of a 'government' than that expressed unofficially by the UK government. An example might be where the UK refuses to deal with a government because of political or ideological differences, but where that government is generally regarded as representing a state in international law. If this does happen, the 'one voice' principle referred to earlier will be no more, at least in relation to governments. All in all then, the decision in *Somalia* was a timely affirmation of the objective nature of personality in international law and puts into practice, at last, the full meaning of the 1980 change in UK practice on recognition of governments. It has been followed, without criticism, in *Sierra Leone Telecommunications* v *Barclays Bank plc* [1998] 2 All ER 821.

5.4.2 **Effects of non-recognition in the United Kingdom**

5.4.2.1 *De facto* or *de jure* recognition

As a preliminary point, it should be noted that because the UK no longer recognises governments formally, the distinction between *de facto* and *de jure* recognition has largely disappeared. Previously, it was possible for two governments of one state to be recognised by the UK at the same time, one *de jure* and one *de facto*, as in *The Arantzazu Mendi* [1939] AC 256. Indeed, the type of recognition which was accorded may have had consequences for the jurisdiction of the court. For example, a *de facto* government appeared to enjoy immunity from the jurisdiction of national courts only in respect of persons or property actually in the territory of the state concerned (*Haile Selassie* v *Cable & Wireless Co. (No. 2)* [1939] Ch 182) and *de jure* recognition was retroactive (i.e. applicable to acts done before the formal act of recognition) only in spheres within the actual control of the *de jure* government (*Gdynia Ameryka Linie* v *Boguslawski* [1953] AC 11), unless it was unlawful under the local law of the *de facto* government (*Civil Air Transport* v *Central Air Transport* [1953] AC 70). These distinctions, which were primarily based on practical and political considerations, are now largely irrelevant.

5.4.2.2 General effects

In the UK, the fact that a state or government is 'recognised' is of vital importance in determining its right to be treated as a sovereign authority within the UK national legal system. (In respect of governments, 'recognised' means accepted as a sovereign government by the courts under the *Somalia* principle.) If a state or government is not recognised or accepted as a sovereign authority it will not be able to sue in its own name (*City of Berne* v *Bank of England* 9 Ves. 347), many (if not all) of its laws and administrative acts may not be accepted as valid (*Carl Zeiss Stiftung* v *Rayner & Keeler (No. 2)*), it may not claim immunity from the execution of judgments and it will not be immune in appropriate cases from the exercise of civil or criminal jurisdiction by UK courts. It is only recognised states and governments of sovereign states that enjoy these privileges automatically. Moreover, it is important to realise that the consequences of non-recognition as a state or non-acceptance as a government can cause particular hardship to individual litigants and may interfere greatly with the normal conduct of inter-state affairs. For example, in *Adams* v *Adams* [1970] 3 All ER 572, a UK court refused to recognise a divorce granted in Southern Rhodesia because the UK did not recognise that country as a sovereign state and the same result occurred in *B* v *B* (2000) 2 FLR 707 in respect of a divorce decree granted in Northern Cyprus. Obviously, this appears rather difficult to justify and, as discussed next, these two decisions need to be qualified because it seems that the UK now will *give* limited recognition to acts taking place in an unrecognised state, at least in respect of purely administrative matters affecting individuals. That said, the practical difficulties caused by non-recognition should not be underestimated, and it is fortunate that a number of developments in UK law have softened the harshness of the non-recognition doctrine.

5.4.2.3 Acts of perfunctory administration

In *Hesperides Hotels* v *Aegean Turkish Holidays* [1978] QB 205, the claimants claimed damages for trespass in respect of two hotels owned by them, but now occupied by the Turkish-Cypriot defendants. The hotels were situated in that part of Cyprus under Turkish occupation following an invasion in 1974 and had been handed over to the defendants by the Turkish administration. The Foreign Office had stated in its certificate (issued for governments at that time) that the UK did not recognise the Turkish administration *de jure* or *de facto*. The effect of this should have been that no laws or administrative acts of the Turkish authorities could be considered valid in a UK court. In fact, the action was dismissed because the court lacked jurisdiction over the substantive issue. However, Lord Denning MR went on to challenge the non-recognition doctrine. In his view, the court could take note of certain acts of a foreign sovereign, if it was effective within a territory, even though the sovereign was not formally recognised by the UK. Furthermore, the court could conduct its own inquiry to see whether the body was effective. Obviously, this dictum was not part of the *ratio decidendi* of the case, but it represented a significant departure from accepted doctrine. The acts which the court could take notice of included marriages, divorces and property transactions involving private individuals. Clearly, the purpose was to mitigate, *for the individual*, the consequences of non-recognition.

Lord Denning went further than the other judges in *Hesperides*, but his approach to non-recognition was supported by cases in the USA (e.g. *Texas v White* 74 US 700, 1868) and by an earlier House of Lords decision. In *Carl Zeiss Stiftung v Rayner & Keeler (No. 2)*, Lord Wilberforce had stated that in so far as the East German 'government' was not recognised, he should wish seriously to consider whether this resulted in the absolute invalidity of all its acts. Indeed, he would wish to consider whether 'where private rights, or acts of everyday occurrence, or perfunctory acts of administration are concerned the courts may, in the interests of justice and common sense, where no consideration of public policy to the contrary has to prevail, give recognition to the actual facts or realities found to exist in the territory in question'. Again, this was an obiter dictum but now the issue appears settled by a more recent case involving the so-called Turkish Republic of Northern Cyprus (the TRNC). In *Emin v Yeldag* [2002] 1 FLR 956, the issue was whether a UK court would recognise a divorce obtained in the TRNC, despite the fact that the TRNC was not recognised as a state by the UK. A full application of the non-recognition doctrine would have prevented the court from recognising the divorce, and this was the result in the earlier case of *B v B* [2000] FLR 707, also concerning the TRNC. However, after a careful review of the UK, USA and European Court of Human Rights jurisprudence, Mr Justice Sumner concluded in *Yeldag* that the exception to the principle of non-recognition was well made out in respect of administrative and similar acts such as divorces. He suggested that the judge in *B v B* would have reached the same conclusion had he had the benefit of full argument and (rightly) that the *Resat Calgar Case* (also involving the TRNC) could be distinguished as the substance of the issue in that case was the alleged state immunity of the TRNC itself, not the validity of a private law act. Thus, these private law acts could be recognised as effective in the UK legal system, despite emanating from an unrecognised state, provided that there was no statutory prohibition (as there was in *Adams* v *Adams* because of the constitutional relationship of the UK to Southern Rhodesia) and provided that such recognition did not in fact compromise the UK government in the conduct of its foreign relations. In *R (on the application of) Kibris Türk Hava Yollari v Secretary of State for Transport* (2010), the court refused to apply the 'acts of administration' exception in favour of the TRNC because, to do so would, indirectly, recognise the TRNC as being covered by an international treaty and would directly contradict the UK government's foreign policy objectives. Clearly, in each case the court must assess both the nature of the acts for which limited validity is sought under this exception and the context in which they arise. This, it is submitted, is an eminently sensible approach for it upholds the policy behind the non-recognition doctrine while at the same time mitigating it for individuals in much the same way that the Foreign Corporations Act 1991 does for companies (see section 5.4.2.5).

5.4.2.4 Acts of a delegated sovereign

In 1967, the UK did not recognise the German Democratic Republic (East Germany or GDR) as an independent state. Again, this meant that all legislative, judicial and administrative acts of that country could not be recognised in UK courts. In *Carl Zeiss Stiftung* v *Rayner & Keeler (No. 2)*, the defendants alleged that the claimants had no standing to sue because the administrative act whereby they (the claimants) had been created was an act of an unrecognised sovereign, the GDR. In essence, it was alleged that for a UK court the East German company did not exist. The remarks of Lord Wilberforce on the consequences of non-recognition have already been noted, yet this was not the reason why the court was able to accept the validity of 'East German' laws.

According to their Lordships, the acts of the GDR could be given effect as the acts of a delegated sovereign legislature. As the replies from the Foreign Office indicated, East Germany (the USSR Zone of Occupation after the Second World War), was then legally under the sovereign authority of the USSR. The UK did indeed recognise the USSR as a sovereign body. Therefore, the acts of an East German administration could be accepted as valid in a UK court because they were the acts of a body to whom power had been validly delegated by a sovereign (and recognised) authority, the USSR. Of course, this was something of a legal fiction, because the Soviet Union regarded East Germany as independent, but it did serve to mitigate the harsh effects of the non-recognition doctrine. On the other hand, the decision has been widely criticised because it does seem to cut against the 'one voice' principle and there is some evidence that it was not consonant with UK policy at that time. It was not until 1973 that the UK finally recognised East Germany and now there is a single unified German state, having full sovereignty in its own right.

Subsequently, in *Gur Corp.* v *Trust Bank of Africa*, the concept of delegated authority was applied once again. In this case, the live issue was whether the 'Government of Ciskei' could sue as claimant in its own name in an English court. This was refused at first instance on the ground that the 'government' was not a sovereign authority. On appeal, the court twice requested a certificate from the Foreign office. As we have seen, this was refused on the ground that the UK no longer formally recognised foreign governments. However, the Court of Appeal found in the Foreign office replies enough information to enable them to determine that the 'Government of Ciskei' was acting under the delegated authority of a sovereign legislature, this being the recognised government of South Africa. Applying the *Carl Zeiss Case*, the 'Government of Ciskei' was allowed to sue in its own name because it was a body to whom power had been validly delegated. Once again, there are difficulties with this line of reasoning. First, the Court of Appeal seemed unaware or unable to accept that there had been a change in UK policy. Its reliance on the Foreign Office replies for the finding of delegated authority is unfortunate, both because the replies do not clearly support this conclusion and because the court could have conducted its own inquiry. Now this inquiry will be different because of the *Somalia* case. Secondly, the finding that the 'Government of Ciskei' was an agent of the South African government was entirely contradicted by the Status of Ciskei Act 1981 which, as a legislative Act of a recognised sovereign (South Africa), the court should have respected. In fact, the Court of Appeal ignored that part of the Ciskei Act which granted independence and took note only of that part which accorded with their interpretation of the Foreign Office replies. As we have seen, these should not have been regarded as conclusive. Thirdly, it must be recognised that the delegated authority doctrine is a legal fiction. Its effect in the *Carl Zeiss Case* was to allow an individual claimant to gain a normal remedy against an individual defendant which would have otherwise been lost. There was no question of recognising East Germany as such. In the *Gur Case*, the theory was used to allow a rogue 'government' to sue in its own name *just as if* it were a sovereign body. Surely, this is entirely inconsistent with the whole purpose of the non-recognition doctrine, which is to prevent exactly what happened in the *Gur Case*. In sum, then, the decision in the *Gur Case* is difficult to reconcile with the change in practice in 1980. Moreover, while there may be some merit in using the theory of delegated authority to prevent injustice or hardship to individuals, it should not be taken further.

5.4.2.5 The Foreign Corporations Act 1991

The third way in which the consequences of non-recognition are mitigated in the UK is, perhaps, the most significant. We have seen already that should a state be unrecognised – for whatever reason – it is likely that none of its legislative, executive, judicial or administrative acts will be accepted as valid by a UK court. Consequently, a company incorporated in an unrecognised state would have had no legal personality as far as UK law was concerned and could not sue or be sued in UK courts. Obviously, this could cause unwarranted hardship to individuals as well as being destructive of the confidence necessary to foster international commerce. This was precisely the problem faced in *Carl Zeiss* and it was avoided by the fiction of delegated sovereignty. Now a UK court would not have to go to such lengths. The Foreign Corporations Act 1991 enables companies incorporated under the laws of a territory which the UK does not recognise as a state to be given legal personality within the UK legal system. Simply put, the consequences of UK non-recognition of the company's 'home' state will not apply if that company is incorporated under the laws of a territory that has a 'settled legal system'. The foreign corporation will be able to sue and be sued, whatever the status of its mother country. Moreover, according to the Minister responsible for piloting this Act through Parliament, it was intended to ensure that matters of legal personality within domestic law should not be complicated by matters of foreign policy. Here, then, is explicit recognition that there is no necessary reason why the courts of the UK and the Executive should 'speak with one voice', even in matters relating to statehood.

An early test of the efficacy of the Foreign Corporations Act was provided by *R v The Minister of Agriculture, Fisheries & Food, ex parte S.P. Anastasiou (Pissouri) and Others* (not reported). In this case, a company (Cypfruvex) registered in the Turkish Republic of Northern Cyprus (TRNC), a state not recognised by the UK, sought to intervene in judicial review proceedings in the UK. In applying the Act to determine whether the company had status before a UK court, Popplewell J interpreted it as requiring affirmative answers to three questions: first, was there an identifiable territory not recognised by the UK; secondly, did this territory possess a settled legal system; and thirdly, was the relevant company incorporated by the laws of that territory? As there was little doubt that all three conditions were satisfied, Popplewell J would permit Cypfruvex to intervene. Clearly, this is an interpretation and application of the Act that is entirely consistent with its purpose: viz. to give legal recognition to a company from an unrecognised state irrespective of the UK government's view of that state's legitimacy. It is obvious that although UK government spokesmen repeatedly referred to this Act as settling an issue of 'private international law' only, there is no doubt that this statute embodies a significant change in UK practice and attitudes towards non-recognition in national law. It is, in effect, the next logical step after the UK had ceased to recognise governments. Unfortunately, the pragmatic approach typified by the Foreign Corporations Act is not universal. The main issue in *S.P. Anastasiou* (the acceptance by the UK of TRNC customs certificates) was referred to the European Court of Justice in order to determine whether acceptance of such certificates was a breach of Community law. Subsequent to Popplewell J's decision, the ECJ ruled that such certificates could not be accepted because of the unrecognised status of the TRNC. This European decision, which places a premium on policy, may come to be regarded as a retrograde step given the many other ways in which the role of recognition in national legal systems has been downplayed in recent years.

5.4.2.6 Statutory interpretation

We have already noted that the decision in *Emin* v *Yeldag* confirms that a UK court may accept the validity of private law acts or 'perfunctory acts of administration' even though emanating from a state that the UK does not recognise. This was enough to dispose of the issue in that case. However, Sumner J went on to consider an alternative argument that the terms of ss. 46 and 49 of the Family Law Act 1986 permitted the recognition of a divorce obtained in the TRNC because it was granted under one of the two systems of law (southern and northern territorial areas) operating within a state (Cyprus) that the UK did recognise. This is similar to the 'delegated sovereignty' fiction discussed earlier, but the point here is not to examine whether the judge correctly interpreted the Family Law Act 1986. Rather it is to note that there is nothing to prevent the UK deliberately granting piecemeal recognition under statute to certain types of acts emanating from an unrecognised state. Indeed, there is nothing to prevent a UK court from interpreting a UK statute in this way – even if it appears to stretch the meaning to breaking point.

5.4.2.7 Is the existence of the unrecognised state really material to the dispute?

In *R (on the application of North Cyprus Tourism Centre Ltd)* v *Transport for London* (2005) UKHRR 1231, the court considered whether Transport for London were subject to judicial review of their decision to remove adverts for holidays in Northern Cyprus from their buses. Transport for London submitted that its decision was lawful because the UK did not recognise Northern Cyprus and thus tourism in the territory could not, and should not, be promoted. The court, however, noted that the contracts for the adverts were with UK companies (albeit closely connected with the authorities in Northern Cyprus) and that in reality no rights, obligations or actions of the authorities in Northern Cyprus as such were in issue. In other words, the consequences of non-recognition apply only to acts of the non-recognised entity itself or its agents, not to any matter in which the entity might conceivably be interested or which might affect it. Of course, even the acts of a private party might directly imply that there is validity in the laws or existence of an unrecognised entity, as in *R (on the application of) Kibris Türk Hava Yollari* v *Secretary of State for Transport* (2010), and so in such cases, the effects of non-recognition must be enforced.

5.4.2.8 International organisations or entities

Lastly, it should be remembered that the problems caused by lack of recognition are not confined to entities established under the law of disputed states or governments. The passing of the Foreign Corporations Act was in part motivated by the decision of the Court of Appeal in *Arab Monetary Fund* v *Hashim*. As we have seen, in that case the Arab Monetary Fund was initially denied personality in the UK legal system because it was created by a treaty which had not been transformed into UK law (i.e. it came from an unrecognised legal system – international law). Although subsequently reversed on other grounds, the case highlighted that lack of legal personality, be it because the institution was incorporated under international law or under the law of an unrecognised state, could cause serious and unwarranted interference with international commerce as well as hardship for individual litigants. As discussed in Chapter 4, it is to be hoped that developments in the case law, particularly *Westland Helicopters Ltd* v *Arab Organisation for Industrialisation* [1995] 2 All ER 387, will reduce the circumstances in which constitutional niceties force the UK legal system to reject the legal creations of international law.

As we have seen in the discussion in Part One of this chapter, the matter of recognition is closely bound up with the concept of international personality. As far as states are concerned, 'recognition' of their existence may have some part to play in their emergence as fully operational subjects of international law, but generally it is more relevant to the opening of optional bilateral relations. Recognition of statehood may enhance the exercise of the capacities of statehood, but only rarely does it determine their existence. However, recognition by states of the existence of other types of legal person can be decisive, especially since the degree and extent of personality can vary from subject to subject. Moreover, on the national level, an act of recognition by the state of jurisdiction can determine finally the capacity of the 'state' or 'government' to act within the national legal system. In the UK, non-recognition of statehood still has some consequences for the 'state', so that it may be effectively barred from enforcing any rights and duties in UK courts. Conversely, the position of legal persons created by the unrecognised state has been much improved by developments in common law and statute. In respect of governments, the UK practice of not formally recognising their existence may encourage a relaxation in the effects of the 'non-recognition' doctrine, especially now that the court will determine for itself the substantive issue of whether the alleged government is 'sovereign'. All in all, there is a general trend to scale down the role of recognition in the national legal system, although as the discussion in Part One of this chapter made clear, recognition in international law may grow in importance as it is used as a lever to encourage emerging states to conform with certain regional values.

FURTHER READING

Brownlie, I., 'Recognition in Theory and Practice', (1982) 53 *BYIL* 197.

Crawford, J., 'The Criteria for Statehood in International Law', (1976–77) 48 *BYIL* 93.

Dixon, M., 'Recent Developments in Recognition (The *Gur Case*)', (1988) *International Lawyer* 555.

Koskenniemi, M., 'National Self Determination', (1993) 43 *ICLQ* 241.

Peterson, M. J., 'Recognition of Governments should not be abolished', (1983) 77 *AJIL* 31.

Pomerance, M., *Self-Determination in Law and Practice*, 1st edn. (Martinus Nijhoff, 1982).

Symmons, C. R., 'United Kingdom Abolition of the Doctrine of Recognition', [1981] *PL* 249.

Warbrick, C., 'Kosovo: The Declaration of Independence', (2008) 57 *ICLQ* 675.

Warbrick, C., 'Recognition of Governments', (1993) 56 *MLR* 92.

Weller, M., 'The International Response to the Dissolution of the Socialist Federal Republic of Yugoslavia', (1992) 86 *AJIL* 569.

SUMMARY

Personality, statehood and recognition

- A subject of international law is a body or entity that is capable of possessing and exercising rights and duties under international law.

- The main capacities of an international legal person are the ability to make claims before tribunals; to be subject to some or all of the obligations imposed by international law; to have the power to make valid international agreements; to enjoy some or all of the immunities from the jurisdiction of the national courts of other states.

- States are the most important and most powerful of the subjects of international law. Article 1 of the Montevideo Convention on the Rights and Duties of States 1933 says that the 'state as a person of international law should possess the following qualifications: (a) a permanent population; (b) a defined territory; (c) a government; and (d) a capacity to enter into relations with other states'.

- The relative nature of international personality, whereby a 'subject' may have certain rights and duties for certain purposes, means that states are not the only territorial entities that can be regarded as subjects of international law.

- There are now more international organisations than at any time previously in the history of international law. In order that they may be able to carry out their allotted tasks, they must enjoy some measure of international personality.

- The clearest example of the personality of individuals in modern international law is the responsibility that each individual bears for war crimes, crimes against the peace and crimes against humanity. In addition to the imposition of duties and responsibilities on individuals, international law also grants personality in the form of rights. The most obvious is the law of human rights.

- In the course of their commercial activities, states will deal not only with each other but also with companies and trading concerns from around the world. They may enjoy personality for purposes connected with these activities if their relations are governed by international law.

- According to the declaratory theory of recognition, when an existing state 'recognises' a new state, this is said to be nothing more than an acknowledgment of pre-existing legal capacity. The act of recognition is not decisive of the new entity's claim to statehood, because that status is conferred by operation of international law.

- The constitutive theory denies that international personality is conferred by operation of international law. The act of recognition is seen as a necessary precondition to the existence of the capacities of statehood.

- The UK continues to recognise states officially, but it no longer formally recognises governments. Non-recognition of a 'state' means that the 'state' has no capacity within the UK legal system.

6

Jurisdiction and sovereignty

The concept of 'jurisdiction' in international law can cover a multitude of sins. In this chapter, we shall examine the nature and extent of a state's authority over territory, persons and aircraft. The maritime jurisdiction of a state is considered in Chapter 8 on the Law of the Sea, while the jurisdiction of the International Court of Justice is considered in Chapter 10 in the context of the Peaceful Settlement of Disputes. Immunities from the exercise of territorial jurisdiction by a state are considered in the following chapter.

6.1 General principles of jurisdiction

In the *Lotus Case* (1927) PCIJ Ser. A No. 10, the Permanent Court of International Justice stated that 'the first and foremost restriction imposed by international law upon a state is that – failing the existence of a permissive rule to the contrary – it may not exercise its power in any form in the territory of another state'. In other words, unless it is expressly permitted, State A may not exercise jurisdiction in the territory of State B. However, the Court went on to explain that this did not mean that a state was barred from exercising jurisdiction in its own territory in respect of any acts that took place abroad. In international law, there was no general prohibition against states extending their legislative jurisdiction to persons, property and events taking place outside their territory. In fact, the reverse was true, and in any international dispute it was for the state alleging lack of jurisdiction to prove the existence of a rule of international law specifically curtailing the general power that every state possessed. This general ability to assume prescriptive jurisdiction – the right to legislate for matters beyond the territorial domain – flowed from the absolute sovereignty of the state and could be curtailed only by positive limitation.

It appears from the *Lotus Case*, then, that we have two competing general rules of jurisdiction. On the one hand, the 'first and foremost' rule is that one state may not exercise jurisdiction in the territory of another state. On the other hand, there is an equally general principle that a state is entirely free to project its jurisdiction over any matter taking place outside its territory, so long as this is not prohibited by a contrary rule of international law in a specific case. Can both these statements of principle be correct, for they appear to be mutually exclusive? The answer lies in the fact that the concept of state jurisdiction over persons, property and territory encompasses two distinct ideas.

6.1.1 The jurisdiction to prescribe

The power of a state to bring any matter within the cognisance of its national law is called its prescriptive jurisdiction. The second principle of the *Lotus Case* refers to this. It is the power of a state to assert the applicability of its national law to any person, property, territory or event, wherever they may be situated or wherever they may occur. As we have seen from the dicta in the *Lotus Case*, in the exercise of its prescriptive jurisdiction a state is virtually unlimited by international law, save only that it may have accepted specific international obligations limiting its competence. Two good examples of the prescriptive jurisdiction of the UK are the Broadcasting Act 1990 which makes it an offence under UK law to broadcast from the high seas in a manner which interferes with domestic broadcasting services, and the case of *Joyce* v *DPP* [1946] AC 347, which illustrates that the offence of treason may be committed by any person owing allegiance to the Crown who has done a treasonable act, wherever that act took place. In essence, the jurisdiction to prescribe comprises a generally unfettered power to claim jurisdiction over any matter. However, the practical effect of this jurisdiction is curtailed by the first of the principles outlined in the *Lotus Case* – the jurisdiction to enforce.

6.1.2 The jurisdiction to enforce

Whereas a state may have a general power under international law to prescribe jurisdiction, the enforcement of that jurisdiction can generally take place only within its own territory. Specifically, a state cannot, as the quotation from the *Lotus Case* makes clear, enforce its prescriptive jurisdiction in the territory of another state. Consequently, the actual exercise of jurisdiction – the operation of a police force, national courts etc. – is limited to the territory of the state asserting jurisdiction unless there is an agreement that the enforcement jurisdiction can take place elsewhere. So when a person over whom the state has prescribed jurisdiction enters the territory, the state may proceed to exercise its powers, as in *Joyce* v *DPP*. It cannot, in the absence of special permission, seek to enforce its prescriptive jurisdiction outside of its territory. A rare example of such a special permission is the UK/Netherlands Agreement 1999, permitting the trial of the Lockerbie subjects by a Scottish court, according to Scots law, in Dutch territory.

In fact, then, the two principles identified in the *Lotus Case* are not contradictory. They are concerned with two different species of jurisdiction. Under international law, a state may assert, by its national law, a jurisdiction that is virtually unlimited. However, any enforcement of that jurisdiction is confined to its own territory and must not, without special agreement, be exercised in any form in the territory of another state. As we shall see, the territorial exclusiveness of the jurisdiction to enforce is one of the most important principles of international law.

6.1.3 The absolute nature of territorial jurisdiction

Third, and as a corollary to the first of the *Lotus* principles, it is a fundamental rule of international law that the jurisdiction of a state within its own territory is complete and absolute. The state has power and authority over all persons, property and events occurring within its territory. This is a basic attribute of sovereignty and flows from the very existence of the state as an international legal person. Furthermore, no other power, including the United Nations (see UN Charter Art. 2(7)), may exercise an enforcement jurisdiction in state territory and matters arising within 'the domestic jurisdiction' cannot form the subject matter of international claims, save in exceptional cases (such as where a state violates human rights). It is for this reason, for example, that police officers from other states have no authority within the UK and may operate there only with the consent of the relevant UK authorities.

However, it is clear that the absolute and complete nature of territorial jurisdiction can be modified either by general principles of international law or by specific obligations freely undertaken by the territorial sovereign. For example, a state is obliged under international law to refrain from exercising its territorial jurisdiction over diplomats (see Chapter 7) and public vessels of other states (e.g. *Schooner Exchange* v *McFaddon* (1812) 7 Cranch 116). These have 'immunity from jurisdiction'. Similarly, a state may agree by treaty that another state can exercise some form of enforcement jurisdiction within its territory for a specific purpose (e.g. the UK/Netherlands Agreement 1999) or the grant of jurisdiction may be an aspect of the grant of sovereignty (as with the UK sovereign military bases in Cyprus) or of the grant of *de facto* exclusive control (as with the US military base at Guantanamo Bay in Cuba).

To sum up, then, the basic principles of jurisdiction are, first, that a state has authority under international law to apply its national laws to matters arising within and outside its territory, irrespective of the nationality of the object of that jurisdiction: this is its prescriptive jurisdiction. Secondly, this prescriptive jurisdiction is curtailed in practice by the fact that the enforcement of jurisdiction may take place only in a state's own territory unless some special permission has been granted to exercise enforcement jurisdiction in an area under the sovereignty of another state. Thirdly, a state has absolute and exclusive power of enforcement within its own territory over all matters arising therein, unless that power is curtailed by some rule of international law, either general or specific. No other state or international legal person may trespass into the 'domestic jurisdiction' of the territorial sovereign.

6.2 Civil and criminal jurisdiction

In international law, a state may have the right to exercise an enforcement jurisdiction over persons by virtue of a number of different principles. These are 'rights' in the sense that no other state (e.g. the national state of the individual concerned) may object to the exercise of the jurisdiction. Conversely, if the territorial sovereign exercises an enforcement jurisdiction in its territory outside of these principles over a foreign national, this may be effective in local law, but it may also give rise to international responsibility for an *internationally* wrongful exercise of jurisdiction. These principles have been analysed at length in the unofficial 1935 Harvard Research Draft Convention on Jurisdiction with Respect to Crime and considered judicially in a variety of international and national law cases. Generally, the scope of jurisdiction in civil matters is coterminous with criminal jurisdiction, although much of the material considered in this section deals only with the latter. Indeed, there is an argument that civil jurisdiction should depend on some sort of real or direct link between the state asserting jurisdiction and the substance of the civil proceedings, but there is little convincing authority in international law to support this. In any event, the heads of jurisdiction discussed later may well satisfy the 'real or direct link' test and it should always be remembered that a state's enforcement powers may well be the same irrespective of whether the matter arose originally in criminal or civil proceedings. The better view is, then, that the heads of jurisdiction considered later in the chapter can apply equally to civil and criminal matters, unless the contrary is indicated.

According to the Harvard Research Draft, which was based on an extensive survey of state practice, there are five species of jurisdiction over *persons* (natural or legal) in international law, although the extent to which each is accepted as part of customary international law is a matter of debate. For example, while most states will exercise jurisdiction in accordance with the principles discussed in sections 6.2.1 (territorial), 6.2.2 (nationality) and 6.2.3 (universal), a lesser number will rely on that in 6.2.4 (protective) and fewer still on that in 6.2.5 (passive personality). This makes it difficult, if not impossible, to assess accurately the extent to which the less commonly pleaded principles of jurisdiction form part of general international law, especially as in many cases the exercise of jurisdiction in a real case can be justified on more than one of the five grounds. Of course, if a state is party to a treaty embodying any of these principles, it will be bound to follow the jurisdictional rules laid down therein in its dealings with other state-parties.

As previously noted, it is implicit in the identification of permissible heads of jurisdiction that any state that exercises a jurisdiction not justified by these criteria may be acting unlawfully under international law. In this sense, a state owes an obligation to the state of rightful jurisdiction to refrain from acting in respect of matters outside its cognisance. This is not inconsistent with the principle of unlimited prescriptive jurisdiction discussed earlier because we are now considering the circumstances in which it will be lawful under international law for a state to exercise enforcement jurisdiction in its own territory (through its courts etc.) over a specific individual in respect of a specific matter. As will become apparent, the heads of jurisdiction are such that two or more states may well be entitled to exercise jurisdiction over the same person in respect of the same event. This is known as concurrent jurisdiction and can give rise to protracted jurisdictional disputes and litigation (see e.g. *Questions relating to the Obligation to Prosecute or Extradite (Belgium v Senegal)* 2009). Normally, it will be for the state that actually has custody of the individual to deal with the matter, although it is possible that the individual may be sent to another state having jurisdiction, as under an extradition treaty. This occurs most frequently, for example, when the state having custody is not the state in which the crime or civil wrong took place. However, where there are competing claims of jurisdiction, the question arises whether one state may take enforcement action against an individual, even though the matter has been dealt with, or will be dealt with, by the legal system of another state. If this occurs or is likely, it appears that an individual may be subject to a second punishment – otherwise known as being in 'double jeopardy'. Consequently, there is a presumption against double jeopardy in international law, although this might tempt some states to shield individuals from the more penetrating judicial system of another state by asserting that it had already dealt with the matter. See, for example, the *Questions relating to the Obligation to Prosecute or Extradite Case (Belgium v Senegal)* (2009) where one of the issues was whether Senegal had properly exercised its jurisdiction over an alleged war criminal in a way that precluded Belgium from seeking to exercise jurisdiction. With these difficulties in mind, the following sections discuss the traditional five principles of jurisdiction. They are not mutually exclusive, neither do they command universal acceptance among the international community.

6.2.1 Territorial jurisdiction

This principle is the basis of much of what has been discussed previously. It is, simply, that a state has jurisdiction over all matters arising in its territory. This is so whether the individuals concerned are nationals, friendly aliens or enemy aliens. For example, it was the primary ground for Scotland's assertion of jurisdiction in the *Lockerbie Case*. There is no doubt that this rule accords with international practice and the greater part of the criminal and civil jurisdiction exercised by states is based on this principle – *Banković and Others v Belgium and 16 other Contracting States*, ECHR 2001. Some doubts remain as to when an act can be said to have 'taken place' on the territory of a state, but these have been substantially reduced by the development of the 'objective' and 'subjective' approaches to territorial jurisdiction.

(a) *Objective territoriality*. A state will have jurisdiction over offences that are completed in its territory, even though some element constituting the offence (or civil wrong) took place abroad. In the *Lotus Case*, for example, a collision between *The Lotus*, a French ship, and a Turkish vessel resulted in the death of eight persons on the Turkish vessel. France objected to the exercise of jurisdiction by Turkey over the French Officer of the Watch. However, after noting that the Turkish vessel was to be assimilated to Turkish territory, the PCIJ decided that Turkey was entitled to exercise jurisdiction by virtue of the fact that a constituent element in the offence of manslaughter – death – had occurred on Turkish territory.

(b) *Subjective territoriality*. This is simply the converse of the principle just discussed. Thus, a state has jurisdiction over all offences and matters commencing in its territory, even if some element – or the completion of the offence – takes place in another state. In the UK, the territoriality of jurisdiction is regarded as of fundamental importance, as made clear in *Compania Naviera Vascongado v Steamship 'Cristina'* [1938] AC 485, when the court emphasised the absoluteness of the court's reach within the territory. So, by way of corollary, in *R v Governor of Belmarsh Prison, ex parte Martin* [1995] 2 All ER 548, the Court of Appeal refused in the absence of clear words to construe an Act of Parliament as operating extraterritorially, that is in respect of acts occurring outside the territory, as this was contrary to the normal UK presumption about the reach of its jurisdiction (but see what follows). More importantly, the UK once took the general view that as a matter of common law a crime did not 'occur' within state territory (so did not trigger an exercise of jurisdiction) unless the last event constituting the crime took place within the UK. There was a self-imposed presumption against subjective territoriality, even though international law permitted just such an approach, although it could be waived by clear statutory provision. When transnational crime was little known this was not a serious limitation. However, in the 'global village', the fact that an individual might escape UK jurisdiction because an offence was completed abroad, even if all preliminary steps in the commission of the 'crime' were undertaken within the territory, became more difficult to justify. Consequently, the Law Commission reviewed the matter and its modified proposals resulted in the enactment of the Criminal Justice Act 1993, ss. 1–3. This preserves the principle of territoriality in criminal matters – in the sense that there is no general modification of the principle that jurisdiction does not exist for acts occurring outside the territory – but authorises courts in England and Wales to exercise jurisdiction over certain crimes where a constituent element of the crime occurred within UK territory, whether or not the final element was completed therein. It is a move to subjective territoriality. This is perfectly in conformity with international law and is a pattern already followed in other states. A specific example is provided by s. 59 of the Terrorism Act 2000 that gives jurisdiction over incitement to commit certain terrorist offences, if the incitement occurs within the UK, even if the completed crime occurs outside the territory.

(c) *Extra-territorial jurisdiction.* An exercise of jurisdiction is extra-territorial where it provides that acts taking place abroad may be offences within the local jurisdiction and individuals may be made subject to local courts in respect of those acts. It is an unusual jurisdiction, for often it causes conflict with the exercise of other states' jurisdiction. However, in the UK an extraterritorial jurisdiction may be exercised where such is specifically provided for by Act of Parliament (e.g. Civil Aviation (Amendment) Act 1996) or where justified by the other international principles of jurisdiction considered immediately below. In the UK an example is provided by ss. 62 and 63 of the Terrorism Act 2000, which provide for jurisdiction over certain acts related to terrorism even if they occur abroad, provided they would have been offences if they had been committed within the UK.

(d) *Extra-territorial reach of legislation.* A different, though related, question is whether domestic legislation has an extra-territorial effect, rather than does it create an offence which may be committed abroad. As noted earlier, in *R* v *Governor of Belmarsh Prison, ex parte Martin*, the Court of Appeal for England & Wales noted that generally UK legislation would not have extra-territorial effect (unless specifically provided for) in the sense that it could not criminalise actions taking place abroad (in that case interception of telecommunications). However, it is clear that UK legislation may have an extra-territorial reach in that it can cover actions taking place abroad. So, in *Al Skeini and others* v *Secretary of State for Defence* (2009), the House of Lords decided that the Human Rights Act 1998 did have extra-territorial effect in the sense of regulating the actions of UK public authorities abroad (being UK armed forces in Iraq). The House was clearly influenced by the fact that the legislation was protective in nature and that such extra-territorial reach was entirely consistent with the human rights obligations under the European Convention on Human Rights that the statute was designed to support. While the House emphasised that the question of extra-territoriality must be one of the construction of the legislation in the light of its purpose, this demonstrates a relaxation of the UK's once hostile attitude to extra-territoriality, at least where this is beneficial to individuals.

6.2.2 Nationality jurisdiction

It is clear that international law permits (but does not require) a state to exercise jurisdiction over its nationals, wherever they may be when the offence or civil wrong is committed. A national is entitled to the diplomatic protection of his or her state at all times and, as a corollary, he or she is subject to its civil and criminal jurisdiction. Necessarily, the jurisdiction will not be exercised until the national physically comes within the territory of his or her home state and it may be that the state takes no action because the matter has been dealt with by the state in whose territory the events did occur. However, there is a recognised legal right to exercise jurisdiction on the basis of nationality, and this is now exercised by the UK in respect of offences of a serious nature as provided by the common law or more usually by statute (e.g. murder, some sexual offences). Thus, in the *Trial of Earl Russel* [1901] AC 446, the defendant, a UK national, was convicted of bigamy even though the second act of marriage took place outside the UK. This case is also an early example (and at that time rare) of the subjective territorial principle in operation in the UK.

6.2.3 Universal jurisdiction

Under international law, there are certain crimes that are regarded as so destructive of the international order that any state may exercise jurisdiction in respect of them. This is a jurisdiction that appears to exist irrespective of where the act constituting the crime takes place and the nationality of the person committing it. It is a jurisdiction that depends solely on the nature of the offence that the individual is alleged to have committed. For example, universal jurisdiction exists in respect of the crime of piracy, that being a crime against all mankind and in respect of which an individual places himself beyond the protection of any state (in *Re Piracy Jure Gentium* [1934] AC 586). Similarly, in *A-G of Israel* v *Eichmann* (1961) 36 ILR 5, the District Court of Jerusalem had to decide whether Israel had any jurisdiction in respect of the alleged atrocities committed by the defendant during the Second World War. In its opinion, 'the abhorrent crimes are not crimes under Israel law alone. These crimes … are grave offences against the law of nations itself (*delicta jurius gentium*). The jurisdiction to try crimes under international law is universal.' In *Demjanjuk* v *Petrovsk* (1985) 776 F.2d. 571, a US court applied this principle in a hearing to decide whether to extradite the accused to Israel and decided that it was irrelevant that Israel did not exist at the time of the offences, because jurisdiction was not dependent on any link with the prosecuting state, although in practice the individual usually would be extradited to the state most affected by his acts. The precise reach of universal jurisdiction has not yet been considered in detail by the International Court of Justice. In the *Case Concerning the Arrest Warrant of 11 September 2000 (Congo* v *Belgium)* 2002 ICJ Rep, Belgium had issued a warrant for the arrest of the Congolese Foreign Minister for grave violations of human rights and based the exercise of this jurisdiction on the universal principle. In the end, the decision on the merits turned on whether the Foreign Minister could claim immunity (he could, on which see Chapter 7) and a majority of the Court followed the parties' lead and assumed for the purposes of the case that universal jurisdiction was established as a principle of customary law. In fact, however, as the Joint Separate Opinion of Judges Higgins, Kooijmans and Buergenthal illustrates, although many states have adopted a version of the universal principle in national legislation or judicially, this has invariably been in those situations where there is *also* a tie of some kind to the state exercising the jurisdiction: for example, that the individual was a national or the event occurred on state territory or peculiarly affected the state's interests. Thus, there were few examples from state practice of 'pure' universal jurisdiction where a state was prepared to act when there was no connection at all to itself other than that it had physical custody of the individual. These judges conclude, therefore, that although there are international treaties where a pure universal jurisdiction is provided for, the absence of examples of enabling national law meant that international law is neutral on the existence of the purest form of universal jurisdiction, or at best that it is a developing principle rather than a developed one. This is, of course, a highly positivist approach to international law and the three judges do not mean to deny the validity of the universal principle per se: rather they seek to clarify its precise ambit and are not opposed to the exercise of universal jurisdiction if such can be said to exist according to the normal rules for the creation of rules of international law.

As noted, the essence of universal jurisdiction (whatever its precise scope) is that any state may exercise jurisdiction over those offences that are so serious as to qualify as crimes under international law. These include genocide, torture, war crimes, piracy, crimes against humanity and, less certainly, hostage-taking and hijacking. In *DPP* v *Doot* [1973] AC 807, Lord Wilberforce was clearly of the opinion that drugs-related offences were crimes of universal jurisdiction and in *US* v *Yunis* (1988) 681 F.Supp 896, the US court indicated that both air piracy and hostage-taking were susceptible to the jurisdiction of any state, even if the act was committed by a non-national (an 'alien') abroad. By way of contrast, the United States Court of Appeals in *United States v Yousef* (2003) were of the view that terrorism was not a crime susceptible to universal jurisdiction. Of course, states can provide by treaty that the jurisdiction to try offenders should not be limited to the territorial or nationality principles, and this is reflected in the treaties considered later dealing with aircraft-related offences.

The existence of crimes of universal jurisdiction is, of course, inextricably linked with the historical absence of *international* judicial bodies having jurisdiction over individuals. The Nuremberg and Tokyo War Crimes tribunals (post-Second World War) were early examples of such bodies, but clearly these were unique and limited to the alleged misdeeds of nationals of those states that had lost the war. Their lasting importance lies in the impetus they gave to the development of general principles of humanitarian law. More recently, the Security Council established the Yugoslavian and Rwandan War Crimes Tribunals (SC Res. 827 (1993) and SC Res 955 (1994) respectively) and a similar court exists for Sierra Leone (established by the UN and Sierra Leone in 2002). These have tried their first cases, and their value should not be underestimated. For example judgments of the Yugoslav Tribunal are relied on in the *Case Concerning the Application of the Convention on the Prevention and Punishment of the Crime of Genocide (Bosnia and Herzegovina v Serbia & Montenegro)* (ICJ 2007). Of more widespread importance, however, is the establishment in 2002 of the International Criminal Court (ICC) that has a general jurisdiction over individuals in respect of 'the most serious crimes of concern to the international community' (ICC Statute Art. 5), being genocide, crimes against humanity, war crimes and the crime of aggression. At 1 September 2012 there were 121 state-parties and currently the Court has indicted twenty-nine people, one of whom has been convicted and sentenced. Of course, it remains to be seen how active the Court will be in the exercise of its jurisdiction as it is clear that it is not intended to supplant a state's existing rights of jurisdiction over persons as currently provided by international law (ICC Statute Art. 17). Indeed, it is arguable that the existence of a general and effective international jurisdiction over persons exercised by the ICC will precipitate the collapse of the principle of universal jurisdiction, but at present this is merely speculative. Of course, the ICC as an international tribunal is likely to be free of the taint of bias and may be able to escape the bonds of political expediency that can so easily accompany the exercise of jurisdiction by local courts. This more than anything else may encourage states voluntarily to surrender jurisdiction to the ICC as it establishes its reputation as an effective and impartial judicial body.

6.2.4 Protective jurisdiction and the 'effects' doctrine

The essence of jurisdiction based on the protective principle is that a state may assert its authority over matters which produce a deleterious effect on 'the state', irrespective of where those acts take place or by whom they are committed. National laws based on this principle are said to operate extraterritorially – that is, in respect of acts that take place wholly outside state territory. Usually they also refer to activities of non-nationals. The difference between this head of jurisdiction and the universal principle is that the latter exists only in respect of certain offences of an international character, whereas the former subsumes any matter harmful to the particular state. For example, in *DPP v Joyce*, one ground of jurisdiction was that the acts of the defendant while he was in Germany were harmful per se to the UK. Again, the protective principle was cited as additional justification for Israel's assumption of jurisdiction in the *Eichmann* Case, although it is difficult to see how Israel's vital interests were harmed at the time of the offences given that the State of Israel did not then exist. A better example is the UK case of *R v Sansom* [1991] 2 All ER 145, where jurisdiction was asserted on the basis of an extraterritorial conspiracy which, if carried out, would produce effects within the UK and a similar view was taken in *R v Abu Hamza* [2006] EWCA Crim 2918 based on the Offences Against the Person Act 1861. It should be noted, however, that these cases (and the similar *Liangsiriprasert v US* [1990] 2 All ER 866) may also be justified on the territorial principle as it applies to inchoate offences because it often happens that one element of the crime over which jurisdiction is asserted (e.g. a conspiracy) will take place on the territory of the 'target' state.

The Harvard Research team (see the Harvard Research Draft (1935) noted earlier in section 6.2) established that examples of jurisdiction based on the protective principle were to be found in the national laws of most states (see e.g. in the USA the Anti-Apartheid Act 1988, and in the UK the Broadcasting Act 1990). This suggests that the protective principle can be regarded as an accepted head of jurisdiction under customary international law. Indeed, it serves a useful purpose in that it permits a state to combat extra-territorial acts, done by aliens, which have an adverse effect on its welfare or security. However, over the last two decades, some states have enacted legislation designed to give themselves jurisdiction over *any* matters which produce an effect in their territory. This is the so-called 'effects' doctrine, and it goes beyond the protective principle in that what is 'protected' by legislation is not limited to some public or national interest. The most widely cited example of this jurisdiction – which has been resisted by many states, including those of the European Union – is the anti-trust legislation of the USA. Under this legislation, a foreign company having partial operations in the USA may become liable to heavy penalties under US law for engaging in anti-competitive practices, even if the actual activities complained of take place outside US territory (see e.g. *Laker* v *Sabena Airways* (1984) 731 F.2d. 909). It is obvious that any increase in the volume of national law having extraterritorial effect in this way is likely to lead to disputes with those states whose nationals are subject to such laws. The difficulty is particularly acute if the acts over which jurisdiction is claimed are lawful under the law of the state where they took place. For example, the US anti-trust legislation could penalise UK companies trading lawfully in the UK but who have some minimal operating activity in the USA. It is because of the long reach of such jurisdiction that many states like the UK believe extensive extraterritorial jurisdiction to be contrary to international law and some have enacted 'blocking legislation' to meet the threat. The UK has passed the Protection of Trading Interests Act 1980, whereby the relevant Secretary of State may prohibit compliance with US anti-trust decisions by legal persons of UK nationality. Similar measures have been adopted by other EU states. These difficulties, and the tensions they produce between trading partners, mean that negotiation and self-restraint among states will be necessary if jurisdictional disputes of this nature are to be minimised. Towards this end, it was hoped that US practice would accept that jurisdiction should be asserted under the 'effects doctrine' only if the main purpose of an anti-competition agreement between companies was to interfere with US commerce and such interference actually occurred (*Restatement, Third, Foreign Relations Law of the United States*, 1987). Necessarily, this calls for a measure of self-restraint by local courts when faced with an opportunity for the exercise of an extraterritorial jurisdiction. Unfortunately, the US Supreme Court decision in *Hartford Fire Insurance Co.* v *California US Supreme Court* 113 S. Ct 2891 (1993) illustrates just how tempting it is for local courts to assert an effects jurisdiction. In this case, the defendants (UK insurers) did not deny that their activities had had an 'effect' within the USA, but rather claimed that the US court should decline jurisdiction because their acts were lawful in the state where they took place (the UK) and, in any event, any balance of the competing interests of US justice and international comity clearly favoured declining jurisdiction. By a 5:4 majority, the Supreme Court found in favour of exercising jurisdiction, apparently on the ground that no real conflict existed with UK legislation (because UK law did not compel the UK companies to act in the way they did) and so no balancing between the interests of justice and the interests of international comity needed to be undertaken. This is a remarkable decision, at least on the finding of lack of conflict between the two jurisdictions, and it would have been more defensible had the US court accepted the existence of a conflict and the need to balance competing interests, but simply balanced those interests in favour of the USA, as explained in the US case *Timberlane Lumber Co.* v *Bank of America*.

The USA is particularly active in creating grounds of extraterritorial jurisdiction, and there is no doubt that this has been used to further the economic and foreign policy goals of the USA as well as for genuinely 'protective' reasons. The USA has clashed repeatedly with Europe over the extraterritorial application of US anti-trust (anti-competition laws), although an accommodation has been reached with the conclusion of the US/EU Agreement on the Application of Competition Laws ([1995] OJ 95/45). Even more controversial was the adoption by the USA of the Cuban Liberty and Democratic Solidarity Act 1996 (LIBERTAD or Helms-Burton Act) and the Iran-Libya Sanctions Act 1996 (D'Amato Act). Essentially, these imposed penalties on individuals or companies investing in the embargoed countries, irrespective of the nationality of the 'offender' or their place of business activity. Clearly, they were designed more to further US foreign policy than to protect the USA per se and they aroused considerable opposition in the international community. Many states adopted legislative measures blocking the effect of this far-reaching legislation (e.g. Canada, Mexico, the EU). To some extent the disagreement between the USA and the EU has been nullified by the willingness of the US government to suspend parts of the Helms-Burton Act and to be sensible of international concerns in its application of D'Amato. More importantly, the USA and EU have reached an agreement (see Understanding with Respect to Disciplines for the Strengthening of Investment Protection 1998) on the application of these Acts that has done much to limit their practical impact. Nevertheless, concerns remain that the USA *believed* it appropriate (and lawful?) to enact these measures that could hardly be justified under current international principles of jurisdiction.

Of course, it is important that a state should be able to protect itself adequately, but it is equally important not to create too many areas of concurrent jurisdiction. For example, both the protective and the effects doctrines are liable to cause overlap with the territorial principle, leading to a dispute between the state that has custody of the person and the state that wants custody. The existence of cross-border terrorism, funded out of many states and paying no heed to international jurisdictional boundaries, is a prime example of why states believe that more extra-territorial legislation is needed and also a prime example of how this can generate jurisdictional conflicts. The long-running dispute between the USA and many other countries concerning the detainees at Guantanamo Bay is also a jurisdictional dispute as well as one concerning fundamental human rights. One solution would be to adopt the proposal of the Harvard Research Draft that in cases where an act is lawful under the state where it takes place, but unlawful by the law of another state claiming jurisdiction, the latter state should not be permitted to prosecute aliens, only nationals (Draft Art. 14). At least this would give the state some extraterritorial competence and does not inhibit the assumption of jurisdiction where the act is *not* lawful in the state where it takes place. As yet, however, there is no agreement whether this proposal represents customary law, although it is likely to be regarded as too restrictive in today's interdependent world. As the international community becomes more integrated, with activities in one state quite capable of seriously affecting another, the greater will be the temptation for a state to turn to protective jurisdiction of this type to safeguard its own interests. With this in mind, the USA has issued guidelines to companies engaging in international operations on when it will seek enforcement of extra-territorial jurisdiction and has passed the International Anti-Trust Enforcement Assistance Act 1994 to facilitate the location of evidence of anti-trust activities on a reciprocal basis with other states (see 34 ILM 494 and 1081, 1995). Lastly, one word of caution. We must be aware that if it is left to the state itself to decide what 'vital interests' may be protected by extraterritorial legislation, there is the danger that jurisdiction may be asserted over acts for purely political or partisan reasons that have nothing to do with ensuring the political, social or economic safety of the state.

6.2.5 Passive personality jurisdiction

Like jurisdiction based on nationality, the passive personality principle focuses on the identity of the person involved in a criminal offence. However, whereas the former is concerned with the identity of the perpetrator of a crime, the latter is concerned with the identity of the victim. Under passive personality, a state would have jurisdiction over all crimes where the victim was a national, irrespective of the place where the crime was committed or the nationality of the offender. In the *Lotus Case*, for example, Turkey claimed jurisdiction on the additional ground that the persons killed were Turkish nationals. The principle is a further extension of the idea that every national is entitled to the diplomatic protection of his own state. It will be apparent that this principle is primarily a ground for criminal jurisdiction, although there is no necessary reason why it could not be applied to civil matters where there could be said to be a 'victim', such as torts or breach of trust.

In the *Lotus Case*, the Court did not find it necessary to consider the validity of the passive personality principle in international law (nor in *Questions relating to the Obligation to Prosecute or Extradite (Belgium* v *Senegal)* 2009), although it was applied by a Mexican court in respect of a matter occurring wholly within the USA in the *Cutting Case* (1887) (Moore, Digest of International Law vol. ii 228). Similarly, it was cited as an additional ground for jurisdiction in *US* v *Yunis*, where the defendant was tried for offences connected with the hijacking of a TWA aircraft in Lebanon and seems to have been applied in *US* v *Neil* (2002) in respect of sexual offences against an American national. This was despite previous US reluctance to utilise this method of gaining jurisdiction. However, several objections can be raised to this as a ground of jurisdiction and there is some doubt whether it is part of customary international law. First, the occasions on which a state would wish to exercise jurisdiction under this head will be limited. The great majority of criminal matters will necessarily fall within the jurisdiction of at least one other state under one of the four principles previously discussed. To decline passive personality jurisdiction would not produce a significant 'gap' in the system of international law enforcement and rarely will it be necessary to assert jurisdiction beyond those heads of jurisdiction that exist already. Second, the practical effect of the passive personality rule is that a national carries the protection of the law of his home state with him wherever he goes. This means that all those persons who came into contact with him are themselves subject to the laws of his state of nationality. Not only is this an unnecessary extension of state jurisdiction, it may cause considerable practical problems – for example, if the act which is an offence under the law of the state of nationality of the victim is not an offence under the law of the state where it took place or the law of the state of nationality of the perpetrator.

It is doubtful then, whether the passive personality principle is needed in order to maintain a comprehensive system of jurisdiction under international law. The territorial principle, in both forms, the nationality principle and the universal principle are firmly established and the protective and effects principles are increasing in importance. There is no doubt, however, that passive personality has been gaining ground as a potential head of jurisdiction in recent years, predominantly in response to perceived failures by states holding alleged war criminals to bring them to trial. In such cases, the states of nationality of the alleged victims (e.g. Belgium, France) are beginning to assert their right to exercise jurisdiction.

6.2.6 The exercise of jurisdiction over persons apprehended in violation of international law

The previous sections analyse those circumstances in which a state may exercise an enforcement jurisdiction over persons within its custody. These are especially important given that a state may not exercise such a jurisdiction in the territory of another state without its consent. However, difficult questions arise when the presence of the defendant in the state seeking to exercise jurisdiction is brought about in a manner which itself violates international law. The most obvious example of this is provided by the *Eichmann Case*, where Eichmann's presence in Israel was achieved only by his forceful abduction from Argentina, in violation of Argentina's territorial integrity. Israel apologised, but its courts did not decline to exercise jurisdiction because of this violation of international law.

In the UK, courts have taken a rather different approach to the exercise of jurisdiction over persons brought into the UK by unlawful or unconventional means. In *R v Horseferry Magistrates' Court, ex parte Bennett* [1993] 3 All ER 138, Bennett alleged that he had been forcibly removed to the UK by South African police, at the instigation of UK police, in a manner which sidestepped the Extradition Act 1989 and which appeared to amount to a violation of international law. The House of Lords was clear that when a defendant's presence before the court had been procured by abuse of process, by executive lawlessness in another state or in violation of international law, the UK court should decline to exercise such jurisdiction as it might otherwise have. This mirrors the practice of a number of other countries, including South Africa itself (*State v Ebrahim* (1991) 31 ILM 888) and upholds the integrity of international legal standards and principles of jurisdiction. It is unfortunate, therefore, that the UK courts have drifted somewhat from this position. In *R v Staines Magistrates' Court, ex parte Westfallen* [1998] 4 All ER 2101, the court held that the *Bennett* principle applied (jurisdiction to be declined) only if the UK authorities had participated in, or procured or connived at the violation of international law that had led to the defendant's presence within the territory. This seems unwarranted, for it is debatable whether jurisdiction should be declined only when the national authorities were in some way 'responsible for' or 'involved in' the breach of international law. Of course, the line is a fine one. In *R v Mullen* [1999] 3 All ER 777, the Court of Appeal found that Mullen's conviction was unsafe – some ten years after his trial and imprisonment – because of the action of UK authorities in procuring his return from Zimbabwe on terrorist charges in violation of a number of principles of international law. Nevertheless, it remains this author's view that a UK court should decline jurisdiction in all cases where international law has been violated if such violation is the reason why the defendant is before the court irrespective of the degree of involvement of UK authorities in that violation. However, this reluctance to give international law the full respect it deserves is but nothing compared to US practice (*United States v Alvarez-Machain* (1992) 31 ILM 902). In *Alvarez-Machain*, the US Supreme Court held that the abduction of the defendant from Mexico in violation of international law did not require a US court to decline to exercise jurisdiction over him, apparently because it was the Executive that was concerned with breaches of international law by the USA, not its courts. This US decision is somewhat breathtaking, especially as it postulates a very narrow view of the functions of a court of law and seems to dismiss the relevance of international law despite the provisions of the US Constitution. It is submitted that the UK/South Africa position is the more principled approach (without the *Westfallen* gloss), and ultimately will prove to be the more pragmatic given the very serious damage to foreign relations that could be generated by the US court's view of the matter. Indeed, UK courts have been prepared to extend their application of this principle. So in *R v Charrington* (unreported), the unlawful interference by the UK authorities with a foreign vessel on the high seas was sufficient to prevent the trial of those arrested on drugs charges.

6.3 The acquisition of sovereignty over territory

In this section we are concerned with another aspect of jurisdiction, namely the acquisition of sovereignty over territory in international law. Sovereignty is the most extensive form of jurisdiction under international law. In general terms, it denotes full and unchallengeable power over territory and all the persons from time to time therein. It may be subject to certain limitations established under international law, such as guarantees of human rights and diplomatic privileges, but apart from exceptions that are positively established, a state's sovereignty over its territory is absolute and complete. In the following pages we shall consider how a state acquires sovereignty over territory. Or, to put the question slightly differently, how does a state acquire lawful title to territory in international law?

A traditional exposition of this area of international law emphasises that there are several recognised methods or 'modes' by which a state may gain title to a piece of territory. These are considered later. However, as Professor Brownlie has pointed out (*Principles of International Law*, 4th edn. (1998), p. 129), the identification of these various modes should not be used as a substitute for analysis. Of course, they retain validity as a working tool (so, for example, they cannot be displaced by looser concepts such as 'historical consolidation of title' which have no foundation in international law (*Cameroon v Nigeria* 2002)), and they offer a convenient method of exposition, but it is more important to concentrate on the precise reasons why, in any given case, a state can be said to have acquired sovereignty over territory, rather than fitting the claim into a preconceived category. The categories should not be regarded as mutually exclusive or as completely explaining the nature of acquisition of sovereignty over territory. If we keep this in mind, it may be possible to discover whether there is a central thread running through these cases or whether there really are several distinct grounds for the acquisition of sovereignty in international law.

6.3.1 The exercise of effective control – occupation and prescription

The control of territory and the peaceful and effective exercise of the functions of a state therein is the primary means of acquiring title to territory in international law. This can be subdivided into two classes. When the exercise of authority takes place in a territory that does not belong to any other state (*terra nullius*), we may say that title is based on effective 'occupation'. When the exercise of authority takes place in a territory that formally belongs to another state, we may say that title is based on 'prescription'. However, the difference between these two concepts is only one of degree and the essential element of both is the exercise of state functions, which many of the cases refer to loosely as *effectivités*. In fact, whether any given case is classed as one of 'occupation' or 'prescription' may well depend on whether we recognise that some other state did indeed have a valid title at an earlier time, and this can be a matter of judgment rather than fact. In both cases, then, the crucial point is whether there has been effective exercise of state functions without objection. In the *Kasikili/Sedudu Island Case (Botswana v Namibia)*, Namibia and Botswana agreed that the four conditions for a successful claim of prescription were that: (i) the possession had to be exercised in the character of a sovereign; (ii) the possession must be peaceful and uninterrupted; (iii) the possession must be public; and (iv) the possession must endure for a length of time. Although the Court itself refrained from commenting on the role of prescription in international law, and avoided approving this formula, these 'conditions' do indicate what is required for a successful prescriptive claim. Importantly, as noted, they illustrate that 'effective control' underlies prescription in much the same way as occupation but with the added complication of an existing sovereign who must be displaced or acquiescence (*Cameroon v Nigeria* 2002, and see the judgment in the *Sovereignty over Pedra Branca/ Pulau Batu Puteh, Middle Rocks and South Ledge (Malaysia/Singapore) Case* 2008). This should be borne in mind during the following discussion.

The leading case on effective control is the *Island of Palmas Case* (1928) 2 RIAA 829. By the Treaty of Paris 1898, Spain had ceded the Philippines to the USA and the latter believed the Island of Palmas to be included. However, in 1906, the USA discovered that The Netherlands had established a presence on the Island. When the dispute was submitted to arbitration, the USA based its title on cession from Spain under the treaty, whereas The Netherlands contended that it was entitled to sovereignty by virtue of a peaceful and continuous display of state power in the territory. The arbitrator, Judge Huber, found in favour of The Netherlands and his judgment is regarded as a classic statement on the nature of sovereignty and the acquisition of territory. In his view, sovereignty implied independence and this meant the power to exercise the functions of a state within a defined area of territory. Therefore, for the acquisition of territory, the crucial issue was whether a state actually displayed sovereignty within that territory at the 'critical date'. If it did, this was sufficient to defeat other claims to title. In his words, 'the continuous and peaceful display of territorial sovereignty ... is as good as title'.

6.3.1.1 Apparent display of sovereignty

This requirement is, perhaps, at the heart of acquisition of sovereignty in international law. It means, quite simply, that the state claiming title must have exercised the powers of a state within the territory. The state may be required to show that it has set up an effective local administration, that it can control and protect the population (if any) or that it has established a system of national law. The state claiming title must establish that it has behaved *as a state* with respect to the territory although as the *Land, Island and Maritime Frontier Dispute Case (El Salvador v Honduras) (Merits)* 1992 ICJ Rep 35 makes clear, not every state function will be relevant for this purpose. Similarly, in the *Case Concerning Sovereignty over Pulau Ligitan and Pulau Sipadan (Indonesia v Malaysia)* 2002 ICJ Rep, the Court was quick to point out that the relevant acts had to be specifically referable to the territory in question (Indonesia's were only generally applicable to a wide area), to have been done with an intention and will to act as sovereign and to be regulatory, legislative, administrative or judicial in character (Malaysia's were on both counts). Clearly then, some activities will be too trivial or too unconnected with 'sovereignty' to count as acts demonstrating control and independence. In *Botswana v Namibia*, for example, Namibia was unable to claim title by prescription as the acts of occupation were not 'functions of state authority' but intermittent acts related to cultivation and agriculture.

It is also clear that the extent or degree of display of state power required may vary according to the type of territory in question. It is a question of fact in each case. Thus, in the *Clipperton Island Arbitration (France v Mexico)* (1932) 26 AJIL 390, the dispute was over a small uninhabited coral reef. The arbitrator found French title established, even though the acts of effective occupation were limited to minimal acts of the French Navy and subsequent proclamations of sovereignty in various public journals. These acts, when coupled with an intention to exercise sovereignty, were sufficient in respect of this territory. Again, in the *Eastern Greenland Case (Denmark v Norway)* (1933) PCIJ Ser. A/B No. 53, Denmark's claim to sovereignty was upheld even though the display of state sovereignty consisted mainly of the granting of trading concessions over the territory and minimal acts of administration. The Court realised that 'in many cases [a] tribunal has been satisfied with very little in the way of the actual exercise of sovereign rights'. The extent of the display of state powers is relative to the nature of the territory in dispute and so in the *Sovereignty over Pedra Branca/Pulau Batu Puteh, Middle Rocks and South Ledge (Malaysia/Singapore)* (2008), the ICJ recognised that small islands having little or no commercial or economic importance may require very little by way of sovereign acts to establish title, provided that the acts were of sufficient sovereign quality *and* done with a will and intention to exercise sovereignty and this was so even though another state might once have been able to claim title under some formal document or agreement. Likewise, the absence of protest by other states would be significant.

It is clear, however, that the ability and will to behave like a state in respect of a territory may not always be enough, especially if another state might be able to claim sovereignty through a paramount 'paper' title. For example, in the *Land Island and Maritime Frontier Dispute Case (El Salvador v Honduras)* 1992 ICJ Rep 92, an ICJ Chamber made it clear that display of sovereignty (i.e. 'effectiveness') would not necessarily be decisive if another state could establish title to territory by some paramount legal title. Thus, effectiveness would not necessarily defeat a claim based on *uti possidetis* (on which see later), although it might act to modify a territorial boundary established in this way, provided that the 'fundamental principle of the stability of boundaries' was not thereby compromised (*Case Concerning the Territorial Dispute (Libya v Chad)* 1994 ICJ Rep 6). So, in the *Frontier Dispute Case (Benin v Niger)* (2005), a Chamber of the ICJ re-affirmed the dicta from *Frontier Dispute (Burkina Faso/Republic of Mali)* that, 'pre-eminence [is] accorded to legal title over effective possession as a basis of sovereignty'. By way of contrast, however, and as noted earlier, in the *Sovereignty over Pedra Branca/Pulau Batu Puteh, Middle Rocks and South Ledge (Malaysia/Singapore)* (2008), the prior title of Malaysia to one of the islands through *uti possedetis* was displaced by the later effective control of Singapore and this had much to do with the remote nature of the territory and (perhaps crucially) that Malaysia appears to have acquiescence in Singapore's assumption of sovereignty (so called *à titre de souverain*). It is a balancing act where the principle of effectiveness, which recognises the reality of international life and politics, competes with ideas of sovereignty based on legal right, legal principle, consensus and self-determination.

6.3.1.2 Intention to acquire sovereignty

In the *Clipperton Island Arbitration*, the *Eastern Greenland Case* and the *Pulau Ligitan and Pulau Sipadan Case* the Court emphasised that the actual display of sovereignty must be accompanied by an *animus* or intention and will to act as sovereign. In many cases, this can be presumed from the simple fact that the state is exercising such authority in the territory. In territories such as Clipperton Island, Eastern Greenland and the Islands around Malaysia, Indonesia and Singapore where extensive display of authority is not possible, it seems that the state must make clear its sovereign intentions by other means – hence the relevance of the publication of notices of sovereignty in various journals in the *Clipperton Island Arbitration*, the declared application of national laws to Greenland by Denmark in the *Eastern Greenland Case*, the environmental protection and navigation measures (e.g. provision of lighthouses) taken by Malaysia in the *Pulau Case* and the regulation of navigation and shipping by Singapore in the *Pedra Branca/Pulau Batu Puteh Case*.

6.3.1.3 Continuous display and the 'critical date'

In the *Island of Palmas Case*, Judge Huber indicated that title to territory could not be established by a 'once and for all' display of sovereignty. It had to be 'continuous'. This seems to encompass two ideas. First, the display of sovereignty must be ongoing, and rarely can it consist solely of a single act. In the *Clipperton Island Case*, for example, an important element was France's continued affirmation of sovereignty in the face of claims by Mexico, although once again the degree of continuity required may vary with each case. Secondly, the display of sovereignty must exist up to 'the critical date'. The critical date is the date at which the question of sovereignty is to be assessed. All matters arising after that date cannot be taken into account in deciding title to territory, for it is the circumstances existing at that date that are important. It is the date at which 'time stops running' and when the relative strength of the parties' claims are to be assessed. In the *Island of Palmas Case*, the critical date was the date of the Treaty between Spain and the USA (1898), for this was the time at which the latter's claim first arose, and in the *Pulau Ligitan and Pulau Sipadan Case* it was 1969, the date at which Indonesia and Malaysia asserted competing claims to the islands. Thus, the Court has observed that 'it cannot take into consideration acts having taken place after the date on which the dispute between the Parties crystallized unless such acts are a normal continuation of prior acts and are not undertaken for the purpose of improving the legal position of the Party which relies on them' (see the Arbitral Award in the *Palena* case, 38 ILR, pp. 79–80). The Court will, therefore, primarily, analyse the '*effectivités* which date from the period before 1969, the year in which the Parties asserted conflicting claims to Ligitan and Sipadan' 2002 ICJ Rep para. 135. Similarly, in *Benin v Niger*, the Chamber recognised that documents and maps produced after the critical date (the moment of independence from France) could not lead to any modification of the 'photograph of the territory' on which the delimitation was to be based unless this was the express wish of the parties. However, the date of origin of the dispute will not be 'critical' in every circumstance, for it is clear that the critical date depends on the facts of each case. For example, in the *Minquiers and Ecrehos Case (France v UK)* 1953 ICJ Rep 47, the critical date was held to be the date at which the dispute was submitted to the Court, in the *Taba Area Boundary Arbitration (Egypt v Israel)* (1988) 27 ILM 1421, it was held to be the date of entry into force of the British Mandate over Palestine, rather than, say, the date of the Israel/Egypt Peace Treaty, in *El Salvador v Honduras* it was the date of independence of the former Spanish colonies of Latin America (1821) and in the *Case Concerning the Frontier Dispute (Benin/Niger)* 2005 it was their dates of respective independence.

In essence, the critical date is the date at which the dispute between the two parties becomes crystallised and after which no acts can be taken into account in determining sovereignty. It performs a useful purpose in that it provides a definite point at which sovereignty is to be finally determined. It would be absurd if a 'continuous' display had to be established ad infinitum. However, while its necessity is not in doubt, it is clear that the 'critical date' is a judicial invention that depends heavily on the Court's assessment of the facts of each case. This lack of objectivity in the choice of the critical date is a cause for some concern, for the choice of the Court may, in effect, determine the destination of title to the territory. For example, while the date of the Treaty of Paris was an obvious cut-off point in the *Island of Palmas Case*, in the *Minquiers Case* the Court could have chosen either of the dates proposed by France and the UK, each of which enhanced their own claim. Similarly, in some cases, the choice of the critical date will determine whether we have a case of 'occupation' or 'prescription'. If the date is set when the territory is *terra nullius*, it is occupation, but if it is set after another state has made some claim to the land, it may be one of prescription. In *El Salvador v Honduras* (1992), the ICJ Chamber recognised that even though the facts of the dispute established a clear critical date (e.g. independence from Spain in 1821), which was accepted by both parties, that date was not absolute for all aspects of the case. It could be altered by various factors, such as a previous binding judicial award, a treaty or even less concrete factors such as recognition and acquiescence. The point is then, that the critical date serves a useful practical purpose in that it provides a reference point for the Court and prevents continual challenges to state sovereignty. On the other hand, it should not be thought that the actual date chosen can always be logically deduced from the facts of a case and even if it is, it may not hold good for all aspects of that case.

6.3.1.4 Peaceful display

The exercise of state power over a territory must be peaceful in the sense that it is not challenged by other states. In terms of territory that is formally *terra nullius* (as in the *Clipperton Island Arbitration*), this means simply that the display of state functions must proceed in uninterrupted fashion. Moreover, in the case of 'occupation', a display of state sovereignty does not lose its peaceful character merely because some other state verbally objects to the claim of sovereignty. There must be some acts by the objecting state, of an extensive nature, before title based on 'occupation' loses its peaceful character.

In contrast, with cases of prescription (i.e. where another state might be thought to have a pre-existing title), the requirement of a peaceful display of sovereignty is much more important. As we have seen, prescription means the acquisition of sovereignty by one state over territory that formally belongs to another. This is achieved by the effective display of state functions within the territory. Therefore, objections by the state ousted from the territory are an important factor and may well prevent the 'new' state from gaining title by prescription, a fact accepted by both states in *Botswana* v *Namibia*.

There is, however, some debate as to what form this objection should take – see e.g. the *Case Concerning the Land and Maritime Boundary Between Cameroon and Nigeria: (Cameroon* v *Nigeria, Equatorial Guinea Intervening)* (2002). Some jurists argue that unless the ousted state refers the matter to a judicial tribunal within a reasonable period of time, the actual exercise of state powers by another state in the territory cannot subsequently be challenged. The opposing view is that the form of objection is irrelevant, so long as the dispossessed state makes clear its opposition to the acquisition of title by someone else. So, objection may consist of diplomatic protests, statements in international organisations, the enactment of national legislation applying to the territory or referral to a tribunal. This is probably the better view and it is supported by the *Chamizal Arbitration (US* v *Mexico)* (1911) 5 AJIL 785, where the arbitrator relied partly on the fact that US possession of the disputed territory had 'been constantly challenged and questioned by the Republic of Mexico, through its accredited diplomatic agents'. Moreover, in the light of the fact that international law has no compulsory judicial machinery for the settlement of disputes, it is unrealistic to insist on referral to a judicial body as evidencing the necessary opposition to a prescriptive claim. If the essence of the matter is that prescriptive title cannot be established in the face of opposition by another state, the precise form of the opposition should be immaterial. For example, should the UK's claim to the Falkland Islands, which rests partly on prescription, be upheld simply because the matter has not been referred to an international tribunal, even though Argentina has on many occasions formally objected to the exercise of UK sovereignty?

However, whatever the correct approach here, the *Cameroon* v *Nigeria* case illustrates that the degree of effective occupation necessary to oust an existing sovereign must be high and that it is unlikely to be effective to 'transfer' sovereignty unless the existing sovereign acquiesces in some way. So, in this case, Nigeria was unable to demonstrate acquiescence by Cameroon in the assumption of title by Nigeria, even assuming sufficient acts of effective occupation by the latter. In consequence, Cameroon's historic title to part of the disputed area based on a 1913 treaty between the former colonial powers was held good. By way of contrast, the lack of objection or acquiescence by the former title holder was vital in establishing title in *Sovereignty over Pedra Branca/Pulau Batu Puteh, Middle Rocks and South Ledge (Malaysia/Singapore) Case* (2008)). Here, Malaysia's lack of objection to Singapore's assumption of sovereignty over one of the islands that had previously been very clearly within the sovereignty of Malaysia meant was determinative of the matter in Singapore's favour. It is a relatively rare example of title being so clearly established and then lost.

6.3.1.5 Intertemporal law

In the *Island of Palmas Case*, Judge Huber discussed the doctrine of intertemporal law. Essentially, all this means is that the law to be applied to a given dispute is the law in existence at the time the dispute is to be settled – the critical date. So, if the critical date is 1898, the dispute is to be decided by reference to the rules of international law existing at that date. When it comes to solving real disputes, this is an important concept. As we shall see, the acquisition of title to territory by the use of force became illegal in 1945 but may have been perfectly acceptable before then. Under the doctrine of intertemporal law, title to territory acquired by conquest prior to 1945 might not now be open to challenge even though it would be illegal under current international law.

Unfortunately, in the *Island of Palmas Case*, Judge Huber placed a gloss on the doctrine of intertemporal law that does not seem workable in practice or acceptable in theory. In his view, a distinction has to be drawn between the creation of a right and the maintenance of that right. Consequently, title to territory may be validly created under the rules of international law existing at the critical date (e.g. in 1898), but whether that title can be maintained has to be assessed according to the rules of international law as they now exist (e.g. in 2004). In other words, as international law changes, each state's title to its territory must be reassessed according to those changes. If this is what Judge Huber did mean, it is clearly unacceptable. The effect of such a doctrine would be to encourage spurious claims and to foster widespread uncertainty as to title to territory. This would be especially acute in those areas where territory had been validly acquired but the display of state functions was not extensive or frequent. It is at odds with the judicial policy, expressed in *Libya* v *Chad*, of preserving the territorial status quo in all but the most clear-cut cases.

6.3.2 Discovery

Discovery is akin to occupation in that it is usually applied in respect of previously uninhabited territories. However, it is clear from the *Island of Palmas Case* that discovery per se gives only an inchoate title to territory. This means that unless the first act of discovery is followed up within a reasonable period of time by acts of effective occupation, the potential title to territory accorded by discovery does not mature into full sovereignty. In practical terms, in the absence of effective occupation, another state may enter the territory and exercise the functions of statehood therein. If this happens, the title based on effective occupation will have priority over the inchoate title based on discovery.

6.3.3 Cession and treaty

It is not uncommon in international law that one state cedes a piece of territory to another by treaty. The situation is rather like the transfer of property in national law, with one state transferring 'ownership' or sovereignty to another. This may be for money, as with the transfer of Alaska from the USSR to the USA, or it may be in settlement of a border dispute or as part of a more general arrangement. An example of the last is the 1984 agreement between the UK and China, whereby the former transferred sovereignty over the Crown Colony of Hong Kong (as distinct from the New Territories) to the latter. Moreover, like national law, the maxim *nemo dat quod non habet* applies – a state cannot transfer what it does not have. In order for the acquiring state to gain title to the territory, the ceding state must be the legitimate sovereign. In the *Island of Palmas Case*, for example, the USA could not acquire sovereignty to the Island under the Treaty of Paris if Spain had no right to the territory at that time. It is also clear that the normal rules relating to the formation and validity of treaties apply to treaties of cession and this is even more important given that territorial adjustments resulting from treaties may bind third parties (see Chapter 3). Thus, there must be no duress, fraud or corruption in the procurement of the treaty. Likewise, the treaty in issue must be clear the sovereignty has been passed when properly interpreted according to the normal rules of treaty interpretation. So in the *Pulau Ligitan and Pulau Sipadan Case*, neither Indonesia nor Malaysia could establish title under treaties that had been concluded by the former colonial powers and the issue had to be settled according to the principle of effective exercise of sovereignty. Significantly, Art. 52 of the Vienna Convention on the Law of Treaties 1969 provides that a 'treaty is void if its conclusion has been procured by the threat or use of force in violation of the principles of international law embodied in the Charter of the United Nations'. That this represents customary international law was confirmed by the Court in the *Fisheries Jurisdiction Case (Jurisdiction) (UK v Iceland)* 1973 ICJ Rep 3 and it means that, as a general rule, a treaty between a victorious state and its defeated enemy, whereby the former acquires title to some or all of the latter's territory is not effective to transfer title. However, this does not prevent treaties that redraw a border, even if this has been a cause of hostilities between two states, so long as its conclusion 'has not been procured' by the use of force. The aim is to outlaw treaties resulting from aggression, not to prevent the peaceful settlement of border disputes.

6.3.4 Use of force – conquest

Prior to 1945, or perhaps 1928 (the date of the Kellogg–Briand Pact, see Chapter 11), the use of force was perfectly lawful and title to territory acquired through conquest was quite common. As previously noted, under the doctrine of intertemporal law, a title acquired by conquest when force was lawful cannot now be challenged, save only if the right of self-determination applies. However, times have changed and we have seen also that a treaty of cession imposed by the use of force is void. Similarly, from the moment aggressive force became unlawful it has been impossible for a state to acquire title to territory by conquest. For example, whether or not Iraq had a valid claim to parts of Kuwait's territory, it could not obtain sovereignty over it by force of arms and Israel cannot obtain lawful title to occupied Palestinian territory on the basis of effective occupation following its unlawful use of force (*Palestinian Wall Advisory Opinion* 2004 ICJ Rep). In similar vein, it is clear that a state that exercises force in (alleged) self-defence is under a duty to return (or retreat from) any territory of the aggressor state which it has occupied, a point finally accepted by Israel when it withdrew from Southern Lebanon in May 2000 and again in 2006. In such circumstances, although the initial use of force by the defending state would not have been 'in violation of the principles of international law embodied in the Charter' (and see Art. 51 of the UN Charter), the subsequent retention of territory when the threat has passed would be unlawful. Simply put, the point is that self-defence is an essentially negative concept – the use of force is lawful only because it is a reaction to some other state's prior unlawful use of force. As a matter of principle, the use of force in self-defence should not be capable of conferring positive territorial benefits on any state after the need for self-defence has passed. This is the position adopted in the *Ethiopia/Eritrea Claims Commission Award* (2005), which noted that 'the practice of States and the writings of eminent publicists show that self-defense cannot be invoked to settle territorial disputes. In that connection, the Commission notes that border disputes between States are so frequent that any exception to the prohibition of the threat or use of force for territory that is allegedly occupied unlawfully would create a large and dangerous hole in a fundamental rule of international law.'

6.3.5 Accretion and avulsion

Unlike the matters considered earlier, accretion and avulsion are not concerned with the acquisition of title over existing territory. Accretion denotes the extension of sovereignty over 'new' territory by reason of a gradual increase in a state's land mass: for example, as a result of soil deposits in river deltas but it can apply with equal force to land reclamation such as that achieved by the Netherlands along its west coast and Hong Kong in its harbour. Avulsion, on the other hand, is concerned with more dramatic increases in state territory, such as the creation of new islands in existing territorial waters as a result of volcanic activity. Title to the 'new' territory thus arises by reason of its relation to territory over which the claimant state already enjoys sovereignty. The legitimacy of this mode of acquisition of sovereignty is not in doubt, but necessarily it must be limited in practice.

6.3.6 Judicial decisions

The decisions of international courts and arbitral panels have a profound impact on the sovereignty of territory in international law. The *Island of Palmas Case, Clipperton Island Arbitration, Eastern Greenland Case, Minquiers and Ecrehos Case,* the 1988 decision in the *Taba Area Boundary* dispute between Israel and Egypt, the Court's judgment in the *Frontier Dispute Case (Burkina Faso* v *Mali)* 1986 ICJ Rep 545, the *Botswana* v *Namibia* Case, the *Pulau Islands* case, *Cameroon* v *Nigeria, Benin* v *Niger* and the long awaited *Territorial and Maritime Dispute between Nicaragua and Honduras in the Caribbean Sea (Nicaragua v. Honduras)* (2007) all settled disputed questions of sovereignty over territory. The imminent judgment in the pending *Frontier Dispute (Burkina Faso/Niger) Case* will do the same.

Of course, in all of these cases, the court or arbitrator's judgment was based on accepted principles of law such as those discussed earlier. Nevertheless, it should not be forgotten that it was not until the judicial body had actually reached a decision that the location of sovereignty was finally settled. In this sense, the decisions of judicial bodies may be regarded as a practical method of acquiring sovereignty over territory for they crystallise a title that has been in doubt.

6.3.7 *Uti possidetis* and other principles relating to territorial acquisition

There are a number of other principles or guidelines that may be used as a means of determining title to territory in international law. The 'continuity' principle suggests that a state is entitled to sovereignty over the land adjacent to and extending from an area of territory already under its control. Thus, a coastal settlement may carry with it prima facie title to the hinterland. In similar vein is the 'contiguity' principle, whereby a state may claim title over territory not forming part of its land mass – such as islands – by virtue of being the nearest sovereign state. In the *Island of Palmas Case,*

Judge Huber doubted whether the acquisition title by means of contiguity alone was an established principle of international law and, in any event, he made it clear that any title gained by this method is liable to be defeated by the effective occupation of some other state. The same is almost certainly true of title by continuity.

A more important principle concerning title to territory is the principle of *uti possedetis*, very much relied on in the *Territorial and Maritime Dispute between Nicaragua and Honduras in the Caribbean Sea (Nicaragua v Honduras)* (2007). Simply, this encompasses the idea that the frontiers of newly independent states are to follow the frontiers of the old colonial territories from which they emerged and, importantly, that they cannot be easily altered, by unilateral action. The principle originated in South America as a consequence of the collapse of the Spanish Empire when the former provinces agreed that the limits of their sovereignty should conform to the limits of the old colonial boundaries. In the *Frontier Dispute Case (Burkina Faso v Mali)*, the ICJ confirmed that *uti possidetis* was a principle of general application, not confined solely to South America. Indeed, the African Union has adopted the principle in its Resolution on the Intangibility of Frontiers (AHG/Res. 16(1)) and it was applied in Africa in the *Burkina Faso v Mali* case and the *Frontier Dispute Case (Benin v Niger)*. Likewise, in *El Salvador v Honduras*, the ICJ Chamber relied heavily on *uti possidetis* in settling the boundary dispute between the two parties, and there is no doubt that the Chamber regarded the rule as of the utmost importance. In fact, the Chamber made it clear that neither effective display of state functions in disputed areas nor the economic inequality generated by old boundaries was sufficient to displace the *uti possidetis* principle *where the boundary was clear*, although they did recognise that its application may be difficult in some cases because of the contentious nature of the facts. Similarly, in *Benin v Niger*, the ICJ Chamber was clear that *uti possidetis* was the determining factor in deciding the line of sovereignty between the two states, and this was to be the boundary existing between the French colonies at the time of their independence. However, the Chamber recognised that in order to determine what the frontier was at this time, it might have to examine which colonial administration was exercising governmental control over the disputed territory. Thus, there was an interplay between *uti possidetis* and effective display of governmental functions when it was necessary to determine where the boundary ran at the critical date that could then be crystallised by *uti possidetis*.

It is also true that frontiers established by *uti possidetis* may be modified by the acquiescence of one state in the effective exercise of control by another over a disputed area – the acquiescence being the crucial factor when coupled with the effective control of the other state. This was the result in the *Sovereignty over Pedra Branca/Pulau Batu Puteh, Middle Rocks and South Ledge (Malaysia/Singapore) Case* (2008), working in Singapore's favour. Furthermore, the *EC Arbitration Commission on Yugoslavia* [1993] 92 ILR 162, decided that the principle also applied to newly independent states formerly part of a federation. So, as a matter of international law, the old federal boundaries of the Yugoslavian states (and those of the USSR also) will be held to form the frontiers of the new sovereign states that have emerged in their wake. Consequently, any action (by use of force or otherwise) designed to alter unilaterally the old federal boundaries will be unlawful. Clearly, this application of *uti possidetis* beyond the colonial situation is an important development, albeit one that is necessary if stability among the international community is to be preserved. Indeed, it only serves to confirm that the principle of *uti possidetis* is now to be regarded as a principle of customary law of general application. It is a principle rooted in pragmatism and an illustration of how the 'effective control' criterion of *Island of Palmas* is not always decisive.

6.3.8 Self-determination

In 1945, when the United Nations was created, there were only fifty-one members. Today, membership of the Organisation stands at 192, the majority of new states being former colonies or former parts of larger states, as with Eritrea and Ethiopia. The move towards independence started immediately after the end of the Second World War, but it was not until the passing of the UN General Assembly Resolution on the Granting of Independence to Colonial Territories and Peoples in 1960 that it became possible to think of self-determination as a legal right rather than a political philosophy. Nowadays, we may regard the development of this principle and its carrying into effect as a legal rule as one of the great achievements of the United Nations, so much so that there remain very few colonial territories which have not achieved independence or some other form of self-government. Today self-determination is a well-established principle of customary international law and may well be a rule of *jus cogens*. In the *Case Concerning East Timor (Portugal v Australia)* 1995 ICJ Rep 90, the Court was of the view that the principle of self-determination 'is one of the essential principles of contemporary international law', in the *Palestinian Wall Advisory Opinion* the Court explained again that 'the right of peoples to self-determination is today a right erga omnes', that is applicable to all and valid against all (2004 ICJ Rep para. 88) and in the *Advisory Opinion on the Accordance with international law of the unilateral declaration of independence in respect of Kosovo* (2010), the Court noted that 'that one of the major developments of international law during the second half of the twentieth century has been the evolution of the right of self-determination'.

Obviously, the right to self-determination bears some relation to the question of title to territory, although the principle is often more concerned with which 'people' are entitled to exercise sovereignty over a piece of territory, rather than how a state acquires that territory in the first place. In the usual case, an exercise of the right of self-determination will result in the territory becoming independent. Of course, there is no necessary reason why this should be so and it is quite possible for a people to choose to affiliate themselves with another state, either in a federal system or simply as an addition to existing territory (*Western Sahara Case* 1975 ICJ Rep 12). The crucial point is that self-determination 'requires a free and genuine expression of the will of the peoples concerned' (*Western Sahara Case*). If the territory does become independent then, as we have seen, its borders may become permanently fixed under *uti possedetis*. That said, there remains the all-important question of which classes of 'people' are entitled to exercise the right of self-determination.

As we have just noted, the principle of self-determination developed as a direct response to the 'evils' of colonialism and there is no doubt that a 'people' under the foreign domination of another state enjoy this right. In the *Advisory Opinion on the Accordance with international law of the unilateral declaration of independence in respect of Kosovo* (2010), the Court was clear that a customary law right of self-determination existed in the 'context of non-self-governing territories and peoples subject to alien subjugation, domination and exploitation'. Thus, the people of Palestine may enjoy the right in full measure and the creation of the Palestine Autonomous Area in Gaza/West Bank may be seen as a step in the process of self-determination. However, the territories to which the right of self-determination in this classical sense can be said to apply are now limited and the real and pressing question is whether self-determination can be exercised by distinct ethnic or religious groups within an already sovereign and independent state. For example, in 1971 the people of East Pakistan broke away from the Federation of Pakistan to form Bangladesh; in 1967 the Ibos Tribe unsuccessfully attempted to secede from Nigeria; and in 1993 Eritrea successfully ceded from Ethiopia, all these peoples claiming in some measure the right of self-determination. Likewise, what of the break up of once stable federations such as Yugoslavia and the USSR?

A traditional analysis of the right of self-determination would deny that it is available under international law to any and every distinct group that could qualify as a 'people'. On this view, the right, as a right guaranteed by law, arises only in specific circumstances. This certainly seems to be the thrust of the early General Assembly resolution referred to earlier and, of course, it partly avoids the difficult question of exactly who are a 'people'. At the other end of the spectrum are those who argue that any distinct ethnic group, whether part of a colonial, federal or unitary state, have the right to self-determine. Under this approach, the people of Gibraltar (colonial territory), of Alaska (federal state) and of Scotland (unitary state) all have the right and it could be exercised, protected and enforced by international law.

Not surprisingly, it is not easy to find an answer to these questions, and no view is free from doubt. As the Court said in the *Kosovo Opinion*, '[w]hether, outside the context of non-self-governing territories and peoples subject to alien subjugation, domination and exploitation, the international law of self-determination confers upon part of the population of an existing State a right to separate from that State is, however, a subject on which radically different views were expressed by those taking part in the proceedings and expressing a position on the question'. Understandably given the context in which this Advisory Opinion was requested, but unhelpfully for our understanding of international law, the Court decided that it did not need to resolve the matter in order to answer the question posed by the General Assembly. The Court took the view that it was being asked about the lawfulness of the *declaration* of independence as an act, not whether Kosovo could be independent under international law.

With that note of caution firmly in our minds, perhaps we can conclude that the right of self-determination has moved on from the very narrow right found in the 1960 General Assembly Resolution, and that state practice has re-shaped the principle of self-determination in a small measure to meet the new circumstances of the postcolonial world. As the EC Arbitration Commission on Yugoslavia has indicated, the right of self-determination now certainly exists beyond the colonial situation and we know from the *Palestinian Wall Advisory Opinion* (2004) that the ICJ regards the right as valid erga omnes – against the world. In the view of the EC Arbitration Commission, self-determination is available to the people of a territory that is part of an existing federal state, provided that they can achieve the factual prerequisites for statehood identified in the Montevideo Convention (see Chapter 5). It is not clear, however, if this is only when they are also subject to 'alien subjugation, domination and exploitation' or simply because they wish to be separate. On the one hand, there is no wish to encourage secessionist movements in reasonably stable states, but on the other, no wish to see cohesive populations suppressed by a central authority. The EC Commission did, however, express considerable doubts as to whether self-determination extended to ethnic groups within existing unitary states, as opposed to peoples linked to a specific territory within a federal arrangement. Hence, it would not apply (for example) to Muslims in India or the *Bosnian* Serbs in Bosnia. While such groups may well enjoy 'second level' self-determination, in that their culture, social organisation and religious preferences should be respected by the state of which they are part, the EC Commission were not prepared to recognise a right to self-determine for all 'peoples' wherever and however they were found. Similar issues faced the Supreme Court of Canada in the *Case Concerning Certain Questions Relating to Secession of Quebec from Canada* 161 DLR (4th) 385, where it was asked to rule on the legitimacy under Canadian law and international law of a possible declaration of independence by Quebec. In the Court's view, there was no right of secession under international law of a political sub-unit of an existing state, provided that the central authorities respected the 'internal' self-determination of the ethnic group, e.g. respect for language, culture, etc. Clearly, this echoes the approach of the EC Arbitration Commission, although whether this view reflects existing customary law is uncertain.

Overall, a balance needs to be struck between protecting the human rights of peoples and individuals and preserving the fabric of international society. Self-determination can foster the former, but might well be destructive of the latter. As the conflict in the former territories of Yugoslavia demonstrates, pleading self-determination is all well and good, but achieving it is another matter. Nevertheless, once the existence and applicability of the right to self-determination is accepted, this generates legal responsibility for other states. As the majority noted in the *Palestinian Wall Advisory Opinion*, '[i]t is also for all States, while respecting the United Nations Charter and international law, to see to it that any impediment, resulting from the construction of the wall, to the exercise by the Palestinian people of its right to self-determination is brought to an end' (2004 ICJ Rep para. 159).

6.3.9 Conclusion

The foregoing sections have identified several 'modes' by which a state may acquire title to territory and have suggested that these are complemented by additional principles such as *uti possidetis* and self-determination. However, as indicated earlier, simple categorisation is no substitute for analysis and, in practice, title to territory may well be decided by a combination of the factors we have considered. This is only to be expected in the complex world of international relations. It is clear from the *Island of Palmas Case* that the effective display of state authority within a territory is to be regarded as the primary means for the acquisition of territory in international law, but that is only the beginning of the story. The effective occupation and control of territory in the period preceding the critical date would seem able to defeat title based on other concepts, such as cession, discovery, conquest, prior occupation by another state, continuity and contiguity, although there is also strong support for upholding the integrity of existing borders through *uti possedetis*. Overall, the actual ability to control a territory carries much weight and this is not surprising in a system of law that relies heavily on state practice for the creation of legal rules. As we have seen in Chapter 5, the existence of an effective government is a precondition of statehood, and the criteria discussed earlier are based on the same need to give effect to the realities of international life. However, since 1945, rules based on the simple ability to exercise state functions within a territory have become less important due to the development of rules based more on notions of 'justice' and 'equity' (natural law). For example, the prohibition of the acquisition of territory by conquest and the development of the principles of self-determination and non-racial discrimination have tempered the primacy of effective control. Similarly, the principle of *uti possidetis* emphasises a need for stability and certainty in matters relating to territorial frontiers by denying that these can be modified solely by the subsequent occupation or control of territory by other states. Finally, it is clear that the rules relating specifically to *acquisition* of territory are now diminishing in importance. This is a reflection of the fact that there are few significant areas of territory around the world to which title itself is undetermined. Obviously, the time will come, perhaps even has come, when acquisition of territory by occupation of *terra nullius* will cease to have any practical relevance. Those problems that do remain – such as frontier disputes and crumbling states – are more likely to be settled by negotiation between the parties than by the application of rules based on physical control. It is equally likely that those rules of international law having a more 'moral' or humanistic content, such as self-determination, non-racial discrimination and prohibition of force, will continue to grow in importance. The successful move to independence of the people of East Timor in 2000, after exercising their right of self-determination in an internationally monitored plebiscite, is a vibrant example.

6.4 **Rights over foreign territory**

It is quite possible for one state to grant limited rights over its territory to another. This may be done by treaty or it may arise by way of customary law. In the *Rights of Passage Case (Portugal v India)* 1960 ICJ Rep 6, Portugal claimed a right of passage between its enclave territories in India. The Court agreed that such a right of passage for peaceful purposes could exist on the basis of local customary law between the two states. What is not clear, however, is whether rights over foreign territory are equivalent to servitudes (or easements) as found in national law. The significance of this point is that if rights over foreign territory do have a 'proprietary' status, they may survive changes in ownership of the territory or changes in sovereignty. Rights over foreign territory would acquire a permanence that could derogate from state sovereignty almost indefinitely. For this reason, there are considerable doubts whether servitudes exist as such in international law. In the *North Atlantic Fisheries Arbitration (US v Great Britain)* (1910) 11 RIAA 167, the Tribunal did not agree with the US claim that Great Britain was bound by a servitude to permit its nationals to fish freely, even though the original liberty had been granted by treaty. On the other hand, the Tribunal did not indicate unequivocally that such rights could not exist and, in the *Wimbledon Case* (1923) PCIJ Ser. A No. 1, the PCIJ left the question open. As a matter of principle, it may be that international law should not recognise such proprietary rights, precisely because they could endure more or less permanently. As indicated earlier, this does not mean that states cannot provide by treaty that other states may exercise limited rights in or over their sovereign territory. Whatever the nature of these rights – be they 'personal' or 'proprietary' – it is certain that the state granting the rights is bound to allow reasonable exercise of such rights for the duration of the grant. In fact, the granting of rights to a foreign state over sovereign territory is not unusual in international law, witness the existence of foreign sovereign military bases in Cuba (USA) and Cyprus (UK). Emphasis should be placed, therefore, on the nature of a treaty as a self-imposed limitation on sovereignty, rather than on a largely theoretical discussion as to the juridical nature of the rights granted.

6.5 Areas outside the exclusive jurisdiction of any state

As well as having jurisdiction over their territory proper, states may exercise some powers of regulation and management over other areas. In such cases, jurisdictional rights may be shared by all states, or just by those having a particular and recognised interest. Similarly, individual states may have exclusive but limited powers of jurisdiction over certain communal areas that must be exercised with reference to other states' rights. It will be apparent that 'jurisdiction' in this section has a meaning different from that used earlier. It does not mean that a state has sovereignty over an area and, in this sense, the areas discussed subsequently are 'beyond the limits of national jurisdiction'. However, within these areas, states may enjoy certain jurisdictional rights, not amounting to sovereignty, either in company with other states or exclusively. It is quite possible that no state can be said to have actual sovereignty over such areas and if this is the case the area is said to be *res communis* (communal). This means that it is not open to acquisition by any state and, perhaps, that it must be used for 'the common heritage of mankind'. An example of this is the Deep Sea Bed, considered in Chapter 8.

6.5.1 Outer space

It is clear that a state enjoys exclusive jurisdiction over the airspace immediately above its territory and territorial sea. In practical terms, this means that it can prohibit overflight by other states, unless prior agreement has been reached (see section 6.6). However, what is not clear is how far up this jurisdiction extends. Does it extend upwards indefinitely, so as to create slices of sovereignty in outer space, or is it limited to, say, the outer edge of the atmosphere? There appears to be a measure of agreement that state sovereignty does not extend upwards ad infinitum and that it ceases where outer space begins. Unfortunately, there is an equal measure of disagreement as to where this boundary actually occurs, although most commentators might accept that outer space (in international law) begins somewhere between 150 and 200 miles up from Earth. Moreover, it should not be thought that the question is unimportant, for although a separate legal regime exists for outer space, a state will have absolute sovereignty above its territory up to that point. So, the legality of overflight by high-flying reconnaissance or military aircraft will depend on where this elusive boundary occurs.

The development of the law of outer space is a product of necessity. As man invents an ever greater capacity to explore and control this environment, it has become apparent that a stable legal regime governing its use is required. In 1963, the General Assembly adopted the Declaration of Legal Principles Governing the Activities of States in the Exploration and Use of Outer Space (GA Res. (XVIII) (1962)) and this was followed by a series of treaties elaborating these Principles. The most important of these are the Treaty on Principles Governing the Activities of States in the Exploration of Outer Space, including the Moon and Other Celestial Bodies (1966) and the Agreement Governing the Activities of States on the Moon and other Celestial Bodies (1979). Other treaties cover the activities of astronauts and satellites and liability for damage caused by space objects. Taken together, these treaties establish that outer space and the celestial bodies are not open to acquisition by any state. States cannot claim sovereignty over them. The area is to endure for the benefit of all mankind and be open for use by all states. Significantly, no weapons of mass destruction (including nuclear weapons) may be placed in space, either in orbit or on celestial bodies, and outer space may generally be used only for peaceful purposes. Thus, while states bear responsibility for their own actions in outer space – and therefore have jurisdiction over their own craft and satellites – the area itself is *res communis*, part of the 'common heritage of mankind'. The UK has enacted the Outer Space Act 1986 in order to ensure compliance with its international obligations under these treaties.

6.5.2 The Antarctic

The area of the Antarctic is generally taken to be that extending south from latitude 608S and it consists of a mix of permanent and temporary ice and, importantly, a frozen land mass. The area is subject to claims of sovereignty by seven states – the UK, Argentina, Chile, France, Australia, New Zealand and Norway – although only the territorial claims of the first three overlap. It is now reasonably certain that Antarctica contains valuable reserves of natural resources, such as coal, oil, gas and precious metals. At present, the prospect of commercial exploitation of these resources is remote, but the time will come when states will look to the Antarctic for new supplies of these non-renewable minerals. It is also clear that such exploitation *could* proceed on the basis of state sovereignty, even though many states do not accept that the area is open to claims of sovereignty at all. Conversely, it has been suggested that all states should be permitted to share in the potential wealth of the continent and that, like outer space and the Deep Sea Bed, Antarctica should be part of 'the common heritage of mankind'. However, whatever view we take on the question of who is entitled to benefit from Antarctica, one thing is clear. If this unique and unspoiled environment is not to be destroyed, the international community must act to ensure that commercial mining, if it takes place at all, is regulated by a comprehensive and effective system of international controls. If individual states were to be given a free hand, the area would not survive in its present form. It is these twin problems of sovereignty and regulation that have led to the development of an international regime governing Antarctica.

In 1959, the Antarctic Treaty was drawn up by those states having an interest in or claim to sovereignty over the area. This recognised the importance of preserving the environment of the Antarctic and established that it could be used for peaceful purposes only. It included a prohibition on nuclear testing and the disposal of nuclear waste. Importantly, the treaty also placed a moratorium on claims of sovereignty and stipulated that 'no acts or activities taking place while the treaty is in force shall constitute a basis for asserting, supporting or denying a claim to territorial sovereignty in Antarctica or create any rights in Antarctica' (Art. 4). Thus, since 1961 when the treaty came into force, claims to sovereignty over the Antarctic have been suspended. At present there are fifty parties, and this includes twenty-eight Consultative Parties who meet every two years (or more frequently in Special Session) and make Recommendations under the treaty. These Recommendations deal with various matters and can become binding on the Consultative Parties. Although the treaty has no formal period of duration, it may be 'reviewed' at any time after it has been in force for thirty years. This provision prompted fears that the regime would fall apart in 1991, but since 1982 the Consultative Parties have met regularly in an effort to continue the progress made by the Treaty of 1959. In 2009, at the 32nd Consultative Meeting in the 50th anniversary year of the treaty, the Consultative Parties decided, by formal declaration 'to continue and extend for the benefit of all humankind their cooperation established in the Treaty and in the Treaty system over the last fifty years'. Thus, the Antarctic Treaty is still in force and, as discussed later, it has acquired new vitality with the addition of a Protocol on Environmental Protection.

The Antarctic Treaty regime has developed both in substance and in importance in recent years. In November 1988, the now defunct Convention on the Regulation of Antarctic Mineral Resource Activities (CRAMRA) was opened for signature, establishing an international regime for 'mineral resource activities' in Antarctica. The Minerals Convention was, at the time, the best that could be hoped for in the face of claims by some states to full-blown sovereignty. In fact, some of these (e.g. Norway) seemed prepared to forgo their claims if a comprehensive international regime could be established. Crucially, the Minerals Convention failed to anticipate the international community's renewed interest in environmental matters and very shortly it became clear that some Consultative States were unhappy at the idea of any exploitation of Antarctica at all. This led to proposals, first mooted by France and Australia at a meeting of the Consultative Parties in Paris in October 1989, to turn Antarctica into a 'wilderness reserve' where all mining and exploitation would be forbidden. This has now found embodiment in the Protocol on Environmental Protection to the Antarctic Treaty that was finally agreed by the Consultative Parties at a Special Session in Madrid in October 1991. This Protocol represents a compromise between those states wishing to follow the Minerals Convention and those proposing an absolute ban on the exploitation of Antarctica. Under Art. 7 '[a]ny activity relating to mineral resources, other than scientific research, shall be prohibited' but provision is made in Art. 25 for modification of these terms either by the special procedure of the Antarctic Treaty itself or by review conference 50 years from the Protocol's entry into force. What this means, and what it was intended to mean, is that all mining activity is to be prohibited for at least 50 years, with the option to continue the ban thereafter. Indeed, the prohibition on mineral resource activity cannot be modified or amended until a 'binding legal regime' on such activities is in place.

It is apparent that this Protocol substantially reduces the chance that there will be commercial mining in Antarctica. For example, the UK has enacted the Antarctic

Act 1994, making those changes to national law necessary for ratification of the Antarctic Protocol. Indeed, the Environmental Protection Protocol is a considerable achievement, even though in formal terms it does not affect the legal claims of states held in abeyance by the 1959 Treaty. It reiterates firmly the uniqueness of the Antarctic and lends support to the idea that the area is part of the 'common heritage of mankind' under customary international law. It may even prevent the destruction of this very special environment.

6.5.3 Arctic

Unlike Antarctica, the Arctic wilderness consists mainly of frozen sea. There are isolated islands, which are the subject of claims of sovereignty (e.g. by Denmark, Norway), but by far the greater area is composed of shifting, though permanent, pack-ice. This has not prevented some states (e.g. Russia and Canada) claiming sovereignty over the frozen sea area, or parts thereof, and has generated resistance by others (e.g. Norway and the USA) on the ground that the Arctic sea is subject to the same legal regime as the high seas. At the present time, therefore, there is some disagreement over the precise status of the Arctic. There is no treaty regime comparable to that found for Outer Space or Antarctica. Undoubtedly, this is a reflection of the fact that the prospect of valuable mineral resources being found in the Arctic area is remote, although it is of considerable military importance.

6.6 Jurisdiction over airspace and aircraft

As has already been indicated, a state has exclusive jurisdiction over the airspace immediately above its territory. Therefore, unless otherwise agreed, a state may prohibit all aircraft movement over its territory and may take any action necessary to preserve its sovereignty. An invasion of airspace is no different from an invasion of territory. Of necessity, however, this position of principle has long since been modified by international treaty and a general set of rules exists concerning freedom of overflight and transit passage.

The basic principles were formulated at the Chicago Conference on International Civil Aviation 1944 and are to be found in the 1944 Chicago Convention on International Civil Aviation. This came into force in 1947 and as at 1 September 2012 there were 191 parties. Article 1 of this Convention reflects the general standard of customary law by affirming that each state has 'complete and exclusive sovereignty over the airspace above its territory'. The Convention then provides certain exceptions to this, which, generally, permit civil aircraft, not engaged in scheduled international air service, to fly into or over the territory of a contracting state. However, by Art. 6, no scheduled international air service may be operated without the authorisation of the state, although under the Chicago International Air Services Transit Agreement 1944, scheduled international air services enjoy the 'two freedoms' of the privilege to fly across the territory of a contracting state without landing and the privilege to land for non-traffic purposes. Together, these treaties set the standard for the control of non-military aircraft, although they make no provision for the actual conduct of scheduled passenger services. This in turn is regulated by a series of bilateral agreements, with general safety standards and navigational matters regulated by the International Civil Aviation Organisation (ICAO).

Under Art. 17 of the 1944 Convention on International Civil Aviation, aircraft have the nationality of the state in which they are registered and they cannot be validly registered in more than one state (Art. 18). Moreover, under the Tokyo Convention on Offences and Certain Other Acts Committed on Board Aircraft 1963, the state of registration is competent to exercise jurisdiction over all offences and acts committed on board while the aircraft is in flight, on the high seas or in any other area outside the territory of another state. However, under the Tokyo Convention, other states may have criminal jurisdiction over offences committed on board when the aircraft is in any of these areas if the offence has an effect on the territory of the state, its security, or has been committed by or against a national of the state or is a breach of flight regulations or is necessary to ensure observance of treaty obligations (e.g. Scotland and the *Lockerbie Case*). Obviously, if the aircraft is present in another state, that state will also have jurisdiction under the territorial principle.

As a result of concern at the increase of hijacking and other acts detrimental to the safety of international air transport, another set of treaties dealing with acts committed on board aircraft has been concluded. The main body of law is to be found in the Hague Convention for the Suppression of Unlawful Seizure of Aircraft 1970 and this is supplemented by the ICAO Montreal Convention for the Suppression of Unlawful Acts against the Safety of International Civil Aviation 1971, the application of which was the issue in the *Libya* v *UK, Libya* v *US* actions in the ICJ. Under the Hague Convention, each contracting party undertakes to make the 'offence' of hijacking 'punishable by severe penalties'. The Convention also creates a series of rules establishing the principles of jurisdiction over such 'offences'. Generally, the parties must take steps to establish jurisdiction over the offence when it takes place on an aircraft registered in their territory, when the aircraft lands in their territory, when the lessee of an aircraft has his place of business or residence in their state or when the offender is present in their territory. Moreover, every state in which an offender is found is under a duty to take him into custody and, if they do not extradite him, to commence prosecution. A similar position on jurisdiction is adopted in the Montreal Convention.

The Hague Convention, then, obliges states to create the offence of hijacking in their national law and the UK has done this by virtue of the Aviation Security Act 1982 (previously the Hijacking Act 1971). In fact, the Hague Convention goes a long way to establishing air piracy as an offence of universal jurisdiction and, for the parties at least, this is ensured by Art. 7. The weakness of the Convention is that it does not impose a positive obligation to extradite an offender, although the offence is to be an 'extraditable offence' within existing treaties. Strictly, of course, extradition would not be necessary if all states exercised their universal jurisdiction. Yet, the fact that hijacking may be seen as a 'political' crime means that some states do not regard hijackers as offenders at all.

The jurisdictional rules contained in the Convention provide a reasonably comprehensive system but, as always, the actual exercise of the jurisdiction depends as much on the will of states as on the granting of rights under international law. An excellent example of the multi-sided problems that can occur in relation to offences committed on board aircraft is the Lockerbie incident.

FURTHER READING

Akehurst, M., 'Jurisdiction in International Law', (1972–3) 46 *BYIL* 145.

Blay, S., 'New Trends in the Protection of the Antarctic Environment', (1992) 86 *AJIL* 377.

Bowett, D., 'Jurisdiction, Changing Patterns of Authority over Activities and Resources', (1982) 53 *BYIL* 1.

Cassese, A., *Self-Determination of Peoples* (Cambridge University Press, 1995).

Lowe, A., 'Blocking Extraterritorial Jurisdiction: The British Protection of Trading Interests Act 1980', (1981) 75 *AJIL* 256.

Lowe, A., 'Problems of Extraterritorial Jurisdiction: Economic Sovereignty and the Search for a Solution', (1985) 34 *ICLQ* 724.

McCorquodale, R., 'International Law, Boundaries and Imagination', in D. Miller and S. Haskins (eds.), *Boundaries and Justice* (2001).

Redgwell, C., 'Antarctica', (1991) 40 *ICLQ* 976.

Roth, P. M., 'Reasonable Extraterritoriality', (1992) 41 *ICLQ* 245.

SUMMARY

Jurisdiction and sovereignty

- The 'first and foremost' rule of jurisdiction is that one state may not exercise jurisdiction in the territory of another state. Secondly, there is a general principle that a state is entirely free to project its jurisdiction over any matter taking place outside its territory, so long as this is not prohibited by a contrary rule of international law.

- The power of a state to bring any matter within the cognisance of its national law is called its prescriptive jurisdiction.

- Whereas a state may have a general power under international law to prescribe jurisdiction, the enforcement of that jurisdiction can generally take place only within its own territory.

- Jurisdiction over persons may be exercised on the following basis: objective and subjective territorial jurisdiction; nationality jurisdiction; universal jurisdiction; protective jurisdiction; passive personality jurisdiction.

- Sovereignty is the most extensive form of jurisdiction under international law. It denotes full and unchallengeable power over territory and all the persons from time to time therein. It may be subject to certain limitations, such as guarantees of human rights and diplomatic privileges, but apart from exceptions that are positively established, a state's sovereignty over its territory is absolute and complete.

- The control of territory and the peaceful and effective exercise of the functions of a state therein is the primary means of acquiring title to territory in international law.

- Discovery is akin to occupation in that it is usually applied in respect of previously uninhabited territories. Discovery *per se* gives only an inchoate title to territory. This means that unless the first act of discovery is followed up within a reasonable period of time by acts of effective occupation, the discoverer's title may be defeated by another state's effective display of state sovereignty.

- It is not uncommon in international law that one state cedes a piece of territory to another by treaty.

- Since 1945, the acquisition of title to territory by the use of force has been unlawful.

- *Uti possidetis* encompasses the idea that the frontiers of newly independent states should follow the frontiers of the old colonial territories from which they emerged and, importantly, that they cannot be easily altered by unilateral action.

- Self-determination is now a principle of international law. In the usual case, an exercise of the right of self-determination will result in the territory becoming independent, but it may apply to give groups within states limited autonomy without becoming independent.

7

Immunities from national jurisdiction

As a general rule, the jurisdiction of a state within its own territory is complete and absolute. The territorial sovereign is the master of all things and every person present in state territory is subject to the jurisdiction of the local courts. However, there is also a rule of international law that a foreign sovereign state is entitled to certain immunities from the exercise of this jurisdiction – generally known as the principle of state (or sovereign) immunity. For example, international law requires that a foreign state be accorded immunity from the jurisdiction of the courts of the UK and from the enforcement of court orders. Similarly, diplomatic staff of a foreign sovereign state are immune from arrest and detention in the UK and diplomatic correspondence will be exempt from normal customs and entry procedures. A violation of any of these immunities by the 'host state' will give rise to international responsibility, as was the case for Italy in the *Jurisdictional Immunities of the State (Germany v Italy: Greece intervening) Case* (2012). In this chapter, we shall examine the scope of, and the reasons for, the principles of state and diplomatic immunity in international law. Reference will be made to the UN Convention on Jurisdictional Immunities of States and Their Property 2004, which although not yet in force was based on extensive analysis of the law by the International Law Commission ('the ILC Draft Articles') and in some respects represents customary law. In addition, several states have enacted domestic legislation in order to ensure that their national law gives effect to both state and diplomatic immunities and there are many cases at national and international level. This chapter will also examine how international rules concerning immunity in its various forms has been put into effect in the UK.

As previously suggested, immunities from national jurisdiction can be split conveniently into two categories. First, state (or sovereign) immunity, which concerns the rights and privileges accorded to a state, its government, representatives and property within the national legal systems of other states. Secondly, diplomatic and consular immunity, which deals with the immunities enjoyed by official envoys of the foreign sovereign state and the duties owed to them by the 'host' state. These will be considered in turn.

Part One: **State immunity**

When State A makes a contract with a company registered in State B, or the property of State A is the cause of a dispute with a national of State B, or where State A acts in any other way within the territory of State B, it is imperative to determine whether State A is subject to the jurisdiction of the courts of State B. Furthermore, if State A is subject to the jurisdiction of these courts, can a court order be enforced against it? These issues raise questions of state immunity. As we shall see, the *precise* rules governing the scope of immunity in any particular state will be determined by the national laws of that state. However, it is quite clear that there is a legal duty under international law to ensure that a foreign sovereign state is accorded immunity in an appropriate case. As the ICJ made clear in the *Jurisdictional Immunities of the State (Germany v Italy: Greece intervening) Case* (2012) the 'Court considers that the rule of State immunity occupies an important place in international law and international relations. It derives from the principle of sovereign equality of States, which, as Article 2, paragraph 1, of the Charter of the United Nations makes clear, is one of the fundamental principles of the international legal order.' In the UK, Lord Millet in the House of Lords in *Holland v Lampen-Wolfe* [2000] 1 WLR 1573, noted that state immunity 'is not a self-imposed restriction on the jurisdiction of its courts which the United Kingdom has chosen to adopt. It is a limitation imposed from without upon the sovereignty of the United Kingdom itself.' Consequently, if immunity is denied when it should be given (as judged by reference to international law), the state denying immunity may be held liable in international law before an international court and certainly incurs international responsibility – *Jurisdictional Immunities of the State (Germany v Italy: Greece intervening) Case* (2012) where Italy was held to have broken in international law in failing to provide Germany with immunity from legal process in its courts.

7.1 **General conception of immunity and rationale in international law**

It is important to realise that a distinction exists between 'non-justiciability' and 'immunity'. When an issue is non-justiciable, this means that the national court has no competence to assert jurisdiction at all. The point is that the substantive issue is of such a nature that it cannot be the subject of judicial proceedings before the national court. In fact, the issue of non-justiciability may arise in a number of ways. First, there are certain matters which cannot properly be raised in the courts of any state other than those of the state directly concerned, such as the validity of certain constitution or legislative acts of the impleaded state save where those acts violate international law (*Kuwait Airways Corp. v Iraqi Airways Co. (No. 3)* 1998 (1999) CLS 31, per Mance J). For example, in *Buck v A-G* [1965] Ch 745, a UK court would not pronounce on the validity of the constitution of Sierra Leone. However, that does not mean that a UK court will always assume the validity of a foreign state's official acts. Thus, a UK court will refuse to give legal validity to the sovereign acts of a foreign state (in so far as they might produce effects within the UK legal system) where those sovereign acts are clearly in violation of international law. Although not technically assessing the legitimacy of those acts, the UK court is in effect denying their status and sidestepping the non-justiciability rule – *Kuwait Airways Corp. v Iraqi Airways Co. (No. 4 & 5)* [2002] UKHL 19. Moreover, not only may a UK court refuse to give effect to the acts of a foreign state that it considers to be internationally unlawful, there are dicta in *R v Secretary of State for Foreign and Commonwealth Affairs, ex parte Abbasi* [2002] EWCA Civ 1598 that suggest that a UK court actually might be persuaded to pronounce on the validity of a foreign sovereign act (as opposed to 'merely' refusing them effect within the UK) if those acts are in contravention of *fundamental* principles of international law *and* such a pronouncement is necessary in order for the court to decide the issue before it. This would indeed conflict with the non-justiciability rule put forth in *Buck v A-G*. In *Abbasi*, which concerned the detention of a UK national without trial by the USA at Guantanamo Bay, the court was stinging in its criticism of the US action and gives the impression that it would have been minded to retreat from the non-justiciability rule *if* such a declaration of unlawfulness of US conduct could have had legal effect on the USA. Secondly, there are some issues which do not raise questions of national law at all, such as the validity of treaties as in *ex parte Molyneaux* [1986] 1 WLR 331. In such cases, it is clear that a UK court 'has no jurisdiction to declare the true interpretation of an international instrument which has not been incorporated into English domestic law and which it is unnecessary to interpret for the purposes of determining a persons rights or duties under domestic law', *CND v Prime Minister* [2002] EWHC 2759, QB per Simon Brown LJ. Thirdly, the courts of most states regard as non-justiciable any actions of a governmental nature taken by a foreign sovereign state in its *own* territory (especially if concerned with only its own nationals) and also actions of other states in the conduct of their own foreign affairs (*Buttes Gas and Oil Co. v Hammer* [1981] 3 All ER 616 and *Kuwait Airways Corp. v Iraqi Airways Co.* [1995] 1 WLR 1147). This is sometimes referred to as the doctrine of non-justiciability for 'acts of state' and should not be confused with state immunity proper, even though both issues may arise in the context of the same dispute, as in *Kuwait Airway Corp*. Fourthly, there is a related non-justiciability principle – not strictly a matter of international law but more a principle of UK constitutional law – which provides that a UK court will not readily examine the validity of acts of the *UK government* in relation to foreign affairs because this may be to undermine the constitutional supremacy of the Executive in such matters. As stated in *CND v Prime Minister*, the court 'will decline to embark upon the determination of an issue if to do so would be damaging to the public interest in the field of international relations, national society or defence'. However, this is clearly not an absolute principle and whether the court refuses jurisdiction in any given case will depend on the substance of the precise matter before it and the reality of whether judicial consideration would indeed undermine the Executive in the conduct of foreign affairs (*Abbasi*).

By way of contrast, immunity from the jurisdiction of the court operates differently. Immunity is where a national court would have had jurisdiction over the subject matter of a dispute, but is not permitted to exercise it in a particular case because one of the parties is a foreign sovereign state or government. Immunity is based in the first instance on the *identity* of the litigant – it is an issue *ratio personae* – whereas non-justiciability is based on the substance of the dispute – it is always an issue *ratio materiae*. We are concerned in this chapter with immunity. Note, however, that once it is clear that the identity of one of the parties to a dispute *may* attract immunity (the *ratio personae* issue), whether in fact that 'person' (i.e. the state) has immunity in the particular case can depend on the substance of what has occurred (a *ratio materiae* issue). Evidently, there is scope for confusion here and many of the cases refer to immunity as raising issues of *ratio materiae* (substance). This is true, but only after it is clear that the 'person' is indeed a 'state' so as to attract the prospect of immunity in the first place.

What, then, is the basis of state immunity? Why should it be given at all? What is so special about a foreign sovereign state that it should be immune from the normal judicial processes of another state, especially when this may cause severe hardship to a national who is thereby deprived of a normal legal remedy? Several theories have been put forward.

(a) Under international law, states are legal equals. This is the sovereign equality of states that may even be a rule of *jus cogens*. The maxim *par in parem non habet imperium* expresses the idea that it is legally impossible for one sovereign power to exercise authority (by means of its legal system) over another sovereign power. Consequently, State A should be immune from the jurisdiction of State B because the former has no authority over the latter, it being of equal status. In *The Schooner Exchange* v *McFaddon* (1812) 7 Cranch 116, the plaintiffs claimed ownership of a ship of the French navy recently put into port. The US Supreme Court dismissed the petition on the ground of French state immunity, stating that there was a 'perfect equality and absolute independence of sovereigns' which meant that one sovereign could not be amenable to the territorial jurisdiction of another. This was also Lord Cooke's preferred explanation of state immunity in *Lampen-Wolfe* and is adopted by Lord Bingham in *Jones* v *Saudi Arabia* (2006). Importantly, the ICJ itself in the *Jurisdictional Immunities Case* (2012) said that state immunity 'derives from the principle of sovereign equality of States, which, as Article 2, paragraph 1, of the Charter of the United Nations makes clear, is one of the fundamental principles of the international legal order'.

(b) It was also pointed out in *The Schooner Exchange* that 'the jurisdiction of the nation within its own territory is necessarily exclusive and absolute. It is susceptible of no limitation not imposed by itself.' The idea here is that state immunity rests on a waiver of jurisdiction by the territorial sovereign by which it forgoes its absolute right, for the simple reason that, without it, no foreign state would be prepared to conduct trade with the nationals of any other state. However, in so far as this suggests that immunity rests on a *voluntary* waiver of jurisdiction by the territorial sovereign, it is not accurate. As Lord Millet said in *Lampen-Wolfe* immunity 'is imposed from without' and is not a matter of self-restraint, and in the *Jurisdictional Immunities Case* (2012) the ICJ said that '[i]mmunity may represent a departure from the principle of territorial sovereignty and the jurisdiction which flows from it'. Perhaps it was once true that immunity rested on a voluntary waiver of absolute territorial sovereignty, but now it is a matter of international legal obligation.

(c) According to Lord Denning MR in *Rahimtoola* v *Nizam of Hyderabad* [1958] AC 379 and reaffirmed by him in *Thai-Europe Tapioca Service* v *Government of Pakistan* [1975] 3 All ER 961, a national court ought not to consider the merits of a dispute involving a foreign sovereign state where questions of policy are in issue. In his view, these are matters that should not be the subject of decision in national courts. While this may well be one practical reason why local judges are reluctant to decide matters involving foreign states, as acknowledged by Lord Clyde in *Lampen-Wolfe*, this is not a convincing explanation of state immunity. Immunity is a loss of jurisdiction because of the status of one of the parties, not because of the complexity or delicacy of the issue.

(d) As we shall see when considering the UK law on state immunity, the general rule is still that a judgment of a domestic court (even if validly given) cannot be enforced against a foreign state. Such was one of Italy's breaches in the *Jurisdictional Immunities Case* (2012). This is so even if the state against whom the order is made had no immunity from the actual exercise of jurisdiction, as opposed to its enforcement. There is, therefore, a very real chance that the decisions of national courts will not be respected by a foreign sovereign and there may be little that can be done to ensure that they are. Indeed, even to attempt enforcement of an adverse court order may be regarded as an unfriendly act. In these circumstances, it has been argued that the better practical course could be to allow a claim of total immunity from the entire court process. If this is our view, immunity is no more than a reflection of the practical difficulties involved in enforcing court orders against foreign states. While this might seem attractive, it would follow that immunity should be given in all cases where a foreign state is a party to a dispute, because all cases raise the same problem of enforcement. Plainly, however, immunity from jurisdiction is not given in all cases and, in fact, the circumstances where it is given have diminished in recent years despite problems of enforcement. State immunity is not, therefore, simply a by-product of necessity.

(e) Another view of state immunity is that it is based on international comity. The grant of immunity by the territorial sovereign is said to result from a desire to foster international cooperation and avoid unnecessary disputes between the state of jurisdiction and other members of the international community. This does not mean that the requirement of state immunity is itself based on comity rather than legal obligation, for it is clear that a territorial sovereign is under an international legal duty to grant immunity. Immunity derives from a rule of binding law and not from some privilege freely granted. What it does suggest, however, is that immunity was originally designed to foster good relations by protecting foreign states from the vicissitudes of domestic legal systems. If this was a motivating factor in the development of the doctrine, it is ironic that the wheel has now turned full circle. Recent developments that have restricted the circumstances in which immunity is accorded have been designed to protect the individual when dealing with a foreign sovereign state and not vice versa. It is true, however, that immunity is a flexible concept that can react to the demands of a changing international society. Thus, the immunity of former heads of state *might* be diminished in the face of gross violations of human rights (*R v Bow Street Metropolitan Stipendiary Magistrate, ex parte Pinochet (No. 3)* [1999] 2 All ER 97, but see the reasoning in *Jones v Saudi Arabia*) and the immunity of a state might be extended into new areas as international relations become more complex (*Lampen-Wolfe* – provision of educational services on foreign military base within the UK).

Of course, the most important point concerning state immunity is that it is supported by the practice of states. Whatever the reason or legal justification for the doctrine, it is clear that state immunity is alive and well in the practice of international and national law. Its importance is illustrated by the time devoted to preparing a comprehensive set of Draft Articles on Jurisdictional Immunities by the ILC, a task considered important in 1948 although not embarked upon until 1978 and only recently brought to some sort of conclusion in the UN Convention on The Jurisdictional Immunities of States and their Property 2004 (itself not yet in force).

7.2 State immunity in international law

For many years, the practice of states was to grant foreign sovereigns absolute immunity from the jurisdiction of their courts. This meant that whenever a foreign state was impleaded, or sued, before a national court, it was able to claim immunity from the exercise of jurisdiction simply because it was 'a state'. Immunity flowed from its status as a recognised foreign sovereign and there was no inquiry into the substance of the dispute. Neither was there any mitigation of the consequences for the individual litigant. For example, if State A entered into a contract with a national of State B for the supply of cement, and then refused to pay the purchase price, the national would have been unable to sue in the national courts of State B for damages. State A had absolute immunity from the jurisdiction of the national courts, as well as absolute immunity from the enforcement of any court order. Obviously, such a strict doctrine was capable of causing substantial hardship to individual litigants. They were denied the protection of their own national law, even in the clearest cases of wrongful action by the foreign state. Of course, in many cases, the state would voluntarily compensate an individual for any loss – in order to prevent friction with the state of nationality – or the state of nationality could take up the matter if it raised an issue of state responsibility (see Chapter 9). Yet, for the individual there remained the uncertainty and risk of dealing with a foreign sovereign state, and when ideological changes and a general expansion in world trade after the First World War caused an increase in direct state involvement in commercial activities, the doctrine of absolute immunity became too high a price to pay for maintaining strict adherence to the theory of the sovereign equality of states. The greater involvement of states in ordinary commercial dealings meant that a greater number of individuals fell foul of absolute immunity. More importantly, absolute immunity was becoming counter-productive as those countries that still adhered to it found themselves facing a decline in their share of world trade because of a failure to safeguard the rights of private citizens and corporations. The result of these changes in the organisation of international commerce, combined with some concern for the rights of the individual, led to the development of the doctrine of restrictive immunity.

Under the doctrine of restrictive state immunity, a state has immunity from the jurisdiction of a local court only in respect of certain classes of acts. A distinction is to be drawn between acts *jure imperii* and acts *jure gestionis*. Acts *jure imperii* are acts of a sovereign nature in respect of which the state is immune, whereas acts *jure gestionis* are commercial acts in respect of which the state is subject to the jurisdiction of the territorial sovereign. Essentially, the distinction is designed to ensure that the state is treated as a normal litigant when it behaves like one, and as a sovereign when it exercises sovereign power. Restrictive immunity recognises, in effect, that the state may act in a variety of capacities and that it should have immunity only when it is acting as a state. It achieves a compromise between the desire to ensure that a foreign sovereign is not unduly restricted by the activities of inferior (national) courts and the desire to provide a forum for the settlement of disputes about national law that happen to involve states. It should be noted, however, that the restrictive theory does not necessarily deal with the question of the enforcement of court orders, as distinct from the 'mere' exercise of jurisdiction. This is a separate issue that is discussed later, where it will be seen that a state still has immunity from enforcement in a wide range of circumstances, even when it is subject to jurisdiction under the restrictive theory.

Today, the restrictive theory is adopted by a great many states, including the UK, the USA and most major trading nations. It is true that some states still follow the doctrine of absolute immunity, at least in theory, but as the work of the ILC has illustrated, there is near unanimity that restrictive immunity should be adopted in practice. Indeed, restrictive immunity has the advantage of providing a remedy for aggrieved individuals while at the same time encouraging the growth of trade and commerce. Given this, it will be appreciated that it is imperative that a reasonably clear distinction can be drawn between acts *jure imperii* and acts *jure gestionis*. If this is not possible, the restrictive theory loses much of its force. Herein lays the great difficulty of the restrictive theory.

It is easy enough to propose an abstract distinction between acts of a commercial nature and acts of a sovereign nature, but how this is to be made in practice is another matter entirely. Let us suppose that State A enters into a contract with a national of State B for the supply of steel. This might be thought to be a commercial transaction. Yet what if the steel is to be used to build an army barracks or a warship. Is it still a commercial act? Again, if State A refuses to pay for banknotes ordered from a company in State B, is this a commercial transaction and does it make any difference if the reason for breaking the contract is to steady the economy or to enable a new company in State A itself to supply the banknotes? As previously indicated, each state may develop its own criteria for distinguishing precisely between acts *jure imperii* and *jure gestionis*, as in the UK with the State Immunity Act 1978, and this makes *general* conclusions about the difference between acts *jure imperii* and *jure gestionis* even more fragile. Bearing this in mind, the following sections discuss some of the grounds upon which such a distinction could be made.

7.2.1 Purpose of the act

One ground of distinction might be the purpose of the transaction in respect of which immunity is claimed. Thus, if the contract for steel is in order to build an army barracks, it is an act *jure imperii*, because equipping the state's armed forces may be regarded as an act done in a sovereign capacity. However, if the steel is for a new office block for the civil service, then it is a commercial transaction, for the state is acting in a private capacity just like any other builder. Using this distinction, if the purpose is to achieve an act of sovereignty, there is immunity. If the purpose of the transaction is non-sovereign, there is no immunity.

Although this might at first sight appear to be an entirely logical way to proceed, a distinction based on the purpose of the act has not found favour with national courts. In this country, in *Trendtex Trading Corp.* v *Central Bank of Nigeria* [1977] 1 All ER 881, the Court of Appeal stated that the purpose of a state's act was immaterial in deciding whether it was *jure imperii* or *jure gestionis*. It was enough if the transaction itself was of a commercial type – such as a *contract* for the supply of goods or services. Similarly, in *I Congreso del Partido* [1981] 2 All ER 1064 the House of Lords thought the purpose of the act was not a sufficiently certain test upon which to base such an important distinction, and this was reiterated by the House in *Kuwait Airways Corp.* v *Iraqi Airways Company* [1995] 1 WLR 1147 when interpreting the scope of immunity under the UK State Immunity Act 1978 and in *Lampen-Wolfe* when considering the common law. In fact, as was made clear in the US case of *Victory Transport Inc.* v *Comisaria General De Abastecimientos y Transpertos*, 35 ILR 110 (1963), the purpose test is unsatisfactory because all the acts of a sovereign can be said to have a 'public' purpose of some sort – as in our example of the steel for the office block for the civil service – and the US court pointed out that a state itself has no 'private' needs because it always acts for the benefit of the country as it sees it. On this basis, all state acts could be classed as *jure imperii* and this is clearly ridiculous. Again, the purpose test is useful only if national courts are able to determine what the proper bounds of state activity actually are, and it is only if a court is able to identify what may properly be regarded as a 'public' or 'sovereign' purpose that this test has any value. This is clearly unrealistic and it is courting disaster to expect a national court to decide – even if it were able – whether the policies or acts of a foreign state were 'for the public good'. The difficulties experienced by the House of Lords in determining whether the acts of Senator Pinochet were part of his 'public function' are a good illustration (see *ex parte Pinochet*). However, despite the drawbacks the purpose test was incorporated in the original version of the ILC Draft Articles on Jurisdictional Immunities, albeit in a subsidiary role, and this is repeated in the UN Convention. Article 2 of the UN Convention allows the purpose of a 'transaction' to be relevant in determining its nature if, in the practice of the state concerned, 'purpose' has been a relevant consideration in the past. In this sense, the Convention attempts to broker a compromise between those states that favour giving 'purpose' the pre-eminent role and those that would exclude it altogether. That this was not universally welcomed was apparent when states were asked to comment on the Draft Articles but the subsidiary role of 'the purpose' of the transaction in defining a 'commercial' transaction seems now to be established. Indeed, this compromise solution is not *just* a reflection of an unresolved disagreement between states. It also recognises that each case is unique and that 'purpose' may or may not be relevant depending on the precise issue before the national court. In other words, that the distinction between sovereign and commercial acts is not two-dimensional (nature *or* purpose) but rather more sophisticated. For example, in the Canadian case *United States* v *The Public Service Alliance of Canada* (1993) 32 ILM 1, the Canadian Supreme Court decided that the 'purpose' and 'nature' tests (see section 7.2.2) for determining whether a transaction was commercial were complementary rather than in opposition. So, at least in so far as distinguishing a commercial transaction under Canadian legislation, '[n]ature and purpose are interrelated, and it is impossible to determine the former without considering the latter'. Although being less helpful when it comes to making the distinction in a concrete case, this rather broader, contextual approach may reflect more accurately the complex nature of the many transactions in which states can become engaged.

7.2.2 Nature of the act

The test proposed here is whether the act in question is of its nature an essentially commercial transaction. A *contract* for the supply of goods is a commercial transaction *par excellence* and, under this test, all such contracts would be *jure gestionis*. In our example, the contract for the supply of banknotes is a commercial transaction, even though the purpose of the transaction – currency supply – is a sovereign matter. The same is true of the steel contract, whether it be for the army, a warship or the civil service.

This seems to be the test adopted in the *Trendtex* case where the court was concerned primarily with the intrinsic nature of the arrangement entered into by the Central Bank. On finding that the transaction was essentially 'commercial', the Bank had no immunity, even if it could be regarded as performing functions and charged with the purposes of an organ of the state. Likewise in *Central Bank of Yemen* v *Cardinal Finance Investments Corp.* [2000] EWCA Civ 266, a promissory note was enforceable between the parties as a commercial transaction even though concluded by a state's central bank. In *Victory Transport*, however, this approach was criticised on the ground that some contracts that are prima facie commercial transactions can only be made by states, as with a contract for the purchase of a warship. In such cases, the 'nature' test does not reflect the exclusively sovereign nature of the transaction. It seems, then, that this test is not entirely satisfactory because it does not accept that some sovereign activities can only be conducted through means that appear essentially 'commercial'. The nature test would not, for example, protect a developing state that sought to boost its economy (a sovereign act) through normal commercial contracts with foreign investors. It was concerns of this type that led the ILC away from a strict 'nature' test and which found expression in the *Public Service Alliance of Canada* Case (section 7.2.3). Likewise, although the House of Lords in *Lampen-Wolfe* refer with approval to the 'nature' test (when considering UK common law), the actual decision makes it clear that 'nature' alone is not a sufficient criterion (see section 7.2.4).

7.2.3 Subject matter

After rejecting both the 'pure' nature and purpose tests, the test proposed by the US court in *Victory Transport* was a pragmatic one. Its solution was to look at different types of acts and classify them according to their subject matter. Thus, administrative acts such as the expulsion of aliens, legislative acts such as the nationalisation of foreign-owned property, acts concerning the armed forces and acts regulating the economy could all be regarded as acts *jure imperii*, irrespective of their purpose or the manner (e.g. by contract) in which they were concluded. The important thing was to draw up a list of acts in advance to which a court could make reference should a dispute arise. There was to be pre-selection of acts *jure imperii* and *jure gestionis* and this was to be conclusive. Neither 'purpose' nor 'nature' could affect the outcome. The merit of this list system is that a court would not have to decide on the nature of a transaction or attempt to divine its purpose. The court could consult its list and decide accordingly without inquiring into the motives of a foreign state or scrutinising its domestic policies. It would be relieved of the burden of determining the merits, or otherwise, of the internal policies of other states. Of course, there is the initial difficulty of assigning each type of transaction to its proper category, but this could be done by prior agreement between states or by domestic legislation. In neither case would the decision be left to a national court. On the other hand, the defect of this system is that it could result in arbitrary or discriminatory choices and, certainly, it could not take account of the particular or peculiar circumstances of individual cases.

7.2.4 The two-stage test: a contextual approach

In *I Congreso del Partido*, the House of Lords developed a two-stage test in order to distinguish between acts *jure imperii* and acts *jure gestionis* for disputes arising under English common law. The case concerned two ships (*The Playa Larga* and *The Marble Islands*) carrying sugar to Chile, both of which were diverted elsewhere on the orders of the Cuban government after a new government came to power in Chile. An action *in rem* was brought by the Chilean owners of the cargo against *I Congreso*, another ship owned by Cuba. Cuba claimed state immunity.

In order to determine whether Cuba was entitled to state immunity, the House of Lords held that the distinction between acts *jure imperii* and acts *jure gestionis* depended on whether the relevant acts of Cuba were acts of private law or acts done by virtue of governmental authority. An act of private law was one that could be performed by a private citizen. However, in applying this test, the court was to look at the whole case, both the initial transaction between the parties and the particular act that gave rise to the dispute between them. In order for the matter to be *jure gestionis*, both of these acts, the initial act and the act giving rise to the claim (the act in breach), had to be private law acts. There was, then, a two-stage test. First, was the initial act between the parties a private law act as could be done by a citizen and, secondly, was the act which caused the dispute also a private law act as could be done by a citizen?

In the case itself, the initial act was a contract for the supply of sugar and this was clearly a private law act because it could have been done by an individual. What, then, of the act that caused the dispute – the second act – this being the diversion of the ships and the discharge of the cargo to third parties? In respect of *The Playa Larga*, which was actually owned by the Cuban state, the act of diverting it was one that any owner exercising normal powers of ownership could have achieved. It was, therefore, a private law act and there was no immunity. In respect of the second vessel, *The Marble Islands*, this was not owned by the Cuban state at the relevant time, and for Lords Wilberforce and Edmund-Davies the order diverting it did not seem to be done as owner but in exercise of sovereign authority. However, a majority of their Lordships thought that the act of discharging the cargo of *The Marble Islands* at another destination was a private law act, being analogous to the tort of conversion in UK law. Therefore, Cuba was not immune in respect of the actions maintained by the owners of the cargoes of both ships. In both cases, the initial act and the act in breach were private law acts.

All of their Lordships in *I Congreso* agreed with this approach in principle, although Lord Bridge did have some reservations. However, the fact that two of their Lordships disagreed as to the outcome in respect of the second ship shows that the application of a two-stage test may be difficult in practice. After all, it will still be necessary to determine which are the relevant acts and whether they were such that a private citizen could accomplish them. Indeed, because the act that caused the dispute is to be examined, as well as the initial transaction between the parties, some states may be able to claim immunity under this test by using their sovereign powers to break commercial contracts. Despite these reservations, the *I Congreso* test does have some advantages and it was applied again in the UK in *Sengupta* v *Republic of India* [1983] ICR 221, in *Littrell* v *United States of America (No. 2)* [1994] 2 All ER 203, and in *Lampen-Wolfe*, all cases falling outside the UK's State Immunity Act. A similar rounded approach has now been explicitly approved in *Egypt* v *Gamal-Eldin* [1996] 2 All ER 237 (see later). Furthermore, a 'two-stage' approach has been adopted by the Canadian Supreme Court in a case concerning the interpretation of their State Immunity Act 1985. In *United States* v *The Public Service Alliance of Canada* [1993] ILM 1, the USA was claiming immunity in respect of a dispute with its Canadian workers employed on a US military base in Canada. A majority of the Court decided that, under the Act, the 'nature' of the disputed transaction was central in deciding whether the transaction was 'commercial' but, as noted previously, that its purpose may well affect what that nature actually is. Furthermore, the Court went on to say that they could look to both the nature of the transaction (an employment contract) and the context in which it operated (on a foreign state's military base). So, while the contract was undoubtedly commercial in nature (even allowing for an element of purpose), the context was undoubtedly sovereign. Hence, the USA had immunity because both 'steps' were not commercial. While this case turns essentially on the meaning of Canadian legislation, it does illustrate that a two-stage test is flexible enough to meet the criticisms of both the 'nature' and 'purpose' tests discussed previously. Explicit reliance on this 'in context' approach is found in the *Lampen-Wolfe* decision, where the provision of educational services (a seemingly non-sovereign act) was held to attract immunity because the services were provided for US military personnel on base in the UK. (See also *New Zealand Banking Group* v *Australia*, noted (1990) 39 ICLQ 950.) Likewise, in *McElhinney* v *Williams and Her Majesty's Secretary of State for Northern Ireland* (1995) the Irish Supreme Court specifically followed a contextual approach to determine the scope of restrictive immunity in the Irish Republic, believing that this was now required as a matter of international law. Consequently, an alleged tortious act committed by a UK soldier within the Irish Republic was a sovereign act because of the circumstances of the claim, even though (like the *Public Service Case*) the impugned act appeared at face value to be anything but 'sovereign'. All of this demonstrates that national courts, at least of trading nations, approach concrete questions of sovereign immunity in the light of the reasons behind the doctrine, whether they be applying common law or statute. This seems entirely appropriate and will avoid a mechanical application of what must necessarily be a flexible set of rules.

These four tests have, at one time or another, been proposed as a means of distinguishing between acts *jure imperii* and acts *jure gestionis*. As indicated earlier, each state may differ in the test it adopts in its national law. The important point is, then, that international law allows a state to offer restrictive immunity, based on the distinction between acts *jure imperii* and acts *jure gestionis*. It may be that some states will still wish to accord absolute immunity to foreign sovereign states and, of course, they may do so given that this is a matter for their national law. However, it is now clear that a state will not incur international responsibility by limiting the immunity of other states to disputes arising in certain specific circumstances. Only if immunity is completely withdrawn (as in the *Jurisdictional Immunities Case* 2012), or restrictive immunity wrongly applied, will responsibility at international law exist.

7.2.5 Immunity and violations of international law

State immunity is essentially a doctrine that allows a state to plead immunity before national courts in respect of the application of local law. The 'state', in its various guises (e.g. to include a government department, and agents such as police officers – see *Jones* v *Saudi Arabia* (2006)), is able to escape the application of national law by the national court. Sometimes, however, a national court may be authorised to apply international law to a particular dispute, as where the court asserts jurisdiction over international crimes of universal jurisdiction (see Chapter 6). In *ex parte Pinochet*, one possible explanation (there were other reasons) for the denial of immunity in that case was that Senator Pinochet was charged with torture contrary to international law. In other words, is it possible that international law might not require states to grant immunity for international crimes, or acts contrary to rules of *jus cogens*, and indeed may require that immunity be denied?

Despite much commentary that this would be a welcome development, it is clear that at present immunity remains available even if the alleged offence is one that might be regarded as a crime for which an individual may be tried under international law and even if it involves a breach of a rule of *jus cogens*. In the *Jurisdictional Immunities Case* (2012), Italian courts had exercised jurisdiction over Germany by allowing civil claims in respect of the actions of Nazi Germany in Italy. There was no doubt (and neither state denied) that the actions of Nazi Germany were illegal under international law and constituted some of the worse incidents of inhumanity that the world had seen. Nevertheless, once it was established that the subject matter of the claims attracted immunity (i.e. they were the actions of a state's armed forces), immunity necessarily followed. As the ICJ pointed out, there is in fact no conflict between rules giving immunity and rules imposing individual criminal responsibility liability for crimes or state actions contrary to rules of cogens. This is because the 'rules of State immunity are procedural in character and are confined to determining whether or not the courts of one State may exercise jurisdiction in respect of another State. They do not bear upon the question whether or not the conduct in respect of which the proceedings are brought was lawful or unlawful.' This confirmed the earlier jurisprudence of the *Case Concerning the Arrest Warrant of 11 April 2000 (Congo v Belgium)* (2002) which had decided that the immunity of diplomatic agents remained in place even where an individual was alleged to have committed crimes against international law for which personal international responsibility existed.

As noted, the Court's conclusion in this regard cannot be challenged as a matter of law. The Court in *Jurisdictional Immunities* conducted a thorough examination of state practice and of the decisions of local courts and found almost overwhelming state practice confirming that immunity should still be given in cases involving breaches of international law, either by states or individuals acting for states. In the UK, for example, the Court of Appeal in *Al-Adsani* v *Government of*

Kuwait 107 ILR 536 had granted immunity under the strict terms of the UK State Immunity Act 1978 for alleged acts of torture and this approach was confirmed by the House of Lords in *Jones v Saudi Arabia* (2006). In *Jones*, the House was very clear that neither UK law, nor more pertinently international law itself, required the denial of immunity 'just because' the alleged offence was contrary to a rule of *jus cogens* or was one that attracted universal jurisdiction. So, the immunity of Saudi Arabia was upheld irrespective of the (unproven) allegations of torture by state officials and the UK's own State Immunity Act 1978. A similar view had been taken prior to *Jones* by the European Court of Human Rights in three decisions: *Al-Adsani v UK* (2002) 34 EHRR 273, *Fogarty v UK* (2001) and *McElhinney v Ireland* (2001).

As this consistent judicial activity demonstrates, immunity is a powerful concept in international law. In cases where the subject matter is a sovereign act, immunity *from national courts* extends to acts contrary to the national law of that state and contrary to international law itself, even to rules of cogens. Note, however, that state immunity is not an 'excuse' or 'defence' to a charge of violation of a rule of *jus cogens* (or any other rule of international law). It simply precludes a national court from trying the matter. There will still be international responsibility, either for the state or for the individual. That responsibility can be enforced in an appropriate international forum, such as the ICJ itself or the International Criminal Court.

7.3 The UN Convention on Jurisdictional Immunities of States and their Property 2004 (the ILC Draft Articles)

The International Law Commission's long work in this area came to fruition in 2004 with the conclusion of the UN Convention on Jurisdictional Immunities of States and Their Property 2004. This was based on extensive work by the International Law Commission and much comment by states on the ILC's Draft Articles. The Convention is not yet in force (requiring thirty parties; as at 1 September 2012, there were thirteen), but it is the result of the most extensive analysis of state practice ever undertaken in this area and is already being relied on as *evidence* of the content of international law – *Jones v Saudi Arabia*. In effect, the UN Convention favours the restrictive approach to immunity. Thus, a state will not be immune in respect of a 'commercial transaction' (Art. 10) nor in relation to a number of specific matters such as employment contracts (Art. 11) and cases of personal injury or damage to tangible property in the forum state (Art. 12 – though it is not clear if the immunity is denied if the acts are *jure imperii*, *Jurisdictional Immunities Case*). In Part IV, the Convention also provides for a separate regime dealing with measures of constraint (i.e. enforcement of court orders).

As noted, the UN Convention is not in force and while some states regard it as reflecting customary law (or at least promoting its development), other states have a number of difficulties. First, the definition of 'commercial transaction' in Art. 2 allows for an element of 'purpose', but this was criticised by some states at the time (including the UK). Secondly, although the UK and others also favour limiting a state's immunity from enforcement as well as from process, Arts 18 and 19 propose relatively far-reaching immunity from the enforcement jurisdiction of local courts. Thirdly, not all states agree with the wide-ranging definition of 'the state' found in Art. 2(1), but favour instead granting immunity to 'political subdivisions' of a state, or separate state entities within a state, *only* when the substance of their activities demands it. Although the UN Convention itself contains a sharper definition of 'the state' than that originally proposed by the ILC, it may not be enough to tempt states like the UK to ratify the Convention. All in all, on these matters of detail, the UK's view is consistent with those of a major trading nation endeavouring to protect its nationals from the loss of normal remedies in other states' national courts. On the other hand, a developing state might well regard the relatively wide immunity postulated in the Convention as a vital part of its programme for economic development through increased trade.

In addition to these matters, it is also clear that the ILC has been divided over the proper theoretical approach to state immunity. On the one hand, it was argued that a general rule of absolute immunity should be postulated (as in the UK legislation) which should then be made subject to a list of specific exceptions (i.e. cases in which there is no immunity). On the other, some ILC members favoured a simple list indicating the circumstances in which there would be no immunity, without expressing any view on the wider question. Indeed, the matter is not entirely academic because if a general rule of absolute immunity is postulated, any state activity that falls outside the list of exceptions (i.e. which is not within a class of case subject to jurisdiction) will necessarily attract immunity. Under the Convention, Art. 5 now provides that a state enjoys immunity 'from the jurisdiction of the courts of another state subject to the provisions of the present Convention' and this lends itself to the UK's general approach. In any event, as can be seen from the UK's legislation and cases decided under it (section 7.4.2), the initial acceptance of absolute immunity in theory is unlikely to affect the working of the real test of restrictive immunity in practice. It should also be noted that problems concerning the compatibility of existing domestic legislation (such as the UK State Immunity Act) with the terms of the Convention have now been overcome. Thus, Art. 2(3) provides that the definition of such matters as 'commercial contracts' and 'the state' in the Convention 'are without prejudice to the use of those terms or to the meanings which may be given to them in other international instruments or in the internal law of any state'. Effectively, this means that the UK's domestic legislation (and that of other states) which denies immunity more effectively than the UN Treaty – e.g. because of a different definition of 'commercial contract' or 'the state' etc. – will not be incompatible with it. Neither will 'other international instruments' such as the European Convention on State Immunity. Finally, it is interesting that whereas Art. 10 denies immunity in 'commercial transaction' cases, it no longer does so by means of the fiction that the foreign sovereign has 'consented' to the local jurisdiction. Such a clause, which was designed to safeguard the notion of the inherent sovereignty and equality of all states, and which was found in earlier Drafts of ILC Articles, has been rejected in favour of a much more honest and practical approach that does not seek to justify the withdrawal of absolute immunity on any theoretical grounds. On a balanced view, then, the current Convention represents a more realistic appraisal of the practical problems involved in immunity issues and may yet be the springboard to a truly global approach to immunity.

7.4 State immunity in the United Kingdom

7.4.1 The common law until 1978

Until the mid-1970s, the UK accorded absolute immunity to all states acting within its jurisdiction. There may have been certain exceptions to this, such as proceedings relating to the title to land within the UK (e.g. *The Charkieh* (1873) LR 4 A & E 59), and matters relating to trust funds and company assets (e.g. *Larivière* v *Morgan* (1872) 7 Ch App 550), but generally a foreign state was able to escape jurisdiction if it was recognised as sovereign by the UK (see Chapter 5 on recognition). It followed that it could also escape enforcement of a court order.

However, in *The Philippine Admiral* v *Wallem Shipping (Hong Kong)* [1977] AC 373, the Privy Council decided that the theory of restrictive immunity should apply to actions *in rem* – that is, where ownership of property such as ships and land can be asserted against the whole world and not just between the parties to a dispute. In the Judicial Committee's view, the restrictive theory was more equitable, although precedent dictated that absolute immunity should continue to apply to actions *in personam*. In reality, of course, there was no real basis for a distinction between actions *in rem* and actions *in personam*, especially since it was unknown in other jurisdictions. Consequently, in *Trendtex Trading Corp.* v *Central Bank of Nigeria*, the Court of Appeal adopted the doctrine of restrictive immunity for acts *in personam* as well as those *in rem*. This brought the UK into line with the majority of major trading countries. The Court's view in *Trendtex* was that international law had developed to such an extent that restrictive immunity was now so firmly established as a rule of customary law that it could be incorporated into English law without an Act of Parliament (see Chapter 4). Finally, in *I Congreso*, the House of Lords confirmed that the doctrine of restrictive immunity was part of the common law and was applicable to all actions involving recognised sovereign states before UK national courts.

7.4.2 The State Immunity Act 1978 – the law after 1978

In 1978, the UK passed the State Immunity Act (SIA). The circumstances in which immunity may be accorded in the UK are governed by this Act, although the common law will be relevant for those matters excluded from the Act (e.g. matters relating to foreign armed forces: *Lampen-Wolfe*). The Act came into force on 22 November 1978 although it does not apply retrospectively to transactions that took place before this date (see e.g. *Hispano Americana Mercantile SA* v *Central Bank of Nigeria* [1979] 2 Lloyd's Rep 277). This is why the *I Congreso* case was decided according to the common law. The Act was passed in order that the UK could ratify the 1926 Brussels Convention on the Unification of Certain Rules relating to the Immunity of State Owned Vessels and the 1972 European Convention on State Immunity. Several sections of the Act are designed specifically to give effect in national law to these treaties, although the Act would probably fulfil the UK's obligations under the UN Convention. Another important consideration was to ensure that the UK remained a centre of world trade and commerce by providing a remedy in national law for the individual trader in disputes with states.

7.4.2.1 General scheme

The Act lays down a general principle of immunity (s. 1), but makes this subject to a list of wide-ranging exceptions (ss. 2–11). In effect, the Act establishes a code of restrictive immunity, although if a case falls within the Act and an 'exception' does not apply, the state's immunity will be assured (s. 1). For example, in *Al-Adsani* where the acts causing injury took place abroad, there was no exception under the Act, and so absolute immunity applied; likewise in *Jones* v *Saudi Arabia* where there was no plausible exception to the rule of immunity found in s. 1 on the facts of the case. In s. 2 it is made clear that a state that would otherwise have immunity under the Act can submit to the jurisdiction after a dispute has arisen or by prior written agreement. This reverses the old common law rule of *Kahan* v *Pakistan Federation* [1951] 2 KB 1003, whereby a state was unable to submit to the jurisdiction of the court in advance. Consequently, in *Svenska Petroleum* v *Lithuania* (2006) and *Donegal* v *Zambia* (2007), the court held that written submissions to the jurisdiction in (respectively) an arbitration agreement and a compromise agreement meant that immunity from enforcement was not available. Similarly, in *A Company* v *Republic of X* (1989) *The Times*, Saville J held that the state had no immunity from the enforcement powers of the court (except in respect of diplomatic property, see section 7.4.2.3) because it had agreed with the claimant in their contract that it had waived 'whatever defence it may have of sovereign immunity for itself or its property'. Moreover, it is clear from these cases that such agreements are not to be construed narrowly just because the defendant was a sovereign state: so they were not simply a waiver of immunity from jurisdiction, but also from enforcement. Waiver may still be made by acting in proceedings, except where this is done for the purpose of claiming immunity or asserting an interest in property (s. 2(3) and (4)), although all waivers must be made by the head of the state's diplomatic mission (*Malaysian Industrial Redevelopment Authority* v *Jeyasingham* [1998] ICR 307 – alleged waiver not effective as not given by Head of Mission). In *Egypt* v *Gamal-Eldin* [1996] 2 All ER 237, a letter sent to an employment tribunal by the Medical Officer of the Egyptian Mission did not, as a matter of interpretation, constitute a waiver or submission to jurisdiction, nor did an uncompleted form in *London Branch of the Nigerian Universities Commission* v *Bastians* [1995] ICR 358. Likewise, in *Ahmed* v *Government of the Kingdom of Saudi Arabia* [1996] 2 All ER 248 a solicitor's letter advising the government that employees might have certain employment rights in UK law could not be interpreted as a 'written agreement' to waive within s. 2 of the Act. In essence, it is for the court deciding the matter to investigate whether a waiver has occurred and if it has been given by the person authorised to do so on behalf of the state – *Farouk* v *Yemen* (2005).

Also by way of general matters, under s. 15 SIA, if the immunities conferred by the 1978 Act are more than, or less than, those accorded by other states or are less than those required by conventions or treaties in force, the immunities under the Act may be extended or restricted as the case may be by Order in Council. So, if the UK becomes a party to the UN Convention, it could, if necessary, bring national law into line by using this power. Lastly, where a claim of immunity is raised by a state, this is to be treated as a preliminary issue, to be settled conclusively before the court addresses any aspect of the merits of the dispute (*Maclaine Watson* v *Dept of Trade* [1988] 3 All ER 257 at 317, CA) and it is an issue which the court should consider of its own motion, even if not pleaded by the allegedly immune state – *Military Affairs Office of the Embassy of the State of Kuwait* v *Caramba-Coker* (2003). It is, however, a matter to be settled in open court and not (simply because a state is involved) in secret session – *Janan* v *King Fahad* (2006).

7.4.2.2 Immunity from jurisdiction

Perhaps the most important provision of the Act is s. 3, for this contains the primary grounds on which a state will *not* be immune from the jurisdiction of the courts of the UK. Under this section, a state is not immune in respect of proceedings relating to 'a commercial transaction entered into by the state' or 'an obligation which by virtue of a contract (whether a commercial transaction or not) falls to be performed wholly or partly in the United Kingdom'. Most significantly, in s. 3(3), the Act defines what is meant by a commercial transaction:

(a) any contract for the supply of goods or services, or

(b) any loan or other transaction for the provision of finance, guarantee, indemnity or other financial obligation, or

(c) any other transaction or activity into which a state enters or engages otherwise than in the exercise of sovereign authority.

It is immediately apparent that if a matter falls within either s. 3(3)(a) or (b) it is by definition a commercial transaction. There is no need for a court to decide whether it arises from sovereign authority and no need to enquire into the nature or purpose of the transaction. In the examples considered previously, the contracts for the supply of steel and banknotes would be commercial transactions, being contracts for the supply of goods or services. So, in *Commissioners of Customs and Excise* v *Ministry of Industries and Military Manufacturing, Republic of Iraq* (see (1994) 43 ICLQ 194), a contract relating to parts for the Iraqi 'Supergun' fell within s. 3(3)(a) and was not immune and in *Central Bank of Yemen* v *Cardinal Finance Investments Corp.*, a promissory note contract did not attract immunity. Importantly, however, in order for immunity to be denied under s. 3(3)(a), the proceedings between the parties must be related to that contract; that is, the disputed matter must arise out of the contract because immunity cannot be denied simply because a contract lurked in the background. So, in *Lampen-Wolfe*, the claimant had concluded a contract with the USA for the provision of services. However, she sued in libel because of comments made about her performance under her contract. This was not, therefore, a suit on the contract itself and, had the Act been applicable, s. 3(3)(a) would not have denied immunity for the USA.

As far as s. 3(3)(c) is concerned, here the court is directed that any other transaction or activity *may* be a commercial transaction if it does not arise from 'sovereign authority'. Obviously, for this subsection, the old common law may still be important as an aid to interpretation, for the court must decide for itself whether the transaction or activity was done as a result of 'sovereign authority'. In *New Zealand Banking Group Ltd* v *Australia*, for example, the claimants alleged that the defendants had committed the tort of negligent misrepresentation during the Tin Council affair. The issue turned on the construction of s. 3(3)(c) and the judge held that the 'activity' for which immunity was claimed (which could actually be a single act) must be looked at in context in order to determine whether it was done by virtue of 'sovereign authority'. In fact, he held that the allegations arose out of the failure of commercial loan contracts and therefore the alleged tort could not have been committed under sovereign authority. He also thought that immunity might be denied by s. 3(3)(b), the alleged tort being an 'obligation' which arose by virtue of contract to be performed in the UK. This case suggests that a tortious activity may be caught by s. 3, as well as by ss. 5 and 6, but in *Lampen-Wolfe*, Lord Millet (obiter) thought that s. 3(3)(c) referred to commercial relationships falling short of contracts rather than 'a unilateral tortious act'. At present, then, the extent to which s. 3(3)(c) does include torts is unclear, but in *Grovit* v *De Nederlandsche Bank* (2005) the trial judge accepted a plea of immunity on behalf of the Bank (as exercising sovereign authority within s. 14 of the Act – section 7.4.2.4) in respect of an alleged libel contained in a letter. In essence, as the *New Zealand Banking* case suggests, perhaps the best view is to accept that the meaning of 'sovereign authority' under s. 3(3)(c) depends on the circumstances in which the dispute arises.

This flexible approach to the interpretation of 'sovereign authority' under the Act has been confirmed by the House of Lords in *Kuwait Airways Corp.* v *Iraqi Airways Company* [1995] 1 WLR 1147, although that case also revealed just how difficult it can be to apply the concept in practice. In *Kuwait Airways Corp.*, the important issue was whether the Iraqi Airways Company (IAC) could claim immunity as being in the shoes of Iraq itself after seizing certain aircraft in Kuwait on the orders of the Iraqi government following the invasion in 1990 (on which see section 7.4.2.4). The issue turned in part on the meaning of 'sovereign authority', with Lord Goff (for the majority) taking the view that the initial seizure was a sovereign act, but subsequent use of the aircraft by IAC was non-sovereign, giving only partial immunity. Lords Mustill and Slynn, dissenting on this point, believed that the IAC's actions could not be dissected in this fashion and that when looked at as a whole, the entire action was based on sovereign authority and was not a commercial transaction and therefore was entirely immune. Underlying the majority view in this case is a desire to ensure that UK jurisdiction reaches as far as possible where the rights of an 'innocent' party are at risk, while the minority are not happy with fine distinctions that subvert the purpose of the state immunity doctrine, albeit that an individual is thereby protected. As we shall see later when discussing IAC's claim to be entitled to immunity as the *alter ego* of Iraq itself, there is much to commend what has been described as Lord Slynn's and Mustill's holistic approach to the interpretation of sovereign authority under the SIA (see e.g. Evans (1996) 45 ICLQ 401). It is suggested that this minority view is more in tune with the two-stage or contextual test of *I Congreso*, *Littrell* and *Lampen-Wolfe* all of which aim to see the imputed activities in the round, as opposed to the piecemeal approach of the majority in *Kuwait Airways Corp.* The preferred global approach was applied by the Court of Appeal in *Egypt* v *Gamal-Eldin*, applying *Littrell*, where Mummery J said that 'the proper approach to the question whether an activity is commercial or in the exercise of sovereign authority, involves looking at all the circumstances in relation to the activities and their context and then consider all the factors together. No one factor is in itself determinative.... It is relevant to look at the nature of the activity, the identity of those who deal with it, and the place where it takes place.' This is an admirable summary of the modern approach to these issues.

Section 4 of the Act deals specifically with contracts of employment because these are not within s. 3. Generally, a state will not be immune in respect of proceedings relating to a contract of employment where the contract was made in the UK and the work is to be wholly or partly performed there. There are limited exceptions to this rule, as for contracts made with nationals of the state claiming immunity provided that the national's contract was not for 'commercial purposes' (e.g. *Egypt v Gamal-Eldin* and what would have been the position in *Sengupta v Republic of India* had the matter not fallen completely outside the Act) or if the parties to the contract have agreed otherwise in writing (s. 4(2)–(4)). In addition, there will be no loss of immunity in respect of proceedings concerning the employment of members of the diplomatic mission or consular post (s. 16(1)(a)) as applied in both *Egypt v Gamal-Eldin* and *Ahmed v Saudi Arabia*. By way of contrast, we may note that the position may be different in other states. For example, under the Canadian State Immunity Act, a contract of employment between a state and a national may be a sovereign and immune act if the context so requires, as where the contract relates to employment on a foreign state's military base in Canada (*United States v The Public Service Alliance of Canada* (1993) 32 ILM 1).

Section 5 provides that there will be no immunity for death or personal injuries caused in the UK (thus allowing immunity for injury committed abroad: *Al-Adsani v Government of Kuwait* 107 ILR 536, *Jones v Saudi Arabia*), or where there is a loss of tangible property; and s. 6 removes immunity for proceedings relating to interests in, or obligations arising from, immovable property situated in the UK (save for matters relating to the diplomatic mission (s. 16(1)(b)) or proceedings in respect of the armed forces of a state while in the UK (s. 16(2), *Littrell v United States of America (No. 2)* [1994] 2 All ER 3 and *Lampen-Wolfe*)). Section 6 also deals with indirect impleading, as where a state is indirectly implicated in a dispute – for example, where Mr A sues Mr B over ownership of a piece of property, and State C, a third party, also has a claim on that property. In such circumstances, s. 6 provides that the state shall not have immunity unless it would have done so had proceedings been brought against it directly. In *Re Rafidian Bank* [1992] BCLC 301, it was held that Iraq's title to money held at the Bank (which was subject to a winding-up order) was not indirectly challenged when the Bank's liquidators refused to pay out the full amount owed in preference to other creditors because Iraq's ownership of their funds was not in doubt, merely the amount which they would eventually receive on distribution of the Bank's assets.

Section 7 deals with questions relating to intellectual property (e.g. trademarks and copyright), s. 8 concerns membership of bodies corporate and s. 9 preserves the court's supervisory jurisdiction over arbitration proceedings into which the state has voluntarily entered in writing. Section 10 is important in practice, for it deals with a state's position in respect of Admiralty proceedings, particularly its liability to jurisdiction in matters affecting ships. Generally, under s. 10, a state is not immune if the ship was used for commercial purposes, as defined by s. 3, with some modifications for those states that are parties to the Brussels Convention referred to earlier. Section 11 deals with customs and excise duties (although not other taxes), again with reference to property used for 'commercial purposes'.

As one can see, the Act presents a fairly detailed scheme regulating the grant of state immunity in respect of the jurisdiction of UK courts. In fact, as a result of the Act, the circumstances in which immunity is refused (and the court therefore has jurisdiction) are now greater than those when immunity is given. The *Kuwait* case is simply the most complicated on a growing list of decisions which interpret the

SIA in a manner which denies immunity, but we should note that UK courts do not seek to subvert the Act and will accord immunity where the Act requires it – even in cases of severe harm to individuals, *Al-Adsani*, *Jones* v *Saudi Arabia*. By way of contrast, when analysing the question of state immunity from the enforcement of court orders, it is clear that the Act leans heavily in favour of the state. Indeed, this is one of the ways that the Act attempts to strike an even balance between the proper concerns of the foreign sovereign and the need to ensure access to UK courts for the individual.

7.4.2.3 Immunity from execution and enforcement

Under the State Immunity Act, a foreign sovereign state may well be subject to the jurisdiction of the court, but this does not necessarily mean that a court order can be enforced against it compulsorily. Immunity from the exercise of jurisdiction is different from immunity from enforcement. So it is that immunity from the execution of judgments and related procedural privileges are dealt with in s. 13. Under this section, a state is not liable to fine or committal for failure to produce a document relating to proceedings in which it is a party and, more importantly, a state cannot be made subject to an injunction, order for specific performance or order for the recovery of land or other property, unless it consents in writing, s. 13(3), *Svenska Petroleum v Lithuania*, *A Company Ltd* v *Republic of X*. Moreover, under s. 13(4), the property of a state may not be subject to the enforcement process in any manner unless it is used for 'commercial purposes' as defined in s. 3. In this regard, the UK Supreme Court in *SerVaas Incorporated (Appellant) v Rafidian Bank and others (Respondents)* (2012) has made it clear that property is 'used' for commercial purposes when that is the purpose the state now puts it to. It does not matter that the property may have been acquired as a result of sovereign activity, it is 'use' at the time of execution that matters. However, the Act also provides in s. 13(5) that the head of a state's diplomatic mission may certify that the property is, or is not, used for commercial purposes and that this will be conclusive unless there is clear evidence to the contrary. So, in *SerVaas* the head of mission had certified that the property (a debt owed to the state) was not for commercial purposes and so it was immune from enforcement.

Quite clearly, these are extensive procedural privileges and unless consent is given or the matter falls within s. 13(4) (commercial property), the individual may be left with a court order which the state cannot be compelled to satisfy. The loss of the injunction is particularly significant because it means that a state cannot be prevented from removing its assets from the jurisdiction in order to frustrate judgment: the freezing injunction awarded by the court in the *Trendtex Case* is no longer available. Similarly, the position of a central bank 'or other monetary authority' is even stronger, for under s. 14(4), their property shall never be regarded as being used for commercial purposes and, even if it be a 'separate entity' (see section 7.4.2.4, s. 14), it has all the other privileges accorded by s. 13 (see e.g. *AIG Capital Partners Inc v Kazakhstan*).

7.4.2.4 Who may claim immunity?

Section 14 deals with the important question of who can claim immunity on behalf of the state. Or, to put it another way, what is a 'state' for the purposes of this Act? The general principle is that whether any territory is a 'state' or a person is a head of state will be settled conclusively by a certificate from the Secretary of State for Foreign and Commonwealth Affairs (s. 21, *R (on the application of HRH Sultan of Pahang)* v *Secretary of State for the Home Department* 2011). This was essentially the position before the Act, as illustrated by *Duff Development Corp.* v *Kelantan* [1924] AC 797. As far as constituent territories of federal states are concerned, these do not have immunity in their own right unless an Order in Council so specifies. This reverses the principle applied in *Mellenger* v *New Brunswick Development Corp.* [1971] 1 WLR 604, where a Canadian province was given immunity as of right under the common law and without express enactment. In *Pocket Kings Ltd* v *Safenames Ltd* (2009), the Court examined s. 14 in detail in respect of constituent territories of federal states (in this case the Commonwealth of Kentucky and the United States). The court concluded, unsurprisingly, that the scheme of the Act meant that a constituent territory could not be regarded as the embodiment of the federal state in immunity proceedings, but neither could it claim to be *separately* sovereign. As the court said, it is not possible under the Act 'for an entity to be both a constituent territory of a federal state and a state in its own right'. Further, if the constituent territory claimed immunity because it was exercising 'sovereign authority' as a separate entity (see immediately below), that must be a claim to be exercising the sovereign authority of the federal state, rather than sovereign authority in some abstract sense. Thus, Kentucky was not immune as they were not equivalent to the United States, or sovereign in their own right, or (on the facts) exercising the sovereign authority of the United States.

Clearly, the 1978 Act itself provides one mechanism for deciding when an entity may be regarded as a 'state'. However, a UK court must still determine which institutions or entities comprise 'the state' and so are entitled to immunity in appropriate cases. Under s. 14, immunity may be claimed in an appropriate case by the sovereign or head of state acting in a public capacity, the government of the state and any department of the state. This seems clear enough and it may include entities which the UK would not otherwise regard as part of the state, *Propend Finance* v *Singh* (1999) (Australian police officer equivalent to Australian state on the facts) and *Jones* v *Saudi Arabia* (applying *Propend* and confirming state immunity for the acts of Lieutenant-Colonel Aziz of the Saudi police). However, the SIA is also concerned with 'separate entities', being those bodies that might claim to be part of 'the state'. A separate entity is a body 'distinct from the executive organs of the government of the state and capable of suing or being sued' (s. 14(1)). Normally, a separate entity will not be immune from the jurisdiction of the court, for the simple reason that it is not part of the state. Examples may include a Board of Trade, a state-run industry (see e.g. *Wilhelm Finance Inc* v *Ente Administrator Del Astillero Rio Santiago* 2009) or a state-owned public utility. Again, however, the Act recognises that some 'separate entities' may occasionally undertake 'state' functions, and it therefore provides that such bodies may have immunity if, but only if, the proceedings relate to anything done by it (the separate entity) in exercise of 'sovereign authority' and in circumstances in which the state itself would have had immunity had it acted directly. In effect, this means that a 'separate entity' will be entitled to immunity if it can show first that it was exercising the 'sovereign authority' of the state (*Pocket Kings Ltd* v *Safenames Ltd*) and secondly if the actual acts under consideration fall outside ss. 3 to 11 (i.e. immunity is not taken away). The matter is therefore one both of procedure (in what capacity was the entity acting) and of substance (what did they do). Clearly, this is a very limited immunity, designed only to ensure that the 'state' is protected even if it is not acting through a recognised arm of government. The reference to 'sovereign authority' means that the issues raised in connection with s. 3 (section 7.4.2.2) will be relevant here also.

Judicial consideration of s. 14 has been limited, but it seems there are two questions in play. First, is the entity in question a 'separate entity' (as opposed to an arm of the state) within the legislation and, secondly, if it is, was it exercising sovereign authority? As to the first question, the court in *Wilhelm Finance Inc v Ente Administrator Del Astillero Rio Santiago* focused on the status of the shipyard as revealed by the documents establishing it in order to determine whether it was a separate entity or an arm of the Argentine state. There was thus an emphasis on the formal position of the shipyard in Argentinian law. As to the second issue, in *Kuwait Airways Corp.* v *Iraqi Airways Co.* [1995] 1 WLR 1147, the House of Lords had to determine whether the Iraqi Airways Company (IAC) had seized and used Kuwait Airways' aircraft 'in the exercise of sovereign authority' (s. 14(2)(a)) and in circumstances where a state would be immune (s. 14(2)(b)). As we have seen, the majority found in favour of partial immunity only, although all five Lords of Appeal decided that IAC had at some time been acting as a sovereign authority. Lord Goff for the majority decided that the question whether a separate entity was acting in the exercise of sovereign authority was to be decided by asking whether it had engaged in a commercial transaction or not, using the definition in s. 3 of the Act. This approach *appears* quite sound, but it is submitted that it misses the point. If the question whether a separate entity is behaving as a 'sovereign' is to be answered by asking whether its acts were commercial or not, in reality this already assumes that the entity is *entitled* to claim immunity, because the 'commercial transaction' test addresses what the entity has done, not its status when it did it. Lord Goff's approach actually provides an answer to the question asked by s. 14(2)(b) of the Act: viz. were the acts of a kind as to attract immunity if they had been undertaken by a state? It does not tell us whether we need bother to ask that question. A different view was taken by Lords Mustill and Slynn who thought the issue was whether, first, the entity was acting on the basis of sovereign authority (i.e. on behalf of the state, s. 14(2)(a)) and, secondly, when it so acted whether its activities were 'commercial' or not within the Act. This seems more in tune with the general scheme of the SIA and has the merit of recognising that both limbs of s. 14(2) have a role to play. It appears to be the interpretation adopted in *Re Rafidian Bank* and *Grovit* v *De Nederlandsche Bank*.

Of course, it might still be difficult to know when a separate entity was acting on the basis of sovereign authority (i.e. on behalf of the state), but Lords Mustill and Slynn thought this was a question that could be answered only by analysing in full the circumstances in which the dispute took place. Consequently, it is apparent that the *Kuwait* case has revealed that 'sovereign authority' is used in two distinct senses in the 1978 Act. First to determine whether a separate entity can be treated as if it was the state it claims to represent (s. 14(2)(a)) and secondly to assess the nature of a disputed transaction (s. 3 and s. 14(2)(b)).

The preceding discussion assumes that it is possible to decide in the first place whether a litigant really is the state (in which case go straight to ss. 3–11), or whether it is a separate entity (s. 14, then perhaps ss. 3–11). This is crucial, for the 'state' may claim immunity as of right (in an appropriate case) whereas the separate entity must prove that it was nonetheless acting in the exercise of sovereign authority before any issue of immunity arises. The Act itself draws the distinction by reference to the national law of the claimant body – hence the reference to whether the body is capable of suing or being sued in its own right. This can be settled by evidence from a representative of the state or expert, but it is open to challenge (*Wilhelm Finance Inc* v *Ente Administrator Del Astillero Rio Santiago*). To this extent, the question of immunity in a UK court may rest on the provisions of the domestic law of another state. If, under that domestic law, the claimant is not a 'separate entity' that appears to conclude the matter and immunity is considered on the basis that it is part of 'the state'. It would seem, however, that this test is different from the old common law approach adopted in *Trendtex* where the court looked to the extent of state control and the functions of the entity in deciding whether it formed part of the 'state'. Under the common law, a body incorporated in a foreign state could not claim to be 'part of' that state simply by pleading that this status was granted by its own national law. There had to be some element of 'sovereignty' in the functions that were delegated to it: it was a question of substance, not form. It is to be hoped that the statutory test will not result in artificial claims to immunity by bodies that are in reality distinct from the state, even though *de jure* they appear not to be. In *Re Rafidian Bank*, two Iraqi companies – the Iraqi Reinsurance Company and Iraqi Airways Ltd – claimed to be part of the state of Iraq for immunity purposes. As neither had distinct governmental functions and both had legal personality in their own right, the judge determined that they were separate entities. He then went on to hold that they were not entitled to immunity under s. 14. Contrast this with *Grovit* v *De Nederlandsche Bank* where the defendant was clearly exercising sovereign authority for the purposes of banking and currency issues and consequently did have immunity.

7.4.2.5 Specific problems

The State Immunity Act has done much to clarify the law of immunity in the UK. By laying down a series of circumstances in which a state does not have immunity the Act promotes certainty and allows both states and individuals to know in advance when a UK court will have jurisdiction. Furthermore, the adoption of restrictive immunity in statutory form has helped to promote the UK as a centre of world trade and commerce. Section 3 is particularly important because it provides the court with a clear definition of a commercial transaction and, in many cases, without requiring it to conduct its own inquiry into the meaning of 'sovereign authority'. Similarly, the certainty that exists in relation to central banks, waivers, federal states and state ships is to be welcomed. However, it would be surprising if the Act had resolved all difficulties and a few problems remain.

Most importantly, it is clear that in a limited number of circumstances, the court will have to decide for itself what is 'an exercise of sovereign authority'. Thus, under s. 3(3)(c), s. 14(2) and where 'commercial purposes' are referred to, as in ss. 10 and 13, the court will have to make its own assessment of the nature of a foreign state's activity, although it is not at all certain that the court is asking the same question in each case (see *Kuwait Airways*, section 7.4.2.4). At least in respect of s. 3 and references to it, the *New Zealand Banking* case, and the minority in *Kuwait Airways*, suggest that the court should adopt a rounded approach to this problem, looking at the whole context in which the dispute arose in very similar fashion to the *I Congreso* 'two-stage' test under the common law and the decisions in *Littrel, Gamel-Eldin* and *Lampen-Wolfe*. Again, this is highly desirable given the almost limitless circumstances in which claims to immunity may arise. Perhaps the rather more piecemeal approach adopted by the majority in *Kuwait Airways* can be justified by the exceptional circumstances of that case.

In addition, there are still considerable problems with the execution of judgments and court orders against unwilling states. Whereas the Act goes a long way in denying states immunity from the jurisdiction of the court, it does not go nearly as far in providing that any subsequent award can be compulsorily enforced. For example, only property used for 'commercial purposes' can be used to satisfy a court order, and not then if the defendant is a central bank. In *Alcom* v *Republic of Colombia* [1984] 2 WLR 750, the claimants were unable to obtain execution of a court order against monies held in a bank account belonging to the state because the funds therein were used for the day to day expenses of the embassy. In *Alcom* the monies were not being used for 'commercial purposes', rather like the result in *SerVaas Incorporated (Appellant) v Rafidian Bank and others (Respondents)* (2012). But, in *Re Rafidian Bank* (a different case), the fact that the state's money held in a bank was used to pay the costs of running the state's Embassy did not prevent enforcement, and this despite s. 16(1) SIA which preserves such diplomatic immunities (on which see section 7.8) as the state may enjoy. Clearly, the relationship between state immunity and diplomatic immunity in UK courts is another area where some confusion remains. Similarly, the protected position of central banks, even if they are 'separate entities', undermines much of the restrictive theory where they are concerned, although perhaps this is not surprising given the vital role they play in managing a state's economy. Again, the loss of the availability of the court orders of specific performance and injunction may prove important in practice, especially if states do remove their assets from the jurisdiction in order to avoid satisfying a judgment creditor. Moreover, it appears from *Westminster CC v Islamic Republic of Iran* [1986] 3 All ER 284, and now confirmed by *Kuwait Airways*, that unless a writ initiating proceedings can be served in the manner prescribed by s. 12 of the Act, the court cannot proceed to try the substantive issue. In *Westminster*, the UK had broken off diplomatic relations with Iran and consequently the summons could not be served through the Foreign Office as required by the Act, and in *Kuwait Airways* the same happened with Iraq. In both cases the claimants were deprived of access to UK courts through a procedural defect not of their own making.

As we have also seen, there may be problems in determining what is a 'separate entity' under s. 14 of the Act. It seems that a certificate from the Secretary of State is not available in this regard and this could be an unfortunate omission. The court will have to look to the local law of the entity to see if it is 'separate' and the help of a state representative may be required. It remains unclear how far the functions of the body may be taken into consideration in resolving this issue, but *Wilhelm Finance Inc v Ente Administrator Del Astillero Rio Santiago* suggests that functions are important in similar fashion to the approach taken in *Trendtex* before the Act. Moreover, even if it is decided that the body is a separate entity, the court may then have to consider whether it acted in exercise of 'sovereign authority' and would have otherwise attracted immunity. In this regard at least, the court may examine the functions of the entity within its own state's governmental system but, as *Kuwait Airways* illustrates, there is no consensus on how the requirements of s. 14 are to be satisfied.

Another difficulty is that certain matters are outside the scope of the Act altogether, and not simply because the dispute related to matters occurring before the Act came into force (as *was* the case in *I Congreso* and *Sengupta* v *Republic of India*). For example, by virtue of s. 16(5), the Act does not regulate immunity in proceedings relating to taxation, other than in respect of those taxes specified in s. 11. Proceedings relating to income tax and advanced corporation tax are outside the Act and fall to be dealt with by the common law (see e.g. *R* v *IRC, ex parte Camacq Corp.* [1990] 1 All ER 173). Likewise, in *Littrell* v *United States of America (No. 2)* [1994] 2 All ER 3, an action by a US serviceman claiming negligent medical treatment by US medical staff on a base in the UK was outside the Act under s. 16(2) as being a proceeding relating to the armed forces of a foreign state within the UK. The common law applied and the state was immune. A similar result was achieved in *Lampen-Wolfe*, where a broad interpretation of s. 16(2) meant that the provision of education on a US military base in the UK was 'in relation to' armed forces. Again, most matters concerning the staff of diplomatic missions are outside the scope of the Act, being issues raising questions of diplomatic immunity, as in *Egypt* v *Gamal-Eldin* and *Ahmed* v *Saudi Arabia*. This is so even if the matter might otherwise not have attracted immunity, as where a 'pure' employment issue would not have generated immunity (SIA 1978, s. 4) but did so because the complainant was a member of a foreign embassy and the state had immunity under 'diplomatic law' (*Kuwait* v *M.S. Fenzi* (1999)).

Finally, for completeness, one should note those areas in which the Act goes beyond or changes the old common law. Clearly, the most significant change is s. 3, which defines 'commercial transaction' and so dispenses with the need to apply any other test except in the limited case of s. 3(3)(c). Also, a state may now waive immunity from jurisdiction in writing in advance. Similarly, there are changes in respect of federal states, remedies and central banks.

7.5 Heads of state

Whether a person is a 'head of state' for the purposes of these rules can be determined conclusively by a certificate from the Foreign Office – s. 21 SIA, *The Queen on the Application of HRH Sultan of Pahang v SSHD*. The position of heads of state acting in a public capacity is dealt with by s. 14(1)(a) of the SIA 1978. This provides for immunity in the same circumstances as the state simply because the head *is* 'the state' in such cases. The position of a head of state and family who are in the UK for reasons other than the public purposes of their country is governed by s. 20. This provides that the head of state and family shall have all the immunities conferred on a head of diplomatic mission by the Diplomatic Privileges Act 1964, save only that minor restrictions placed on the immunities of the head of mission do not apply. Generally, the scope of these immunities is wide and unchallengeable, and they are designed to protect the person, property and dignity of the head of state. However, following *ex parte Pinochet*, it appears that these immunities may be subject to an important qualification. On leaving office, a (now) ex-head of state (as with an ex-head of mission) enjoys continuing immunity in respect of acts done while in office only if those acts were part of his official functions. Private acts done while in office lose immunity once the head of state ceases to be head of state and they can then be made the subject of an action in national courts. Necessarily, this is a large restriction on the immunity of a head of state, illustrating that in some respects it is transient (i.e. existing while in office only). The principle was doubted by Lord Goff, in the minority, in *ex parte Pinochet*, as having no basis in international practice as well as requiring a national court to make difficult decisions about what is, or is not, an official act of the head of state.

7.6 **The European Convention on State Immunity 1972**

The European Convention 1972 is very much like the UK Act to which it gave rise. There is a statement of absolute immunity for all signatories that is then qualified in certain specified circumstances. It entered force in 1976 and as at 1 September 2012 there were eight parties, including the UK. The major advance that the Convention makes on the general provisions of the UK State Immunity Act is that it requires states to give effect to judgments made against them (Art. 20), with only limited exceptions. Under s. 18 of the UK Act, a judgment given against the UK in a court of another state which is a party to the Convention, not being a matter in which the UK had immunity from jurisdiction, is to be recognised by the courts of the UK as conclusive, save in the exceptional circumstances of s. 19. Furthermore, there is an Additional Protocol to the Convention that establishes a European Tribunal on matters of State Immunity, with six parties at 1 September 2102, not including the UK. This establishes a tribunal for the determination of certain disputes arising under the Convention.

7.7 **State immunity in the UK and human rights**

It is a necessary consequence of a successful plea of immunity that an individual will be denied access to justice. The state is immune and the individual will be denied a chance to prove his or her case. Article 6 of the European Convention on Human Rights (ECHR), enacted in UK national law by the Human Rights Act 1998 (in force 2 October 2000), affords an individual the right to a fair trial to determine his civil rights and obligations. In *Lampen-Wolfe*, the claimant argued that the granting of immunity violated this fundamental right. If correct, this would be a serious, perhaps terminal, blow to the doctrine of state immunity. In fact, in *Lampen-Wolfe* Lord Millet rejected this plea on the ground that Art. 6 ECHR guaranteed the right to a fair trial only where the national court had jurisdiction in the first place. In his view, Art. 6 was not actually engaged if the national court lacked jurisdiction because of immunity. In that event, Art. 6 ECHR could not give the individual a right that he or she did not otherwise possess. This view has subsequently been approved, obiter, by Lord Bingham in *Jones v Saudi Arabia*. However, in *Jones*, Lord Bingham felt obliged by the European Court of Human Rights decision in *Al-Adsani* to suppose that Art. 6 *was* engaged and so for the moment we should operate on the (questionable) basis that it is.

As we have noted, this issue arose directly in a trio of cases before the European Court of Human Rights and there is clear authority in one of these (*Al-Adsani* v *UK*) that Art. 6 of the Convention is engaged by a plea of immunity. That being so, questions then arise as to whether a successful plea of immunity infringes the Article per se (it clearly does because access to the court is factually limited – *Jones* v *Saudi Arabia*) and, more importantly, whether a successful plea of immunity is a legitimate and proportionate response that justifies the apparent infringement. In all three cases before the ECH – *Al-Adsani* v *UK*, *Fogarty* v *UK* and *McElhinney* v *Ireland* – the Court denied that a violation of the Convention had occurred simply by reason of the fact that immunity had been granted by the host state. This was so even though – as in *Al-Adsani* – the acts for which immunity was claimed would have constituted a crime under international law. In essence, the grant of immunity was proportionate to the legitimate aim of the host state in seeking to comply with its international obligations to grant immunity. Similarly, in the *Case Concerning the Arrest Warrant of 11 April 2000 (Congo* v *Belgium)* 2002 ICJ Rep 14, the ICJ determined that the immunity of diplomatic agents remained in place even where the individual was alleged to have committed crimes against international law for which personal responsibility existed. This view has now been adopted in the UK in *Jones* v *Saudi Arabia*. In that case, the House of Lords held that, assuming Art. 6 ECHR was engaged, acceptance of the plea of immunity was proportionate and legitimate and, moreover, that there was no reason for a different conclusion simply because the immunity was pleaded in respect of a rule of *jus cogens* or in respect of a crime for which international law provided universal jurisdiction. In fact, the point was made that immunity does not conflict with rules of *jus cogens* nor justify their violation – rather it means that the local court may not hear the matter.

Part Two: **Diplomatic and consular immunities**

In Part One, we examined the immunities from jurisdiction and enforcement that were available to a state in international law and in the UK in particular. In this section, consideration will be given to the immunities and privileges enjoyed by official representatives of a foreign state when they are within the territory of another state. Again, we shall consider the general position under international law and then examine how this has been put into effect in the law of the UK.

Diplomatic and consular immunities are personal in the sense that they are enjoyed by individuals, rather than by the state itself. However, as we shall see, the purpose of these immunities is not to benefit the individual as such, but to enable him to carry out his designated functions on behalf of the state. Furthermore, it will become apparent that the law on diplomatic immunities is double edged. On the one hand, the individual is given certain privileges within the legal system of the state to which he is accredited (the 'receiving' state) and, on the other, the receiving state is under certain obligations to protect the diplomat and his property in order that he may carry out his functions effectively. The law on diplomatic and consular immunities encompasses both privileges for the diplomat/consular official and obligations for the receiving state.

The importance of the diplomatic representative in world affairs cannot be emphasised too strongly. Even in the modern age of direct and instantaneous communications, nothing can rival the personal and confidential liaison between a diplomat and the government of the receiving state. Consequently, the law on diplomatic immunities is one of the most important areas of international law. As the ICJ pointed out in the *US Diplomatic and Consular Staff in Tehran Case (US v Iran Hostages Case)* 1980 ICJ Rep 3, these rules are of a 'fundamental character', perhaps even *jus cogens*, and their integrity is 'vital for the security and well-being of the complex international community of the present day'. So it was in that case that Iran was strongly condemned by the Court for its failure to protect the US embassy in Iran prior to its occupation by students in November 1979. In the *Diplomatic Claim, Ethiopia's Claim 8, (2006), Eritrea/Ethiopia Claims Commission*, the Commission noted that it 'does not accept that the Parties could derogate from their fundamental obligations under the Vienna Convention on Diplomatic Relations, notably those relating to the inviolability of diplomatic agents and premises, because of the exigencies of war'. These are rules which are essential to the smooth running of the international community.

7.8 International law

In international law, the legal principles of diplomatic and consular immunities are to be found primarily in two multilateral conventions – the Vienna Convention on Diplomatic Relations 1961 (at 1 September 2012 187 parties) and the Vienna Convention on Consular Relations 1963 (at 1 September 2012 173 parties). In this section we are concerned primarily with the Convention on Diplomatic Relations and references to 'the Convention' should be taken as references to this treaty. Although consular officials perform vital administrative functions in respect of nationals present in the state to which they are accredited, the major policy and representative work falls to diplomatic staff. As a general rule, immunities and privileges of consular officials are less extensive than those of diplomatic staff.

The Vienna Convention on Diplomatic Relations came into force on 24 April 1964 and as noted earlier at 1 September 2012 there were 187 contracting parties. The Convention was the outcome of a UN Conference on Diplomatic Intercourse and Immunities 1961 and was based on a series of Draft Articles prepared by the International Law Commission. It is one of the more successful attempts at codification by the ILC. Following the normal rule for international treaties, only parties are bound by the specific obligations of the Convention and it is unclear just how much of the Convention was originally a codification of existing law, as opposed to progressive development. However, as the Court indicated in *US v Iran*, a great part of the Convention now reflects customary international law and it is clear that virtually all of the disputes over diplomatic law can be resolved by reference to this treaty or the obligations contained therein.

The basis of diplomatic privileges was once thought to be parasitic on the dignity and status of the head of state. Consequently, a diplomat was seen as a representative or alter ego of the sovereign and entitled to all the immunities that he or she would have enjoyed. Similarly, the rules relating to the protection and inviolability of the diplomatic mission – the embassy – were said to rest on the idea that it constituted part of the sovereign territory of the sending state. However, it is now clear that both of these ideas misinterpret the role of diplomatic and consular immunities. The purpose of these immunities is to enable diplomatic staff to represent their home state effectively without fear of harassment or hindrance by the authorities of the receiving state. The basis of diplomatic immunities is functional, and to this end the diplomat is given certain privileges and immunities and the receiving state is placed under certain obligations. This rationale is no less correct even though certain immunities extend to those occasions on which the diplomat is not fulfilling his official duties, as where he enjoys immunity in private or personal matters. Again, this is to ensure that the diplomat is not subject to any form of pressure by the receiving state. As the Preamble to the Vienna Convention makes clear, 'the purpose of such privileges and immunities is not to benefit individuals but to ensure the efficient performance of the functions of diplomatic missions in representing states'.

7.8.1 Immunities relating to the person

The Vienna Convention deals with several categories of person who may enjoy some or all of the immunities specified therein (Art. 1). These include the 'head of the mission' (e.g. the ambassador or chargé d'affaires), 'the members of the diplomatic staff' (diplomats proper), 'the members of the administrative and technical staff' (secretaries etc.), 'members of the service' (e.g. kitchen staff, butlers) and 'private servants' (e.g. a personal valet). Generally, the most extensive immunities are accorded to the head of mission and his diplomatic staff, with a descending scale in respect of the other categories. Members of the families of the head of mission, diplomats and administrative and technical staff may also be entitled to those immunities enjoyed by the primary recipient. However, unless there is special agreement, if a person is a national of the receiving state, immunity will be restricted to matters arising in the performance of his official functions or, for the lesser categories of staff, lost altogether.

The main personal immunities are to be found in Arts 29 and 31 of the Convention. The person of a diplomat (henceforth to include the head of mission) is inviolable and he may not be arrested or subjected to any other form of detention. The receiving state is under a duty to protect him and prevent any attack on his person, freedom or dignity (Art. 29). Under Art. 31, a diplomat is completely immune from the criminal jurisdiction of the receiving state and immune from the civil and administrative jurisdiction, save in respect of actions relating to private real property, succession under a will or an action relating to any 'professional or commercial activity outside his official functions'. For example, a diplomat will enjoy immunity in respect of parking tickets, shoplifting, rape and every other criminal offence and in the majority of civil actions. A diplomat will not, however, have immunity in respect of civil actions arising out of, say, a private consulting business or other unofficial 'commercial activity'. Generally, the members of a diplomat's family enjoy the same immunities, so long as they are not nationals of the receiving state.

Administrative and technical staff and their families enjoy similar immunities to the diplomat, save that immunity from civil jurisdiction extends only to acts done in the course of their official functions (see e.g. *Empson* v *Smith* [1966] 1 QB 426). These immunities are lost if they are nationals of, or permanently resident in, the receiving state (Art. 37). The immunities of other categories of persons become progressively less extensive. Other immunities, again varying in degree with each category, include exemption from taxes, customs duties and public service, such as conscription and jury service.

7.8.2 Immunities relating to property

The premises of the mission (the embassy) are inviolable and agents of the receiving state may not enter them without the consent of the head of mission (Art. 22). These 'premises' include any buildings and ancillary land, irrespective of ownership, which are used for the purposes of the mission, including the residence of the head of mission (Art. 1). Likewise, the property and means of transport of the mission are immune from search and seizure (Art. 22) and the archives and documents of the mission are inviolable even if they are not on the premises (Art. 24). The receiving state is under a duty to protect the mission (Art. 22) and it will be responsible under international law if it fails to do so, as with Iran in the *Hostages Case*. These immunities and the obligation to protect continue even if diplomatic relations are broken off or armed conflict occurs (Art. 45), but not if the mission premises cease to be used for diplomatic purposes (see e.g. *Westminster CC* v *Islamic Republic of Iran*). The private residence of a member of the diplomatic staff enjoys the same inviolability as the mission proper, as do his papers and correspondence, except if they relate to matters for which he is subject to civil jurisdiction (Art. 30). Similar immunities are accorded to administrative and technical staff, not being nationals or permanently resident in the receiving state.

7.8.3 Freedom of communication

Under Art. 26, the receiving state is under an obligation to ensure freedom of movement for all members of the mission and this may be curtailed only in respect of 'zones entry into which is prohibited or regulated for reasons of national security'. Furthermore, in Art. 27, there is perhaps one of the most important provisions of the Convention. The receiving state is obliged to permit and protect free communication for all official purposes and the use of codes to communicate with the home state is expressly authorised. A wireless transmitter may be used with the consent of the receiving state. All correspondence relating to the mission and its functions is inviolable and, importantly, the 'diplomatic bag' must not be opened or detained. It is clear, moreover, that the 'bag' may vary in size, from an aircraft full of wooden crates to a small pouch, but, as long as the 'bag' bears visible external markings it is immune from normal entry procedures.

In recent years, this provision on the sanctity of the diplomatic bag has been a cause of grave concern for many states. There have been several examples of the bag being used to smuggle drugs, weapons, art treasures and even individuals into or out of the receiving state. Yet, despite the provision in Art. 27(4) that the bag 'may contain only diplomatic documents or articles intended for official use', the better view is that the receiving state cannot require the bag to be opened for inspection. Reservations to Art. 27 permitting inspection have not generally been accepted.

Moreover, while some states follow a practice of requesting permission to open the bag in the presence of an official of the mission and then refusing entry if this is denied, this would also seem to be a breach of Art. 27. The receiving state must permit free communication and the bag may not be detained.

Not surprisingly, disquiet over misuse of the bag has led to calls for reform and the ILC has completed a thorough examination of the law on diplomatic correspondence. They have now produced a set of Draft Articles on the Diplomatic Courier and the Diplomatic Bag which are intended to lay down a comprehensive scheme and which may form the basis of a multilateral treaty. The most important Draft Article is Dr. Art. 28 that deals with 'protection of the diplomatic bag'. There was a considerable amount of debate in the ILC concerning this provision, with some members preferring the rule of absolute inviolability and others the 'request or return' approach. The Draft Article substantially adopts the former of these in that the 'diplomatic bag shall be inviolable wherever it may be; it shall not be opened or detained and shall be exempt from examination directly or through electronic or other technical devices'. Notably, Dr. Art. 28(2) preserves the 'request or return' rule for the consular bag, as it now stands in Art. 35(3) of the Vienna Convention on Consular Relations.

After considerable debate, the ILC opted for maintaining absolute inviolability of the diplomatic bag and, as a general rule, the Draft Articles as a whole favour increased protection for diplomatic communications. It remains to be seen whether this is acceptable to states, especially since the Draft Articles do not address the problem of abuse. The UK, for example, opposes a strict inviolability rule – preferring the 'request or return' approach – and has proposed that Dr. Art. 28 be renegotiated. However, it must also be remembered that the diplomatic bag is a vital form of communication between the sending state and its representatives. Its inviolability works for the benefit of all states, even more so if the state has a large number of overseas missions, as with the UK. In addition, there is considerable evidence to suggest that the diplomatic bag and the luggage of diplomatic staff (protected under Art. 30) are subject to deliberate delay and sometimes search at the point of entry in some countries. Violations of the Convention are not limited to unscrupulous diplomats of the sending state.

7.8.4 Abuse

Under Art. 41 of the Convention, it is the duty of all persons enjoying immunities and privileges to respect the laws of the receiving state. Similarly, the premises of the mission may not be used in any manner incompatible with its functions and members of the mission are under a duty not to interfere in the internal affairs of the receiving state. This provision makes it clear that immunities and privileges are granted not for the personal benefit of members of the mission, even though many apply outside official duties, but to ensure the proper functioning of the mission and the effective discharge of the diplomat's duties. Does this mean that the scope of the immunities may be limited in cases of deliberate abuse by the diplomat – for example, repeated parking offences or shoplifting? In the UK, for example, in 1996, twenty-nine diplomats were found to be responsible for 'serious offences' (meriting a custodial sentence). Yet, despite arguments to the contrary, Art. 41 is quite clear. This provides that the diplomats' obligation to obey and respect the laws of the receiving state is 'without prejudice to their privileges and immunities'. In other words, abuse of the privileges contained in the Convention does not entail a loss of those privileges. At first sight, this might appear unjust, for if the purpose of immunities is to facilitate the proper functioning of the mission, why do such immunities persist when the diplomat is clearly 'on a frolic of his own'? Again, the reason is to protect the diplomat from false charges, deliberate fabrication of evidence and all manner of other practices that the receiving state might resort to in order to embarrass another state or engineer a diplomatic incident. If a diplomat or member of the mission persistently abuses his privileges or commits what would be a particularly grave offence under national law, the receiving state can request that his immunity be waived under Art. 32 of the Convention. In the last resort, the receiving state may declare a diplomat *persona non grata*, so that the sending state is obliged to recall the individual or terminate his functions. This power may be used at any time and without giving reasons. It is exercised most often in the case of diplomats and other staff engaging in 'activities incompatible with their status', as in May 1996 during a spying row between the UK and Russia when four diplomats on each side were expelled.

As has been stated previously, the great majority of disputes concerning diplomatic law will be settled by reference to the Vienna Convention. Indeed, it is probable that the great majority of its provisions also represent customary international law. It is no surprise, however, that in recent years an apparent increase in the abuse of diplomatic privileges by individual diplomats has led to calls for a less absolute approach to the granting of immunities, although this clearly did not find favour with the ILC when adopting the Draft Articles on the diplomatic bag. In fact, it is by no means clear that a weakening of these immunities in favour of the receiving state really is desirable. It would be acceptable if we could be certain that states would not attempt to use any changes in the law to achieve their own, unauthorised ends. This is clearly not the case. To restrict the immunities of diplomats and those attaching to diplomatic property would serve only to encourage those states already flouting the law. As the ICJ emphasised in the *Hostages Case*, the 'frequency with which at the present time the principles of international law governing diplomatic and consular relations are set at naught by individuals or groups of individuals is already deplorable'. It seems clear that a relaxation in the uncompromising nature of the Vienna Convention would only facilitate these unwelcome incidents.

7.9 The United Kingdom

The UK is a party to both the Vienna Convention on Diplomatic Relations and the Vienna Convention on Consular Relations. As a consequence it is bound in international law to ensure that the immunities and privileges contained therein are afforded to diplomatic and consular staff within the jurisdiction of the UK. However, because of the constitutional rule that treaties made by the UK government do not have direct effect in national law, it is necessary that those provisions of the Conventions that absolve individuals from normal legal process be transformed into UK law. There are, therefore, a number of Acts of Parliament giving diplomatic staff and consular officials immunity from the local jurisdiction. These include the

Consular Relations Act 1968, transforming much of the Vienna Convention on Consular Relations; the International Organisations Acts 1968 and 1981, regulating the privileges and immunities of international organisations and connected persons (see e.g. *Standard Chartered Bank* v *International Tin Council* [1987] 1 WLR 641); the Diplomatic and Consular Premises Act 1987, providing that the consent of the Secretary of State for Foreign Affairs is required before land can become diplomatic or consular premises and giving him certain powers in respect of disused premises (see e.g. *R* v *Secretary of State for Foreign and Commonwealth Affairs, ex parte Samuel*, *The Times*, 17 August 1989); and the Diplomatic Privileges Act 1964, transforming much of the Vienna Convention on Diplomatic Relations.

The major piece of legislation is the last of these, the Diplomatic Privileges Act 1964. In effect, this ensures that most of the privileges and immunities of the Vienna Convention form part of the law of the UK. The Articles having this effect are contained in Schedule 1 to the Act, namely Arts 1, 22–24, 27–40. The Diplomatic and Consular Premises Act 1987 also transformed Art. 45. The net effect is that nearly all those provisions of the Convention that require a change in national law in order to be effective have been so transformed. Of course, in respect of the other provisions of the Convention, the UK will be liable in international law if it fails to fulfil the obligations contained therein. Lastly, it should be noted that under s. 3 of the 1964 Act, the UK may restrict any immunities and privileges granted by it, if it appears that these are greater than those granted to a mission of the UK in another state. Similarly, under s. 7, any extension of immunities beyond the scope of those guaranteed by the Convention which have been effected by bilateral agreement between the UK and another state are to form part of the national law of the UK for as long as the bilateral agreement continues in force.

7.10 A note on the immunities of international organisations

Many international organisations have legal personality in international law, and many of these have personality in UK law, one way or another (see Chapter 4). These organisations have functions to perform and need to act within local legal systems to be able to achieve their aims. As with states and their diplomats, international organisations and their staff are entitled as a matter of international law to certain privileges and immunities. These privileges and immunities exist to enable the international organisation to achieve its ends without hindrance by local authorities. A good example is the Convention on the Privileges and Immunities of the United Nations 1946 that establishes a code of immunity for the Organisation itself and its staff, designed to be effective in the local law of state-parties to the Convention. It encompasses immunity from legal process, immunity from tax and extensive immunity from criminal and civil liability (see e.g. the ICJ *Advisory Opinion on the Difference Relating to Immunity from Legal Process of a Special Rapporteur of the Commission of Human Rights*, 20 April 1999). Following accepted theory on the relationship of UK law to international law, the privileges and immunities of international organisations have to be made manifest in UK law by legislation if the UK is to meet its international obligations. The International Organisations Acts 1968 and 1981 exist to give effect to the privileges and immunities of those international organisations (and their staff) recognised by the UK and operating within the UK as legal persons. These international organisations have privileges and immunities within the UK legal system to the extent of the enacting legislation.

FURTHER READING

Caplan, L, 'State Immunity, Human Rights, and *Jus Cogens*: A critique of the normative hierarchy theory', (2003) 97 *AJIL* 741.

Denning, Lord, *Landmarks in the Law* (Butterworths, 1984), pp. 143–53 (abuse of diplomatic privileges).

Douglas, Z., State Immunity for the Acts of State Officials, 2012 *BYIL*, at http://bybil.oxfordjournals.org/content/early/2012/05/29/bybil.brs002.

Greig, D., 'Forum State Jurisdiction and Sovereign Immunity under the ILC Draft Articles', (1989) 38 *ICLQ* 243.

Greig, D., 'Specific Exceptions to Immunity under the ILC Draft Articles', (1989) 38 *ICLQ* 560.

Higgins, R., 'UK Foreign Affairs Committee Report on the Abuse of Diplomatic Immunities and Privileges: Government Response and Report', (1986) 80 *AJIL* 135.

Marks, S., 'Torture and the Jurisdictional Immunity of Foreign States', [1997] *CLJ* 8.

Sinclair, I., 'The European Convention on State Immunity', (1973) 22 *ICLQ* 254.

Stewart, D., 'The UN Convention on Jurisdictional Immunities of States and Their Property' (2005) 99 *AJIL* 194.

Whomersley, C., 'Some Reflections on Immunity of Individuals for Official Acts', (1992) 41 *ICLQ* 848.

The ILC Draft Articles on the Jurisdictional Immunities of States and Their Property, (1991) 30 *ILM* 1563.

SUMMARY

Immunities from national jurisdiction

- The jurisdiction of a state within its own territory is complete and absolute. However, there is also a rule of international law that a foreign sovereign state is entitled to certain immunities from the exercise of this jurisdiction – generally known as the principle of state (or sovereign) immunity.

- There are several competing justifications of state immunity – states are legal equals; the local state voluntarily waives its jurisdiction; policy requires states to refrain from exercising jurisdiction over other states; enforcement of judgments is difficult; international comity justifies state immunity.

- Immunity under international law is not absolute, but restrictive, usually based around the nature of the act, but sometimes including the purpose of the act or the general context in which the act takes place. There is a UN Convention on Jurisdictional Immunities that is not yet in force but much of which represents customary law.

- Immunity is available even if the act is in violation of a fundamental rule of international law.

- Immunity in the UK is governed by the State Immunity Act 1978, which gives immunity except where it is denied. The overall effect is restrictive, based around a 'commercial transaction'.

- Enforcement of judgments in the UK comes close to absolute immunity.

- Section 14 of the Act stipulates what constitutes 'the state' for the purposes of the 1978 Act.

- Diplomatic and consular immunities are personal in the sense that they are enjoyed by individuals, rather than by the state itself. However, as we shall see, the purpose of these immunities is not to benefit the individual as such, but to enable him to carry out his designated functions on behalf of the state. They are governed by two Vienna Conventions.

8

The law of the sea

This chapter is concerned with those rules of international law usually referred to as the 'law of the sea'. Generally, this will involve consideration of matters of state sovereignty, state jurisdiction and state rights over the waters, sea bed, subsoil and airspace of the 'sea'. It is vital to appreciate at the outset the fundamental importance of this area of international law. Not only are the seas a primary medium for international commerce and communication, they are rich in living and non-living natural resources such as fish, oil, gas and minerals, as well as providing opportunities for wind and wave power generation. In view of the increasing dependency of states on marine resources and the growing interdependence of international society in general, it is imperative that international law develops a set of consistent and coherent rules governing this whole area. Stability and predictability are at a premium in the international law of the sea (*Barbados/Trinidad & Tobago Maritime Delimitation Arbitration*, April 2006). In fact, it is one of the major achievements of the United Nations that a large measure of agreement now exists among the international community about much of the legal framework necessary for effective regulation of the law of the sea, many principles of which are to be found in the 1982 Law of the Sea Convention. As we shall see, this wide-ranging multilateral treaty sets the tone and provides much of the content for the law of the sea, and will continue to do so for the foreseeable future. Obviously, however, with such a diverse and vital topic there are some matters upon which there is no clear universal rule and there is still a little way to go before international law can be said to have developed a *completely* consistent set of rules governing maritime affairs.

In addition to discussing rules of a general nature in this chapter, we shall also examine some of the specific legal regimes that govern use of the sea by coastal and non-coastal states. Thus, consideration will be given to the territorial sea and contiguous zone, the Exclusive Economic Zone (EEZ), the continental shelf, the deep sea bed, the high seas and, finally, to a miscellaneous category of matters such as pollution control, archipelagos, islands and international straits. Of necessity, this is not a complete list and such matters as navigation, landlocked states, vessel seizure and marine research are omitted or not considered in great detail.

8.1 Sources of the law of the sea

It should not be thought that the 'law of the sea' is to be found in one place. The current law is a mix of customary law and treaty law, both bilateral and multilateral.

8.1.1 The 1958 Geneva Conventions

As a result of the First United Nations Conference on the Law of the Sea, four multilateral conventions were concluded covering various aspects of the law of the sea.
These are the 1958 Geneva Conventions on The Territorial Sea and Contiguous
Zone, on The Continental Shelf, on The High Seas and on The Fishing and
Conservation of Living Resources of the High Seas. All these Conventions are in
force, although in many respects (but not all) they have been superseded by the
1982 Convention on the Law of the Sea. This 1982 Convention is of general application (i.e., it is not confined to one specific aspect of the law of the sea). Note,
however, that for non-parties to the 1982 Convention (such as the USA), and for
those matters on which the 1982 Convention is silent, the 1958 Conventions will
continue to govern the relations of states that have signed them. This is considered
in more detail later. For states that are parties to neither the 1958 Conventions nor
the 1982 Convention, the relevant law is customary. Not surprisingly, however, it
is perfectly possible for the principles contained in the 1958 and 1982 Conventions
to have become part of customary law, and despite the warning in the *North Sea
Continental Shelf Cases* 1969 ICJ Rep 3 that this is not to be presumed lightly (see
Chapter 2). Recent case law has confirmed that much of the 1982 Convention has
indeed passed into customary law (*Case Concerning Maritime and Territorial Questions
between Qatar and Bahrain* 2001 ICJ Rep; *Eritrea/Yemen Arbitration* 1999).

8.1.2 The 1982 Convention on the Law of the Sea and the 1994 Agreement on the Deep Sea Bed

The Law of the Sea Convention 1982 (LOS 1982; see Appendix to this chapter)
is one of the most comprehensive and complex multilateral treaties ever concluded. It entered into force in revised form on 16 November 1994 and as at 1
September 2012 there were 163 parties, including the UK, but not the USA. The
Convention deals with almost every aspect of the law of the sea and it is intended
to lay down a universal code for the use of the sea and marine resources. It was
the product of nine years of work by the Third United Nations Conference on the
Law of the Sea and it contains 320 Articles and nine Annexes, plus the addition
of an important supplementary agreement in 1994. The Convention is designed
to operate as an integrated whole and, to that end, the Conference proceeded on
the basis of consensus whereby there was no vote on the adoption of individual
articles. The Convention is a 'package deal' and very much the result of a bargain
between states with different priorities. Unfortunately, however, the Conference
was unable to adopt the Final Text of the Convention by consensus due to a US
request for a vote because of its opposition to Part XI of the Convention relating to the Deep Sea Bed. In the end, the final text was adopted by a vote of 130
to 4, with 17 abstentions, with Turkey, Venezuela and Israel joining the USA in
voting against. The 17 abstentions came largely from the states of western and
eastern Europe, including the UK. Moreover, it soon became clear that neither
the USA nor the western allies were prepared to ratify the Convention in its original form. Their objections to Part XI on the Deep Sea Bed were insurmountable.
While this would not prevent the Convention from entering into force eventually, the absence of major maritime powers would have seriously compromised

the authority of the Convention regime. Fortunately, the desire for a truly universal code of the law of the sea, the recognition that the western powers were the leaders in deep sea mining technology and the imminent entry into force of the Convention among a small number of states provided powerful incentives for compromise. Under the good offices of the UN Secretary-General, several conferences were held and a solution was thrashed out. The result was the 1994 Agreement Relating to the Implementation of Part XI of the Convention, adopted by the UN General Assembly on 28 July 1994. This Agreement, which forms an integral part of the 1982 Convention and which can be ratified by states only in consequence of ratification of the Convention, modifies Part XI on the Deep Sea Bed to meet many of the concerns of the western allies. It came into force on 28 July 1996 (at 1 September 2012 with 143 parties) and modifies the Convention for those accepting the Agreement from that date. Its conclusion meant that ratifications of the Convention proper increased dramatically. The 1982 Convention, as modified, truly can now be regarded as a comprehensive statement of the law of the sea for the twenty-first century.

Importantly, because of the comprehensive nature of the Convention and its development over nine years, and the wait of twelve years before its entry into force, it has had, and will have, a significant impact on customary law. So, even if some states decide not to ratify and remain outside the Convention regime (such as the USA), many of the principles codified or developed therein will be binding on them as a matter of customary international law. For example, in the *Continental Shelf Case (Libya v Malta)* 1985 ICJ Rep 13, both parties and the Court agreed that the 1982 Convention substantially reflected customary law on continental shelf delimitation and in the *Continental Shelf Case (Tunisia v Libya)* 1982 ICJ Rep 18, the Court accepted that the Exclusive Economic Zone, developed at the Third Conference, was now a recognised part of customary law. Again, in the *Delimitation of Maritime Areas Arbitration (France/Canada)* (1992) 31 ILM 1145, a Court of Arbitration relied on Art. 121 of the 1982 Convention when considering the status of islands and in *Qatar v Bahrain* (2001), the ICJ noted that both states agreed 'that most of the provisions of the 1982 Convention which are relevant for the present case reflect customary law', at para. 167. These provide examples of how rules of customary law can run in parallel to treaty obligations in international law and confirm the vital importance of the 1982 Convention – even for non-parties.

It is also important to be aware of the precise relationship between the 1982 Convention and the four Geneva Conventions of 1958. Many of the Articles of the 1982 Convention repeat verbatim, or with minor modifications, the text of corresponding Articles of the 1958 Conventions. However, there is overlap between the treaty regimes. Consequently, the relations inter se of states both of whom are parties to the 1982 Convention are governed by the 1982 Convention, irrespective of whether either was a party to any of the 1958 Conventions. In other words, the 1958 Conventions are superseded by the 1982 Convention between parties to the latter (Art. 311, LOS 1982). However, the relations inter se of states both of whom are parties to a 1958 Convention, but where only one is a party to the 1982 Convention, will continue to be governed by the 1958 Convention. This simply follows the general rule that states are not bound by treaties to which they are not a party. Finally, if a state is not a party to any of these Conventions, its relations with every other state will be governed by customary law.

8.1.3 Customary law, bilateral treaties and other multilateral treaties

In order to complete the picture, reference must be made to customary law, bilateral treaties and other multilateral treaties. As regards the first of these, we have already noted that the 1958 and 1982 Conventions have contributed to the development of customary international law. Similarly, many of the provisions of these Conventions simply codified customary law existing at the time they were drafted. In addition, there are other rules of customary law that may not be precisely reflected in any Convention text nor owe their origin to incorporation in such a text. These, as with all customary rules, bind states in the normal way. Secondly, many states have concluded bilateral treaties regulating their relations with other states in particular areas of mutual concern. Again, these are binding in the normal way. Thirdly, there are other multilateral treaties besides the Conventions considered previously. The International Convention for the Safety of Life at Sea 1974 and the International Convention for the Prevention of Pollution from Ships 1973 both regulate specific matters under a multilateral umbrella. These are just examples of the many multilateral (and bilateral) treaties which regulate use of the sea and its resources. Generally, they deal with very specific or technical matters and, for this reason, this chapter will focus primarily on the 1958 Conventions, the 1982 Convention and the complementary customary rules.

8.2 The territorial sea and contiguous zone

8.2.1 Territorial sea

8.2.1.1 Nature and rights

According to Art. 1 of the Territorial Sea Convention 1958 (TSC 1958), the 'sovereignty of a State extends beyond its land territory and its internal waters, to a belt of sea adjacent to its coast'. This is the territorial sea and the definition is substantially repeated in LOS Art. 2. It is clear that this belt of water is assimilated for most purposes to the land itself; thus the state also has sovereignty over the airspace and subsoil of the territorial sea. In essence, the rights of the coastal state in the area are not merely functional – that is, they are *not* purely for limited purposes as is the case for EEZ and Continental Shelf rights – but are territorial and 'entail sovereignty over the sea-bed and the superjacent waters and air column', *Qatar* v *Bahrain* 2001 ICJ Rep para. 174. Moreover, as was made clear by Judge McNair in the *Anglo-Norwegian Fisheries Case* 1951 ICJ Rep 116, the territorial sea is inherent in statehood and does not have to be claimed by the coastal state. In this one sense, it is similar to the continental shelf, although as we shall see the coastal state does not have 'sovereignty' over the latter.

The fact that a state has sovereignty over the territorial sea means that it has full legislative jurisdiction therein in the same way as land territory. However, because territorial waters may be used regularly by other states international law has placed limitations on the exercise of this jurisdiction in certain circumstances. So, under TSC 1958 Art. 19, a state 'should not' exercise its criminal jurisdiction over foreign vessels in the territorial sea except in certain specified situations and, under Art. 20, a state 'should not' stop or divert foreign ships for the purpose of exercising civil jurisdiction. These provisions are substantially reproduced in LOS Arts 27 and 28. What they establish is that while a state is legally entitled to exercise such jurisdiction – because the territorial sea is under its sovereignty – it should not do so for reasons of international comity. It should be added that warships and other governmental ships in the territorial sea will have sovereign immunity in the normal way (see Chapter 7).

Additionally, the coastal state is under a more onerous obligation to grant all ships the right of 'innocent passage'. Under LOS Art. 17 (and see TSC Art. 14), 'ships of all States' are to enjoy the right of innocent passage through the territorial sea, although this may be suspended by the coastal state if essential for the protection of its security (except that innocent passage is non-suspendable through straits used for international navigation: *Corfu Channel Case* 1949 ICJ Rep 4; LOS Art. 45; TSC Art. 16(4)). In order for a ship to avail itself of this right, it must be both in 'passage' and 'innocent'. Progress through the territorial sea amounts to 'passage' if it is for the purpose of traversing the sea or entering internal waters and includes anchorage when necessary for normal navigation and, under LOS Art. 18(2), it must be 'continuous and expeditious'. Whether passage is 'innocent' would seem to be a matter of fact in each case and the Court in the *Corfu Channel Case* indicated that this was to be determined by the 'manner' of passage, rather than, say, intent or purpose. In TSC Art. 14(4), passage is innocent so long as it is 'not prejudicial to the peace, good order or security of the coastal state', although under LOS Art. 19 this is supplemented by a list of activities which are *ipso facto* deemed to be prejudicial to good order and security. Importantly, these include 'any fishing activities', 'any act aimed at collecting information to the prejudice of the defence or security of the coastal state', 'the carrying out of research or survey activities' and 'any other activity not having a direct bearing on passage'. All in all, the effect of LOS Art. 19 is to favour the coastal state by increasing the chances that passage will not be innocent. If passage is not innocent, the coastal state may take steps necessary to prevent such passage, although in the case of warships the appropriate remedy is to require them to leave the territorial sea immediately. As well as being binding on the parties, to a large extent these treaty provisions represent customary law and they were specifically treated as such in a 1989 US/USSR Joint Statement on Innocent Passage, (1989) 28 ILM 144. Importantly, this clarification by two powerful maritime nations, neither of whom were parties to the 1982 Convention at the time of the statement, notes that 'Article 19 of the Convention of 1982 sets out in paragraph 2 an exhaustive list of activities that would render passage not innocent'.

8.2.1.2 Delimitation

One of the great controversies in the law of the sea has always been the permissible width of the territorial sea. The 1958 Convention has no provision on the breadth of the territorial sea and a Second UN Conference in 1960 failed narrowly to agree on a compromise solution. Until 1988, the UK had claimed a territorial sea three miles wide and disputed broader claims, this being regarded by traditional maritime nations as the rule in customary law. However, a more accurate view is that there never had been any truly consistent state practice, with states claiming anything between three and 200 nautical miles, the latter being pursued by several Latin-American countries such as Peru and Ecuador. Traditionally, this controversy has been seen as a contest between maritime states – who wish to keep the coastal states' jurisdiction to a minimum – and coastal states who wish to gain exclusive control over the sea adjacent to their coast for fishing or mineral resource activities. In this respect, the development of the 'continental shelf' and Exclusive Economic Zone (EEZ) has removed much of the heat from the argument. At the Third Conference, therefore, there was a measure of agreement and LOS Art. 3 now provides that each state has the right to a territorial sea not exceeding 12 nautical miles in width. Of course, this provision will bind parties to the 1982 Convention, although once again very many states had adopted the 12-mile standard before the Convention entered into force. At 1 July 2011, 144 states had claimed a territorial sea of 12 miles or less, with only six states or territories claiming more. For the UK, the Territorial Sea Act 1987 extended the territorial sea to 12 miles and it is now the UK view that this is a principle of customary law. This was confirmed by the Arbitration Panel in the *Guinea/Guinea-Bissau Maritime Delimitation Case*, 77 ILR 636. That does not mean, of course, that states must claim 12 miles and it is more accurate to say that a state may have a territorial sea for any distance up to this maximum. (As at 1 July 2011, three had claimed less.) Consequently, the claims of states to a territorial sea extending beyond 12 miles will be valid (opposable) only against other states that have specifically recognised its validity.

In the usual case, the landward edge of the territorial sea will be the low-water mark on the coast and it will extend seaward from this point. This is known as the *trace parallèle* method of delimitation, with the outer edge of the territorial sea following the general shape of the coast. However, problems with this method of delimitation have occurred for states which have rugged or severely indented coastlines where it may be impossible or impractical to be able to adopt the 'tracing' method. Examples include the broken coastlines of Scandinavia and Scotland. In such cases, it is now clear that a state may be able to adopt a system of straight baselines as the landward edge of the territorial sea. These baselines are simply straight lines drawn between fixed points on the coast, so providing a geometric base from which to calculate the seaward limit of the territorial sea. In practical terms, the use of straight baselines means that more coastal waters will be 'internal waters' (i.e. on the landward side of the baseline) with a consequent seaward extension of the territorial sea. This is the case whatever rule governs the width of the sea, because moving the starting line (the baseline) seaward increases automatically the area of state jurisdiction.

In the *Anglo-Norwegian Fisheries Case*, the UK challenged the use of the system of straight baselines by Norway as being contrary to international law. The ICJ decided that not only was the system opposable to (enforceable against) the UK because it had not objected to its implementation by Norway, but also that straight baselines were generally valid under international law in appropriate cases. In the majority view, if the coast of a state was deeply indented, then a system of straight baselines was permissible if the lines did not depart to an appreciable extent from the general direction of the coast and if the waters on the landward side of the baselines were sufficiently closely connected to the land to be properly regarded as internal waters. Moreover, when assessing the validity of particular baselines, the Court would consider the historic economic interests of the region in which they were used in order to judge whether the waters enclosed should be reserved as 'internal waters' for sole use by the coastal state.

The principle of straight baselines, plus the criteria identified by the Court, were incorporated in TSC Art. 4 and this now represents customary law. The provision is repeated in LOS Art. 7, with only a minor modification in respect of 'low tide elevations' (rocks visible only at low tide). Today, ninety states use the straight baseline system at some point along their coasts and it is employed by the UK in parts of Scotland. Of course, the fact that states may use a system of straight baselines does not mean that every application of it is necessarily lawful. As the Court emphasised in the *Anglo-Norwegian Fisheries Case*, while actual delimitation will be left to the state itself, 'the validity of the delimitation with regard to other states depends upon international law'. Similarly, in *Qatar v Bahrain*, the ICJ noted that the system of straight baselines is an exception to the normal rule for the determination of baselines and may only be applied if a number of conditions are established, judged objectively. Thus, in that case, Bahrain was not entitled to apply the straight baseline method. Finally, it should be noted that the baselines of the territorial sea, whether drawn by *trace parallèle* or straight baselines, have added significance in the 1982 Convention because they are the point from which other maritime zones are measured.

As regards the delimitation of the territorial sea between opposite and adjacent states, the general rule is that the territorial sea may not extend beyond the median line which is equidistant from the nearest points of the baselines of the coastal states (the equidistance-median rule), except by agreement between the parties or where historic title or other special circumstance indicates otherwise, in other words halfway between the coasts unless special factors apply: TSC Art. 12; LOS Art. 15. In the usual case, such delimitation will be done by agreement, as with the UK/France Territorial Sea Boundary Agreement 1988 concerning the boundary in the Dover Strait where it is less than 24 miles wide. In recent times, delimitation has been made by a judicial tribunal, as with the *Guinea/Guinea-Bissau Arbitration* where the Tribunal utilised the boundary previously agreed by the former colonial authorities of the two states, in the *St Pierre and Miquelon Case (Canada/France)* where an ad hoc Court of Arbitration was asked to draw a single maritime boundary to include in part division of the territorial sea and by the International Tribunal for the Law of the Sea in the *Dispute Concerning Delimitation of the Maritime Boundary between Bangladesh and Myanmar in the Bay of Bengal, (Bangladesh/Myanmar)* (2012). As ITLOS says in this latest case, citing the ICJ decision in the *Maritime Delimitation in the Black Sea (Romania v Ukraine) Case* (2009), the equidistance-median rule is now well established as the starting point (under a three-phase approach, see section 8.3.4) in cases of maritime delimitation, including those involving the territorial sea. The ICJ was also asked to draw a single maritime boundary (i.e. concerning the territorial sea and other maritime zones) in the earlier *Qatar v Bahrain* and, because the delimitation concerned a single zone for all purposes, declined to use the equidistance-median line rule to delimit parts of the territorial sea. That decision attracted a strong dissent from Judge Oda who suggested that the Court had erred by departing from the well-established median rule. This dissent is indeed persuasive, and its force borne out by later cases, but perhaps we might conclude from the case law that the equidistance-median rule is the presumptive starting point for delimitation of the territorial sea and will be applied save only where the need to delimit a single maritime boundary means that it may be departed from in order to achieve practical consistency across all the relevant maritime zones.

8.2.2 The contiguous zone

It has been the practice of states in the past to claim certain jurisdictional rights in a zone of waters beyond the outer edge of the territorial sea. Until the institution of the EEZ, this would have been an area of high seas and generally would not otherwise have been susceptible to the jurisdiction of the coastal state. Consequently, such jurisdictional rights were exceptional and had to be positively established before they could be exercised. Such 'contiguous zones' (contiguous to the coast and territorial sea) were recognised in Art. 24 of the 1958 TSC as being available for customs, fiscal, immigration or sanitary purposes up to a maximum of 12 miles from the baseline of the territorial sea and necessarily implied enforcement rights against foreign registered ships. Although not material to the decision in the case, the International Tribunal for the Law of the Sea confirmed that a coastal state has the power to enforce customs law in its contiguous zone in the *MV Saiga (No. 2) Case (St Vincent and the Grenadines v Guinea)* (1999) 38 ILM 1323. Obviously, with the extension in customary and treaty law of the territorial sea to 12 miles, the 1958 TSC definition of the contiguous zone became redundant, and in LOS Art. 33 the permitted width of the contiguous zone is extended to 24 nautical miles from the baseline of the territorial sea. This probably reflects customary law.

The use of contiguous zones gives the coastal state an additional area of jurisdiction for limited purposes. However, because of the extension of the territorial sea and the seaward push of coastal jurisdiction exemplified by the EEZ, the contiguous zone has lessened in practical importance. Moreover, a certain amount of doubt surrounds the claim of some states to a contiguous zone for 'security purposes'. This particular claim of jurisdiction is not recognised by either the 1958 or 1982 Convention, despite some states asserting that such zones are lawful under customary law. The use of 'security' contiguous zones is disputed by many maritime nations, not least because the definition of 'security purposes' is highly subjective and could be used as a cover for the assertion of jurisdiction over foreign ships in all manner of unwarranted circumstances. As at 1 July 2012, eighty-nine states had claimed a contiguous zone, all of which were 24 miles or less. This does not include the UK or any of its dependent territories.

8.3 The Exclusive Economic Zone

8.3.1 Origin

If it were necessary to identify one feature of the 1982 Convention that has had a really profound impact on customary international law, it would be the development of the Exclusive Economic Zone (EEZ). Although the EEZ has its origins in the Exclusive Fisheries Zones (EFZ), recognised by the ICJ as legitimate in the *Fisheries Jurisdiction Cases (UK v Iceland)* 1974 ICJ Rep 3, its development was largely the result of negotiations at the Third UN Conference and its subsequent adoption in the national legislation of several states. In the *Continental Shelf Case (Tunisia v Libya)* 1982 ICJ Rep 18, the ICJ was clear that the concept of the EEZ had by then become rooted in customary law, and this was confirmed by the Tribunal in the *Guinea/Guinea-Bissau Maritime Delimitation Case* 77 ILR 636 (1983). At 1 July 2011, over 105 states had declared an EEZ, including the initially hostile USA. Most of the others claim an EFZ, probably because their current needs are met by a combination of fisheries zone and continental shelf rights. The UK claims an EEZ for some of its dependant territories but an EFZ for the mainland proper. The EEZ is dealt with at length in Part V LOS 1982. As we shall see, the Convention contains obligations as well as benefits for the coastal state and has a level of detail that simply could not have been matched had the EEZ remained only a creature of customary law.

8.3.2 Nature and extent

The EEZ is a belt of sea, adjacent to the coast, extending up to 200 miles from the baselines of the territorial sea (i.e. 188 miles in width). Within this area, the coastal state is given 'sovereign rights' for the purpose of exploring and exploiting the living and non-living natural resources of the area. In addition, it is given certain rights to establish artificial islands, conduct research and utilise the super-adjacent waters (LOS Art. 56). Importantly, although the territorial sea ends at 12 miles, the 188 miles of the EEZ are not 'high seas'. It seems that the waters of the EEZ are to be regarded as *sui juris*, wherein the coastal state has certain exclusive rights for the functional purpose of enjoying EEZ rights but where many of the freedoms of the high seas are preserved. However, given that the coastal state has 'sovereign rights' over natural resources, other states have lost the freedom to fish.

The coastal state has, then, sovereign rights over all the natural resources (e.g. fish, oil, gas, lobsters, crabs, etc.) up to 200 miles. The EEZ provides the coastal state with an exclusive share of the wealth of the sea and it is not surprising that it has found favour with so many states. What coastal states do not have is 'sovereignty', as witnessed by the preservation in the LOS legal regime of other states' rights. 'Sovereign rights' denotes exclusivity but it does not give the coastal state dominium over the EEZ. Consequently, it has only those rights given by the Convention and cannot interfere with commercial activity by other states in the EEZ unless such activity directly challenges the coastal state's sovereign rights. For example, the coastal state cannot enforce its customs laws in the EEZ or exercise a broad, undefined jurisdiction based on 'self-protection' (*MV Saiga (No. 2)*, rejecting Guinea's claim to this effect). However, it is clear that the coastal state can arrest foreign vessels that are violating its exclusive rights to the natural resources, subject to the 'prompt release' provisions of LOS Art. 73 – see *The Volga Case (Russian Federation v Australia)* (2002). Similarly, under the Convention, the coastal state is under a number of obligations that are inconsistent with the grant of full sovereignty. For example, the coastal state must conserve the natural living resources of the EEZ (Art. 61) and must determine the 'allowable catch' of such resources and if thereafter the coastal state does not have the capacity to harvest the total allowable catch it 'shall' give other states access to the living resources up to the limit of the allowable catch (LOS Art. 62(2)). In practical terms, this means that for living resources, the coastal state must conserve and must share in appropriate cases. Of course, if the coastal state wishes to deny all other states access to the EEZ, there is little that can be done to stop it from setting the allowable catch at the level of its own capacity. Yet the simple fact that the coastal state is under binding legal obligations, enforceable according to the mechanisms of the Law of the Sea Convention, illustrates that it does not have complete control over the EEZ, as it would have if it were actually sovereign territory. It is also to be noted that the EEZ, unlike the continental shelf, is not 'inherent' in statehood. It has to be specifically claimed by states. It is a legal construct permitted by international law rather than a natural extension of land-based sovereignty.

8.3.3 Other states' rights in the EEZ

What, then, is the nature of other states' rights in the EEZ? As we have just seen, other states may be able to share in the living resources of the EEZ under the 'allowable catch' mechanism, even though the right to fish freely has been lost. In addition, under LOS Art. 58, those freedoms of the seas such as navigation, overflight, laying of submarine cables 'and other internationally lawful uses of the sea related to these freedoms' are still available, except as modified by the Convention in respect of coastal state jurisdiction. These include commercial activities not part of the coastal state's exclusive rights (*MV Saiga (No. 2)*). As a counterweight, other states 'shall have due regard' to the rights and duties of the coastal state and 'shall comply' with the coastal state's laws and regulations adopted in accordance with the Convention (LOS Art. 58(3)). In this regard, it is clear from the *MV Saiga (No. 2) Case* that restrictions on other states' rights in the EEZ that are not specifically laid down by LOS 1982 are not to be presumed lightly. There is no general power in the coastal state to regulate commercial activity, unless this is in direct pursuit of the rights granted by the EEZ regime. Consequently, in the *MV Saiga* case, while the foreign ship was in Guinea's EEZ, it was not subject to Guinea's general customs laws and the coastal state could not take measures to prevent what it regarded as smuggling of fuel oil. What this adds up to is a regime where the coastal state is given those rights and ancillary powers which are necessary in order to enable it to utilise the resources of the EEZ but, after that, the rights of other states remain intact. For example, because the EEZ is not territorial waters, it may be that other states have the right to conduct military manoeuvres in the EEZ, so long as this does not interfere with the coastal state's exploration and exploitation of resources. This is certainly the view of the major maritime powers that see the EEZ as a grant of rights to the coastal state rather than as a zone over which coastal states have pre-existing legal rights. This is disputed by some coastal states who do regard the EEZ as akin to sovereign territory for all practical purposes. The 1982 Convention avoided this issue by the use of 'sovereign rights' which is more than 'jurisdiction' but less than 'sovereignty'.

8.3.4 Delimitation

Under the Convention, delimitation of the EEZ between opposite and adjacent states 'shall be affected by agreement on the basis of international law ... in order to achieve an equitable solution' (Art. 74). As we shall see, this open-ended provision is identical to that applicable to the continental shelf and it will be considered in more detail later. Generally, it should be noted that since the EEZ and shelf overlap within 200 miles, usually it will be desirable to draw a common maritime boundary for both zones between opposite or adjacent states. This was emphasised by Judge Oda and Judge ad hoc Evensen in their Dissenting Opinions in *Tunisia* v

Libya and since then it has been the default position. It was achieved in the *Guinea/ Guinea-Bissau Arbitration*, the *Delimitation of Maritime Areas Between Canada and France (St Pierre and Miquelon) Case* (1992), the *Maritime Delimitation and Territorial Questions between Qatar and Bahrain (Qatar v Bahrain)* (2001), the *Barbados/Trinidad & Tobago Maritime Delimitation Arbitration*, (2006), the *Territorial and Maritime Dispute between Nicaragua and Honduras in the Caribbean Sea (Nicaragua v Honduras)* (2006), *the Maritime Delimitation in the Black Sea (Romania v Ukraine)* (2009) and the first delimitation case decided by the International Tribunal for the Law of the Sea, the *Dispute Concerning Delimitation of the Maritime Boundary between Bangladesh and Myanmar in the Bay of Bengal, (Bangladesh/Myanmar)* (2012).

However, while a common maritime boundary may be desirable, it is not mandatory, because an 'equitable result' for the shelf may be different from an 'equitable result' for the EEZ. Judge Gros in his Dissenting Opinion in the *Gulf of Maine Case (Canada v USA)* (1984), suggested that a common continental shelf/fisheries zone boundary might not have been appropriate given the different legal regimes of each area; and in the *Maritime Delimitation in the Area Between Greenland and Jan Meyen Case (Denmark v Norway)* (1993), Vice-President Oda (dissenting) emphasised that the separate and independent legal regimes of the shelf and EEZ (which he claimed the majority had overlooked) meant that a common maritime boundary should never be presumed, even if it was eventually adopted. It is usually, therefore, at the request of the parties that such a delimitation is achieved and, in such cases, the Tribunal does seem prepared to overlook differences in the legal regime and delimitation rules of the different maritime zones in order to achieve the 'greater good' of a single line delimitation. However, we must be clear that a tribunal may insist on a common maritime boundary as the most equitable solution to the problem of maritime delimitation even if the parties do not request this or agree to it – provided of course that the Tribunal has jurisdiction to make any award. Thus, in the *Barbados/Trinidad & Tobago Maritime Delimitation Arbitration*, (2006) the Arbitral Panel recognised that the EEZ and Continental Shelf were of different legal origin but insisted on drawing a common maritime boundary even though this was not requested jointly by the parties.

8.3.5 Overlap with the continental shelf

As we shall see, the continental shelf extends in law to a minimum of 200 miles, within which the coastal state is given rights over the non-living natural resources, such as oil and gas. Obviously, there is a geographical overlap within the 200-mile limit with the EEZ in respect of these particular resources. The relationship between the two zones is considered in detail later, but for now it should be noted that extraction of non-living resources from the EEZ is to be carried out in conformity with those provisions of the Convention concerning the continental shelf (LOS Art. 56(3)). As indicated previously, even if these two zones do share a common maritime boundary and even though they do overlap considerably geographically, they remain juridically distinct. They are parallel but separate, and it is difficult to disagree with Vice-President Oda in the *Jan Meyen Case* when he bemoans the tendency to regard the relatively immature EEZ regime as absorbed by the more mature and pre-1982 Convention regime of the continental shelf.

8.4 The continental shelf

The continental margin as a physical (geomorphological) feature consists of a relatively shallow plateau of land adjacent to the coast (the shelf proper), followed by a steep slope going to near the ocean floor (the continental slope) and then a gradual incline going to the ocean floor itself (the continental rise). Generally, these three features constitute the 'continental shelf' although as we shall see, the legal definition of the shelf does not necessarily correspond with its physical limits.

The origin of the continental shelf as a juridical concept lies in customary law, even though today it is governed largely by treaty law. Traditionally, the starting point in the history of the shelf is seen as the Truman Proclamation 1945, wherein the USA claimed 'the natural resources of the subsoil and sea bed of the continental shelf beneath the high seas but contiguous to the coasts of the United States as appertaining to the United States, subject to its jurisdiction and control'. This was followed by similar claims by other states, all wishing to gain access to the oil, gas and mineral deposits believed to exist in the shelf. By 1958, the practice of states had developed to such an extent that the First UN Conference on the Law of the Sea adopted the Convention on the Continental Shelf (CSC 1958). For most purposes, this has now been superseded by Part VI of the 1982 Convention, although many of the two treaties' provisions are similar in substance. In fact, Part VI of LOS is one of its least controversial aspects. Once again, it is also true that customary law has developed in parallel to the Conventions, as made clear by the ICJ in the *Continental Shelf Case (Libya v Malta)*.

8.4.1 Nature and extent of shelf rights

It is now firmly established that continental shelf rights are 'inherent' in statehood. The rights which a coastal state exercises over the shelf exist as an extension of the statehood of the coastal state and do not have to be claimed or recognised by other states (*North Sea Continental Shelf Cases*; CSC Art. 2(2); LOS Art. 77(3)). However, the coastal state does not have sovereignty over the shelf, but 'sovereign rights' for the purpose of exploring and exploiting its natural resources (CSC Art. 2; LOS Art. 77). Consequently, the waters above the shelf prima facie retain their status as high seas (CSC Art. 3; LOS Art. 78), although this will be modified for waters within the 200-mile limit where the EEZ regime will operate.

The coastal state has, then, exclusive rights to explore and exploit the 'natural resources' of the shelf area. If the coastal state does not undertake such exploration or exploitation, then no other state may do so without its permission (LOS Art. 77(2)). Natural resources are defined in both the 1958 and 1982 Conventions as all non-living resources (e.g. oil, gas) of the sea bed and subsoil plus certain 'sedentary species'. These are living organisms which are either immobile on or under the sea floor or which are unable to move except in constant physical contact with the sea floor. They include such creatures as coral, oysters and sponges, and possibly lobsters and crabs. The precise definition of such species may well prove to be important in respect of resources lying beyond the 200-mile EEZ limit, for if they are within the legal regime of the shelf they fall exclusively to the coastal state (cf. the *Barbados/Trinidad & Tobago Maritime Delimitation Arbitration* (2006)).

8.4.2 Delimitation of the shelf – seaward limit

As indicated earlier, the shelf as a physical feature comprises the shelf, slope and rise, which together make up the 'continental margin'. The end of the rise is the seaward limit of the shelf as a matter of physical fact. However, we are concerned with the shelf as a legal institution and the seaward limit of this may not correspond exactly to the physical feature, even though LOS 1982 brings them closer together than the 1958 Convention.

In Art. 1 of the 1958 Convention, the shelf was defined as the submarine area adjacent to the coast but outside the territorial sea 'to a depth of 200 metres or, beyond that limit, to where the depth of the super-adjacent waters admits of the exploitation of the natural resources'. Under this treaty, the inner limit of the shelf was the outer edge of the territorial sea but the seaward limit was a depth of 200 metres or any area capable of exploitation. Obviously, this is a very open-ended provision, for it envisages the extension of coastal state jurisdiction in direct relation to its ability to extract natural resources. Taken to extremes, this definition means that the deep ocean floor could become part of the 'shelf' if it became possible to exploit it. This definition had been criticised at the First Conference in 1958 and it became clear during the Third UN Conference that it was unsuitable given the development of the principle of 'common heritage of mankind' in relation to the ocean floor (see section 8.5). Consequently, under Art. 76 of LOS 1982, the seaward limit of the shelf is to be determined by the following rules:

(1) All states, regardless of the physical shape of the shelf, have a continental shelf in law up to 200 nautical miles from the baselines of the territorial sea. This is so even if there is no physical shelf or if it stops short of 200 miles (Art. 76(1)).

(2) If the physical extent of the shelf goes beyond 200 nautical miles, the coastal state has a shelf in law 'throughout the natural prolongation of its land territory to the outer edge of the continental margin' (Art 76(1)). In other words, where the shelf goes beyond 200 miles as a physical feature (as it did in the *Dispute Concerning Delimitation of the Maritime Boundary between Bangladesh and Myanmar in the Bay of Bengal, (Bangladesh/Myanmar)* (2012)), the coastal state has shelf rights to the outer edge of the continental rise except as provided in rule (3).

(3) The continental shelf in law cannot extend beyond 350 nautical miles from the baselines of the territorial sea or 100 nautical miles from the 2,500 metre isobath (depth line) (Art. 76(5)). This seaward maximum limit, which applies even if the shelf is physically greater, was adopted at the Third Conference as a result of an Irish/Soviet proposal designed to ensure that coastal state jurisdiction had a definite limit.

It can be seen, then, that although there is a greater correlation between the 'physical' and 'legal' shelf in the 1982 Convention than was found in the 1958 Convention, the match is not perfect. Importantly, all states have a shelf up to 200 miles irrespective of physical conditions and there is a seaward limit even if the physical shelf does continue further. At the Third Conference, there was some suggestion that the EEZ and shelf regimes should be merged, with the consequent curtailing of the shelf at 200 miles. However, states such as the UK and the USA, which have natural shelves extending beyond this limit, objected to this restriction and so the regimes have remained juridically separate – a point emphasised by Vice-President Oda in the *Jan Meyen Case*. By way of compromise, the 1982 Convention does recognise that shelf rights beyond 200 miles constitute a derogation from the 'common herit-age' principle of the deep sea bed discussed later. Consequently, in respect of exploi-tation of the resources of the shelf where it extends beyond 200 miles, the coastal state 'shall' make payments to the International Sea Bed Authority for distribution among other states (LOS Art. 82). This illustrates the 1982 Convention view that coastal state jurisdiction beyond 200 miles is exceptional, even where there is a strong geological claim to more extensive rights.

The entry into force of the 1982 Convention now means that for state-parties the governing rules for delimiting the outer edge of the *juridical* continental shelf will be those found in Art. 76. As most major maritime and coastal states are already parties to LOS 1982, the existence of a competing rule in the 1958 Convention is likely to have little practical importance. It is, perhaps, more con-troversial whether the 350 mile/2,500 metre maximum limit is a rule of customary law, but again significant maritime non-LOS states are going to be few in number (perhaps only the USA). In any event, the reality is that few states actually possess a shelf with such a large seaward reach, and many of these are subject to compet-ing claims by 'opposite' states who share the same shelf. Likewise, the establish-ment of an effective regime for the management of the sea bed and other areas 'beyond the limits of national jurisdiction' (i.e. beyond the juridical shelf) means that coastal states lack a compelling motive to attempt to extend their jurisdiction beyond defensible limits. Fortunately, many of these matters fall within the remit of the Commission on the Limits of the Continental Shelf (CLCS). Established under LOS 1982, its purpose is to facilitate the implementation of LOS 1982 in respect of the outer limits of the shelf beyond 200 nautical miles. It is concerned with all aspects of shelf-delimitation beyond the 200-mile limit and offers advice and assistance to states, including scientific and technical guidelines on delimi-tation, and receives submissions from states on the delimitation of their shelf beyond these limits.

8.4.3 Delimitation of the shelf – opposite and adjacent states

8.4.3.1 Questions of principle and judicial uncertainty

In many areas of the sea, the physical continental shelf will be shared between two or more states. This can occur where states share a land border running to the sea (adjacent states, e.g. Tunisia/Libya, Bangladesh/Myanmar) or where states share a shelf because it runs under the sea which divides them (opposite states, e.g. Libya/Malta, Barbados/Trinidad & Tobago)). In this section, we shall examine how inter-national law seeks to divide up the shelf between these states so that each may share profitably in the shelf regime. In fact, there has been considerable judicial activity in this area and there are a number of examples of the application of the criteria of the 1958 Convention, customary law and LOS 1982 to concrete cases. The relatively recent entry into force of the 1982 Convention has meant that the specific law in issue has, in the past, been customary law. However, as we shall see, judicial deci-sions have established that the 1958 Convention criteria and the rules of customary law are broadly similar in effect and, in turn, that both sets of rules broadly assimi-late to the criteria of the 1982 Convention. Consequently, even though it is clear that LOS 1982 will now govern the shelf (and EEZ delimitation) in most disputes (as in *Barbados/Trinidad & Tobago Maritime Delimitation Arbitration* and the *Dispute*

Concerning Delimitation of the Maritime Boundary between Bangladesh and Myanmar in the Bay of Bengal, (Bangladesh/Myanmar)), the 'old' cases will continue to be very important. Additionally, as indicated previously, the question of shelf delimitation is bound up with that of the EEZ, especially as the provisions of LOS 1982 dealing with the delimitation of each are virtually identical. Therefore, many of the principles discussed later will be relevant for EEZ delimitation, both when the parties ask the tribunal to indicate a single maritime boundary for both shelf and EEZ areas (e.g. *Canada/France Delimitation*, 1992), when they do not but the tribunal finds a common maritime boundary appropriate (*Barbados/Trinidad & Tobago Maritime Delimitation Arbitration*, 2006) and in those rare cases where only EEZ delimitation is requested.

In the *North Sea Continental Shelf Cases*, the ICJ was asked to consider the principles and rules applicable to delimitation of the shelf between West Germany/Netherlands and West Germany/Denmark in the North Sea. Under Art. 6 of the CSC Convention 1958, delimitation was to be by agreement or, failing that, by a median line equidistant from the nearest points of the baselines of the territorial sea of each state, subject only to variations for special circumstances. This is known as the 'equidistance-special circumstance' rule. However, West Germany was not a party to the 1958 Convention and, as we have seen in Chapter 2, the Court decided that the Art. 6 rule was not part of customary law; it is binding only on those parties to the Convention. What then was the customary rule?

It was recognised by the Court in the *North Sea Continental Shelf Cases* that the equidistance-special circumstance rule could result in an inequitable delimitation in certain cases, especially where a state had a concave coast which would distort the median line. Therefore, in its view, delimitation under customary law was to be effected by the application of equitable principles in order to achieve an equitable result, with the ultimate aim of ensuring that each state had as much continental shelf as was a 'natural prolongation' of its land territory. No single method of delimitation was obligatory, but particular consideration should be paid to the general configuration of the coast, the physical shape of the shelf and the relative lengths of the coastlines of the claimant states. All in all, the shelf was to be divided on the basis of natural prolongation, in order to achieve an equitable result. Some years later, in the *Anglo-French Continental Shelf Case* (1979) 18 ILM 397, a Court of Arbitration considered the delimitation of the shelf between the UK and France in certain stretches of the English Channel. In this case, both states were parties to the 1958 Convention and were subject to the rule in CSC Art. 6. Nevertheless, the Tribunal emphasised that the purpose of the equidistance-special circumstance rule was also that an equitable delimitation should be achieved, a view confirmed in the *Jan Meyen Case (Denmark v Norway)* 1993 ICJ Rep 38, the first case where the ICJ was required to apply only Art. 6 of the 1958 Convention for shelf delimitation. This assimilation of customary law and Art. 6 of the 1958 Convention is supported by the reference in Art. 6 to 'special circumstances' which indicated that each case was heavily dependent on its particular facts – a view confirmed by *Canada/France Maritime Delimitation* (1992) 31 ILM 1145, albeit in a case where a multi-zone delimitation was requested. So, while it may be true that the 1958 CSC rule and customary law are not absolutely identical, it is clear that both may be applied only in a way likely to achieve an equitable result. For parties to the 1958 Convention only (i.e. where one or both disputing states are not parties to LOS 1982) the initial delimitation will usually be by means of an equidistant median line, but this will be varied quite readily if special circumstances (e.g. a concave coast) require a more equitable solution, as in the *Jan Meyen Case*. Likewise, in customary law, the *North Sea Cases* indicate that natural prolongation leading to an equitable result is the key.

It will be appreciated that the need to ensure equitable delimitation gives the court or tribunal a great deal of flexibility when faced with a concrete case. This was borne out by a series of cases dealing with delimitation under customary law which moved away from the relatively formalistic approach of the *North Sea Cases*. In *Tunisia v Libya*, for example, the ICJ was asked to identify the principles which the parties should use in delimiting their adjacent continental shelves. According to the Court, the basic rule of customary law was that, in the absence of agreement, delimitation should be by equitable principles designed to achieve an equitable result. Such equitable principles would vary from case to case but still encompassed the use of 'rules of law', rather than delimitation *ex aequo et bono*. Furthermore, even though natural prolongation had been emphasised in the *North Sea Cases*, this was said to be subordinate to the overriding aim of an equitable result. A delimitation according to natural prolongation was not, in itself, necessarily equitable. So in *Tunisia v Libya*, attention was paid primarily to geographical features, such as the proportionality of the lengths of the coast to the area of the shelf, the change in direction of the Tunisian coast and the existence of offshore islands. The court would not, however, act on the basis of 'distributive justice', whereby one state 'should' receive more shelf because it was 'poorer' than another.

Tunisia v Libya represented a shift of emphasis in shelf delimitation away from 'natural prolongation' to flexible criteria designed to achieve a just result in the circumstances of each case. It confirmed the rejection of an inflexible equidistance principle in customary law, a point that was reiterated by the majority in the *Continental Shelf Case (Libya v Malta)*. In that case, the ICJ rejected Libya's reliance on the natural prolongation method as a means of delimitation between opposite states but preferred instead the 'distance' principle. This idea, closely related to EEZ delimitation, accepts that as far as possible states should have a continental shelf of 200 miles width, irrespective of physical features. Again, delimitation was to be by equitable principles taking account of all relevant circumstances, with an enhanced role going to the proportionality principle. Similarly, in *Guinea/Guinea Bissau*, the Arbitration Court applied the 'relevant rules of international law' in order to achieve an equitable solution, noting that the equidistance method was just one possibility and that there was no compulsion to use it as a matter of customary law. Finally, in the *Gulf of Maine Case* – the first where a court was asked to determine a single boundary line delimiting both the shelf and another maritime zone (fisheries) between the competing states – an ICJ Chamber described the 'fundamental norm' of customary law as 'delimitation by agreement or by the application of equitable criteria to achieve an equitable result'. Indeed, in the *Gulf of Maine Case*, the 'equidistance-special circumstance rule' was rejected by the Chamber, even though both states were parties to the 1958 Continental Shelf Convention, on the ground that the issue before it was not simply one of shelf delimitation. The rejection of Article 6 as a basis for delimitation for parties to the 1958 Convention when a single maritime boundary for several zones is desired was then adopted by a Court of Arbitration in the *Canada/France Maritime Delimitation Case*, where the

Tribunal applied its own rule of equity to achieve a just result when drawing a shelf/fisheries boundary between the two states.

The result of this considerable judicial activity was then, that customary international law seemed to require nothing more than that an equitable result be achieved. The court or tribunal was to have considerable latitude, with (it seemed) few concrete rules, and there was a reluctance to over-conceptualise. Of course, there is the fundamental principle that there are to be no unilateral delimitations (*Gulf of Maine*) and, as the *Tunisia* and *Malta* cases show, the court may use the relative lengths of each state's coastline as the ratio for the area of each state's continental shelf (i.e. proportionality). For example, if the ratio of the length of coastline of State A and State B bordering the shelf is 2:1, State A may be awarded twice as much shelf as State B. However, the *Canada/France Arbitration* illustrated clearly that proportionality was not critical, as in that case the court rejected both equidistance and comparative coastal lengths as direct criteria for delimitation, but chose instead to use the proportionality rule (and natural prolongation) only in order to 'check' the equity of a delimitation after it had been made. It was not clear, however, whether the equidistance principle was also to be downgraded in delimitations between *opposite* states, especially because it is less likely to achieve an inequitable result (*Gulf of Maine Case*). Certainly, it was used as a basis for a delimitation between opposite states under LOS 1982 in the *Barbados/Trinidad & Tobago Maritime Delimitation Arbitration Case*, but it is not clear whether this was because LOS 1982 applied (and not the 1958 Convention) or because equidistance is to be preferred in 'opposite delimitations'. Likewise, these cases do not tell us how far 'natural prolongation' is still relevant (see e.g. its use as a 'safety net' in *Canada/France* and more directly in *Barbados/Trinidad & Tobago Maritime Delimitation Arbitration*).

Of course, throughout all of this, we must remember that delimitation is supposed to be made on the basis of law. As the 1982 Convention requires, delimitation between opposite or adjacent states must 'be effected by agreement on the basis of international law … in order to achieve an equitable solution' (Art. 83(1)). Yet, the very terms of Art. 83(1) only perpetuate the apparent uncertainties identified earlier – states are placed under an obligation to reach an equitable solution, but are not told how. As we have seen, this was the way customary law was developing, and so these cases are relevant to delimitation under Art. 83 of LOS 1982, but that does not take us much further.

This brings us to what may turn out to be a very significant decision in the law of maritime delimitation, the *Barbados/Trinidad & Tobago Maritime Delimitation Arbitration*, where both states were parties to LOS 1982 and delimitation was entirely under its provisions. In this case, the Arbitral Panel was determined to follow an approach that led to stability and predictability and thus proceeded to delimit the common maritime boundary between the parties' EEZ and the shelf in a traditional and highly positivist manner. In the Panel's view, delimitations should start with a provisional line based on equidistance, which should be modified in the light of relevant criteria in order to achieve an equitable result. One important factor in testing the equidistance line was natural prolongation and the litmus test of 'equity' was a broad notion of proportionality. Clearly, if this was to become the benchmark for delimitation between (at least) states under the Convention, it hearkens back to a more fixed formula for delimitation. For many commentators, this would not be unwelcome and the most recent case law seems to be taking this path.

8.4.3.2 A pragmatic way forward

The reliance in the *Barbados/Trinidad & Tobago Maritime Delimitation Arbitration* on a rather more tightly drawn set of criteria (similar to those favoured in the very early cases on shelf delimitation) was, perhaps, driven by a desire to identify more clearly what principles of *law* operated in shelf and maritime delimitation. This was the point being made by those that had dissented in the cases discussed previously. The issue came to a point in the *Maritime Delimitation in the Black Sea (Romania v. Ukraine) Case* (2009) where the ICJ itself returned to maritime delimitation. These adjacent and opposite states sought a single maritime delimitation of their shelf and EEZs (but not their territorial seas) and both were parties to the 1982 Convention which therefore provided the applicable law. According to the Court, such a delimitation should proceed in three stages. First, a median (or equidistance) line should be drawn, there being no difference between the two. This line would be 'heavily dependant' on the physical shape of the coasts and is to be based on objective data. Secondly, 'the Court will at the next, second stage consider whether there are factors calling for the adjustment or shifting of the provisional equidistance line in order to achieve an equitable result'. Finally, 'and at a third stage, the Court will verify that the line (a provisional equidistance line which may or may not have been adjusted by taking into account the relevant circumstances) does not, as it stands, lead to an inequitable result by reason of any marked disproportion between the ratio of the respective coastal lengths and the ratio between the relevant maritime area of each State by reference to the delimitation line'. This is because a 'final check for an equitable outcome entails a confirmation that no great disproportionality of maritime areas is evident by comparison to the ratio of coastal lengths'.

This is a statement of considerable importance, for it locates the search for an equitable solution in objective facts and provides a process for principled maritime delimitation. In short, one draws an equidistance line according to the physical geography; one adjusts it for special circumstances; and then one checks it to see if the result is disproportionate. This gives an equitable result within the meaning of LOS 1982, and, more likely than not, customary law. The formula has been applied, and confirmed, by ITLOS in the *Dispute Concerning Delimitation of the Maritime Boundary between Bangladesh and Myanmar in the Bay of Bengal, (Bangladesh/Myanmar)* (2012). It represents a return to a more principled approach to delimitation.

To sum up then, the factual matrix of a delimitation dispute may be the delimitation of the shelf alone or the delimitation of several maritime zones (e.g. shelf/EEZ; shelf/EFZ; shelf/territorial sea, or any combination thereof) between opposite or adjacent states. In the multi-zone case, the disputing states may request the tribunal to establish a single line to delimit the boundaries of all the disputed maritime zones – the 'common maritime boundary'. Even if no such request is made, the tendency has been to propose a single line as a boundary for all zones, which some critics allege ignores the different juridical origin of the various zones. The governing law for future maritime disputes usually will be LOS 1982, but this mirrors existing customary law in its emphasis on reaching an equitable solution. However, it now seems that this equitable solution is to be the product of the application of a three-stage test incorporating clear rules, rather than what is abstractly fair. If by some chance the 1958 Convention should apply (*Jan Meyen* may be the first and the last case), then the tribunal is bound to apply equidistance and then 'shift' the line by reason of special circumstance to reach an equitable result. This now mirrors the requirements under the LOS/customary law formula, as explained in *Romania* v *Ukraine* and *Bangladesh* v *Myanmar*.

8.4.4 Relationship with the Exclusive Economic Zone

As we have seen, both the EEZ and continental shelf give the coastal state sovereign rights to explore and exploit the natural resources of a sea area adjacent to its coast. At the Third UN Conference there was a move by some states to set aside the shelf regime altogether and subsume it within the EEZ or, alternatively, to use the shelf as a supplement to the EEZ such that there would be no separate shelf regime within 200 miles of the coast. Eventually, the proposal now found in the 1982 Convention was adopted, wherein the shelf starts at the outer edge of the territorial sea and encompasses mineral resources and only those living resources that are linked to the shelf bed. The shelf and EEZ are legally autonomous even though within the 200-mile limit they operate with respect to the same area and similar non-living resources. What then are the differences between the two regimes?

(a) The most obvious difference is that the shelf may extend beyond 200 miles, whereas the EEZ has a fixed limit.

(b) Shelf rights are 'inherent'; an EEZ is optional and must be claimed by the state. However, both confer sovereign and exclusive rights.

(c) The waters of the EEZ are *sui juris*, whereas the waters above the shelf where it extends beyond 200 miles remain as high seas. The waters of the shelf within 200 miles are comprised within the EEZ, if one has been claimed.

(d) The shelf covers non-living resources and only those living resources which are 'sedentary species'. The EEZ covers all resources within the 200-mile limit.

(e) There is an obligation to conserve the living resources of the EEZ and, in certain cases, an obligation to share those resources with other states. There is no obligation to conserve shelf resources (including the living sedentary species) and no obligation to share those resources (but see (f)). There is no obligation to share or conserve the non-living resources of the EEZ, for they are to be utilised in conformity with the shelf regime (LOS Art. 56(3)).

(f) For shelf rights beyond the 200-mile limit, the 1982 Convention obliges coastal states to contribute a percentage of its revenue to the International Sea Bed Authority.

(g) The criteria for delimitation of the two zones between opposite and adjacent states are expressed in identical terms and a single boundary for both zones between competing states is usually the most sensible result. It is possible, though not likely to be common, that the application of the common criteria could lead to a different boundary for each zone because of the need to reach an 'equitable result' in each case.

In the *Jan Meyen Case*, Vice-President Oda in his dissent had much to say about the way judicial tribunals had reacted to the existence of these two overlapping maritime zones. First, he makes the point that a 'fishery zone' is not to be equated with the EEZ, correctly asserting that the former has no place in LOS 1982. He might have added, however, that a fisheries zone appears to be recognised in customary law as a 'single issue' zone, parasitic upon the acceptance of the EEZ. After all, a 200-mile fishery zone is much less intrusive of the rights of other states than a 200-mile EEZ. Secondly, he bemoans the failure of the Tribunal (and other courts) to recognise the independent existence of the shelf and EEZ regimes and its subsequent failure to give effect to their distinct juridical qualities. With reference to delimitation, he believes that the 'practical identity' between Art. 74 (EEZ) and Art. 83 (shelf) does not mean that actual delimitation of the EEZ and shelf between the same disputing states will be identical. It may be, but need not be. As a matter of law, Judge Oda must be right, because a tribunal need not 'presuppose a single delimitation for two separate and independent regimes' and such delimitation should proceed on the basis of an independent application of the delimitation criteria to each zone. In practice, however, the reality of maritime exploration and exploitation means that jurisdictional boundaries should be as certain and uncluttered as possible. Consequently, although it may be permissible for State A and State B to have one line delimiting their 200-mile EEZ and a different one delimiting their 200-mile shelf, is this practical? The Panel in *Barbados/Trinidad & Tobago Maritime Delimitation Arbitration*, clearly thought not.

(h) Other states' commercial and shipping activities are not hindered in the waters above the shelf if those waters are high seas. If those waters are within the EEZ, other states' activities may be controlled by the coastal state *only* as an adjunct to the exercise of EEZ sovereign rights.

8.4.5 Single maritime zone delimitation

It is apparent from what has been said already that there is a tendency to delimit the overlapping maritime zones of opposite or adjacent states by reference to a single maritime boundary. Often this is at the request of the parties, or construed by the tribunal to be the desirable outcome of the parties' submission to the jurisdiction (e.g. *Eritrea/Yemen, Barbados/Trinidad & Tobago Maritime Delimitation Arbitration*). Obviously, such an approach has advantages, not least that it minimises future jurisdictional conflicts by providing a single maritime boundary that is easily and clearly located. Similarly, it minimises the possibility of conflict over the exercise of the different substantive rights that undoubtedly exist in, say, the territorial sea, EEZ and continental shelf zones. However, the fact that there *are* separate and different legal regimes for these zones must lead us to question whether a single maritime boundary is always consistent with the rights and obligations of the coastal states within these zones. Different substance can lead to different form. Likewise, as Judge Oda (again!) points out in his dissent in the *Qatar* v *Bahrain Case*, the application of the specific rules for the delimitation of each zone (e.g. the median line for the territorial sea, but the three stage approach for shelf and EEZ) should not be discarded unless that is justified as a matter of international law as applied to the facts of the immediate case. That said, the recent case law confirms a trend towards single line maritime delimitation, not least because states seem to value it.

8.5 The deep sea bed

In recent years, it has become possible for states to exploit the mineral resources of the deep sea bed. Currently, interest is focused on polymetallic nodules which lie on the sea bed and which are rich in minerals such as manganese, cobalt and copper as well as traditional extraction of oil from deep sea wells. With advances in technology, it is becoming possible for large-scale mining or drilling in the deep sea bed, although as yet there is uncertainty as to the actual mineral wealth available. Traditionally, the exploitation of the sea 'beyond the limits of national jurisdiction' (formerly, this meant beyond the territorial sea), was governed by the doctrine of the high seas. While this meant that the sea and ocean floor were not open to acquisition by any state (i.e. no state had or could gain sovereignty), it also permitted any state to take whatever resources it was capable of harvesting, so long as it did not interfere unduly with the legitimate uses of the sea by other states. The high seas and ocean floor were *res communis* (belonging to the community at large). Following the First and Second UN Conferences on the Law of the Sea, many states became disturbed at the prospect of deep sea mining being governed by the one-dimensional doctrine of freedom of the seas. In essence, it would mean that those states capable of exploiting the sea bed would monopolise its resources to the detriment of others.

In 1969, the UN General Assembly, at the instigation of developing states, adopted the 'moratorium resolution' on sea bed mining. This resolution declared an intention to establish an international regime for the sea bed area and, pending this, declared that states 'are bound to refrain from all activities of exploitation of the resources of the area of the sea-bed and ocean floor and the subsoil thereof, beyond the limits of national jurisdiction' (GA Res. 2574D (XXIV)). This resolution was opposed by many industrialised states but was followed in 1970 by the Declaration of Principles Governing the Sea-Bed and The Ocean Floor, and the Subsoil Thereof, Beyond the Limits of National Jurisdiction (GA Res. 2749 (XXV)). This second resolution declared that the sea bed etc. was the 'common heritage of mankind', to be used for 'the benefit of mankind as a whole' and not open to the acquisition or sovereignty of any state. It declared further that all mineral activities should be governed by an international regime and that the area should be used for peaceful purposes only. These were landmark resolutions and, not surprisingly, there is some debate about the precise effect they have in customary law. Developed states once argued (and some still do) that the 'moratorium resolution' was no more than a statement of intent which does not prohibit unilateral mining of the area under the high seas principle, especially since they voted against it. On the other hand, the 1970 resolution was adopted 104 to 0, with 14 abstentions, which does suggest that at least the principle of 'common heritage' has now passed into customary law, even if there is no agreed method of achieving it. Fortunately, the entry into force of the 1982 Convention, albeit in amended form, has made this debate less pressing.

8.5.1 The 1982 Convention

Part XI of the Convention as *originally* drafted contained a detailed legal regime providing for the exploitation and management of the 'Area' for the benefit of all mankind. It remains the longest part of the Convention and the one to which most time was devoted. It was also the Part to which some of the industrialised countries most strongly objected and was the reason why the USA voted against adoption of the Conference text, and why the UK would not have ratified the Convention in its original form. Obviously, the certain absence of these and other influential states from the Convention regime because of Part XI would have been a serious blow, not only because of the effect this would have on the Convention as a whole but also because these were the states most able to fund and participate in deep sea-bed mining. The establishment by these states of a Reciprocating States Regime, a scheme whereby each participating state (e.g. UK, USA, France, Japan, Belgium, Italy, The Netherlands, Germany) would license its nationals for deep sea-bed mining and recognise the licences granted by others, was a practical expression of this opposition. Clearly something had to be done and the imminent entry into force of the Convention consequent upon its 60th ratification in November 1993 (by Guyana) provided the final impetus. Under the auspices of the UN Secretary-General, exploratory discussions began between interested parties covering the whole range of the objections of the dissenting states (on which see later in the chapter). Several mechanisms for compromise were put forward: that LOS 1982 should come into force minus Part XI but with the ratification of the objecting states; that the Convention should be frozen in its entirety without entering into force; or that an amending/additional instrument should be drafted consequent upon which the Convention should come into force as amended and with the ratification of the objecting states. It was this last solution that was adopted.

On 27 July 1994, the UN General Assembly was presented with an Agreement Relating to the Implementation of Part XI of the United Nations Convention on the Law of the Sea. This was adopted on 28 July by a vote of 121 to 0, with 7 abstentions. It was then opened for signature and ratification and is now in force. In essence, although the Agreement is not cast formally as an amending instrument, in practice that is exactly what it has achieved. The entry into force of the 1994 Agreement has modified substantially the provisions of Part XI of the Convention. The Agreement is to be regarded as an integral part of the Convention and the two instruments are to be interpreted and applied as one, the Agreement prevailing in cases of conflict. So, no state can become bound by the Agreement unless it first becomes bound by the Convention. Its adoption and entry into force prompted the UK and other objectors to ratify the Convention (and Agreement) although the USA remains outside both. In this sense, the 1994 Agreement is a remarkable achievement and there is much to be said for the view that it provides a workable and equitable regime for deep sea-bed mining. It also ensured that many more states would accept the remainder of the 1982 Convention and thus has done much to make it a truly global treaty.

8.5.2 General scheme of Part XI

The Area is defined as the 'sea-bed and ocean floor and subsoil thereof beyond the limits of national jurisdiction' (LOS Art. 1(1)), which for practical purposes means the sea bed starting at the outer edge of the juridical continental shelf. The whole system will be overseen by the International Sea Bed Authority with its headquarters in Jamaica. This has a number of organs such as a Secretary-General, the Assembly (which comprises all parties to the Convention and has general supervisory functions), the Council (having thirty-six elected members and which exercises considerable practical power), various commissions which are under the control of the Council, the Secretariat and (under Section 9 of the 1994 Agreement) a Finance Committee.

The basic principle is that the Area is to be used for the common heritage of mankind and is not open to acquisition by any state (LOS Arts 136–7). In essence, the Convention establishes a system of 'parallel access' for exploitation of the Area, although the Agreement has toned down the original scheme substantially (1994 Agreement, Section 2). All activities will be controlled by the International Sea Bed Authority, but mining may be carried out by states (or groups of states) or the 'Enterprise', the mining arm of the Authority, initially in joint ventures with other miners (1994 Agreement, Section 2). Authorisation from the Authority is required before mining by states or by the Enterprise in joint venture can go ahead. States will pay a levy to the Authority in respect of their operations as well as a proportion of the market value of the minerals extracted, again in much modified form from that originally envisaged (1994 Agreement, Section 8). Both the income from state activity and the revenue obtained by the Enterprise will be distributed among parties to the treaty by the Authority on an 'equitable' basis (LOS Art. 140). Other features of the regime include protection for 'pioneer investors', that is, those states who have already invested considerably in deep sea mining (under Res. I and Res. II appended to the Convention and under Section 1 of the 1994 Agreement), regulation of marine research (Art. 143), protection of the marine environment (Art. 145), the retention of the existing status of waters above the Area (Art. 135) and, notably, provisions regarding the transfer of technology from developed states to the Enterprise and developing states (Art. 144 as modified by Section 5 of the 1994 Agreement).

8.5.3 Specific concerns met by the 1994 Agreement

As we have seen, the original scheme of Part XI was so objectionable to a number of states that they felt compelled to resist ratifying the 1982 Convention. The nub of these objections is that the unmodified Part XI established a bureaucratic, expensive international institution, which denied a decisive say to those financing it, which proposed to exploit the ability of developed states to undertake deep sea-bed mining operations and which distributed its funds on an inappropriate basis. According to the objectors, the original scheme was not market orientated, but policy driven. The specific objections of the US-led protestors were: that the institutions of the International Sea Bed Authority were unwieldy and, in any event, downgraded the decision-making influence of states fundamental to the regime's success; that decision-making in the Council of the Authority was inappropriately weighted against industrialised nations; that the scheme whereby mining sites were reserved for the Enterprise to exploit alone was commercially unviable and unfair; that the provisions for review of the Deep Sea-Bed Regime were inadequate and too extensive in that they could be used to override the legitimate concerns of active mining states; that protection of land-based mineral producers by subsidy and protectionist measures was too extensive and commercially unsound; that the obligation to transfer mining technology to other states penalised developed states and should be done only on commercial principles; and that certain existing investors were not protected. Most of these concerns have been addressed in the 1994 Agreement, so much so that the Part XI of the Convention now in force bears only scant resemblance to that originally envisaged.

There is no doubt that the Convention has established a comprehensive and detailed regime for the management of the Deep Sea Area. As originally conceived, Part XI of the Convention emphasised the communal aspects of deep sea mining and minimised the benefits which a state (or its nationals) could take for itself, even if it had injected much finance and toil over many years. It was led by altruism, not economics, and placed an undue burden on those states which might actually mine and which might actually have had real costs. The modified regime is, in essence, a market-led regime with less subsidy and less protection for non-mining states and less scope for intervention in mining activities by the International Sea Bed Authority. That is not to say that the regime is not truly communal – it is – but the principle of common heritage is suffused with commercial considerations that (some would say) actually make mining more likely and may mean that profits for all states do eventually emerge.

8.5.4 Summary of the legal status of the deep sea bed

The legal rules governing the status and use of the deep sea bed are to be found in LOS 1982 and the 1994 Agreement, supported for non-parties by customary law. The Agreement modifies the Convention and takes precedence over it. Salient features include the following:

(a) The deep sea bed (the Area) – starting from the outer edge of the continental shelf – is not susceptible to the sovereignty of any state. It cannot be owned. It is within the common heritage of mankind. This was the position in customary law and is encapsulated in the 1982 Convention, Arts 136, 137 and 140.

(b) The deep sea bed may be used for peaceful purposes only. This excludes such matters as the installation of nuclear weapons on the ocean floor, but probably does not exclude the installation of defensive detection systems. Again, this is the position in customary law and under Art. 141 LOS.

(c) All states, whether coastal or landlocked, have access to the Area under LOS 1982 Art. 141 and in customary law.

(d) The resources of the deep sea bed are to be used for the common heritage of mankind and are subject to an international legal regime. Unilateral mining without prior authorisation is prohibited. The International Sea-Bed Authority will regulate deep sea mining, although there is now greater latitude and greater incentives for individual states or their nationals acting within the international regime. Mining by the Authority entirely on its own will not occur (at least initially), but will be effected through joint ventures with others. Some of the profits of deep sea mining are to be shared among all states, but with considerable protection for the rights and profits of those actually undertaking the mining activity.

(e) As explained by the Seabed Disputes Chamber of ITLOS in its first ever (and unanimous) Advisory Opinion, *Responsibilities and obligations of States sponsoring persons and entities with respect to activities in the Area* (2011), States have two types of legal obligation in respect of entities (e.g. companies) that they have sponsored for exploitation of the resources of the Area. First, the obligation to ensure compliance by sponsored contractors with the terms of the contract and the obligations set out in the Convention and related instruments. This is an obligation of 'due diligence' so that the sponsoring State is bound to make best possible efforts to secure compliance by the sponsored contractors with

Convention requirements. Secondly, direct obligations with which sponsoring States must comply independently of their first obligation. This direct obligation includes the obligation to assist the Authority, the obligation to apply a precautionary approach, the obligation to apply the best environmental practices, the obligation to adopt measures to ensure the provision of guarantees in the event of an emergency order by the Authority for protection of the marine environment; and the obligation to provide recourse for compensation.

8.6 The high seas

The 1958 Convention on the High Seas was said to 'codify the rules of international law relating to the high seas' (Preamble). In Art. 1, the high seas were defined as those parts of the sea not within the internal waters or territorial sea of a state. Today we have to revise this definition, for the waters of the EEZ are no longer part of the high seas, although many high seas freedoms remain. Consequently, Art. 86 of the 1982 Convention defines 'high seas' as all parts of the sea except internal waters, the territorial sea, the EEZ and archipelagic waters of an archipelagic state. This reflects customary law. The general principle of the high seas is that they are *res communis*. They are open to the enjoyment of every state, whether coastal or landlocked, and may not be subject to the sovereignty of any state (LOS Art. 220 HSC Art. 2). The high seas must be used for peaceful purposes only, although weapons testing and military exercises are permitted. In this respect, however, the atmospheric testing of nuclear weapons is now prohibited under the Nuclear Test Ban Treaty 1963, although the position under customary law remains unclear following the indecisive outcome of the *Nuclear Test Cases* 1974 ICJ Rep 253 and *Nuclear Test Case* 1995 ICJ Rep 288.

Given that the high seas are *res communis*, it is a basic principle of customary law (perhaps even of *jus cogens*) that all states, whether coastal or landlocked, may enjoy the 'freedom of the seas'. This bundle of rights comprises several distinct freedoms, such as the freedom of navigation and overflight, the freedom to fish, the freedom to lay submarine cables and pipelines, the freedom to conduct scientific research and the freedom to construct artificial islands (LOS Art. 87). Of these, only the first four are mentioned specifically in the 1958 High Seas Convention (HSC Art. 2), but the expanded definition of LOS 1982 almost certainly represents customary international law and in any event binds parties to it. As a corollary of this, all freedoms must be exercised with due regard to the rights of other states. In addition, under LOS 1982, the freedoms must be exercised with due regard to the special regime established for the deep sea bed.

As far as state jurisdiction over ships on the high seas is concerned, both the 1958 and 1982 Conventions provide that the flag state (i.e. the state in which the ship is registered) shall generally have exclusive jurisdiction (HSC Art. 6; LOS Art. 92). This means that the state of nationality, and only that state, may exercise criminal and civil jurisdiction in respect of the ship. However, there are certain exceptions to this, both customary and conventional. These include:

(a) cases of piracy (HSC Art. 145; LOS Art. 100);

(b) cases of unauthorised sound and television broadcasting (LOS Art. 109 and see the UK Broadcasting Act 1990);

(c) cases of 'hot pursuit' from the territorial sea or contiguous zone (HSC Art. 23; LOS Art. 111). In this regard, see the UK case of *R v Mills* (1995) 44 ICLQ 949, where the national court discussed the conditions for a lawful exercise of hot pursuit and decided that Art. 23 of the 1958 Convention (and therefore almost certainly Art. 111 LOS 1982) reflected customary law. This has been reinforced by the *MV Saiga (No. 2) Case*, where the Tribunal makes it clear that all of the conditions of Art. 111 LOS must be fulfilled before hot pursuit is legitimate;

(d) cases in respect of certain pollution matters (LOS Art. 221);

(e) as a residual right in cases of collisions on the high seas (HSC Art. 11; LOS Art. 97);

(f) under the 'right of visit' in cases of ships of unknown nationality (HSC Art. 22; LOS Art. 110); and

(g) where treaty provides otherwise (e.g. as authorised by the Convention against Illicit Traffic in Narcotic Drugs and Psychotropic Substances 1988, at issue in *R v Charrington*, unreported).

In these situations, the flag state shares jurisdiction with other states, generally that which is specifically interested or harmed by the actions of the ship. In the case of piracy, all states share jurisdiction because this is a crime under international law giving universal jurisdiction.

8.7 Miscellaneous matters

8.7.1 International straits

If the navigable channel in an international strait is comprised of high seas, then there is no difficulty with the right of states to proceed through the strait unhindered. It would be an exercise of the freedom of navigation. However, problems arise when the waters of a strait consist of the territorial sea (or other maritime zone) of a coastal state, as is now the case in the Dover Strait in the English Channel. In such circumstances, is there a right of navigation and may it be restricted by the coastal state?

In the *Corfu Channel Case*, the ICJ made it clear that if the waters of a strait which was used for international navigation were comprised of territorial sea, there existed a non-suspendable right of innocent passage for all ships through the strait. This was confirmed and embodied in the 1958 Territorial Sea Convention, Art. 16(4) and still exists for some straits under LOS Art. 45. However, the extension of coastal state jurisdiction after 1958, especially the extension of the territorial sea and the emergence of the EEZ, provoked a re-examination of the right of ships to pass through straits used for international navigation. This was of particular concern to major maritime powers for whom the guarantee of navigation rights was part of the 'package deal' of the Convention. Thus, the 1982 Convention defines an entirely new right called 'transit passage' (Part III).

The right of transit passage exists through 'straits used for international navigation between one part of the high seas or an [EEZ] and another part of the high seas or an [EEZ]'. It applies only to those straits which pass through the territorial sea and not to straits where the waters are actually high seas or EEZ. Similarly excluded are territorial sea straits formed by a coast and an island where a suitable navigable route exists round the island in the high seas or EEZ (LOS Arts 36, 38). Again, 'transit passage' will not apply to those straits that are already governed by 'long-standing international conventions in force', such as the Montreux Convention 1936 governing the Bosphorus and Dardenelles.

In essence, transit passage encompasses 'freedom of navigation and over-flight solely for the purpose of continuous and expeditious transit of the strait' (Art. 38(2)) and, although the coastal state may make regulations for various purposes (Art. 42), the right of transit passage may not be suspended (Art. 44). In this respect transit passage is wider than innocent passage, for the latter does not include 'innocent overflight'. In practice, the right is unlikely to be tested (e.g. what is meant by 'continuous and expeditious'?) until a case arises where a coastal state specifically denies passage which would be authorised under the Convention. In so far as 'transit passage' is not yet a customary right and the disputing states are not parties to the 1982 Convention, the right of non-suspendable innocent passage will still govern passage through the territorial sea strait, as it will continue to do for other sea straits not governed by treaty or transit passage.

8.7.2 Archipelagos

The 1982 Convention lays down a specific regime for archipelagic states; that is, a state 'constituted wholly by one or more archipelagos'. An 'archipelago' means 'a group of islands, including parts of islands, interconnecting waters and other natural features which are so closely interrelated that [they] form an intrinsic geographical, economic and political entity, or which historically have been regarded as such' (LOS Art. 46). The most obvious archipelagic states under this definition are Indonesia and the Philippines, both of whom did much to push for a specific regime at the Third UN Conference. However, it is clear that the definition is wide enough to include many states that would not normally regard themselves as archipelagos, such as the UK and Iceland. Part IV of the Convention provides that archipelagic states may use straight baselines to join the outer islands of the archipelago, so enclosing the state within a geometric configuration. These baselines will then serve as the baselines from which the territorial sea is measured. Waters inside the baselines are known as 'archipelagic waters' and the state has full sovereignty over them. Obviously, however, the effect of this system is to redefine as 'archipelagic waters' a large area of sea that was formerly high seas or territorial waters and, for this reason, the Convention provides that the right of innocent passage shall exist in archipelagic waters, although suspension is possible in order to avert a threat to security (Art. 52). In addition, a right of 'archipelagic sea lane passage' also exists through archipelagic waters in respect of routes normally used for international navigation. This includes overflight and is very similar to transit passage. Archipelagic sea lane passage is not suspendable (Art. 54).

8.7.3 Islands

Under the 1958 Convention on the Territorial Sea, an island is defined as 'a naturally formed area of land, which is above water at high tide' (TSC Art. 10). It is clear that islands may have a territorial sea of their own and, if they are close to the coast of a state, this will involve a seaward extension of the main territorial sea. Additionally, islands may be used as points from which to draw straight baselines (as in the *Anglo-Norwegian Fisheries Case*) and they are intrinsic to the archipelagic system just described. Again, islands can have a significant effect on the delimitation of the continental shelf between opposite and adjacent states, as in the *Anglo-French Continental Shelf Case* and *Tunisia v Libya*, where groups of islands were given 'half-effect' in extending the continental shelf of the mother state. Likewise, they were at the heart of the delimitations in the *Jan Meyen Case*, the *Canada/France Maritime Delimitation* and *Qatar v Bahrain* being islands of one state off the coast of another. The sovereignty of islands is a matter on which the ICJ has pronounced on a number of occasions – recently for example, the *Territorial and Maritime Dispute between Nicaragua and Honduras in the Caribbean Sea (Nicaragua v Honduras)* (2007) and the *Case Concerning Sovereignty over Pedra Branca/Pulau Batu Puteh, Middle Rocks and South Ledge (Malaysia v Singapore)* (2008).

Obviously, sovereignty over islands can be important for any number of reasons, but the issue may be even more significant where the island would have an impact on the other maritime zones of the parties or where they might support an EEZ or continental shelf of their own. Under LOS Art. 121, an 'island' is defined in exactly the same way as in the Territorial Sea Convention and it is confirmed that all islands may have a territorial sea. However, under LOS Art. 121(3), 'rocks which cannot sustain human habitation or economic life of their own shall have no economic zone or continental shelf'. This represents an attempt to prevent unwarranted extensions of state jurisdiction arising from the effect of what may be no more than a tiny land mass and means, for example, that following the UK's ratification of the LOS 1982, it cannot use Rockall (an isolated 'island' of just rock) as a basepoint for its fisheries zone. Yet, while the conventional rule is clear in principle, it may be very difficult to determine in practice what amounts to 'human habitation or economic life'. Moreover, it is not at all clear that non-parties to the 1982 Convention will accept that this restriction has become part of customary law, although it was apparently taken as such by the Arbitrators in *Canada/France*. In that case, the majority opinion confirmed the view that islands capable of sustaining 'human habitation or economic life' (LOS Art. 121(3)) may have the same juridical continental shelf (and presumably, therefore, an EEZ) as a mainland coastal state. In fact, in *Canada/France* the Tribunal rejected the Canadian argument that, because of the shorter coastline and political status of the islands in this case, the seaward reach of their shelf should not be presumed to be 200 miles from the coast. The court treated the islands as having equivalent effects as 'mainland' territory – a view not contradicted by LOS 1982 or state practice. In *Jan Meyen*, the ICJ took the view that the length of coastlines of the mainland and the island was so different that any delimitation which ignored this would be inequitable and so was a 'special circumstance' relevant to delimitation under Art. 6 of the 1958 Convention on the Continental Shelf. Again, this shows how varied may be the circumstances considered relevant by judicial tribunals charged with maritime delimitation. Lastly, it should be noted that in *Jan Meyen* (a 1958 Convention case), Denmark alleged that the island could not sustain human habitation or economic life, but did *not* thereby deny that it could have a shelf or fishery zone. It is unclear, therefore whether LOS Art. 121(3) does indeed reflect customary law on this point although this may be of less significance given widespread ratification of LOS 1982 itself.

8.7.4 **Bays**

Large indentations along a state's sea coast may cause particular problems in the law of the sea. If a bay can be enclosed by a baseline across its mouth, this is advantageous to the coastal state in that it results in an extension of the territorial sea and means that waters on the landward side of the 'closing line' are classified as 'internal waters'. If, however, the starting point for measurement of the territorial sea is the low-water mark around the coast of the bay, the area of the territorial sea and internal waters is correspondingly reduced.

Customary international law has long recognised that 'bays' can be enclosed by a straight baseline across their mouth. This was confirmed by the *Anglo-Norwegian Fisheries Case*, where the Court also rejected the UK contention that such closing lines could not be more than 10 miles long. In the Court's view, there was no agreed customary limit on the length of such lines. Moreover, in Art. 7 of the TSC 1958 there are detailed rules relating to baselines and bays. A 'bay' is defined as a well-marked indentation which is more than a mere curvature of the coast, although an indentation is not a 'bay' in international law unless the area of its waters is as great as or greater than the area of a semi-circle whose diameter is a line drawn across the mouth of the indentation. This is simply a mathematical formula designed to ensure that a bay is an area of real penetration of the coast. Under TSC Art. 7, a bay closing line cannot exceed 24 miles and, if the mouth of the bay is wider than this, the state may draw a closing line of 24 miles so as to enclose as much water area as possible. These provisions are repeated in LOS Art. 10, although under both Conventions the rules do not apply to 'historic bays' (i.e. those established in customary law as belonging solely to one state) or bays bordering more than one state. In respect of the latter, these may not be capable of enclosure under customary law, unless a local custom or treaty between the neighbouring states establishes otherwise.

8.7.5 **Protection of the marine environment**

The 1982 Convention devotes considerable attention to this question in Part XII. Generally, these rules give primacy to the flag state to legislate for and enforce pollution control measures against ships of their nationality, but they also provide for coastal state jurisdiction in respect of pollution control and management. The Law of the Sea Preparatory Commission has considered Draft Regulations on the Protection of the Environment which will take effect under Part XII of LOS 1982 and which are designed to prevent 'serious harm' to the marine environment. Similarly, Arts 24 and 25 of the High Seas Convention 1958 contain general obligations to prevent pollution from ships or by dumping of radioactive waste. In addition to these Conventions there are limited customary rules dealing with responsibility for acts injurious to other states and a host of multilateral and bilateral treaties concerning international standards and the rights of non-flag states to avert pollution disasters. The most important of these in relation to pollution from ships is the International Convention for the Prevention of Pollution of the Sea by Oil 1954 (amended 1962), the International Convention for the Prevention of Pollution from Ships 1973 and Protocol 1978 and, in the case of accidental oil spillages, the International Convention on Intervention on the High Seas in Cases of Oil Pollution Casualties 1969. Other treaties include those regulating liability for pollution damage, such as the International Convention on Civil Liability for Oil Pollution Damage 1969. There are, in fact, many international treaties controlling pollution of the sea and the entry into force of the 1982 Convention may go a significant way to ensuring a more enforceable code for the protection of the marine environment.

8.7.6 Peaceful settlement of disputes

As we have seen in the previous sections, many states have used the ICJ and arbitration tribunals to settle law of the sea issues. This is particularly true in respect of the delimitation of maritime boundaries between opposite and adjacent states. In addition to this, one of the great successes of the 1982 Convention is the inclusion in Part XV and Arts 186–191 (special provisions relating to the deep sea bed) of a comprehensive procedure for dispute settlement. Essentially, there is the expected obligation to settle disputes by peaceful means (Art. 279) but also a system of compulsory settlement involving reference to either the International Tribunal for the Law of the Sea (whose first case was the *MV Saiga (No. 1)* and *(No. 2)*), the ICJ or certain arbitral tribunals established for various parts of the Convention (e.g. as in *Barbados/Trinidad & Tobago Maritime Delimitation Arbitration*). There are procedural exceptions to this form of compulsory settlement, as where states have agreed to settle their law of the sea disputes in another forum (e.g. the European Court of Justice for EU states). In addition, a number of substantive matters may be excluded, such as certain disputes relating to coastal states' sovereign rights in the EEZ, disputes concerning maritime delimitation (although these may be subject to compulsory conciliation) and, significantly, matters relating to the 'allowable catch' and sharing provisions in the living resources of the EEZ. On the whole, however, LOS 1982 provides a good model for any future multilateral treaty contemplating compulsory settlement of disputes and we should recognise that the inclusion of an obligation to settle disputes compulsorily is a real achievement in a multilateral treaty of this magnitude.

8.8 Conclusion

It should be apparent from the earlier analysis that the law of the sea is a burgeoning and vital area of international law. The 1958 Conventions did much to create orderly and predictable rules for the use and management of this common resource and many of the rules contained in these Conventions have now passed into customary law. The great achievement, however, was the conclusion of the comprehensive 1982 Convention. It deals with almost all law of the sea issues and it does so in a way that has commanded a considerable amount of support. Again, many of its provisions either reflect existing customary law or will crystallise into new law in due course. Moreover, now that the 1982 Convention has entered into force, and with most of the major maritime and industrialised states as parties, there is the prospect of a comprehensive, coherent and realistic international regime for management of the oceans and their resources.

FURTHER READING

Anderson, D., 'Further Efforts to Ensure Universal Participation in the United Nations Convention on the Law of the Sea', (1994) 43 *ICLQ* 866.

Anderson, D., 'Legal Implications for the Entry into Force of the UN Convention on the Law of the Sea', (1995) 44 *ICLQ* 313.

Anderson, D., *Modern Law of the Sea: Selected Essays* (Oxford University Press, 2008).

Anderson, D., 'Oceans Policy and the Law of the Sea Convention', (1994) 88 *AJIL* 733.

Caminos, H., and Molitor, M., 'Progressive Development of International Law and the "Package Deal"', (1985) 79 *AJIL* 87.

Charney, J., 'The EEZ and Public International Law', (1985) 15 *OCDI* 233.

Evans, M., 'Delimitation and the Common Maritime Boundary', (1994) 64 *BYIL* 283.

Evans, M., 'The Law of the Sea', in M. Evans (ed.), *International Law* (Oxford University Press, 2003).

Harrison, J., *Making the Law of the Sea: A Study in the Development of International Law* (Cambridge University Press, 2011).

Hutchinson, D., 'The Seaward Limit to Continental Shelf Jurisdiction in Customary International Law', (1985) 56 *BYIL* 111.

Nelson, L., 'The Roles of Equity in the Delimitation of Maritime Boundaries', (1989) 84 *AJIL* 837.

Paolillo, F., 'Arrangements for the International Sea Bed', (1988) 188 *Rec. de Cours* 135.

SUMMARY

The law of the sea

- The 'law of the sea' involves consideration of matters of state sovereignty, state jurisdiction and state rights over the waters, sea bed, subsoil and airspace of the 'sea'.

- Four multilateral conventions were concluded covering various aspects of the law of the sea in 1958. All these Conventions are in force, although in many respects they have been superseded by the 1982 Convention on the Law of the Sea.

- The sovereignty of a state extends beyond its land territory and its internal waters, to a belt of sea adjacent to its coast. This is the territorial sea.

- It has been the practice of states in the past to claim certain jurisdictional rights in a zone of waters beyond the outer edge of the territorial sea. Until the institution of the EEZ, this would have been an area of high seas and generally would not otherwise have been susceptible to the jurisdiction of the coastal state and is known as the contiguous zone.

- The EEZ is a belt of sea, adjacent to the coast, extending up to 200 miles from the baselines of the territorial sea. Within this area, the coastal state is given 'sovereign rights' for the purpose of exploring and exploiting the living and non-living natural resources of the area.

- It is now firmly established that continental shelf rights are 'inherent' in statehood. The rights that a coastal state exercises over the shelf exist as an extension of the statehood of the coastal state and do not have to be claimed or recognised by other states.

- The deep sea bed is the common heritage of mankind but the 1982 Convention establishes a system of 'parallel access' for the international community and for individual states.

- The high seas are *res communis* and it is a basic principle of customary law (perhaps even of *jus cogens*) that all states, whether coastal or landlocked, may enjoy the 'freedom of the seas'. This bundle of rights comprises several distinct freedoms, such as the freedom of navigation and overflight, the freedom to fish, the freedom to lay submarine cables and pipelines, the freedom to conduct scientific research and the freedom to construct artificial islands.

- The 1982 Convention includes comprehensive procedures for dispute settlement including a system of compulsory settlement involving reference to either the International Tribunal for the Law of the Sea, the ICJ or certain arbitral tribunals established for various parts of the Convention.

APPENDIX: GUIDE TO THE 1982 CONVENTION ON THE LAW OF THE SEA
AND 1994 AGREEMENT ON THE DEEP SEA BED

1982 Convention on the Law of the Sea

Part II: The territorial sea and contiguous zone

Art. 2	Nature of the territorial sea
Art. 3	Breadth
Art. 5	Normal baseline, low-water mark
Art. 7	Straight baselines
Art. 10	Bays
Art. 15	Delimitation between opposite and adjacent states
Art. 17	Right of innocent passage
Art. 18	Definition of passage
Art. 19	Definition of innocent
Art. 27	Criminal jurisdiction
Art. 28	Civil jurisdiction
Art. 33	Contiguous zone

Part III: Straits used for international navigation

Art. 36	Alternative routes, not transit passage
Art. 37	Availability of transit passage
Art. 38	Definition of transit passage
Art. 44	Non-suspendable

Part IV: Archipelagic states

Art. 46	Definition of archipelagic state
Art. 47	Straight baselines
Art. 49	Archipelagic waters
Art. 52	Innocent passage through archipelagic waters
Art. 53	Archipelagic sea lanes

Part V: Exclusive Economic Zone

Art. 56	Coastal state rights in the EEZ
Art. 57	Breadth
Art. 58	Rights and duties of other states
Art. 61	Conservation of living resources
Art. 62	Allowable catch and sharing provisions
Art. 74	Delimitation between opposite and adjacent states

Part VI: The continental shelf

Art. 76	Definition and seaward limit
Art. 77	Coastal state rights
Art. 78	Waters above to retain status
Art. 82	Payments in respect of shelf rights beyond 200 miles
Art. 83	Delimitation between opposite and adjacent states

Part VII: High seas

Art. 86	Definition
Art. 87	Freedoms
Art. 92	Flag state jurisdiction
Art. 105	Right to seize pirate ships
Art. 109	Unauthorised broadcasting
Art. 110	Right of visit
Art. 111	Right of hot pursuit

Part VIII: Islands

Art. 121	Regime of islands

Part XI: Deep sea bed (The Area)

Art. 136	Common heritage of mankind
Art. 137	Legal status
Art. 140	Benefit of mankind
Art. 141	Peaceful purposes
Art. 144	Transfer of technology
Art. 145	Protection of environment

Part XII: Protection of marine environment

Part XV: Settlement of disputes

Part XVII: Final provisions

Art. 308	Entry into force
Art. 309	Prohibition of reservations
Art. 311	Relationship to earlier conventions

1994 Agreement Relating to the Implementation of Part XI of the United Nations Convention on the Law of the Sea, General Assembly Resolution and Annex

Art. 1	Implementation of Part XI of LOS to be in accordance with this Agreement
Art. 2	This Agreement to prevail in cases of conflict, although an integral part of the Convention
Art. 7	This Agreement to be applied provisionally pending its own entry into force
Section 1	Phasing in of International Sea-Bed Authority institutions
Section 2	Enterprise to operate in joint ventures, with no cross subsidy
Section 3	Modification of decision-making provisions of LOS 1982
Section 4	Provisions relating to a review conference
Section 5	Modification of transfer of technology provisions of LOS 1982
Section 6	Minerals production policy to be based on market forces
Section 7	Modification of compensation provisions of LOS 1982 for land based producers of minerals
Section 8	Modification of financial arrangements of LOS 1982 relating to mining contractors
Section 9	Establishment of a Finance Committee

9

State responsibility

It is intrinsic in every legal system that violation of a legally binding obligation involves legal responsibility. In this respect, international law is no different from national law. The rules of 'state responsibility' indicate the circumstances in which a state will be fixed with legal responsibility for the violation of an international obligation and the consequences this entails. In this chapter, therefore, we are not generally concerned with the type of conduct that gives rise to responsibility, because this will depend greatly on the substance of the legal obligation binding the state and the circumstances in which it is alleged to have been broken. However, in respect of responsibility for the treatment of foreign nationals ('aliens' in the early jurisprudence), some indication will be given of the type of conduct that will cause a state to be in violation of its international responsibilities. In the following analysis, then, 'state responsibility' is used in two senses: first, to denote the procedural rules which apply to the establishment of responsibility for a violation of any and every international obligation; secondly, to denote the procedural and substantive rules relating to the particular case of responsibility for injury to foreign nationals.

In recent years, the principles of state responsibility have been the subject of extensive consideration by the International Law Commission and much of the material in this chapter revolves around their proposals. It should be noted, however, that the ILC Draft Articles on State Responsibility do not deal with the specific topic of state responsibility for injury to foreign nationals. They are concerned with general principles only. However, the ILC has commenced a separate project on one aspect of the law concerning injury to foreign nationals: the Draft Articles on Diplomatic Protection 2006, being the procedural rules applicable when a state makes a claim on behalf of injury to one of its citizens abroad.

In respect of the general rules of state responsibility, the ILC original plan of work resulted in a set of Draft Articles divided into various Parts, and in 1996 a complete set of Articles (sixty Articles in three Parts) was adopted on a First Reading. It soon became clear, however, that there was much in this First Reading that was controversial or did not enjoy the support of large numbers of states. Many states filed objections both to the content and philosophy of this initial attempt and the draft was subject to criticism in both the ILC and the 6th (Legal) Committee of the General Assembly of the UN. Consequently, since 1996 much work has been done to reshape the original scheme, or at least to re-assess its content, and in 2001 a final set of Draft Articles was adopted by the ILC on Second Reading. This final version of the Draft Articles shares much with its predecessor, although there are also significant differences that have been incorporated to take account of state practice and the developing jurisprudence of the law of state responsibility. This final set of *Draft Articles on the Responsibility of States for Internationally Wrongful Acts* consists of fifty-nine Articles in four Parts and has been commended by the General Assembly for further consideration by states. It is now unlikely that these Draft Articles will be adopted in a formal treaty or Convention, but they remain of critical importance. Many of the Draft Articles have been approved judicially and it is clear that a great portion of the Draft represents existing customary law. Those that do not, will, inevitably, shape future state practice and some will mature into customary law over time.

Part One of the Draft Articles contains twenty-seven Articles and deals with general principles, the identification of the elements of international responsibility, the nature of international responsibility, the circumstances in which liability can be imputed to the state through the acts of organs and individuals and general defences (known as 'circumstances precluding wrongfulness'). Part Two is concerned with the Content of the International Responsibility of a State and deals with the consequences of a finding of responsibility for the state in breach (i.e. obligations of reparation owed to the injured state), as well as considering the consequences of serious breaches of international law that may entail obligations to the international community as a whole (Draft Arts 40 and 41). Part Three considers how the injured state (or states) may invoke state responsibility, as well as the invocation of responsibility by states other than the injured state. This distinction has important consequences for the type of countermeasures that may be taken against the offending state and this also is covered in Part Three. Part Four essentially ties up loose ends, but contains the important provision that the current Articles are without prejudice to any question of individual responsibility for a breach of international law (Draft Art. 58).

Unlike the first set of Draft Articles, the final version makes no distinction between responsibility giving rise to 'state crimes' and 'ordinary' examples of state responsibility. Of course, the final Draft does recognise that serious breaches of international law may give rise to different kinds of consequences than other less serious breaches – e.g. a serious breach may trigger or justify response from the community as a whole, rather than just the injured state (see Draft Art. 40) – but the abandonment of a concept of 'state crime' will meet the objections of many states to the original draft. As noted earlier, there is no doubt that the Draft Articles will do much to promote the development of a comprehensive body of law on state responsibility and much that is contained in (at least) Part One of the final Draft already represents existing customary law (see, for example, dicta in the *Military and Paramilitary Activities in and against Nicaragua Case (Nicaragua v USA) (Merits)* 1986 ICJ Rep 14 and the acceptance of Draft Arts 4, 8 and 16 as embodying customary law in the *Case Concerning the Application of the Convention on the Prevention and Punishment of the Crime of Genocide (Bosnia and Herzegovina v Serbia & Montenegro)* (ICJ 2007)).

As well as these Draft Articles, the law of state responsibility also has been developed through case law, both that of the PCIJ and ICJ, as well as that provided by Mixed Claims Commissions set up to resolve disputes between states and the nationals of the other states operating in their territory. An example is the Iran–US Claims Tribunal that deals with claims arising out of the breakdown in relations between the USA and Iran in 1979. In essence, then, the law of state responsibility is to be found in customary law (whose development is aided and reflected by the Draft Articles), judicial pronouncements, bilateral treaties and UN General Assembly resolutions dealing with specific topics.

To recap then, this chapter will first examine the general principles of state responsibility (section 9.1). Secondly, we shall consider one particular aspect of state responsibility that has always been of considerable practical importance, namely the treatment of foreign nationals by the state in which they reside or in which they have their business interests (section 9.2). This will include reference to the substantive rules that determine when responsibility may arise in that type of case. In addition, as a particular example of responsibility for injury to foreign nationals, we will consider the rules relating to the expropriation (nationalisation) of property owned by them (section 9.3), including an indication of the means by which foreign nationals may protect themselves from this type of conduct (sections 9.4 and 9.5). Finally, brief mention will be made of two other forms of responsibility or liability under international law (section 9.6).

9.1 General issues of state responsibility

State responsibility occurs when a state violates an international obligation owed to another state. In the words of Art. 1 of the ILC Draft Articles, '[e]very internationally wrongful act of a State entails the international responsibility of that State' and this cannot be avoided simply by reason of the fact that the act is lawful under internal law (Draft Art. 3, and see *Questions relating to the Obligation to Prosecute or Extradite (Belgium* v *Senegal)* ICJ (2012)). The obligation may be derived from a treaty or customary law or may consist of the non-fulfilment of a binding judicial decision. It may also consist of aid or assistance in the commission of an internationally wrongful act by another state or even non-state (Draft Art. 16, *Case Concerning the Application of the Convention on the Prevention and Punishment of the Crime of Genocide (Bosnia and Herzegovina* v *Serbia & Montenegro)* (ICJ 2007)). In addition, responsibility may occur when a state ill-treats the nationals of another state or acts contrary to a legally binding decision of a competent international organisation, such as the Security Council. The origin of the international obligation is irrelevant for the purposes of state responsibility (Draft Art. 12).

In general terms, state responsibility comprises two elements: an unlawful act, which is imputable to the state. Necessarily, responsibility may be avoided if the state is able to raise a valid defence (what the Draft Articles call a 'circumstance precluding wrongfulness'). If not, the consequence of responsibility is a liability to make reparation and/or suffer the consequences of being internationally responsible (Draft Arts 28, 31). Examples include the payment of damages (e.g. *Eritrea Ethiopia Claims Commission, Final Award, 17 August 2009 (Ethiopia's Damages Claims), Permanent Court of Arbitration, The Hague*) or action by a competent international body (e.g. SC Res. 687, which creates a compensation fund, financed by Iraq's oil revenues, out of which payments are made for all damage caused as a result of Iraq's unlawful invasion of Kuwait in 1992). It is clear however, that injury or damage is not a precondition to a finding of responsibility, although it may well be a precondition to the obligation to make reparation. Thus, international responsibility not causing injury (moral or material) may still involve consequences for the delinquent state. For responsibility to arise it is enough that there has been an internationally unlawful act attributable to the state. For example, in *The I'm Alone Case* (see section 9.1.4), the Joint Arbitration Commission ordered the USA to apologise to Canada and awarded a substantial sum in recognition of the unlawfulness of the act of sinking *The I'm Alone*, even though no compensation was payable in respect of the actual damage caused. Of course, in most practical examples, the claimant state will be alleging actual damage and this is certainly true in the majority of the cases concerning injury to foreign nationals considered later.

9.1.1 An illegal act

It is axiomatic that whether an act of a state gives rise to responsibility is to be judged according to international law. As Draft Art. 3 of the Draft Articles makes clear, 'the characterisation of an act of a State as internationally wrongful is governed by international law. Such characterisation is not affected by the characterisation of the same act as lawful by internal law.' This is simply yet another example of the rule that conduct in international law is judged by international rules. Consequently, international responsibility cannot be avoided by pleading that the disputed actions were lawful in national law – *Questions relating to the Obligation to Prosecute or Extradite (Belgium v Senegal)* (ICJ 2012).

As noted earlier, this chapter is not concerned with an analysis of the very many circumstances in which responsibility can arise. That can be done only by reference to the substantive rules discussed in other chapters. On a general level, however, it is clear that responsibility can arise from either an act or an omission, so long as this causes a breach of an international obligation. For example, a state will be responsible for the use of unlawful force by its military forces against a neighbouring state (e.g. Iraq/Kuwait), but it will also be liable if it fails to prevent autonomous armed groups from using its territory as a base for unlawful attacks against that neighbouring state. This duality is confirmed by Art. 2 of the ILC Draft Articles and by several judicial decisions, such as the *Janes Claim (US v Mexico)* (1926) 4 RIAA 82, the *Corfu Channel Case* 1949 ICJ Rep 4 and *Asian Agricultural Products Ltd (AAPL)* v *Republic of Sri Lanka* (1991) 30 ILM 577, where responsibility consisted of a failure by Sri Lanka to exercise due diligence in protecting AAPL's property from attacks by Tamil Tigers.

If responsibility is to arise, it is essential that the act or omission causes a breach of an international obligation that is binding on the state at the time of the act or omission (Draft Art. 13). Obligations not yet in force have no legal effect. In addition, there is also the question of whether responsibility arises simply because the state has committed an act or omission which violates one of its obligations, or whether responsibility arises only if there is some element of blameworthiness in the conduct of the state. By analogy with UK law, the question is whether international responsibility is a matter of strict liability, so that it arises by virtue of the simple fact of a broken obligation, or whether responsibility is dependent on the state having acted intentionally or negligently. These are known respectively as the 'objective' and 'subjective' theories of responsibility. The 'objective' or 'risk' theory of responsibility supposes that once a breach of obligation is established, the state bears all the risk irrespective of any fault. The 'subjective' or 'fault' theory denies that responsibility arises even if there is conduct in violation of a binding obligation, unless the state is in some way subjectively to blame.

This issue is not addressed by the ILC, and customary law offers support for both theories. Cases such as the *Caire Claim* (1929) 5 RIAA 516, *Neer Claim* (1926) 4 RIAA 60, and *Roberts Claim* (1926) 4 RIAA 77, all support the objective theory. In contrast, the *Home Missionary Society Case* (1920) 6 RIAA 42, possibly the *Corfu Channel Case* and *AAPL* v *Sri Lanka* support the subjective theory. At the heart of the matter is the choice between fixing states with responsibility for all breaches of obligation that can be imputed to them, or requiring an additional element of fault, such as intent, recklessness or negligence. In practice, it may be that the most sensible solution is not to have a general rule at all, but to impose strict liability or require fault according to the subject matter of the obligation broken. Responsibility for violations of rules of *jus cogens* might be strict, but responsibility for violations of commercial treaties might be based on fault. In *AAPL* v *Sri Lanka*, for example, it is entirely appropriate that Sri Lanka's responsibility for failing to protect an installation against rebel attack should be triggered only by lack of due diligence (negligence). It would impose impossible duties on the host 'state' were this liability to be strict. The existence of different levels of 'fault' (or none at all) is how the problem is tackled in national law, although as yet it cannot be said that this is being adopted in the international system. At the moment, the objective theory is most widely applied, on the grounds that any other approach might provide yet another loophole in an already imperfect system of international justice. It also means that an international tribunal does not have to deal with difficult questions of fact and fault that are beyond its competence. For purely pragmatic reasons, therefore, responsibility usually arises by reason of the simple fact of a broken obligation, without more, save perhaps where the substantive content of the state's obligation is only to take 'reasonable care' rather than achieve an absolute standard, as in *AAPL* v *Sri Lanka*.

As previously noted, the original ILC draft attempted to divide wrongful acts into state crimes and other forms of responsibility, the idea being that state crimes against international law should be dealt with in a different way e.g. they might generate different consequences. This distinction has now been abandoned and it finds no place in the final Draft. As a result, the final Draft has secured considerably more support from states than the earlier versions. Indeed, it was never clear that such a distinction had any roots in state practice (as opposed to legal theory) and very many of the adverse comments by states on the initial first draft focused on the provisions advancing this alleged distinction. However, that it is not to say that the final Draft does not recognise that there may well be a need for the community as a whole to respond to certain kinds of wrongful act, rather than leaving this just to the injured state or states. It is not necessary to have some preconceived notion of a 'state international crime' in order to understand that, for example, the unlawful use of force by State A against State B might well require a different response from the international community than the breach of a bilateral treaty concerning import quotas between State A and State B.

In Part Two of the final Draft, there are a number of provisions dealing with the consequences of a finding of responsibility for wrongful acts. Necessarily they cover such matters as the requirement to continue to perform an international obligation that is breached (Draft Art. 29), the duty to cease and not repeat wrongful conduct (Draft Art. 30), the duty to make reparation for moral or material injury (Draft Art. 31) and the irrelevance of internal law as a justification for failure to perform any intentional obligations. However, Draft Art. 33 also makes it clear that 'obligations of the responsible State may be owed to another State, to several States, or to the international community as a whole, depending in particular on the character and content of the international obligation and on the circumstances of the breach' and Draft Art. 40 contains the important provision that 'international responsibility which is entailed by a serious breach by a State of an obligation arising under a peremptory norm of general international law' may generate particular and special consequences. Here then is recognition that grave breaches of international law can trigger a community response. Clearly, in such circumstances it is vital to know when this form of responsibility arises – not because it is 'criminal' – but because of the possibility of a community response in addition to the duties owed by the wrongdoer to the injured state. The trigger for such responsibility is both formal and of substance. Thus, the responsible state must have engaged in a *serious* breach of a rule of *jus cogens*. It now seems possible to identify a core set of rules that have the status of *jus cogens* – e.g. *inter alia*, the prohibition of the use of force, prohibition of genocide – and Draft Art. 40(2) indicates that 'a breach of such an obligation is serious if it involves a gross or systematic failure by the responsible State to fulfil the obligation'. It remains to be seen whether this is sufficiently clear and unambiguous to apply in practice, but of course we should not forget that the application of any rule of law to a given set of facts will involve questions of judgement and so no provision can be watertight. The consequences of such a serious finding of responsibility are dealt with in Draft Arts 41, 48 and 54. Thus, states must cooperate to bring an end to such a breach of international law and must not recognise any situation (e.g. seizure of territory) arising from such a breach (Draft Art. 41); non-injured states may invoke the responsibility of the state in breach (Draft Art. 48); and under Draft Art. 54, any countermeasures taken by the injured state are without prejudice to 'the right of any State, entitled under art. 48, para. 1 to invoke the responsibility of another state, to take lawful measures against that state to ensure cessation of the breach and reparation in the interest of the injured State or of the beneficiaries of the obligation breached'. In other words, collective action can be taken in the event of these serious breaches.

This reformulation of the Draft Articles is much more than an exercise in cosmetic drafting: it is not merely the removal of the language of criminal responsibility while maintaining the concept. The final version of the Draft in relation to these matters is different in substance as well as form from the original and we should not underestimate the power of language – or incorrect language – in hindering or promoting the development of substantive changes to international law. States may be willing to accept that certain types of responsibility may trigger collective action, but that is different from being willing to accept a finding that their conduct was, in the first place, 'criminal'. Finally, for the avoidance of doubt, we should note that the issue (or rather now non-issue) of state criminal responsibility has nothing to do with the personal international criminal responsibility of individuals that may arise under international law and which may be dealt with by the International Criminal Court or similar tribunal. That is unaffected by these Draft Articles (Draft Art. 58).

9.1.2 Attributability

In order for a state to be fixed with responsibility, not only must there be an unlawful act or omission, but that unlawful act or omission must be attributable to the state. It must be an unlawful act of the state itself and not of some private individuals acting for themselves. In the simple case, as where a state refuses to honour a treaty commitment, there may be no doubt that the act is an 'act of the state'. However, in cases where the acts complained of are committed by specific individuals or organs within the state, it is essential to know whether they are acting (or can be treated as acting) on behalf of the state so as to give rise to international responsibility. If they are not, then no breach of international law has occurred for which the state is responsible.

Whether an act or omission perpetrated by institutions or individuals is to be attributed to the state is a matter of international law. While international law may well use rules of national law to help make this decision (such as those national rules defining the status of individuals or organs), the final determination is for the international system. It is perfectly possible, therefore, for an act to be attributable to the state in international law, even though in national law it would not be so regarded. Articles 4 to 11 of the ILC Draft deal with the question of attributability and, on the whole, they reflect existing customary law – see the approval given to Arts 4 and 8 in the *Case Concerning the Application of the Convention on the Prevention and Punishment of the Crime of Genocide (Bosnia and Herzegovina v Serbia & Montenegro)* (ICJ 2007).

9.1.2.1 Activities of organs of the state

The general rule is that any act or omission of an organ of a state, 'shall be considered an act of that State under international law, whether the organ exercises legislative, executive, judicial or any other functions, whatever position it holds in the organization of the State and whatever its character as an organ of the central government or of a territorial unit of the State' and this 'includes ... any person or entity which has that status in accordance with the internal law of the State' (Draft Art. 4). This is one of the cornerstones of the law of state responsibility – *Case Concerning the Application of the Convention on the Prevention and Punishment of the Crime of Genocide (Bosnia and Herzegovina v Serbia & Montenegro)* (ICJ 2007). This rule makes the state responsible for the activities of all its organs, such as the army, police, judiciary (e.g. *Paraguay v USA (Provisional Measures)* (1998) 37 ILM 810), departments of state and security services (see e.g. *Rainbow Warrior Arbitration* (1987) 26 ILM 1346). Furthermore, the acts of these organs are still attributable to the state even if they are outside the sphere of competence granted to them by national law. So, if a policeman, acting as such, causes injury to a foreign national, the state will be responsible even though the policeman is acting outside his powers as defined in national law. The simple fact that the organ exceeded its powers is not enough to excuse the state from responsibility, so long as the organ was acting on behalf of the state at the time. This is the rule encapsulated in Art. 7 of the Draft Articles and it was applied in substance in the *Youmans Claim (US v Mexico)* (1926) 4 RIAA 110, where Mexican soldiers participated in violence directed against US nationals despite being ordered to protect them. Again, in *Southern Pacific Properties (Middle East) Ltd v Arab Republic of Egypt* (1993) 32 ILM 933, Egypt could not avoid responsibility by pleading that the acts of government officials were null and void under Egyptian law. The rule reflects the general principle that responsibility is a matter for international law and it prevents a state from deliberately and artificially limiting the competence of its organs so as to minimise its potential international liabilities. Importantly, it is also clear that a person or group or entity may be equated with an organ of the state even if it does not have that status officially under internal law. Internal law is not the sole arbiter of what or who is an 'organ' for the purposes of the law of state responsibility. Thus, as was made clear in the *Case Concerning the Application of the Convention on the Prevention and Punishment of the Crime of Genocide (Bosnia and Herzegovina v Serbia & Montenegro)* (ICJ 2007), a group etc. can be equated to an organ of the state, even if it lacks that status officially, provided that it is completely dependent on the state and a mere instrument through which the state works. However, in that case, the Court noted that such a finding would be exceptional and would have to be supported by clear evidence of total dependency. Thus, the perpetrators of the genocide in Bosnia did not have the official status of organs of the Serbian state within Draft Art. 4 and neither could they be equated with such under the 'complete dependency' rule. Finally, for the sake of clarity we should note that, if the state organ is *not* acting *as a state organ* at the time of the act or omission, there is no responsibility, as where an off-duty policeman injures a foreign national in a street fight or even where an organ is brought into existence by the state but does not actually exercise state functions (*Schering v Iran* (1984) 5 Iran–US CTR 361).

It is to be noted also that Draft Art. 7 imposes responsibility for *ultra vires* acts whether or not the organ of state's lack of authority was manifest or undiscoverable. It matters not that it was crystal clear that the organ was acting outside the competence granted to it by national law. The organ merely has to be acting in the capacity of an organ of state and there is no requirement of 'apparent authority' before responsibility can arise. This is a strict approach to attributability, which some commentators doubt reflects customary law. However, it is in tune with the general rule that states should not escape liability at international law through provisions of their national law and this alone makes it commendable. Finally, this rule of attributability applies in equal measure to all government organs, whether high-ranking or minor, and irrespective of their judicial, legislative, administrative or executive character (Draft Art. 4). It also applies to local administrations that exercise governmental authority over part of state territory and to provincial authorities within a federal state (Draft Art. 4).

9.1.2.2 Activities of private individuals

It is clear from the preceding analysis that individuals (e.g. policemen, soldiers, court officials, local administrators) can be regarded as 'organs of the state'. If so, their acts are dealt with according to the rules discussed earlier. For example, in the *Case Concerning the Application of the Convention on the Prevention and Punishment of the Crime of Genocide (Preliminary Objections) (Bosnia and Herzegovina v Yugoslavia)* 1996 ICJ Rep 1, the Court accepted that in principle a state could be held liable for genocide through the acts of its functionaries, such as soldiers and police forces. However, in this section we are concerned with the attributability of acts of private individuals who are not formally part of 'the state'.

In most cases, of course, the activities of individuals or groups will not normally be attributable to the state, simply because they are the acts of private citizens. However, there are circumstances in which acts of private citizens (irrespective of their *de jure* status) may be attributable to the state such that international responsibility arises. In general terms, this will be where, for whatever reason, private individuals do *in fact* act on behalf of the state. That is, that their conduct is such that they take on the role of a state representative. Whether this has occurred is largely a matter of fact in each case, but a good example is provided by *Yeager* v *Iran* (1987) 17 Iran–US CTR 92, where 'Revolutionary Guards' (who probably were not formally 'organs of the state') had caused the unlawful expulsion of the plaintiff from Iran. The Tribunal found, as a fact, and relying on the original ILC Draft Articles, that these acts were attributable to Iran, especially since Iran could not prove that it was unable to control the guards had it wished to do so. In other words, Iran could have avoided the attribution of the guards' actions had it been able to show a bona fide repudiation of those acts, coupled with a genuine attempt to avert them. These eventualities now appear to be covered by Draft Arts 5 and 9 of the final version. First, the acts of the individuals or groups can be attributable if they are empowered by local law to act on behalf of the state and are so doing (Draft Art. 5). For example, the acts of private individuals may be attributable where private citizens are utilised by state agencies for police, public order or other state functions as where private citizens are enlisted for a police search and then cause injury to a foreign national. The ILC gives the *Zafiro Case (Great Britain* v *US)* (1925) 6 RIAA 160 as an example of this type of situation, where a private ship was utilised by the USA during its war with Spain in 1898. Secondly, attribution to the state will arise if the group etc. is acting on the instructions of, or under the control of, the state (Draft Art. 8). This provision was also considered in the *Case Concerning the Application of the Convention on the Prevention and Punishment of the Crime of Genocide (Bosnia and Herzegovina* v *Serbia & Montenegro)* (ICJ 2007) and was said to reflect customary international law. In that case, the question arose whether the acts of the perpetrators of the genocide were attributable to Serbia under Draft Art. 8 and the ICJ noted that it was necessary to show something akin to 'complete dependence' of the group (echoing the view taken in *Military and Paramilitary Activities in and against Nicaragua Case (Nicaragua* v *USA)*), amounting to 'effective control', if state responsibility were to be engaged. This was, essentially, a question of fact and the Court reached the conclusion that attributability to the state was not established in that case despite the opposite view being taken in the Yugoslav War Crimes tribunal which had applied a weaker test of 'overall control' (see *Tadic Case* (1999 ILM 1518)). Thirdly, if in the absence of official authorities, private individuals actually exercise governmental authority in circumstances that justified the exercise of such authority, the activities can once again be attributable to the state (see Draft Art. 9.) So, if private citizens take on public order responsibilities after serious internal disturbances have incapacitated the official police force, their acts may be attributable to the state. According to the ILC, this is exemplified by *A-G of Israel* v *Eichmann* (1961) 36 ILR 5, where it was not clear whether the abductors of Eichmann were actually Israeli agents or private citizens *de facto* acting on Israel's behalf. Indeed, the key to all these situations is that private citizens may in fact act on behalf of the state in such circumstances that primary responsibility for their actions or omissions should lie with the state itself. In such cases, the acts are attributable to the state even though the individuals were not formally 'an organ of the state'.

Where, however, individuals neither constitute an 'organ' of the state nor act on behalf of the state in the sense just discussed, their activities are not attributable to the state and there is no international responsibility. This is simply a statement of the rule that a state cannot be internationally responsible for the acts of private citizens even if they take place within its territory. For example, if a private citizen assaults a foreign national, the state will not be internationally responsible for this act, as in the *Noyes Claim (US v Panama)* (1933) 6 RIAA 308. It should be noted, however, that the situation created by the act of the private citizen may give rise to a separate and independent cause of state responsibility if the state subsequently fails to fulfil one of its own international obligations – see section 9.1.2.5.

9.1.2.3 Activities of revolutionaries

Draft Art. 10 of the final Draft deals with the attributability of acts or omissions of revolutionary movements to the state in which they occur. Assuming no attributability under any of the other rules discussed in this section, the question arises whether the acts of such a movement can be attributed to the state even though the purpose of the movement was to overthrow the established authorities. Draft Art. 10 implies (though is not explicit) that there is a general rule that the conduct of an insurrectionist movement is not to be considered an act of the state. The state is not responsible for the actions of its rebellious subjects, as in the *Sambaggio Case (Italy v Venezuela)* (1903) 10 RIAA 499 and *AAPL v Republic of Sri Lanka*. However, different considerations apply if the insurrectionist movement succeeds in becoming the new government of the state. In that circumstance, as Draft Art. 10(2) indicates, 'the conduct of an insurrectionist movement which becomes the new government of a state shall be considered as an act of that state under international law', as in the *Bolivar Railway Case (Great Britain v Venezuela)* (1903) 9 RIAA 445. As a matter of principle, this must be the correct approach, but *Short v Iran* (1987) 16 Iran–US CTR 76, illustrates that this is not an absolute rule. In *Short*, the Iran–US Claims Tribunal had to consider the alleged unlawful expulsion of Short from Iran by Iranian revolutionaries, who then went on to overthrow the existing authorities. The Tribunal concluded for two reasons that the new Iranian government was not internationally responsible for the acts of the revolutionaries who had helped to establish it. First, because there was no evidence to suggest that any agents of the revolutionary authorities had actually caused the expulsion of Short from Iran (i.e. the facts were in doubt), and secondly, on the ground that the new revolutionary government was not actually in control of Iran when Short's expulsion took place. This opinion is noteworthy because it does suggest that circumstances can arise where no defined governmental group will be responsible for an internationally wrongful act. So, if the 'old' regime is overthrown it will not be responsible because it may not exist, but neither will the 'new' authorities until they have actually asserted control over the state. Putting aside the question of whether the revolutionaries actually caused Short's expulsion, it was into this interregnum that he fell, although it must be said that the absence of an effective *government* would not normally vitiate the responsibility of the *state*, which could then pass to the succeeding authorities under the rules of state succession.

Finally, two further points may be noted. First, if a rebellion results in the establishment of an independent state in part of the territory of an old state (i.e. a successful secession), the acts of the 'revolutionaries' can be attributed to the 'new' state and this is made clear in Draft Art. 10(2). This is precisely the position with the states that have emerged from the former Yugoslavia. Secondly, it is possible for one state to be internationally responsible for the acts of revolutionaries who are seeking to overthrow another state. For example, although not established on the facts, it could have been possible in law for the USA to be responsible for the acts of the *Contra* rebels as they fought to overthrow the Nicaraguan government (*Nicaragua* v *USA* 1986 ICJ Rep 14; and see section 9.1.2.4).

9.1.2.4 Activities of groups acting in another state's territory

We have seen earlier that a state may be internationally responsible for the activities of individuals or groups in respect of acts or omissions taking place within its own territory, for example when harm is caused to a foreign national. Similarly, as explained later, a state may be responsible in its own right (primary responsibility) for failing to prevent individuals or groups using its territory from committing wrongful acts against foreigners within the territory. A different situation arises, however, where it is claimed that State A is internationally responsible for the activities of groups – usually armed groups – that occur on the territory of State B. A typical example would be if State A 'supports' the activities in State B of a guerrilla movement determined to overthrow the existing government of State B. In the *Nicaragua Case*, the ICJ considered the relevant principles for determining the responsibility of State A in such situations. In the Court's view, it was not enough to establish the responsibility of State A for the acts of the armed group if it 'merely' encouraged, supported, supplied, trained, assisted with planning, financed or organised the group. What was necessary was a degree of direct and effective control that effectively meant that the group were agents of State A and were dependent on it. Obviously, this is a high burden of proof and there has been some criticism that the 'effective control and dependency' test is too strict, especially as it could leave the victim state (State B) without an effective international remedy. Thus, in the appeal in the *Tadic Case* (1999), the Appeals Chamber of the Yugoslav War Crimes Tribunal preferred a weaker test of 'overall control' in assessing whether the actions of the Bosnian Serb forces in Bosnia could be attributed to the Federal Republic of Yugoslavia (Serbia and Montenegro).

Clearly this is a difficult area, overlain with political considerations. The 'effective control and dependency' test of the *Nicaragua Case* has now been confirmed by the ICJ in the *Case Concerning the Application of the Convention on the Prevention and Punishment of the Crime of Genocide*, rather than the weaker 'overall control' in *Tadic*. Moreover, we have been considering the responsibility of State A for the actions *of the armed group* in State B. It remains possible in addition that State A might be responsible *in its own right* for failing to prevent the armed group using its territory as a base for attacks against State B. This is primary responsibility under international law and is distinct from the difficult questions of attribution just considered (see for example the allegations in *Certain Activities carried out by Nicaragua in the Border Area (Costa Rica* v *Nicaragua)* (2010)).

9.1.2.5 Primary responsibility of the state

In this section we have been considering whether the acts of organs or individuals can be said to be those of the state itself. If they cannot then no international responsibility arises. However, irrespective of the question of attributability, a state may incur primary responsibility because of a breach of some other international obligation, even though this obligation arose out of the situation created by a non-attributable act. For example, the acts of a private individual are not normally attributable to the state, so that if a private citizen murders a foreign national, the state cannot be held responsible for this act. If, however, the state fails to fulfil one of its *own* duties arising in connection with this non-attributable act, there will be responsibility under international law. In the *Noyes Claim* Panama was not responsible for the injuries to Noyes on the simple ground that they were committed by private individuals. However, the USA claimed in addition that Panama was responsible in its own right for failing to protect Noyes from such injury. In the event, this claim was disallowed on the facts, but in the *Janes Claim*, Mexico was held responsible not for the death of Janes at the hands of private individuals, but because it had failed to apprehend and punish those individuals. Likewise in *AAPL v Sri Lanka*, Sri Lanka was not responsible for the acts of destruction of the Tamil Tigers, but was responsible for failing in its own duty to act with due diligence to protect the installations. In these types of case, the state is responsible because it has violated an additional primary obligation of its own, even though the trigger for that obligation lay in the non-attributable act of an individual. It must not be forgotten, therefore, that 'state responsibility' can arise even in cases where the initial act is not attributable to the state. Another example is the *Hostages Case (US v Iran)* [1980] ICJ Rep 3, where Iran was not responsible for the acts of the individuals who stormed the US embassy, but was responsible because it failed in its own duty to protect the embassy.

9.1.3 Legal consequences of an internationally wrongful act

It is axiomatic that breach of an international obligation entailing responsibility gives rise to legal consequences and this is a principle which – not surprisingly – is rooted in customary law: see, for example, the *Chorozow Factory Case (Merits) (Germany v Poland)* (1928) PCIJ Ser. A No. 17. These consequences are dealt with in Part Two of the ILC final Draft. In fact, as the Draft Articles make clear, the 'legal consequences' of responsibility can take many forms and, as we have seen earlier, may not be limited to claims or action by the directly injured state alone.

Perhaps the most common consequence of state responsibility is the obligation to make reparation and this is codified in Draft Art. 31. This codifies a rule of customary law and stipulates that the 'responsible State is under an obligation to make full reparation for the injury caused by the internationally wrongful act'. Reparation is, however, a generic term and in most cases the injured state will be looking for some concrete manifestation of the wrongdoing state's liability. In fact, reparation can take many forms. It may, for example, consist of apology (*The I'm Alone (Canada v US)* 3 RIAA 1609) (see Draft Art. 37), restitution of the property unlawfully taken (*Temple of Preah Vihear Case* 1962 ICJ Rep 6), restitution in kind (*Texaco v Libya* (1977) 53 ILR 389) or any combination thereof (see Draft Art. 35). By far the commonest form of reparation is monetary compensation for the injury suffered (see Draft Art. 36). This may be calculated by reference to the actual value of the damage done or property lost and it may also include an element of lost profits, as discussed (although not awarded on the facts) in the *Amoco Finance Case* 15 Iran–US CTR 189 (1987) and interest (see Draft Art. 38). In *The Lusitania Claims* 7 RIAA 32, the Court assessed the compensation due to the USA by reference to the loss suffered by the claimants as a result of the deaths of their relatives when *The Lusitania* was sunk in 1914, an approach that reflects the states role in 'diplomatic protection' cases where it acts on behalf of its injured nationals. Significantly, in the *Eritrea Ethiopia*

Claims Commission, Final Award, 17 August 2009 (Ethiopia's Damages Claims), the Arbitration Panel considered that the amount of compensation awarded must bear some relation to the particular circumstances of the state claiming, and being held to pay, compensation. Mindful of the crippling effect reparations payments can have (and explicitly mentioning the settlements at the end of the First World War), the panel noted that the 'difficult economic conditions found in the affected areas of Ethiopia and Eritrea must be taken into account in assessing compensation there. Compensation determined in accordance with international law cannot remedy the world's economic disparities.' The panel reminded us that compensation has a limited function (see the *Chorzów Factory Case*) and its 'role is to restore an injured party, in so far as possible, to the position it would have occupied but for the injury. This function is remedial, not punitive.'

However, the obligation to make reparation in any of these forms – restitution, compensation or satisfaction – is not the only legal consequence arising from an internationally wrongful act. There are, of course, the necessary duties either to perform the obligation breached or desist from conduct in breach (Draft Arts 29 and 30), but also the possibility of countermeasures designed to induce the delinquent state to comply with its international obligation to make reparation (see Draft Art. 49). These countermeasures must be proportionate with any injury suffered (Draft Art. 51) and may be resorted to only if a number of pre-conditions are met (Draft Art. 52). Importantly, countermeasures must not comprise action which itself is generally unlawful, such as the use or threat of force, violation of fundamental human rights or violation of other rules of *jus cogens* (Draft Art. 50). In addition, as noted previously, some forms of international responsibility may give rise to a response from the international community as whole, as where responsibility arises from a serious breach of a rule of *jus cogens*.

The identification of specific remedies and countermeasures was a cause of much controversy in the ILC and today it is not certain to what extent these Draft Articles represent customary international law. Some states are unhappy with a 'list' of remedies on the ground that the draft may not encapsulate the variety of rights, remedies and countermeasures that may be claimed or employed by the injured state as a result of a breach of an international obligation. Others are concerned that by being overly specific we might arrest the development of international law for what is – when compared to national law – an unsophisticated set of principles. There remains further doubt about the extent of the legal ability of the community at large to respond to serious breaches of international obligation.

9.1.4 Defences

As in national law, it is not every prima facie breach of a legal obligation that gives rise to legal responsibility. International law recognises that the state may have a valid defence to a charge of unlawful conduct. In the ILC rubric, these are known as 'circumstances precluding wrongfulness', which suggests that the matters considered later in this chapter prevent responsibility from ever arising, as opposed to providing the state with a defence once responsibility is otherwise made out.

Articles 20–26 of the ILC Draft Articles list a number of 'circumstances precluding wrongfulness'. These include: the consent of the potential victim state to the commission of an otherwise unlawful act, except in cases of rules of *jus cogens* (Arts

20, 26); situations where the act complained of was a legitimate countermeasure to an internationally wrongful act of the complaining state (Art. 22); *force majeure* or unforeseen event making it materially impossible to fulfil the international obligation which is violated (Art. 23); cases where the perpetrator of the allegedly unlawful act was in a situation of extreme distress where no other means was available to save his life or that of persons entrusted to him (Art. 24); a narrow ground of state necessity (Art. 25 and see the *Danube Dam Case*) and lawful self-defence (Art. 21).

In the *Rainbow Warrior Case*, an arbitral tribunal suggested that these general defences could be raised in *all* cases where it is alleged that a state has violated international law, even if the source of the obligation binding the state is a treaty, and even if the particular defences of the law of treaties are not available (see Chapter 3). Furthermore, in considering the French defences of *force majeure* and distress, the tribunal relied heavily on the original ILC Draft Art. 32, suggesting that this now represented customary law. In the end, France was only partially successful in raising these defences. The claim that the breach of treaty was *force majeure* was dismissed, as that concept was applicable only where circumstances made the performance of an international obligation impossible, not where circumstances made it more difficult. However, the defence of distress was more sympathetically received, with the tribunal making it clear that it was applicable in cases of a serious threat to life or the integrity of a state organ if the result was a situation of extreme urgency and emergency. On the facts, 'distress' was made out in part. The defence of necessity was also considered in the *Palestinian Wall Advisory Opinion*, (2004), where the ICJ considered whether a state of necessity (in that case civil unrest) could preclude the wrongfulness surrounding Israel's construction of the wall. In the result, the ICJ reiterated that a 'state of necessity is a ground recognized by customary international law' that 'can only be accepted on an exceptional basis, [it] can only be invoked under certain strictly defined conditions ... and the State concerned is not the sole judge of whether those conditions have been met'. Adopting the language of Draft Art. 25, this meant that the act in breach for which the defence is claimed must have been 'the only way for the State to safeguard an essential interest against a grave and imminent peril'. Israel could not meet this strict test.

The general jurisprudence of the *Rainbow Warrior Case* in respect of these 'circumstances precluding wrongfulness' was later adopted by the ICJ itself in the *Danube Dam Case*. In that case, the Court confirmed that the 'defences' of the law of state responsibility are applicable to breaches of all international obligations and specifically are in addition to those that might arise under the rubric of the law of treaties if it is a treaty that has been violated. International law does not have specific 'defences' that are applicable according to the source of the particular rule of international law that has been broken. This must be correct. If international law is to be regarded as a homogenous system of law, the particular method by which an international obligation came into existence should not determine which defences a state may raise. However, the Court in the *Danube Dam Case* did go on to explain that, in their view, 'treaty defences' go to the initial validity of a treaty whereas 'responsibility defences' determine the consequences if a valid treaty is broken. This is superficially attractive, and as noted, it is no doubt correct that the availability of defences should not be determined by the type of international obligation that has been broken. However, the Court's explanation presupposes that a state's conduct can be dissected into conduct relating to treaty validity (treaty defences) and conduct relating to performance (responsibility defences), but in reality this may be difficult to achieve and may well misrepresent the true factual situation. As the *Danube Dam Case* illustrates, the availability of *any* defence will depend on the Court's interpretation of the extent of the obligation that may have been broken, the standard of performance required from the alleged malefactor and the peculiar facts surrounding the alleged breach. It is not straightforward, and each case is unique. Nevertheless, the general position – now firmly established – that types of defences are not earmarked for particular types of obligation is greatly to be welcomed.

9.2 The treatment of foreign nationals

In general, every state is under an international obligation not to ill-treat foreign nationals present in its territory. If the state violates this obligation in any way it may incur international responsibility to the state of whom the person is a national. In fact, state responsibility arising from the treatment, or rather ill-treatment, of foreign nationals is one of the commonest forms of responsibility that arises in international law today. In this section we shall consider both the procedural and substantive rules applicable to this particular type of international responsibility.

9.2.1 Examples of ill-treatment giving rise to responsibility

Mistreatment of foreign nationals giving rise to international responsibility can occur in any number of ways. For example, it can result from the mistreatment of foreign nationals in the custody of judicial authorities (*Roberts Claim*; *Paraguay v USA*), from the unlawful expropriation of foreign-owned property (section 9.3, but note *Texaco v Libya*), from a failure to punish those individuals responsible for attacks on foreign nationals (*Janes Claim* and *Massey Claim* (1927) 4 RIAA 155) or from direct injury to foreign nationals by state officials (*Youmans Claim*). In addition, responsibility may arise by reason of a 'denial of justice', as where a foreign national is denied due process of law in respect of a legal dispute arising in the state, whether civil or criminal. In the *Chattin Claim* (1927) 4 RIAA 282, Mexico was held responsible for inadequacies and unfairness in the trial and prosecution of Chattin on charges of embezzlement and in *The Loewen Group, Inc. and Raymond L. Loewen* v *United States of America* (2006), NAFTA Arbitration Tribunal, the discriminatory and biased way in which an action between Loewen and a US national had been conducted in a local court amounted to a denial of justice and a breach of international law. It must be appreciated, however, that in respect of responsibility arising from an alleged denial of justice, not every defect in the administration of justice in the local state can give rise to international responsibility, so that, for example, mere error by the local court is insufficient. It seems that there has to be some element of arbitrariness or unfairness in the court's proceedings, such as a refusal to afford the foreign national a right to be heard, corruption of the judge, deliberate manufacture of evidence and the like. According to Art. 9 of the Harvard Research Draft on State Responsibility 1929 (an early attempt to codify aspects of state responsibility) a denial of justice exists 'where there is a denial, unwarranted delay or obstruction of access to courts, gross deficiency in the administration of justice or remedial process, failure to provide those guaranties which are generally considered indispensable to the proper administration of justice or a manifestly unjust judgment. An error of a national court which does not produce manifest injustice is not a denial of justice.' This may be a wider definition than some commentators are prepared to accept, but it does, at the very least, capture the essence of the doctrine. It should be noted, finally, that what constitutes a 'denial of justice' may well depend on the appropriate standard of conduct which international law requires a state to adopt in its dealings with foreign nationals. This is discussed subsequently.

9.2.2 The appropriate standard of conduct in dealing with foreign nationals

Whether or not a state is internationally responsible for the way it treats foreigners depends on the standard of treatment which international law obliges that state to adopt. It is only if the state falls below this standard that it becomes internationally responsible. Unfortunately, there is considerable debate as to the correct standard of treatment which international law does require.

On the one hand, many states, mostly those of the 'developed' world, maintain that the treatment of foreign nationals is governed by an 'international minimum standard'. This means that every state must treat foreigners within its territory by reference to a minimum international standard, irrespective of how national law allows that state to treat its own citizens. Of course, the required standard of treatment will vary according to the facts of each case, but the important point is that the treatment must conform to an international norm. The standard is not satisfied by pleading the provisions of national law, unless they match up to the international minimum standard. The test of the international minimum standard has been applied in a number of cases, such as the *Chattin Claim* and the *Neer Claim*.

The contrary view is that the treatment of foreign nationals is to be judged by reference to the 'national standard' pertaining in the state alleged to have violated its obligations. So, under this test, the state is responsible only if it fails to accord foreign nationals the same standard of treatment afforded to its own nationals. This standard is adopted in Art. 9 of the Montevideo Convention on Rights and Duties of States 1933, which specifies that 'foreigners may not claim rights other or more extensive than those of the nationals' of the allegedly delinquent state. The national standard was championed by the states of Latin America as a way of preventing unwarranted interference in their affairs by more powerful states. Today, it is favoured by 'developing' states for similar reasons, especially in that it allows them to establish an economic and social system of their own design. The 'national standard' would, for example, allow a state to nationalise property owned by foreigners, without fear of international responsibility, if its national law allowed it to nationalise the property of its own citizens in similar circumstances. Likewise, it would allow the state to impose severe criminal penalties on foreigners (e.g. whipping for drinking alcohol) if its own nationals were subject to the same penalties for the same offence.

Not surprisingly, there is no real consensus about which standard is obligatory under customary law. As we shall see, this has caused particular problems in the field of expropriation of foreign-owned property. Generally, proponents of the 'national standard' argue that nationals of other states entering their territory must be prepared to take the host state as they find it – that voluntary presence in another state amounts to acceptance of the standards of that state and that responsibility arises only if there is discrimination against the foreigner. This is said to be especially true in respect of economic activities carried on by the foreigner, from which presumably he or she expects to benefit. On the other hand, the national standard pays no regard to such matters as fundamental human rights. It is hardly credible that a state can escape international responsibility for, say, brutal torture of foreigners simply because its national law allows it to abuse its own citizens. Of course, much of the problem is caused by the fact that there is no agreement as to the content of the international minimum standard and, in this respect, national legislation does have the advantage of certainty. At least it is known in advance. A rather more pragmatic approach is that neither 'standard' should be applied universally but that the standard of care should vary with the type of obligation in question. So, for example, alleged breaches of human rights could be judged by an international minimum standard, but the lawfulness of an expropriation of property might be assessable by the national standard. As we have said before, national legal systems do not have one standard of care for all types of legal obligation and there is no reason of principle why international law should either. However, whatever the correct approach, it is clear that international law alone may specify which standard is to be adopted; i.e. that international law specifies whether the 'national standard' or the 'international minimum standard' is appropriate for the type of case before the tribunal. Simply because international law may use rules of national law to set the content of the required standard does not mean that it has abdicated its authority. Therefore, if a state falls below the required standard, whatever that may be, it incurs international responsibility.

9.2.3 Admissibility of claims of state responsibility for the treatment of foreign nationals

9.2.3.1 Nationality of claims

State responsibility concerns the liability of one state to another. This is no less true in cases of the ill-treatment of foreign nationals even though the 'damage' is actually done to an individual. Under international law, every state has the right of 'diplomatic protection' of its nationals. This means that when a national suffers an injury at the hands of another state, his state of nationality may take up the claim. Moreover, it is clear that if a state decides to take up a matter concerning the ill-treatment of one of its nationals, the claim becomes that of the state itself, although compensation may be assessed by the actual loss caused suffered by the individual. In the *Mavrommatis Palestine Concessions Case (Jurisdiction)* (1924) PCIJ Ser. A No. 2, the Permanent Court noted that it is an elementary rule of law that a state is entitled to take up a claim in respect of injury to its nationals and, when it does, 'a state is in reality asserting its own rights – its right to ensure, in the person of its subjects, respect for the rules of international law'. So, although a state is under no obligation to exercise its right of diplomatic protection in this way (see e.g. *R (Abbasi)* v *Secretary of State for Foreign and Commonwealth Affairs and Secretary of State for the Home Department* [2003]), if it chooses to do so, it claims in respect of an injury to itself that has been perpetrated through the person of one of its nationals. This is so even though compensation may be awarded in direct proportion to the injury suffered by the national, for the latter is simply the method of calculating the damage to the state, not the basis of responsibility. Indeed, there is no obligation in international law requiring the state to pass on the compensation to the national.

It will be evident from the above that 'nationality' is a vital concept in this area of state responsibility. It is only in respect of injury to such persons that the state may enforce its own rights. Generally, international law takes the view that whether an individual is a 'national' is to be determined by the national law of the claimant state. However, as the *Nottebohm Case* 1955 ICJ Rep 4 makes clear, whether the grant of that nationality is sufficient to found a claim in international law must be judged by international criteria. Consequently, the *Nottebohm Case* suggests that before a state can make a claim in international law, there must be a 'genuine link' between that state and the individual/national who has been injured. In this very case Liechtenstein was not permitted to bring a claim in respect of alleged injury suffered by Nottebohm at the hands of Guatemala, even though Nottebohm had been granted naturalisation and nationality by Liechtenstein. The Court did not dispute Nottebohm's nationality but declined to allow it to have an effect in international law because there was no real connection between the individual and the claimant state. Similarly, in the *Grand Prince Case (Belize v France)*, Case No. 8, 2001, a case before the International Tribunal for the Law of the Sea concerning the nationality of a ship (which raises similar questions), a majority of the Tribunal decided that it had no jurisdiction to hear the case because it was not convinced (on the documents before it) that Belize was the flag state of the vessel. This was despite evidence from the Belize Ministry of Foreign Affairs and the Belize shipping registry that the *Grand Prince* was a Belize registered vessel.

The requirement of a 'genuine link' as a precondition to the exercise of the right of diplomatic protection has been criticised in many quarters and there was a powerful joint dissent by nine judges in the *Grand Prince* case based on the propriety of the Tribunal raising the issue of jurisdiction itself. Indeed, the minority adhered to the principle that each state had exclusive jurisdiction over the question of the nationality of its ships (see Art. 91 LOS 1982) and noted that 'the statements of the competent Belize authorities that the *Grand Prince* was registered in Belize suffice to discharge the initial burden of establishing that it had Belize nationality'. Importantly, the introduction of a 'genuine link' or similar test could mean that an individual or vessel went without the protection of any state simply because of the absence of a *de facto* link with the state that had formally granted them nationality, and this is a lacuna that should be avoided. It has to be appreciated, however, that the Court in *Nottebohm* was dealing with a claim by one state (the *de jure* state of nationality) against the state that actually had the closest connection with the individual (though this was not the case in *Grand Prince*). It was in Guatemala that Nottebohm primarily lived and worked and hence unacceptable that his *de facto* 'home state' should be treated as if it were truly 'foreign' to him. It is clear that the ICJ in *Nottebohm* was influenced by the weakness of Liechtenstein's position vis-à-vis Guatemala. It is open to question, therefore, whether the Court would have disallowed the claim on the ground of 'no genuine link' had the defendant state been one with which Nottebohm did not have a real connection. In the *Flegenheimer Claim* (1958) 25 ILR 91, this was recognised by the Conciliation Commission who noted, obiter, that it was 'doubtful that the [ICJ] intended to establish a rule of general international law in requiring, in the *Nottebohm Case*, that there must be an effective link between the person and the State in order that the latter may exercise its right of diplomatic protection on behalf of the former'. This is supported by the earlier decision in the *Salem Case (Egypt v US)* (1932) 2 RIAA 1161, where the defendant state objected that the individual in question was a national of two states and that the 'genuine link' was not with the present plaintiff but with the other state of nationality. This argument was not accepted and the right of the state of *de jure* nationality to bring a claim was upheld. In contrast, in the *Mergé Claim* (1955) 22 ILR 443, a tribunal of three Commissioners, including two who were to sit in the *Flegenheimer Case*, applied the effective link test to a case where the individual had nationality under the laws of both the claimant and defendant state. The result was that the state of 'effective nationality' would have been entitled to proceed if such nationality had been made out on the facts, the converse of the *Nottebohm* decision.

There is, then, some confusion as to the status of the genuine link test, although some commentators argue that the *Mergé Claim* can be distinguished because it concerned a special procedure established by the 1947 Italian Peace Treaty. This is not entirely convincing, for the *Flegenheimer Case* was decided under the same rubric. Perhaps the better view is to regard the whole topic of nationality of claims as turning on the *relative* relationship of the plaintiff (or claimant) and defendant state to the individual concerned. Thus, the state of nationality will prima facie be entitled to exercise diplomatic protection and bring a claim of state responsibility. Nationality is to be determined by reference to the laws of the claimant state and these prevail in normal circumstances. However, the prima facie rule may be displaced if the individual has no real link with the state of formal nationality but, rather, a close connection with the defendant state (as in *Nottebohm*). In cases of dual nationality, where one national state is claiming against the other, it seems from the *Mergé Claim* that the genuine link test will apply. On the other hand, if one of the states of nationality is claiming against a third state, as in the *Salem Case*, the relative strength of nationality lies with the claimant state and the effective link test cannot oust the normal presumption.

We also need to be aware that particular problems can arise in this field in respect of limited companies. When a company is maltreated at the hands of another state, this may give rise to international responsibility just as if a natural person had been injured. In fact, many of the most significant cases of state responsibility involve companies, not individuals. The company is a legal person and so entitled to diplomatic protection. However, it is necessary once again to determine which state is the state of nationality of the company. Usually, this issue resolves itself into a contest between the state in which the company is registered and the state (or states) of nationality of the shareholders of that company. This was the issue facing the ICJ in the *Barcelona Traction Case (Belgium v Spain)* 1970 ICJ Rep 3. The Barcelona Traction Light and Power Company was registered under Canadian law and it suffered various injuries at the hands of Spanish authorities. Belgium brought a claim against Spain on the grounds that the majority of shareholders in the company (about 88 per cent) were Belgian citizens. In rejecting the Belgian claim, the majority judgment indicated the following principles:

(a) If a separate and exclusive right of the *shareholders* is damaged by governmental action, then the state able to pursue the claim is the state of nationality of the shareholders. This is simply an application of the normal nationality of claims rules and was confirmed by the ICJ in the *Case Concerning Ahmadou Sadio Diallo (Republic of Guinea v Democratic Republic of the Congo) Preliminary Objections,* (2007) where part of the admissible claim concerned injury to Mr Diallo personally, in addition to the companies which he owned. Of course, in practice, when a company suffers injury it is usually the legal person or rights of the company per se which are damaged rather than some separate rights of the shareholders. Companies are, after all, legally distinct from their owners.

(b) When, as is the usual case, the company itself is injured, then the prima facie rule is that the state of nationality of the company alone is entitled to make a claim – *Case Concerning Ahmadou Sadio Diallo (Republic of Guinea v Democratic Republic of the Congo) Preliminary Objections* (2007). Consequently, it is essential to determine which is the state of nationality of the company. This is usually the state in which the company is incorporated; that is, where it has its registered office. In exceptional cases, however, the state of nationality of the company may be determined either by examining where real control of the company lies (which may mean identifying the majority shareholders) or assessing where the seat of business of the company is located. Yet whatever means we use to determine the state of nationality of the company, the important point is that this state alone may bring the claim. In this regard, it is interesting to note the provision in the US–Iran Claims Settlement Declaration 1981 (establishing the Iran–US Claims Tribunal) that for either state to be able to bring a claim in respect of a company, that company has to be both incorporated in the state and 50 per cent or more of its ownership must be in the hands of nationals of that state. Under this rubric, the normal rule applies that claims can only be brought by the state of nationality, but the test for determining it is a compromise formula.

(c) According to one view of the *Barcelona Traction Case,* it might be possible, in exceptional cases, for the state of nationality of the shareholders to bring a claim even though it is indeed the company itself that has been injured. This is the so-called idea of substitution of claims. These special cases are: first, if the company no longer exists as a distinct legal person. This is a pragmatic rule (otherwise nobody could claim); secondly, if the state of nationality of the company is unable to protect the company, but only where that state is *incapable* of offering diplomatic protection, rather than being merely unwilling to do so; thirdly, if it is the state of nationality of the company that caused the injury in the first place, especially if the state of nationality of the company acted against the company precisely because it was *de facto* owned and controlled by foreign nationals. However, while these seem pragmatic exceptions to the normal rule, it is not certain if all (or any) are valid under international law. In the *Case Concerning Ahmadou Sadio Diallo (Republic of Guinea v Democratic Republic of the Congo) Preliminary Objections,* Guinea sought to rely on the third of these exceptions (harm caused by the state of nationality of the company), but the existence of such a principle as a matter of customary law was rejected by the Court in clear terms. In so doing the Court reiterated the primacy of the company-nationality rule so it is uncertain whether even the first two alleged expcetions in *Barcelona Traction* are valid.

To sum up then, the position in respect of companies is relatively clear. The paramount rule is that it is the state of nationality of the company that enjoys the right to bring a claim. Moreover, such nationality will normally be determined by reference to the location of the company's registered office and not by reference to the location of *de facto* control. To this extent, the Court in the *Barcelona Traction Case* disapproved of the 'effective link test', at least in so far as corporations are concerned. Lastly, it is interesting to note how questions of nationality were indirectly relevant in *The I'm Alone Case*. In that case, the tribunal refused to award compensation for the physical damage inflicted by the US navy on a Canadian registered ship on the grounds that it was '*de facto* owned, controlled and ... managed' by US nationals. Such payments as were made reflected only the notional injury to Canada of having one of 'its' ships sunk. This international tribunal gave effect to the 'genuine link' principle by reducing the damages, rather than denying the original claim. This is understandable because the owners of *The I'm Alone* had deliberately acquired Canadian nationality for the ship as a matter of convenience only (in fact in order to facilitate their illicit purposes) and it is hardly surprising that the tribunal applied the 'genuine link' test to reduce the liability of the defendant state.

9.2.3.2 Exhaustion of local remedies

According to Art. 44 of the ILC Draft, the responsibility of a state may not be invoked if the 'claim is one to which the rule of exhaustion of local remedies applies and any available and effective local remedy has not been exhausted'. This means that foreign nationals must utilise such measures as are available in the local law to achieve a satisfactory vindication of their rights before their state of nationality can successfully maintain a claim in international law. The purpose of the rule is essentially practical in that it ensures that international tribunals are not engulfed by inter-state claims that could have been more easily and more profitably dealt with at the local level. It is also, as Judge Anderson pointed out in his dissent in *The Camouco Case (Panama v France)*, ITLOS, to prevent 'forum hoping' and to encourage the efficient administration of justice. As he says, an 'international tribunal can best adjudicate when the national legal system has been used not partially ... but completely and exhaustively'. However, it is clear that the rule requiring exhaustion of local remedies applies only to cases founded on diplomatic protection and injury to foreign nationals. If there is direct state-to-state responsibility, as in the case of a breach of treaty involving state rights, the matter is immediately and without more on the international plane. Similarly, states can by agreement exclude the operation of the local remedies rule to cases involving their nationals, although only if this is clearly expressed (*Elettronica Sicula Case*). This is sometimes the case where a treaty establishes a Claims Commission whose purpose is to consider a large number of cases of state responsibility, and it is the *de facto* position under the US–Iran Claims Settlement Declarations 1981 which established the US–Iran Claims Tribunal.

In the *Ambatielos Arbitration (Greece v UK)* (1956) 12 RIAA 83, Greece brought a claim on behalf of one of its nationals allegedly injured by acts of the UK. Ambatielos had made limited use of the UK national legal system, but had not conducted his original hearing with due diligence and had failed to pursue an appeal to the House of Lords. In upholding the UK's objections on the ground of non-exhaustion of local remedies, the Court noted that 'the state against which an international action is brought for injuries suffered by private individuals has the right to resist such action if the persons alleged to have been injured have not first exhausted all the remedies available to them under the municipal law of that state'. Similarly, the ICJ dismissed the claims in the *Interhandel Case* 1959 ICJ Rep 6, and the *Panevezys Railway Case (Estonia v Lithuania)* (1939) PCIJ Ser. A/B No. 76.

On the other hand, the local remedies rule cannot be used to shield a state from an otherwise proper attempt to bring an international claim. The rule is satisfied if the individual has sought to exhaust all *effective* local remedies. If the structure of the judicial system of a state is such that further progress through national courts is useless, then the state of nationality is not barred from making a claim because its citizen failed to take all possible procedural steps, as in the *Finnish Ships Arbitration (Finland v Great Britain)* (1934) 3 RIAA 1479 where the inability of the Court of Appeal to overturn findings of fact crucial to the individuals' claims meant that local remedies had been effectively exhausted. Likewise, in the *Case Concerning Ahmadou Sadio Diallo (Republic of Guinea v Democratic Republic of the Congo) Preliminary Objections* (2007), the ICJ emphasised that whether effective local remedies were available was a question of substance not form and that, in particular, administrative processes would rarely be an effective substitute for a judicial process for the vindication of the claimant's rights.

It is also clear that the individual will not fall foul of the local remedies rule where the judicial or executive authorities of the state have deliberately attempted to frustrate his claims, as noted by the Court in the *Barcelona Traction Case (Preliminary Objections)* 1964 ICJ Rep 6, and by the tribunal in the *Brown (R.E.) Case (US v Great Britain)* (1923) 6 RIAA 120. In both these cases, not only did the conduct of the state mean that the local remedies rule was satisfied – because there was no hope of redress – it also involved a 'denial of justice' giving rise to further responsibility. Similarly, in the *Elettronica Sicula Case*, a Chamber of the ICJ indicated that the local remedies rule is satisfied if the substance of a matter has been litigated in local courts, even though every variation and nuance of the argument had not been presented and even if, as in this case, the local litigation was not pursued directly by the national alleged to have been injured. It is enough if the particular legal and factual issues that the injured foreign national would have raised have been fully litigated already. This is entirely in keeping with the purpose behind the local remedies rule: viz. the reduction of *unnecessary* litigation on the international plane, not the duplication of litigation on the national plane.

There is also some debate over the precise effect of the local remedies rule within the law of state responsibility. Does it mean that no state responsibility arises at all until the local remedies have been exhausted, or does it mean that responsibility exists from the moment of breach but is not justiciable before an international tribunal until those remedies are exhausted? The original version of the ILC Draft Articles (1996 Draft, Art. 22) seemed to take the former approach, but Draft Art. 44 of the final version groups the local remedies rule under a section about 'admissibility' and this implies that failure to exhaust local remedies makes the dispute inadmissible before the tribunal, rather than that the responsibility of the state does not arise. This latter view is consistent with the opinion in the *Ambatielos Arbitration*, where the Arbitration Commission suggested that failure to exhaust local remedies was a procedural bar preventing the state of nationality from pursuing an otherwise *existing* claim of responsibility. Indeed, this does seem to be the better view because it is not clear why the failure of an individual to take action in local courts should prevent responsibility for *the state* from arising, although we might accept that it should bar action to enforce the responsibility in an international tribunal. Perhaps, however, the point is moot and unlikely to have practical consequences save only – possibly – for the calculation of interest on damages. In this connection we should note that for the purpose of assessing whether local remedies have been exhausted, an international tribunal will assume the truth of the facts upon which the claimant bases its claim (*Finnish Ships Arbitration*). This does suggest that the rule has a procedural rather than a substantive effect. It is a bar to an existing liability not a trigger for that liability.

Finally, for the sake of clarity, we should remind ourselves that the rule requiring exhaustion of local remedies is a rule that applies when a state brings a claim of responsibility because of an injury to a national. If the claim is that the *state itself* has suffered injury, then the local remedies rule does not apply. Indeed, in some cases, the state will make a claim on the dual ground that its nationals have suffered injury and that it has suffered injury to its own rights. So, in the *Case of Avena and Other Mexican Nationals (Mexico v United States)* 2004 ICJ Rep. Mexico alleged breaches of international law causing injury to its nationals (and thus exhaustion of local remedies applied) and breaches of international law causing damage to its own rights (and thus exhaustion of local remedies did not apply). In consequence, and following the *La Grand Case* (2001 ICJ Rep) the United States' objection based on non-exhaustion of local remedies could not apply to the claims that Mexico itself had suffered injury and the United States' objection to admissibility on this ground was dismissed.

9.2.3.3 The Calvo clause

A Calvo clause is a clause inserted into an agreement between a foreign national and a state whereby the foreign national agrees in advance to submit all disputes to the local law and, furthermore, to forgo his right of diplomatic protection. The purpose of a Calvo clause (named after an Argentinian jurist) is to prevent the state of nationality bringing a claim of state responsibility at international law due to an alleged waiver of such rights by the national.

Obviously, there is a close connection between such clauses and the exhaustion of local remedies rule discussed earlier. If the purpose of a Calvo clause is merely to reinforce the obligation to resort to the national law before an international claim is brought, then such clauses are both unobjectionable and unnecessary. However, if they purport to go beyond this and exclude diplomatic protection altogether, their validity (i.e. effectiveness) is open to doubt. In the *North American Dredging Company Case (US v Mexico)* (1926) 4 RIAA 26, a Calvo clause insisting on resort to local remedies and precluding the right of diplomatic protection was partially upheld. The Commission gave the clause effect in so far as it required the individual to resort to Mexican law. In the circumstances of this case, this was not surprising because the 'local remedies rule' had already been excluded by treaty for cases within the Commission's jurisdiction. The Calvo clause merely reinstated the local remedies rule; it did not operate to deny the right of diplomatic protection. It is also clear that the Commission reiterated the general rule that diplomatic protection is based on an injury to the state of nationality, not to the national themselves. Hence, an obligation entered into by the national (i.e. not to seek diplomatic protection) could not destroy the right of the state itself to seek a remedy at international law.

9.3 Expropriation of foreign-owned property

The expropriation (or nationalisation) of property owned by foreign nationals is one particular example of the rules relating to the treatment of aliens. It is treated separately only because it is one of the most contentious areas of state responsibility wherein there is considerable disagreement between developed and developing states.

In general terms, 'expropriation' denotes the taking of property by a state from the ownership of private individuals. This may be a single asset, as in a rubber plantation or building development, or it may be an entire industry. 'Nationalisation' is best regarded as a species of expropriation, referring to the second situation. As has been frequently pointed out, however, expropriation is not simply limited to the taking of property per se. It may also include any state activity that is destructive of the property rights of the foreign national, such as the imposition of a punitive tax, imposition of local management (without loss of ownership) or permanent prohibition of sale. For example, in *Starrett Housing Corp* v *Iran*, Interlocutory Proceedings, (1984) 23 ILM 1090, a chamber of the Iran–US Claims Tribunal decided that the effective assumption of the rights of management of a foreign-owned company by an Iranian government appointee amounted to a 'taking' of property that could require the payment of compensation. In this respect it is also clear that 'property' is not limited to tangible assets, but may include valuable intangible assets such as contractual rights (e.g. *Amoco Finance* v *Iran* 15 Iran–US CTR 189 (1987)), intellectual property rights, rights of shareholders (*Shahin Shane Ebrahim* v *Iran*, 1995 Iran–US Claims Tribunal) and rights of management and control. Of course, the acts of the expropriating state must actually cause the damage to the foreign-owned asset and if this causal link is not established, the expropriating state cannot be liable, as with Italy in the *Elettronica Sicula Case* where it was not proven that the acts of the local authority had caused the bankruptcy of ELSI, the foreign-owned company.

In general terms, then, and following the standard rules on the treatment of foreign nationals, if the 'host' state expropriates foreign-owned property contrary to the principles of international law, it will be liable in international law to the state of nationality of the injured party. As we shall see, however, it is clear that international law does not impose an absolute bar on expropriation and the key issue is to identify the circumstances in which an expropriation will in fact be 'contrary to the principles of international law'.

9.3.1 Conditions for lawful expropriation

In 1962, the UN General Assembly adopted a Resolution on Permanent Sovereignty over Natural Resources: GA Res. 1803 (XVII). This stated, *inter alia*, that expropriation 'shall be based on grounds or reasons of public utility, security, or the national interest which are recognised as overriding purely individual or private interests, both domestic and foreign. In such cases the owner shall be paid appropriate compensation in accordance with the rules in force in the state taking such measures in the exercise of its sovereignty and in accordance with international law.'

This resolution is closely connected with the principle of self-determination and it is important to note that it characterises expropriation as a right inherent in sovereignty. This means that expropriation is prima facie lawful, provided the conditions established by international law are met. According to the resolution, an expropriation is lawful if it is made on grounds of public policy, security or in the national interest and only if 'appropriate' compensation is paid. Importantly, whether the compensation actually paid is 'appropriate' is to be judged by reference to the national law of the expropriating state *and* international law. Moreover, in addition to these requirements, case law also suggests that a lawful expropriation must not be discriminatory, in the sense of being deliberately directed against the nationals of one state only. This was one of the grounds on which the arbitrator found the expropriation to be unlawful in *BP* v *Libya* (1974) 53 ILR 329. Again, in the *Liamco Case* (1977) 20 ILM 1, the arbitrator stated categorically that it 'is clear and undisputed that non-discrimination is a requisite for the validity of a lawful expropriation' and the tribunal in the *Aramco Case* (1963) 27 ILR 117 took the same view.

Yet, despite these reasonably clear statements of principle, subsequent General Assembly resolutions and other case law suggests that some, or all, of these conditions are no longer relevant. This is certainly the view of the states of the developing world. Following the 1962 resolution, the General Assembly has adopted a number of other instruments in which there is a definite tendency to regard expropriation as a matter for the national law of the expropriating state rather than as a matter of international law. In 1974, the Assembly adopted the Declaration on the Establishment of a New International Economic Order (GA Res. 3201 (S–VI)) and the Charter of Economic Rights and Duties of States (GA Res. 3281 (XXIX)). Both of these affirm the legality of expropriation and go on to provide that the 'appropriateness' of compensation is to be judged solely by reference to national law and they omit references to 'non-discrimination' and 'public purpose'. Similarly, in the *Liamco Case*, the arbitrator denied that 'public purpose' was a condition of lawful expropriation and this is despite its inclusion in the 1962 resolution and judicial authority as far back as the *Certain German Interests in Polish Upper Silesia Case* (1926) PCIJ Ser. A No. 7 and as recently as the *Amoco Finance Case*.

All in all, it is difficult to reach any firm conclusions about the conditions which customary international law requires to be satisfied before an expropriation can be regarded as lawful, thereby precluding a claim of state responsibility. As discussed later, there is a large measure of agreement that compensation must be paid (as recognised by all three GA resolutions), but there are doubts about how that compensation is to be measured. Similarly, although the requirement of non-discrimination has been affirmed by many judicial authorities, it is not mentioned in any of the Assembly resolutions, including the important 'Permanent Sovereignty' resolution. Likewise, it is difficult to see what is added by a requirement of 'public purpose', especially since this necessitates an examination of the motives of a state and an assessment of their 'validity' by outside authorities. Is any judicial authority competent to dispute the expropriating state's assertion that it acted in what it believed to be the best interests of its country? These difficulties have not, however, prevented several judicial tribunals applying some test of 'public purpose' (albeit one that can be easily satisfied – *Amoco Case*) and although the 1974 Charter does not mention this requirement, the Charter itself is not widely regarded as reflecting customary law. Again, many bilateral investment agreements do oblige the 'host' state to refrain from expropriation except for reasons of public necessity, a public purpose related to internal needs or on a non-discriminatory basis (e.g. UK/Peru

Agreement 1994, UK/India Agreement 1994 and UK/Ukraine Agreement 1993). Of course, these bilateral agreements, binding on the parties, do not necessarily reflect general customary law, but at least they suggest that the imposition of conditions for lawful expropriation in bilateral treaties is not prohibited by international law, even if they are not mandatory.

Clearly, these are difficult questions, but perhaps we should remember that these 'natural resources' are declared to be under the 'permanent sovereignty' of the territorial sovereign. If this is true, can another state legitimately complain about a reassertion of ownership of those resources – for whatever reasons – provided, of course, that some 'compensation' is paid to the person suffering actual loss? Indeed, given that the restitution of the expropriated property to the foreign national is hardly ever going to occur – irrespective of whether the expropriation was technically unlawful – it may be more realistic to concentrate on the level of compensation than to attempt to distil 'conditions for lawful expropriation'. This was the view taken by the Iran–US Claims Tribunal in *Shahin Shane Ebrahim* v *Iran* (1995), where the Tribunal declined to decide whether the appropriation was lawful or unlawful, concentrating instead on the measure of compensation. In this sense, a tribunal concerned at the 'unfairness', 'arbitrariness' or even 'discriminatory' nature of the expropriation can make its point in the level of compensation awarded rather than with largely hortatory statements about legality.

With this in mind, the next section considers the issue of compensation for expropriation as this is where the developing states (usually the expropriators) and the developed states (usually the claimant states) disagree most fundamentally. As already indicated, there seems little doubt that customary law requires compensation to be paid in order that an expropriation be lawful. This is stated clearly in the 1962 resolution and the 1974 Charter of Economic Rights and Duties and it has been confirmed in nearly every judicial award (e.g. *Chorzow Factory Case*, *BP* v *Libya* and the *Animoil Case* (1982) 21 ILM 976). However, the simple assertion that compensation must be paid in order for an expropriation to be lawful does not address the issues at the heart of the problem.

9.3.2 The standard by which to measure compensation

According to the industrialised nations, the standard of compensation required by international law is 'the international minimum standard'. In effect, this means that the adequacy of compensation is to be judged by reference to international criteria rather than the provisions of the national law of the expropriating state. It will be remembered that the 1962 resolution supports this, in that it requires compensation to be paid having regard to 'the rules in force in the state taking such measures ... and in accordance with international law'. Developing states, on the other hand, claim that compensation is to be judged by the 'national treatment' standard and that if the compensation matches up to that guaranteed to nationals under national law, it is *ipso facto* 'appropriate'. So, the only rule of international law of relevance for developing states is that which allows compensation to be definitively measured by national law provided, of course, that it is paid. Substantive international rules about the standard of compensation have no part to play. This view is supported by the Assembly resolutions of 1974, although not surprisingly the developed nations do not regard these as reflecting customary law. However, the practical importance of this uncertainty should not be overestimated. The argument focuses on the procedural question of which system of law (international or national) sets the standard for compensation: it is not necessarily an argument about the amount of compensation that must actually be paid. So, if in practice national courts and international tribunals reach sensible compromise solutions about the level of compensation, rather than adopting the polarised arguments of 'developed' or 'developing' states, this question becomes much less pressing. Fortunately, this seems to be the case.

9.3.3 The measure of compensation

According to the 1962 resolution, expropriation must be accompanied by 'appropriate' compensation. This is generally accepted to reflect customary law (e.g. the *Animoil Case* (1982) 21 ILM 976) and it seems to require consideration of all the circumstances of the case. However, this still does not take us very far. In fact, the question of the measure of compensation is the area where theoretical disputes between developed states (capital-exporting) and developing states (nationalising/capital-importing) have practical consequences. According to the 'Hull formula' adopted by industrialised nations, compensation must be 'prompt, adequate and effective'. This means, in essence, that the nationalising state should pay in a form of currency that can be readily used (not, for example, devalued local currency), that it should reflect the full value of the property taken, perhaps incorporating an element for future lost profits, and that it must be handed over within a reasonable time after the expropriation and, if not, interest should be paid (see e.g. the *Anglo-Iranian Oil Co. Case*). Obviously, this is a strict and arduous standard. Not surprisingly, developing states have objected to this formula, not least because it requires them to pay out a substantial capital sum when the very reason for the expropriation may have been that they were in serious financial difficulties. Consequently, developing states argue that 'appropriate' means compensation assessed by reference to the economic viability of the nationalising state, the importance of the expropriated property and the benefits which the foreign nationals have already acquired through commercial activities in the state. This will almost certainly not be the market value of the property and will not include an amount for future lost profits.

This disagreement over legal principle is also a reflection of political and ideological differences. It is not surprising, therefore, that actual awards tend to steer a middle course. In the *Amoco Finance Case*, the tribunal thought that compensation for lawful expropriations should be 'just', which in the context of the governing treaty meant the value of the expropriated asset as a going concern, and in *Southern Pacific Properties (Middle East) Ltd* v *Arab Republic of Egypt* (1993) 32 ILM 933, the arbitrators thought that 'fair' compensation was required for a lawful expropriation. A similar middle way was taken in the *Animoil Case*. As far as the UK is concerned, bilateral investment protection agreements do tend to oblige the host state to pay 'prompt, adequate and effective' compensation (e.g. UK/Peru, UK/Ukraine), but there is also some reliance on 'fair and equitable' compensation (UK/India). In effect, the customary law requirement to pay 'appropriate compensation' is so flexible that it encompasses both the 'equitable' and the 'Hull formula' approaches, as witnessed by the disagreement among the tribunal in *Shahin Shane* v *Iran* with the majority favouring the former and the minority the latter.

9.3.4 **Damages and remedies for unlawful expropriations**

As indicated previously, an expropriation might be regarded as unlawful for a number of reasons. *Assuming* that preconditions for lawful expropriation do exist, this might be because it was discriminatory, not for reasons of public policy, in violation of a treaty obligation (e.g. *Certain German Interests in Polish Upper Silesia Case*) or because of a failure to provide any compensation or failure to provide compensation up to the international standard (whatever that may be). In the event that the nationalising state fails to observe any of the first three conditions, it is clear that the expropriation could never have been lawful (it would be 'unlawful per se'). On the other hand, if the illegality stems from a failure to pay 'appropriate' compensation, this renders the expropriation unlawful from the date at which the obligation to pay arises. In both cases, however, any monetary sum later awarded can be characterised as 'damages' for unlawful conduct, rather than as 'compensation' for a lawful expropriation although, as discussed earlier, it might be preferable to avoid such labels. Despite the difficulties, a distinction between 'lawful' and 'unlawful' expropriation was drawn in the *Amoco Finance Case* (although it was not adopted in *Starrett Housing* v *Iran* 4 Iran–US CTR 122 or in *Shahin Shane* v *Iran*), where the tribunal emphasised that the measure of damages for *unlawful* expropriation should be assessed according to the normal standard for damages applicable in all cases of state responsibility. In effect, this means that a state claiming that the expropriation was unlawful (as opposed to arguing about the amount of compensation offered) may be entitled to different remedies, including an enhanced monetary sum. For example, in cases of illegality the tribunal could order restitution of the entire property to the injured party (very unlikely) or its full monetary equivalent (as in *Texaco* v *Libya*) and this may include an element for future lost profits as in *Amco* v *Indonesia* (1985) 24 ILM 1022. In practice, therefore, a state that offers compensation, however derisory, may be in a better position than a state that offers no compensation or whose expropriation is unlawful on other grounds. The former may find that the level of 'compensation' is actually increased by the tribunal, but the latter may find that the level of 'damages' is even greater than that. This is simply a reflection of the illegality of the latter state's conduct.

9.3.5 **The mathematics of compensation awards**

In the preceding sections we have examined the questions of principle that arise from an expropriation: what is the standard by which to judge expropriation and the compensation it gives rise to, what is the measure of that compensation and what, if any, is the difference between lawful and unlawful expropriation? A very different question – but probably the most important – is how the compensation is actually calculated. The rubric adopted by a tribunal for arriving at a sum to be paid will often subsume and incorporate the issues raised by our questions of principle. The mathematical calculation may, or may not, reflect one standard or the other, or give effect to the lawfulness or unlawfulness of the expropriation, and this may be made explicit, or not.

(a) *The discounted cash flow (DCF) approach.* This calculates the compensation by reference to the value of the enterprise at the time of the expropriation in terms of its projected revenues over the period for which the investment was expected to last, minus (i.e. discounting) revenue flow from its inception to that date. This method may be useful where the project has been in existence for some time, but not where there are no data to make a meaningful DCF calculation (*Southern Pacific* v *Egypt*).

(b) *The net book value method.* This calculates the compensation by reference to the paper value of the assets that the company holds. It is essentially an accounting exercise. It can exclude factors such as goodwill, know-how and experience and it regards the asset as an amalgamation of disposable items that could be sold separately. It minimises the value of the enterprise as an operating 'whole' and therefore is not universally favoured (*Amoco Finance* v *Iran*). It may provide a starting point for an assessment of compensation.

(c) *The 'going concern' method.* This calculates compensation by reference to the physical and financial assets of the undertaking, but with the addition of intangible values such as existing commercial contracts and contacts, goodwill and commercial prospects. Liabilities of a similar kind are deducted. It stresses the value of the asset as a functioning undertaking and consequently can include an element for lost future profits. It is the method most likely to be adopted if there is some suggestion of 'unlawfulness' in the expropriation, especially if the unlawfulness stems from something other than a failure to offer compensation in the first place (*Amoco Finance* v *Iran*).

(d) *Does the fact of expropriation affect the value of the asset and thereby reduce the compensation?* It should be clear enough that the 'value' of the asset (however calculated) should be its value pre-expropriation. In most cases, the fact of expropriation will reduce commercial prospects for the immediate future and may well disrupt cash flow, effective management, trading performance and ability to attract new business. In this sense, its value decreases, but only because the expropriation has occurred and such reduction should be ignored. Somewhat strangely, in *Shahin Shane Ebrahimi* v *Iran*, the majority (2–1) concluded that a valuation of the company on the basis of its past performance was not appropriate because its prospects had been adversely affected by the changes accompanying the Islamic Revolution. Therefore, its value for compensation purposes was less than the value of its tangible assets because of a deduction for so-called 'negative goodwill'. As the judge in the minority pointed out, this appears to violate the principle that the value of an expropriated asset is to be assessed without any reference to the acts causing the expropriation or its effects. To follow the majority view could allow the expropriating state to plead its own actions as a reason why it should not pay so much for the asset it has just taken and devalued.

(e) *Lump sum settlements.* In cases where the expropriating state is subject to many claims arising out of a series of connected incidents, the claims to compensation may be settled by the payment of a lump sum to the host state of the nationals concerned. This sum, which is invariably less than the value of all individual claims combined, may then be distributed by the host state to its nationals on a pro rata or other basis. It is an efficient means of dealing with interlinked claims. Examples in the UK include the UK/Latvia Agreement 1993 relating to losses of UK assets in the Baltic states in 1940–45, and the Foreign Compensation (Amendment) Act 1993 (amending the Foreign Compensation Act 1950) concerning sums that might be received from abroad or from an international organisation in respect of losses to UK nationals arising from another state's unlawful actions (e.g. funds distributed by the UN Compensation Commission dealing with losses arising from Iraq's invasion of Kuwait).

9.4 The internationalisation of contracts

Generally, when an individual or a company enters into a contract with a state, that contract is governed by the national law of one of the parties, usually the state in which the investment is occurring. If the state then breaches the contract, this does not give rise to state responsibility per se. The contract is governed by national law and the individual's remedy lies in a normal action for breach of contract. However, in certain circumstances, it seems that contractual relations between a foreign national and a state can give rise to international responsibility for that state.

(a) The first and clearest case is if the individual is prevented from obtaining due process of law in pursuit of his contractual claim. In this case, there will be a 'denial of justice' so as to allow the state of nationality of the company to make an international claim against the delinquent state. There is nothing special in this form of responsibility and it can arise if the foreign national is denied due process in respect of a contractual claim against any person, not necessarily the state itself.

(b) Additionally, it seems that contractual rights may be regarded as 'property' that may be unlawfully expropriated. This was recognised by the arbitrator in the *Liamco Case* in respect of concession contracts between a company and a state. A similar approach lies behind the *Jalapa Railroad Claim* (1948) 8 Whiteman 908, where the contract between the American company and the Mexican state of Veracruz was rendered useless by a legislative act of the contracting state. Again, there is no necessary reason why a state should not be regarded as having expropriated the contractual rights of a foreign national arising out of their contract with an ordinary citizen as well as under a contract with the state itself.

(c) The most startling circumstance in which a contract between a company and a state can be taken out of the national sphere and placed in the realms of international law is under the doctrine of the 'internationalisation of contracts'. In *Texaco* v *Libya*, the American oil companies had concluded concessionary contracts with the Libyan state for the exploitation of oil. Libya then nationalised all the property and rights of the companies. The subsequent dispute was referred to arbitration under an arbitration clause in the contract. In his award in that case, the arbitrator suggested that certain contracts between states and individuals (including companies) could be 'internationalised'. This could be done in various ways. Specifically, a contract could be internationalised where it made reference to a system of law, other than the law of the state itself, as in this case where the award was to be made by reference to 'the principles of the law of Libya common to the principles of international law and then ... by and in accordance with general principles of Law' (*Texaco* v *Libya*). Secondly, where the contract provided for disputes to be settled by international arbitration. Thirdly, where the contract was within the class of 'international development agreements' that involved long-term assistance to a state in an area of essential economic activity.

The effect of a contract between an individual and a state becoming internationalised is clearly to place the contract in the domain of international law. In this sense, the company becomes subject to international law and can enforce its rights on the international plane. Importantly, the fact that the state has voluntarily agreed to internationalise the contract in the first place may mean that there can be no lawful expropriation of property connected with it. Crucially, this seems to depend on whether the contract contains a 'stabilisation clause' (which possibly might, of itself, internationalise the contract). A stabilisation clause is a contractual term by which the state agrees that it will not terminate the contract, although following *Animoil* and *Texaco* it seems that the clause must be clear and unequivocal and must only seek to restrict the power to terminate for a reasonable period of time: it cannot operate indefinitely. Once again, however, there is considerable disagreement as to the precise effect of a stabilisation clause in an internationalised contract. One view is that, irrespective of the alleged conditions for lawful expropriation, if a state promises to give effect to a contract, and this obligation takes effect in international law, it is bound by that obligation in the same way as it would be bound by a treaty. Internationalisation precluded expropriation. Therefore, any purported expropriation of an internationalised contract would be unlawful and the measure of damages would reflect this, perhaps even justifying a very rare order for restitution. In the *Animoil Case*, however, the majority took a different line and gave effect to the stabilisation clauses only by way of an increased award of compensation without regarding the clauses as precluding expropriation per se, although this may have been because the clauses were regarded as being insufficiently precise. This approach, which treats a stabilisation clause as a factor to be regarded when computing compensation rather than as an indicator that the state has behaved unlawfully, is consonant with the view that expropriation of natural resources is a right derived from sovereignty and can rarely be unlawful. Of course, in practice, the difference between a monetary award that is comprised of compensation plus damages for unlawful action and a monetary award that comprises 'higher' compensation because of the existence of a stabilisation clause may be difficult to grasp. However, should a tribunal ever feel itself competent to order actual restitution of the property expropriated, it may do so only if it has first determined that the expropriation was indeed unlawful. Then, should this possibility ever come to pass, the true effect of a stabilisation clause will be crucial.

Clearly then, the concept of the internationalised contract may offer considerable protection to a company contracting with a state. The contract is removed to the international plane and the existence of a stabilisation clause, even if it does not preclude expropriation altogether, will make the state wary of taking precipitate action if enhanced compensation has to be paid. Of course, the state must first agree to have these terms in its contract with the company and it is no longer true that multinationals are in a dominant bargaining position *vis-à-vis* the major oil exporting countries. In this sense, the internationalised contract may be a thing of the past. On the other hand, the international community is not always stable and predictable and, to take but one example, the break up of the Soviet Union has produced oil-rich states that have to rely on western expertise if they are to exploit their natural resources. Whether this results in new forms of contracts between states and foreign nationals remains to be seen.

9.5 **Protection for private investors**

If, as we have seen, states enjoy a great deal of liberty in the field of expropriation, the question arises whether foreign investors can take any steps to safeguard their rights. The following is an indication of the possibilities, although it must be realised that in the end they may operate only to ensure adequate compensation or damages rather than to prevent expropriation altogether.

(a) The company can attempt to internationalise the contract, although it is debatable whether this precludes expropriation altogether. Internationalisation may increase the measure of damages and/or compensation.

(b) The company can ensure that the contract does not contain a Calvo clause. Again, however, following the general rule that state responsibility is a matter of international law, the inclusion of such a clause cannot preclude the right of diplomatic protection and the presence of such a clause will not be fatal to the company's position.

(c) The company can seek to have the 'prompt adequate and effective' rule concerning compensation incorporated into the terms of the contract. Whether this would be effective at international law is open to question.

(d) The company may seek registration (i.e. nationality) in a state willing and able to exercise its right of diplomatic protection. This is particularly important given that a state can legitimately refuse to make a claim on behalf of its nationals and may do so if it wishes to preserve good relations with the nationalising state.

(e) The company can attempt to persuade its state of nationality to enter into a treaty with the state in which it is investing. This should guarantee the terms of the contract and any breach of the contract will then be a breach of the treaty. In some circumstances, this could involve the direct responsibility of the delinquent state, although as the *Elettronica Sicula (ELSI) Case* makes clear, this will occur only if the treaty confers additional and independent rights on the plaintiff/claimant state. In the *ELSI Case*, the treaty did not have this effect and the rules of state responsibility (e.g. the requirement to exhaust local remedies) still applied. Another example of the state of nationality seeking to mitigate in advance the consequences of expropriation of property belonging to its nationals (and therefore to protect its companies) is provided by the UK's Investment Promotion and Protection Agreements. IPPAs are treaties between the UK and foreign states whereby the state in which investment is made guarantees the independent settlement of disputes arising under a contract with a national of the other party. They also promise to pay compensation in the event of expropriation, although this is not always 'prompt, adequate and effective'. Currently, there is a large number of IPPAs in force and these are very effective in both encouraging investment in foreign states and protecting the interests of UK companies trading abroad.

(f) The company could bring the matter within the regime of the International Convention for the Settlement of Investment Disputes 1964, if its state of nationality and the expropriating state have signed the Convention. This provides a formal mechanism for the settlement of investment disputes between contracting states and nationals of contracting states, subject to prior consent. In fact, the Convention regime is proving to be an effective mechanism for the protection of companies (and states) and has brought a large measure of stability and certainty to foreign investment matters. It was the applicable regime in *AAPL v Sri Lanka* and *Southern Pacific v Egypt*.

9.6 Other forms of responsibility in international law

In this chapter we have considered the law relating to state responsibility for acts contrary to international law. In addition to this, we should note the international responsibility of individuals for acts contrary to international law. These may be prosecuted in national courts, special international tribunals (e.g. the Yugoslav and Rwandan War Crimes Tribunals) or in the International Criminal Court. The ILC is also considering a set of Draft Articles on international liability for injurious consequences arising out of acts not prohibited by international law.

FURTHER READING

Allot, P., 'State Responsibility and the Unmaking of International Law', (1988) 29 *Harvard Int LJ* 1.

Amerasinghe, C. F., 'Issues of Compensation for the Taking of Alien Property in the Light of Recent Cases and Practice', (1992) 41 *ICLQ* 22.

Bederman, D., 'Nationality of Individual Claimants before the Iran–US Claims Tribunal', (1993) 42 *ICLQ* 119.

Crawford, J., *The International Law Commission's Articles on State Responsibility: Introduction, text and commentaries* (Cambridge University Press, 2002).

Crawford, J. and Olleran, S., 'The Nature and Forms of International Responsibility', in M. Evans (ed.), *International Law* (Oxford University Press, 2003).

Dixon, M., 'The ELSI Case', (1992) 41 *ICLQ* 701.

Greenwood, C., 'State Contracts in International Law: The Libyan Oil Arbitrations', (1982) 53 *BYIL* 27.

Lillich, R., 'Duties of States regarding the Civil Rights of Aliens', (1978) 161 *RC* 329.

Nollkaemper, A., 'Concurrence between Individual Responsibility and State Responsibility in International Law', (2003) 52 *ICLQ* 615.

Paasivirta, E., 'Internationalisation and Stabilisation of Contracts versus State Sovereignty', (1989) 60 *BYIL* 315.

Schacter, O., and Mendelson, M., discussing compensation for expropriation in (1984) 78 *AJIL* 121; (1985) 79 *AJIL* 414, 1041; (1985) 79 *AJIL* 420.

Staker, C., 'Diplomatic Protection of Private Business Companies: Determining Corporate Personality for International Law Purposes', (1990) 61 *BYIL* 155.

Weiss, E., 'Invoking State Responsibility in the Twenty-First Century', (2002) 96 *AJIL* 798.

SUMMARY

State responsibility

- The rules of 'state responsibility' indicate the circumstances in which a state will be fixed with legal responsibility for the violation of an international obligation and the consequences this entails.

- State responsibility comprises two elements: an unlawful act, which is imputable to the state. Responsibility may be avoided if the state is able to raise a valid defence. If not, the consequence of responsibility is a liability to make reparation and/or suffer the consequences of being internationally responsible.

- Whether an act or omission perpetrated by organs or individuals is to be attributed to the state is a matter of international law. While international law may well use rules of national law to help make this decision, the final determination is for the international system.

- It is axiomatic that breach of an international obligation entailing responsibility gives rise to legal consequences and this is a principle that is rooted in customary law.

- Not every prima facie breach of a legal obligation gives rise to legal responsibility. International law recognises that the state may have a valid defence to a charge of unlawful conduct. These are known as 'circumstances precluding wrongfulness'.

- Every state is under an international obligation not to ill-treat foreign nationals present in its territory. If the state violates this obligation in any way it may incur international responsibility to the state of which the person is a national.

- The expropriation (or nationalisation) of property owned by foreign nationals is one particular example of the rules relating to the treatment of aliens that may give rise to international responsibility.

10

The peaceful settlement of disputes

According to Art. 2(3) of the United Nations Charter, all members 'shall settle their international disputes by peaceful means in such a manner that international peace and security, and justice, are not endangered'. While this obligation is addressed primarily to members of the Organisation, there is no doubt that this principle is one of the central obligations of international law which all states must observe (*Legality of the Use of Force Case (Provisional Measures) Yugoslavia* v *Belgium etc.* (1999) 39 ILM 950). It is the natural counterpart to the prohibition of the use of force and may also have acquired the status of *jus cogens*. The forceful resolution of disputes, the use of force by one state to impose its will on another, is now legally obsolete and the obligation to settle disputes by peaceful means is a corollary of this.

The precise scope of the obligation is, however, that states should settle disputes peacefully, not that they should *settle* them. In other words, there is no general rule requiring a state to settle its grievances. Rather, the rule is that if a state does decide to settle, this must be done in a peaceful manner. As we shall see, the absence of a general obligation to settle disputes is reflected in the fact that the jurisdiction of the International Court of Justice (and most other tribunals) is not compulsory. A state cannot be compelled to submit a dispute with another state to a third party for settlement unless it has given its consent in some form or other. The only exception to this is the obligation under Art. 33 of the United Nations Charter to settle disputes which are likely to endanger international peace and security. Furthermore, the obligation to settle disputes peacefully applies to international disputes only. There is no explicit rule in general international law requiring a state to settle internal grievances peacefully. A state may, therefore, use force in its relations with its own citizens in its own territory, subject only to limitations imposed by human rights law or other specific obligations, such as the requirements of a mandatory resolution of the Security Council. Of course, an internal dispute may well become 'international' if it has consequences outside of its borders or otherwise impinges on the international community and this may well trigger Security Council involvement, as with the initially internal dispute in Libya in 2012. Similarly, it is also clear that a dispute may be 'international' even though the parties (or some of them) are not states. Recent examples are the dispute between the Bosnian Muslims, Serbs and Croats and the disputes between rival groups in Sudan (which led to the creation of a new state – South Sudan). Consequently, the obligation to settle disputes peacefully encompasses all disputes occurring on the international plane, including those considered in the previous chapter arising between a state and a foreign company over an internationalised contract (e.g. *Texaco* v *Libya* (1977) 53 ILR 389).

It is vital that the obligation to settle disputes peacefully should be supported by practical means. In fact, international law knows many methods of dispute settlement and it is important to remember that the International Court of Justice is only one piece in this jigsaw. There are many other tribunals – international, regional and bilateral – which resolve disputes 'judicially', as well as several ways in which disputes can be resolved 'diplomatically'. While there are no set criteria by which to identify a 'judicial' means of settlement, generally this is taken to mean the settlement of a dispute according to international law, usually by an impartial third party, the outcome of which is legally binding on the disputants. The growing list of cases settled by the International Tribunal for the Law of the Sea (ITLOS) is a good example, as are the Arbitral Panels established under the auspices of the Permanent Court of Arbitration. However, even in modes of dispute settlement that are essentially 'diplomatic', international law is not irrelevant. In direct negotiations, for example, each side will have a battery of legal principles with which to support its economic and political arguments. Consequently, it should not be thought that any of the various methods of dispute settlement are exclusively 'judicial' or 'diplomatic'. International disputes are complex and international law will play a role in most methods of resolution, varying from being the sole criterion before the ICJ to one of several in 'negotiations' and 'mediation'. Similarly, there is no exclusive method by which any particular dispute, or any aspect of it, need be resolved, as seen by the many methods specified in the Law of the Sea Convention 1982. In practice, the means of dispute settlement are cumulative and they do not operate in isolation.

10.1 Negotiation

As in national law, the most common method of settlement is direct negotiations between the parties. This 'method' accounts for the great majority of settlements between states and appears to be the one most preferred. There is no set procedure for negotiations and these may be at arm's length, through an intermediary or face to face. Necessarily any negotiated settlement will be *legally* binding only if this is the wish of the parties, and then it may be encapsulated in a treaty. Otherwise, the terms of the agreement may be recorded in an exchange of notes or diplomatic memoranda having no legal effect but obviously effective as a practical solution to a problem. Further, while international law may play a significant part in the negotiations between the parties, as with the dispute between Congo and Uganda concerning alleged acts of aggression and intervention 1999/2000, it is clear that political, economic and social considerations are also important. This is not surprising given that international law does not operate in a vacuum. Direct negotiations between the parties enable the states concerned to reach a comprehensive settlement, having regard to all the factors, of which international law may be one.

Occasionally, a state may be able to underpin its negotiations with the threat of legal proceedings. This is not as potent a weapon as it is in national law because of the general absence of compulsory judicial settlement of disputes. However, where available, the threat or reality of judicial settlement may be used to crystallise an issue between the states and force a resolution. Nevertheless, it is often the case that neither party wishes to use judicial means precisely because of the narrow focus this entails. It has been suggested that once a state has voluntarily entered into negotiations, it is under a binding legal obligation to negotiate in good faith. If this were a rule of international law, it would seem to require states to act honestly and reasonably and to make a genuine attempt to reach a settlement. It would not mean that they had to settle the dispute, but that having made an attempt, they should carry it through in good faith. In reality this obligation is probably too vague to be of any practical value although it should be remembered that it is quite possible for states to bind themselves by treaty to proceed to negotiations should a dispute arise (see the Law of the Sea Convention 1982) and in such specific cases there is both a legal obligation to negotiate and, perhaps, an obligation to make genuine and reasonable efforts to reach a solution.

10.2 Mediation and good offices

Although it is possible to distinguish mediation and good offices from negotiation, in practice they are very much part of the same process. 'Good offices' are a preliminary to direct negotiations between the parties. The person offering his 'good offices' – usually a neutral trusted by both sides – will attempt to persuade the parties to negotiate. Such was the task of the US Secretary of State, Alexander Haig, in the days preceding the UK's reoccupation of the Falkland Islands, and has been the role of the African Union in many disputes in Africa, such as the dispute between Congo and Uganda. Mediation is simply a continuation of this, and often the mediator will be the person who originally brought the parties together. A mediator is a person, again approved by both parties, who takes part in the negotiations and whose task is to suggest the terms of a settlement and to attempt to bring about a compromise between the two opposing views. In recent years, the UN Secretary-General has offered his 'good offices' in a variety of situations and has then gone on to mediate when the parties have come together. An example was the dispute between the Soviet Union, Pakistan and Afghanistan concerning the presence of Soviet troops in the latter's territory. A similar function seems to have been served by the EU's various special representatives to the Middle East Peace Process.

10.3 Inquiry

The use of commissions of inquiry is most often intended to establish the factual basis for a settlement between states. The parties to a dispute will agree to refer the matter to an impartial body whose task is to produce an unbiased finding of facts. It is then up to the parties to negotiate a settlement on the basis of these facts. While it is rare that the parties agree to be legally bound to accept the findings of such an inquiry, in practice it is just as rare for their conclusions to be ignored. The commission of inquiry is invaluable in the present system of international law where no compulsory fact-finding machinery exists and where, in reality, many disputes are compounded by the simple truth that neither party is prepared to accept the other's version of events.

10.4 Settlement by the United Nations

The United Nations has a variety of institutionalised and informal methods through which states may settle disputes. Obviously, the 'good offices' of the Secretary-General and judicial settlement by the ICJ (an organ of the UN) fall into this category. (These are dealt with separately; see sections 10.2 and 10.8.)

10.4.1 The General Assembly

The General Assembly has wide-ranging authority to make recommendations for the settlement of disputes. Subject to the primacy of the Security Council in matters comprising a threat to or breach of the peace, the Assembly 'may recommend measures for the peaceful adjustment of any situation, regardless of origin, which it deems likely to impair the general welfare or friendly welfare among nations' (UN Charter Art. 14). However, as with the great majority of Assembly resolutions, these 'recommendations' are not legally binding and the Assembly has no power to make authoritative and binding determinations of fact. It cannot impose a settlement on the parties, although it may often provide the impetus that is needed for a negotiated solution. In practice, the effect of Assembly discussions and resolutions is variable. Any formal determination or recommendation must necessarily carry some weight, but it is also true that the Assembly is a political body that makes decisions according to bloc allegiances rather than impartial judgment. The Assembly contributed significantly to the solution of the problem of the former South-West Africa (now Namibia) and buttressed the Secretary-General in his efforts to bring peace to Iraq. Yet it has had little success with the dispute between India and Pakistan over Kashmir and the prospects for a solution for the divided island of Cyprus – once rosy – now look less promising. Much depends, as always, on the will of the parties to a dispute, rather than on the will of the Assembly. Indeed, the political nature of the Assembly means that questions of international law are not always at the front of its concern and it would seem more suited to the solution of political and economic disputes, especially those in which the Assembly itself has an interest. Thus, the Assembly will play a critical role in matters concerning statehood and membership, as it was with China in 1974, the states of the former Yugoslavia in 1992–2000 and in East Timor in 2002. These are issues having considerable legal significance in respect of which the Assembly has particular expertise.

10.4.2 The Security Council

Under Chapter VI of the Charter (Pacific Settlement of Disputes), the Security Council has various powers and responsibilities in respect of the settlement of disputes. First, if all other means have failed, the parties to a dispute which is likely to endanger international peace and security are under an obligation to refer it to the

Security Council. Secondly, any member or non-member of the Organisation may, without the parties' consent, refer any dispute to the Council to see if it is likely to endanger the maintenance of international peace and security. In both cases, the Council may recommend appropriate procedures or methods of settlement, as well as the actual terms of a compromise. In practice, the procedural aspects of these provisions are quite readily invoked, especially the reference power enjoyed by uninvolved states. Generally, the Council is reluctant to make a concrete recommendation without the participation of all interested parties, as was the case with the India/Pakistan conflict in 1971. It is also clear that the Security Council cannot actually impose a settlement on the parties, save only that its residual power to deal with threats to the peace and acts of aggression remains intact (e.g. the Congo/Uganda/Rwanda Resolution, 16 June 2000, SC Res. 1304 (2000)) and this could conceivably lead to the Council imposing a settlement if the preconditions of Art. 39 were established (breach of the peace, threat to the peace, act of aggression). Again, however, the Security Council is primarily concerned with political, not legal matters, and its task is to keep the peace rather than to judge the rights and wrongs of a dispute. According to Art. 36(3) of the Charter, the Council must bear in mind that 'legal disputes should as a general rule be referred by the parties to the International Court of Justice', although it has no power to force states to submit to this jurisdiction.

In this respect, note must be taken of a number of ICJ decisions which bear on the relationship between the Council and the Court. In the *Lockerbie Case* one of the grounds upon which the ICJ decided not to grant 'interim measures of protection' to the plaintiff state (on which see later in the chapter) was that the Security Council had taken concrete measures in respect of the dispute after determining that the matter fell within Art. 39. This illustrates not only that most disputes have both a legal and a political dimension, but also that the Security Council can assume paramount responsibility for dispute settlement in such cases as it deems appropriate. Conversely, in the *Case Concerning Armed Activities on the Territory of the Congo (Congo v Uganda) (Provisional Measures)*, 1 July 2000, the ICJ did grant interim measures of protection to Congo, which in terms were very similar to those 'demanded' in SC Res. 1304 of 16 June 2000. Apparently, in contrast to Security Council action in the *Lockerbie Case*, in the Congo situation the Council had not reached a decision determinative of the rights which Congo now claimed deserved protection. No doubt this is a logically defensible distinction, but it requires a fine judgment by the Court. Thirdly, in the *Advisory Opinion Concerning the Legal Consequences of the Construction of a Wall in the Occupied Palestinian Territory* 2004 ICJ Rep, the Court again touched on the relationship of the UN with the Court (including, but not specifically, the Security Council). In this Advisory Opinion, the Court was clear that the mere fact that other UN bodies are considering a dispute is no bar to the Court considering the legal aspects of the same dispute. The cases concerning the former Yugoslavia before the Court – particularly the *Legality of the Use of Force Cases* (2004) and the *Case Concerning the Application of the Convention on the Prevention and Punishment of the Crime of Genocide (Bosnia and Herzegovina v Serbia & Montenegro)* (ICJ 2007) – are also good examples of where the ICJ may reach a determination act even though the Council and Assembly are active.

The Court's willingness to consider matters even though the Council (or other UN body) is dealing with the case now seems to be firmly established, and perhaps the

Lockerbie Case (with two of the Council's permanent members intimately involved) can be regarded as the exception rather than the rule. So, in the *Advisory Opinion on the Accordance with international law of the unilateral declaration of independence in respect of Kosovo* (2008), the Court issued a strong statement about its ability and willingness to rule on a legal question even if this concerned contentious matters before the Assembly and Security Council and in respect of a dispute where the Security Council had indeed taken concrete measures. Neither is this willingness limited to Advisory Opinions, because in the *Application of the Interim Accord of 13 September 1995 (The Former Yugoslav Republic of Macedonia v Greece)* (2011), the ICJ decided that the case was admissible despite the fact that aspects of the dispute between Greece and the Former Yugoslav Republic of Macedonia were subject to the Security Council attempts at a negotiated settlement.

10.4.3 Other agencies

A number of specialised agencies operating under the general aegis of the United Nations may also assist in the resolution of disputes between states. These agencies deal with a variety of matters of a specific nature and they provide a forum for discussion and an impetus to settlement in much the same way as the General Assembly. Included in this category are the International Labour Organisation, the International Monetary Fund, the International Civil Aviation Authority and the International Atomic Energy Agency.

10.5 Conciliation

Conciliation can be regarded either as a 'non-judicial' or a 'semi-judicial' procedure for the settlement of disputes. Once again the process of conciliation may deal with a variety of questions, including matters of international law. Bearing this in mind, conciliation denotes the reference of a dispute to a third party, often a commission or committee, whose task is to produce a report recommending proposals for settlement. Conciliation commissions are different from commissions of inquiry because the latter do not produce concrete proposals. In this regard, conciliation is similar to arbitration. However, here also there is one vital difference. Generally, the reports of conciliation commissions are not legally binding on the parties, although the simple fact that the matter has been referred to a third party combined with the force of a formal recommendation means that the great majority of proposed settlements are not ignored. The report and the proposed solution of the conciliation commission may, of course, form the basis for future negotiations. Conciliation is, then, the middle ground between inquiry and arbitration. A settlement is proposed by a neutral third party, but it is not binding. Conciliation commissions were established by the 1899 and 1907 Hague Conventions for the Pacific Settlement of Disputes and by the General Act for the Pacific Settlement of Disputes 1928. A more recent example is provided by the *Jan Meyen Conciliation Commission (Iceland v Norway)* (1981) 20 ILM 797 on maritime delimitation. Conciliation commissions may be used as one of the dispute settlement procedures established by the 1982 Convention on the Law of the Sea.

10.6 Settlement by regional machinery

There is a great variety of regional organisations that are instrumental in the peaceful settlement of disputes. These range from political bodies such as the Organisation of American States and the African Union to economic forums such as the Caribbean Community and Common Market (Carricom) and the World Trade Organisation (formerly GATT), to more judicial bodies such as the European Court of Human Rights, the Central American Court of Justice and Inter-American Court of Human Rights. In this context, note must also be taken of the political-legal Dispute Settlement Mechanism of the Organisation for Security and Co-operation in Europe (formerly the CSCE). This Organisation has increased in importance following the massive political changes in Eastern Europe in the late twentieth century. Obviously, these forums are eminently suitable for the resolution of local disputes, and their precise terms of reference will vary accordingly.

10.7 Arbitration

The International Law Commission has defined arbitration as 'a procedure for the settlement of disputes between states by a binding award on the basis of law and as a result of an undertaking voluntarily accepted'. It is the most commonly used 'judicial' means for the settlement of disputes much more so than reference to the International Court of Justice. Arbitration awards have contributed significantly to the development of many areas of international law, and this has not diminished even now that we have more established courts. The decisions of the US–Mexican Claims Commission 1926, for example, did much to clarify the law of state responsibility, and the arbitral award in the *Island of Palmas Case* (1928) 2 RIAA 829, is the *locus classicus* on acquisition of territory. The US–Iran Claims Tribunal resolved many of the disputes that arose out of the rupture of relations between these two states in 1979 and has made significant pronouncements on the law relating to expropriation of foreign-owned property (e.g. the *Amoco Finance Case* 15 Iran–US CTR 189 (1987)).

Like all methods of pacific settlement in international law, arbitration is voluntary. States must consent beforehand to the exercise of jurisdiction by the arbitrators. This may be done on an ad hoc basis, as with the *Guinea/Guinea-Bissau Maritime Delimitation Case* 77 ILR 636 and the *Canada/France Maritime Delimitation* (1992) 31 ILM 1145, or consent may be given in advance to a specific procedure, as with the Permanent Court of Arbitration (PCA) although the submission of actual disputes may depend on further consent. This last body, established by the 1899 and 1907 Hague Conventions on Pacific Settlement, provides an institutionalised procedure for the settlement of disputes by arbitration and it has been revived in recent years as an effective mechanism for the judicial settlement of disputes. A recent example is the *Barbados/Trinidad & Tobago Maritime Delimitation Arbitration* (April 2006) and the PCA has a number of other arbitrations pending including *The Republic of Ecuador* v *The United States* (2011) on certain matters relating to investment disputes. It must also be remembered that arbitration proceedings are not limited to the determination of disputes between *states*. An important function of arbitration, and one which the ICJ cannot undertake, is to settle disputes between states and other bodies having international personality. Typically, such arbitrations involve states and multinational corporations (e.g. the pending NAFTA arbitration between Bilcon of Delaware and the Government of Canada), although exceptionally individuals may be given the right to claim directly against a state. One of the most important examples of an arbitration procedure for non-states and states is the International Centre for the Settlement of Investment Disputes, established by International Convention in 1964, which provides a forum for the settlement of disputes between states and corporations arising out of capital investment in the former's territory. Two examples of arbitrations heard under this framework are *AAPL v Sri Lanka* and *Southern Pacific v Egypt*, both important in the law of state responsibility. In addition, there is now a set of Model Rules for International Commercial Arbitration (28 ILM 231) again reflecting the practical importance of arbitration in the world of commerce.

Moving away from the machinery of arbitration, what are its legal characteristics? In general parlance, 'arbitration' can denote any settlement achieved by reference to a third party. However, as the Permanent Court of Justice indicated in its Advisory Opinion on the *Interpretation of the Treaty of Lausanne Case* (1925) PCIJ Ser. B No. 12, arbitration in international law has a more specific meaning. First, arbitration is a procedure for the settlement of a *legal* dispute. Arbitration is concerned with the rights and duties of the parties under international law and a settlement is achieved by the application of this law to the facts of the case. This is not to say that political or economic factors are irrelevant, but rather that they, of themselves, cannot affect the outcome. Like the procedure before the ICJ itself, arbitration is concerned primarily with questions of international law.

Secondly, as a general rule, arbitration awards are legally binding on the parties. Once a state has committed itself to arbitration, it is under a legal obligation to give effect to the result. In fact, despite the absence of enforcement machinery, the majority of arbitral awards are adhered to. Like decisions of the ICJ, they have an inherent force because they represent an adjudication of binding legal obligations. Of course, some awards will be ignored, as with the *Beagle Channel Arbitration (Chile v Argentina)* 17 ILM 638 which proved unacceptable to Argentina, or the parties can determine in advance that the award should not be binding. However, this last is rare and generally arbitration is a formal process leading to a legally binding settlement between the parties.

Thirdly, in arbitration proceedings, the parties may choose the arbitrators or 'judges'. Unlike disputes submitted to the International Court (but note the Chamber system considered below), parties to arbitration have direct control over both the composition of the panel and its procedure. This ensures that the panel enjoys the confidence of the parties and adds to the force of its final award. Usually, the panel will comprise an equal number of arbitrators from each disputant, plus one 'neutral' who may act as chairperson. However, it is quite possible that a single arbitrator may be appointed, again agreed by the parties, and this may be a foreign sovereign who then delegates the task to an expert, as in the *Clipperton Island Arbitration (France v Mexico)* (1932) 26 AJIL 390. Indeed, there is nothing to stop the parties appointing judges of the International Court, as happened in *Guinea/ Guinea-Bissau*, or a judge of a foreign state, as in the *Tinoco Arbitration* (1923) 1 RIAA 369. Again, arbitration panels dealing with specialised matters may include non-legal experts or lawyers with special expertise, as in the *Canada/France Maritime Delimitation Arbitration* (1992) 31 ILM 1145.

The prevalence of arbitral awards and procedures testifies to the success that this form of dispute settlement enjoys within the international community. It has the same advantages as settlement by the International Court, in that its awards are binding and made on the basis of international law, plus the added advantage that states are reassured by the fact that they can nominate arbitrators of their own choice. A panel may include technical experts and the parties may be encouraged to go to arbitration by stipulating that the award be unpublished, although this also means that public pressure to adhere to the final award is forfeited. On a practical level, the use of arbitration as a means of dispute settlement has contributed greatly to the peaceful resolution of disputes between states, as well as the development of international law. Its contribution has been felt more readily in specific areas, such as state responsibility and maritime delimitation, but the fact that the parties have a greater control over the entire proceedings means that many states prefer it to ICJ settlement if a dispute cannot be settled by negotiation.

Finally, we should also note that the ICJ itself may be used in order to review an arbitration award with which one of the disputant states is unhappy. An example is the *Senegal/Guinea-Bissau Arbitral Award Case* (1992) 31 ILM 32, where Guinea-Bissau challenged the legitimacy of a previous arbitral award made between itself and Senegal. However, as the ICJ made clear in this case, its function in such circumstances is not to hear an appeal from the arbitral award (unless, of course, such is specifically agreed to), but rather to act in a supervisory function to ensure compliance in matters of procedure and propriety etc. In similar fashion to proceedings for 'judicial review' in the High Court in the UK, if the ICJ considers the legitimacy of an arbitral award, it is not commenting on the merits of the dispute but on the legality of the award made. It was for this reason that the ICJ refused Guinea-Bissau's application for interim measures of protection in the *Senegal/Guinea-Bissau Arbitral Award Case*.

10.8 The International Court of Justice

The International Court of Justice is often thought of as the primary means for the resolution of disputes between states. As we have seen, this is not so in purely numerical terms, and only a few cases a year are referred to the Court for judicial settlement. On the other hand, the Court does command the greatest respect and even one case can have enormous political and legal consequences. The *Case Concerning the Application of the Convention on the Prevention and Punishment of the Crime of Genocide (Bosnia and Herzegovina v Serbia & Montenegro) (2007)* and the *Advisory Opinion on the Accordance with international law of the unilateral declaration of independence in respect of Kosovo (2010))* are prime examples. Of course, the extent to which the Court becomes *the* paramount judicial body, both qualitatively and quantitatively depends ultimately on the desire of states to utilise it in full measure. The development of the Chamber procedure and states' increasing acceptance of the jurisdiction of the Court indicates that it is gaining in stature the longer it operates. While there are a number of tribunals having jurisdiction over specific matters (e.g. the various settlement mechanisms under the Law of the Sea Convention 1982, the International Criminal Court and the single issue war crimes tribunals), the International Court of Justice is one of only three general, universal and permanent judicial institutions for the settlement of disputes (the others being the Permanent Court of Arbitration and the International Criminal Court). As explained in Chapter 2, it has made a significant contribution to the development of international law that should not be underestimated.

The Court is composed of fifteen judges of different nationalities, who are elected by the General Assembly and Security Council. As a matter of practice and politics these will include one judge from each of the five permanent members of the Council, although the veto does not apply in the election process. Judges are elected from candidates proposed by the national groups of the Permanent Court of Arbitration, although again in practice there is always equitable distribution among the various geographical and political groupings of UN members. In addition, any party to a dispute which does not have a national as a member of the Court may appoint an ad hoc judge, with equal powers, for the duration of any particular case in which it is involved (ICJ Statute, Art. 31). In the end result, the regular composition of the Court should represent the 'main forms of civilisation and the principal legal systems of the world' and the judges must be 'persons of high moral character, who possess the qualifications required in their respective countries for appointment to the highest judicial offices or are jurisconsuls of recognised competence in international law' (ICJ Statute, Art. 2). As a permanent member of the Security Council, the UK has always provided an ICJ judge, which included the first female judge.

Up to 1982, every dispute submitted to the Court had been heard by the full complement of fifteen, sixteen or seventeen judges. Since then, the Court has been willing to act under Art. 26 of its Statute, which provides that three or more judges may hear a case acting as a Chamber of the Court. The first such example was the *Gulf of Maine Case (US v Canada)* 1982 ICJ Rep 3, where there was a Chamber of five, and the procedure has been adopted subsequently in a number of cases, including the *Frontier Dispute Case (Burkina Faso v Mali)* 1985 ICJ Rep 6, the *Land and Maritime Boundaries Case (El Salvador v Honduras)* 1987 ICJ Rep 10 and 1992 ICJ Rep 92, the *Elettronica Sicula Case (US v Italy)* 1989 ICJ Rep 15 and the *Application for Revision of the Judgment of 11 September 1992 in the Case Concerning the Land, Island and Maritime Frontier Dispute (El Salvador v Honduras)* 2003 ICJ Rep. It is not clear whether the use of Chambers will be maintained, although they might be thought to be attractive to states in that the parties are able, in practice, to exert great influence over the choice of judges. However, no Chamber constituted under Art. 26 is currently active and in 2006 the ICJ decided not to hold elections to fill the places in its Chamber for Environmental Matters (which must therefore be regarded as defunct). It may be that the Chamber system was divisive within the ICJ, with certain judges being regarded as more appropriate than others.

10.8.1 Access to the Court

It is a basic principle of the ICJ system that 'only states may be parties in cases before the Court' (ICJ Statute Art. 34), and consequently only states may be parties in contentious cases (for Advisory Opinions see later in the chapter). However, just because a state has 'access' to the Court does not imply that the Court necessarily has *jurisdiction* to settle a dispute between it and another state with access. The question of access to the Court is completely separate from the question of whether the Court has jurisdiction over a dispute referred to it. Access is logically prior to the question of jurisdiction and a lack of access means that a submitted case is, without more, unable to proceed (*Legality of the Use of Force Cases* (2004)). However, if a state is a party to the Statute, or otherwise has access, it has the *potential* to refer any dispute to the Court and the Court will then go on to decide whether all parties to that dispute have accepted the Court's jurisdiction (see sections 10.8.4 and 10.8.5).

In many cases, questions of access pose no real problems. First, the ICJ is one of the principal organs of the United Nations and its Statute is an integral part of the Charter. Consequently, all members of the United Nations are *ipso facto* parties to the Statute and therefore have access to the Court and this is the primary method by which access is obtained (ICJ Statute, Art. 35(1)). Secondly, non-members of the United Nations may be parties to the Statute in its own right (Art. 35(1)) and thirdly, non-parties to the Statute may have access to the Court under special conditions laid down by the Security Council (Art. 35(2)), as with Albania in the *Corfu Channel Case* 1949 ICJ Rep 4. Fourthly, Art. 35(2) also permits access under 'special provisions contained in treaties in force' and the ICJ has confirmed in the *Case concerning the Application of the Convention on the Prevention and Punishment of the Crime of Genocide (Bosnia and Herzegovina v Yugoslavia (Serbia & Montenegro)) (Indication of Provisional Measures)* 1993 ICJ Rep 325, that this gives a right of access to the Court independent of a state being party to the Statute and independent of special conditions laid down by the Security Council. In other words, a clause in a treaty referring a matter arising under the treaty to the ICJ operates as an independent access clause for the parties to that treaty.

This may seem simple enough, but in practice Art. 35(2) has generated much judicial comment. In a series of cases concerning the former Yugoslav constituent republics, Bosnia-Herzegovina has claimed that both it and Serbia have access to the court (and indeed that the Court has jurisdiction) under Art. IX of the Genocide Convention 1948, being a special provision of a treaty in force. In the *Case concerning the Application of the Convention on the Prevention and Punishment of the Crime of Genocide (Bosnia and Herzegovina v Yugoslavia (Serbia & Montenegro)) (Indication of Provisional Measures)* 1993 ICJ Rep 325, the ICJ considered that Art. 35(2), operating on Art. IX of the Genocide Convention, did indeed provide a basis for access and jurisdiction and thus Serbia was susceptible to the Court's control. However, in the *Legality of the Use of Force Cases* (2004) (Serbia v NATO countries) a majority of the Court decided that 'special provisions contained in treaties in force' within Art. 35(2) meant *only* treaties actually in force when the Statute of the ICJ itself entered into force – being treaties in force in 1945. Thus, a provision in any treaty entering into force after the Statute (of which there are very, very many) could not confer access (or jurisdiction) via Art. 35(2). It must be said that this narrow interpretation was subject to a powerful dissent by seven judges in the *Legality of the Use of Force Cases* and their alternate view – that Art. 35(2) operated on any treaty in force, regardless of when that treaty came into force – appears to be consistent with the drafting history of Art. 35(2) and previous ICJ practice. Consequently, when the Court tried the merits in the *Case Concerning the Application of the Convention on the Prevention and Punishment of the Crime of Genocide (Bosnia and Herzegovina v Serbia & Montenegro)* (ICJ 2007), a majority (including many of the minority in the *Legality of the Use of Force Cases*), made it clear that they believed the decision in the 1993 *Genocide Case* (Provisional Measures) to be correct and that Art. 35(2) should *not* be interpreted narrowly and should operate on all treaties containing a jurisdictional clause. It goes without saying that this uncertainty as to the scope of the Article is unhelpful, although it should be remembered that the vast majority of states have access to the Court under one of the other provisions. Nevertheless, this argument over the scope of Art. 35(2) – i.e. to what treaties does it refer? – will have consequences for the *jurisdiction* of the Court (see section 10.8.4).

In addition to this lingering uncertainty, the *Genocide Cases* also revealed another disagreement between members of the ICJ. Serbia had been suspended from the rights of membership of the United Nations from 1992–2000 in the sense that it could not exercise the rights of 'Yugoslavia'. In 2000, it was admitted to membership under its own name. Consequently, Serbia argued that it was not a member of the UN during 1992–2000, and hence not a party to the ICJ Statute, and hence could not be subject to the control of the Court in any cases arising in this period. In the 1993 *Genocide* decision, the ICJ indicated, without formally deciding, that this hiatus (1992–2000) did *not* prevent Serbia being treated as party to the Statute and thus subject to the Court. Nevertheless, in the *Legality of the Use of Force Cases* (2004), the ICJ appeared to change its mind and regarded Serbia as *not* being a party to the Statute during this period (the Court thus dismissed the case), having become a party only on admission in its own name in 2000. When then, in 2007, the ICJ considered the merits in the *Genocide Case*, it might be thought that it would follow the *Legality of the Use of Force Cases* and decide that Serbia was not a party to the Statute during the relevant time, and indeed Serbia argued this very point. In fact, the majority in the 2007 decision decided that it had already dealt with this point in its 1993 judgment and so the matter was *res judicata* – already being decided by a binding decision of the Court. Thus, in 2007, Serbia could be a party to a dispute before the Court. As with the argument over the scope of Art. 35(2) considered previously, these different views of a state's status before the Court, emanating from differently composed panels of judges, does little either for the credibility of the Court itself or the credibility of the judgments in the cases. On the matter of substance, it may well be that the 1993 judgment is correct and that the *Legality of the Use of Force* judgment wrongly equates the suspension of the membership of Serbia with a loss of its status under the ICJ Statute. However, whatever the correct answer, it is the integrity of the Court that is damaged by these inconsistent findings.

Finally, we should note that non-state entities might request an Advisory Opinion from the Court in the exercise of its functions, as provided for in Art. 96 of the UN Charter. These agencies include the General Assembly (see e.g. *Advisory Opinion on the Legality of the Use of Nuclear Weapons* (1996) and the *Palestinian Wall Case* (2004)), the Security Council, the IAEA and all the specialised agencies except the Universal Postal Union. In fact, the Secretary-General of the UN has mooted the idea that he be authorised to request an Advisory Opinion, but this has met with a lukewarm response from some states, including the UK.

10.8.2 Admissibility in contentious cases

It is a general principle that a dispute must be admissible before the Court will exercise jurisdiction. As a court of law, the ICJ has an inherent power to decline to exercise jurisdiction for it must safeguard the judicial function. Consequently, before the Court will act, it must establish 'first, that the dispute before it is a legal dispute, in the sense of a dispute capable of being settled by the application of principles and rules of international law, and secondly, that the Court has jurisdiction to deal with it, and that that jurisdiction is not fettered by any circumstance rendering the application inadmissible': *Border and Transborder Armed Actions Case (Nicaragua v Honduras) (Jurisdiction and Admissibility)* 1988 ICJ Rep 69.

The concept of 'admissibility' can arise in many contexts, although it will be triggered by an objection to the exercise of jurisdiction by a state that wishes to avoid settlement by the ICJ: for example, the USA raised five objections to admissibility (and four to jurisdiction) in the *Case Concerning Avena and other Mexican Nationals (Mexico v United States of America)* 2004 ICJ Rep, none of which were successful. As a general principle, when considering issues of admissibility the Court is astute to ensure that its judgment will have practical consequences, in the sense that it should affect a state's legal obligations or resolve some area of uncertainty or contention. The Court may make a declaratory judgment but only if this is consistent with the judicial nature of its function (*Northern Cameroons Case* 1963 ICJ Rep 15). On a more specific level it is clear that the Court will not decline jurisdiction merely because the dispute between the parties has 'political' or 'military' overtones. The Court is not concerned with the political inspiration which may have led a state to choose pacific settlement (*Nicaragua v Honduras*) and may accept jurisdiction even though the legal issue has political consequences, as with the matter of apartheid in the *South-West Africa Cases (Preliminary Objections)* 1962 ICJ Rep 319. The simple fact that a dispute has 'political' aspects does not make it non-justiciable (*Nicaragua v Honduras*). Similarly, in *Nicaragua v USA*, the Court held the dispute admissible despite the fact that the Security Council was seised of another aspect of the dispute. This last point, however, must be read in the light of more recent decisions. In the *Lockerbie Case (Libya v UK)* 1992 ICJ Rep para. 22, the Court declined to exercise aspects of its jurisdiction (e.g. to indicate interim measures of protection) because the Security Council had taken concrete enforcement action under the Charter (as opposed to simply discussing one aspect of the situation). However, in the *Congo Case* (1 July 2000) interim measures were granted, on terms very similar to those adopted by the Security Council in a previous resolution (SC Res. 1304, 16 June 2000), because the Council had not actually taken a binding decision. This rather narrow ground of distinction between *Lockerbie* (binding Council resolution) and *Congo* (solution 'demanded' by Council but not binding formally) illustrates that the relationship between Court and Council in matters touching international peace and security is not yet settled although the *Congo Case* rationale was adopted in the *Palestinian Wall Advisory Opinion* (2004). In fact, the Court in recent years has adopted a more robust attitude to admissibility that goes back to its early days pre-*Lockerbie Case*. So, in the *Advisory Opinion on the Accordance with international law of the unilateral declaration of independence in respect of Kosovo* (2008), the Court was prepared to rule on a legal question even if this concerned contentious matters before the Assembly and Security Council and in respect of a dispute where the Security Council had indeed taken concrete measures. Moreover, in the contentious case, the *Application of the Interim Accord of 13 September 1995 (The Former Yugoslav Republic of Macedonia v Greece)* (2011), the ICJ decided that the case was admissible despite the fact that aspects of the dispute between Greece and the Former Yugoslav

Republic of Macedonia were subject to the Security Council attempts at a negotiated settlement and clearly involved matters of high politics.

An objection based on admissibility can also cover alleged procedural defects in a state's application to the Court. For example, in the *Case concerning Certain Phosphate Lands in Nauru (Nauru v Australia) (Preliminary Objections)* 1992 ICJ Rep 240, Australia used the inadmissibility umbrella to allege, *inter alia*, that Nauru's claim should be dismissed as being out of time or because Australia had been discharged of all possible responsibility by termination of the Nauru Trusteeship by the General Assembly. Neither objection was upheld on the merits. Similarly, in the *Avena Case*, Mexico objected to the US objections to jurisdiction and admissibility (i.e. a claim that the objections to admissibility were themselves inadmissible!) on the ground that the US objections had been filed out of time. Once again however, the Court interpreted its Charter – with some justification – in the manner that both preserved the judicial function and permitted the Court to consider all aspects of the dispute.

As these cases illustrate, questions of admissibility can arise for a variety of reasons. Alleged failure to exhaust local remedies, undue interference with the domestic affairs of states, lack of legal subject matter, lack of the right of diplomatic protection over the injured persons (i.e. they are not nationals) and undue delay have all been alleged as grounds on which the Court should declare an application inadmissible. However, as the *Avena Case* illustrates, the Court is always astute to prevent states from escaping from judicial settlement of their disputes by spurious or ill-conceived admissibility claims. In the *Avena Case* itself, the Court rejected all five of the US admissibility objections and in so doing followed a pattern set from its earliest days.

10.8.3 Interim measures of protection

The Court has an inherent jurisdiction to take such action as is necessary to ensure that its exercise of jurisdiction over the merits of a dispute will not be frustrated, if and when such jurisdiction is established. Article 41 of the ICJ Statute provides that, before deciding the question of jurisdiction, the Court has the power 'to indicate ... any provisional measures which ought to be taken to preserve the respective rights of either party'. Given that these measures may be indicated before any disputed question of jurisdiction is settled, this is a form of involvement in the affairs of states that does not depend on their consent, apart from original signature of the Statute. Indeed, this may be the reason why interim measures of protection are 'indicated' rather than 'ordered' and this terminology was thought to ensure that they were not legally binding in the classic sense. However, it now appears from the *La Grand Case (Germany v United States)* 2001 ICJ Rep, that failure to take action to preserve the status quo of a dispute as 'indicated' by provisional measures itself amounts to a breach of international obligation, a decision confirmed. Thus, in that case, the USA failed to observe the provisional measures indicated against it and the Court found that it was thereby in breach of the obligations incumbent on it. Likewise, in *Case Concerning the Application of the Convention on the Prevention and Punishment of the Crime of Genocide (Bosnia and Herzegovina v Serbia & Montenegro)* (ICJ 2007), Serbia was found to have violated its obligations to comply with the provisional measures indicated in 1993 and thus to have incurred international responsibility. In other words, the 'indication' of provisional measures can involve a binding obligation to comply with the Court's order and this makes them effectively legally binding.

One of the most urgent questions in this regard is the degree to which the Court must be satisfied of at least the prospect of jurisdiction over the merits of the dispute before interim measures can be indicated. According to the *Nuclear Test Cases (Interim Protection)* 1973 ICJ Rep 99, the Court 'ought not to indicate such measures unless the provisions invoked … appear, prima facie, to afford a basis on which the jurisdiction of the Court might be founded' and this was reaffirmed in the *Prevention of Genocide Case* (1993), in the *Pulp Mills on the River Uruguay Case (Uruguay v Argentina)* (2007) and the *Certain Activities carried out by Nicaragua in the Border Area Case (Costa Rica v Nicaragua)* (2010). However, if there is no such prima facie case (sometimes called a manifest lack of jurisdiction – *Fisheries Jurisdiction Case (UK, Federal Republic of Germany v Iceland)* (1972)), interim measures cannot be indicated as in the *Case Concerning Armed Activities on the Territory of the Congo (New Application: 2002) (Democratic Republic of the Congo v Rwanda)* (2002). In this regard, note also the view taken in the *Passage Through the Great Belt Case (Finland v Denmark) Provisional Measures* 1992 ICJ Rep 3, where the Court was faced with a Danish argument (upon which it did not adjudicate directly because provisional measures were not thought appropriate) that no measures should be indicated because, although there may have been a prima facie case for jurisdiction (which in fact was not disputed), there was no prima facie evidence that Finland had any *rights* which could be protected. What this illustrates is that a balance has to be struck between preserving the rights of an injured (or potentially injured) state and the right of the other state not to be hamstrung by an indication of measures by the Court in a case where it is not clear whether it has consented to the exercise of the Court's powers. Of course, this question now has more practical significance because interim measures are effectively legally binding, and we should not forget that the political pressure to conform to the Court's 'indication' will be great. Unfortunately, this pressure has not always proved effective and the indication of interim measures has been ignored in a number of cases, such as the *Fisheries Cases*, the *Nuclear Test Cases*, the *US Diplomatic and Consular Staff in Tehran Cases (US v Iran)* 1979 ICJ Rep 7, *Nicaragua v USA* 1984 ICJ Rep 169 and the *Case Concerning the Application of the Convention on the Prevention and Punishment of the Crime of Genocide (Bosnia and Herzegovina v Serbia & Montenegro)* (ICJ 2007).

The Court is not bound to order interim measures and there are several examples where it has refused a request. As noted previously, interim measures were refused in the *Lockerbie Case* because the Security Council was actively dealing with the dispute, and they were also refused in *Guinea-Bissau v Senegal* 1990 ICJ Rep 64 and the *Pulp Mills on the River Uruguay Case (Uruguay v Argentina)* (2007). Notably, the Court refused to indicate interim measures in the *Great Belt Case* because there was no factual possibility that Denmark would infringe any of Finland's rights before the merits of the case could be heard, and refused Uruguay's request in the *Pulp Mills Case* because there was no risk of irreparable prejudice to Uruguay's rights. Nevertheless, in these cases the Court reaffirmed the general principles that any action taken by a state while a dispute was pending before the Court which affected the merits of that dispute could not improve its legal position and reminded the parties of their general obligations to settle disputes according to international law.

By way of contrast, interim measures were indicated in the *Prevention of Genocide Case* (1993) where the statehood of the disputants was in doubt, where the jurisdiction of the Court was marginal, where the Security Council was dealing with a very similar issue and where the measures indicated came very close to blaming one of the parties. Likewise, in the *Request for interpretation of the Judgment of 15 June 1962 in the case concerning the Temple of Preah Vihear (Cambodia v Thailand) (Cambodia v Thailand)* (2011), the Court indicated provisional measures in respect of a case that it had considered first in 1962 and where the basis of the Court's jurisdiction to indicate measures seemed to be only that a request had been made to interpret that earlier judgment.

Of course, each case is different and sweeping generalisations are best avoided. So interim measures were granted in the *Land and Maritime Boundary Case (Cameroon v Nigeria) (Provisional Measures)* 1996 ICJ Rep 13, the *La Grand Case*, the *Avena Case* and in the *Congo Case* (1 July 2000) and the *Certain Activities carried out by Nicaragua in the Border Area (Costa Rica v Nicaragua)* (2011), the last two of which both involved the alleged ongoing use of force. They were refused in the *Legality of the Use of Force Case (Yugoslavia v Belgium)*, and the *Congo Case (New Application: 2002)* primarily because of a lack of prima facie jurisdiction and also refused in the *Arrest Warrant Case (Congo v Belgium)* because on the facts that prevailed at the time of the hearing, they were no longer necessary and in the *Pulp Mills Case* because the applicant's rights were not at risk of serious harm. Lastly, the *Great Belt Case* also makes it clear that the state asking for interim protection is not under an obligation to undertake to compensate the object of an interim order for any damage caused by observance of that order should the claim be dismissed on the merits. However, it is not clear whether this can remain the position now that the Court has determined that interim measures of protection can be effectively binding. If they are legally binding and complied with, it would seem to follow that the state making the (successful) request should compensate the other party should it emerge on the merits that there was no violation of international law.

10.8.4 Jurisdiction in contentious cases

'When considering the jurisdiction of the International Court of Justice in contentious cases, I take as my point of departure the conviction that the Court's jurisdiction must rest upon the free will of sovereign States, clearly and categorically expressed, to grant the Court the competence to settle the dispute in question', (Judge Oda: *Nicaragua v Honduras (Jurisdiction and Admissibility)* 1988 ICJ Rep 69 at 109).

It is a general principle of international law that a state cannot be compelled to undertake the settlement of a dispute, least of all by submission to a third party. As far as the International Court is concerned, this means that its jurisdiction in contentious cases depends on the consent of states, *Legality of Use of Force (Yugoslavia v Belgium), Provisional Measures* 1999 (I) ICJ Rep, *Congo Case (New Application: 2002) (Congo v Rwanda)* 2002 ICJ Rep 1999 (I). As we have seen, such consent is not given merely by a state becoming a party to the Statute of the Court or otherwise having access. There are, however, a variety of ways by which a state may signify its consent to jurisdiction, including an optional system whereby consent is given in advance of any dispute arising. These are examined subsequently (sections 10.8.5.1–10.8.5.9).

In theory at least, the requirement of consent is a strict one, as indicated by Judge Oda earlier. For example, if a third state's international responsibilities are closely tied to the dispute between the 'plaintiff/claimant' and 'respondent', the Court cannot decide the matter unless this third party also consents (*Monetary Gold Removed from Rome Case (Preliminary Question)* 1954 ICJ Rep 19). However, as a Chamber of the Court emphasised in the *Frontier Dispute Case (Burkina Faso v Mali)*, the Court should not decline to exercise its jurisdiction merely because the rights of a third state would have to be considered at some later stage. In such circumstances, the third state is protected by Art. 59 of the Statute (award does not bind non-parties to the hearing) and by its ability to intervene under Art. 62 or Art. 63 as in the *Land and Maritime Boundary Case (Cameroon v Nigeria)* 2002 ICJ Rep. It seems, then, that the Court will not decline jurisdiction because the interests of a third state may be affected unless they are so central as to make it impossible to settle the actual matter outstanding between the parties to the dispute (see e.g. *Cameroon v Nigeria (Application for Intervention)* (21 October 1999)). Clearly, the line can be a fine one. In the *Nauru Case (Nauru v Australia)*, a majority of the Court refused to dismiss Nauru's application even though both New Zealand and the UK were members with Australia of the Administering Authority of Nauru whose actions were being impugned. The Court did not believe that the obligations of New Zealand and the UK formed the subject matter of the dispute, at least in so far as Australia's own responsibility was concerned. This is open to the criticism that it is hardly credible that New Zealand and the UK could avoid international responsibility if Australia was held internationally liable for the acts of the Administering Authority, an Authority in which all three states played an equal part. The Court in this case has used Art. 59 effectively to sidestep the *Monetary Gold* principle. In contrast, in the *Case Concerning East Timor (Portugal v Australia)* 1995 ICJ Rep 89, the Court declined jurisdiction on the ground that Australia's alleged responsibility to Portugal (being the administering power of East Timor) for concluding certain agreements with Indonesia concerning East Timor, could not be determined without reference to the position of Indonesia, with whom Australia had dealt as the *de facto* power in the territory. Indonesia was not a party to the proceedings. As the Court said, the legality of Australia's behaviour could not be assessed without entering into the question of the legality of Indonesia's assumption of power over East Timor. The difference between this and the *Nauru* case seems to be that in *East Timor* an assessment of the absent third state's rights was a precondition to the liability of the defendant, whereas in *Nauru* the absent third states' rights might be called into question but would not affect the defendant's position at all. Many critics would argue that the *Monetary Gold* principle should operate to deny jurisdiction in both these situations.

It is also clear, as the *Monetary Gold Case* again illustrates, that it is not for the state-parties to decide whether consent has been validly given. This is a question of law to be resolved in the light of the relevant facts. The Court has the power to determine the limits of its own jurisdiction and its decision in this regard is binding. This is inherent in its nature as a Court and in a sense is thus independent of the consent of the parties. As reiterated by the Court in the *Fisheries Jurisdiction Case (Spain v Canada)* 1998 ICJ Rep, 'the establishment or otherwise of jurisdiction is not a matter for the parties but for the Court itself'. Consequently, the raising of a preliminary objection to jurisdiction does not destroy a state's consent, for it is up to the Court to determine whether the objection is valid. In practice, in recent years the Court has been called upon to decide a wide range of preliminary matters but it is apparent that it has been reluctant to decline jurisdiction unless this is unavoidable. In *Nicaragua v USA*, a majority of the Court appeared willing to stretch the concept of jurisdiction to breaking point and this was followed up by interesting acceptances of jurisdiction in the *Prevention of Genocide Case*, the *Maritime Delimitation and Territorial Questions Case (Qatar v Bahrain)* 1994 ICJ Rep 112, 1995 ICJ Rep 6 and the *Nauru Case*. These cases are evidence of a positive approach whereby the Court will seek to assert jurisdiction if at all possible (some would say plausible) and deny it only in the clearest cases, as in *East Timor*. That said, the *Fisheries Jurisdiction Case* saw the Court decline to accept jurisdiction because of its interpretation of Canada's Declaration under the Optional System, and the Court has decided that it should decline jurisdiction in the *Certain Property Case (Lichtenstein v Germany)* (2006) because of its interpretation of when the dispute between the parties actually arose. Likewise, jurisdiction was declined in the *Legality of the Use of Force Cases* on a variety of grounds, both contentious and non-contentious. In addition, as we shall see, the assertion of jurisdiction may depend on fine questions about the meaning and scope of a state's Declaration under the Optional System, as well as difficult questions of treaty interpretation (*Qatar v Bahrain* and *Avena Case*) or issues about the sources of international law (*Nicaragua v USA*) or even of the capacities of international personality (*Legality of the Use of Force Cases*). In all this, it should be remembered that the Court exists and operates only with the agreement and approval of states. It was intended to play a limited role in the system of international law, and then only at the clear behest of states. Should the Court attempt to usurp or disregard the sovereign will of states by an over-zealous assertion of jurisdiction, it will lose their respect and cease to be a significant force in the development of international law and in the peaceful settlement of disputes. It is better that the Court remain true to the principle of jurisdiction based on consent and decide only a few cases a year, than seek to expand its jurisdiction and decide none. At the same time, it must not allow states to escape the consent they have given simply because they *now* object to the Court having power over their dispute. It is a balancing act.

10.8.5 The acquisition of jurisdiction by the ICJ

10.8.5.1 As provided in the UN Charter

Under Art. 36(1) of the Statute, the Court has jurisdiction over 'all matters specifically provided for in the Charter of the UN'. This provision was designed to trigger a jurisdictional clause (i.e. a referral to the ICJ), which was included in preliminary drafts of the Charter. If the clause had survived, it would have provided for compulsory jurisdiction for all UN members for certain types of dispute. However, such a provision was never inserted in the final text of the Charter and the better view is that this phrase now has no meaning. In the *Corfu Channel Case*, the UK argued that these words could be interpreted to refer to a Security Council resolution which recommended that the parties submit their dispute to the Court. If this argument had been accepted, it would have created a compulsory jurisdiction exercisable by the Council at will and without the consent of the parties. While a majority of the

Court in this case found it unnecessary to decide the point, there are weighty dicta in the Separate Opinions of seven judges rejecting the UK argument. Their view was that the Security Council could make only 'recommendations' and they affirmed that the basic principle of jurisdiction was that it was fundamentally consensual. This is clearly the correct view and it must be that this part of Art. 36 is otiose. In the *Case Concerning the Aerial Incident of 10 August 1999 (Pakistan v India) (Jurisdiction)*, 2000 ICJ Rep, Pakistan attempted to rely on Art. 36(1) without success, its argument being rejected swiftly by the court on the simple (and correct) ground that the UN Charter itself contains no jurisdictional clause.

10.8.5.2 Consent ad hoc

Article 36(1) of the Statute also stipulates that the Court is to have jurisdiction over 'all cases which the parties refer to it'. Ad hoc consent to the jurisdiction of the Court is an express form of consent, given by the parties at the time of a particular dispute and in respect of that dispute alone. The classic method of consent ad hoc is by special agreement (or *compromis*), whereby the parties agree by treaty to refer a specific matter to the Court. It is, however, possible to achieve jurisdiction under this head by means of an initial unilateral application by one state, provided always that the 'respondent' state signifies its acceptance of jurisdiction with a separate act of consent. Both these methods are simply examples of the wider principle that voluntary submission to the jurisdiction is not to be restricted by requirements of form. The only test is whether such consent has actually been given. In practice, the usual method is the *compromis*, for this usually avoids doubt and presents a defined issue to the Court, as in the *Minquiers and Ecrehos Case (France v UK)* 1953 ICJ Rep 47, *El Salvador v Honduras* (1987), *Sovereignty over Pulau Ligitan and Pulau Sipadan Case (Indonesia v Malaysia)* 2002 ICJ Rep, the *Case Concerning Sovereignty over Pedra Branca (Malaysia v Singapore)* 2003 ICJ Rep and the *Frontier Dispute (Burkina Faso/ Niger)* (2010).

In similar fashion, a state may give ad hoc consent to the exercise of jurisdiction unilaterally, as where the other party already is subject to the jurisdiction of the Court and the unilateral consent is a way of creating a consensual jurisdictional bond – as in the *Certain Criminal Proceedings in France Case (Congo v France)* (2003) and the *Certain Questions Concerning Mutual Assistance in Criminal Matters (Djibouti v France)* (2006) where France gave ad hoc consent. Even here, however, things can go wrong. In the *Maritime Delimitation and Territorial Questions Case (Qatar v Bahrain)*, there was considerable doubt about the precise circumstances in which the parties' agreement to confer jurisdiction on the Court could be triggered. While both accepted that they had agreed that their dispute should be submitted to the Court, Qatar argued that the agreement permitted this to be done by means of a unilateral application, while Bahrain argued that the agreement permitted only a joint-submission. By interpreting the agreement liberally (on which see Chapter 3) the Court agreed with Qatar, but the case illustrates that even the completion of a specific agreement to confer jurisdiction is not watertight.

10.8.5.3 Consent post hoc (*forum prorogatum*)

It is possible that the Court may be invested with jurisdiction subsequent to the initiation of proceedings by one of the parties. This may occur if, while the Court is considering the unilateral application of one state, the other expressly or impliedly signifies its consent to the jurisdiction. In such circumstances, jurisdiction is by consent post hoc or prorogation. This is a perfectly acceptable doctrine if it is applied only in those cases where it is certain that consent has been given. In this sense, it is no more than a particular example of the general principle considered earlier that no particular form of consent is required. Generally, however, the Court should be slow to infer consent simply by reason of some communication between the Court and the respondent state. In the *Corfu Channel Case*, Albania was taken to have consented to the exercise of jurisdiction, after a unilateral application by the UK, by reason of a letter which was fairly clear. Similarly, in the *Mavrommatis Palestine Concessions Case (Jurisdiction)* (1924) PCIJ Ser. A No. 2, the UK was held to have consented to jurisdiction over matters which had previously been excluded by her, by reason of her subsequent written pleadings on those very points. However, it is certain that simply appearing before the ICJ to argue that a case referred to it is either inadmissible or that the ICJ does not have jurisdiction *cannot* be taken to be a submission to the jurisdiction – *Case Concerning Armed Activities on the Territory of the Congo (New Application: 2002) (Democratic Republic of the Congo v Rwanda)*, and the *Case Concerning the Application of the Convention on the Prevention and Punishment of the Crime of Genocide (Bosnia and Herzegovina v Serbia & Montenegro)* (ICJ 2007). It would be absurd to think otherwise and for this reason it will be only rarely that the ICJ has jurisdiction by this route.

10.8.5.4 Consent ante hoc – treaties

A third head of jurisdiction under Art. 36(1) is 'all matters specially provided for ... in treaties or conventions in force'. Many multilateral and bilateral treaties contain clauses granting the Court jurisdiction in advance over the subject matter of the treaty. In a sense, this is a form of 'compulsory' jurisdiction. If a state has accepted a jurisdictional clause in a treaty, when a dispute arises concerning that treaty, it is subject to the jurisdiction of the Court at the suit of other treaty-parties whether it likes it or not. However, like the optional system considered later, the ultimate basis of jurisdiction is the consent which the state gives when it signs the treaty and, indeed, some of these 'jurisdictional clauses' are also optional, in that a state may be permitted to sign the treaty without accepting the additional obligation to submit future disputes to the Court. Examples of jurisdiction arising under a clause in a multilateral treaty include *Nicaragua v Honduras*, where Art. XXXI of the Pact of Bogota provided for reference to the ICJ (see also the *Certain Activities carried out by Nicaragua in the Border Area (Costa Rica v Nicaragua)* (2010) and the *Construction of a Road in Costa Rica along the San Juan River (Nicaragua v Costa Rica) Case* (2011)), the *Prevention of Genocide Case* 1993 and 2007 where the Court's jurisdiction arose under Art. IX of the Genocide Convention and the *Avena Case* where the Court's jurisdiction arose under the Optional Protocol to the Vienna Convention on Consular Relations 1963. An example of jurisdiction arising under a jurisdictional clause in a bilateral treaty is the *Territorial Dispute Case (Libya v Chad)* 1994 ICJ Rep 6.

In the *Certain Property Case (Liechtenstein v Germany)* (2006), Liechtenstein sought to found jurisdiction on the European Convention for the Peaceful Settlement of Disputes 1957. Ultimately, this was unsuccessful because the treaty itself limited the circumstances in which the ICJ could have jurisdiction and the facts of this dispute fell outside the jurisdictional clause. Thus, as with every other provision in a treaty, a jurisdictional clause is open to interpretation and may even be made subject to a reservation – provided the reservation is not prohibited and does not conflict with the object and purpose of the treaty – *Armed Activities on the Territory of Congo Case (New Application 2002: Congo v Rwanda).*

It is also clear that for states not otherwise having access to the court, Art. 35(2) of the Statute may provide both a right of access and a ground for jurisdiction. This provision has already been considered in the context of access, but all that has been said there about the interpretation of the article applies with equal force when the clause gives jurisdiction. Thus, in the *Genocide Cases* 1993 and 2007, it was possible that Serbia could be held subject to the jurisdiction of the ICJ under Art. 35(2), in its reference to 'treaties in force' as an alternative ground to holding that Serbia was a party to the state and thus subject to jurisdiction under Art. 36(1).

10.8.5.5 Consent ante hoc – the Optional System – Article 36(2)

Under Art. 36(2) of the Statute of the ICJ, states may accept, in advance, the jurisdiction of the Court. Acceptance of jurisdiction is by means of a unilateral Declaration of Acceptance, deposited with the UN Secretary-General. The system is optional in the sense that states may become parties to the Statute without making Declarations of Acceptance. However, states accepting jurisdiction in this manner are then bound vis-à-vis all other states declaring acceptance under the system. Once acceptance is deposited, the state enters into a consensual bond with all other members of the system, irrespective of the time at which Declarations were made. The consensual bond exists from the first moment of deposit and not at the later date that other states are informed of the acceptance (*Case Concerning the Land and Maritime Boundary (Cameroon v Nigeria) (Preliminary Objections)* 1998 ICJ Rep 275). For example, when Japan declared acceptance in 1958, it came under the jurisdiction of the Court in respect of potential disputes with the UK (1963, renewed 2004 in a different form) and then with respect to Barbados who accepted in 1980. Article 36(2) was invoked both by Nauru and Portugal when they began proceedings against Australia in 1989 and 1991 respectively. It was also invoked by Denmark to bring Norway before the Court in the *Jan Meyen Case* 1993 ICJ Rep 38, the first example of compulsory jurisdiction in a maritime delimitation case. Again, the Optional System is a form of compulsory jurisdiction (although it rests ultimately on consent), for a state is bound by its acceptance in respect of future disputes, regardless of its views at that later time.

The effect of acceptance of jurisdiction under the Optional System is well illustrated by the *Rights of Passage over Indian Territory Case (Preliminary Objections)* 1957 ICJ Rep 125. Portugal and India were in dispute over certain territories in Asia and whereas India had accepted the jurisdiction of the Court under the Optional System, Portugal had not. However, on 19 December 1955 Portugal deposited a Declaration of Acceptance of jurisdiction and on the 22nd made an application to the Court. In objecting to jurisdiction, India protested that it had no notice of Portugal's intention to join the system and therefore no chance of consenting to jurisdiction vis-à-vis her. If the Indian government had known of Portugal's plans it would have withdrawn its own Declaration or at least deposited a reservation. In rejecting India's argument, the Court explained that a consensual bond was created as soon as Declarations were deposited and potential jurisdiction existed from that point. This was reiterated to Nigeria's disadvantage in *Cameroon v Nigeria*, where Nigeria's claim that it was bound to jurisdiction only when it was informed of

Cameroon's acceptance was rejected. Moreover, since the Court is seised of jurisdiction on the day an application is filed (confirmed in *Cameroon* v *Nigeria*), the unilateral action of one party in withdrawing its Declaration after this date is without effect. Consequently, India's substitution of a more restrictive Declaration on 7 January 1956 to escape jurisdiction in the *Rights of Passage Case* was ineffective.

It is also clear that the consensual bond created by deposit of a Declaration has full legal effect in much the same way as a treaty obligation. Thus, in *Nicaragua* v *USA*, the USA had specified in its Declaration of 1946 that acceptance of compulsory jurisdiction was terminable on six months' notice, but then sought to exclude a certain class of case without giving such notice. The Court held that the proposed modification was equivalent to a termination and that the USA was bound by its own stipulation and could not therefore withdraw before expiry of the notice period. This was so even though the Declaration of Nicaragua contained no such provision concerning notice. Indeed, some members of the Court went further and suggested that Declarations generally could not be terminated without reasonable notice, by analogy with the requirements of good faith in the law of treaties. The plain effect of the *Nicaragua* decision is that although the deposit of a Declaration is a voluntary act, once it is made it places the state under a binding legal obligation which can be altered only in accordance with its own terms. Potentially, then, the Optional System provides a powerful and effective method by which the Court may gain jurisdiction in advance over disputes between states. Of course, much depends on the take up of the System and, as at 1 September there were 68 Declarations (including 7 PCIJ 'transfers'), not including the USA which had withdrawn in October 1985 after the *Nicaragua* case and France which withdrew in 1974. This is very promising but, as we shall examine, because the system is based on consent, there are several reasons why a state's potential liability to jurisdiction under the Optional System may be limited in practice.

10.8.5.6 Reservations under the Optional System

The Statute of the Court makes it clear that Declarations of Acceptance may be made unconditionally or subject to reservations. In practice, most states depositing Declarations incorporate some form of reservation, the effect of which is to limit the matters over which the Court may exercise jurisdiction. There are several types of reservations which a state may use, including the reservation of specific matters, as with the Philippines and its reservation (i.e. exclusion) of disputes concerning its continental shelf. Likewise, many states reserve matters pertaining to their land or maritime borders and many Commonwealth countries reserve disputes with fellow members, as do the UK, Canada and India, the last relying on the reservation successfully in *Pakistan* v *India* (2000). Perhaps the most common reservations are those made *ratione temporis*, that is, those dealing with the time frame in which disputes must arise before jurisdiction exists. Thus, a Declaration may exclude disputes arising before the Declaration made, as with India's declaration of acceptance. Declarations may be for a renewable term of years, as with Denmark, or in respect of disputes arising after a specific date, as with Finland. Provisions relating to termination, such as the six months provision in *Nicaragua* v *USA*, are within this category, although the Court's ruling in that case on the requirement of good faith is relevant here. Likewise, states may reserve disputes with states whose own Declaration has not been in force for twelve months, so avoiding India's problem in the *Rights of*

Passage Case. Most states also reserve matters of 'domestic jurisdiction' from consideration by the Court (e.g. Canada). Strictly speaking, these may be unnecessary,
for if a matter does fall within the domestic jurisdiction or competence of a state,
ex hypothesi it is not a matter of international law and not admissible before an
international court. What is clear, however, is that without more these reservations
leave it to the Court itself to decide whether a matter falls exclusively within the
domestic jurisdiction of a state and its own views are irrelevant, as in the *Rights of
Passage Case.*

The most troublesome reservations are the so-called 'automatic' or 'self-judging'
reservations. These reservations reserve a state's competence over domestic matters
as before, but add that the state itself is to be the sole judge of what is a domestic
matter. In the *Norwegian Loans Case (France v Norway)* 1957 ICJ Rep 9, for example,
the French Declaration contained a reservation excluding all 'differences relating to
matters which are essentially within the national jurisdiction as understood by the
Government of the French Republic'. The alleged effect of such a reservation is to
give the state itself the power to decide whether the Court may hear a case, because
what constitutes a 'domestic matter' (and is therefore reserved) is apparently left
entirely to the state's own judgment. Hence, it is self-judging or automatic and
was applied as such in the *Norwegian Loans Case.* However, despite this authority,
there is a body of judicial and academic opinion that believes such reservations
to be unlawful. According to Judge Lauterpacht in the *Norwegian Loans Case* and
the *Interhandel Case (Switzerland v USA)* 1959 ICJ Rep 6, automatic reservations are
unlawful and invalid because they are contrary to Art. 36(6) of the Statute which
provides that it is the Court which has the power to determine the limit of its own
jurisdiction. Moreover, because jurisdiction is liable to be defeated on the word
of the state at the time of submission of a dispute to the Court, they create only a
contingent acceptance of jurisdiction and this is contrary to the principle of the
binding legal effect of Declarations under the Optional System. In his view, and
that of Judge Spender in the *Interhandel Case* and Judge Schwebel in the *Nicaragua*
case, the existence of such reservations renders the entire Declaration of Acceptance
invalid.

The invalidity of such reservations was also argued by Judge Guerrero in *Norwegian
Loans* and by President Klaestad and Judges Carry and Armand in *Interhandel*,
although they drew different conclusions about the effect of such illegality. In their
view, the Declaration as a whole remained valid because the illegal automatic reservation could be severed. It is submitted that this is the better view, because otherwise the state making the (illegal) self-judging reservation would be in exactly the
same position as if the reservation had been lawful: that is, it would escape jurisdiction either under the valid reservation or because of an entirely invalid Declaration.
Thus, the better view is that invalid reservations can be severed without compromising the legal effect of the Declaration as a whole. For the present, however, it must
be accepted that there is no consensus either as to the status of such reservations or
the effect on a state's Declaration should they be invalid. In the *Fisheries Jurisdiction
Case (Spain v Canada)*, the Court decided that the Canadian reservation was not
'automatic' in the sense of depriving the Court of the power to determine whether
it had jurisdiction, and so no issue arose. This does imply that a reservation which
did seek to deny the Court's ability to decide the jurisdictional question would be
unlawful, but it is not conclusive. In this connection it is interesting to note that the

USA did *not* attempt to rely on its automatic reservation when seeking to resist the jurisdiction of the Court in *Nicaragua* v *USA*. Indeed, the dispute was very plainly not within the USA's domestic jurisdiction and it could be that the USA never seriously considered pleading the reservation. A more cynical (but totally speculative) view is that the USA did not plead the reservation in such an undeserving case for fear the Court would indeed declare such reservations unlawful as a matter of principle. This would have negated their effect for the future in cases where the substance of the dispute was more arguably a matter of domestic jurisdiction.

It is obvious that Declarations deposited under the Optional System are central in any discussion concerning the Court's jurisdiction. Given that jurisdiction is granted in advance and without precise knowledge of any claim that may arise against the state in the future, Declarations are worded with care. In many cases coming before the Court, a state will raise 'preliminary objections' to the assertion of jurisdiction which do not deny that a valid Declaration under the Optional System has been made, but rather contend that the terms of the Declaration (and its reservations) do not cover the substance of the claim made against it. This requires the Court to interpret the Declaration for, as we have seen, it is for the Court to decide whether jurisdiction exists. The *Fisheries Jurisdiction Case (Preliminary Objections) (Spain* v *Canada)* 1998 ICJ Rep raised just such an issue and the Court gave some valuable guidance on the general approach to interpreting Declarations containing reservations. First, because it is for the Court to determine whether jurisdiction exists under a Declaration, the parties are not under a burden of proof as to proving, or disproving, the existence of jurisdiction. The parties must prove facts on which they rely, but the Court will balance the scales of jurisdiction. Secondly, although a Declaration results in a binding obligation on a state, the 'regime relating to the interpretation of declarations under Art. 36 of the Statute is not identical with that established for the interpretation of treaties by the Vienna Convention on the Law of Treaties'. The 'treaty rules' may apply analogously, but the unique character of Declarations as unilateral acts means that such rules must not be imported wholesale. Thirdly, following from this, in interpreting reservations made in Declarations, the Court should *not* start from the position that jurisdiction has been prima facie given which is then taken away by a reservation. Reservations are an integral part of the Declaration and there is no rule that in cases of doubt a reservation must be interpreted against the state making the reservation (no *contra preferentum* rule). In other words, a reservation defines the limits of a state's consent to jurisdiction, it does not seek to detract from a jurisdiction already given. This is important as it means in practice that the Court should not seek to 'interpret away' the effect of a reservation as a matter of course. Fourthly, given that the whole purpose of a reservation is to deny the Court's jurisdiction in a case where a state *may* (or may not) have been acting unlawfully, the Court cannot interpret a reservation so that it excludes from jurisdiction only conduct which is lawful. If it were otherwise, there would be no point in having reservations because unlawful conduct would automatically fall within the Court's jurisdiction. Fifthly, because Declarations are essentially unilateral acts (not treaties), in interpreting a Declaration particular weight must be given to the intention of the state making the Declaration and reservations. The primary rule of interpretation is that reservations must be interpreted 'in a natural and reasonable way, with appropriate regard for the intentions of the reserving state and the purpose of the reservation'. This is a key finding, as it re-emphasises that consent is at the heart of the Optional System. So, the Court should not adopt a strained construction of a reservation, but should (in so far as is compatible with the express provisions of the Declaration) give it the effect intended by the state at the time it made the reservation. Of course, the Court cannot ignore the clear words of a Declaration. Thus, in the *Legality of the Use of Force Case*, Yugoslavia intended by its Declaration to give the Court jurisdiction over the legal issues arising from NATO air attacks against its territory while at the same time excluding jurisdiction over the events which led to those air attacks (its alleged violation of human rights in Kosovo). However, the express reservation employed by Yugoslavia actually denied jurisdiction over both events and Yugoslavia's purpose was thwarted. Nevertheless, the *Fisheries Jurisdiction* principles – especially the repeated emphasis on the import-ance of the intention and purpose of the state making the Declaration – demonstrate that the Court has recognised the reality that a consent-based system of jurisdiction must command the respect of the parties who are to use it.

10.8.5.7 The principle of reciprocity

Under Art. 36 of the Statute of the Court, states accept the jurisdiction of the Court by their Declaration on condition of reciprocity. This has two aspects:

(a) The Optional System applies only between participating states. In other words, a state which has not made a Declaration cannot rely on another state's membership of the system in order to bring a dispute with it before the Court even if the plaintiff (or claimant) state is happy to make a one-off submission to jurisdiction. States have to make a Declaration before they can rely on Art. 36, because the system operates only between the participants inter se. Indeed, some Declarations, such as that of the UK, deny jurisdiction in respect of states that join the Optional System for the purpose of one dispute only, or whose Declarations have not been in force for a minimum period, usually one year. This is to remove the danger of abuse by those wishing to avail themselves of the Court for a particular case, but who are not prepared to participate fully in the 'consensual bond' which is created. As indicated previously, such a provision would have prevented the problems experienced by India in the *Rights of Passage Case* and it proved its value for the UK in the *Legality of the Use of Force Case*, where Yugoslavia made a Declaration under Art. 36(2) on 26 April 1999 and issued proceedings on 29 April. As regards the UK, Yugoslavia could not rely on Art. 36(2).

(b) The second and more subtle operation of the principle of reciprocity concerns the subject matter over which the Court may have jurisdiction. The principle of reciprocity means that the Court exercises jurisdiction only to the extent to which the Declarations of the parties to a dispute coincide. The Court has jurisdiction over the areas common to both states' Declarations. In practice, this means that one state may rely on the reservations contained in another state's Declaration. For example, State A reserves all disputes concerning its land and maritime boundaries. State B reserves all disputes relating to the activity of its armed forces. In a dispute between States A and B, the Court will not have jurisdiction over either land/maritime boundaries or actions of armed forces, irrespective of who is plaintiff. So, if State A attempts to refer a dispute with State B to the Court concerning their common continental shelf, State B will be able to deny jurisdiction on the basis of the reservation contained in State A's own Declaration. The Court has jurisdiction only to the extent to which the Declarations coincide and they must coincide both as to subject matter (jurisdiction *ratione materiae*) and where the reservation concerns the time at which disputes arise (*ratione temporis*). In the *Norwegian Loans Case*, France had made an 'automatic' reservation and Norway had not. The Court held that Norway was entitled to utilise the automatic reservation and consequently there was no jurisdiction because Norway then deemed the matter to be within her domestic competence. Norway relied on the 'automatic' reservation in France's Declaration.

The principle of reciprocity is a powerful one, but it is not unlimited. It appears that reciprocity applies only to the substance of reservations, not to their procedural aspects. In *Nicaragua* v *USA*, the USA had stipulated that it would give six months' notice before termination of its Declaration. Nicaragua's Declaration contained no similar provision and appeared to be terminable without notice. The USA contended that it was able to terminate its own Declaration without notice in a dispute with Nicaragua, because of the principle of reciprocity. The Court rejected this argument, because reciprocity was concerned with substance not form. However, for some critics, the overpowering force of this argument is not immediately self-evident, for if reciprocity is truly designed to ensure the equality of states before the ICJ, it is not obvious why such equality should be denied in procedural matters. After all, the very existence of jurisdiction may turn on such an issue, as in this case, and if Nicaragua could have terminated its Declaration without notice (or possibly with only reasonable notice) if sued by the USA, why could not the USA when sued by Nicaragua. This decision does compromise the effect of certain types of reservations *ratione temporis* and makes it clear that they at least operate unilaterally (i.e. not on condition of reciprocity), irrespective of the Declarations of other states. Nevertheless, the *Nicaragua* principle has been confirmed in *Cameroon* v *Nigeria*, with the Court citing dicta from the *Nicaragua Case* to the effect that 'reciprocity is concerned with the scope and substance of the commitments entered into, including reservations, and not with the formal conditions of their creation, duration or extinction'.

10.8.5.8 Transferred jurisdiction

Under Art. 36(5) of the Statute, Declarations of Acceptance of Jurisdiction under the Optional System of the Permanent Court of International Justice which are still in force are to be deemed to be acceptances of jurisdiction under the Optional System of the ICJ, on the same conditions. There are seven such 'transfers' at present. This is a procedural device intended to ensure that the ICJ lost none of the jurisdiction of the PCIJ simply by reason of its reconstitution as an organ of the United Nations instead of the League of Nations. Article 36(5) was the basis of Nicaragua's claim to jurisdiction in *Nicaragua* v *USA*. However, Art. 36(5) will transfer jurisdiction from one Optional System to the other only for those states that became parties to the ICJ Statute before the dissolution of the Permanent Court. In practice, this means that jurisdiction is transferred only for those who were parties to the ICJ Statute in 1945 and have not withdrawn since. Thus, in the *Aerial Incident Case (Israel v Bulgaria) (Preliminary Objections)* 1959 ICJ Rep 127, Bulgaria's acceptance of PCIJ jurisdiction did not revive when it eventually became a party to the ICJ Statute in 1955, because by that time the PCIJ had been dissolved. There was no continuity in the acceptance of jurisdiction. In the *Aerial Incident Case*, Judges Lauterpacht, Wellington Koo and Spender dissented from this limited view of Art. 36(5), but it was implicitly confirmed by the Court in the *Barcelona Traction Case (Preliminary Objections)* 1964 ICJ Rep 6, where Art. 36(5) was distinguished from Art. 37.

Under Art. 37 of the Statute, where a treaty provides that a dispute shall be referred to the PCIJ or to a tribunal constituted by the League of Nations, this shall be taken as between parties to the ICJ Statute to be a reference to the International Court of Justice. Several pre-1945 treaties, such as the International Air Transport Agreement 1944, provide that disputes shall be settled by the Permanent Court, in much the same way as treaties now refer specific matters to the International Court. The purpose of Art. 37 is to ensure that this jurisdiction is not lost by reason of the substitution of one judicial body for the other. In order for this transfer of jurisdiction to operate, the treaty containing the jurisdictional clause must be in force and all parties to the dispute must be parties to the ICJ Statute (*Ambatielos Case (Jurisdiction)* 1952 ICJ Rep 28). In *Pakistan* v *India* (2000), India escaped jurisdiction under Art. 37 because it had ceased to be a party to the relevant treaty before the dispute with Pakistan arose. However, following the *Barcelona Traction Case*, it is clear that Art. 37 will transfer jurisdiction to the ICJ so long as all parties to the dispute are *currently* members of the Statute. There is no requirement, as there is under Art. 36(5), that states must have been signatories to the ICJ Statute before the dissolution of the PCIJ. The date at which states sign the Statute is irrelevant.

10.8.5.9 Interpretation of previous decisions

Under Art. 60 of the Statute of the ICH, as supplemented by Art. 98 of the Rules of the Court, a state may request interpretation of a previous judgment. Where such an interpretation is requested, the Court has jurisdiction to do so by reason of Art. 60 and does not have to find a new or continuing basis for jurisdiction. This is so even if the basis for the original exercise of jurisdiction has lapsed. So, in the *Request for interpretation of the Judgment of 15 June 1962 in the case concerning the Temple of Preah Vihear (Cambodia* v *Thailand) (Cambodia* v *Thailand)* (2011), the ICJ determined that the 'Court's jurisdiction on the basis of Article 60 of the Statute is not preconditioned by the existence of any other basis of jurisdiction as between the parties to the original case; [and that] it follows that, even if the basis of jurisdiction in the original case lapses, the Court, nevertheless, by virtue of Article 60 of the Statute may entertain a request for interpretation'. This jurisdiction is limited to interpreting the judgment if there is 'dispute as to the meaning or scope' of the judgment, so it is not wide ranging. However, it does demonstrate that the Court will act to ensure that it asserts jurisdiction where this is necessary to protect its essential judicial function in respect of disputes over which it once had jurisdiction and which it has dealt with.

10.8.5.10 Intervention

At this point it is also convenient to mention another matter relating to the jurisdiction of the Court, namely the power of a third state to intervene in proceedings between two others by virtue of Arts 62 and 63 of the ICJ Statute. Under Art. 63, a state has the *right* to intervene in proceedings before the Court if the dispute concerns the construction of a treaty to which it is a party, This has occurred only rarely, in the *Haya de la Torre Case* (1951) ICJ Rep 71 and the *Cameroon* v *Nigeria Case (Equatorial Guinea intervening)* but this infrequency is not surprising given that, if a state exercises this right, it becomes bound by the construction which the Court places on the treaty at issue. Of much greater interest is Art. 62, by which a state may *request* permission to intervene if it considers it has an 'interest of a legal nature' in a dispute before the Court. For some time, the Court had refused all requests to intervene under this Article (e.g. the refusal of Italy's application in the *Continental Shelf Case (Libya/Malta)* 1984 ICJ Rep 3) but in the *Land, Island and Maritime Frontier Dispute Case (El Salvador v Honduras)* (1992) ICJ Rep 92, a Chamber of the Court granted Nicaragua permission to intervene in certain aspects of the El Salvador/Honduras dispute. Not only was this the first occasion on which such permission was granted, it was granted in the face of opposition by one of the actual parties. The Chamber's judgment is of the utmost importance for questions of intervention and a number of principles have emerged. First, the state requesting intervention bears the burden of proof to demonstrate convincingly that it has an interest of a legal nature which may be affected by the dispute. General fears are not enough. Secondly, however, it need only demonstrate that its legal interests *may* be affected, not that they will or must be affected. Thirdly, the competence of the Court to grant permission to intervene does not depend on the consent of the states who are actually the parties to the dispute before the Court. The Court's competence flows from the consent to Art. 62 which each state gives when it first signs the Statute. Consequently, the opposition of either or both of the disputing states is not a bar to permitting third-party intervention. Fourthly, if permission to intervene is granted, the intervener does not thereby become a party to the proceedings. The purpose of intervention is to inform the Court that the legal rights of the intervener may be prejudiced, not to trigger a binding judicial determination of its rights. So, importantly, the existence of a jurisdictional link between the intervener and the disputing states (e.g. under the Optional System, a treaty in force or ad hoc consent) is not required. The intervener is not a party, so questions of a jurisdictional link with the parties and their consent do not arise. Indeed, as the final award in this case now makes clear (*El Salvador v Honduras* 1992 ICJ Rep 92), the fact that the intervener is not a party to the dispute means that it is not bound by the Court's final judgment. Furthermore, the intervener cannot agree to be bound by that judgment unilaterally. It must formally become a party if it wishes to be bound (via a pre-existing jurisdictional link or with the consent of the disputants) because otherwise the actual parties would have been propelled into a binding legal settlement with a state that had not needed to show jurisdiction in order to intervene, and to whom *they* may have objected. Once again, while the non-binding nature of the award for the intervener follows logically from the Court's opinion that no jurisdictional link is required for a successful intervention, it appears somewhat unrealistic. As Judge Oda makes clear in his Dissenting Opinion on this point, is it really true that Nicaragua, after intervening, is not bound by the Court's determination as to the sovereignty of various islands and the delimitation of various maritime zones in the disputed area? To hold that it is not simply ignores the real force which a binding judicial determination by the ICJ has in practice. Despite these criticisms, however, the principles put forward in *El Salvador v Honduras* have now been endorsed by the full Court in the *Land and Maritime Boundary Case*. In allowing Equatorial Guinea to intervene under Art. 62 of the Statute, the Court confirmed both that no jurisdictional link was needed with the two main parties and that the intervener did not become a party to the dispute and so would not be bound by a judgment. The fact that neither Cameroon nor Nigeria objected to the intervention does not diminish this precedent, and the matter must now be regarded as settled despite the doubts raised earlier. In the *Jurisdictional Immunities of the State (Germany v Italy) Case* (2008), the ICC granted Greece permission to intervene, although neither party formally objected. The Court did, however, make it clear that intervention could be limited to particular aspects of a case (as was the decision in relation to Greece) and this is consistent with the intervener being a non-party.

10.8.5.11 The future of the Court

The use of the Court in contentious cases has not been as widespread as originally intended. Certainly, the number of cases going to the Court in the 1970s and 1980s was no greater than two or three per annum. Moreover, periodically, the Court has been faced with the problem of the absent defendant. In *US Diplomatic and Consular Staff in Tehran Case* 1980 ICJ Rep 3, and then in *Nicaragua v USA*, Iran and the USA respectively objected to the Court's jurisdiction and, having failed to avoid compulsory jurisdiction, refused to appoint counsel or to appear before the Court to argue the merits. In such cases, the Court is in some difficulty, although the Statute provides that judgment for the plaintiff may be entered in default. Fortunately, in the interests of justice and in order to maintain its credibility, it seems that the Court will not order judgment in default but will endeavour to consider all of the argument that the defendant state would have presented had it been in attendance. This is not an easy task, although the presence of a judge of the nationality of the absent state is a considerable help, as in *Nicaragua v USA*. Obviously this is not an ideal solution, and in both of these cases, the state that declined to appear then lost and then refused to carry out the Court's judgment. While it may be that the Court itself has contributed to this problem by being too eager to find jurisdiction in some cases, this is no excuse for the rejection of the legally binding obligations which arise from consensual jurisdiction.

Whether the Court will survive as an effective institution for the settlement of disputes remains to be seen, although the regular referral of cases – while not a torrent – is encouraging. Likewise, the geographical and political mix of the judges has altered considerably since 1945 and the Court seems to have recovered its prestige in the eyes of the developing world after the widely criticised *South-West Africa Cases* of the 1960s. Of course, the different approaches of the Court to the question of Serbia's standing in the *Legality of the Use of Force Cases* (2004) (no standing) and then the *Case Concerning the Application of the Convention on the Prevention and Punishment of the Crime of Genocide (Bosnia and Herzegovina v Serbia & Montenegro)* (ICJ 2007) (standing and jurisdiction) illustrate that the Court will never be able to operate in a vacuum and that there is always the risk of perceived bias.

However, we should remember that it is only rarely that states have refused to carry out the judgments of the Court and, as we have seen with Iran and the USA, this may be more of a rejection of *any* kind of peaceful settlement rather than of the Court itself. Of course, if acceptance of jurisdiction is by ad hoc *compromis* or is otherwise mutually acceptable, there is every possibility that the Court's judgment will be respected by both parties and that it will bring the dispute to a close. In the law of the sea, for example, where it is vital that states reach agreement on the allocation of mineral and other resources, the Court has played a significant role, as in *Tunisia v Libya* 1982 ICJ Rep 18, *Libya v Malta* 1985 ICJ Rep 13, the *Gulf of Maine Case* 1984 ICJ Rep 246 and the *Jan Meyen Case* 1993 ICJ Rep 38. It seems that it is only where there is an element of contested compulsory jurisdiction that serious problems of non-appearance or non-compliance arise. In such circumstances it may be that a negotiated settlement is more likely to be effective than one imposed by a third party and the Court must be astute to preserve this possibility while at the same time preserving the integrity of the consensual jurisdictional system. Of course, it would be better if states were prepared to accept that the peaceful resolution of disputes per se was in everybody's interest, irrespective of whether they won or lost a particular case. Yet, in the real world, the fear of losing, the prospect of objective determination by third parties over whom the state has no control, the cost of litigation and the legally binding effect of the award all contribute to the relatively scant use made of the Court. On the positive side, as long as the Court can maintain a reputation for impartiality and competence, it will continue to contribute in some measure to the resolution of disputes between states and more frequent use of the Chamber system may facilitate this. Ultimately, its success depends on the political will of states.

10.8.5.12 The Court and the Security Council

As will be seen in Chapter 11, the powers of the Security Council are extensive and there is no doubt that in matters concerning international peace and security it may make a determination of factual, political and legal issues that is legally binding on the parties to whom it is addressed. This is in addition to the Council's general responsibility to consider and discuss all incidents likely to endanger international peace. In these circumstances, it is not surprising that there have been a number of cases before the ICJ where one or other of the parties has sought to persuade the Court that it should decline to exercise jurisdiction over a dispute either because the Council is currently considering the matter (or aspects of it), or because the Council has already made a determination in respect of it.

As a general principle, just because the Council is seised of a matter will not prevent the Court from hearing a case – see for example the *Case Concerning the Application of the Convention on the Prevention and Punishment of the Crime of Genocide (Bosnia and Herzegovina v Serbia & Montenegro)* (ICJ 2007). Indeed, in the *United States Diplomatic and Consular Staff in Tehran Case (United States v Iran)* 1980 ICJ Rep 3, the Court made it absolutely clear that it would not decline jurisdiction over a legal dispute just because the Council was considering certain aspects of it. The Court was the principal judicial organ of the United Nations and it was not enough to deny jurisdiction that the Council was fulfilling its own functions in parallel. This must be correct. However, it is clear that the Court is subject to some limitation. In the *Case Concerning Questions of Interpretation and Application of the 1971 Montreal Convention arising from the Aerial Incident at Lockerbie (Libya v United States; Libya v United Kingdom) (Request for the Indication of Provisional Measures)* 1992 ICJ Rep 114, the Court decided not to order interim measures of protection against the UK and USA because the Council had made a binding determination under Chapter VII of the Charter which effectively removed any factual basis Libya might have had for its allegations – in essence, Libya was requesting interim protection contrary to certain rights of the UK and USA that the Council had determined should be protected. This decision has not been welcomed universally, with some critics arguing that the Court abdicated its judicial role and that it sets a dangerous precedent.

In fact, however, these fears have proved unfounded, and in the *Congo Case* the ICJ did order interim measures even though the Security Council had passed a resolution demanding (but *not* deciding) a cessation of hostilities. Indeed, as Judge ad hoc Lauterpacht made clear in the *Prevention of Genocide Case* 1993, the Court has not abdicated its powers to act when the Council is also acting and neither does the *Lockerbie Case* mean that the Court is incapable of reviewing or challenging Council action. The Council's powers stem from the Charter and are not without limit, and it is inconceivable that the Court could not review a binding Council decision that authorised action contrary to (say) a norm of *jus cogens*. The *Lockerbie Case* is important, and it does provide an example of the Court restraining itself in deference to another UN organ. Yet it is also unusual and, as the *Congo Case* showed subsequently, it did not spell the end of the Court's independence and effectiveness when faced with an active Security Council. Indeed, the Court has further made clear that it will not desist from the judicial function just because other organs of the UN system may be dealing with some aspect of a dispute. In the *Palestinian Wall Advisory Opinion* 2004 ICJ Rep, the Court noted that neither consideration by the General Assembly nor by the Security Council of the same issue would deter it from giving its view on legal issues where it was validly seised of the question under the terms of the Statute and the UN Charter. This has been followed by the *Advisory Opinion on the Accordance with international law of the unilateral declaration of independence in respect of Kosovo* (2008) where the Court was determined to rule on a legal question even if this concerned contentious matters before the Assembly and Security Council and in respect of a dispute where the Security Council had taken concrete measures, and significantly in the contentious case of the *Application of the Interim Accord of 13 September 1995 (The Former Yugoslav Republic of Macedonia v Greece)* (2011) where neither the fact of Security Council involvement nor the highly political nature of the dispute prevented the Court from reaching a judgment.

10.9 Advisory Opinions

Under Chapter IV of the Statute and Art. 96 of the Charter, the Court may give an Advisory Opinion 'on any legal question' at the request of any body duly authorised by the United Nations. As noted previously, Advisory Opinions may be requested, *inter alia*, by the General Assembly, the Security Council, ECOSOC, the IAEA and all of the specialised agencies, except the Universal Postal Union. States may not request Advisory Opinions, but along with international organisations they may participate in such proceedings before the Court as did the UK in the *Legality of the Use of Nuclear Weapons Case*. Indeed, in the *Palestinian Wall Advisory Opinion*, a large number of states, international organisations and the 'pre-state' of Palestine itself all made representations and this was repeated in the *Advisory Option on the Accordance with international law of the unilateral declaration of independence in respect of Kosovo* (2008). Advisory Opinions are not binding in law, but in practice if they concern the rights and duties of states, generally they are acted upon. Three notable failures in this regard, however, were the *Certain Expenses of the United Nations Case* 1962 ICJ Rep 151 on the payment of financial contributions to Assembly peacekeeping operations, the *Namibia Case* 1971 ICJ Rep 16 on the legal effects of the termination of the South African Mandate over South West Africa/Namibia and the *Palestinian Wall Advisory Opinion* that construction of the Wall is contrary to international law. We should note, however, that the Court is mindful in giving Advisory Opinions that it is not its role to settle disputes between states. So, in the *Kosovo Opinion*, the Court is very clear that it is determining whether the *making* of the declaration of independence by Kosovo was lawful: it is not determining thereby that Kosovo is a state or what (if any) consequences arise from that declaration.

The range of matters on which the Court has delivered an Advisory Opinion is varied. In addition to the *Palestinian Wall* and *Kosovo Declaration of Independence* opinions, it has delivered an opinion on the legality of the use or threat of nuclear weapons (at the request of the UN General Assembly), and an *Advisory Opinion on the Applicability of Art. VI, section 22 of the Convention on the Privileges and Immunities of the United Nations (Immunities Case)* following a first ever request by ECOSOC. This opinion concerns the privileges of a UN staff member under the General Convention on the Privileges and Immunities of the Specialised Agencies of the UN 1947, and is significant because under section 30 of that Convention the opinion 'shall be decisive' of the dispute. In other words, this is the first example of a *formally* binding Advisory Opinion, albeit a rare beast because of the special terms of section 30 of the 1947 Convention. In Chapter 2, we considered the role of judicial sources in the formation of international law and there is no doubt that Advisory Opinions contribute significantly to this.

10.9.1 The issue of consent

As noted previously, Advisory Opinions may deal with a wide variety of issues, including membership of international organisations (*Conditions for the Admission of a State to Membership in the UN Case* 1948 ICJ Rep 57), the interpretation of treaties (*Interpretation of Peace Treaties Case* 1950 ICJ Rep 65), the payment of financial contributions (*Certain Expenses Case*) and the status of territory (*Western Sahara Case* 1975 ICJ Rep 12, *Namibia Case* and the *Palestinian Wall Case*). Moreover, it is quite clear that Advisory Opinions may have a significant impact on the rights and duties of states. In the *Western Sahara Case*, for example, the Advisory Opinion on the status of the territory effectively decided the claims of sovereignty made by Morocco and Mauritania and the legal consequences for Israel of the *Palestinian Wall Case* are clear enough. Yet where does this leave the principle discussed earlier in the context of contentious cases that a state's rights should not be determined without its consent? Does the same requirement apply when the effect of an Advisory Opinion is to resolve an inter-state dispute?

In the *Eastern Carelia Case* (1923) PCIJ Ser. B No. 5, the PCIJ stated that if an Advisory Opinion would be decisive of a controversy between two states, the Court should decline to give such an opinion unless all of the states concerned had given their consent. So, in this case, the Court refused to give an opinion on the status of Eastern Carelia because Russia had not consented to the resolution of the issue. However, some years later in the *Interpretation of Peace Treaties Case*, the ICJ adopted a less strict approach and stated that an Advisory Opinion would not be refused, even if an interested state objected to the proceedings, so long as that state's legal responsibilities were not actually an issue. In effect, the Court distinguished *Eastern Carelia* on the ground that the case before it did not relate to the main point of the dispute between two states, even though as a matter of fact it would resolve one area of conflict.

In subsequent years, it became apparent that the ICJ was willing to pull back even further from the full rigour of the *Carelia* decision. In the *Western Sahara Case*, the

Court held that it was now established that Advisory Opinions did not depend on the consent of interested states, even when the case concerned a legal question pending between them. Moreover, as a general rule, only 'compelling reasons' should lead to a refusal to give an opinion and, in any event, a signatory of the Statute and Charter (such as Spain in the *Western Sahara Case*) had agreed in advance to the exercise of advisory jurisdiction. This formidable jurisprudence was confirmed in the *Palestinian Wall Case* and the *Kosovo Opinion*. Similarly, in its *Advisory Opinion on the Applicability of Art. VI, section 22 of the Convention on the Privileges and Immunities of the United Nations (Immunities Case)* (1989) ICJ Rep 177, the Court refused to give effect to a reservation to the Privileges Convention entered by Romania which attempted to prevent the Court from determining disputes under it. The Court's simple reason was that the matter had been referred to the Court by the General Assembly under the latter's general powers to request an Advisory Opinion, as manifested in the UN Charter and Statute of the Court, to which Romania was a signatory. Thus, Romania's reservation to the Convention itself was irrelevant, as was its general lack of consent. As we have seen, there is a similar willingness to downplay the role of consent in contentious cases, although this is more justified for Advisory Opinions because of the special function they perform within the international legal order.

In *Western Sahara*, the Court also emphasised that Advisory Opinions were designed to give guidance to international organisations on the exercise of their functions and were not intended to resolve any questions pending between the parties. While this may be true in theory, the position in practice is somewhat different. Whatever the non-binding status of Advisory Opinions (but note the exception of the *Immunities Case*), it is clear that if they relate to the legal responsibilities of states, they may effectively crystallise those responsibilities at the date of judgment – the *Palestinian Wall Case* could not be clearer in this regard. Indeed, should it not be so, for Advisory Opinions are delivered according to international law and have the full authority of the highest judicial body known to the system? It is unrealistic to maintain that they do not resolve legal disputes between states in certain cases, although they may be crafted carefully to avoid doing so, as in the *Kosovo Opinion*. Indeed, the present position seems to be that the Court will not automatically refuse to give an Advisory Opinion even if, as a fact, a state's rights will be determined, so long as it is not the only area of uncertainty. Likewise, it is not always the case that an Advisory Opinion will simply give guidance to an international organisation. In the opinion on the *Legality of the Use of Nuclear Weapons*, the Court comes very close to answering an abstract question of international law. It is very similar to a declaratory judgment.

10.9.2 What is a legal question?

The Court is empowered to give opinions on any 'legal question'. Like proceedings in contentious cases, this raises an issue of admissibility. In the *Eastern Carelia Case*, another reason for dismissing the application was that the question raised factual rather than legal issues which the Court was not competent to resolve. While this may be a bar in extreme cases, the *Western Sahara Case* now makes it clear that the Court will not refuse to adjudicate on factual issues if this is necessary for a thorough examination of the 'legal question'. As the Court said, 'a mixed question of law and fact is nonetheless a legal question within the meaning of Art. 96(1)' of the Charter.

It is clear, then, that the definition of a 'legal question' is flexible and can be resolved only on a case by case basis. It matters not that the question is framed abstractly (*Admissions Case*) but the Court will not pronounce on the moral duties of states (*South West Africa Case* 1950 ICJ Rep 128), for it is essential that the Court safeguards the judicial function by undertaking primarily judicial tasks. On the other hand, the Court will not decline to give an opinion because the legal issues are intertwined with political considerations or because they have political significance as the *Legality of the Use of Nuclear Weapons Case*, the *Palestinian Wall Case* and the *Kosovo Case* illustrate. The Court is not concerned with the motives for a request, even if these are political. Indeed, if it were otherwise virtually every Advisory Opinion dealing with the functions of the United Nations would be 'inadmissible'. The Court is loathe to refuse to give an Advisory Opinion because it sees them as an indispensable part of its responsibilities within the United Nations system. It will do so only when the reasons are compelling, as with the WHO's request in the *Legality of the Use of Nuclear Weapons Case* which had to be denied due to the WHO's lack of standing in respect of the subject matter. Even then, in that case, the UN General Assembly was held to have power to request the opinion on the same subject matter.

FURTHER READING

Ago, R., '"Binding" Advisory Opinions of the ICJ', (1991) 85 *AJIL* 224.

Bowett, D., 'Contemporary Developments in Legal Techniques in the Settlement of Disputes', (1983) 180 *Rec. de Cours* 169.

Brownlie, I, The Peaceful Settlement of International Disputes, (2009) 8 *Chinese Journal of International Law* 267.

Caron, D., 'The Nature of the Iran–US Claims Tribunal and the Evolving Structure of International Dispute Resolution', (1990) 84 *AJIL* 104.

Chinkin, C., 'Third Party Intervention before the ICJ', (1986) 80 *AJIL* 495.

Crawford, J., 'The Legal Effect of Automatic Reservations to the Jurisdiction of the ICJ', (1979) 50 *BYIL* 63.

Evans, M., '*El Salvador* v *Honduras*, The Nicaraguan Intervention', (1992) 41 *ICLQ* 896.

Franck, T., '*Nicaragua* v *USA*: Jurisdiction and Admissibility', (1985) 79 *AJIL* 373.

Franck, T., 'The Good Offices Function of the UN Secretary-General', in Roberts, A. and Kingsbury, B. (eds), *The United Nations in a Divided World* (Clarendon Press, 1980).

Greig, D., '*Nicaragua* v *USA*: Confrontation over the Jurisdiction of the ICJ', (1991) 62 *BYIL* 119.

Higgins, R., 'A Babel of judicial voices? Ruminations from the Bench' (2006) *ICLQ* 791.

Llamzon, A., 'Jurisdiction and Compliance in Recent Decisions of the International Court of Justice' (2007) 18 *EJIL* 815, 850–851.

Mendelson, M., 'Interim Measures of Protection in Cases of Contested Jurisdiction', (1972–73) 46 *BYIL* 259.

Redfern, A., and Hunter, J., *International Commercial Arbitration* (Sweet & Maxwell, 1987).

Schwebel, S., 'Chambers of the ICJ formed for Particular Cases', in Y. Dinstein (ed.), *International Law at a Time of Perplexity* (Nihoff, 1989).

SUMMARY

The peaceful settlement of disputes

- According to Art. 2(3) of the United Nations Charter, all members 'shall settle their international disputes by peaceful means in such a manner that international peace and security, and justice, are not endangered'. There is no doubt that this principle is one of the central obligations of international law.

- The most common method of settlement is direct negotiations between the parties. This 'method' accounts for the great majority of settlements between states and appears to be the one most preferred.

- 'Good offices' are a preliminary to direct negotiations between the parties. Mediation is a continuation of this, and often the mediator will be the person who originally brought the parties together.

- The United Nations has a variety of institutionalised and informal methods through which states may settle disputes.

- Arbitration is 'a procedure for the settlement of disputes between states by a binding award on the basis of law and as a result of an undertaking voluntarily accepted'. It is the most commonly used 'judicial' means for the settlement of disputes.

- The International Court of Justice exercises an important jurisdiction based on the consent of states. This consent may be given in advance of a dispute arising, but only states may be parties before the Court.

- Under Art. 36(2) of the Statute of the ICJ, states may accept, in advance, the jurisdiction of the Court. Acceptance of jurisdiction is by means of a unilateral Declaration of Acceptance, deposited with the UN Secretary-General. The system is optional in the sense that states may become parties to the Statute without making Declarations of Acceptance and is based on reciprocity.

11

The use of force

As with every other legal system, international law must seek to prevent its subjects from using violence to settle their differences. In this chapter, we shall examine how the use of armed force is regulated by international law. As emphasised by the International Court in *Nicaragua* v *USA* 1986 ICJ Rep 14, these rules encapsulate some of the most fundamental of all international obligations and there is little doubt that as noted by a number of judges in that case, the primary obligation not to use force has attained the status of *jus cogens*. Unfortunately, however, this important area of international law is also one of the most troublesome. While every state agrees that the use of force is generally impermissible, there is considerable disagreement over the precise circumstances in which it may lawfully be used. Of course, this is not surprising given that armed force has traditionally played such a central role in international relations. Yet it is a sad fact that many states are not prepared to relinquish their ability to impose a settlement forcefully in favour of a system where disputes are settled on the basis of legal principle. In their view, such idealism is misplaced precisely because international law does not provide an adequate, effective and compulsory machinery for the peaceful resolution of disputes or for the punishment of those bent on destroying international peace and security.

The rules of international law regulating the right to use force (the *ius ad bellum*) will be considered in two sections. First, consideration will be given to those rules controlling the use of armed force by individual states or groups of states acting on their own initiative. This is often referred to as the 'unilateral' use of force, although the same general rules apply whether one state or twenty states resort to armed action. Secondly, and by way of contrast, there are those rules indicating when force may be used by a competent international organisation, such as the United Nations. This is commonly referred to as the 'collective' use of force, because it results from a collective decision by a duly authorised body. Usually, this type of armed action will involve a number of states, as with the multinational action against Iraq in 1991 following its invasion of Kuwait, but the essence is that force is used on behalf of all states in support of community goals. Thus, the distinction between a 'unilateral' and 'collective' use of force is not one of numbers, but of authority and purpose. Irrespective of the number of states involved, the first is the result of a unilateral decision and is designed primarily to achieve goals personal to the acting state(s), whereas the latter is the result of the decision of a competent international organisation and is taken on behalf of the community at large.

Before proceeding to the substantive law, one more introductory point should be noted. This chapter is concerned with international law and the use of *armed* force;

that is, the use of deliberate military action by one state against another. This may be 'direct', as with the deployment of a state's regular armed forces (e.g. Iraq against Kuwait, USA against Iranian oil platforms, US/UK against Afghanistan and Iraq, Eritrea against Ethiopia), or 'indirect', as where armed groups of irregulars (such as guerrillas) operate on a state's behalf, either with or without a purpose of their own. We are not concerned with measures that do not involve actual physical violence, such as 'economic aggression' or destructive anti-government propaganda. These other forms of coercion may or may not be unlawful, but the better view is that they do not fall within the general meaning of 'force' as used in Art. 2(4) of the UN Charter. It is clear, for example, that 'aggression' as defined by the General Assembly's Resolution on the Definition of Aggression 1974 (GA Res. 3314, 29th Session) is limited to acts of armed force. For the purposes of this chapter, therefore, 'force' means military violence and does not include other types of injurious conduct.

Part One: **The unilateral use of force**

11.1 **The law before 1945**

The *ius ad bellum* of today is not simply a product of the United Nations Charter. Prior to 1945, there was a web of customary and treaty law which regulated the unilateral use of force by states. Indeed, perhaps the most difficult question of all is the extent to which pre-1945 rules still affect the scope of a state's rights and obligations under current international law. Furthermore, even if the Charter did usher in a completely new era – and many would dispute this – this would not diminish the relevance of pre-Charter law. It is only through an awareness of the historical development of the law of force that the current law can be properly understood.

In the early days of international law, the use of force by states was governed by the Just War doctrine. As developed by writers such as St Augustine and Grotius, the Just War theory stipulated that war was illegal unless undertaken for a 'just cause'. A just cause encompassed a variety of situations, but essentially involved a wrong received or a right illegally denied. War outside of these circumstances was illegal and there are obvious parallels with the system of today. By the late seventeenth century the rise of the nation state in Europe had produced a change of direction. At first, the Just War doctrine was refined, so that a state could be said to be acting legally if it believed it had a just cause, irrespective of whether it actually had one. There was no objective legal test of a state's right to use force. Then, as state practice came to be regarded as the primary source of international law (i.e. legal positivism) even this watered-down version of the Just War theory disappeared. By the eighteenth century, the governing doctrine was the sovereign right to resort to war. Every state had a perfect legal right to resort to war for any reason. International law regulated the actual conduct of war, but it did not interfere with a state's right to pursue it. This development was of crucial importance in the history of the *ius ad bellum*. In essence, the existence of unlimited legal competence meant that no express rights to use force for particular purposes needed to be established. Consequently, at this time, it was legally meaningless to talk of a 'right' of self-defence or a 'right' of reprisal, simply because there was no general prohibition to which these 'rights' could be an exception.

The sovereign right to resort to war, founded on state practice, governed international relations until the birth of the League of Nations in 1919. Although it was not legally unnecessary, by this time states had begun to classify the use of force by reference to the purpose it was intended to achieve. So, there were examples of the use of force in 'self-defence', for the 'rescue of nationals abroad' and in 'reprisal' for injury suffered. More importantly, states began to claim that force used for these purposes did not amount to a 'state of war', so avoiding the obligations of formal belligerency. This led to the development of certain criteria whereby the legality of 'force short of war' could be judged. Here then, is the legal origin of concepts such as self-defence, reprisals and protection of nationals. Of course, this development should not be exaggerated because there was at this time no general prohibition of the use of force, and in many cases the classification was for political consumption rather than legal justification. However, the seed had been planted.

The Covenant of the League of Nations introduced a limited restriction on the sovereign right to resort to war. Under the Covenant, war was lawful only if the procedural safeguards laid down in Arts 10 to 16 were observed, although if this was done a state remained perfectly entitled to achieve its objectives through formal war. Moreover, the Covenant did not place any conditions on the use of 'force short of war' and since the categorisation of any particular forceful act as 'war' (or not) was for the acting state alone, the Covenant was not effective in prohibiting resort to violence to any great degree. In a more general sense, however, the Covenant did have two significant consequences. First, the right of self-defence began to emerge more clearly as a genuine legal exception to the procedural restraints on the right to resort to war. In other words, going to war 'in self-defence' exempted a state from even the minimal restrictions of the Covenant. Secondly, the categories of 'force short of war', already developed prior to the Covenant, began to appear more clearly as legal claims or rights, rather than as political justifications. Both of these developments could not have occurred without the procedural restriction on a state's unlimited legal competence to go to war.

In 1928, the Covenant was supplemented by the General Treaty for the Renunciation of War, otherwise known as the Kellogg–Briand Pact. This treaty, which is still in force, represented the first attempt to outlaw war completely. In Article I, the parties 'condemn recourse to war for the solution of international controversies and renounce it as an instrument of national policy in their relationship with one another'. This was a vital development in the law of force, for it demonstrated that a general ban on 'war' was politically and legally possible. Again, however, since the prohibition applied only to 'war' (and not 'force'), the Pact was as flawed as the Covenant, although some commentators have argued that subsequent state practice reveals the ban to have been reasonably extensive. Nevertheless, whatever view one takes of the impact of the Kellogg–Briand Pact, the general prohibition of war it contained ensured that the use of force in self-defence emerged as an independent legal right. Although the Pact itself makes no reference to self-defence, the *travaux préparatoires* indicate that this was because the existence of such an exception was taken for granted.

To sum up, in the period immediately preceding the Charter, the right of states to use armed force was regulated by a mix of customary and treaty law. In customary law, there was no general prohibition on the use of force as such, although the Kellogg–Briand Pact did stipulate a ban on the right to resort to war. Moreover, by 1945, self-defence had emerged as a claim of right, an exception even if there was a general prohibition on war or the use of force. Furthermore, the conditions for lawful self-defence were emerging in customary law. Likewise, such matters as reprisals, rescue of nationals and humanitarian intervention were seen as legitimate examples of the 'use of force short of war' or, alternatively, if all force was outlawed, as legitimate exceptions to the general ban itself.

11.2 The law after the UN Charter

One of the primary purposes of the United Nations Charter is the 'suppression of acts of aggression or other breaches of the peace' (Art. 1). In Art. 2(4), the Charter gives substance to this statement of intent by providing that:

> All members shall refrain in their international relations from the threat or use of force against the territorial integrity or political independence of any state, or in any other manner inconsistent with the Purposes of the United Nations.

This is one of the central obligations of the Charter and, in terms, it stipulates a general prohibition of the unilateral use of force. Since 1945, the principle of Art. 2(4) has been reaffirmed many times, most notably in a number of General Assembly resolutions such as the Declaration on the Inadmissibility of Intervention in the Domestic Affairs of States (GA Res. 2131 (XX) (1965)), the Declaration of the Principles of International Law (GA Res. 2625 (XXV) (1970)), the Definition of Aggression (GA Res. 3314 (XXIX) (1974)) and the Resolution on Enhancing the Effectiveness of the Prohibition of the Use of Force (GA Res. 42/22, 18 November 1987) but also judicially inside the ICJ and elsewhere, as in the *Armed Activities on the Territory of the Congo (Democratic Republic of the Congo v Uganda) Case* 2005 ICJ Rep, the *Palestinian Wall Advisory Opinion* 2004 ICJ Rep para. 87, the Eritrea Ethiopia Claims Commission *Partial Award, Jus Ad Bellum* Ethiopia's Claims 1–8 ((*The Federal Democratic Republic of Ethiopia v The State of Eritrea*) (2006) 45 ILM 430) and the *Guyana v Suriname*, Arbitral Award, 17 September 2007, para. 445. Moreover, as is apparent from *Nicaragua v USA*, this general prohibition does not exist in treaty law alone. The ICJ in that case made it quite clear that a general ban on the use of force exists in customary law also, running parallel to the Charter.

There is no doubt that all states recognise and accept the fundamental importance of the primary ban on resort to force. In every example of the use of force in recent years, including Iraq's invasion of Kuwait, the NATO bombing of Serbia, and the US-led invasions of Iraq and Afghanistan, the states using violence have acknowledged that international law raises a *presumption* that force is unlawful and have never claimed that *all* uses of force are lawful. Unfortunately, this consensus is not matched by agreement over the precise scope of the prohibition, or of the explicit exception of self-defence found in Art. 51 of the Charter. In fact, the 'aggressor' state usually tries to mask its aggression by pleading a claim of right, such as self-defence, legitimate invitation or multilateral treaty authorisation. In general terms, this debate about the extent of the ban on force focuses on a 'permissive' or 'restrictive' interpretation of the relevant legal principles. The permissive school takes the general view that the Charter did not fundamentally change the direction of international law and, therefore, that reference may be had to pre-1945 rules in determining both the ambit of the primary prohibition of force and the explicit exception of self-defence. The restrictive school takes the view that the Charter brought about a radical alteration in states' rights, so that Art. 2(4) lays down a total and uniform ban on the unilateral use of force, and that a right of unilateral action survives only in so far as the Charter explicitly preserves one. In practice, the restrictive approach argues that unilateral force may be used only for self-defence under Article 51 and under (the now obsolete) Art. 107 provision for action against 'ex-enemy' states.

It should come as no surprise to learn that proponents of both the restrictive and permissive schools rely on policy considerations and value judgements in order to support their interpretation of the Charter and customary law. The permissive school sees a total ban on the use of force as an emasculation of a state's ability to protect itself against the illegal conduct of other states and groups of individuals (terrorists, insurgents etc). This, they argue, would be particularly foolish in an international society that has no police force and no reliable machinery for the vindication of rights illegally denied. They would point to the impotence of the United Nations during the Serbian/Kosovan crisis in 1998/9 and the Syrian civil war in 2012 as examples of the failure of collective responsibility and to the need for a state to protect itself and innocent victims against new forms of international violence. On the other hand, the restrictive school argues that the maintenance of international peace and security is the primary aim of international law and that the use of force can be permitted only in the most exceptional circumstances. In their view, the harm caused to the fabric of international society, both materially and psychologically, by an outbreak of violence nearly always outweighs the 'evil' it was intended to counter. Moreover, they see permissive rules as favouring powerful states and as being 'a signpost for abuse'. This itself, they point out, cannot be checked in a decentralised system such as international law.

There is no 'right' answer to the questions posed by this clash of ideas about the purpose of international law and the importance of the rights of individual states. It is a matter of judgement. However, in the following analysis, particular attention will be paid to the interpretation favoured by states themselves. These are to be found principally in the debates of the Security Council and General Assembly after an actual resort to violence has occurred and in the formal pronouncements of these bodies, although occasionally a state may make an ad hoc pronouncement about its view on an incident or problem (see, for example, the National Security Strategy issued by President Bush in September 2002 in which, *inter alia*, the USA's asserted a right of anticipatory self-defence).

11.2.1 Article 2(4)

Although Art. 2(4) appears absolute in its prohibition of the use of force, some commentators question whether this is an accurate interpretation. In terms,

Art. 2(4) prohibits the use of force 'against the territorial integrity or political independence' of any state or 'in any other manner inconsistent with the purposes' of the United Nations. This rather elliptical phraseology has led to the argument that Art. 2(4) prohibits only that use of force which is, in fact, directed against 'territorial integrity' or 'political independence' or is, in fact, contrary to the purposes of the UN. According to this permissive view, if the use of force does not result in the loss or permanent occupation of territory, if it does not compromise the 'target' state's ability to take independent decisions and if it is not contrary to UN purposes, it is not unlawful. In practice, therefore, a use of force that is designed to rescue nationals by means of a swift surgical strike, as with Israel at Entebbe airport in 1976, is not unlawful. Neither, on this view, was the United States' limited intervention in Panama in 1989 to kidnap the 'undemocratic' and 'criminal' General Noriega, nor the NATO action against Serbia for humanitarian purposes, nor the intervention in Afghanistan and Iraq to remove the oppressive, terrorist-like regimes. These actions (it is alleged) were not intended to, and arguably did not, compromise the 'territorial integrity' or 'political independence' of the 'victim' state although it is difficult to see why this is not the very outcome in Iraq and Afghanistan.

This very literal interpretation of Article 2(4) has been put forward in a number of instances of the actual use of force, most notably by Israel in 1976 and by the UK before the International Court in the *Corfu Channel Case* 1949 ICJ Rep 4. In Bowett's his view, because the right to use force for certain 'non-aggressive' purposes existed before the Charter, and because there is no clear abrogation of it in the Charter, the limited use of force for certain purposes must still be valid.

The particular purposes that are alleged to be lawful under this interpretation of Art. 2(4) are discussed later in greater detail. Necessarily, this interpretation does not allow a state to resort to force in every circumstance and even permissive doctrine accepts that Art. 2(4) goes beyond the prohibition of 'war' found in pre-Charter treaties. Yet, it still permits the use of force in a variety of situations. This in itself is enough to persuade proponents of the restrictive view that such an interpretation of Art. 2(4) should not be adopted. Moreover, in so far as the permissive interpretation places the distinction between lawful and unlawful force on the subjective intention or aim of the acting state, it may go too far. If the use of force is to be regulated at all, surely it must be on the basis of objective legal criteria.

According to the restrictive view of the use of force (e.g. Brownlie, *International Law and the Use of Force by States* (1963), and Kelsen, *The Law of Nations* (1950)), the effect of Art. 2(4) is to prohibit totally a state's right to use force, unless some specific exception is made by the Charter itself. Customary law rules, in so far as they give a wider freedom of action, are no longer relevant. In this sense, the right of self-defence under Art. 51 and action against ex-enemy states (Art. 107) are the only permissible exceptions involving unilateral force to the general ban in Art. 2(4). As to the effect of the disputed words in Art. 2(4) ('territorial integrity' etc.), it is argued that they were not intended to qualify the obligation not to use force but merely to describe the totality of a state's existence under international law. Consequently 'territorial integrity' and 'political independence' comprise all that a state is; they do not afford loopholes for action against that state. Likewise, the final words of Art. 2(4) prohibiting use of force against the purposes of the UN were not intended to allow force to be used to *achieve* those purposes, but rather as a safety net to ensure that force could never be used against non-state entities, such as colonies and protectorates. The net effect of the argument is, therefore, that Art. 2(4) prohibits all force, for all purposes, unless a specific Charter provision says otherwise.

An analysis of the *travaux préparatoires* of the San Francisco Conference that gave birth to the Charter confirms that the disputed phrases in Art. 2(4) were inserted in preliminary drafts in order to strengthen the obligation not to use force rather than to weaken it. Furthermore, although there have been many examples of the use of force since the birth of the United Nations, only Israel after the Entebbe raid has relied primarily on the permissive view of Art. 2(4). In all other cases, such as the US invasions of the Dominican Republic (1965) and Grenada (1983), the bombing of the Iraqi Nuclear Reactor in 1981, the Indian invasion of East Pakistan in 1971, the Tanzanian invasion of Uganda in 1979, the NATO action against Serbia in 1998/99, the invasions of Iraq and Afghanistan, the destruction of Iranian oil platforms and Ugandan operations in the Democratic Republic of the Congo, the states resorting to force have relied on alleged exceptions to the general principle prohibiting armed force rather than interpreting that prohibition narrowly. While these exceptions might be widely drawn, this is very different from claiming that the primary obligation is itself inherently flexible.

To conclude, the consensus among the international community, as evidenced by consideration of instances of the use of force, is that Art. 2(4) is not to be interpreted in the way claimed by protagonists of the permissive view. This is supported by the drafting history of the provision, the general purposes of the Charter and an analysis of the types of arguments used by those states actually using force. It would be strange indeed if the Charter was to repeat the mistakes of the League Covenant and the Kellogg–Briand Pact by providing a loophole based on an artificial and self-serving interpretation of Art. 2(4). Therefore, the important question is, are there any exceptions to Art. 2(4)?

11.2.2 Self-defence

As already indicated, the concept of self-defence as a legal right has no meaning unless there is a corresponding general duty to refrain from the use of force. A prohibition was achieved in some measure under the Kellogg–Briand Pact and taken further by the Charter. That is not to say that claims of 'self-defence' were not made before this, for the classic definition of customary self-defence arose out of an incident occurring in 1837. What we must bear in mind, however, is that self-defence as an 'inherent right' dates back only to the time when war and the use of force generally became unlawful.

The customary right of self-defence is taken to have been definitively expressed in the diplomatic correspondence between US Secretary of State Webster and British officials over *The Caroline* incident. In 1837, British military forces seized *The Caroline* while it was berthed in an American port and sent her over the Niagara Falls. During subsequent British attempts to secure the release from US custody of one of the individuals involved in the action, the US Secretary of State indicated that Great Britain had to show 'a necessity of self-defence, instant, overwhelming, leaving no choice of means and no moment for deliberation'. Further, it had to be established that, after entering the USA, the armed forces 'did nothing unreasonable or excessive; since the act justified by the necessity of self-defence must be limited by that necessity and kept clearly within it': *The Caroline Case*, 29 Brit. & For.

St. Papers 1137. This statement effectively defines the use of force in self-defence as lawful under customary law if it is made in response to an immediate and pressing threat, which could not be avoided by alternative measures and if the force used to remove that threat was proportional to the danger posed. So, if the crisis can be avoided by diplomatic representations, or if the 'danger' is so remote as to be nothing more than a feeling of suspicion, self-defence is not justified. Similarly, an attack against a naval vessel cannot be used as an excuse for the occupation of the territory of the offending state, for this would not be a proportionate response. It remains uncertain, however, whether the use of nuclear weapons or other weapons of mass destruction could be a proportional defensive measure in response to either a nuclear or a conventional attack. The matter was left unresolved by the *Advisory Opinion on the Legality of the Threat or Use of Nuclear Weapons*. That said, if the flexible conditions of *The Caroline Case* are satisfied, the customary right of self-defence permits the use of force in any of the following circumstances:

(a) in response to and directed against an ongoing armed attack against state territory e.g. by Kuwait against Iraq in 1990;

(b) in anticipation of an armed attack or threat to the state's security, so that a state may strike first, with force, to neutralise an immediate but potential threat to its security, e.g. as alleged by Israel as justification for its strike against an Iraqi nuclear reactor in 1981;

(c) in response to an attack (threatened or actual) against state interests, such as territory, nationals, property and rights guaranteed under international law. If any of these attributes of the state are threatened, then the state may use force to protect them e.g. by Israel against Uganda (Entebbe) in 1977 and the US-led invasions of Afghanistan and Iraq to counter the terrorist threat;

(d) where the 'attack' does not itself involve measures of armed force, such as economic aggression and propaganda. All that is required is that there is an instant and overwhelming necessity for forceful action.

It is apparent from the preceding analysis that the customary right of self-defence is not a narrow exception to the general ban on the use of force. It allows an armed response in a variety of situations, so long as there is some element of 'defence' of the 'state'. Importantly, however, customary self-defence may go beyond the right guaranteed by the Charter, and for this reason it has become essential to determine whether customary self-defence has survived the Charter. In many examples of the unilateral use of force in recent years, such as the US invasion of Grenada in 1983, the destruction of the Iraqi nuclear reactor by Israel in 1981 and the USA attack on Iranian oil platforms in 1987 and 1988 the customary right of self-defence, based on *The Caroline* formula, has been pleaded by the state resorting to force and its supporters.

By way of contrast, under the restrictive approach to the use of force, it is argued that this wide right of self-defence is no longer available. In the Charter, Art. 51 stipulates that nothing 'shall impair the inherent right of individual or collective self-defence if an armed attack occurs against a member of the United Nations'. As we have seen, Art. 2(4) is said to prohibit all armed force, so, reading Arts 2(4) and 51 together, the conclusion is reached that the only right of self-defence now available is that found in Art. 51. The old customary law is superseded, with the practical result that a state may resort to self-defence 'if an armed attack occurs' but not otherwise. Specifically, this would seem to preclude the right to use force in self-defence in anticipation of an attack, or when the threat is not an 'armed attack', or when the violence is directed at state interests rather than state territory. Indeed, if we take the view put forward in the *Palestinian Wall Advisory Opinion* (ICJ Rep 2004 at para. 139) at face value, it is available only when the armed attack emanates from another state, as opposed to groups of insurgents operating from other states but not under the control of the 'host' state. However, this view of Art. 51 as a 'state-to-state only' rule was put forward by the majority in the Advisory Opinion without full analysis and it is not clear whether this narrowest interpretation of self-defence is either justified as a matter of law or serves the practical needs of modern international society. It is discussed more fully later. What is clear, however, is that Art. 51 is generally narrower than the right that some alleged to exist under customary law. At its most restrictive, this would mean that of the four situations permissible under pre-1945 customary law, only (a) remains lawful.

There is, then, some doubt as to the extent of self-defence under current international law and a wide variety of arguments have been used in support of a wider right than that apparently postulated in Article 51. First, it is argued as before that Art. 2(4) did not take away the right to use force absolutely, therefore the customary right of self-defence has never been abolished. It remains extant. Secondly, it is contended that Art. 51 was never intended to be a definitive statement of the right of self-defence. Indeed, the *travaux préparatoires* of the San Francisco Conference suggest that Art. 51 was included in the Charter in order to clarify the relationship of regional organisations to the Security Council, rather than to define self-defence. For example, such organisations may take armed action, without Security Council authorisation, if it is a matter of self-defence, but they do need Council approval if they propose 'enforcement action' (see section 11.3). Thirdly, it is argued that the customary right is actually preserved by Art. 51, because of the reference therein to the 'inherent' right. This is taken to mean 'pre-existing in customary law', although it could also mean that self-defence is an inalienable right of statehood that can never be denied. Finally, it is rightly pointed out that Art. 51 does not say that self-defence is available *only* if an armed attack occurs and it does not indicate that the 'armed attack' must be made by a state. In any event, when considering anticipatory action, it is also noted that an attack may 'occur' before troops cross a frontier, as when missiles are launched or aircraft deployed.

These are powerful arguments and they do support the view that Art. 51 was never intended to narrow such right of self-defence as pre-dated the Charter. On the other hand, there is a great deal of evidence to suggest that states themselves interpret the right of self-defence in the strictest possible way. For instance, in those examples previously noted where the state resorting to force relied on an expanded concept of self-defence, this was hotly disputed by the majority of other states. Considerable reliance was placed by 'uninvolved' states on the precise terms of Art. 51. Furthermore, as Brownlie argues, there is some evidence to suggest that the scope of customary law in 1945 was not as wide as the permissive doctrine suggests. Again, if customary law and Charter law on the use of force exist in tandem, as decided by the Court in *Nicaragua* v *USA*, this could mean that the scope of the former has changed to become more restrictive. The counter argument advanced by Judge Jennings in that case, that state practice cannot have had the effect of redefining the customary right because such practice is referable to the Charter and not customary law, is artificial and proves only that it is the Charter after all which now governs international conduct.

The safest but least satisfactory conclusion is that the precise ambit of the right of self-defence is open to debate. The key points of contention are these.

(i) What is meant by an 'armed attack'? It seems clear from judicial considera- tion of the right that not all armed activities can amount to an armed attack sufficient to trigger the right of self-defence. In the Eritrea Ethiopia Claims Commission, Partial Award, *Jus Ad Bellum Ethiopia's Claims 1–8 (The Federal Democratic Republic of Ethiopia* v *The State of Eritrea)* (2006), the Commission made the point that '[l]ocalized border encounters between small infantry units, even those involving the loss of life, do not constitute an armed attack for purposes of the Charter' and this is echoed in the *Armed Activities on the Territory of the Congo (Democratic Republic of the Congo* v *Uganda) Case.* So, there is a point at which the use of force is unlawful, but nevertheless it does not constitute an armed attack so as to justify a response in self-defence. Presumably, the state suffering the unlawful use of force is entitled to take countermeasures falling short of the use of force. Is this realistic?

(ii) Can an 'armed attack' occur through a series of events rather than a major episode? So, does an armed attack occur if the state is subject to repeated, relatively small scale incidents over a period of time, such as rocket launches, isolated attacks, small armed incursions? This was the argument advanced by the United States in the *Oil Platforms (Islamic Republic of Iran* v *United States of America) Case* (2003) when asserting that it had attacked and destroyed Iranian oil installations in self-defence because of a pattern of small scale attacks against its vessels and personnel. The ICJ found that the United States could not prove that these incidents were attributable to Iran, so it did not consider whether self-defence was justified on an 'accumulation of events' approach to an armed attack. On the other hand, in that case the ICJ avoided deciding that such events could not, in principle, trigger the right of self-defence, and some see the judgment as offering tacit support for the United States' view of the law.

(iii) Does the 'armed attack' have to be perpetrated by, or be the responsibility of, a state, or can it arise from acts of insurgents, armed groups and similar simply using the territory of the state that is then subject to measures of self-defence? This was one of the issues raised in *Nicaragua* v *USA* and the ICJ did not present a wholly convincing answer. In the majority view in that case, the provision of weapons, finance, training facilities and general encouragement for armed forces operating against another state (State B) was indeed an unlawful use of force against that state committed by the supplier (State A). This is not surprising and is greatly to be welcomed, for it properly gives 'force' a very wide meaning. However, although it is an unlawful use of force to supply rebels in this fashion, apparently this does not amount to an 'armed attack' by the supplier against the threatened state so as to justify the use of force in self-defence. A similar view is found in the *Palestinian Wall Advisory Opinion* where the Court assumes that Art. 51 is available only in the event of a *state's* armed attack on another. (Assuming, of course, that the supply etc. does not mean that the state is indeed committing the armed attack.) The issue is left unresolved by the decision in the *Armed Activities on the Territory of the Congo (Democratic Republic of the Congo* v *Uganda) Case* (2005) because Uganda could not establish factually that 'armed attacks' of sufficient magnitude had occurred. Thus, the Court had 'no need to respond to the contentions of the Parties as to whether and under what conditions contemporary international law provides for a right of self-defence against large-scale attacks by irregular forces'. In fact, Art. 51 itself, in its own terms, does *not* say that an armed attack must be made *by* another state before the right to self-defence can arise. It talks only of an armed attack *against* a state.

(iv) Is self-defence available in anticipation of an armed attack occurring, or is it lawful only if reactive to an armed attack that has already occurred? In *Nicaragua v USA*, the issue of the legitimacy of anticipatory self-defence was expressly reserved by the Court (this being a case of an alleged actual armed attack), and while the majority tended to favour the restrictive view, Judges Jennings and Schwebel clearly felt that the Charter had not removed the customary right to take pre-emptive action.

(v) In order to justify self-defence, must the armed attack be against state territory, or is an attack against state interests, such as economic assets or nationals abroad sufficient? Again, a number of states argue that aggression can take many forms, not only the classic attack against territory, especially in the modern age. Such attacks can be equally as destructive as sending troops over the border. Generally, however, it seems that most states would not accept this as sufficient to trigger a forceful response in self-defence, although there has been little judicial consideration of the point. It is discussed more fully later in relation to an alleged right to use force to protect nationals or property abroad, or to protect human rights.

(vi) Is the use of force in self-defence available in response to indiscriminate attacks by terrorist and similar groups? These, generally, do not emanate from a specific 'enemy' state but are perpetrated by groups that span borders and sometimes continents. Recent years have seen far too many examples of such incidents, and they have been met with overwhelming force by the victims, particularly the United States and its allies. Such a view of self-defence – typified by US President Bush's National Security Strategy of September 2002 – has not been decisively rejected by the international community.

(vii) There is widespread agreement that to be lawful, the use of force in self-defence must be proportionate the events that triggered. This is true, and uncontested, in customary law (*Caroline Case*) and under the Charter (*Armed Activities on the Territory of the Congo (Democratic Republic of the Congo v Uganda)*), if they be different. Critically, whether this obligation is met, will depend on the facts of each case and it is impossible to lay down any guidance. The tendency of the acting state will be to use such force as removes the threat and any future prospect thereof. However, in both the *Oil Platforms Case* and the *Congo Case*, the ICJ indicates that, had the right of self-defence been available, the responses would have been held to be disproportionate. We should, of course, be wary of encouraging violence in international affairs, but the Court should reflect before proposing a concept of proportionality that requires the defensive state to deal only with the immediate threat without permitting it also to safeguard the future. If that is the sense of these recent decisions – and in fairness it is not clear – it will not reflect the reality of how states will respond. It might be better to see 'proportionality' as providing an outer limit to what is permissible rather than as a prescriptive concept specifying what is.

(viii) Under Art. 51, states are obliged to report an exercise of self-defence to the Security Council, as did the United States when taking the action that led to the *Oil Platforms Case*. Clearly, the point is both to alert the Council, and to give it an opportunity to take collective action. Nevertheless, it is not clear what the consequences of a failure to report are. In both the *Congo* and *Ethiopia* cases, there was a failure to report and this was noted in the judgments, but given that the claims of self-defence were not made out on the facts, there is no further discussion. It is conceivable that a failure to report might be regarded as rendering an otherwise lawful self-defence unlawful, although that does seem an unlikely conclusion.

11.2.3 Other legitimate uses of force

11.2.3.1 Collective self-defence

The use of force in collective self-defence is also preserved by Art. 51 and essentially it will be lawful in the same circumstances as individual self-defence – i.e. in response to an armed attack or, if customary law survives, in the wider situations indicated earlier. However, there is some debate as to what 'collective' self-defence means. Obviously, on a factual level, what is envisaged is the use of force in self-defence by two or more states. Yet, does this mean that all the states exercising the right of self-defence must have been subject to individual attacks, or can states that have not been attacked come to the aid of the victim? In other words, for collective self-defence, who must be attacked – all the states taking action or just one?

The latter interpretation of collective self-defence is the basis for military alliances such as NATO, for they envisage that all members of the alliance will use force if any one of them is subject to an unlawful use of force. This was why NATO was involved in warning Syria when Turkey was hit by missiles fired from Syria during the civil war in 2012 and it was the initial basis for action against Iraq following its invasion of Kuwait in 1990. In the *Nicaragua* case, the majority of the judges took this view, although they also suggested that the attacked state must 'request' assistance before action by others in its aid can be lawful. This is, perhaps, an unrealistic procedural requirement, not found in the language of Art. 51 itself, although it does prevent a third party from taking military action simply because it thinks that collective self-defence is justified. More controversially, Judge Jennings in his Dissenting Opinion in *Nicaragua* v *USA* criticised this approach, pointing out that 'collective' self-defence was not a concept found in customary law and further, that there was then no substantial evidence to support the majority's conclusions. In his view, 'collective' self-defence was simply the joint exercise of individual rights – in other words, all states joining in the defensive action must be able to claim self-defence in their own right.

One must note at this point that Judge Jennings' narrow view of collective self-defence may be linked to his opinion that individual self-defence is not limited to the simple 'armed attack' situation. Consequently, when one state is attacked, it is quite possible on the expanded concept of individual self-defence that other states will be threatened – 'attacked' in the wider customary law sense. They will, then, have an individual right and any action will be a joint exercise by joint victims. On the other hand, if we take the view that individual self-defence is available in the event of an armed attack only (narrowly defined), it would seem that we should see collective self-defence as a device whereby 'non-attacked' states can come to the aid of a victim. Certainly, the majority view in *Nicaragua* v *USA* seems to be tied to the belief that the individual right of self-defence is narrowly drawn. If it was otherwise, under Judge Jennings' view of collective self-defence, an aggressor could 'pick off' his targets without incurring collective action. It is this author's opinion that the better view on the meaning of collective self-defence is that of the majority in *Nicaragua* and it is implicit in most of the treaties that establish defensive military alliances. Consequently, collective self-defence is not the joint exercise of individual rights, but is collective action in response to an actual armed attack against one state, with the *possible* additional criterion that the victim should formally request assistance through its recognised representatives.

11.2.3.2 Invitation and civil wars

It is quite clear that one state may request the deployment of another state's military forces in its territory. In 1958, for example, Jordan requested the deployment of UK forces because of serious internal disorder encouraged by the United Arab Republic. Likewise, a state may give permission for the use of force on its territory for any lawful purpose, as where a state seeks to secure the safety of its nationals as alleged by the USA when it invaded Grenada in 1983. These are not violations of international law because they occur with the consent of the territorial sovereign, provided of course that the purpose is not unlawful in itself (e.g. genocide). Often, the objects of such consensual interventions are entirely altruistic, as where the military forces of one state form a 'peacekeeping force' in a territory with the consent of the territorial sovereign. This appears to have been the origin of the peacekeeping force in Bosnia, present in that territory initially with the consent of all three disputing populations. Of course, as the Grenada case illustrates, it can be difficult to determine whether real consent actually has been given and by the body or person competent to act for the state in international law. In the *Armed Activities on the Territory of the Congo (Democratic Republic of the Congo* v *Uganda) Case*, the Court notes that an intervention that is lawful through consent will become unlawful if that consent is withdrawn, as in that case.

Apart from the obvious factual difficulties in determining when consent has been given genuinely (or withdrawn), there are further problems because of the general principle of non-intervention: see, for example, the General Assembly Resolution on the Declaration on the Inadmissibility of Intervention in the Domestic Affairs of States, GA Res. 2131 (XX) (1965). It is clear that each state has the right to determine its own internal policies and that no other state may intervene or interfere in any way. Thus, under international law, civil war is perfectly lawful and it is extremely unlikely that third-party military intervention can be justified by, say, a desire to assist the 'democratic' faction. Yet, this bald statement of principle hides two very real problems. First, when *exactly* does internal disorder amount to a civil war so that the 'established' government is no longer competent to request outside assistance to help put down the rebellion? Secondly, what is the position when, as typically happens, both sides in a civil war establish rival governments and both request assistance from different third parties?

Taking the second question first, it is reasonably clear that once a civil war is in progress, no other state may respond to a request for military assistance from either party. If it does, it will be using force unlawfully, as was the case when the former

Soviet Union invaded Afghanistan in pursuance of an invitation from the allegedly legitimate government. Simply put, in a civil war there is no authority competent under international law to invite assistance from other states, although there is a possible exception in respect of assistance given to a group fighting for self-determination (see section 11.2.2.4). Until the Security Council decided to act, this was the position in respect of Libya during the civil war of the 'Arab Spring' in 2011.

The first question is, by comparison, much more difficult to answer. As we have seen, the established authorities in a state are competent to invite military assistance from other states, at least where this is not in order to deny its population some internationally protected right of its own (e.g. self-determination). But when do those 'established authorities' cease to be competent because the rebellion now amounts to an internationally recognised civil war? It is of little help, but probably true, that it boils down to a question of fact in each case, with determinations by international agencies (such as the UN and concerned regional organisations) providing powerful evidence of the true nature of the crisis. Obviously, this gives those states that would like to intervene considerable latitude. One state's civil war that requires non-intervention is another state's small rebellion which friendly states can help suppress. This unfortunate duality is borne out in practice and there are many examples of invitations to intervene being issued by entities that almost certainly have no right to do so, either because the crisis has evolved into civil war (no intervention permitted) or because the invitation comes from a minor rebel group that has requested assistance in order to overthrow the genuinely established authorities. Examples of the former include the USA invasion of Grenada and of the latter, the Vietnamese intervention in Cambodia in 1978 and the USSR intervention in Afghanistan in 1979. For this reason many commentators suggest that, as a matter of principle, invitation should cease to be a lawful ground for the use of force, at least in all situations of internal disorder. The counter-argument is that it is the right of every state to conduct its domestic affairs as it wishes, and in practice many states have agreed to the stationing of foreign troops on their soil and to the assistance of foreign forces for certain purposes (e.g. ending a hostage situation). Moreover, as demonstrated by the situation in Syria in 2012, absolute adherence to the principle of non-intervention can lead to humanitarian crises and a drawn out and bloody internal struggle. To conclude, then, if we accept that intervention by invitation is lawful as an aspect of state sovereignty, we must also accept that it might be used as a loophole through which states can jump in order to perpetrate the most serious violations of international peace and security.

11.2.4 The use of force for other purposes

At various times, states have made claims that the use of force is lawful if intended to achieve certain 'approved' purposes. We must be clear where the alleged validity of these 'rights' springs from. The most common explanation offered by the state resorting to force for one of the purposes discussed subsequently is that it is legitimate as an aspect of the customary right of self-defence. Essentially, all this means is that the state is claiming the expanded version of the right just considered, legitimate under *The Caroline* formula. Alternatively, the state may claim that the use of force is lawful because it does not violate the precise terms of Art. 2(4), if interpreted literally as by the permissive school. This has also been discussed previously.

Finally, and most controversially, the state may claim that new customary rules have developed since 1945 which permit the use of force for the particular purpose undertaken.

11.2.4.1 Reprisals

The use of force in reprisal regards violence as the proper legal procedure for the vindication of rights illegally denied or as the proper method for inflicting punishment for harm suffered. Recent examples include the attack by the USA on Iraq in 1993 in retaliation for an alleged assassination attempt against former President Bush (although the USA would plead self-defence), Israel's bombing of Lebanon in response to attacks by guerrillas and the USA's fatal attempt to capture Osama Bin Laden in Pakistan in 2011. According to the *Naulilaa Case* (1928) 2 RIAA 1012, a 'reprisal is an act of self-help by the injured state responding to an act contrary to international law by the offending state'. The legality of the reprisal was said to depend on a prior illegal act being committed against the state now using force and, under pre-Charter law, the use of armed force was permitted only if it was a proportionate response to the prior illegality. Armed reprisals were a method of gaining satisfaction and redress in a system that could not otherwise provide it. It is generally accepted that Art. 2(4) has outlawed armed reprisals, especially since the Charter was intended to provide more effective machinery for the peaceful settlement of disputes.

However, the reluctance of the community at large to utilise the machinery of collective security for much of the last sixty-five years and the inability of the current system to punish, let alone prevent, even the most serious breaches of international law (see e.g. the Bosnian situation and the US-led interventions in Iraq and Afghanistan) have led many writers to question whether the ban on armed reprisals is still desirable, at least where the prior illegality itself involved the use of armed force. Bowett, for example, has argued forcefully that certain types of reprisal may be legitimate under 'an accumulation of events' theory of self-defence (66 *AJIL* 1), a view favoured by the USA in the *Oil Platforms Case*. Thus, if a state has been subject to repeated armed attacks in the past and these are likely to continue sporadically in the future, this may amount or 'accumulate' to an attack against the state so as to trigger self-defence. In fact, this is really another way of arguing for a wider right of self-defence to meet the challenges of modern-day terrorist and guerrilla warfare. Yet as we have seen, the international community is largely against any expansion in self-defence and it is unlikely that they would accept its *de facto* merger with the doctrine of reprisals. The better view is, then, that armed reprisals are illegal under international law, even where the prior illegality itself involved the use of force and even where the right of self-defence may not arise, as in the case of past and anticipated attacks. In the Declaration on the Principles of International Law (GA Res. 2625 (XXV)), the General Assembly notes that states must refrain from acts of reprisal involving the use of force.

11.2.4.2 Protection of nationals at home and abroad. Terrorism and the use of force

The right to use force to protect nationals abroad has been claimed several times in the last twenty-five years. It was the linchpin of the Israeli claim of justification for the use of force at Entebbe airport, the US action in Grenada in 1983, in Panama in 1989 and against Iraq in 1993. It is accepted by the UK as a lawful reason for the use of force. Essentially, it involves the use of force on the territory of another state, without the permission of the territorial sovereign, in order to rescue nationals who are in serious danger. In the Suez crisis of 1956, the UK also claimed that state property could be protected in this way, but no more recent claims have been made.

If this is a lawful ground for the use of force – and that is uncertain – customary practice appears to have identified four conditions. First, the 'host' state must be unable or unwilling to protect the nationals. Secondly, the nationals must be in serious and immediate danger of life-threatening harm. Thirdly, force must be the weapon of last resort. Fourthly, the acting state may use only such force as is reasonably necessary and must vacate the territory of the 'host' state as soon as is practicable. Thus, the continued occupation of territory, as happened in the Grenada and Panama cases, is not justifiable on the basis of this doctrine. It will be apparent, moreover, that this theory shares much with the right of self-defence and it is frequently justified under that general rubric – the nationals being the 'state' for the purpose of the actual or threatened armed attack. It is also possible to argue that this is not a use of force 'against the territorial integrity or political independence' of the state and so not prohibited by Art. 2(4), at least where the intervening state does withdraw promptly.

Whether international law knows of such a right is a matter of debate. If valid, it would seem that it is better seen as within the rubric of self-defence and this was essentially the view of the USA in the Grenada case, in the bombing of Libya in 1986 and when Baghdad was attacked in 1993. In respect of this last incident, the UK offered unqualified support for the US legal position, arguing that protection of nationals came within self-defence when '(a) there is good evidence that the target attacked would otherwise continue to be used by the other State in support of terrorist attacks against one's nationals; (b) there is, effectively, no other way to forestall imminent further attacks on one's nationals; (c) the force employed is proportionate to the threat' (Foreign Secretary, House of Commons, 28 June 1993). It will be appreciated that this justification is valid only if the right of self-defence is itself taken to be the wider right unconstrained by the language of Art. 51. Of even greater interest is the way in which the 'right' to protect nationals allegedly has evolved from the swift, Entebbe-style rescue mission in the 'host' state's territory and now encompasses the right to use force against a malefactor in order to counter isolated terrorist attacks against nationals wherever they may be. The examples par excellence are the US-led invasions of Afghanistan and Iraq in response to terrorist attacks but which were not even 'surgical' and have instead led to the overthrow of the governing regimes in both countries and the occupation of state territory by the 'liberators'. It is difficult to see how this 'defence against terrorism' can be within the rubric of protection of nationals and self-defence, even if the more traditional rescue missions are. To most objective observers this new claim looks like punitive reprisals, or at best long range pre-emptive self-defence, and in reality it is the pursuance of foreign policy by force and illustrates why the existence of these permissive rights to use force is so controversial.

Thus, while it may be possible to justify the surgical use of force in a target state to rescue nationals under an immediate threat followed by an immediate withdrawal (e.g. an Entebbe-style operation), most states dispute the existence of an extended right to use force to combat threats to nationals and state interests from terrorism (whether justified as self-defence or otherwise), not least because it provides a tempting opportunity to interfere in the domestic affairs of 'target' states, either by occupation of their territory or by intimidatory 'reprisal type' strikes (e.g. the USA action in the *Oil Platforms Case*). Moreover, even if responsive action against another state using force is initially justified because, say, of the fear of imminent further terrorist attacks, there is scant – if any – justification for using the opportunity as an excuse for engineering a change of government in the target state and the occupation of its territory, as happened in both Iraq and Afghanistan. Nothing is added by asserting that the action will lead to the capture and punishment of those responsible for terrorist outrages or widespread violations of human rights because there is no rule of international law that authorises the use of force for these purposes.

Once again then, there is a dichotomy here between the requirements of international law generally prohibiting the use of force – which itself is a rule of *jus cogens* – and the ability and willingness of powerful states to achieve their goals by the use of aggressive force. While most of the international community were outraged by the terrorist attacks against the property and the nationals of all countries in the USA in 2001, few have gone on to agree that the actual military response was lawful, whether that be on grounds of self-defence, legitimate reprisal, the apprehension of terrorists or as a means of averting a potential threat to the peace and security of mankind (i.e. the search for weapons of mass destruction). There is simply no law that permits a state to take *unilateral* action in these circumstances. Certainly, it is difficult to explain why such action is not in violation of the 'territorial integrity or political independence' of the target state and not contrary to the purposes of the United Nations.

11.2.4.3 Humanitarian intervention

Under the 'doctrine' of humanitarian intervention it is alleged that one state (State A) may use force in the territory of another state (State B) in order to protect the human rights of individuals in State B, usually being nationals of State B. It is similar in purpose to the protection of nationals by means of a surgical strike just considered, except that now there is no necessary link between the acting state and the individuals in danger, and is an alleged general right to intervene with force for humanitarian purposes without the consent of the territorial sovereign, as where a government is systematically murdering whole sections of its own population. This is the alleged basis of the NATO action against Serbia (Yugoslavia) in 1998/99, an issue that will not now be resolved by the ICJ given that it has declined jurisdiction over Serbia's complaint in the *Legality of the Use of Force Cases* (2004). However, certain 'conditions' have been postulated for the lawful exercise of this 'right'; for example, that the intervention must be authorised by a competent international organisation and that the use of armed force is legitimate only in cases of extreme deprivation of fundamental human rights, such as genocide.

That said, it is reasonably clear that neither the existence of the right itself, nor the conditions for its exercise, are supported by unequivocal state practice. Although there have been suggestions that 'humanitarian intervention' was the basis of India's intervention in East Pakistan in 1971 and Tanzania's intervention in Uganda in 1979, this was not the position adopted by either of the states actually using force. Moreover, while Vietnam appears to have claimed this 'right' in respect of its intervention in Cambodia in 1978, this was specifically rejected by the great majority of states participating in the Security Council debates on the affair. This is significant, especially since the Vietnamese invasion halted perhaps the worst violations of human rights by a government against its own population since 1945. A claim of 'humanitarian intervention' appears to have been made by the USA and the UK as justification for their maintenance of 'no-fly' zones in southern and northern Iraq (now superseded by the US-led occupation) the purpose of which was to project the local populations from the excesses of the Iraqi government. However, while there may have been a humanitarian motive for these interferences with Iraq's sovereignty (as with that of Libya in 2011), and while the action may have achieved a humanitarian purpose, it is a far cry from accepting that this was in pursuance of a *right* to intervene. In fact there were other possible justifications for these no-fly zones, not least that they were a continuance of the collective security action against Iraq duly authorised by the Security Council, and this appears to have been more to the fore in later UK and US pronouncements. When these no-fly zones were superseded by the general attack on Iraq and its subsequent occupation, humanitarian considerations – that is the need to remove a murderous dictator – were to the fore of the political and public justification, but no clear claim of humanitarian intervention as of right has been made. Of more significance for the development of state practice was the widespread bombing of Serbia by NATO in 1998/99 in order to prevent Serbian atrocities in Kosovo. Although the UK government avoided explicit reliance on humanitarian intervention, this is generally taken to be the only tenable ground for the use of force. Undoubtedly, the NATO action was motivated by a genuine desire to protect the Kosovars, but this may not be enough to make it legal. In sum, the legitimacy of humanitarian intervention is debatable. Indeed, unless we again read Art. 2(4) very literally or assume that it has been 'remodelled' by some overriding state practice, 'humanitarian intervention' runs directly counter to the whole purpose of Art. 2(4) and many General Assembly resolutions adopted in the last fifty years. This is especially true when we realise that it is nearly always necessary to remove the offending government, or at least seriously compromise its freedom of action (as with Serbia and Libya), in order to stop the violations of human rights. Such a result would surely be against the 'political independence' of the 'target' state and it is no answer that the purposes so achieved are themselves an aim of the UN Charter.

In conclusion, then, there still appears to be little evidence that states have accepted a *right* of humanitarian intervention although, as some commentators have suggested, the Iraqi and Serbian episodes may be the first steps in the formation of a new customary exception to Art. 2(4). Yet the fragility of this state practice is illustrated by the fact of a *lack* of intervention in the Rwanda, Sudanese and Syrian crises, all examples of very serious and widespread violations of human rights. It is also important that the dangers of accepting this doctrine, based as it is on subjective opinions about the internal policies of other states, should not be underestimated. Likewise, on a practical level is it really true that one state will be prepared to expend money and effort and the lives of its own citizens for no gain for itself? The possibilities for abuse are manifest. This may be a depressing and cynical conclusion and it doubtless contradicts the modern emphasis on human rights generally but, as harsh as it may seem, states appear to value their independence and political freedom more highly than they prize the protection of human rights. Finally, should it be true that a right of humanitarian intervention is in the making, we must remember that for the international lawyer who believes in a theory of the 'sources' of international law, such a right can exist only if it is based in treaty or found in state practice supported by adequate *opinio juris*. There is no moralistic magic that can manufacture the right simply because it ought to exist.

11.2.4.4 Self-determination and national liberation movements

The use of force to achieve self-determination and for the assistance of national liberation movements has been claimed as legitimate on the ground that it furthers the principles of the Charter. The General Assembly in its Definition of Aggression (Art. 7) and Declaration of Principles of International Law (Principle 5) has dealt with the issue in a deliberately ambiguous fashion, stating only that such peoples have the right to achieve self-determination and to receive unspecified assistance. The same circumspection is evident in the *Palestinian Wall Advisory Opinion* when the ICJ observes that it 'is for all States, *while respecting the United Nations Charter and international law*, to see to it that any impediment, resulting from the construction of the wall, to the exercise by the Palestinian people of its right to self-determination is brought to an end' (emphasis added).

The issue may arise in three ways. First, may the 'colonial' power use force to suppress the self-determination movement? This would seem to be unlawful, being contrary to customary and Charter law. Thus, according to the Declaration of Principles of International Law (GA Res. 2625 1970), 'every state has the duty to refrain from any forcible action which deprives peoples ... of their right to self-determination and freedom and independence' and there is no doubt that this represents customary law (*Palestinian Wall Advisory Opinion* (2004)). Similarly, Art. 2(4) prohibits the use of force 'in any manner inconsistent with the purposes of the United Nations' and this may have been designed specifically to protect peoples who have not yet achieved statehood. In 1999, Indonesia seemed to be prepared to use force to prevent the people of East Timor exercising their right to self-determination under UN auspices. The Security Council responded by authorising states to use 'all necessary measures' to protect the rights of the East Timoreans (SC Res. 1264 (December 1999)). Although this was a 'collective' use of force, it does suggest that it would have been unlawful for Indonesia itself to use force to prevent the people of East Timor exercising their right of self-determination.

Secondly, may national liberation movements use force to overthrow the 'colonial' power and thereby achieve self-determination? This is more problematic, although many developing countries argue that the 'right' is implicit in the Assembly resolution referred to previously. However, Assembly resolutions are not binding and it is unclear whether state practice supports the right as a matter of customary law. In a survey of state practice, the evidence was found to be inconclusive, although the 'right' was favoured by the majority of Afro-Asian countries (see Wilson, *International Law and the Use of Force by National Liberation Movements* (1988)). Again, if we recognise this right, does that mean that the colonial power is not able to take defensive measures to protect itself and *its* people, because this would be tantamount to suppressing self-determination as indicated earlier? Moreover, how do we identify which groups are authorised to use force for this purpose? We might all agree that it included the South West Africa People's Organisation in Namibia, and Palestine Liberation Organisation in the Middle East but what of the Kurds in Turkey or the Basques in Spain? These are serious practical difficulties and they serve only to reinforce the reservations based on legal principle. The third difficulty is whether an established state may use force to assist a national liberation movement in its fight for self-determination, as claimed by India after its invasion of East Pakistan. Once again, several states have argued that the obligation in Art. 2(4) does not prohibit force for this 'beneficial' purpose and, further, that it is implicitly recognised by the Definition of Aggression and other General Assembly resolutions. Yet, where does this leave the primary obligation in Art. 2(4) not to use force? There is, moreover, no evidence that a customary practice has developed permitting armed assistance to national liberation movements and it is hotly disputed by countries such as the UK and USA. It was no surprise that the ICJ in the *Palestinian Wall Advisory Opinion* was circumspect, as they were when discussing generally the concept of self-determination in the *Advisory Opinion on the Accordance with international law of the unilateral declaration of independence in respect of Kosovo* (2008).

Of course, there are competing principles and values in play here. The international community places great importance on self-determination and on the prohibition of the use of force. Both may well encapsulate principles of *jus cogens*. Logically, because international law permits a qualifying group to exercise self-determination, and prohibits states from preventing its exercise, does not mean that it may be achieved by violating another fundamental norm – the prohibition of the use of force. The better view is, then, that third states may assist politically and economically in the fight for self-determination, but not militarily. An example of how external intervention can distort an internal, self-determination conflict is provided by the Bosnia crisis. In the end, the Security Council passed mandatory resolutions prohibiting outside assistance to any party, thus reinforcing the obligation of non-intervention to which this section has just referred. Thus, if the international community is seeking to use force to support self-determination, this should be done only after authorisation by a competent international organisation as a 'collective action': for example, the Security Council action in support of the people of East Timor.

11.2.4.5 Hot pursuit

The question here is whether the police or military forces of State A may cross the frontier into State B, without permission, in order to pursue and capture persons who have committed offences or other acts on the territory of State A. In terms of the use of force, the alleged right of 'hot pursuit' is used to justify armed incursions into the territory of neighbouring states for the purpose of destroying the military bases of guerrillas who have launched, or will launch, attacks against the state. It was claimed most frequently by South Africa and the former territory of Southern Rhodesia to justify their operations in the territories of neighbouring African states prior to the dismantling of apartheid.

Generally, this type of action has been justified on the basis of expanded self-defence, although its purpose is often punitive rather than defensive. In this sense, it is similar to reprisals. Moreover, it is obvious that land-based pursuit is very different from the maritime version, for the former requires pursuit into another state's jurisdiction, whereas the latter is permissible only into the high seas. South Africa also put forward the argument that action against guerrillas was not directed against the territorial integrity of the neighbouring state, but only against forces operating from it. However, in the Southern Africa context, the Security Council on many occasions condemned the practice of hot pursuit and the states resorting to force found no support for their claims. Generally such action was believed to be an 'aggression' or otherwise contrary to Art. 2(4). Although this determination was in part tied up with the fight for majority rule in these territories and the political disapproval of the minority regimes, it is reasonably clear that international law does not accept the principle of land-based hot pursuit on any of the grounds put forward. That is not to say, of course, that a national court necessarily must refuse to exercise local criminal jurisdiction over an individual brought before it as a result of an unlawful incursion into another state's territory. In the USA, such jurisdiction has not been refused (*US* v *Alvarez-Machain* 31 ILM 902 (1992): see also Israel and the *Eichmann Case*), although in South Africa itself the local court has set aside a conviction on the ground that the defendant was brought into custody in violation of the territorial integrity of a neighbouring state (*State* v *Ebrahim* 31 ILM 888 (1991)).

In sum, it is extremely doubtful whether a right of hot pursuit across land borders exists in international law, although the local courts of the state resorting to force might take a more lenient view for the purposes of their own legal system. Of course, a state is always permitted to take defensive measures on its own territory in the event of an attack by guerrillas, but must desist as soon as the protection of the state is accomplished. This is simply an application of the restrictive theory of self-defence that is favoured by a majority of the international community.

11.2.4.6 Monroe, Johnson and Brezhnev doctrines

The Monroe, Johnson and Brezhnev doctrines are statements of political philosophy. The Monroe doctrine was advanced by the USA as a reason for forcibly resisting any attempt by non-American states to establish a foothold in the western hemisphere. The Johnson doctrine, relied on by the USA at the time of the invasion of the Dominican Republic in 1965, is a refined version of this. It indicates that the USA and other American nations will resist with force any attempt to establish communism in the western hemisphere. Similarly, the Brezhnev doctrine was designed to preserve regional solidarity in Eastern Europe and maintained that the socialist states had limited sovereignty and that their allegiance to the socialist model could be lawfully compelled by the use of force, as with Czechoslovakia in 1968. It is now defunct.

It is clear, moreover, that none of these three 'rights' has any grounding in international law whatsoever. They are motives for action rather than valid legal justifications and any actual use of force would have to be justified under the rules already discussed. Significantly, in 1989 the Soviet Union (as it then was) renounced the Brezhnev doctrine as contrary to the right of self-determination and the sovereign equality of states. The same is also true, whether acknowledged or not, of the Monroe and Johnson doctrines and any other version of a policy that is designed to maintain one state's control over the region in which it operates.

Part Two: **The collective use of force**

In this section we shall examine the powers of the United Nations and other international organisations to authorise the use of armed force against delinquent states. This is what is meant by the collective use of force or, more properly, 'collective security'. It is the use of force on behalf of the community at large, as opposed to action in pursuance of individual states' rights. It should be remembered that the powers considered here are in addition to any rights which individual states may have under the unilateral rules just discussed, save in so far as these are not abrogated by the actual exercise of collective security. Particularly, it should be noted that the right of collective *self-defence* does not depend on the prior authorisation of any international organisation, although it must be lawful under the general law. In situations where an international organisation coordinates the joint response to an unlawful armed attack on a state, the international organisation is simply the umbrella under which collective self-defence is organised. So, for example, in the Grenada crisis, members of the organisation of Eastern Caribbean States claimed to be engaging in lawful collective self-defence that had nothing to do with the collective security provisions of the Charter. Consequently, it would not need to be authorised by the United Nations, being legitimate under the general law. There is, however, one important restriction on the right of collective (and individual) self-defence that comes into play when an action of collective security is also contemplated as a response to an unlawful use of force. According to Art. 51 of the Charter, the right of self-defence is available 'until the Security Council has taken measures necessary to restore international peace and security'. This is discussed more fully later with reference to the Kuwait–Iraq affair, but for now this overlap between unilateral rights and collective security should be noted.

11.3 The United Nations

11.3.1 The Security Council

11.3.1.1 The maintenance of international peace and security

Under the UN collective security system as originally envisaged, the Security Council was to be the organ through which international peace and security was to be maintained. The Council was given specific powers in Chapter VII of the Charter to act on behalf of all states, even if this meant using force itself. Until recently this was not how the system had worked in practice and even now, at a time when the Security Council is more active in the maintenance of international peace and security, the original Charter scheme is not applied in full measure.

Under Art. 39 of the Charter, if the Security Council determines that there is any 'threat to the peace, breach of the peace, or act of aggression' it may take such measures as are specified in Arts 41 and 42, although under Art. 40 it may indicate provisional measures pending a determination under Art. 39. It is of considerable importance, therefore, to know what types of conduct may fall within Art. 39 for this is the precondition to the exercise of these 'enforcement' powers. In this regard, the General Assembly Definition of Aggression will be of assistance, although it cannot add to or detract from the terms of the Charter itself. Clearly, armed military action or threats thereof are encompassed by Art. 39, but as the South African, Southern Rhodesian, Liberia, Haiti, Rwanda, East Timor, Liberia, Congo and Libya (in 2011) cases illustrate, 'threats to the peace' are not limited to military situations or international conflicts. In these cases, the *internal* situation in the territories gave rise to action under Chapter VII. A similar approach was taken in 1992/3 when

Chapter VII resolutions were directed against Libya because of its alleged promotion of international terrorism. In fact, it seems that the Council itself is the final judge of when a problem falls within Art. 39, perhaps (but only perhaps) with the possibility of review by the ICJ. It is, after all, the Council that has the 'primary responsibility' for the maintenance of international peace and security.

The measures envisaged in Art. 41 of the Charter involve non-military sanctions, such as a trade boycott (e.g. against Haiti, now lifted), an arms embargo (e.g. against Liberia, Rwanda), an embargo on international air flights (e.g. against Libya, now lifted), measures designed to prevent nuclear proliferation by isolating the target state (e.g. against North Korea in 2006, still in force) or a no-fly zone (Libya 2011). They may include the total interruption of economic and diplomatic relations, as well as more limited measures. Decisions taken under Art. 41 are binding on member states that are usually required to report to the Secretary-General on the measures they have taken to comply with the resolution. Obviously, in the case of trade boycotts etc. domestic law may have to be amended in order to prevent nationals trading with the delinquent state and in the UK this is done under the United Nations Act 1946. An example of this is the UK Order in Council imposing a UK arms embargo against Rwanda in pursuance of SC Res. 918 (1994) (SI 1994 No. 1637).

Until the Kuwait–Iraq affair and the end of the cold war, the power of the Council to impose non-military sanctions under Art. 41 had been used sparingly. In 1968 the Council had imposed comprehensive mandatory sanctions on Southern Rhodesia (SC Res. 235 (1968) and see SC Res. 232 (1966)) and in 1977 the Council imposed a ban on the provision of arms and war material to South Africa (SC Res. 418 (1977)), both now lifted. In fact, prior to the reform programme in South Africa, repeated attempts to widen the sanctions against that country (and to impose sanctions on Israel) had failed due to the veto of either the USA or the UK. In the last few years, of course, this has changed somewhat and there have been mandatory Chapter VII resolutions imposing non-military sanctions against Iraq, Libya, the territories of the former Yugoslavia, Haiti, Liberia, Angola (UNITA), Somalia, Sierra Leone, Rwanda and North Korea and also against non-state entities such as the Taliban and Al-Qaida (1999). Undoubtedly, this is a reflection of the new understanding between the USA and Russia and the apparent unwillingness of China to wield its veto power. Indeed, with the imposition of limited sanctions against Libya (after the Lockerbie incident, now lifted) many would argue that the Council had reached the height of its powers, because they seemed to have been motivated by the powerful national interests of the five permanent members rather than by a desire for a 'New World Order'. Indeed, a sharp reminder of the reality of international politics is provided by the UN response to the Syrian crisis in 2012. While few doubt the suffering of the Syrian people on all sides, and the likely commission of war crimes and crimes against humanity, a draft resolution authorising action under Chapter VII of the Charter has been vetoed three times by Russia and China. So, while the recent past has witnessed a revival in the powers of the Council to order sanctions in order to restore international peace and security, this does not mean that the Council will act in every, or all, situations.

Although non-military sanctions may well be an effective remedy in some cases, the Charter recognises that some acts of aggression etc. may be so serious as to warrant the collective use of armed force. Under Art. 42, the Council may take such military action 'as may be necessary to maintain or restore international peace and security'. Here is the heart of the collective security system: the Council's power to use (or authorise) armed force against a malefactor. It should be noted, however, that this power does not exist in order to redress breaches of international law per se. The Council acts to restore peace and security, and this is not necessarily the same as allocating international responsibility or redressing a prior illegality even if such objectives coincide.

Under the original scheme, the use of armed force by the Council under Art. 42 was dependent upon satisfactory agreements having been concluded under Art. 43. Agreements under Art. 43 between the Council and UN members were intended to establish an organised military force to be at the Council's disposal. Due to disagreements between the five permanent members in the early days of the UN, no such agreements have ever been concluded. Consequently, the Council has never been able to authorise and require the use of force under Art. 42. Fortunately, by using different powers, and by following different procedures, the Security Council has been able to *authorise* the use of armed force against a state as a means of restoring international peace and security, most notably following Iraq's invasion of Kuwait. Similarly, the Council has authorised NATO to take 'all necessary measures' (including the use of force) to implement the Bosnian Peace Plan (SC Res. 1031 (1995)), has authorised states to use all necessary measures to support the people of East Timor in the vindication of their right of self-determination (SC Res. 1264 (1999)) and, in SC Res 1973 (2011) authorised 'Member States that have notified the Secretary-General, acting nationally or through regional organizations or arrangements, and acting in cooperation with the Secretary-General, to take all necessary measures ... to protect civilians and civilian populated areas under threat of attack in the Libyan Arab Jamahiriya'.

As these cases illustrate, collective security is possible, but not in the way originally envisaged by the drafters of the Charter. This power to authorise states to use force on the Council's behalf is said to arise by implication from the Council's general responsibilities under Chapter VII for international peace and security (see e.g. Art. 39). In any event and whatever its merits, it is now clearly established in the practice of the Council. In fact, the implied power to authorise force against a state in circumstances where that force might otherwise be unlawful has the great advantage that states are *permitted* to use force; they are not required to do so, as would seem to have been contemplated by the original scheme of Arts 42 and 43. In sum, the Council has developed a practice whereby it permits, requests or authorises states to use force to restore international peace and security, it does not require them to do so.

Two recent episodes illustrate how the Council now proceeds. First, the Security Council's action in response to Iraq's invasion of Kuwait in 1990 is the most effective enforcement action undertaken so far and the most widely supported, both politically and materially. The key resolution was SC Res. 678 which authorised UN members to take 'all necessary means' to restore Kuwait's sovereignty and which clearly contemplated the use of armed force. In the end, some twenty-nine countries sent military or associated forces to assist in the action against Iraq. This action was collective security *par excellence* and, apart from acting under its implied powers instead of Art. 43, this was the Council doing exactly that which it had been designed to do. Of course, there were cogent political reasons why this enforcement action was possible where so many others were not and it is the absence of a Russian or Chinese veto that is the most significant political aspect of this episode. However, the ejection of Iraq from Kuwait, by a UN sponsored force, illustrated that collective security could work if the members of the international community had the political will to make it work. Secondly, in 1993 the Security Council authorised states to use 'all necessary measures' in response to the killing of UN soldiers engaged in humanitarian relief in Somalia, and it is to be noted that the use of force which followed in June 1993 was directed against a Somali leader in his own country. This was collective enforcement in respect of an internal situation, albeit with international implications. Like the later resolution in respect of East Timor this demonstrates that the Council is prepared to take a wide view of its enforcement powers.

What is obvious, however, is that collective security can be a one-sided affair. Whatever the legal merits of the US-led invasions of Afghanistan and Iraq, one certainty was that there was no prospect of Security Council action unless it met the concerns of USA and the UK. The same is true of action against Syria because of Russia and China. The existence of the veto ensures that the Council is frozen until these states decide that UN-sponsored multilateral action serves their purposes. These cases provide a most telling illustration of the reality of collective security: it works when the powerful members of the United Nations put forth their collective will, but never in the face of opposition from those who wield either the constitutional or military power to prevent it. Consequently, we must temper our enthusiasm and acclaim for the success of collective security in the post-cold war world with the recognition that, where collective security is concerned, there is one law for the weak, and another law for the strong.

11.3.1.2 Collective security and collective self-defence

We have already noted that there is the potential for overlap between situations where collective self-defence would have been justified and situations where collective security would have been desirable. Iraq's invasion of Kuwait was, however, the first situation since Korea in 1950 where this was manifested in a concrete case. Clearly, the western allies' immediate assistance to Saudi Arabia and Kuwait was taken on the basis of collective self-defence, and there is little doubt that had the Council not acted, armed force could have been used to expel Iraq from Kuwait's territory on a collective self-defence basis. There had been an armed attack against a sovereign state and a request for assistance from a legitimate government had been made. Other states were perfectly entitled in the first instance to come to Kuwait's aid with military force. Yet, as already noted, self-defence under Art. 51 may be taken only 'until the Security Council has taken measures necessary to restore international peace and security'. This seems to imply that while the use of force in self-defence will be lawful as an immediate response to an armed attack, it will cease to be so if the collective security mechanism is properly activated. Necessarily, this does assume that the Council is able to restore international peace and security and many states would argue that the simple fact that a Council resolution has been passed does not amount to 'measures *necessary*' to restore that peace and security. They would say that something concrete has to be done. We must remember also that the purposes of self-defence and collective security are different. Self-defence is an emergency response to an emergency situation, but it also implies that the 'defender' is entitled to use force for so long as it is threatened and for so long as its territory remains occupied. Collective security, on the other hand, is concerned with the maintenance of international peace and security and this may or may not mean the complete vindication of the rights of the state that was unlawfully attacked. It is often forgotten that the goals of collective self-defence and collective security are neither practically nor legally identical. In the Kuwait case, this potential difference of aim and emphasis had little actual impact as the collective security action did not stop short of completely evicting Iraq from Kuwait. Yet, the problem still remains: what does it mean to say that self-defence may be undertaken 'until' the Council has taken the measures necessary to restore international peace and security? One potential, but speculative, answer is that the right of self-defence is superseded by Council action under Chapter VII only if such enforcement action results in the restoration of the *status quo ante* the unlawful use of force by the aggressor. That is, that in this context 'peace and security' are not actually 'restored', and the 'measures necessary' have not been taken, until the state subject to the armed attack is restored to its position before the attack. This at least has the merit of creating an identity between collective security and collective self-defence in the most serious cases of a breach of the peace: the armed attack against state territory. It also has the added advantage that it nullifies the practical importance of the veto power of a permanent member who decides to agree to initiating enforcement action but who is not prepared to see it through to its logical conclusion. In such a case, collective security might well be thwarted, but self-defence would remain.

11.3.1.3 The diverse powers of the Security Council

Although we have concentrated on the use of force by the Security Council as part of its collective security function, it has become apparent in recent years that the Council has assumed the authority to recommend or authorise a wide range of measures in pursuit of collective security. Many of these do not fit neatly into the categories of 'military' or 'non-military' sanctions but nevertheless are instituted under Chapter VII by virtue of the implied powers developed in the practice of the Council. Thus the Council may initiate and regulate the operations of peacekeeping forces, both those sent with the consent of the disputing parties (which does not need a decision under Chapter VII) or those imposed on the parties under Chapter VII without their consent (e.g. Somalia). Likewise, the Council appears to be able to impose all manner of ancillary obligations on a delinquent state after it has been subdued by enforcement action. So, for example, the Council imposed acceptance of a peace settlement on Iraq, including within it the demarcation of its frontier with Kuwait, the destruction of its chemical and ballistic weapons and the mandatory establishment of a compensation fund from its oil revenues. Indeed, Iraq's non-compliance with all of its ancillary obligations under these resolutions has been used to justify the US-led invasion and we must wonder whether the Council will, in future cases, be so unspecific in its requirements if such resolutions can then be used to justify – however weakly – the use of force against the defaulting state. All this, plus the sanctions against Libya for its alleged sponsorship of terrorism, the action in East Timor in support of self-determination and the Council's involvement in the internal strife in Somalia, Liberia, Rwanda, Angola, Haiti, Burundi and Côte d'Ivoire is a far cry from the cold war days when the Council had difficulty in passing just one resolution that had any meaningful content. Obviously, the power of the five permanent members has been enhanced by these developments and there is some criticism that the Council is now too narrow in ideology and outlook. It is already apparent that many non-aligned states feel uneasy about the cosy relationship that exists among four of the 'Big Five' (with China not opposing), and the trumping of the ICJ by the Council in the Libyan affair (see Chapter 10) did nothing to dispel this fear. Perhaps the re-emergence of *disagreement* in the Council over the Syria crisis will temper some of these fears, although it is doubtful whether the people of Syria would see it that way. However, in all of this we need to remember that it is not the Council's powers that are the issue. It is the members' willingness to use those powers in the manner and for the purposes specified in the UN Charter.

11.3.2 The General Assembly

The failure of the collective security system in the early years of the UN because of the widespread use of the veto in the Security Council led the General Assembly to play a more active role in the maintenance of international peace and security. In 1950, the Assembly passed the Uniting for Peace Resolution (GA Res. 377 (V) (1950)). This resolved that if the Council could not discharge its primary responsibility because of the use of a veto by a permanent member, the Assembly 'shall consider the matter immediately with a view to making appropriate recommendations to members for collective measures, including in the case of a breach of the peace or act of aggression, the use of armed force when necessary, to restore international peace and security'.

This landmark resolution has been invoked by the Assembly on many occasions to justify its consideration of cases where force has been used unlawfully against a state, as with Korea in 1950, Afghanistan in 1980 and in respect of the situation in Palestine that led to the *Advisory Wall Opinion*. To date, this procedure has not led to the use of coercive force against an aggressor state, for that is the sole preserve of the Security Council, but the Assembly has used this resolution as the basis for the formation of a peacekeeping force (UNEF), which operated on Egyptian soil with that state's consent after the Suez crisis in 1956. As was made clear in the *Certain Expenses Case* 1962 ICJ Rep 151, the deployment of such a force did not constitute 'enforcement action', because it operated with the consent of the territorial sovereign, and thus did not require Security Council authorisation. In recent years, the Uniting for Peace Resolution has been used more as a means of bringing a matter before the Assembly for debate, rather than for instigating specific measures of collective action but it was at the heart of the Assembly's request in the *Palestinian Wall Case*, and led indirectly to that important judgment. Nevertheless, as discussed subsequently, even the peacekeeping function of the UN has largely passed out of the Assembly's hands.

However, the importance of this resolution in the history of the UN and the impact it had in 1950 should not be underestimated. In its Advisory Opinion in the *Certain Expenses Case*, delivered after some UN members had refused to pay their financial contributions to the expenses of UNEF on the grounds that peacekeeping forces were *ultra vires* the Assembly's powers, the Court confirmed that Arts 11 to 14 of the Charter empowered the Assembly to make recommendations for the peaceful resolution of disputes in matters affecting international peace and security. The authority of the Council in this regard was 'primary' (Art. 24), not exclusive (see also the *Palestinian Wall Case*). Similarly, the Court confirmed the constitutionality and legality of peacekeeping forces, whether instigated by the Assembly or Council, on the grounds that these could operate only with the consent of the territorial sovereign and were not enforcement action within the meaning of Chapter VII.

Although the original scheme of collective security has not been used to anything like its potential, this does not mean that the UN as a whole has been unable to contribute significantly to the maintenance of international peace and security. Apart from providing a valuable forum for debate and compromise, the UN has been able to adopt more concrete measures. The assertion by the Assembly of competence in security matters was a great step forward and the significance of the first peacekeeping force is considerable. Furthermore, although the Assembly has not recently instigated actual measures (discounting the request for an opinion in the *Palestinian Wall Case*) the Council has taken on the mantle of providing peacekeeping forces where these are requested or consented to by disputing states and, as the Somalia case shows, this can develop into peace enforcement.

11.4 Regional organisations

Under Art. 53 of the Charter, the Security Council may utilise regional organisations, such as the OAS, OAU and NATO, for 'enforcement action'. This is essentially a delegation of function by the Council to the regional organisations, although the authority clearly remains with the former. As stated in Art. 53, 'no enforcement shall be taken under regional arrangements or by regional agencies without the authorisation of the Security Council'. Of course, this does not impair measures of collective self-defence by regional organisations but it does ensure that they cannot take punitive action against a state, even if within their sphere of influence, without community approval given through the Council.

Until the 1990s, the Council had been very reluctant to utilise regional agencies under Art. 53, sometimes because of a threatened or actual veto and sometimes because it recognised the inherent dangers of employing an independent organisation that might have its own agenda. In 1992, in SC Res. 787, the Council took a tentative step forward and authorised states 'acting nationally or through regional agencies' to use appropriate measures to enforce the UN economic sanctions against Serbia and Montenegro. Then, in December 1995, the Council authorised member states acting in concert with NATO to take 'all necessary measures' to oversee the General Framework Agreement for Peace in Bosnia and Herzegovina (SC Res. 1031). This resolution also transferred the authority and responsibilities of UNPROFOR (the UN force) to IFOR (the NATO force), including the functions assigned by numerous previous Council resolutions. In strict terms this is not an Art. 53 delegation of responsibility because the Council formally authorises 'members' (not 'a regional organisation') to act in pursuance of international peace and security. Nevertheless, for all practical purposes this is the first time the Council has deliberately utilised a specific regional agency for the fulfilment of its primary functions. Subsequently in 2003, the Council welcomed the deployment of French and ECOWAS forces (Economic Community of West African States) in Côte d'Ivoire (SC Res. 1464) as a vital step in stabilising the situation in the country and this led, in 2004 (SC Res. 1528), to a transfer of functions from the ECOWAS forces to a fully fledged UN peacekeeping force (UNOCI – UN Operation in Côte d'Ivoire). Also, as we have seen, SC Res. 1973 (2011) in respect of Libya authorised members 'acting nationally or through regional organizations or arrangements' to take necessary measures and this led to the multinational coalition intervention in the Libyan civil war.

The Council's limited use of Art. 53 has led some countries, most notably the USA, to argue that regional organisations are permitted to take measures for the maintenance of international peace and security, including the use of armed force, without Council authorisation, so long as this does not amount to 'enforcement action' within Art. 53. For example, at the time of the invasions of the Dominican Republic (1965) and Grenada (1983), the USA argued that intervention designed to restore peace, as opposed to punish a delinquent state, was not 'enforcement action' and did not require Council authorisation. Obviously, such a narrow interpretation of 'enforcement action' would give regional organisations considerable power to intervene for all manner of purposes, as in both these countries where the object was to remove socialist regimes. So long as the action could be described as essentially 'peacekeeping' it would not be 'enforcement'. This gives 'enforcement action' a very limited meaning, being appropriate to describe only that armed action against a 'target state' that has committed some prior illegal act and where the community wishes to compel observance of some international obligation.

A number of points can be made about this argument. First, if the regional action is with the consent of the state in whose territory it occurs, there is no difficulty. In those circumstances the military operation is on a par with other consensual operations and involves no illegality because of the consent of the territorial sovereign. Such a claim was made in both the Dominican Republic and Grenada cases, but in both instances it is not supported by the evidence. Secondly, there is no indication in the *travaux préparatoires* of the San Francisco Conference that drafted the Charter that 'enforcement action' was to have the limited meaning attributed to it by the USA. On the contrary, it is clear that the purpose of Art. 53 was to ensure that the Security Council had sole responsibility for maintaining international peace and security, especially where this involved military action against a state without its consent. Indeed, Art. 51 on self-defence was inserted in Chapter VII specifically to make clear there was but one exception to this monopoly of power. Thirdly, there is no other provision in the Charter from which the power of regional organisations to undertake armed 'peacekeeping' operations can be implied. Chapter VIII on regional arrangements provides that all measures must be in conformity 'with the Purposes and Principles of the United Nations' (Art. 52). Fourthly, even if the constituent treaty of a regional organisation allows it to take armed action against a member, that action must still be in conformity with the fundamental obligations of the Charter (Art. 103, UN Charter) and rules of *jus cogens*. Thus, a regional organisation cannot by its own treaty authorise an otherwise unlawful use of force against a member of the organisation because the Charter and *jus cogens* take precedence over that regional treaty; *a fortiori*, if the action is taken against a non-member.

The crux of the issue is that regional organisations cannot employ armed force in or against a state without its consent, unless it amounts to lawful self-defence (or some other limited right). All other action is a violation of Art. 2(4) on either the permissive or restrictive interpretation of that provision. During the UN debates over the Dominican Republic and Grenada crises, the right of organisations to take this kind of armed coercive action was not generally accepted. This must be correct. Otherwise, regional organisations would be able to use force to ensure that all states conformed to the orthodox political orientation of the region, as happened in the Dominican Republic and Grenada. This is contrary to all the norms on non-intervention as well as the sovereign equality of states. The better view is, then, that apart from self-defence, regional organisations can undertake armed action only on the express authorisation of the Security Council although regional peacekeeping operations with the consent of the territorial sovereign (or warring factions) are lawful.

11.5 Peacekeeping

In simple terms, peacekeeping denotes the inter-position of armed forces, usually of a multinational character, in a territory with the consent of the territorial sovereign or internal factions. Its purpose is usually to act as a buffer between warring states or factions, to supervise (without enforcing) a peace or merely to observe a cease-fire line. The impetus for such forces may come from the UN Secretary-General, General Assembly, Security Council or even regional agencies, but their essential external legal validity lies in the consent to their presence given by the competent territorial sovereign or sovereigns. In this sense, peacekeeping is conciliatory not confrontational. In times past, the creation and financing of a peacekeeping force by the UN led to internal constitutional wrangles about which organ – Council or Assembly – had the power to act for the Organisation. As a result of the *Expenses Case* it is settled that both the Assembly and the Security Council have competence to establish peacekeeping operations, although in recent years the Council has effectively monopolised the UN's peacekeeping functions. This should come as no surprise given the jealousy with which the Council – and its five permanent members – guards its powers. However, the essentially consensual nature of peacekeeping means that the UN – or regional organisation – is merely the umbrella under which the peacekeeping operation is organised. The UN Charter or regional treaty is not the origin of the external legitimacy of the peacekeeping force: that lies in the consent of the territorial sovereign. Of course, the Security Council (and only the Council) can move from consensual peacekeeping to non-consensual enforcement action (e.g. peace enforcement) by changing the mandate of a peacekeeping force (e.g. in Yugoslavia, Somalia), but this is not a step to be taken lightly.

There is no doubt that the recent past has seen a rapid growth in the number of peacekeeping operations and the diverse nature of the responsibilities entrusted to them. In Mozambique, UNMOZOZ supervised a ceasefire and general demobilisation of forces; in Cambodia, UNTAC supervised a ceasefire, arranged elections and supervised the protection of human rights; in Cyprus, UNFICYP acts as a buffer between Greek and Cypriot; in Somalia, UNOSOM protects aid workers; in El Salvador, ONUSAL monitored the implementation of the peace accords and ensured observance of human rights guarantees; in The Sudan, UNMIS supported steps towards a peaceful political solution and in Côte d'Ivoire, UNOCI took over regional peacekeeping operations from ECOWAS in conjunction with French forces. This is by no means a complete list of even the UN's peacekeeping missions and demonstrates just how much peacekeeping has taken over from collective security and enforcement action as the mainstay of international peace and security.

The use of armed force is one of the most emotive areas of international law. On the one hand, it is argued that while the use of force generally should be unlawful, international law must permit states to use force whenever their vital interests, their security or their international rights are at risk. This is necessary, it is said, because the system of international law does not adequately protect states from the illegal acts of others. Thus, force may be used for a variety of purposes, one of which is a reasonably extensive right of self-defence. This approach places a premium on certain 'values' that may take precedence over the territorial inviolability and the sovereign equality of states. The contrary view sees Art. 2(4) as prohibiting all force except in the limited circumstance of self-defence against an armed attack, as defined in Art. 51 of the UN Charter. Any more permissive rules are said to be an invitation to abuse, whereby the rights of the weak may be overridden by the actions of the powerful. Generally, and bearing in mind that states often say one thing and do another, the majority of states favour the latter view, especially since most are incapable of using violence to achieve their own political ends. For this author, the strict approach to the use of force is probably the better view on an objective basis, although this does leave nationals, 'human rights' and 'democracy' often unprotected in the face of a determined aggressor. However, it also ensures that states cannot violate the equally important rights of independence and sovereign equality with impunity and without committing an illegal act even if the result is only a verbal condemnation. Without a guarantee of these basic principles, which touch the very essence of statehood, there is no international community and no international law.

As far as collective security is concerned, there is no doubt that the Security Council has the power under the Charter to act in a variety of situations. Historically, lack of agreement among the permanent members and free use of the veto made this a rare event. Instead, the General Assembly adopted a higher profile and consensual peacekeeping operations supervised by both Council and Assembly played a vital role. Now, the picture is less clear. The Council's prompt and effective action in response to the invasion of Kuwait showed that collective security could work. Unfortunately, the Council's slow and inadequate response to the Yugoslavian situation and its non action when Iraq and Afghanistan were invaded and in the Syrian crisis, remind us that the UN is helpless if individual states lack the political will to take action or if the protagonists wield insuperable power – either legal or military. It is true, however, that the Council has become more *involved* in disputes which threaten international peace and security, even if it does not always achieve a great deal. This is significant in itself for at least the emphasis has changed. It is now accepted and recognised that both inter-state and internal disputes are matters with which the Council may legitimately be concerned and in respect of which it may legitimately respond on behalf of the community. An excellent example of the Council's involvement in nominally 'internal' affairs was its sanctions against Haiti, made entirely with the aim of forcing the government of that state to return to 'democracy' after a *coup d'état*. This was almost exclusively an internal matter and no other state was endangered by the situation, but the Council still felt competent to act; likewise, with the action in East Timor and Libya (2011). In conclusion then, there is no doubt that the system of collective security has progressed in recent years, although we must wait and see how extensive and how permanent are recent achievements.

FURTHER READING

Akehurst, M., 'The Use of Force to Protect Nationals Abroad', (1976/77) 5 *International Relations* 3.

Bowett, D., 'Reprisals Involving Recourse to Armed Force', (1972) 66 *AJIL* 1.

Brownlie, I., 'Humanitarian Intervention', in Moore, J. N., *Law and Civil War in the Modern World* (Johns Hopkins University Press, 1974).

Franck T., 'What Happens Now? The United Nations after Iraq' (2003) 97 *AJIL* 607.

Franck, T., 'Who Killed Article 2(4)?' (1970) 64 *AJIL* 809.

Gray, C., 'After the Ceasefire: Iraq, the Security Council and the Use of Force', (1994) 65 *BYIL* 135.

Gray, C., *International Law and the Use of Force* (Oxford University Press, 2008).

Greenwood, C., 'New World Order or Old? The Invasion of Kuwait and the Rule of Law', (1992) 55 *MLR* 153.

Greig, D., 'Self-Defence and the Security Council: What Does Article 51 Require?', (1991) 40 *ICLQ* 366.

Hargrove, J., 'The Nicaragua Judgment and the Future of the Law of Force and Self-Defence', (1987) 81 *AJIL* 135.

Henkin, L., 'The Reports of the Death of Article 2(4) are Greatly Exaggerated', (1971) 65 *AJIL* 544.

Lillich, R., 'Forcible Self-Help by States to Protect Human Rights', (1967–68) 53 *Iowa LR* 325.

Rostow, N., International Law and the Use of Force: A Plea for Realism, (2009) 34 *Yale J. Int'l L.* 549.

Schachter, O., 'The Rights of States to Use Force', (1984) 82 *Michigan Law Review* 1620.

Warbrick, C., 'The Invasion of Kuwait by Iraq', (1991) 40 *ICLQ* 482 and 965.

White, N., 'Libya and Lessons from Iraq: International Law and the Use of Force by the United Kingdom', (2012) 42(2) *NYIL* 215.

SUMMARY

The use of force

- 'All members shall refrain in their international relations from the threat or use of force against the territorial integrity or political independence of any state, or in any other manner inconsistent with the Purposes of the United Nations' – Art. 2(4) UN Charter. This is one of the central obligations of the Charter and, in terms, it stipulates a general prohibition of the unilateral use of force. It is a rule of *jus cogens*.

- States have the right to use force in self-defence. There is a debate as to whether this is limited to the conditions of Art. 51 of the UN Charter or is available in wider circumstances. It is also permissible to use force in collective self-defence.

- One state may request the deployment of another state's military forces in its territory. Likewise, a state may give permission for the use of force on its territory for any lawful purpose.

- Under the 'doctrine' of humanitarian intervention it is alleged that one state (State A) may use force in the territory of another state (State B) in order to protect the human rights of individuals in State B, usually being nationals of State B. This is controversial in international law.

- Under the UN collective security system, the Security Council is given specific powers in Chapter VII of the Charter to act in the maintenance of international peace and security, even if this means using force itself.

- Under Art. 53 of the Charter, the Security Council may utilise regional organisations for 'enforcement action'. This is essentially a delegation of function by the Council to the regional organisations, although the authority clearly remains with the former.

12

....

Human rights

Throughout this book we have concentrated primarily on the international rights and duties of states. International law has been presented as a system of rules governing the relations between sovereign and independent states. This is undoubtedly correct. However, one of the most significant advances of international law since the creation of the United Nations in 1945 is the development of rules and principles governing the rights and obligations of individuals. We have seen already that individuals may be under certain international duties for which they can be made responsible before national and international courts. These may give rise to personal responsibility for, among other things, war crimes, crimes against the peace, crimes against humanity, and piracy. In this chapter we shall examine another aspect of the personality of individuals – the rules of international law affording protection to individuals under the law of human rights.

As discussed in Chapter 2, the greater part of the rules of international law are derived from treaty or custom. The same is true for the law of human rights. It is only because of their incorporation in treaty form or customary law that states have accepted concrete obligations in the area of human rights. Yet it is clear that there is an added dimension to human rights law that is often absent from other topics. Although the binding force of human rights obligations must rest ultimately in treaty or custom, the inspiration for these obligations lies in 'morality', 'justice', 'ethics' or a simple regard for the dignity of Mankind. The law of human rights cannot be explained solely by reference to the traditional 'positivist' approach to international law. Indeed, even if the law of human rights has not had any direct impact on the everyday lives of people – and this is clearly not the case – the simple fact that international law now recognises that individuals may fall within its jurisdiction is an achievement of considerable significance. Above all else, it is an acknowledgement that the 'state' is no longer the supreme, ungovernable entity that pure positivism suggests that it is.

12.1 The role and nature of human rights law

This chapter is concerned with the procedures which exist in international law for the promotion, protection and vindication of the 'human rights and fundamental freedoms' of individuals. For this purpose, reference will be made to both the substance of the 'rights' guaranteed and to the institutional mechanisms that exist for the promotion, protection and vindication of those rights. However, this chapter is not devoted primarily to an examination of the detail of individual types of 'human rights' or to the mechanisms for their protection in UK law (e.g. the Human Rights Act 1998). We are concerned here with issues of an international character relating mainly to procedural matters i.e. with the *system* of international human rights protection. Of course, there will be some consideration of types of 'right' for, as we shall see, the nature or substance of a 'human right' might vary according to the political, social or economic orientation of the state or group of states in which it is said to exist – so-called 'cultural relativism'. It is quite possible, for example, for the substantive law and institutional procedures concerning human rights in Europe to be significantly different from those found in Africa or the Americas. Of course, few would doubt (although some do) that there are some 'fundamental' or 'universal' human rights which can and do cross social, economic and political boundaries, and it is also true that too much 'relativism' simply opens the door to abuse, with states pleading their own 'special circumstances' as an excuse for flagrant human rights abuses. Good examples of such universal rights are the right to life, the prohibition of torture and the prohibition of genocide and it may well be that these – especially the last two – have attracted the status of *jus cogens* (see e.g. *A* v *Secretary of State for the Home Department* [2006] 2 AC 221 and the *Case Concerning the Application of the Convention on the Prevention and Punishment of the Crime of Genocide (Bosnia and Herzegovina* v *Serbia & Montenegro)* ICJ 2007 respectively). Nevertheless, despite profound advances in the law and practice of human rights, we must be wary of making broad generalisations and statements of 'high moral principle'. The 'protection of human rights' as an abstract moral concept will do little to enhance the everyday existence of even one individual unless it is firmly rooted in the day-to-day experience of the people who are to be protected and of the governments who are supposed to be doing the protecting.

In a similar vein, it is important for the international lawyer concerned with human rights to draw a clear distinction between substantive rules of law and rules of morality, no matter how much the latter might be thought desirable or necessary. As with other areas of international law, no amount of pure rhetoric can ensure that a state will observe an international human rights obligation, but there is considerably more chance if that obligation can be shown to flow from a recognised 'source of law'. That does not mean that every human right must be based in treaty or custom, for as we have seen in Chapter 2, 'general principles of law' may add considerably to the purely positivist stock of international legal obligations. It does mean, however, that before *legal* mechanisms can be used to constrain a state's behaviour (e.g. through procedures stipulated in a binding treaty), we must be sure that the 'right' being enforced also has the quality of a legal rule. In this respect, reference should be made to the discussion in Chapter 1 on the nature of international law, methods of enforcement and the impact that rules of law can have on state behaviour outside formal enforcement procedures. Similarly, although most institutional procedures for the protection of human rights do concentrate on 'pure' legal obligations, a state's general behaviour in the field of human rights can be influenced by many other factors, not least public opinion and 'soft law'. In other words, when talking about the *law* of human rights, we must be sure that the substance of what is being promoted resides in legal obligation and not only in moral principle. However, when talking about the nature of human rights generally and the way in which such concepts affect state behaviour, it is quite appropriate to make reference to a broad range of principles, some of which will not yet have attained the status of rights guaranteed by international law per se, and some of which may influence state behaviour even though not embodied in a legal-type mechanism.

In practice, the bulk of human rights law operates to oblige a state to refrain from causing 'harm' to its own nationals or other persons within its territorial jurisdiction. Such obligations are not limited in scope to the outlawry of physical harm, but can encompass obligations seeking to prevent a denial of economic, social, legal or intellectual rights. In this sense, the law of human rights is an exception to the absolute and exclusive territorial jurisdiction which a state otherwise possesses (Chapter 6). Furthermore, any denial of the human rights of nationals of other states may give rise to a further claim of state responsibility for injury to aliens. In practice, however, by far the greatest impact of human rights law has been to erode the absolute control which a state once exercised over its nationals, and it is one of the most significant achievements of international law that a state may now be internationally responsible for acts done in its own territory to its own citizens. Human rights law is one area where the state cannot rely on the reserved domain of 'domestic jurisdiction'. Thus, Art. 2(7) of the Charter, which provides that '[n]othing contained in the present Charter shall authorise the United Nations to intervene in matters which are essentially within the domestic jurisdiction of any state' has not inhibited the UN in its attempts to develop a comprehensive code of human rights. Quite simply, developments since 1945 have lifted the question of human rights out of the domestic plane and removed it to the jurisdiction of international law, so much so in fact that human rights may now be a relevant factor when the Security Council considers the need for enforcement action under Chapter VII of the Charter (e.g. Iraq/Kuwait, Yugoslavia, East Timor).

The purpose of the law of human rights is, then, to ensure that individuals are protected from the excesses of states and governments. How could this operate in practice? As an ultimate goal, it might be possible to operate a comprehensive and compulsory machinery for the protection of human rights in concrete cases. As we shall see, this has been achieved to a limited extent and the successful establishment of the International Criminal Court is part of this ongoing process. However, in general, effective protection for specific individuals in respect of personal violations of their human rights is the exception rather than the rule and this *apparent* defect in the enforcement of human rights obligations has led many commentators to lament the 'ineffectiveness' of human rights law and to castigate states for not being prepared to accept compulsory enforcement machinery. Yet is this really so surprising given that it is only relatively recently that states have accepted the basic principle of protecting human rights? Until 1945, international law was generally concerned only with the rights and duties of states and it is easy to forget just how great a change of emphasis was required before states were prepared to accept even the abstract principle that international law could protect the human rights of individuals within their own territory. Moreover, it is evident that states are reluctant to accept the compulsory settlement of disputes in a whole range of circumstances, even when the opposing party is another sovereign state (see Chapter 10). Why, then, should we be surprised if sovereign states are at least as reluctant to accept compulsory settlement of disputes in the law of human rights, especially since the opposing party is likely to be one of its own nationals? Regrettably, but not surprisingly, the reality is that states are even more hostile to compulsory enforcement in human rights matters, with the notable exception of the protection of human rights in Europe.

Even though the protection of human rights in concrete cases is not as vigorous as we might like, it is important to appreciate that this is only one way in which international law can challenge and control the excesses of sovereign states. On another level, the existence of international obligations to respect human rights generally and the emergence of common obligations in respect of specific, identifiable rights (such as the prohibition of genocide) should be recognised as considerable achievements per se. Likewise, the existence of genuine legal obligations means that we can describe a state's conduct as 'unlawful' or 'illegal' and this is a most powerful form of criticism. The simple fact that many of the moral principles concerning human rights have been transformed into a series of legal obligations, even if they only ever exist in the abstract without the support of effective enforcement mechanisms, may actually inhibit states in their conduct towards individuals. For example, although the international community was powerless to prevent the violations of human rights in Peking in 1989 (the Tiananmen Square incident), the opprobrium directed at China, plus the curtailment of diplomatic and economic ties by other states is, in itself, a partial deterrent against similar conduct in the future. If human rights were not protected under international law, such conduct may have been deplored, it may even have been 'immoral', but it could not have been 'illegal'.

12.2 The development of the law of human rights

Prior to the United Nations Charter, individuals were not a major concern of international law. As previously noted, there were certain areas where they could be made directly responsible for criminal acts, but there was little in the way of rules geared to their protection. There were some exceptions to this, such as the rules protecting combatants and civilians in time of war, the Mandate provisions of the League of Nations Covenant and certain rights accorded under the Peace Treaties ending the First World War, but usually international law left individuals to seek their protection in national law. This was often no protection at all.

These perceptions were radically altered by the experiences of the Second World War and the protection of human rights has been one of the primary purposes of the United Nations ever since. The preamble to the Charter, in its second paragraph, reaffirms a 'faith in fundamental human rights, in the dignity and worth of the human person, in the equal rights of men and women and of nations large and small'. Likewise, in Article 55, the United Nations is committed to promoting, *inter alia*, 'universal respect for, and observance of, human rights and fundamental freedoms for all without distinction as to race, sex, language, or religion'. Under Article 56, all members of the Organisation pledge themselves to take 'joint and separate action in co-operation with the Organisation for the achievement of the purposes set forth in Article 55'.

Taken together, these provisions represented a bold statement of intent and it may be that Art. 56 places states under a legal obligation to take practical steps for the protection of human rights. However, whatever the precise legal effect of these general provisions, the sentiments they express were taken seriously by the members of the fledgling Organisation. In 1948, at its third session, the General Assembly adopted Resolution 217A, being a Universal Declaration of Human Rights. There was no opposition to this resolution, although eight states did abstain, primarily because of the then uncertain standing of human rights in international law and the effect that such obligations could have on state sovereignty. The Declaration contains a list of economic, social, cultural and political rights and provides in Article 2 that 'everyone is entitled to all the rights and freedoms set forth in this Declaration, without distinction of any kind'. It should be noted, however, that the Declaration was not intended to create binding legal obligations, nor could it, following the general rule for Assembly resolutions discussed in Chapter 2.

The precise effect of the Declaration was, therefore, to urge states to establish procedures for the future protection of human rights. It did not, and could not, place states under an immediate binding obligation to protect them. Yet, such a simple analysis fails to do justice to the dynamic effect that the Declaration has had on the law of human rights. In a general sense, the simple fact of the adoption of the Declaration illustrated that there was broad agreement in principle about the importance of human rights, as well as a consensus as to the kind of rights that should be protected. More importantly, the Declaration provided the impetus for the development of customary law and the more comprehensive treaty regimes discussed later in the chapter. In the US case of *Filartiga* v *Pena-Irala* (1980) 630 F. 2nd 896, the court stated its belief that the Declaration had assumed a force and validity in customary law all of its own and, further, that it had given rise to a specific customary rule prohibiting torture. In fact, the Declaration is one of the most significant resolutions ever adopted by the Assembly, both in terms of its effect on the development of international law and because of its subject matter. It is a standard by which the behaviour of states, ethnic groups, individuals and even multinational corporations is judged. In 1993, the United Nations' commitment to human rights was further reinforced by the Vienna Declaration and Programme of Action. Again, although not binding in law, this Declaration, adopted by consensus after a World Conference on Human Rights, proclaimed the universal nature of human rights and set the promotion and protection of human rights as a priority objective of the UN. It is the successor to the Universal Declaration and, together with the operations of the UN High Commissioner for Human Rights, is a further step towards effective, universal protection for human rights.

In this regard, it is important to realise that the law of human rights is not static. Many commentators talk of 'generations' of human rights, which is another way of describing how the substance of human rights has become more refined as the very concept of 'human rights' has become more entrenched in the system of international law. So, 'first generation' rights comprise those civil and political rights that are now at the core of most human rights treaty regimes. They include such matters as the right to life, the abolition of slavery, the right to a fair trial, the prohibition of torture and the right to recognition before the law. So-called 'second generation' human rights generally relate to matters of social and economic significance, such as the right to work, the right to social security, the right to an adequate standard of living and the right to education. Obviously, these are rights of a more amorphous nature, and this is an important element in the distinction between these and 'first generation' rights. Confusingly, that distinction does not reside in the fact that 'second generation' rights developed later (see e.g. the two International Covenants referred to later in the chapter, both of 1966); rather it is that the enforcement mechanisms for second generation rights tend to be more flexible and less powerful than those available to the individual claiming a violation of their civil and political rights. This is not surprising given that the attainment of economic and social rights depends greatly on the particular social organisation within each state, whereas civil and political rights do have a more 'universal' flavour. Finally, there is some academic support for so-called 'third generation' rights. 'Third generation' rights may include very general concepts such as rights of development, the right to a protected environment, rights of peace and a wide-ranging right of self-determination. Clearly, these are 'rights' which belong more appropriately to groups or 'peoples' rather than individuals, and many jurists would argue that they are 'rights' in a moral or philosophical sense and that they do not yet connote the existence of legal obligations and correlative legal rights. There is some strength in this view, not least when we realise that some states would not yet accept the legal quality of some 'second generation' rights. Indeed, this is a good example of the problem identified above: viz. the need to differentiate between human rights susceptible of vindication as a matter of international law and those human rights that exist for the moment in the realm of morality and humanity. On the other hand, if we do not take the law of human rights forward, we run the risk of never achieving effective protection for even very basic rights. Some commentators would argue that a continuing reappraisal of the reach of human rights law is the only way to ensure their protection in a rapidly changing world. Practice will always lag behind theory, and if theory does not advance, neither will practice.

12.3 The protection of human rights under the United Nations

An optimistic view of the effect of the Universal Declaration of Human Rights is that it generated a general principle of customary international law to the effect that states were bound to respect the human rights of persons within their jurisdiction. This might be thought too vague to be of any practical significance, but even if this criticism is true, it is to the credit of the UN that it has been able to take this general principle and put it into practice in a number of concrete ways. Some commentators go further and argue that the impact of the UN and related treaty regimes has been so powerful that a general obligation to respect human rights is now a rule of *jus cogens*. Perhaps there is not enough evidence for this yet, especially as some states still do not accept the full personality of individuals in international law, but the binding legal nature of the *specific* regimes instituted under the auspices of the UN cannot be doubted.

The most significant of the UN-administered treaty regimes are those established by the two International Covenants which will be discussed later. Together, these form a reasonably comprehensive code of universal human rights and provide for some level of enforcement against delinquent states. In addition, the UN has instituted a number of other procedures and reference will be made to these also. Moreover, it should not be forgotten that the General Assembly, its committees and other organs of the UN regularly consider questions of human rights as a necessary adjunct to their political activities. For example, the questions of Namibia, apartheid in South Africa and the situation in the Middle East have all given rise to discussion and action in the field of human rights. In 1977, the Security Council imposed mandatory sanctions on South Africa partly because of 'its resort to massive violence against and killings of the African people, including schoolchildren and students and others opposing racial discrimination': SC Res. 418 (1977). A similar desire to promote civil and political rights appeared to be part of the motive for the imposition of economic sanctions against Haiti in June 1993 and against territories of the former Yugoslavia in 1992–95 and The Sudan in 2005. The Security Council Resolutions concerning East Timor in 1999/2000 were explicit in their aim of promoting the right of self-determination.

12.3.1 The International Covenant on Civil and Political Rights 1966

The International Covenant on Civil and Political Rights (ICCPR) entered into force in 1976 and, as at 1 September 2012, there were 167 parties, including the UK. In similar fashion to the Universal Declaration, a party to the Covenant undertakes 'to respect and to ensure to all individuals within its territory and subject to its jurisdiction the rights recognised in the present Convention, without distinction of any kind'. Unlike the Declaration, however, this Covenant is a legally binding treaty and the state-parties are legally bound to give effect to its provisions. Importantly, each state undertakes to adopt such legislative measures within their domestic jurisdiction as may be necessary to give effect to the rights listed in the Covenant (Art. 2(2)) and also to provide an effective remedy should a violation occur (Art. 2(3)). Moreover, because these obligations are binding in international law, a violation of the Convention gives rise to international responsibility, although as we shall see, the procedure for enforcement of the obligations in concrete cases is not as rigorous as it might be.

The Covenant establishes a code of civil and political rights similar to those found in the Universal Declaration. They include, *inter alia*, the right to life (Art. 6), the prohibition of torture (Art. 7), the prohibition of slavery (Art. 8), the right to liberty of the person (Art. 9), the prohibition of retroactive criminal legislation (Art. 15), the right of peaceful assembly (Art. 21) and the protection of minority rights (Art. 27). Furthermore, although a state may derogate from certain rights 'in time of public emergency which threatens the life of the nation' (Art. 4), no derogation may be made in respect of the more fundamental rights protected by Arts 6–8, 11 (prohibition of imprisonment for inability to fulfil a contractual obligation), 15, 16 (right of recognition as a person before the law) and 18 (freedom of conscience and religion). All in all, the effect of the Covenant is to provide a framework for the protection of those civil and political rights most commonly regarded as being essential for the dignity and liberty of Man and Woman.

The parties to the Covenant are under a clear legal obligation to respect the human rights defined therein. Unfortunately, the system of enforcement is not really designed to provide a remedy for individuals in concrete cases, although recent years have seen the Human Rights Committee (on which see later) take a more vigorous approach to such complaints. On becoming a party, a state is automatically bound by Art. 40 to submit periodic reports (every five years) to a Human Rights Committee established under Part IV of the Covenant. This Committee is made up of eighteen individuals elected from among the contracting parties, but they do not formally represent their states. Reports submitted to the Committee should indicate the measures undertaken to implement the terms of the Covenant and there may be limited cross-examination of a state representative. The Committee is reluctant on the basis of these reports (and some would argue not empowered) to identify particular malefactors or to criticise the conduct of states too severely. It sees its function as supervisory rather than investigatory; and of course, a government official writes these reports and it is unlikely that they will contain admissions of violation of the treaty. However, the legal duty to submit reports is significant in that it places a burden on the state to explain positively the steps it has taken to fulfil its international obligations. The Human Rights Committee is also empowered to issue 'General Comments' discussing at large compliance with the Covenant. These are valuable public statements that may, *inter alia*, elaborate on the Covenant's specific human rights or indicate those actions that the Committee believes states should take to protect those rights.

More concrete measures are provided for in Art. 41. This establishes a procedure for inter-state complaints, whereby a party may declare, at its option and on a basis of reciprocity, that it recognises the competence of the Human Rights Committee to receive complaints from other states. Subject to the exhaustion of local remedies and after a prescribed period of direct negotiation, if an inter-state complaint is referred to the Committee, it will attempt to mediate in order to achieve a settlement. If this is not possible, the Committee may, with the further consent of the parties, refer the matter to an ad hoc Conciliation Commission. The report of this body, as with the finding of facts produced by the Committee, is not binding. It may, of course, result in political pressure to remedy the alleged violation of human rights – for example, by changing domestic law – but it does not give rise to a secondary legal obligation in the same way as a binding decision of the ICJ. In essence, then, the procedure for inter-state complaints is both voluntary – at two stages – and also does not result in an award legally binding on the state. As at 1 September 2012, forty-eight states had made optional declarations under Art. 41, accepting the possibility of inter-state complaints, including the UK.

In addition to this system, the 1966 Optional Protocol to the Covenant provides for the possibility of individual complaints to the Human Rights Committee in respect of personal violations of human rights. As its name suggests, this procedure is entirely optional and, as at 1 September 2012, 114 of the parties to the Covenant had signed the Protocol. This does *not* include the UK, but does include many other European states (e.g. Spain, France, Italy, Hungary), as well as several from Central and South America (e.g. Argentina, Uruguay, Nicaragua, Panama). Individual applications are subject to the local remedies rule and may be declared inadmissible. In theory, the Committee does not act judicially when considering complaints made by individuals under the Optional Protocol and it remains true that state-parties cannot be compelled to provide information or make representations. In fact, most do, and the public records of applications heard by the Committee reveal that the proceedings are becoming more 'judicial' in character. The Committee has, for example, made it clear that the burden of proof in respect of complaints does not lie solely on the applicant and that the Committee may conclude that a violation has occurred 'in the absence of satisfactory evidence and explanations to the contrary submitted by the state' (*Bleir* v *Uruguay*, 1 Selected Decisions HRC 109, 1982). This must be correct, or else the state charged with a violation could hide behind its monopoly of official information. Again, although in theory a finding by the Committee that a state has violated the Covenant is not binding on it, in practice such decisions are treated by objective observers as decisive of a state's legal obligations. The more widespread publication of awards in recent years reinforces this. The Committee has also adopted the practice of asking states found responsible for a breach of the Covenant to submit information within a set time on the measures adopted by them in respect of the Committee's findings (e.g. *Leroy Simmonds* v *Jamaica* (1994) 1 IHRR 94) and this has encouraged states to carry out the Committee's recommendations for redress.

As a whole, the International Covenant on Civil and Political Rights provides a reasonably comprehensive list of civil and political rights and fixes state-parties with a definite legal obligation to respect them. This was supplemented in 1989 by the Second Optional Protocol aiming at the Abolition of the Death Penalty, which came into force in 1991 and now (1 September 2012) has seventy-five parties including the UK. As we have seen, the procedure for enforcement of these obligations is not particularly strong, although for those states accepting the First Optional Protocol concerning the possibility of individual complaints there is more bite. Unfortunately, one major defect is that a state may sign the Covenant and accept only the obligation to submit a report at five-yearly intervals and even then reports are routinely late, lacking in detail or not submitted at all. In fact, it is those states that have least to fear from the Human Rights Committee that are most regular in the submission of reports. Many would argue that the Human Rights Committee spends a great deal of its time preaching to the converted. In this vein, two general criticisms are, unfortunately, easily made. First, it is axiomatic that a more comprehensive system of enforcement for specific violations of the human rights of particular individuals would have been preferable. While the protection of rights in the abstract is to be welcomed, the ultimate goal must be to see this work in practice on a more systematic basis. Secondly, the Covenant regime allows a state to *appear* to be protecting human rights, whereas in fact it may be committing the most serious violations. Signature of the Covenant is good publicity and it is instructive that not all state-parties accepting the general obligation to protect human rights are prepared to take the next logical step and undertake even the very limited enforcement obligations of the Covenant and the First Optional Protocol. Such opportunistic (but lawful) sidestepping of an optional enforcement regime does not occur with other human rights regimes, such as the European Convention (see section 12.4) where nearly all signatories to the primary instrument have accepted some machinery for enforcement. This gulf between the apparent and real nature of a state's obligations under the International Covenant has led some commentators to question whether it would have been better to have established a fairly strict enforcement machinery for the International Covenant that would have at least identified those states unwilling to do anything practical about human rights. On the other hand, the Covenant may never have come into force had it contained more rigorous enforcement procedures, and then the general legal obligations contained therein would have been of no use at all.

12.3.2 The International Covenant on Economic, Social and Cultural Rights 1966

This is the counterpart to the Covenant on Civil and Political Rights considered previously. Originally it was intended that there should be only one treaty, covering the whole range of human rights, but in view of the rather more subjective nature of economic and social rights (hence 'second generation') it was rightly considered preferable to deal with them separately. This Covenant also entered into force in 1976 and, as at 1 September 2012, there were 160 parties, including the UK.

There is no doubt that this second Covenant, being a treaty governed by international law, does impose binding legal obligations on the parties to it. However, as already noted, the substance of the rights guaranteed is relatively diffuse and this has made the particular obligations of Covenant much less specific. Consequently, the tenor of the Economic Covenant is promotional rather than mandatory. Thus, each party 'undertakes to take steps, individually and through international assistance and co-operation, especially economic and technical, to the maximum of its available resources, with a view to achieving progressively the full realisation of the rights' (Art. 2), rather than, as before, being under an immediate obligation to do so. In addition, some rights are relative, so that states may determine the extent to which they guarantee economic rights to non-nationals (Art. 3). This is a reflection of the very nature of the rights protected in the Covenant, but also recognises the diverse social and economic conditions prevailing in different countries – so-called cultural relativism. The Covenant is designed to promote economic and social welfare, not to hinder it by placing states under obligations that prevent widespread economic and social reform.

For similar reasons, the enforcement machinery of this Covenant is not as 'strong' as its counterpart. States are under an obligation to submit reports every five years to the Committee on Economic, Social and Cultural Rights (CESCR), effectively a body of eighteen members (who do not formally represent their state of nationality) operating under the auspices of the UN's Economic and Social Council (ECOSOC). These reports are intended to fulfil a similar purpose to the reports submitted to the Human Rights Committee of ICCPR, although their examination is often a political rather than a legal exercise. In consequence, the machinery for 'enforcement' is not likely to discover any serious breaches of the Covenant, although there are signs that the CESCR is developing a slightly more rigorous approach to the Covenant now that many 'first generation' human rights have been secured. Nevertheless, we should not be surprised at the existence of weaker enforcement machinery given the promotional nature of the obligations contained in the Economic Covenant. Generally, and for understandable reasons, this treaty is not intended to interfere with a state's control over its own nationals (and the nationals of other states within its territory) to the same degree as the Covenant on Civil and Political Rights.

Originally, there was no right of individual or group petition, or inter-state complaints under the Economic and Social Covenant. However, in 2008, the General Assembly adopted and recommended an Optional Protocol to the International Covenant on Economic, Social and Cultural Rights which gave a right of individual or group petition to CESCR that may in turn adopt a variety of strategies to resolve the petition (assuming it is admissible – Arts 2 and 3). Similarly, under Art. 10 of the Protocol inter-state complaints are possible and a 'State Party to the present Protocol may at any time declare under the present article that it recognizes the competence of the Committee to receive and consider communications to the effect that a State Party claims that another State Party is not fulfilling its obligations under the Covenant'. This is of course similar to the provision under the Civil Covenant. As at 1 September 2012, there were eight parties to this Protocol, and it enters force three months after deposit of the 10th instrument of ratification. So, the Optional Protocol is not yet in force.

12.3.3 **ECOSOC and the Human Rights Council**

By its nature, the UN Economic and Social Council has a wide remit in matters of human rights. It is particularly active, for example, in relation to the work of the UN High Commissioner for Refugees and, as we have seen, ECOSOC oversees compliance with the International Covenant on Economic, Social and Cultural Rights.

In 1948, ECOSOC made a significant contribution to the development of human rights law by establishing the Human Rights Commission. Over the next forty odd years, the Commission did achieve much in terms of the general promotion of human rights, but by the beginning of the twenty-first century it was clear that the Commission had outlived its effective usefulness and that a new structure was needed. Consequently, in March 2006, the General Assembly abolished the Commission and replaced it with a Human Rights Council which started operations in June 2006. The Council reports directly to the General Assembly and its forty-seven members are elected for three-year terms on the normal geographical basis employed at the United Nations. The Council's remit is wide and it has adopted a Universal Periodic Review procedure under which it monitors human rights matters in *all* UN member states, not merely those which are brought to its attention by reason of a complaint. The Council also has adopted a Complaints Procedure under which it may receive – and consequently investigate – complaints from groups and individuals concerning a violation of human rights and fundamental freedoms. They are admissibility criteria, but the focus is meant to be 'victims oriented' and initial contact is made through the office of the Office of United Nations High Commissioner for Human Rights. The Council, through its Periodic Review process and the Complaints Procedure is tasked with identifying consistent patterns of gross and reliably attested violations of human rights and fundamental freedoms, and of course helping to resolve them. One significant mechanism used by the Council is the 'Special Procedures' process whereby thematic issues or specific country matters are referred to a Special Rapporteur or Independent Expert who monitors, advises and publicly reports on human rights matters. As at 1 September 2012 there were thirty-six thematic and twelve country mandates. Examples of the former include the Special Rapporteur on the promotion and protection of the right to freedom of opinion and expression, and the Independent Expert on the issue of human rights obligations relating to the enjoyment of a safe, clean, healthy and sustainable environment; of the latter, the Special Rapporteur on the situation of human rights in Eritrea and the Independent Expert on the situation of human rights in Haiti.

12.3.4 **The International Convention on the Elimination of All Forms of Racial Discrimination 1966**

This international treaty establishes a specific regime in the field of racial discrimination. As at 1 September 2012, there were 175 parties to the Convention, including the UK. As regards enforcement of the obligations of the Convention, there is a procedure similar to that existing under the International Civil and Political Covenant, although the more limited nature of the rights protected means that its enforcement provisions are slightly stronger. States are under an obligation to submit reports to a Committee on the Elimination of Racial Discrimination. These are examined and general recommendations made. In addition, by signing the Convention, each state automatically accepts the possibility of an inter-state complaint. In such an event, and unless the disputants can settle the matter by negotiation, the Committee may refer the matter to an ad hoc Conciliation Commission. Its findings are not binding, but they may provide essential factual material on the degree of state compliance with the Convention. There is also an optional system of individual complaints under Art. 14, which may prove effective in specific cases even though an 'award' is not binding. As at 1 September 2012, fifty-four states had made a declaration under Art. 14, not including the UK, but including France, Italy, Norway, the Netherlands, Sweden and Russia.

12.3.5 UN agencies and other multilateral instruments

A number of the specialised agencies and subsidiary organs of the UN are also concerned with the promotion and protection of human rights. Chief among these is the International Labour Organisation that has done much in the field of forced labour, equal pay and the right to work. Members are under an obligation to submit reports and there is a procedure for inter-state complaints to the International Labour Office. These may be referred to a Commission of Inquiry and although its report is not binding as such, a party may refer the matter forward to the ICJ. Similarly, the United Nations Educational, Scientific and Cultural Organisation (UNESCO) and the United Nations Relief and Works Agency (UNRWA) all deal with various aspects of human rights. The last of these has field officers and legal advisers stationed in the Israeli-occupied territories of Palestine whose function is to protect the human rights of Palestinian refugees on a day-to-day basis.

There are, in addition to these bodies, many other treaties covering specific human rights matters. Examples include the 1948 Convention on the Prevention and Punishment of the Crime of Genocide, the Convention against Torture referred to earlier, the Convention on the Elimination of All Forms of Discrimination Against Women 1979, the 1973 Convention on the Suppression and Punishment of the Crime of Apartheid and, in the field of personal responsibility, the 1945 Agreement for the Prosecution and Punishment of Major War Criminals and Charter of the International Military Tribunal at Nuremberg, the Yugoslav, Somalia and Rwanda War Crimes Tribunals and of course the International Criminal Court. In a slightly different vein, we can note the 1949 Geneva Conventions and 1977 Protocols concerning the protection of military and civilian personnel in time of armed conflict. In a sense, these last treaties protect the 'human rights' of individuals in a situation of extreme distress.

12.4 The European Convention on Human Rights and Fundamental Freedoms 1950

In 1950, the member states of the Council of Europe signed the European Convention on Human Rights. This entered into force in 1953 and as at 1 September 2012 there were forty-seven parties, including the UK. The Convention represents a comprehensive statement of the civil and political rights believed to be common to the peoples of Europe. Although originally a creation of the nations of Western Europe, the Convention is open to signature by all members of the Council of Europe and since the end of the 'cold war' many of the former socialist European states have become parties to the system (e.g. Poland, Hungary). The Convention is similar in scope to the International Covenant on Civil and Political Rights although its provisions for enforcement are considerably more effective. The basic obligation is found in Art. 1, wherein the parties 'shall secure to everyone within their jurisdiction the rights and freedoms' defined in Section I. As is evident, this provision obliges states to protect the human rights of any person within their jurisdiction, be they a national, a national of another contracting party or a national of a third state (as in *Berrehab* v *Netherlands* (1989) 11 EHRR 322 where the rights of a resident Moroccan were violated).

The usual way in which a contracting party will meet its obligations will be to ensure that its national law does not violate the rights protected in the Convention. For this reason, many states have formally incorporated the Convention into their national law, often as an element of their constitution. The UK has adopted this approach with the entry into force of the Human Rights Act 1998 on 2 October 2000. This implements (albeit in a unique way) many of the Convention rights in UK law. In addition, the government has established special procedures within the executive, legislature and judiciary to ensure that both existing law and new legislation comply with the substantive rights of the Convention. Even after just over twelve years, it is clear that the 1998 Act is having a profound impact on the procedure and substance of UK law. It also appears to have had the welcome side benefit of reducing the occasions on which the UK is brought before the European Court of Human Rights in Strasbourg for an alleged violation of the Convention. Thus, it appears that local UK courts are able to offer a relatively quick and effective remedy, with resort to Strasbourg being reserved for the exceptional cases.

The rights protected by the Convention are detailed in Arts 1–12 and these are supplemented substantively and procedurally by fourteen Protocols, all of which are in force, save Protocol 10 which has been superseded by Protocol 11. They include the right to life (Art. 2), prohibition of torture or inhumane or degrading treatment (Art. 3), prohibition of slavery (Art. 4), the right to liberty (Art. 5) and the right of due process of law in respect of criminal or civil proceedings (Art. 6). Generally, the purpose of the Convention is not to prevent or punish wholesale violations of human rights (although it would operate in such circumstances) but to close gaps in the domestic law of the parties. In similar fashion to the International Covenant, states are permitted to derogate from certain provisions 'in time of public emergency threatening the life of the nation' (Art. 15), except that no such derogation may be made in respect of Arts 2, 3, 4(1) and 7 (no retrospective criminal legislation). The UK, for example, entered a derogation to Art. 5(3) following the decision in *Brogan* v *UK* (1989) 11 EHRR 117, where it was held that the UK was in violation of the Convention in so far as the Prevention of Terrorism (Temporary Provisions) Act 1984 authorised detention contrary to the right of every person 'arrested or detained to be brought promptly before a judge'. This derogation itself has been confirmed as lawful by the court in *Brannigan and McBride* v *United Kingdom* ECHR Series A (1993) No. 258-B.

A breach of the Convention entails international responsibility. This may mean that the state concerned is obliged to bring its national law into line with the Convention or, as happened after the *Brogan* case, the state may act to prevent future liability by effecting a lawful change in those obligations. In appropriate cases, usually of specific injury to individuals, the European Court of Human Rights may award 'satisfaction' under Art. 50. This may take the form of a monetary award, as in the *Young, James and Webster Case* (1983) 5 EHRR 201, following a breach of Art. 11 (freedom of association) by the UK.

Originally, the application of the European Convention was overseen by three bodies: the European Commission of Human Rights, the Committee of Ministers and the European Court of Human Rights based in Strasbourg. Although effective in its own way, this procedure became cumbersome and expensive and it became clear that an overhaul was needed if the Convention was to blossom into an effective guarantee of human rights for the whole of Europe. This was achieved by the adoption of the Eleventh Protocol to the Convention, concluded in May 1994 and entering into force on 1 November 1998 (with further changes made by the Fourteenth Protocol, in force 1 June 2010). In formal terms, the Eleventh Protocol has amended Sections II to IV of the Convention. The Commission is abolished and the role of the Committee of Ministers (which was always of a political nature) reduced. The aims were to simplify the procedures by which a case may be brought before the Court, to strengthen the judicial elements of the system and to speed consideration of specific cases. These have been largely achieved. The Court itself has been re-organised so that there now exist single judge formations (see Protocol 14) and Committees of the Court (both single judges and Committees may decide questions of admissibility in cases brought by individuals), Chambers of the Court (seven judges, to decide questions of admissibility in some cases brought by individuals and in those brought by states and to hear cases) and a Grand Chamber (seventeen judges, to hear some cases at first instance and some on appeal from a Chamber). Necessarily, the use of Chambers – instead of the full Court for every case – has speeded up the judicial process.

12.4.1 Access to the Court

As an international treaty, the European Convention is open for ratification by state members of the Council of Europe. Acceptance of the Convention imposes a primary obligation for states to guarantee protection of the rights contained therein for all persons within their national jurisdictions. Failure entails international responsibility. In addition, however, under the reforms of the Eleventh Protocol, parties to the Convention automatically accept the right of other state-parties and individuals (including non-governmental organisations) to bring a case under the enforcement mechanisms: see Arts 33 and 34 of the Convention. This replaces the previous optional system. Consequently, if a breach of the Convention is suspected, either another state or the individual directly affected may bring the alleged delinquent state before the Court.

12.4.2 The procedure for bringing a claim

The restructuring of the Court into single-judge formations, Committees, Chambers and the Grand Chamber is an attempt to streamline the process by which claims can be made and assessed. Necessarily, not all claims will be 'admissible', and under

Art. 35 both individual and inter-state complaints can be declared inadmissible if domestic remedies have not been exhausted, the application is anonymous, substantially the same matter has been dealt with previously or the application is incompatible with the provisions of the Convention, is manifestly ill-founded or an abuse of the process.

In respect of individual petitions under the Convention, a single judge or Committee of the Court (three judges) will consider questions of admissibility (Art. 27 and Art. 28 respectively). Decisions of the single judge or Committee on admissibility usually are final, but there is a mechanism for referring the question of admissibility to a Chamber under Art. 29. Admissible applications from individuals are open to 'friendly settlement', but failing this are considered on the merits by a Chamber. In the normal course of events, a decision on the merits by a Chamber will be final, but in exceptional circumstances a party to the case may refer the Chamber's decision to the Grand Chamber which may hear the case if it raises a serious question affecting the Convention or a serious issue of general importance (Art. 43). Further, in certain cases a Chamber may relinquish its jurisdiction in favour of the Grand Chamber without first giving judgment. This can occur if the issue raises a serious question affecting the Convention or might result in an inconsistency with a judgment previously delivered (Art. 30). The judgment of the Chamber or the Grand Chamber (as the case may be) is final and execution is supervised by the Committee of Ministers (Art. 46).

Inter-state complaints are submitted to a Chamber for a decision on their admissibility (Art. 29). Admissible applications are open to 'friendly settlement', but failing this the Chamber will also consider the merits. Once again, however, one of the parties may refer a decision of a Chamber to the Grand Chamber in the exceptional circumstances of Art. 43, or the Chamber may relinquish jurisdiction to the Grand Chamber under Art. 30. The award (of Chamber or Grand Chamber as the case may be) is binding and again supervised by the Committee of Ministers under Art. 46. We should also note at this point that the Committee of Ministers may request the Grand Chamber to give an Advisory Opinion within fairly narrow limits (Art. 47).

Finally, under Protocol 14, Article 46 of the Convention dealing with binding force and execution of judgments has been amended and strengthened for all cases. The Committee of Ministers has been given a new power in the event that a State refuses to abide by a final judgment. Such cases are rare, but now the Committee of Ministers 'may, after serving formal notice on that Party and by decision adopted by a majority vote of two thirds of the representatives entitled to sit on the Committee, refer to the Court the question whether that Party has failed to fulfil its obligation under paragraph 1'.

12.4.3 Conclusion

There is no doubt that the European Convention has had a significant impact on the law of human rights in Europe since its entry into force in 1953. The procedures of the Convention have done much to remedy general defects in the national law of the contracting states, as well as providing individuals with concrete remedies for specific violations of their human rights. This represents a great advance on the International Covenants discussed in the previous sections. The overhaul of the system effected by the Protocols (particularly the Eleventh and Fourteenth) will speed up the process of justice and is to be greatly welcomed. Of course, problems remain, particularly the ability to derogate from certain Convention rights consequent upon a proven violation but any criticisms are minor when compared to the relative lack of progress made elsewhere in the field of human rights protection.

12.5 Other regional machinery

12.5.1 Other European initiatives

It is tempting to think of human rights in Europe only in terms of the European Convention discussed previously. However, there are several other European initiatives that have done much to protect the rights of peoples on the European continent. On one level, there are the human rights provisions of the treaties establishing the European Communities and the European Union and these can have 'direct effect' in the national law of the Member States. Obviously, the 'rights' themselves are more economic than political, but the implementation of the Treaty on European Union (the Maastricht Treaty) and its Social Chapter has had a significant effect on the economic and social welfare of the nationals of most Member States. In similar vein is the European Social Charter 1961, a multilateral treaty, binding in international law, to which the UK is a party. Of perhaps more political significance is the process initiated by the Final Act of the Conference on Security and Co-operation in Europe 1975 (the Helsinki Final Act of the CSCE). The Organisation for Security and Co-operation in Europe (OSCE, as it is now called) is the product of this process and involves nearly every European state, including those of the former socialist bloc, and the USA, Canada and Russia. It has spawned a number of more specific agreements dealing with human rights issues and there are limited procedures for monitoring human rights violations within Europe (see e.g. OSCE activities in Kosovo). Indeed, although this may seem very vague, the OSCE has been quite effective in raising the profile of human rights in Europe and illustrates again the extra-legal dimension of international law.

12.5.2 The western hemisphere: American Convention on Human Rights

In 1948, the Ninth Conference of American States adopted the American Declaration of the Rights and Duties of Man. Although it contained no enforcement provisions, this acted as an impetus to human rights law in the western hemisphere. Then, in 1969 the Organisation of American States adopted the American Convention on Human Rights including provision for an Inter-American Court of Human Rights. On signing this Convention, states *ipso facto* accept the right of individual complaint to the Inter-American Commission of Human Rights (established separately in 1959/60). Conversely, the right of inter-state complaint is optional under Art. 45. Furthermore, the jurisdiction of the Court is optional under Art. 62 and only the Commission and/or the state concerned may refer a matter to it following unsuccessful attempts by the Commission to reach a negotiated settlement. The rights protected by the Convention are broadly similar to those of the European model. As at 10 September 2012, there were twenty-three parties, not including the USA, with Venezuela withdrawing with effect from 10 September 2012.

12.5.3 African Charter on Human and Peoples' Rights 1981

In 1979, a UN Seminar on the Establishment of Regional Commissions on Human Rights with Special Reference to Africa was held in Monrovia, Liberia. This proved to be the final impetus for the adoption of an African system for the protection of human rights. Thus, on 24 June 1981, the 18th Organisation of African Unity (now called the African Union) Assembly of Heads of State and Government adopted the OAU Charter on Human and Peoples' Rights (the Banjul Charter). This entered into force in October 1986 when a simple majority of OAU states (the Organisation is now called the African Union) had ratified it. At 1 September 2012, there were fifty-three parties.

Under Art. 1 of the Charter, state-parties 'shall recognise the rights, duties and freedoms enshrined in this Charter and shall undertake to adopt legislative or other measures to give effect to them'. This obligation is less absolute than that found in the European Convention, although this is probably a sensible approach given that many African states see political independence and economic stability as the most important national goals. The Charter does, however, cover a wider range of rights than its European counterpart, dealing with political, civil, economic, social and cultural rights. Significantly, the Charter does not always emphasise individual rights, but stresses certain community values. Thus, Art. 18 provides that 'the family shall be the natural unit and basis of society' and Arts 19 to 24 affirm the rights of 'peoples' to self-determination, 'existence' and conditions of satisfactory environment. Likewise, Arts 27, 28 and 29 impose duties on the individual in respect of the family and society. Enforcement of the Charter is through the African Commission on Human and Peoples' Rights, which has general supervisory functions as well as jurisdiction under a compulsory system of inter-state complaints.

12.6 Success and failure

As noted at the beginning of this chapter, the simple fact that there now exists a comprehensive body of human rights law is an achievement in itself. International law will intervene to protect individuals from the excesses of their own, or any other, government. Moreover, in the concrete application of these principles, the European Convention regime represents a major step forward. It does remedy human rights abuses arising from specific cases, and although it is largely an *ex post facto* system of justice the new procedures have done much to speed the award of a remedy. In addition to this, the United Nations has done much promotional work in the human rights area and perhaps the greatest achievement of the UN in the field of human rights is the raising of consciousness and the placing of human rights firmly on the plane of international law (see e.g. the Vienna Declaration 1993). In specific areas also the United Nations has made some headway, as with the right of self-determination, the provisions on racial discrimination, crimes of personal responsibility and in the work of specialised agencies such as the International Labour Organisation.

As far as the international protection of human rights in concrete form is concerned, there have not been great advances outside the European regional model.

The enforcement procedures of the International Covenants are not rigorous and they are often nullified by their purely voluntary nature. In one sense this is not surprising. The search for *universal* human rights is always going to be fraught with difficulty. States are diverse and have different moral, political and economic values. Is it possible in such circumstances to agree on a general pattern of human rights that all states will protect? Is the European view of 'democracy', 'liberty' and 'justice' any more correct than those of African, Asian or Arab states? Similarly, the UN itself is a political body and the emotive issue of human rights can become a political football. Why, for example, did the UN fail to take action over the massive violations of human rights in Cambodia when at the same time Canada was held responsible in the *Lovelace* decision for a violation that paled into insignificance? Of course, it is no surprise that those states with the least to fear accept the toughest obligations.

If, then, the *universal* protection of a significant number of human rights is unattainable (and many would dispute this), perhaps the best way forward is to focus on establishing effective regional machinery. The European model is an excellent example, but others exist. Yet even here there are difficulties. The effective protection of human rights by a regional code is necessarily dependent upon a cultural, economic and political homogeneity among the participating states that simply may not exist. The states of Europe by and large do share such a common heritage (but note the former Yugoslavia), but is this true of states of the western hemisphere or Africa? On the other hand, it is easy to be negative. We should not overlook the fact that the cause of human rights has advanced considerably since 1945, both internationally and regionally. International law now has the potential to help individuals in cases where their national law may be ineffective or may even be the instrument of their oppression. States may be reluctant to accept the full force of international human rights law in concrete cases, but all are subject to some level of general and binding legal obligations not to maltreat their nationals or any other persons within their jurisdiction. Whatever else may be criticised, this should be recognised as an achievement of the highest order.

FURTHER READING

Alston, P., 'Reconceiving the UN Human Rights Regime: Challenges Confronting the New UN Human Rights Council' (2006) 7 *Melbourne Journal of International Law* 187.

Baderin, M. and McCorquodale, R., *Economic, Social and Cultural Rights in Action* (Oxford University Press, 2007).

Claude, R., and Weston B., *Human Rights in the World Community* (University of Pennsylvania Press, 1992).

Falk, R. Stevens, J. and Rajagopal, B., *International Law and the Third World: Reshaping Justice* (Routledge, 2008).

Gearty, C., 'The European Court of Human Rights and the Protection of Civil Liberties: An Overview', (1993) 52 *CLJ* 89.

Hannum, H. (ed.), *Guide to International Human Rights Practice* (University of Pennsylvania Press, 1992).

Hannum, H., 'Minorities, Indigenous Peoples, and Self-Determination', in Henkin and Hargrove (eds), *Human Rights: An Agenda for the Next Century* (American Society of International Law, 1994).

McCorquodale, R., 'Self-determination: A Human Rights Approach', (1994) 43 *ICLQ* 857.

McCorquodale, R., with R. Fairbrother, 'Globalization and Human Rights', (1999) 21 *Human Rights Quarterly* 735.

Meron, T. (ed.), *Human Rights in International Law: Legal and Policy Issues* (Clarendon Press, 1986).

Schmidt, M., 'Individual Human Rights Complaints Procedures Based on the United Nations Treaties and the Need for Reform', (1992) 41 *ICLQ* 645.

Sweeney, J., 'Margins of Appreciation: Cultural Relativity and the European Court of Human Rights in the Post-Cold War Era', (2005) 54 *ICLQ* 459, 462–3.

SUMMARY

Human rights

- It is important to draw a clear distinction between substantive rules of law and rules of morality, no matter how much the latter might be thought desirable or necessary. No amount of rhetoric can ensure that a state will observe an international human rights obligation, but there is considerably more chance if that obligation can be shown to flow from a recognised 'source of law'.

- 'First generation' rights comprise those civil and political rights that are now at the core of most human rights treaty regimes. 'Second generation' human rights generally relate to matters of social and economic significance, such as the right to work, the right to social security, the right to an adequate standard of living and the right to education. 'Third generation' rights may include very general concepts such as rights of development, the right to a protected environment, rights of peace and a wide right of self-determination.

- An optimistic view of the effect of the Universal Declaration of Human Rights is that it generated a general principle of customary international law to the effect that states were bound to respect the human rights of persons within their jurisdiction.

- The International Covenant on Civil and Political Rights (ICCPR) entered into force in 1976 Covenant and is a legally binding treaty. Each state-party undertakes to adopt such legislative measures within their domestic jurisdiction as may be necessary to give effect to the rights listed in the Covenant and also to provide an effective remedy should a violation occur.

- The International Covenant on Economic, Social and Cultural Rights 1966 is the counterpart to the Covenant on Civil and Political Rights and deals with so-called 'second generation' rights.

- A number of the specialised agencies and subsidiary organs of the UN are also concerned with the promotion and protection of human rights.

- In 1950, the member states of the Council of Europe signed the European Convention on Human Rights. The Convention represents a comprehensive statement of the civil and political rights believed to be common to the peoples of Europe. The usual way in which a contracting party will meet its obligations will be to ensure that its national law does not violate the rights protected in the Convention.

- Other regional machinery exists for the protection of human rights in the Americas and in Africa.

GLOSSARY

Arab League Established in 1945 as a loose association of independent states geared to cooperation in a variety of economic and political affairs.

Customary international law International law developed through the practice of states.

de facto As a fact.

de jure As of right.

ex aequo et bono A decision of the ICJ based not on strict rules of international law but on such general principles as seem appropriate to the Court.

International Law Commission The body charged by the UN with the development and codification of international law. It consists of thirty-four independent members representing the major legal systems of the world. Proposals are drawn up by a Special Rapporteur and then modified and adopted as Draft Articles.

jure gestionis Acts *jure gestionis* are state acts of a commercial nature.

jure imperii Acts *jure imperii* are state acts of a sovereign or governmental nature.

jus cogens Certain fundamental rules of customary international law incapable of being modified by treaty.

opinio juris A necessary component in the formation of customary law: the belief that a practice is obligatory rather than habitual.

Organisation of African Unity (OAU) Established in 1963 as a forum for political, economic and social cooperation in Africa. Its main organ is the Assembly of Heads of State or Government which meets annually. Now called the African Union.

Organisation of American States (OAS) Formally established by the Pact of Bogotá in 1948, the Organisation grew out of a series of inter-American conferences held over the previous fifty years.

pacta sunt servanda The rule that treaties are binding on the parties, often said to be a rule of customary law.

par in parem non habet imperium Expresses the idea that one sovereign state cannot exercise jurisdiction over another sovereign state because of their legal equality.

res communis A description applied to areas of territory indicating that they are not open to acquisition by any state but may be enjoyed by any member of the international community.

terra nullius Territory which does not belong to any state or people. It may therefore be acquired by occupation.

travaux préparatoires The preparatory material containing the negotiating history of a treaty or international conference.

Treaties or international conventions Agreements between states or other subjects of international law creating rights and duties enforceable in international law.

United Nations (UN) The UN is the successor to the League of Nations with its Headquarters in New York and offices around the world (e.g. Geneva, Vienna). At the time of writing, membership stands at 188. The UN Charter is the Organisation's constitution, but as a treaty it is also a major source of the current rules of international law. The UN has six principal organs:

General Assembly Each member of the UN is a member of the Assembly, with one vote. The Assembly is the main policy making body of the UN and it can instigate initiatives covering all the UN's activities. Resolutions are adopted by majority vote, although most are not binding in law. It meets annually, usually in New York.

Security Council Technically the most powerful organ of the UN, the Council is charged primarily with the maintenance of international peace and security. At any one time, there are fifteen members of the Council, including the five Permanent Members – China, France, UK, USA and Russia – who have the power to veto any substantive resolution. The Council may impose economic or military sanctions on delinquent states.

Trusteeship Council Responsible for the supervision of non-self governing territories with a view to their eventual independence. No Trust Territories remain.

Economic and Social Council Responsible for UN activity in the field of economic and social welfare, including general responsibility for human rights.

Secretariat Responsible for the day-to-day running of the Organisation. Its head is the Secretary-General, the head of the Organisation. It is tantamount to an international civil service.

International Court of Justice (ICJ) The primary judicial organ of the UN, charged with the peaceful resolution of disputes according to international law. It is the successor to the Permanent Court of International Justice.

uti possidetis The principle that the frontiers of newly independent states should conform to the frontiers of the colonial territories from which they emerged.

INDEX

Acceptance of ICJ jurisdiction 306–7
Accepted law *see Opinio juris*
Accretion and
      avulsion 169
Ad hoc tribunals
  competence to deal with individuals 129
  dispute settlement 11
  judicial decisions as source of law 48
  judicial enforcement of international law 9
  rationale for system of law 6
  trial of individuals 128
Advisory Opinions
  Charter provisions 316–17
  issue of consent 317–18
  relevant legal questions 318–19
Afghanistan
  defined territories 119
  limitations on enforcement by Security
    Council 8
  perception of failed international law 1
  political cost of violating international
    law 13
  prevalence of vital interests 15
  use of force 322, 324, 326–8, 334–7, 345,
    347, 351
African Union
  Charter on Human and Peoples' Rights 1981
    370
  collective security provisions 348–50
  role of international law 3
  subject of international law 127
Agencies of states 125
Aggression
  General Assembly as source of law 50–1
  maintenance of peace by Security
    Council 342
  rationale for system of law 5
Airspace jurisdiction 178–9
Amendment of treaties 80–1
Antarctica 176–8
Arab League
  role of international law 3
  source of law 52
Arbitration 292–4
Archipelagos 243
Arctic 178
'Armed attacks' 330–1

Berlin (territorial entity) 125
Bosnia *see* Former Yugoslavia
Brezhnev doctrine 341

Calvo clauses 274
Cessation of territory 167–8

China
  approach to Taiwan 118, 134
  human rights violations 6, 357
  rationale for system of law 6
  Security Council veto 8, 343, 345
  transfer of sovereign UK territory 57, 79, 167
'Circumstances precluding wrongfulness' 264–6
Collective security provisions
  overview 341–2
  peacekeeping forces 351
  United Nations
    General Assembly 347–8
    Security Council 342–7
Collective self-defence
  general principles 332–3
  no requirement for prior authorisation 342
  overlap with Security Council powers 345–6
  requests to third states 333–4
Comity between nations
  maritime jurisdiction 221
  opinio juris 36
  rationale for immunities 186–7
Command theory of international law 16–17
Common heritage of mankind
  Antarctica 176, 178
  continental shelf 229–30
  deep seabed 237, 239, 240
  outer space 176
  res communis 175
Compensation
  expropriation of foreign property
    appropriateness in accordance with
      customary law 278
    calculation 279–81
    international minimum standard 277–8
    unlawful appropriations 279
  sources of law
    general principle common to all systems 43
    soft law 52
Conciliation 291
Concurrent jurisdiction 151
Conquest of territories 168–9
Consent
  consensual theory of international
    law 17–18
  customary international law 17
  defence to state responsibility 264–5
  diminishing role of publicists 49
  ICJ jurisdiction
    ad hoc 304
    Advisory Opinions 317–18
    forum porogatum 304–5
    Optional system 306–7
    with reservations 307–10

Consent (*cont.*)
   treaties 305–6
  inception of treaties 66–7
  termination of treaties 81
  treaties as source of law 28–9
Constitutive theory of recognition
  declaratory theory compared 135–6
  general principles 133–5
Contiguous zones 242
Continental shelf
  defined 228
  impact on claims to territorial seas 222
  nature and extent of rights 228
  opposite and adjacent states
    pragmatic approach 234–5
    uncertainty 230–3
  origins 228
  overlap with EEZ 222
  preference for single maritime boundary 236
  relationship with EEZs 235–6
  seaward limit 229–30
Contractual obligations
  concessionary agreements and treaties
    distinguished 61
  national law and treaties distinguished 55
  state immunity 190
  state responsibility 282
  treaties as source of law 30–1
Corporations
  dispute resolution 97
  effects of non-recognition in UK 143–4
  entitlement to immunity 204–6
  impact of absolute state immunity 187
  international personality 130
  jurisdiction of ICC 21
  multiple personalities 102
  peaceful settlement of disputes 293
  prohibition of torture 358
  protection of foreign investors 283–4
  state responsibility for foreign
    nationals 270–2
  supervisory jurisdiction over arbitration
    proceedings 200
Countermeasures
  defence to state responsibility 265
  enforcement through loss of rights and
    privileges 9
  role of Security Council 7
  termination of treaties 85
Crimes against humanity
  human rights responsibilities 354
  humanitarian intervention 343
  individual responsibility 128
  jurisdiction of the ICC 129
  jus cogens 41
  relationship with national law 90
  role of international law 13
  universal jurisdiction 155
Crimes against the peace
  human rights responsibilities 354

  individual criminal responsibility 128
Croatia *see* Former Yugoslavia
Customary international law
  codification by treaty 29–30
  consensual theory of international law 17–18
  creation of legally binding obligations 61
  development through General
    Assembly 50–1
  future prospects 21
  incorporation into UK law 108–10
  law of the sea
    bays 245
    high seas 241
  matters for ICC to consider under
    Art 38 24
  process of law creation 47–8
  relationship with VCLT 1969 63–4
  self-defence 327–8
  source of law
    foundation of law of nations 32
    relationship with treaty law 39–42
    state practice 32–9
  state responsibility 253
    compensation for expropriation 278
    fundamental principle 263
  state responsibility for foreign
    nationals 267–8
  theoretical basis 17
  unilateral use of force 322–4

Damages *see* Compensation
Danzig (territorial entity) 125
De facto recognition 140–1
De jure recognition 140–1
De lege ferenda 52
Declarations 57–8
Declaratory theory of recognition
  constitutive theory compared 135–6
  general principles 132–3
Deconstructionist theories 19–20
Deep seabed
  Convention 1982
    concerns met by 1994 Agreement 239–40
    difficulties with original draft 237–8
    general scheme under Part XI 238–9
  exploitation of mineral resources 236–7
  summary of rules 240–1
Derived personality 116
Dignity of individuals
  heads of state 206, 209
  human rights 354, 357, 360
  personal immunity 210
  role of international law 3
Diplomatic and consular immunities
  duty not to abuse 212–13
  embassies and property 211
  enforcement through loss of rights and
    privileges 9
  freedom of communication 211–12
  legal principles of international law 209–10

personal to individuals 208–9
relevant persons 210–11
role of international law 3–4
UK approach 213–14
Discovery of new territories 167
Dispositive treaties 18, 78–9
Dispute settlement *see* Peaceful settlement of
   disputes
'Double jeopardy' 151–2
Dualism
   approach to subject matter 93
   incorporation doctrine 100
   practical application 94
   relationship between national and
      international law 92–3

East Timor
   cession of territory 118
   human rights 360
   humanitarian intervention 342
   powers of the Security Council 346
   role of international law 7
   self-determination 2
   use of force 346
Effectiveness principle 74
'Effects' doctrine 156–8
Enforcement
   see also Peaceful settlement of disputes
   central questions about international law 1
   command theory of law 16–17
   effectiveness 14
   future prospects 21
   hallmark of system of law 6–7
   judgments against foreign states 186
   jurisdiction 149
   jurisdiction over persons state in custody
      analysis of principles in Harvard Research
         Draft 150–2
      nationality jurisdiction 153–4
      passive personality jurisdiction 159
      persons apprehended in violation of
         international law 160–1
      protective jurisdiction 156–8
      territorial jurisdiction 152–3
      universal jurisdiction 154–6
   loss of legal rights and privileges 8–9
   maintenance of peace by Security
      Council 342–4
   rationale for system of law 6
   role of human rights 356
   state immunity 201
   weaknesses of international law 15–16
Entry into force of treaties
   effect of reservations 71–2
   Vienna Convention on the Law of
      Treaties 1969 67–8
Environmental protection
   central questions about international
      law 1
   law of the sea 242, 245–6

promotion of common good 12
role of international law 3
Equity 44
European Court of Human Rights (ECtHR)
   access to Court 367
   claims procedure 367–8
   establishment 367
   role as institutional mechanism for system
      of law 6
   settlement of disputes 292
   significant impact 368–9
European Union (EU)
   enforcement through loss of rights and
      privileges 9
   human rights
      European Court of Human Rights (ECtHR)
         367–9
   human rights protection
      ECHR 1950 365–7
      other regional initiatives 369
      successes and failures 370–1
   state immunity 207
   state recognition 135–6
   subject of international law 127
Evidence
   application of international law in domestic
      courts 111–12
   application of national law in international
      courts and tribunals 96–7
   general principles common to all
      systems 43
Ex aequo et bono decisions 24, 44
Exceptio non adimpleti contracus 84–5
Exclusive Economic Zones (EEZ)
   delimitation 226–7
   impact on claims to territorial seas 222
   nature and extent 225–6
   origins 224–5
   other states' rights 226
   overlap with continental shelf 227
   relationship with continental
      shelf 235–6
Executive certificates 112
Exhaustion of local remedies 272–4
Exiled governments 130
Expropriation of foreign property
   conditions for lawful expropriation 275–7
   meaning and scope 275
   measure of compensation
      appropriateness in accordance with
         customary law 278
      calculation 279–81
      international minimum standard 277–8
      unlawful appropriations 279
   soft law 52
Extinction of statehood 124–5
Extra-territorial jurisdiction 153
Extradition
   judicial decisions as source of law 48
   role of international law 3

Flag states 241–2
Force *see* Use of force
Force majeure 265
Former Yugoslavia
  establishment of ad hoc tribunal 155
  extinction of statehood 124
  humanitarian intervention 337
  need for international rules 4
  non-military sanctions 343
  peaceful settlement of disputes 286
  peacekeeping forces 350
  protection of human rights 365
  scope of Security Council action 8
  trial of individuals 11, 128
  UN failures 1
  War Crimes Tribunal 6
Forum porogatum 304–5
Freedom of the high seas 80, 241
Fundamental change of circumstances 83

General Assembly
  collective security provisions 347–8
  conditions for lawful expropriation 276
  'moratorium resolution' on sea bed
    mining 237
  peaceful settlement of disputes 289
  resolutions and treaties distinguished 57–8
  source of law 25, 50–1
General principles
  descriptive function only 43
  equity 44
  inclusion within ICC Statute 45
  matters for ICC to consider under Art 38 24
  source of law
    ICC Statute 42
    natural law doctrines 42–3
    rules and principles common to all
      systems 43–4
'Generations' of rights 358–9
Genocide
  customary international law 42
  individual responsibility 128
  judicial enforcement of international law 10
  jurisdiction of the ICC 129
  jus cogens 80
  rationale for system of law 5
  universal jurisdiction 155
Genuine link test 269–72
Good offices 288
Government
  see also States
Governments
  see also Immunities; States
  acceptance by the community 124
  calls for collective security 345
  control over the disputed territories 170
  effect of entering into contract 124
  executive certificates 112
  in exile 130
  factual prerequisite 123

  grounds for humanitarian
    intervention 337–8
  invitations to use force 333–4
  opinio juris 37
  peaceful settlement of disputes 293, 306,
    308
  practitioners of international law 4, 12
  precondition of statehood 174
  recognition
    constitutive theory 133–5
    declaratory theory 132–3
    UK national law 136–45
  relationship between national and
    international law 92, 101, 109–10
  requirement for statehood 129
  sovereign immunity for ships 221
  state responsibility
    expropriation 275–81
    officials 258–9
    revolutionaries 261–2
  treaties
    authority to conclude treaties 65–6
    as contracts 30–1

Harvard Research Draft 150–2, 156, 266
Heads of state
  African Union 370
  diplomatic and consular immunities 209
  granting of state immunity 186, 206–7
  treaty representatives 66
High seas 241–2
Hosti humani generis 128
Hot pursuit 242, 337–9
Human rights
  European Union (EU)
    ECHR 1950 365–7
    European Court of Human Rights (ECtHR)
      367–9
    other regional initiatives 369
  groundbreaking work of ICC 2
  history and development
    'generations' of rights 358–9
    League of Nations 357
    UN Charter provisions 357–8
    Universal Declaration in 1948 358
  humanitarian intervention 337–9
  rationale for system of law 4
  regional initiatives
    African Charter on Human and Peoples'
      Rights 1981 370
    American Convention on Human Rights
      1948 369
    European Union (EU) 369
    successes and failures 370–1
  rights granted to individuals 129
  role of international law 3
  role on international law 354–7
  sources of law 354
  state immunity 207–8
  successes and failures 370–1

UN treaty regimes
  International Convention on the
    Elimination of All Forms of Racial
    Discrimination 1966 364–5
  International Covenant on Civil and
    Political Rights 1966 360–2
  International Covenant on Economic,
    Social and Cultural Rights 1966 362–4
  Universal Declaration in 1948 359–60
  US denial at Guantanamo Bay 1–2
Humanitarian intervention 337–9

ICC Statute
  see also International Criminal Court (ICC)
  general principles 45
  matters for ICC to consider under Art 38 42
  recognition of local custom 35
  source of law
    formal and material sources
      distinguished 26–7
    material and evidentiary sources
      distinguished 27
    matters for Court to consider 24–6
  subsidiary approach to judicial
    decisions 45–6
Immunities
  see also Jurisdiction
  diplomatic and consular immunities
    duty not to abuse 212–13
    embassies and property 211
    freedom of communication 211–12
    legal principles of international law 209–10
    personal to individuals 208–9
    relevant persons 210–11
    UK approach 213–14
  international organisations 214–15
  judicial decisions as source of law 48
  overview 182
  rationale for system of law 4–5
  state practice 33
  states
    adoption of restrictive theory 187–8
    classification of acts according to subject
      matter 190–1
    commercial transactions 190
    distinctions found on purpose of act 188–9
    European Union (EU) 207
    heads of state 206–7
    ILC Draft Articles 194
    overview 182
    relationship with Art 6 (fair trial) 207–8
    two stage test to distinguish acts jure imperii
      and jure gestionis 191–3
    UK approach 196–206
    underlying concept and rationale 183–7
    violations of national law 193–4
Inception of treaties
  authority to conclude treaties 65–6
  consent 66–7
  entry into force 67–8

framework of rules 64–5
Incorporation doctrine
  customary law into UK law 108–10
  theoretical perspectives 98–100
Individuals
  diplomatic and consular immunities
    duty not to abuse 212–13
    embassies and property 211
    freedom of communication 211–12
    legal principles of international law 209–10
    personal right 208–9
    relevant persons 210–11
    UK approach 213–14
  international personality 128–30
  jurisdiction of ICC 21
  responsibility for illegal acts 284
  role of human rights 356
  state responsibility 259–61
'Innocent passage' 221
Inquiries 288–9
Institutions
  see also International courts and
    tribunals
  courts and tribunals 9–11
  enforcement role of Security Council 7–8
  future prospects 21
  future prospects for development 2
  lack of institutions 14–15
  national and international law
    compared 5–6
  non-statist theories of international
    law 20–1
  peaceful settlement of disputes
    General Assembly 289
    other agencies 291
    Security Council 289–91
  sources of law 24
Intemporal law doctrine 166–7
Interim protection measures 299–301
International Court of Justice (ICJ)
  access to Court 295–7
  admissibility in contentious cases 297–9
  Advisory Opinions
    Charter provisions 316–17
    issue of consent 317–18
    relevant legal questions 318–19
  impact on use of world's oceans 2
  interim protection measures 299–301
  interpretation of previous judgments 312
  judicial composition 295
  judicial decisions as source of law
    doctrine of stare decisis 47
    process of law creation 47–8
    subsidiary source under ICC Statute 45–6
  judicial enforcement of international
    law 9–11
  jurisdiction by consent 304–7
  jurisdiction in contentious cases 301–3
  jurisdiction under UN Charter 303–4
  jurisdiction with reservations 307–10

International Court of Justice (ICJ) (*cont.*)
  legally binding effect of declarations 58–9
  primary means of dispute settlement 294–5
  reciprocal jurisdiction 310–11
  relationship with Security Council 315–16
  third state interventions 312–14
  transferred jurisdiction 311–12
  uncertain future of Court 21, 314–15
  use of equitable principles 44
International courts and tribunals
  ad hoc tribunals
    competence to deal with individuals 129
    dispute settlement 11
    judicial decisions as source of law 48
    judicial enforcement of international law 9
    rationale for system of law 6
    trial of individuals 128
  European Court of Human Rights (ECtHR)
    access to Court 367
    claims procedure 367–8
    establishment 367
    role as institutional mechanism for system of law 6
    settlement of disputes 292
    significant impact 368–9
  International Court of Justice (ICJ)
    access to Court 295–7
    admissibility in contentious cases 297–9
    Advisory Opinions 316–19
    doctrine of *stare decisis* 47
    impact on use of world's oceans 2
    interim protection measures 299–301
    interpretation of previous judgments 312
    judicial composition 295
    judicial enforcement of international law 9–11
    jurisdiction by consent 304–7
    jurisdiction in contentious cases 301–3
    jurisdiction under UN Charter 303–4
    jurisdiction with reservations 307–10
    legally binding effect of declarations 58–9
    primary means of dispute settlement 294–5
    process of law creation 47–8
    reciprocal jurisdiction 310–11
    relationship with Security Council 315–16
    stare decisis 47
    subsidiary source under ICC Statute 45–6
    third state interventions 312–14
    transferred jurisdiction 311–12
    uncertain future of Court 21, 314–15
    use of equitable principles 44
  International Criminal Court (ICC)
    future prospects 21
    groundbreaking work 2
    judicial enforcement of international law 9–11
  Nuremberg Military Tribunal
    body with universal jurisdiction 155
    protection of human rights 365
    trial of individuals 128
  settlement of disputes 292
  Tokyo Military Tribunal
    body with universal jurisdiction 155
    trial of individuals 128
International crimes
  aggression
    General Assembly as source of law 50–1
    maintenance of peace by Security Council 342
    rationale for system of law 5
  crimes against humanity 128
    human rights responsibilities 354
    humanitarian intervention 343
    individual responsibility 128
    jurisdiction of the ICC 129
    jus cogens 41
    relationship with national law 90
    role of international law 13
    universal jurisdiction 155
  crimes against the peace
    human rights responsibilities 354
    individual criminal responsibility 128
  genocide
    individual responsibility 128
    judicial enforcement of international law 10
    jurisdiction of the ICC 129
    rationale for system of law 5
    universal jurisdiction 155
  International Criminal Court (ICC)
    future prospects 21
    groundbreaking work 2
    judicial enforcement of international law 9–11
  piracy
    hostis humani generis 128
    human rights responsibilities 354
    state jurisdiction 241–2
    universal jurisdiction 154–5, 179
  rationale for system of law 5
  state responsibility 253
  torture 193
    customary international law 42
    denial of state immunity 193
    dualist approach to national law 92
    human rights 358, 360, 365–6
    jus cogens 40, 80
    national law 96
    sources of law 30
    sovereign immunity 95
    state immunity 193–4
    state responsibility 268
    treaty interpretation 74
    UK jurisdiction 103–4, 110–12
    universal jurisdiction 155
  war crimes
    human rights responsibilities 354
    humanitarian intervention 343
    individual responsibility 128
    judicial enforcement of international law 10

jurisdiction of the ICC 129
jus cogens 41
universal jurisdiction 155
International Criminal Court (ICC)
  see also ICC Statute
  future prospects 21
  groundbreaking work 2
  judicial enforcement of international
    law 9–11
International Labour Organisation (ILO)
  human rights protection 365, 370
  resolution of disputes 291
  source of law 50, 52
International law
  application in domestic courts 111–12
    executive certificates 112
    statutory authority 111–12
  comparison with national law 2
  consensual theory 17–18
  effectiveness
    acceptance by official practitioners 12
    assumed validity 12
    enforcement 14
    flexibility 12–13
    political cost of violation 13
    promotion of common good 11–12
  enforcement
    effectiveness 14
    hallmark of system of law 6–7
    judicial enforcement 9–11
    loss of legal rights and privileges 8–9
    role of Security Council 7–8
  existence as a *system of law* 2–3
  existence as system of law 4–6
  future prospects 21
  high-profile successes and failures
    1–2
  incorporation of customary law into UK
    law 108–10
  juridical bases
    command theory 16–17
    deconstructionist theories 19–20
    natural law theory 18–19
    non-statist theories 20–1
    realist theories 20
    ubi societas, ubi jus 19
    'value' orientated theories 20
  relationship with national law
    overview 90–1
    theoretical perspectives 91–4
  role 3–4
  role of human rights 354–7
  sources
    customary international law 32–42
    general principles 42–5
    ICC Statute 24–7
    international organisations 49–52
    judicial decisions 45–8
    overview 24
    soft law 52
    treaties 28–31

writings of publicists 49
theoretical and practical criticisms 1
transformation into UK law 108–10
transformation of treaties into UK law
  enacted treaties 104–5
  general rule 100–4
  unenacted treaties 105–8
weaknesses
  lack of certainty 15
  lack of institutions 14–15
  obedience and enforcement of vital
    rules 15–16
  prevalence of vital interests 15
  underlying problems 14
International Law Commission
  Draft Articles on state immunity 194–5
  progressive development of
    VCLT 1969 64
  state responsibility 252–3
International organisations
  see also United Nations
  acceptance of international law by official
    practitioners 12
  application of VCLT 1969 63
  creation of legally binding obligations 61–2
  effects of non-recognition in UK 145
  human rights agencies 365
  immunities 214–15
  jurisdiction of ICC 21
  multiple personalities 102
  non-governmental organisations (NGOs)
    access to ECtHR 367
    practitioners of international law 5, 12
    pressure for reform 14
    role of international law 2–3
  omission from ICC Statute 25
  personality
    criteria for achieving international
      personality 116–17
    main capacities 116
  rationale for system of law 4
  reservations 71
  role of international law 2, 4
  sources of law 25
    General Assembly 50–1
    overview 49–50
    Security Council 51–2
  subjects of international law 126–7
  Vienna Convention on the Law of Treaties
    between International Organisations 1986
    86–7
International personality
  see also Subjects of international law
  corporations 130
  defined by reference to rules 115–16
  individuals 128–30
  international organisations 126–7
  main capacities 116
  miscellaneous bodies 130–1
  relative concept 117
International straits 242–3

International trade
  General Assembly as source of law 51
  role of international law 3
Interpretation of treaties
  effectiveness principle 74
  intention of parties 74
  literal approach 73–4
  overlapping of principles 74–7
  overview 73
  teleological approach 74
Iraq
  defined territories 119
  humanitarian intervention 338
  limitations on enforcement by Security
    Council 8
  non-military sanctions 343
  perception of failed international law 1
  political cost of violating international
    law 13
  prevalence of vital interests 15
  rationale for system of law 4–5
  role of international law 4
  role of Security Council 7
  use of force 322
  weaknesses of international law 16
Islands 243–4
Israel
  abduction of Eichmann 260, 341
  Advisory Opinions of ICJ 317
  conquest of Palestine 168
  defence of necessity 265
  protection of human rights 365
  reprisals 335
  use of force 326–8, 335
Ius ad bellum 321

Johnson doctrine 341
Judicial decisions
  acquisition of sovereignty 169
  ad hoc tribunals 48
  doctrine of stare decisis 47
  process of law creation 47–8
  subsidiary source under ICC Statute
    45–6
Jure gestionis
  basis for immunity claim 190
  two-stage test 191–3
Jure imperii
  basis for immunity claim 188
  two-stage test 191–3
Jurisdiction
  see also Immunities; Sovereignty
  airspace 178–9
  application of national law in international
    courts and tribunals 97
  deep seabed 237
  enforcement over persons state in
    custody
    analysis of principles in Harvard Research
      Draft 150–2
    nationality jurisdiction 153–4

passive personality jurisdiction 159
  persons apprehended in violation of
    international law 160–1
  protective jurisdiction 156–8
  territorial jurisdiction 152–3
  universal jurisdiction 154–6
European Court of Human Rights (ECtHR)
  367
general principles
  absolute nature of territorial
    jurisdiction 149–50
  enforcement jurisdiction 149
  first rule of international law 148
  prescriptive jurisdiction 149
high seas 241
International Court of Justice (ICJ)
  interpretation of previous judgments 312
  jurisdiction by consent 304–7
  jurisdiction in contentious cases
    301–3
  jurisdiction under UN Charter 303–4
  jurisdiction with reservations 307–10
  reciprocal jurisdiction 310–11
  third state interventions 312–14
  transferred jurisdiction 311–12
liberty to make reservations 70
non-exclusive rights
  Antarctica 176–8
  Arctic 178
  outer space 175–6
relationship between customary and treaty
  law 39
'sovereign equality of nations' 45
territorial seas 224
Jus cogens
  consensual theory of international law 18
  high seas 241
  natural law theory 19
  no defence to state responsibility
    264–5
  relationship between customary and treaty
    law 40, 41–2
  scope of legal obligations under VCLT 1969
    79–80
  sovereign equality of states 185

Law of the sea
  application of international law in domestic
    courts 111
  archipelagos 243
  bays 245
  burgeoning and vital area of law 246
  continental shelf
    defined 228
    impact on claims to territorial seas 222
    nature and extent of rights 228
    opposite and adjacent states 230–5
    origins 228
    overlap with EEZ 222
    preference for single maritime
      boundary 236

relationship with EEZs 235–6
    seaward limit 229–30
deep seabed
    Convention 1982 237–40
    exploitation of mineral resources 236–7
    summary of rules 240–1
environmental protection 245–6
Exclusive Economic Zones (EEZ)
    delimitation 226–7
    impact on claims to territorial seas 222
    nature and extent 225–6
    origins 224–5
    other states' rights 226
    overlap with continental shelf 227
    relationship with continental shelf 235–6
flexibility of international law 13
guide to Convention 1982 249–50
high seas 241–2
impact of ICJ on use of world's oceans 2
international straits 242–3
islands 243–4
overview 217
peaceful settlement of disputes 246
promotion of common good 12
sources
    Convention 1982 218–20
    Geneva Conventions 1958 218
territorial seas
    contiguous zones 224
    'hot pursuit' 242
    nature and rights 220–1
    permissible width 221–3
League of Nations
    dissolution 127
    early human rights 357
    ICJ jurisdiction 137
    Mandated territories 126
    peaceful settlement of disputes 312
    protection of human rights 357
    treaty in international law 57
    unilateral use of force 323
Lebanon
    enforcement as underlying hallmark of
        system of law 6
    prevalence of vital interests 15
    role of international law 4
Legally binding obligations
    application of national law in international
        courts and tribunals 94–5
    capacity as a requirement of statehood
        manner of attainment 121–3
        meaning 'independence' 120–1
    declarations 58–9
    effect of state practice 61
    international organisations 61–2
    national laws 60–1
    treaties
        essential requirement 56–7
        other acts and agreements
            distinguished 57–8
    unilateral statements 59–60

Vienna Convention on the Law of Treaties
    1969
    fundamental rule 68
    inconsistent treaties 79
    interpretation 73–7
    jus cogens 79–80
    reservations 68–73
    third states 77–9
Lex specialis 51–2
Liberation movements
    international personality 130–1
    international personality of PLO 130
    state responsibility 261–2
    unilateral use of force 339–40
Liberia
    humanitarian intervention 342
    non-military sanctions 343
    powers of the Security Council 346
    use of force 346
Libya
    humanitarian intervention 338, 342
    judicial enforcement of international law 10
    maintenance of peace by Security
        Council 342
    non-military sanctions 343
    powers of the Security Council 346
    rationale for system of law 4
    role of international law 4
Literal interpretation of treaties 73–4

Maritime law *see* Law of the sea
Material breaches of treaty 81–2
Mediation 288
Monism
    approach to subject matter 93
    incorporation doctrine 100
    practical application 94
    relationship between national and
        international law 91–2
Monroe doctrine 341

National law
    see also Immunities
    absolute nature of territorial jurisdiction 149–50
    application in international courts and
        tribunals
        binding legal obligations 94–5
        defining concepts for dispute resolution 96
        evidence of 'facts' 96–7
        jurisdictional basis for decision 97
        source of law 94
        theoretical perspectives 98–100
    application of international law in domestic
        courts
        executive certificates 112
        exercise of discretionary powers 112–13
        statutory authority 111–12
    assumed certainty of enforcement 7
    authority to conclude treaties 65–6
    comparison with international law 2
    general principles common to all systems 44

National law (*cont.*)
  judicial decisions as source of law 48
  legally binding obligations on states 60–1
  prescriptive jurisdiction
    apparent displays of sovereignty 162–4
    continuous displays over time 164–5
    effective control 162
    intemporal law doctrine 166–7
    intention to acquire sovereignty 164
    peaceful displays 165–6
  relationship with international law
    overview 90–1
    theoretical perspectives 91–4
  UK approach to recognition
    effects of non-recognition 139–45
    governments 137–9
    states 137
Nationalisation *see* Expropriation of foreign
    property
Nationality
  jurisdiction 153–4
  protection of nationals by force 335–7
  role of international law 3
  state responsibility for foreign nationals
    admissibility of claims 268–74
    appropriate standard of conduct 267–8
    ill-treatment giving rise to
        responsibility 266–7
Natural law theory
  basis for general principles 42–3
  juridical basis for international law 18–19
Necessity
  defence to state responsibility 265
  ubi societas, ubi jus 19
  weakness of international law 15
Negotiated settlements 287–8
'New World Order' 343
Non-governmental organisations (NGOs)
  access to ECtHR 367
  practitioners of international law 5, 12
  pressure for reform 14
  role of international law 2, 3
Non-justiciability
  customary international law 108
  immunities distinguished 183–5
  peaceful settlement of disputes 298
  state responsibility 273
  treaty obligations 101–2, 104, 106
Non-military sanctions 342–3
Non-registered treaties 57–8
Non-state actors
  see also Corporations; International
      organisations; 'Peoples'
  application of VCLT 1969 63
  jurisdiction of ICC 21
  scope of international law 2
  Security Council sanctions 7
  sources of law 25, 27
Non-statist theories 20–1
North Atlantic Treaty Organisation (NATO)

'all necessary measures' 344, 348
  collective security provisions 348–50
  collective self-defence 332
  humanitarian intervention 337–8
  intervention in Former Yugoslavia 310, 324,
      326–7
  role of treaties 42
North Korea
  non-military sanctions 343
  Security Council decisions 7
Nuremberg Military Tribunal
  body with universal jurisdiction 155
  protection of human rights 365
  trial of individuals 128

Objective territoriality 152
Opinio juris
  process of law creation 47–8
  state practice 36–8
Organisation of American States (OAS)
  collective security provisions 348–50
  peaceful settlement of disputes 292
  role of international law 4
  subject of international law 127
Original personality 116
Outer space 175–6

Pacta sunt servanda
  consensual theory of international law 17
  fundamental rule of VCLT 1969 68
  treaties as source of law 31
Pacta tertiis nec nocent nec prosunt 77–8
Palestine
  Advisory Opinions of ICJ 316
  Autonomous Area in Gaza/West Bank 171–2
  British Mandate 165
  claims to statehood 122
  conquest by Israel 168
  international personality of PLO 130
  protection of human rights 365
  state recognition 135
  territorial claims 119
  territory per se 126
  use of force 339
Par in parem non habet imperium 185
Passive personality jurisdiction 159
Peaceful settlement of disputes
  ad hoc tribunals 11
  arbitration 292–4
  Calvo clauses 274
  conciliation 291
  direct negotiations 287–8
  European Court of Human Rights (ECtHR)
      368
  inquiries 288–9
  International Court of Justice (ICJ)
    access to Court 295–7
    admissibility in contentious cases 297–9
    Advisory Opinions 316–19
    doctrine of *stare decisis* 47

impact on use of world's oceans 2
interim protection measures 299–301
interpretation of previous judgments 312
judicial composition 295
judicial enforcement of international
    law 9–11
jurisdiction by consent 304–7
jurisdiction in contentious cases 301–3
jurisdiction under UN Charter 303–4
jurisdiction with reservations 307–10
legally binding effect of declarations 58–9
primary means of dispute settlement 294–5
process of law creation 47–8
reciprocal jurisdiction 310–11
relationship with Security Council 315–16
subsidiary source under ICC Statute 45–6
third state interventions 312–14
transferred jurisdiction 311–12
uncertain future of Court 21, 314–15
use of equitable principles 44
law of the sea 246
mediation and good offices 288
rationale for system of law 5
regional bodies 292
UN Charter provisions 286–9
UN institutions
    General Assembly 289
    other agencies 291
    Security Council 289–91
Peacekeeping
    collective security provisions 350–2
    role of international law 3
'Peoples'
    African Charter on Human and Peoples'
        Rights 1981 370
    migration across territorial boundaries 119
    national liberation movements 339
    'non self-governing peoples' 126
    protection of human rights 369–70
    right to self-determination 121–2, 171–3
    scope of international law 2
    'third generation' rights 359
'Persistent objector' rule 34
Personality *see* International personality
Piracy
    hostis humani generis 128
    human rights responsibilities 354
    state jurisdiction 241–2
    universal jurisdiction 154–5, 179
Political independence *see* Self-determination
Population
    displays of sovereignty 162
    existence not enough for statehood 122–3
    factual prerequisite 123
    humanitarian intervention 334, 337–8
    requirement for statehood
        government over 120
        permanence 119
    right to separate from state 172
Positivism 49

Pre-emptive self-defence 331
Precedent 47
Prescriptive rights
    acquisition of sovereignty
        apparent displays of sovereignty 162–4
        continuous displays over time 164–5
        effective control 162
        intemporal law doctrine 166–7
        intention to acquire sovereignty 164
        peaceful displays 165–6
    jurisdiction 149
Protective jurisdiction 156–8
Publicists *see* Writings of publicists

Ratio personae issue 185
Realist theories 20
Rebus sic stantibus 83
Reciprocity principle 310–11
Recognition
    effect on statehood 123–4
    states
        formal requirements 131–2
        theoretical perspectives 132–6
        UK national law 136–45
Reprisals *see* Countermeasures 335
Res communis 176, 241
Reservations
    effectiveness 69–70
    entry into force of treaties 71–2
    ICJ jurisdiction 307–10
    international organisations 71
    liberty to make reservations 70
    meaning and scope 68–9
    parties to treaty 70
    primacy to terms of treaty 72–3
Responsibility
    corporations 270–2
    individuals 284
    to protect 337–9
    states
        admissibility of claims 268–74
        appropriate standard of conduct 267–8
        attributability 257–62
        breaches of ECHR 366–7
        concessionary agreements and treaties
            distinguished 61
        contractual obligations 282
        defence to breach of treaty 83–4
        defences 264–6
        expropriation of foreign property 275–81
        ill-treatment giving rise to
            responsibility 266–7
        illegal acts 255–7
        judicial decisions as source of law 48
        legal consequences 263–4
        meaning and scope 252–4
        necessary elements 254–5
        primary responsibility 262–3
        protection of foreign investors 283–4
Restrictive state immunity doctrine 187–8

Revolutionaries *see* Liberation movements
Rules
  central questions about international law 1
  enforcement as underlying hallmark of
    system of law 7
  evidence for existence 5
  future prospects for international law 21
  natural law theory 19
  personality 115–16
  role of international law 3–4
  sources of law 24
  treaties 55
  weaknesses of international law
    lack of certainty 15
    obedience and enforcement of vital
      rules 15–16
Russia
  human rights violations 6
  limitations on enforcement by Security
    Council 7–8
  rationale for system of law 6
  Security Council veto 8, 343, 345
Rwanda
  establishment of ad hoc tribunal 155
  humanitarian intervention 338, 342
  need for international rules 4
  non-military sanctions 343
  peaceful settlement of disputes 290
  protection of human rights 365
  trial of individuals 11, 128
  use of force 346
  War Crimes Tribunal 6

Seabed *see* Deep seabed
Security *see* Peacekeeping
Security Council
  collective security provisions
    diverse powers of Council 346–7
    non-military sanctions 342–4
    overlap with collective self-defence 345–6
    use of armed force 344–5
    use of regional organisations 348–50
  enforcement role 7–8
  non-military sanctions 343
  peaceful settlement of disputes 289–91
  rationale for system of law 4
  relationship with ICJ 315–16
  reports of self-defence 332
  source of law 51–2
Self-defence
  collective self-defence
    general principles 332–3
    overlap with Security Council
      powers 345–6
    requests to third states 333–4
  rationale for system of law 4
  unilateral use of force
    anticipatory action 331
    'armed attacks' 330–1
    collective self-defence 332–4

customary international law 327–8
extent of right 328–30
proportionality 331
reports to Security Council 332
terrorism 331
weakness of international law 15
Self-determination
  acquisition of sovereignty 171–3
  collective self-defence
    no requirement for prior authorisation 342
  criteria for statehood 121–2
  East Timor 2
  impact on future prospects for international
    law 21
  jus cogens 80
  opinio juris 51
  relationship with expropriation 275
  UN success in East Timor 2
  unilateral use of force 325–7, 339–40
Self-interest
  'persistent objector' rule 34
  role of international law 4
  weakness of international law 15
Serbia *see* Former Yugoslavia
Ships
  'freedom of the seas' 241
  'innocent passage' 221
  international straits 242–3
  piracy
    hostis humani generis 128
    human rights responsibilities 354
    state jurisdiction 241–2
    universal jurisdiction 154–5, 179
  'right to visit' 242
Sierra Leone
  establishment of ad hoc tribunal 155
  non-military sanctions 343
  powers of the Security Council 346
Soft law 52
Somalia
  effect of civil war 132
  extinction of statehood 124
  non-military sanctions 343
  peacekeeping forces 348, 350
  protection of human rights 365
  scope of Security Council action 8
  state recognition 138–40, 142
  UN failures 1
  use of force 345–6
  War Crimes Tribunal 6
Sources of law
  customary international law
    foundation of law of nations 32
    relationship with treaty law 39–42
    state practice 32–9
  general principles
    ICC Statute 42
    human rights 354
  ICC Statute
    formal and material sources 26–7

formal and material sources
distinguished 26–7
material and evidentiary sources
distinguished 27
matters for Court to consider 24–6
international organisations
General Assembly 50–1
overview 49–50
Security Council 51–2
judicial decisions
ad hoc tribunals 48
doctrine of *stare decisis* 47
process of law creation 47–8
subsidiary source under ICC Statute 45–6
law of the sea
Convention 1982 218–20
Geneva Conventions 1958 218
national and international law
compared 2
national law 94
overview 24
soft law 52
treaties
governing principles 28–30
as 'law' or 'obligation' 30–1
overview 28
relationship with customary law 39–42
writings of publicists 49
Sovereignty
see also Jurisdiction
acquisition
accretion and avulsion 169
cessation and treaty 167–8
conclusions 173–4
conquest 168–9
control and prescription 161–7
discovery 167
judicial decisions 169
overview 161
self-determination 171–3
uti possidetis 169–71
Exclusive Economic Zones (EEZ) 225–6
impact on future prospects for international
law 21
re-casting of international law 2–3
recognition of delegated sovereigns 142–3
relationship with expropriation 275, 277
rights over foreign territory 174–5
'sovereign equality of nations' 45
territorial seas 220–1
Stare decisis 47
State practice
creation of legally binding obligations 61
diminishing role of publicists 49
essential requirements
consistency 33
general application 34–5
opinio juris 36–8
passage of time 35–6
support for change 38–9

evolution of customary law 32
meaning and scope 32–3
process of law creation 47–8
supervening impossibility 82–3
State responsibility
attributability
individuals 259–61
necessary elements 257–8
organs of state 258–9
revolutionaries 261–2
breaches of ECHR 366–7
concessionary agreements and treaties
distinguished 61
contractual obligations 282
defence to breach of treaty 83–4
defences 264–6
expropriation of foreign property
conditions for lawful expropriation 275–7
meaning and scope 275
measure of compensation 277–81
foreign nationals
admissibility of claims 268–74
appropriate standard of conduct 267–8
ill-treatment giving rise to
responsibility 266–7
judicial decisions as source of law 48
legal consequences 263–4
meaning and scope 252–4
necessary elements
attributability 257–8
illegal acts 255–7
overview 254–5
primary responsibility 262–3
protection of foreign investors 283–4
Statehood
continental shelf 228
difficulties of definition 117–19
extinction 124–5
granting of immunity by UK 201–4
recognition 123–4
requirements of Montevideo
Convention 1933
capacity to enter into legal relations 120–3
defined territory 119
government 129
permanent population 119
States
acceptance of international law by official
practitioners 12
immunities
adoption of restrictive theory 187–8
classification of acts according to subject
matter 190–1
commercial transactions 190
distinctions found on purpose of act 188–9
European Union (EU) 207
heads of state 206–7
ILC Draft Articles 194
overview 182
relationship with Art 6 (fair trial) 207–8

States (*cont.*)
two stage test to distinguish acts *jure imperii* and *jure gestionis* 191–3
UK approach 196–206
underlying concept and rationale 183–7
violations of national law 193–4
personality
criteria for achieving international personality 116–17
defined by reference to rules 115–16
main capacities 116
rationale for system of law 4
recognition
formal requirements 131–2
theoretical perspectives 132–6
UK national law 136–45
role of international law 3
Subjective territoriality 152–3
Subjects of international law
corporations 130
individuals 128–30
international organisations 126–7
miscellaneous bodies 130–1
multiple personalities 102
overview 115
personality
criteria for achieving international personality 116–17
defined by reference to rules 115–16
main capacities 116
relative concept 117
states
difficulties of definition 117–19
extinction of statehood 124–5
recognition 123–4
requirements of Montevideo Convention 1933 119–23
territorial entities other than states
agencies of states 125
territories *per se* 125–6
treaty creations 125
Succession of states 85–6
Sudan
humanitarian intervention 338
UN failures 1
Supervening impossibility 82–3
Syria
defined territories 119
enforcement through loss of rights and privileges 9
humanitarian intervention 343
limitations on enforcement by Security Council 8
rationale for system of law 6
weaknesses of international law 16
System of law
assumed validity 12
deconstructionist theories 19–20
enforcement as underlying hallmark 6–7
essential debate 2–3
general principles 43–4

monist and dualist approaches 93–4
rationale for international law 4–6

Teleological interpretation 74
Termination of treaties
by consent 81
countermeasures 85
fundamental change of circumstances 83
inconsistent treaties 79
material breaches 81–2
non-performance by other party 84–5
purpose achieved 81
state responsibility defences 83–4
supervening impossibility 82–3
Terra nullius 161, 165, 172
Territorial jurisdiction
absolute nature of territorial jurisdiction 149–50
enforcement over persons state in custody
extra-territorial jurisdiction 153
objective territoriality 152
subjective territoriality 152–3
underlying principle 152
Territorial seas
contiguous zones 224
'hot pursuit' 242
nature and rights
'innocent passage' 221
sovereignty 220–1
permissible width 221–3
Territory
acquisition of sovereignty
accretion and avulsion 169
cessation and treaty 167–8
conclusions 173–4
conquest 168–9
discovery 167
exercise of effective control 161–7
judicial decisions 169
overview 161
self-determination 171–3
uti possidetis 169–71
customary right of transit 35
dispositive treaties 18
dualist approach to national law 95
duty to protect foreign nationals 33
factual prerequisite 123
law of treaties 55
prohibition on unilateral force 325–7
requirement for statehood 119
rights over foreign territory 174–5
role of treaties 28
scope of international law 2
'sovereign equality of nations' 45
subjects of international law other than states
agencies of states 125
territories *per se* 125–6
treaty creations 125
succession of states 78, 85–6

Terrorism
  judicial enforcement of international law 10
  limitations on enforcement by Security
    Council 8
  perception of failed international law 1
  protection of nationals by force 335–7
  protective jurisdiction 158
  self-defence against armed attacks 331
Textual interpretation of treaties 73–4
Theoretical perspectives
  application of national law in international
    courts and tribunals 98–100
  command theory of law 16–17
  consensual theory 17–18
  deconstructionist theories 19–20
  natural law theory 18–19, 42–3
  non-statist theories 20–1
  realist theories 20
  relationship between national and
    international law 91–4
  restrictive state immunity doctrine 187–8
  state recognition
    alternative theories compared 135–6
    constitutive theory 133–5
    declaratory theory 132–3
    importance 132
  ubi societas, ubi jus 19
  'value' orientated theories 20
Third states
  binding effect of treaties 77–9
  intervention into ICJ proceedings 312–14
  requests to provide collective self-
    defence 333–4
Tokyo Military Tribunal
  body with universal jurisdiction 155
  trial of individuals 128
Torture
  customary international law 42
  denial of state immunity 193
  dualist approach to national law 92
  human rights 358, 360, 365–6
  jus cogens 40, 80
  national law 96
  sources of law 30
  sovereign immunity 95
  state immunity 193–4
  state responsibility 268
  treaty interpretation 74
  UK jurisdiction 103–4, 110–12
  universal jurisdiction 155
Transferred jurisdiction 311–12
Transformation doctrine
  theoretical perspectives 98–100
  treaties into UK law
    doubts over underlying analysis 110
    enacted treaties 104–5
    unenacted treaties 105–8
Travaux préparatoires 75–7, 105, 323, 327, 329, 349
Treaties
  cessation of territory 167–8
  consensual theory of international law 17

consent to ICJ jurisdiction
  matters provided for 305–6
  with reservations 307–10
creation of territorial entities 125
future prospects 21
human rights protection
  cover for specific rights 365
  ECHR 1950 365–7
  International Convention on the
    Elimination of All Forms of Racial
    Discrimination 1966 364–5
  International Covenant on Civil and
    Political Rights 1966 360–2
  International Covenant on Economic,
    Social and Cultural Rights 1966 362–4
  Universal Declaration in 1948 359–60
intention to create legally binding
  relations 56–7
matters for ICC to consider under Art 38 24
other acts and agreements distinguished
  acts of international organisations 61–2
  national laws 60–1
  state practice 61
  unilateral statements 59–60
overview 55–6
source of law
  governing principles 28–30
  as 'law' or 'obligation' 30–1
  overview 28
  relationship with customary law 39–42
transformation into UK law
  enacted treaties 104–5
  general rule 100–4
  unenacted treaties 105–8
unilateral use of force 322–4
Vienna Convention on the Law of Treaties
  1969
  amendment and modification 80–1
  definitions and exclusions 62–3
  inception of treaties 64–8
  preservation of customary law 63–4
  scope of legal obligations 68–80
  successes 62
  termination 81–5
  validity 80
Vienna Convention on the Law of Treaties
  between International Organisations 1986
  86–7
Vienna Convention on the Succession of
  States 1978 85–6
Trusteeship territories 125–6

Ubi societas, ubi jus 19
Unilateral statements 59–60
Unilateral use of force
  Brezhnev doctrine 341
  customary and treaty law prior to 1945
    322–4
  Johnson doctrine 341
  Monroe doctrine 341
  UN Charter provisions

Unilateral use of force (*cont.*)
  to achieve self-determination 339–40
  'approved' purposes 334–5
  collective self-defence 332–4
  hot pursuit 337–9
  humanitarian intervention 337–9
  protection of nationals 335–7
  reprisals 335
  self-defence 327–32
  statement of intent 324–5
  territorial integrity and political
    independence 325–7
United Kingdom
  application of international law in domestic
    courts
    executive certificates 112
    statutory authority 111–12
  diplomatic and consular immunities 213–14
  enforcement of international law 6
  enforcement through loss of rights and
    privileges 8
  granting of state immunity
    common law rules prior to 1978 196
    general principle of immunity 197–8
    immunity from execution and
      enforcement 201
    immunity from jurisdiction 198–201
    specific problems 204–6
    standing to claim 201–4
    statutory rules after 1978 196
  incorporation of customary law 108–10
  judicial enforcement of international law 10
  political cost of violating international
    law 13
  recognition
    effects of non-recognition 139–45
    governments 137–9
    states 137
  territorial sea 221
  transfer of sovereign territory to China 57,
    79, 167
  transformation of treaties
    doubts over underlying analysis 110
    enacted treaties 104–5
    general rule 100–4
    unenacted treaties 105–8
  Vienna Convention on the Law of Treaties
    between International Organisations
    1986 87
United Nations
  see also Law of the sea
  acceptance of international law by official
    practitioners 12
  collective security provisions
    General Assembly 347–8
    Security Council 342–7
  enforcement as underlying hallmark of
    system of law 6–7
  General Assembly
    collective security provisions 347–8

conditions for lawful expropriation 276
  'moratorium resolution' on sea bed
    mining 237
  peaceful settlement of disputes 289
  resolutions and treaties distinguished 57–8
  source of law 25, 50–1
  high-profile successes and failures 1–2
  human rights agencies 365
  human rights treaties
    history and development 357–8
    International Convention on the
      Elimination of All Forms of Racial
      Discrimination 1966 364–5
    International Covenant on Civil and
      Political Rights 1966 360–2
    International Covenant on Economic,
      Social and Cultural Rights 1966 362–4
    Universal Declaration in 1948 359–60
  peaceful settlement of disputes
    Charter provisions 286–9
    General Assembly 289
    ICJ jurisdiction 303–4
    other agencies 291
    Security Council 289–91
  personality
    criteria for achieving international
      personality 116
    main capacities 116
  recognition of statehood 117–18
  role of international law 3, 4
  Security Council
    enforcement role 7–8
    peaceful settlement of disputes 289–91
    rationale for system of law 4
    relationship with ICJ 315–16
    reports of self-defence 332
    source of law 51–2
  subject of international law 126–7
  unilateral use of force
    to achieve self-determination 339–40
    'approved' purposes 334–5
    collective self-defence 332–4
    hot pursuit 340–1
    humanitarian intervention 337–9
    protection of nationals 335–7
    reprisals 335
    self-defence 327–32
    statement of intent 324–5
    territorial integrity and political
      independence 325–7
  Vienna Convention on the Law of Treaties
    between International Organisations
    1986 87
United States
  American Convention on Human
    Rights 1948 369
  denial of human rights at Guantanamo
    Bay 1–2
  enforcement as underlying hallmark of
    system of law 6

enforcement through loss of rights and
    privileges 8–9
judicial enforcement of international law 10
limitations on enforcement by Security
    Council 7–8
political cost of violating international
    law 13
protective jurisdiction 157–8
Universal jurisdiction 154–6
Use of force
    collective security provisions
        overview 341–2
        United Nations 342–8
    conquest of territories 168–9
    overview 321–2
    peacekeeping forces 350–2
    perception of failed international law 1
    rationale for system of law 5
    role of international law 3
    role of Security Council 7–8
    unilateral use of force
        Brezhnev doctrine 341
        customary and treaty law prior to 1945
            322–4
        Johnson doctrine 341
        Monroe doctrine 341
        UN Charter provisions 324–41
Ut res magis valeat quam pereat 74
Uti possidetis 169–71

Validity of treaties 80
'Value' orientated theories 20
Vienna Convention on the Law of Treaties
    1969
    amendment and modification 80–1

definitions and exclusions 62–3
inception of treaties
    authority to conclude treaties 65–6
    consent 66–7
    entry into force 67–8
    framework of rules 64–5
preservation of customary law 63–4
scope of legal obligations
    fundamental rule 68
    inconsistent treaties 79
    interpretation 73–7
    jus cogens 79–80
    reservations 68–73
    third states 77–9
successes 62
termination 81–5
validity 80
Vienna Convention on the Law of Treaties
        between International Organisations
        1986 86–7
Vienna (territorial entity) 125

War crimes
    human rights responsibilities 354
    humanitarian intervention 343
    individual responsibility 128
    judicial enforcement of international law 10
    jurisdiction of the ICC 129
    jus cogens 41
    universal jurisdiction 155
World public order 20
World Trade Organisation (WTO) 292
Writings of publicists
    matters for ICC to consider under Art 38 24
    source of law 49